Computers in Business Management
An Introduction

IRWIN SERIES IN
INFORMATION AND DECISION SCIENCES

Editors Robert B. Fetter   Claude McMillan
          Yale University   University of Colorado

Computers in
Business Management

An Introduction

JAMES A. O'BRIEN

Professor of Finance and Management Information Systems
School of Business and Administration
Eastern Washington State College

 1975

RICHARD D. IRWIN, INC. Homewood, Illinois 60430

Irwin-Dorsey Limited, Georgetown, Ontario L7G 4B3

7 8 9 0 K 5 4 3 2 1 0 9 8

ISBN 0-256-01671-2
Library of Congress Catalog Card No. 74–18707
Printed in the United States of America

To Sandi . . .
For the joys and burdens we share

Preface

This book is designed for courses which introduce students to computers in a *business management* context, rather than in a context of computer science, computer programming, or computers-in-society. Introductory computer courses are required in the business curriculums of most two-year and four-year colleges and universities. Such courses have been moving away from an emphasis on the details of data processing, computer hardware, and computer programming, and moving toward the emphasis of this text which views the computer as a valuable tool and resource for business management. (A concurrent trend finds the emergence of "computers in society" courses for liberal arts and social science curriculums.)

This trend recognizes that most students in collegiate business programs will be future *computer users* not *computer professionals.* As future computer users in business, students need a basic understanding of computers and how they can be applied to the management and operations of a business enterprise. Therefore, they need to be introduced to: (1) the fundamentals of computers and electronic data processing, (2) the wide range of hardware and software that is available to computer users, and (3) the process of computer programming and the "high-level" programming languages that are utilized by computer-using business firms. However, (*and more importantly*) they need to be introduced to the basic concepts of: (1) systems analysis and design, (3) management information systems, (3) computer applications in business, and (4) the management of the computer.

Objectives of the Text and the Course

The goal of this text is to provide a teaching-learning resource which supports the attainment by students of *two overall course objectives.* Students should be able to demonstrate:

1. A basic understanding of computers and how they can be applied to the management and operations of business firms.
2. A basic understanding of EDP concepts, terminology, and techniques in business.

Attaining these objectives should result in the fulfillment of what should be *the primary goal* of introductory computer courses in business curriculums: "Helping students to become knowledgeable *business users* of the computer resource, as opposed to knowledgeable *technicians* in electronic data processing and computer programming."

How can students demonstrate the attainment of the *"basic understanding"* required by the course objectives? In this text, such understanding can be demonstrated by successful completion of a majority of the assignments at the end of each chapter. Thus, chapter assignments are in reality carefully chosen *"performance objectives"* or *"behavioral objectives."* The assignments demand that the students "do something" which demonstrates and contributes to the basic understanding required by the overall course objectives. Also, instructors can tailor the course to their unique circumstances by selective use of the performance objectives of each chapter.

Structure and Content of the Text

The text material is organized into six parts which can be treated as separate modules. Once the first part is covered, the other parts may be assigned in any order, depending on the preferences of the instructor, the amount of computer programming instruction desired, and the number of credit-hours assigned to the course. A brief summary of each module follows.

Part One, "Fundamentals of Computers and Data Processing," introduces students to the fundamental functions and types of data processing systems and computer systems. It analyzes the representation, organization and processing of data in computers and data processing. The development of computers is surveyed and the student is introduced to the important types and capabilities of modern electronic data processing systems.

Part Two, "Computer Hardware, Software and Programming," surveys the wide range of hardware and software available to computer users and analyzes their functions, benefits, and limitations. It then introduces the student to the functions and techniques of each stage of the computer programming process.

Part Three, "Developing Business Information Systems," introduces students to the concept of information systems development by analyzing each stage of the systems development life cycle. The origins, functions, and techniques of systems analysis and design are also covered. These chapters emphasize that business information systems "do not just happen," but must be conceived, designed, and implemented.

Part Four, "Applying the Computer to Business Management," emphasizes the "systems approach" to introducing students to the business uses of the computer. This approach requires that business applications of computers be viewed as subsystems of the operational and management information systems of business firms. Therefore, the first chapter of this section discusses basic systems concepts and how they relate to the components and requirements of management information systems in business. Chapter 10 discusses the basic computer applications utilized by most computer-using business firms, while Chapter 11 focuses on computer applications utilized by specific business functions and industries.

Part Five, "Managing the Computer," emphasizes the challenges of managing the computer in a computer-based environment. This section illustrates that the use of computers in business does not take place in a vacuum and that it imposes serious responsibilities on business management. The impact of computers and the computer industry on business and society is discussed as well as the acquisition, management, and control of the computer as a valuable business resource. Finally, the challenge of the computer to business management is explored in order to tie together the concepts of the book.

Part Six, "Fundamentals of Computer Programming Languages," consists of four chapters that were designed for courses which require some instruction in computer programming. The chapters of this module discuss the fundamentals of the FORTRAN, COBOL, BASIC, PL/1, and RPG languages.

The primary purpose of the first three chapters of this part is to provide business students with a basic understanding of computer programming by enabling them to write simple programs in *one* of the three most widely used programming languages. This is accomplished by introducing students to the basic types of instructions and rules of a specific language and by illustrating the programming of a few simple data processing problems. The student should then be able to write simple programs in the language he studies. Chapter 18 provides a brief introduction to PL/1 and RPG for those instructors who wish to acquaint their students with these languages. Most instructors will utilize *only one* of the chapters in Part Six, depending on the languages used by their computer centers and their own personal preferences.

Computer Programming Instruction Alternatives

This text supports several alternative methods of computer programming instruction, if such instruction is desired. Programming instruction should begin with Chapter 6 which analyzes the various stages of the computer programming process, describes the construction and use of flowcharts and decision tables, and briefly describes the five popular programming languages. The instructor can then require students to complete *one* of the following alternatives:

1. Review the sample computer programs contained in one or more of the chapters of Part Six. (Recommended for courses which do not require any computer programming experience, or when no computer facilities are available.)
2. Learn how to write a few simple programs in one of the programming languages of the text.
3. Learn how to write simple programs in several of the programming languages provided.
4. Learn how to write complex as well as simple programs in one of the programming languages by supplementing the text with a programming text or manual that offers an in-depth coverage of the programming language selected.

Most instructors will probably commence computer programming instruction after Parts One and Two are completed, but instructors who are anxious to begin computer programming even earlier could begin the course with Chapter 6 and then move immediately to one of the chapters in Part Six. Other instructors may prefer to wait until Parts Three or Four are covered before making computer programming assignments.

Other Instructional Features of the Text

The text is designed as its own "study guide." Each chapter begins with a *chapter purpose* and *chapter outline,* and ends with a *summary,* a *listing of key terms and concepts* and *chapter assignments.* The text begins with a detailed *table of contents,* and ends with an extensive *glossary* of data processing terms and a selected *bibliography* which is organized to correspond to the major parts of the book. The bibliography also includes a listing and brief description of *major periodicals* in the fields of computers, data processing, and information systems. Finally, an extensive *index* indicates the page numbers where key terms or concepts are defined or utilized.

The style of the text is deliberately straightforward, simple, and concise, and it is organized for a logical, nonredundant progression of topics from computer basics, to computer applications, to computer management, with computer programming instruction encouraged anytime after computer basics are covered. Important concepts are described in flow diagrams and tables, and photographs of hardware are provided.

January 1975   JAMES A. O'BRIEN

Acknowledgments

This text would not have been possible without the contributions and cooperation of many persons. In particular, the author wishes to acknowledge the assistance of the reviewers of the manuscript: Claude McMillan of the University of Colorado, and Alden C. Lorents of Northern Arizona University (representing the four-year university viewpoint), and Edward H. Rategan of the College of San Mateo and Gene R. Watkins of C. S. Mott Community College (representing the two-year college viewpoint). Their constructive criticism and generous praise helped shape the final draft of the manuscript.

I wish to acknowledge the many persons who have contributed to my ideas on computer usage in business. They include the authors of books and articles which are specifically acknowledged in the footnotes and bibliography of the text. Not specifically mentioned, but just as important, are the many persons I have worked with at the General Electric Company, the IBM Corporation, and on several consulting assignments. These experiences have shaped my views on the vital need for a "computers in business management" approach for introductory computer courses for business students.

The author is indebted to the President and Board of Trustees of Eastern Washington State College, and the Dean and faculty of the School of Business and Administration for supporting and approving my request for a sabbatical leave to develop this text. The author acknowledges the assistance of Steven O. Rundell, who tested most of the sample programs of the programming chapters and developed sample solutions for several of the programming problem assignments which are provided in the teacher's manual. Special thanks also goes to Ruth Kembel and her daughter Karlene who typed most of the manuscript. The author also acknowledges the contributions of computer manufacturers and others who provided photographs and illustrations used in the text.

Finally, I wish to acknowledge the substantial contribution of my wife, Sandi, whose assistance and support were essential to the successful completion of this work. Special thanks also goes to my mother, Eileen O'Brien, for her support of this project, and to my children, David, Susan, and Michael for the time which their father spent "working on the book" instead of being with them. The debt I owe to these members of my family, I can never fully repay.

J. A. O.

Contents

Determining Information Needs. Determining System Objectives. Identifying Systems Constraints and Criteria. System Feasibility. Economic Feasibility. System Costs. System Benefits. Cost/Benefit Analysis. The Feasibility Study Report. Systems Analysis. Systems Design. Programming. Systems Implementation: *Acquisition. Training. Testing. Documentation. Operation.* Systems Maintenance.

Introduction. Origins of Systems Analysis and Design: *Methods and Procedures. Systematic Analysis. Operations Research. The Systems Approach. The Systems Development Cycle.* Systems Analysis: *Analysis of the Organization System. Major Subsystem Analysis. Present Information Systems Analysis. Proposed Information System Requirements Analysis. System Requirements Development.* Systems Design: *Basic System Design. Detailed System Design. System Implementation Planning. System Specifications Development.* Systems Analysis and Design: Additional Topics: *Techniques of Systems Analysis and Design. The Human Factor in Systems Analysis and Design. Mathematical Models in Systems Analysis and Design. System Simulation. Forms Design and Control.* Checklist for Systems Analysis and Design.

part four
Applying the Computer to Business Management

Introduction. The Cybernetic Systems Concept: *Feedback and Control. Adaptive Systems. Cybernetic Systems.* The Business System: *Operational Systems. Management Systems. Operational Information Systems. Management Information Systems. The Business Environment.* Information Requirements of Operational Systems. Information Requirements of Environmental Systems: *Customer Systems. Competitor Systems. Supplier Systems. Labor Union Systems. Stockholder Systems. Financial Institution Systems. Governmental Systems. Community Systems.* Information Requirements of Management Systems: *The Functions of Management. The Management System. Management Information Requirements.* Management Information Systems: *The Management Information System. MIS Information Output. Internal Information from an MIS. External Information from an MIS.* Business Information Systems: *Production/Operations Information Systems. Marketing Information Systems. Financial Information Systems. Accounting Information Systems. Personnel Information Systems. Other Information Systems.* Integrated Information Systems: *Common Data Flows. The Common Data Base. The Total Information System.*

Introduction. Types of Computer Applications. Trends in Computer Applications. The General Form of Business Computer Applications. The

Managing Computer Operations: *Operations Management. Production Planning and Control.* Controlling Electronic Data Processing: *Data Processing Controls. Input Controls. Processing Controls. Output Controls. Storage Controls. Organizational Controls. Facility Controls. Auditing EDP.*

part six
Fundamentals of Computer
Programming Languages

part one

Fundamentals of Computers and Data Processing

Chapter Outline

Purpose of the Chapter

Introduction
Data versus Information, Data Processing, Data Processing Systems, Information Systems.

Data Processing Functions and Activities
Collection, Conversion, Manipulation, Storage, Communication.

Manual Data Processing Systems
Development, Benefits and Limitations

Mechanical Data Processing Systems
Development, Typing Equipment, Calculating Machines, Bookkeeping Machines, Other Equipment, Word Processing, Benefits and Limitations.

Punched Card Data Processing Systems
Development, The Punched Card, Punched Card Machines, Benefits and Limitations.

Summary

Key Terms and Concepts

Assignments

1

Introduction to Data Processing

Purpose of the Chapter

To promote a basic understanding of data processing systems by analyzing:

1. The fundamental concepts of data, information, data processing systems, information systems, and the functions of data processing,
2. The development, components, benefits and limitations of manual, mechanical, and punched card data processing systems.

INTRODUCTION

Terms such as "data processing systems" and "computer systems" can easily evoke images of mysterious, complicated and technically sophisticated activities. Understanding the concepts behind such activities would seem to be a difficult task. Nothing could be further from the truth. For as you begin to read these opening lines of the first chapter, you are engaged in data processing! In fact, several observations could be made concerning your present book-reading activity.

1. You are gathering *data*.
2. You are storing *information*.
3. You are engaged in *data processing*.
4. You are a *data processing system*.
5. You are part of an *information system*.

3

The purpose of this chapter is to begin to explain the fundamental concepts that underlie such observations. These concepts are essential to an understanding of the present and future uses of the computer. Such an understanding can be acquired without an extensive technical background. Computers, data processing, and information systems will be revealed in this book as important, exciting, but understandable tools that have become essential to the operation and management of modern business firms and other organizations.

Data versus Information

The word "data" is the plural of "datum," though "data" is commonly used as both the singular and plural forms. Data can be defined as any fact, observation, assumption, or occurrence. Data can take the form of numerical or alphabetical characters or special symbols. It can also take forms such as lines on graphs, photographs of phenomenon, or electronic impulses displayed on a cathode ray tube.

The terms "data" and "information" are often used interchangeably. However, a distinction should be made between the two. Data should be viewed as the raw material which is *processed* into the finished product of information. Information can be defined as data that has been transformed into a meaningful and useful form for specific human beings. In some cases data may not require processing before constituting information for a human user. However, data is usually not useful until it has been subjected to a process where its form is manipulated and organized and its content is analyzed and evaluated. Then it becomes information.

What is the difference between data and information?

382436, that's data.

38–24–36, that's information.[1]

Data Processing

The previous sentences mentioned the processing of data to transform it into information. This can be used as a definition of the term "data processing." Data processing can also be defined as any action which makes data usable and meaningful, i.e., transforms data into information. Thus, your reading of this text is one type of data processing. Your eyes are transmitting the *data* of letters and words

---

[1] Charles Wadsworth, *The Orlando* (Fla.) *Sentinel* (April 12, 1971), p. 6.

to your brain which transforms these images into *information* by organizing and evaluating them and storing them for later use.

Data Processing Systems

The activity of data processing can be viewed as a *"system."* A *system* can be defined as *a group of interrelated components that seeks the attainment of a common goal by accepting inputs and producing outputs in an organized process.* Thus, a manufacturing system accepts raw materials as inputs and produces finished goods as output. A *data ·processing system* can be viewed as *a system which accepts data as input and processes it into information as output.* It is in this context that you as a reader of this book are a data processing system. See Figure 1–1.

There are many kinds of data processing systems. They range from a solitary human data processing system to large sophisticated systems utilizing electronic computers. Data processing is classified as *manual data processing* when it uses such simple tools as paper, pencils, and filing cabinets. *Mechanical data processing* utilizes mechanical devices such as typewriters, calculating machines, and bookkeeping machines. Frequently, however, all nonautomatic data processing is classified as manual data processing.

Automatic data processing (ADP) is a term used to identify the use of machines which automatically perform most of the functions of data processing. If this is done by the use of electromechanical machines utilizing punched cards, the term *punched card data processing* is used. This type of data processing is also known as *Electric*

FIGURE 1–1

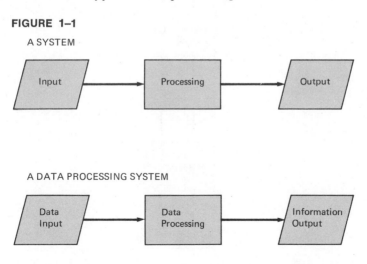

A SYSTEM

A DATA PROCESSING SYSTEM

Accounting Machine (EAM), *Unit Record, Electromechanical,* or *Tabulating Machine* data processing. Finally, *the use of electronic computers to process data automatically* is defined as *Electronic Data Processing* or EDP.

Information Systems

The terms "data processing system" and "information system" are often used interchangeably. However, there is a basis for a distinction between the two terms. An *information system* can be defined as *a system which collects and processes data and disseminates information in an organization.* An information system may utilize several kinds of data processing systems as subsystems in order to collect and process data and disseminate information. (*When a system is a component of a larger system it is called a "subsystem."*)

FIGURE 1–2

A Simplified Marketing Information System

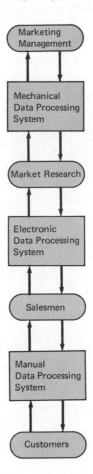

An information system is *organization* and *application* oriented, i.e., *management* information system, *business* information system, *marketing* information system, etc. A data processing system is hardware oriented, i.e., a *manual* data processing system, an *electronic* data processing system, etc. For example, the reader of this book can be considered as one of the *manual* data processing systems that make up an *education* information system.

Figure 1–2 shows a simplified marketing information system as an example of one of the information systems of a business firm. The marketing information system is designed to collect and disseminate information that is necessary for the marketing function of the business. It is evident that the marketing information system of Figure 1–2 is heavily dependent on manual and mechanical data processing systems. If information was not being collected and disseminated adequately, this information system might require a complete redesign, as well as a *conversion* of its manual and mechanical data processing subsystems to EDP. The various information systems of a business firm such as the financial, production, and marketing information systems are analyzed in Part Four of this book.

DATA PROCESSING FUNCTIONS AND ACTIVITIES

Regardless of the type of equipment used, all data processing systems include the performance of certain common functions and activities. Data processing activities can be grouped under the three basic system components of input, processing, and output. They can then be consolidated into the five main functions of collection, conversion, manipulation, storage, and communication. See Figure 1–3.

FIGURE 1–3

Data Processing Functions and Activities

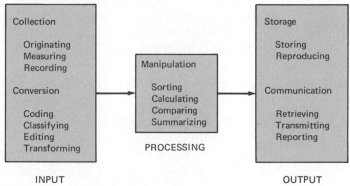

Collection

Data is *originated* as events, transactions, and other phenomena occur and are observed. The observations may take the form of a *measurement* or some other representation of the phenomenon. The data is then *recorded* in a tangible form on a data "medium" such as written *source documents* (sales slips, checks and invoices), or other more machine-usable "media" such as punched cards or magnetic tape. (A "data medium" is a tangible object or device on which data can be recorded.) The data processing function of *data collection* is frequently referred to as *data capture*.

Conversion

Once data is collected, it is frequently converted from its original form to a form that is more suitable for processing. This may involve *coding* the data by assigning identification codes that consist of numbers, letters, special characters, or a combination of these. Thus, a particular person could be represented by a *numeric* code, a social security number such as *575–34–3473;* his academic performance by an *alphabetic* code, the letter grade *A;* his automobile by an alphanumeric code, the automobile license number *CJD–682;* and the amount of money in his possession by a code using both numbers and the special characters of the dollar sign and the decimal point, *$1.42.*

Coding data is particularly useful when data requires *classifying,* i.e., arranging data into groups or classes with like characteristics. For example, sales data may be classified according to customer, salesman, and product. A business firm could assign numerical or alphabetical codes to each customer, salesman, and product. Sales data for a particular time period could then be more easily grouped or "classified" by the customer, salesman, or product involved.

The *editing* activity consists of checking the data for completeness and correctness. The objective of editing is to insure that the collection and conversion of data is done correctly.

The final activity of the conversion function in data processing may be the activity of *transforming* the data from one data medium to another. For example, the data may be transformed from written notations on a sales invoice into holes in a punched card, then transformed into magnetic spots on magnetic tape, and then transformed again into electronic impulses in the circuitry of a computer.

Manipulation

After data is collected and converted it is then ready for the manipulation function in which data is processed into information. First of all, data is "put in order" in the *sorting* activity. This may involve arranging the data in a predetermined sequence or order and grouping the data into several classifications. Sorting may also involve both *merging* data from several classifications into a larger classification or *extraction* where a particular group of data is selected out of a larger data classification. For example, sales data could first be segregated by product classification; within each product classification, sales data could be grouped by customer; the customer groupings of sales data could then be sorted into an alphabetical order.

The data processing activity of *calculating* refers to the manipulation of data by mathematical processes and the creation of new data. For example, multiplying the dollar amount of a sale by a discount percentage would produce a sales discount amount. The *comparing* activity performs comparisons on data in order to discover meaningful facts and relationships. For example, sales data may be analyzed in order to discover whether any of the sales made during a period exceed a certain dollar amount and thus qualify for a volume discount or whether any salesman has failed to make the required minimum amount of sales during a period. The *summarizing* activity condenses data by counting or accumulating totals of the data in a classification or by selecting strategic data from the mass of data being processed. For example, the summarizing activity may be designed to provide a general manager the sales totals by major product line, the sales manager with sales totals by individual salesmen as well as by product line, and a salesman with sales data by customer as well as by product line.

Storage

The output component of any data processing system can be divided into *storage* and *communication* functions. Data and information collected and used by the data processing system is frequently stored for future use. Data may be stored for only a few seconds in a computer system before being retrieved for further processing, or it may be stored for years on microfilm or paper documents. The storing activity includes the concept of storing data and information in an organized manner in order to facilitate the retrieval activity. Another aspect of the storage function is the *reproducing* of data. Data may be stored by simply reproducing or copying the data so that several copies of the data medium are produced. For example, duplicate copies of punched cards may be made. One set of punched cards is then returned to the data processing system for further processing while the duplicate set is used for data storage.

Communication

The final data processing function is *communication*. It involves the transfer of data and information produced by the data processing system to the prospective users of such information or to another data processing system. The *retrieving* activity involves the recovery of stored data and information. The *transmission* activity involves the movement of data or information from one location to another so that it may be conveyed to its ultimate user or introduced as input into another data processing system. The *reporting* activity involves furnishing information produced by the data processing system to the ultimate users of this information. The information may be reported in the form of printed documents such as invoices, statements, and printed reports of all kinds. Information can also be reported in graphic form on charts, maps, and pictures. The reporting activity can also be accomplished by displaying information in visual form on visual display devices such as cathode ray tubes, or in an audible form by word of mouth or by computer audio-response units.

Figure 1–4 summarizes important devices and methods used to perform the data processing functions of collection, conversion, manipulation, storage, and communication in the four major types of data processing systems. We will briefly analyze manual, mechanical, and punched card data processing systems in the remainder of this chapter. The fundamentals of electronic data processing will be discussed in Chapter Three.

MANUAL DATA PROCESSING SYSTEMS

Development

Manual data processing has existed as long as man has walked this planet. It continues to exist today in every organization and is a major form of data processing for many small business firms. The earliest methods of manual data processing included the use of fingers,

FIGURE 1-4

Types of Data Processing Systems

Type of data processing system	Data processing functions—selected methods and devices				
	Collection	Conversion	Manipulation	Storage	Communication
Manual............	Human observation Written records	Manual rewriting, editing, and posting Ledger card Pegboard	Human brain Written Calculations and analysis Abacus Slide rule	Human brain Written records Ledger card Filing cabinets Carbon paper	Human voice Written reports Chalkboard
Mechanical.........	Typewriter Cash register	Bookkeeping machines Cash register Typewritten ledger card	Adding machine Calculator Bookkeeping machines Cash register	Typewritten records Motorized files Microfilm Duplicating machines	Typewritten documents Bookkeeping machines
Punched Card......	Typewriter Cash register Prepunched Cards	Punched cards Paper tape Card and tape punch machines	Card sorter Card collator Electrical accounting machine Card calculator	Punched cards Paper tape Card reproducer	Machine printed documents Card interpreter
Electronic.........	Direct-access terminals Punched card, Magnetic, and optical character readers	Punched cards Paper tape Magnetic tape Card and tape punch machines Key to tape machines	Electronic digital computer	Magnetic core, disks, drums, cards, and tapes Semiconductor storage circuitry	Online terminals: visual display, audio-response and typewriter High-speed printers

stones and sticks for counting, and knots on a string, scratches on a rock, or notches in a stick as recordkeeping devices. The Babylonians wrote on clay tablets with a sharp stick, while the ancient Egyptians developed written records on papyrus using a sharp-pointed reed as a pen and organic dyes for ink. The earliest form of manual calculating device was the abacus. The use of pebbles or rods laid out on a lined or grooved board were early forms of the abacus and were utilized for thousands of years in many civilizations. The abacus in its present form originated in China and is still a widely used calculator. See Figure 1–5.

FIGURE 1–5

Abacus

From an original in the IBM Corporation Antique Calculator Collection.

Manual data processing techniques continued to progress over the centuries due to developments such as Arabic numerals, the decimal system, the manufacture of paper, the printing press, the slide rule, and double-entry bookkeeping, to name a few. Manual data processing systems of today employ tools and materials that have been used for several hundred years, such as pencils, pens, rulers, paper record-keeping forms, folders, and filing cabinets. More recent developments which have increased the efficiency of manual data processing have been tools and materials such as multiple copy forms, carbon paper, accounting pegboards, and edge-notched cards.

Benefits and Limitations

The information systems of any organization can include manual data processing systems if information requirements are simple and the amount of data to be processed is limited. As information requirements become more complex and the volume of data increases, mechanical data processing systems become more efficient and economical. In manual data processing, transactions can be recorded easily in a human-readable form, and changes and corrections to such systems can easily be made. Manual data processing is also quite inexpensive at low volumes. The major limitations of manual data processing include its inability to handle large volumes of work and its reliance on many cumbersome and tedious methods. It is also more susceptible to error and slower than other data processing methods because it depends on human effort for most data processing operations.

MECHANICAL DATA PROCESSING SYSTEMS

Development

Mechanical data processing is the term used to describe a data processing system that uses a combination of manual procedures and mechanical equipment to carry out the basic functions of data processing. The use of machinery to perform arithmetic operations is frequently attributed to Blaise Pascal of France and Gottfried Leibnitz of Germany for their development of the adding machine and the calculating machine, respectively, in the seventeenth century. However, the inventions of Pascal and Leibnitz incorporated some ideas similar to those used in the clockwork mechanism and the odometer, both of which had been developed as far back as the Greek and Roman civilizations. It must also be recognized that the calculators of Pascal and Leibnitz and other early mechanical data processing devices were not reliable machines. The contributions of many men were necessary during the next two centuries before practical, working data processing machines were developed.

Mechanical data processing is widely used today in both large and small business firms. The major machines used in mechanical data processing are typewriters, adding machines, calculators, cash registers, bookkeeping machines, and duplicating machines. When these devices were first introduced, they were manually powered, but later models driven by electric motors were developed. Electronic models were then developed which contained solid state electronic components to carry out many of their functions. However, these devices continue to require considerable human assistance such as the manual entry of data and operating instructions. More recently, developments have occurred which enable several machines to operate more automatically. Thus, typewriters, calculators, and bookkeeping machines have been developed which utilize punched cards, paper tape, and magnetic cards and tape for the input of data and instructions and the output of information. Such advances have blurred the distinction between mechanical, punched card, and electronic data processing equipment. Developments in the technology and application of machines that are used in mechanical data processing systems are summarized below.

Typing Equipment

Manual and electric typewriters are the most widely used office machines and greatly increased the speed and legibility of recording data and reporting information. Automatic typewriters are a recent development which allow letters and documents to be typed without human intervention. The automatic typing process can be controlled by paper tape, punched cards, magnetic tape, or magnetic cards. Automatic typewriters can also produce these paper and magnetic media as by-products of the typing process. The tape or cards can

FIGURE 1–6

Magnetic Tape "Selectric" Typewriter

Courtesy International Business Machines Corporation.

then be filed for future automatic typing of documents. Punched paper tape and cards direct the typing of a document according to a predetermined format, stopping the typewriter at predetermined places when necessary for the manual insertion of variable data. Magnetic tape and cards have the additional capability of allowing error correction, text revision, and insertion of variable information and then automatically adjusting word spacing and line endings. Automatic typewriter systems are used to increase the speed of typing and retyping individual letters and documents, or in the automatic typing of a large volume of letters and documents containing much repetitive information. See Figure 1–6.

Calculating Machines

Manual and electric adding machines and calculators and the more recent electronic calculator are widely used data processing devices. The familiar cash register is an example of a special purpose adding machine. Calculating machines are used to carry out arithmetical operations and print the results on paper tape or display them electronically. Electronic calculators have no moving parts and operate silently at almost instantaneous speeds. The size of these calculators has been greatly reduced by the use of microminiature electronic circuitry. Electronic calculators provide automatic storage for constants and intermediate results that need to be retrieved periodically during a computation process. See Figure 1–7.

Electronic calculators that can read data and operating instructions from various media, store data and instructions internally, and then produce several types of output are the most recent developments in electronic calculators. Such calculators no longer have all of their mathematical capabilities "hardwired" into their circuitry. Instead, they can be "programmed" to carry out several types of mathematical calculations by the insertion and storage of different types of instructions within the machines. These developments have essentially erased the difference between some programmable electronic calculators and the so-called "minicomputer." Some have called the programmable electronic calculator a "subcomputer."

Bookkeeping Machines

Bookkeeping machine systems include several types of equipment also known as accounting, posting, and billing machines. These machines were designed to prepare accounting documents such as ledgers

FIGURE 1–7

Programmable Electronic Calculator (tiny "magnetic cards" can be inserted into the machine for performing complex calculations)

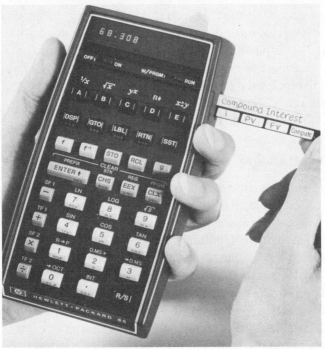

Courtesy Hewlett-Packard

and statements. They can be considered as special purpose machines which combine features of adding machines, calculators, and typewriters in order to perform specific accounting applications such as billing, accounts receivable, and payroll. Electronic bookkeeping machines utilizing features found in the electronic calculator, electronic programmable calculator (and even the electronic computer) are a recent development. These machines not only have magnetic circuitry for calculations and storage but may have magnetic core or magnetic disk storage and may utilize paper tape, punched cards, or magnetic striped ledger cards for input and output. Magnetic ink or tape stripes on the back of a ledger card allow an electronic bookkeeping machine to automatically "read" the account number and account balance from the magnetic stripe, type current transactions and the computed new account balance on the front of the ledger card, and magnetically record the new account balance on the mag-

FIGURE 1–8

Accounting Machine with Electronic Computer Characteristics

Courtesy International Business Machines Corporation.

netic stripe. As in the case of the electronic programmable calculators, these developments have produced a breed of electronic bookkeeping machines that have many of the characteristics of electronic mini-computers. See Figure 1–8.

Other Equipment

Other types of equipment that can be used in mechanical data processing are summarized below.

1. Dictating machines utilizing magnetic belts, cassettes, and other recording media.
2. Copying machines and duplicating machines such as the Xerox machine and the mimeograph machine.
3. Microfilm equipment which can store a microfilm copy of a document, display a full-size image on a screen, and prepare a full-sized paper copy of a microfilmed document.
4. Addressing and postage machines which can automatically address, stamp, and sort documents.

5. Filing systems. The filing cabinets of manual data processing have been mechanized for organizations that must store large volumes of documents. Motor-driven files of several types are available.

Word Processing

The term "word processing" has come into use to describe the automated and centralized typing, addressing, dictating, copying, and filing systems that are part of the latest developments in mechanical data processing. Word processing depends heavily on remote, pooled "dial dictation" by which users may dial a central transcription service and dictate into a recorder by telephone. Word processing can be considered as the input and output components of a mechanical data processing system, with calculating machines and bookkeeping machines making up the processing component.

Benefits and Limitations

Mechanical data processing is superior to manual methods from the standpoint of speed, accuracy, and legibility. However, mechanical data processing systems are more expensive and less flexible than manual data processing systems. Since mechanical methods require manual keyboard entry of data and human intervention during the data processing cycle, they are still quite vulnerable to human error.

PUNCHED CARD DATA PROCESSING SYSTEMS

Development

Punched card data processing refers to the use of electromechanical machines for the processing of data recorded on punched paper cards. Punched cards were developed in France during the eighteenth century to automatically control textile weaving equipment. However, their use in data processing originated with the work of the statistician, Dr. Herman Hollerith, during the 1880s. Dr. Hollerith was hired by the U.S. Bureau of the Census to develop new ways to process census data. The 1880 census report had not been completed until 1887, and it became evident that the processing of the 1890 census might not be completed before the 1900 census would get underway. Dr. Hollerith responded by developing a punched paper card for the recording of data, a hand-operated card punch, a sorting box, and a tabulator which allowed the 1890 census to be completed in less than three years.

Dr. Hollerith's work at the Census Bureau was supplemented by the work of James Powers who developed punched card machines that were used in the 1910 census. Both men left the Census Bureau to found business firms to produce their machines. The International Business Machines Corporation (IBM) is a descendant of Dr. Hollerith's Tabulating Machine Company, while the UNIVAC division of the Sperry Rand Corporation is descended from the Powers Accounting Machine Company founded by James Powers. Improvements in punched card machines led to their widespread use for business and government applications in the late 1930s. They continued to be the major method for large-scale data processing in business and government until the late 1950s, when they were displaced by the development of electronic computers. Punched card equipment is now used as auxiliary equipment to support computer systems that utilize punched cards as a primary data medium.

The Punched Card

The punched card used in punched card machines and in many computer applications is the 80-column punched card also known as the "IBM" card or "Hollerith" card. Up to 80 individual data elements such as alphabetic, numeric, and special characters can be punched into such a card using the Hollerith code shown in Figure 1–9. Notice

FIGURE 1–9

Punched Card Coding: 80-Column Card

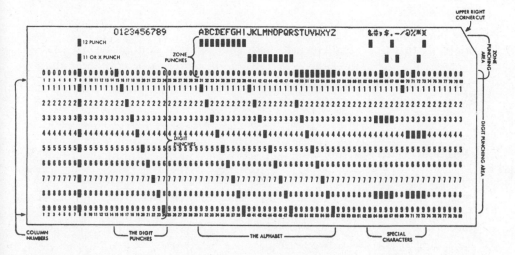

that numeric characters require the punching of only a single hole, while alphabetic and special characters require the punching of two or three holes in a column.

Punched card equipment made by UNIVAC and its predecessor, Remington Rand, utilized punched cards with 90 columns and punched round rather than rectangular holes. However, these machines were never widely used and their production was discontinued by UNIVAC in 1966. In 1969 IBM announced a new small business computer called the System/3 which utilizes a 96-column punched card. See Figure 1–10. Data is punched as round holes in three sec-

FIGURE 1–10

Punched Card Coding: 96-Column Card

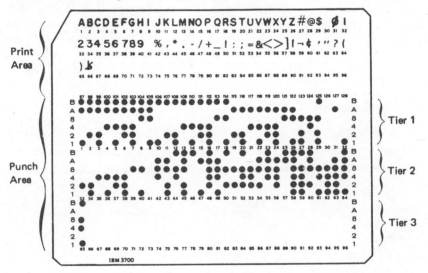

tions of this new smaller card, with each section containing 32 characters. The card uses the EBCDIC code which is a computer data code explained in the next chapter. The computer equipment which utilizes this card is discussed in Chapter Four.

Punched Card Machines

The electromechanical machines used in punched card data processing are shown in Figure 1–11. The following is a description of the functions of these machines.

FIGURE 1–11

Punched Card Data Processing Equipment

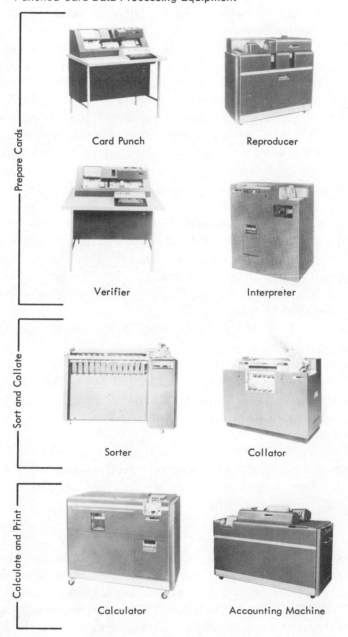

Courtesy of International Business Machines Corporation

Card punch.   This is also known as a keypunch. This machine records data by punching holes in the cards by the use of a keyboard similar to that of a typewriter. "Keypunching" is another name for the card punching operation.

Verifier.   This is similar in appearance to the card punch, but instead of punching holes it electrically senses whether a discrepancy exists between the keys being depressed and the holes punched in the card during the keypunching operation. If a discrepancy exists, a hole is punched in the top of the card above the incorrectly punched column. A hole is punched in the right edge of error-free cards.

Sorter.   This sorts punched cards by sensing the holes in appropriate columns and depositing the cards in the sorter pockets. Cards can be sorted into numeric or alphabetic sequence, into groups, or specific cards can be selected.

Reproducer.   This punches duplicate cards from previously punched cards. All or part of the data on a punched card can be reproduced into one or more cards. Some models can read graphite markings of "mark-sense" cards and produce punched cards. It can also be connected by cable to the accounting machine in order to produce punched card output.

Interpreter.   This reads the data punched into a card and then prints the data onto the card.

Collator.   This merges two sets of punched cards into a desired sequence and can also separate matched and unmatched cards.

Calculator.   This performs addition, subtraction, multiplication and division from data in punched cards and then punches the results into the cards.

The accounting machine.   This is the primary processing unit of most punched card data processing systems. It is also called a tabulator or tab machine. The accounting machine accepts data from punched cards as input, processes the data through addition, subtraction, comparison, and storage operations, and prints reports in various formats as output.

Accounting machines and other electromechanical punched card equipment read the data from punched cards when electrical impulses are generated by the action of metal brushes making electrical contact through the holes punched in a card. The input, processing, and output operations of most punched card machines are controlled by an externally wired removable control panel. See Figure 1–12. Thus, these machines can be "programmed" to perform various data processing applications by different wiring arrangements. Keypunch ma-

FIGURE 1–12

Wired Control Panel for an Accounting Machine

Courtesy International Business Machines Corporation

chines can perform automatic punching and spacing under the control of a "program card" mounted on a small control drum in the machine.

Benefits and Limitations

Speed, accuracy, and the ability to handle large volumes of data are the main advantages of punched card data processing over manual and mechanical methods. Punched card equipment became highly popular for data processing applications with a large volume of repetitive transactions. These benefits are the direct result of the versatility of the punched card as a data input, output, and storage medium, and the automatic nature of the punched card machine. Once data has been accurately punched into a card it can be processed repeatedly in a variety of applications. Unlike manual and mechanical methods, data does not have to be recaptured and reconverted each time it needs to be used. Another benefit of punched card data processing stems from the use of the punched card as a "unit record." In many punched card applications, the data from only one transaction is recorded on a card. This greatly facilitates the ability to produce many types of statistical and business reports since single transactions can be easily grouped or segregated automatically. Thus, punched card data processing is sometimes called "unit record" data processing.

Punched card data processing with electromechanical equipment does have several important limitations. These are especially apparent when compared to the characteristics of electronic data processing. Punched card data processing has speed, accuracy, and flexibility limitations due to a variety of factors. Several machines must be used because each machine performs a special function. Cards must be carried from one machine to the other during the processing operation. Operation by control panel provides limited flexibility. Speeds are limited because of the electromechanical nature of the equipment used, and internal storage of data is limited. Because of these limitations, electronic computer systems have gradually replaced most punched card machine systems.

SUMMARY

Data is the raw material which is transformed into meaningful information by data processing systems. A system is a group of interrelated components that seeks the attainment of a common goal by accepting inputs and producing outputs in an organized process. A data processing system accepts data as input and processes it into information as output. The four major types of data processing systems are manual, mechanical, punched card, and electronic data processing systems. Various data processing systems may be subsystems of an information system, which is a system that collects and disseminates information in an organization. All data processing systems perform common functions and activities. Data is first collected, then converted to a form that is suitable for processing. Then it is manipulated or converted into information, stored for future use, or communicated to its ultimate user.

Manual data processing methods were developed by ancient civilizations and continue to be used today. Mechanical data processing systems, which utilize mechanical, electrical, and electronic machines to process data, continue to be widely used in both large and small businesses. The development of programmable electronical calculating machines, automatic typewriters, and other machines which operate in an automatic fashion, have blurred the distinction between mechanical and electronic data processing. Punched card data processing is the use of electromechanical machines for the processing of data recorded on punched cards. Punched card machines were widely used for data processing until the 1960s when they were displaced by the electronic computer. Punched card equipment is now used as auxiliary equipment in computer systems that utilize punched cards as a primary data medium.

The benefits and limitations of each type of data processing system described in this chapter are directly related to the volume and complexity of the information requirements of an organization. As information requirements become more complex and the volume of data increases, the limitations of each type of data processing system begins to exceed the benefits of its use. Therefore, electronic data processing systems are used by all organizations with complex or high-volume data processing requirements.

KEY TERMS AND CONCEPTS

Data, 4

Information, 4

Data processing, 4

System, 5

Data processing system, 5

Information system, 6–7

Data processing functions, 7–10

Manual data processing, 5, 10–12

Mechanical data processing, 5, 11–14

Word processing, 18

Punched card data processing, 5, 11, 18

Electronic data processing, 6, 11

ASSIGNMENTS

1. Test your understanding of the chapter material by reviewing the *purpose, outline, summary,* and *key terms and concepts* of this chapter. Are you confident that you have attained a basic understanding of the major concepts of the chapter? If not, reread the appropriate material as indicated by the page numbers after each key term and concept.

2. Give an example to illustrate the difference between data and information.

3. "An information system may utilize several kinds of data processing systems as subsystems in order to collect and process data and disseminate information." Explain this statement and give an example to illustrate your answer.

4. Trace the processing of a specific item of data through each of the five functions of data processing.

5. Briefly define manual, mechanical, punched card and electronic data processing.

6. Discuss the benefits and limitations of:
    a. Manual data processing
    b. Mechanical data processing
    c. Punched card data processing

Chapter Outline

Purpose of the Chapter

What Is a Computer?

Computer Characteristics
  Electronic, Speed, Internal Storage, Stored Program,
    Arithmetic and Logic Ability, Program Modification,
    Automated Input/Output.

Computer Classifications
  Type: Analog, Digital, Hybrid; Purpose: Special, General,
    Scientific, Business; Size: Mini, Small, Medium, Large,
    Super; Generation: First, Second, Third, Fourth

The Computer System
  Input, Processing, Storage, Arithmetic-logic, Control,
    Output

How Computers Execute Instructions
  Computer Instructions and Cycles, The Instruction Cycle,
    The Execution Cycle, More Computer Fundamentals

Data Representation
  Binary Number System, Other Number Systems,
    Computer Codes

Data Organization
  Common Data Elements, Computer Data Elements, Other
    Data Organization Concepts

Summary

Key Terms and Concepts

Assignments

2

Computer
Fundamentals

Purpose of the Chapter

To promote a basic understanding of the electronic computer by analyzing:

1. The fundamental properties and types of computers,
2. The functions and components of a computer system,
3. The representation and organization of data in computers and data processing.

WHAT IS A COMPUTER?

There are several varieties of computers and each has a variety of characteristics. However, in electronic data processing, in the computer industry, and in the popular literature the term "computer" refers almost exclusively to a particular type of computer: the "electronic, digital, stored program, general purpose computer." Such computers are used for almost all business applications and are the subject of this book. We can therefore define a computer as "an electronic device that has the ability to accept data, internally store and execute a program of instructions, perform mathematical and logical operations on data, and report the results." Let us examine this definition and the type of computer it describes in order that we can clearly understand its important characteristics.

COMPUTER CHARACTERISTICS

Electronic

The modern computer is an electronic device, while early computers were electromechanical machines. The use of electronic circuitry provides modern computers with fantastic speed and computational abilities. The electronic components of computer systems will be explored in subsequent sections of this book.

Speed

The internal operating speed of electronic computers is often measured by their "storage cycle time," also called the "access cycle time" of computer storage. This is the time necessary for a computer to recall information from one storage position. Storage cycle times are now being measured in the "microsecond" (millionths of a second) and "nanosecond" (billionth of a second) range, with the "picosecond" (trillionth of a second) speed being attained by a few computers. Such speeds seem almost incomprehensible. For example, an average person taking one step each nanosecond would circle the earth about twenty times in one second! Computers operating at such speeds can process millions of instructions per second. See Figure 2–1.

Internal Storage

The computer can store both data and instructions internally in its "memory." This internal storage enables the computer to "remember" the details of many assignments and to proceed from one assignment to another automatically, since it can retain data and instructions until needed. Computer storage is subdivided into many small sections called "storage positions" or "storage locations." Each position of storage has a specific numerical location called an "address" so that data stored in its contents can be readily located by the computer. Each position of storage can usually hold one alphabetical or special, character or two numeric digits. The internal storage of many modern computers consists of magnetic "cores" (which are tiny doughnut-shaped metallic rings) or semiconductor circuits. Groups of these cores or circuits make up each position of storage.

The capacity of computer storage is based on the number of storage positions that it contains. This is usually expressed in terms of the

FIGURE 2–1

Speed and Power of the Computer

In the computer, the basic operations can be done within the order of a

NANOSECOND

One thousandth of a millionth of a second.

Within the half second it takes this spilled coffee to reach the floor, a fairly large computer could —

(given the information in magnetic form)

Debit 2000 checks to 300 different bank accounts,

and *examine the electrocardiograms of 100 patients and alert a physician to possible trouble,*

and *score 150,000 answers on 3000 examinations and evaluate the effectiveness of the questions,*

and *figure the payroll for a company with a thousand employees.*

and a few other chores.

Courtesy International Business Machines Corporation.

number of characters or the number of "bytes" that can be stored. (A byte is a unit of data which will be explained in a later section.) The letter "K," an abbreviation of the word "kilo," is used to describe 1,000 positions of storage. Thus, computer storage capacities of 16,000 or 64,000 positions, for example, would be described at 16 K or 64 K memories. Actually, computer storage usually comes in multiples of 1,024 storage positions, so 16 K is really 16,384 and 64 K is really 65,536 storage positions, but these differences are frequently disregarded in order to simplify descriptions of storage capacity.[1]

Stored Program

The ability of the computer to store its operating instructions internally (the computer program) allows the computer to process data automatically, that is, without continual human intervention. The stored program concept differentiates modern computers from most calculators and early computers.

Arithmetic and Logic Ability

The computer can perform the mathematical operations of addition, subtraction, multiplication and division, can identify whether a number is positive, negative, or equal to zero, and can compare two numbers to determine which is higher than, equal to, or lower than the other. The ability of the computer to make comparisons gives it a logic capability, for it can change from one set of operating instructions to another based on the results of a comparison.

Program Modification

The logical ability of the computer allows it to change or modify its own program based on conditions encountered during processing. With suitable programming, a computer can therefore "learn" from past operations and modify its program accordingly. The logic, program modification, and stored program capabilities of the computer are important characteristics that differentiate the computer from most calculators.

Automated Input/Output

Most computer systems automatically control the flow of data and instructions into the computer from various input devices. This contrasts with the manual keying of data and instructions of most calculators. Most computers can also control a wide variety of output and storage devices.

---

[1] The larger storage capacity of recent computers has resulted in the use of the term "megabyte" to describe one million bytes of storage.

COMPUTER CLASSIFICATIONS

Differences in certain computer characteristics have caused the development of several broad classifications of computers. Frequently used classifications segregate computers by type, by purpose, by size, and by generation.

Type

There are two basic types of computers, the analog and the digital, along with a third type, the hybrid computer, which combines analog and digital capabilities. The basic difference between the analog and the digital computer is that the digital computer *counts* discrete units while the analog computer *measures* continuous physical magnitudes. Thus, a digital computer will perform arithmetic operations and comparisons on numbers (digits) and other characters that have been numerically coded. The analog computer, on the other hand, performs arithmetic operations and comparisons by measuring changes in a continuous physical phenomenon such as electronic voltage, which represents, or is "analogous" to, the numerical values of the data being processed.

✓ *Analog computers.* A slide rule is an example of an analog computing device. The numbers in a mathematical problem are represented by the physical quantity of length. Since the length of the slide rule is marked in a logarithmic scale, mathematical operations can be performed by moving the parts of the slide rule properly. An electronic analog computer converts data into electronic voltages and performs mathematical operations by measuring changes in voltage. Analog computers are typically used to process the data arising from an ongoing physical process, such as scientific or engineering experiments and manufacturing processes and are also used in military weapons systems. For example, the temperature changes of a chemical process can be converted by the analog computer into variations in electronic voltage and mathematically analyzed. The results of the processing could be displayed on dials, graphs, or TV screens or be used to initiate changes in the chemical process.

The major advantage of the analog computer is its ability to analyze the data generated by an ongoing physical process immediately without further conversion to an internal operating code as is necessary for digital computers. Its major disadvantage is that it furnishes only approximate answers, for its accuracy is limited by its ability to accurately represent and measure physical data. For example, it is difficult to maintain precise voltages for long periods of time in an electronic analog computer. Therefore, its accuracy suffers. Going back to our example of the slide rule, most good slide rules are accurate only to three significant digits. Such accuracy is sufficient for many problems; however, many others demand the absolute accuracy that only a digital computing device can provide. Since the analog computer observes and processes data in one operation it has no need for internal storage. This contributes to its great processing speed, but the lack of memory and the necessity for an "external program" of wiring, switches, and control panels severely limits the flexibility of the analog computer.

Digital computers.   The number of digital computers greatly exceeds the number of analog computers. The accuracy of the digital computer is limited only by the size of its memory and the preciseness of its data input. The digital computer can process both numerical and alphabetic data, has internal storage, and has great flexibility because of its stored program characteristic. Digital computers can be used for business and scientific data processing, industrial process control, and many other applications.

Hybrid computers.   The third type of computer mentioned, the "hybrid" computer, combines both analog and digital capabilities in a single computer. This type of computer is used for special applications where data may be collected and measured in analog form and then further analyzed by digital processing.

Purpose

Digital computers can be classified as either special purpose or general purpose computers. A *"special purpose"* computer is designed to process one or more specific applications. Some of these computers are so specialized that part or all of their operating instructions are built into their electronic circuitry. Special purpose computers have been built for both military and civilian applications such as aircraft and submarine navigation, aircraft, missile, and satellite tracking, airline reservation systems, industrial process control, and data communications.

A *"general purpose"* computer is designed to process a wide variety of applications. The applications that can be processed are limited only by the size, speed, and the types of input and output devices of a particular computer. A variety of applications can be processed merely by changing the program of instructions stored in the machine. The versatility of the general purpose computer is accomplished with some sacrifice of speed and efficiency, though this is more than offset by its ability to handle a wide range of applications.

The term "general purpose" computer has taken on a new dimension with the arrival of the third and fourth generation of computers. Computer manufacturers are claiming to have designed general purpose or "multipurpose" computers as opposed to "business" computers or "scientific" computers. For example, the IBM System/360 and System/370 computers have been designed as general purpose computers as opposed to the second generation IBM 1401 computer, which was a business computer, and the IBM 1620, which was a scientific computer.

Scientific computers were designed for the high-speed processing of numerical data involving complex mathematical calculations. Scientific applications typically require a large amount of computations but involve a small volume of input and output data. Thus scientific computers were designed with limited input, output and storage capabilities but had advanced computational power. They were, therefore, capable of high-speed mathematical analyses of numerical data but were inefficient if required to process large volumes of alphabetic input. *Business computers,* on the other hand, were designed to handle the large volumes of numeric and alphabetic data that is required by payroll, billing, inventory and other typical business applications. Thus, business computers had extensive input, output, and storage capabilities, with less emphasis placed on high-speed numeric computation. Scientific applications could be processed on business computers and vice versa but not as efficiently. However, with some exceptions, this problem has been solved with the recent development of truly general purpose computers.

Size

Computers are classified by *size,* which refers not only to their physical size but to their ability to process large volumes of data or handle large computational problems. Computers are frequently classified by size into mini, small, medium, large, and super categories. *Mini computers* are very small computers which can perform all of the functions of a general purpose computer but are limited by their small memories and restricted input/output capabilities. Minicomputers are quite versatile. They are being used, not only for the common business and scientific applications, but as input/output terminals for larger computer systems, as industrial process control computers, as data communications controllers, and as educational devices for computer-assisted learning. A typical minicomputer system sells for around $10,000, though prices can range substantially above and below that figure depending on memory capacity and input/output devices required. Figure 2–2 shows one of the most popular minicomputers, the PDP–8, manufactured by the Digital Equipment Corporation, currently the largest maker of minicomputers.

Small computers are larger and more versatile than minicomputers and have greater input/output and storage capabilities. These small systems are the computers that have finally dislodged electromechanical punched card equipment from even the smallest data processing installation. Punched card-oriented small computers can sell for less than $50,000 and rent for less than $1,000 a month. Magnetic tape and magnetic disk-oriented versions of the small computer are also available. Selling prices range from about $60,000 to $250,000, while monthly rentals vary from $1,200 to $5,000. Wide variations in

FIGURE 2–2

Digital Equipment Corporation PDP–8–e Minicomputer

Courtesy Digital Equipment Corporation

prices are, of course, primarily related to the amount of storage capacity and the number of input and output devices that are included in a particular system. The most popular current small computer is the IBM System/3. See Figure 2–3.

Medium-sized computers are larger, faster, and can handle more input/output and storage devices than the small computer. Selling prices range between $250,000 to $1 million, while rental charges vary between $5,000 to $25,000 per month. See Figure 2–4. *Large-scale computers* have even faster processing speeds, greater storage capacity, a wider selection of input/output devices and greater proeessing capabilities than medium-sized computers. These powerful computing systems are utilized for large and complex data processing assignments in which their ability to handle hundreds of remote input/output terminals and process many applications simultaneously is required. Monthly rentals for large-scale computer systems range from $25,000 to over $100,000, with purchase prices varying from about $1 million to over $5 million. See Figure 2–5.

The term *supercomputer* has been coined to describe a small number of extremely large computer systems that have been built. The IBM STRETCH, the UNIVAC LARC, and the CDC 3600 were

FIGURE 2–3

IBM System/3 Model 6 Small Scale Computer System

Courtesy International Business Machines Corporation

FIGURE 2–4

IBM System/370 Model 155–a Medium-scale Computer System

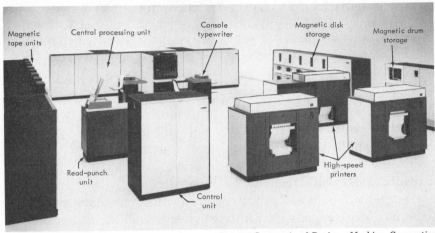

Courtesy International Business Machines Corporation

FIGURE 2–5

UNIVAC 1110 Large-scale Computer System

Courtesy UNIVAC Division of the Sperry Rand Corporation

built during the late 1950s and early 1960s, though only the CDC 3600 was a commercial success. Current supercomputers are the IBM System 370/195 and the CDC 7600. Supercomputers are frequently built under contract for a specific user, such as the Illiac IV built by Burroughs for the University of Illinois at a cost of $24 million. These massive computer systems are extremely large and fast and advance the state of the art for the entire computer industry. Rental prices for the IBM System/370 model 195 range between $165,000 to $300,-000 per month, with a purchase price ranging from $7 million to $12 million.

Generation

Computers are also categorized by describing them as either first, second, third, and currently fourth "generation" computers. These generations correspond to important advances in the development of computers. The generations of computers are frequently simplified by describing them in terms of the electronic components used in their circuitry. Thus, the *first generation* used vacuum tubes, the *second generation* employed transistors, the *third generation* used microelectronic or "integrated" circuits, while the *fourth generation* employs medium-scale and large-scale integration (LSI) technology in its electronic circuitry. However, the concept of computer generations involves more than the development of electronic circuitry, as will be shown in the next chapter.

THE COMPUTER SYSTEM

Like any system, the computer system performs the three main functions of input, processing, and output. Analysis of the processing function of a computer system reveals that it is composed of storage, arithmetic-logic, and control functions. Therefore, we can describe a computer system as being composed of input, storage, arithmetic-logic, control, and output functions. Finally, if we apply these functions to computer equipment or "hardware," we can describe a computer system as being composed of input devices, a central processing unit, storage devices, and output devices. Figure 2–6 illustrates this analysis of the functions and hardware components of a computer system. The concepts on which this diagram is based are essential to a proper understanding of the modern computer. Let us therefore examine them more closely.

FIGURE 2–6

The Computer System

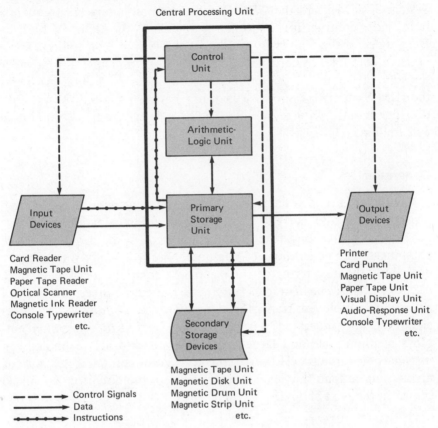

Central Processing Unit

Control Unit

Arithmetic-Logic Unit

Input Devices

Primary Storage Unit

Output Devices

Card Reader
Magnetic Tape Unit
Paper Tape Reader
Optical Scanner
Magnetic Ink Reader
Console Typewriter
etc.

Printer
Card Punch
Magnetic Tape Unit
Paper Tape Unit
Visual Display Unit
Audio-Response Unit
Console Typewriter
etc.

Secondary Storage Devices

Magnetic Tape Unit
Magnetic Disk Unit
Magnetic Drum Unit
Magnetic Strip Unit
etc.

- - - - → Control Signals
———→ Data
•—•—•→ Instructions

Input

Data and instructions are entered into the computer system in the *input* function. Data and instructions may be entered directly into the computer system (through the keyboard of an on-line terminal, for example) but, typically, must first be converted into a machine-readable input medium such as punched cards or magnetic tape. In the later case, "data preparation" equipment such as card punch machines convert data from source documents into punched cards which can then be entered into the computer system through an input device known as a card reader. Input devices convert instructions and data into electrical impulses which are then routed to the primary storage unit where they are held until needed.

Processing

The processing component of a computer system can be subdivided into storage, arithmetic-logic and control components. The primary storage unit, as well as the arithmetic-logic unit, and the control unit make up the *"central processing unit,"* the most important hardware component of any computer system. This unit is also known as the "CPU," the "central processor," or the "main frame." It is this unit that accomplishes the processing of data and controls the other parts of the system.

Storage

The storage function takes place in the *"primary storage unit"* of the CPU and in *"secondary storage"* devices. All data and instructions must be placed in the primary storage unit (also called main memory or main storage) before it can be used in processing. The primary storage unit is also used to hold data and instructions between processing steps, and after processing is completed, but before release as output. Data and instructions can be stored in *secondary storage* devices such as magnetic disk and tape units and thus greatly enlarge the storage capacity of the computer system. However, the contents of secondary storage cannot be processed without first being brought into the primary storage unit.

Arithmetic-Logic

Data held in primary storage is transferred to the *"arithmetic-logic unit"* (or ALU) whenever processing is to take place. Calculation and comparison operations occur in this unit. Depending on the application being processed, data may be transferred from storage to the arithmetic-logic unit and then returned to storage several times before processing is completed. The arithmetic-logic unit also performs such operations as shifting, moving, and temporarily storing data. Through its ability to make comparisons, it can test for various conditions during processing and then perform appropriate operations.

Control

The control arrows in Figure 2–6 should emphasize that every other component of the computer system is controlled and directed by the *"control unit."* The control unit obtains the instructions from the primary storage unit. After interpreting the instructions, the control unit transmits directions to the appropriate components of the computer system, ordering them to perform the required data processing operations. The control unit tells the input and secondary storage devices what data and instructions to read into memory, tells the arithmetic-logic unit where the data to be processed is located in memory, what operations to perform, where in memory the results are to be stored; and, finally, it directs the appropriate output devices to convert processed data into machine or human-readable output media.

Output

The function of *output* devices is to convert processed data (information) from electronic impulses into a form that is intelligible to humans or into a machine-readable form. For example, output devices such as high-speed printers produce printed reports, while card-punch units produce punched cards as output.

HOW COMPUTERS EXECUTE INSTRUCTIONS

Computer users should have a basic understanding of how a computer executes instructions. Such understanding helps users appreciate why a CPU contains special purpose circuitry and devices such as "registers" (which are small temporary storage work areas) and other more specialized circuitry such as "counters," "adders," and "decoders," which are described in Chapter Four. It should also help users appreciate modern "high-level programming languages" which have simplified the task of writing computer programs. It is no longer necessary to write computer instructions utilizing complex "machine language" coding which describes in detail each step of the computer execution process. We will discuss such programming languages in Chapter Five.

Computer Instructions and Cycles

The specific form of a computer instruction depends on the type of programming language and computer being used. However, a computer instruction usually consists of an *"operation code"* which specifies what is to be done (add, compare, read, etc.) and one or more *"operands,"* which specify the primary storage addresses of the data or the type of devices to be utilized. A fixed number of electrical pulses emitted by the CPU's timing circuitry or "electronic clock" determines the timing of each basic CPU operation. This period of time is called a *"machine cycle."* The number of machine cycles required to execute an instruction varies with the complexity of the instruction.

We will see in the next section how data and instructions are represented by the magnetic or electronic characteristics of computer storage circuitry. During each machine cycle, electrical pulses from several special purpose circuitry elements sense and interpret specific instructions and data and move them (in the form of electrical pulses) between various subunits of the CPU.

The Instruction Cycle

The execution of an instruction can be divided into two segments, the *"instruction cycle"* (I-Time) and the *"execution cycle"* (E-Time). Figure 2–7 is a simplified illustration of what happens in a CPU during the instruction cycle. At the beginning of a computer program, an *"instruction counter"* in the control unit is set to the address of the first instruction in the program. I-time begins when the instruction counter transfers the address of an instruction to an *"address register."* This instruction is "fetched" from storage and placed in a *"storage register."* The operation code portion of the instruction is transferred to an *"instruction register,"* while the operand is transferred to the

FIGURE 2–7

The Instruction Cycle

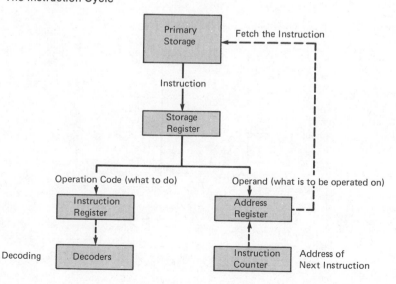

address register. The operation code is then decoded by the *"decoders"* of the control unit, which analyzes the contents of the instruction register and the address register and prepares the electronic circuitry of the CPU to carry out the required operations.

The final operation in the instruction cycle is the determination of the next instruction to be executed. Usually, the instruction counter automatically "steps" to the address of the next instruction stored in memory. Sometimes, however, a *"branch instruction"* is brought from storage whose operand indicates that the next instruction to be executed is in another part of the program. The contents of the instruction counter will then be reset to the address of this instruction, and the CPU will branch to that part of the program.

The Execution Cycle

Figure 2–8 briefly illustrates the execution cycle of a simple addition instruction. One or more machine cycles occur during E-time, depending on the instruction to be executed. The execution cycle begins when data is transferred to a storage register from the location in storage indicated by the address register. Then the operation specified by the operation code in the instruction register is performed. In this example, the data is a number which is placed in the *"adders"* of the arithmetic-logic unit and combined with a number from the *"accumulator,"* which is a register in the ALU. The resulting sum is then returned to the accumulator. The computer repeats such instruction

FIGURE 2–8

The Execution Cycle of an ADD Instruction

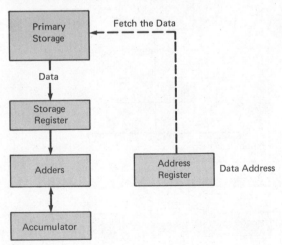

and execution cycles millions of times per second until the final instruction of a program is executed.

More Computer Fundamentals

The previous sections have given a brief but important description of the components, functions, and internal operations of a computer system. Fundamentals of the development and use of computers for electronic data processing are discussed in Chapter Three. Input, output, storage, and processing equipment and media (*computer hardware*) will be examined in detail in Chapter Four. Types of computer programs, or "software," and how each type directs the computer hardware to perform the processing of data will be discussed in Chapter Five. These chapters will emphasize that computer hardware and software are not just a collection of diverse components but are input, output, processing, storage, and control equipment and programs which can be assembled to constitute the components of modern *computer systems* and *electronic data processing systems*.

Before we can proceed with the material in subsequent chapters, we should first analyze several additional concepts which are concerned with the form in which data and instructions exist and are organized both inside and outside of the computer. These topics are known as "data representation" and "data organization."

DATA REPRESENTATION

The letters of the alphabet in this book are symbols that when properly organized or "coded" into the English language will "represent" data that you, the reader, can process into information. Thus, we can say that words, numbers, and punctuation are the human-sensible code by which data is represented in this book. Similarly, data must be represented in a machine-sensible code before it can be processed by a computer system. For example, data is represented by the Hollerith code of small holes punched in specific locations of the punched card. Each of the many types of input media requires a code to represent data. These codes will be described in Chapter Four.

Data is represented in a computer by either the presence or the absence of electronic or magnetic "signals" in certain sections of its circuitry. This is called "binary" or "two-state" representation of data since the circuitry of the computer is indicating only two possible states or conditions. For example, transistors and other semiconductors are either in a conducting or nonconducting state, while devices such as magnetic cores can be magnetized in either clockwise or counter-clockwise direction. Thus, we say that the electronic and magnetic circuitry of a computer operates in a "binary mode" since something is "binary" if it is made up of two parts or conditions. The binary characteristics of computer circuitry are the primary reasons why the binary numbering system is the basis for data representation in modern computers.

Binary Number System

The binary number system has only two symbols, 0 and 1, and is, therefore, said to have a "base" of two. The familiar decimal system has a base of ten, since it uses ten symbols (0 through 9). In the binary numbering system, all numbers, letters of the alphabet, and special characters are expressed as a sequence of either zeros or ones. The binary symbols 0 and 1 are called "binary digits" or more commonly *"bits."*

Like the decimal system, the binary system utilizes the concept of position value or place value. In the decimal system the place value of the decimal digits signifies units, tens, hundreds, thousands, etc. However, in the binary system, place value signifies units, twos, fours, eights, sixteens, etc. Figure 2–9 shows the binary number equivalents of the decimal numbers zero through 16. Using the information in

FIGURE 2–9

Equivalents of Decimal Numbers

Decimal	*Binary*	*Octal*	*Hexadecimal*
0	0	0	0
1	1	1	1
2	10	2	2
3	11	3	3
4	100	4	4
5	101	5	5
6	110	6	6
7	111	7	7
8	1000	10	8
9	1001	11	9
10	1010	12	A
11	1011	13	B
12	1100	14	C
13	1101	15	D
14	1110	16	E
15	1111	17	F
16	10000	20	10

Figure 2–9, you should be able to determine that the decimal number 17 would be expressed by the binary number 10001, 18 by 10010, and so on. Thus, any decimal number can be expressed in a binary form.

Other Number Systems

The *"octal"* (base 8) and the *"hexadecimal"* (base 16) number systems are used as a shorthand method of expressing the binary data representation within many modern computers. The binary number system has the disadvantage of requiring a large number of digits to express a given number value. The use of octal and hexadecimal number systems which are proportionately related to the binary number system provides a shorthand method of reducing the long "string" of ones and zeros which make up a binary number. This simplifies the jobs of programmers and computer operators who frequently have to determine the data or instruction contents of the computer. For example, like most modern computers, the IBM System/370 utilizes the binary number system to represent data internally. However, if a request was made to the computer to display the contents of its primary storage, a listing of the contents of storage in a hexadecimal notation would be produced. Figure 2–9 shows the relationship between the octal, hexadecimal, binary, and decimal systems.

It is not necessary for the average computer user to become an expert at converting decimal values into various number systems, nor is it necessary to become proficient in performing arithmetic computations based on such systems. It is sufficient to understand that data, instructions, and operations are represented in a computer by codes based on binary and other number systems.

Computer Codes

Though the internal circuitry of the computer utilizes only binary ones and zeros, several coding systems have been devised to make the job of communicating with a computer easier and more efficient. These codes should be considered as "shorthand" methods of expressing the binary patterns within a computer. These computer codes can also be thought of as methods of organizing the binary patterns within a computer in order to more efficiently utilize its arithmetic, logic, and storage capacities.

The most basic computer code would be the use of the "pure"

binary number system as the method of data representation for all computer operations. Some scientific and special purpose computers do utilize the pure binary code as their only method of internal data representation. However, most modern computers, though they may use a pure binary code for some operations, use special codes based on the binary, octal, or hexadecimal number systems.

Most common computer codes are versions of the *"binary coded decimal"* (BCD) coding system. In this system, decimal digits are expressed in a binary form using only the first four binary positions. Referring back to Figure 2–9 we see that the decimal digits 0 through 9 can be expressed by four binary positions. Therefore, any decimal number can be expressed by stringing together groups of four binary digits. For example, the decimal number 1975 would be expressed in BCD form as shown below.

Decimal Form	1	9	7	5
BCD Form	0001	1001	0111	0101

The three most common computer codes are based on the BCD system. These codes are shown in Figure 2–10 for the ten decimal numbers and the letters of the alphabet. The *Standard BCD Interchange Code* was used by second generation computers and is a six-bit alphameric code. It is an "alphameric" code because it can represent the letters of the alphabet as well as numbers and special characters. Sixty-four different characters could be represented by varying the combinations of the six bits in this code. However, this did not provide sufficient capacity for data representation, so eight-bit alphameric codes were deviced for use in third and fourth generation computers.

The *Extended BCD Interchange Code* (EBCDIC) is used by most current computers and can provide 256 different coding arrangements. Figure 2–10 shows that this eight-bit code consists of four "numeric" bits and four "zone" bits. The zone bits of this code perform a function similar to the zone positions on a punched card. The letters of the alphabet or special characters can be represented when combinations of zone and numeric bits are used. The other popular eight-bit code is the *American Standard Code for Information Interchange,* which has an eight-bit code version called ASCII–8. It is a standardized code developed primarily for data transmission devices but is also used by some computers.

Most computer codes include an additional bit called the *"check bit."* The check bit is also known as a "parity" bit and is used for verifying the accuracy or validity of the coded data. Many computers have a built-in checking capacity to detect the loss or addition of bits during the transfer of data between components of a computer system. The check bit allows the computer to determine automatically whether the number of bit positions representing a character of data is in agreement with the computer code being used.

Figure 2–11 concludes this section on data representation with an illustration of how data is physically represented in many modern computers. Assuming the use of the eight-bit EBCDIC code, Figure 2–11 reveals that one alphabetical or special character or two decimal

FIGURE 2–10

Common Computer Codes

Character	Standard BCD interchange code	Extended BCD interchange code (EBCDIC)	ASCII-8
0	00 1010	1111 0000	0101 0000
1	00 0001	1111 0001	0101 0001
2	00 0010	1111 0010	0101 0010
3	00 0011	1111 0011	0101 0011
4	00 0100	1111 0100	0101 0100
5	00 0101	1111 0101	0101 0101
6	00 0110	1111 0110	0101 0110
7	00 0111	1111 0111	0101 0111
8	00 1000	1111 1000	0101 1000
9	00 1001	1111 1001	0101 1001
A	11 0001	1100 0001	1010 0001
B	11 0010	1100 0010	1010 0010
C	11 0011	1100 0011	1010 0011
D	11 0100	1100 0100	1010 0100
E	11 0101	1100 0101	1010 0101
F	11 0110	1100 0110	1010 0110
G	11 0111	1100 0111	1010 0111
H	11 1000	1100 1000	1010 1000
I	11 1001	1100 1001	1010 1001
J	10 0001	1101 0001	1010 1010
K	10 0010	1101 0010	1010 1011
L	10 0011	1101 0011	1010 1100
M	10 0100	1101 0100	1010 1101
N	10 0101	1101 0101	1010 1110
O	10 0110	1101 0110	1010 1111
P	10 0111	1101 0111	1011 0000
Q	10 1000	1101 1000	1011 0001
R	10 1001	1101 1001	1011 0010
S	01 0010	1110 0010	1011 0011
T	01 0011	1110 0011	1011 0100
U	01 0100	1110 0100	1011 0101
V	01 0101	1110 0101	1011 0110
W	01 0110	1110 0110	1011 0111
X	01 0111	1110 0111	1011 1000
Y	01 1000	1110 1000	1011 1001
Z	01 1001	1110 1001	1011 1010

FIGURE 2–11

Data Representation, EBCDIC Code

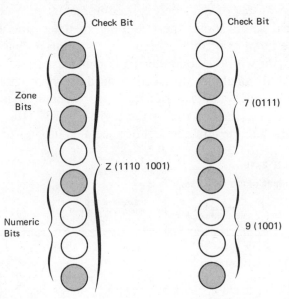

numbers can be represented by an eight-bit code. The circles represent magnetic cores, semiconductor devices, or other forms of computer storage circuitry. The shaded circles represent an electronic or magnetic "on" state, while the nonshaded circles represent the "off" state of binary devices. Thus, the first column of circles represents the letter *"Z"* while the second column of circles is called the "packed decimal" format, since two decimal numbers, in this case a seven and a nine, are represented by only eight bits. In both illustrations, the ninth or check bit is in an "off" state, signaling that the correct number of bits are present.

DATA ORGANIZATION

Once data is effectively represented by a meaningful coding system, it must then be organized in some logical manner so that it can be processed efficiently. Several levels of data have been devised which differentiate between the most simple elements of data and more complex data elements. Thus, data is organized into "characters," "fields," "records," and "files" just as writing may be organized in letters, words, sentences, and paragraphs. Examples of the *common data elements* are shown in Figure 2–12.

FIGURE 2–12

Examples of Common Data Elements

Data Element	Example
Character.............	The letter "J"
Field................	The "Name Field"—Jones, Thomas A.
Record..............	A "Payroll Record"—Jones, Thomas A., Social Security No. 575-32-3874, Salary $10,000, etc.
File.................	A "Payroll File"—contains records similar to that shown above for all employees of a firm
Data Base...........	"Personnel Data Base"—consolidates data formerly segregated in several files such as the Payroll file, Social Security file, Employee Skills file, Personnel Action file, Employee Name and Address file, etc.

Common Data Elements

The most basic data element is the *character,* which consists of a single alphabetic, numeric, or other symbol. The next higher level of data is the *field* which consists of a grouping of characters, such as the grouping of alphabetical characters to form a "name field," or the grouping of numerical characters to form a "sales amount field." The field is sometimes also called an *item* or *word.* Related fields of data are grouped to form a *record,* such as the payroll record for a person which consists of data fields such as his name, social security number, rate of pay, etc. "Fixed-length" records contain a fixed number of data fields, while "variable-length" records may contain a variable number of fields.

A group of related records is known as a *file* or *data set.* Files are frequently classified by the data processing application for which they are primarily used, such as a "payroll file" or an "accounts receivable file." Files are also classified by their permanence, such as the payroll "master file" as opposed to the payroll "weekly transaction file." A transaction file would therefore contain records of transactions during a period which are used periodically to update the permanent records contained in the master file. A level of data organization known as the *data base* has become very important due to recent developments in data processing. A data base consolidates many previous records and files so that a common pool of data records serve as a single "superfile" for many data processing applications.

Computer Data Elements

The organization of data within a computer is a function of the internal design of the computer circuitry and the coding system utilized. Since most current computers are designed to utilize the EBCDIC coding system, we will confine our discussion to data organization based on that coding system. Computers that use other schemes of data organization differ in the size and names of the data elements used, rather than in the basic concepts required.

Figure 2–13 illustrates the hierarchy of data elements used by many computers, including the IBM System/360 and System/370. The smallest element of data is the *bit,* or binary digit, which can have a binary value of either zero or one. The grouping of eight bits required by such coding systems as EBCDIC is called a *byte.* Remember that a byte can contain either one alphabetical or special character or can

FIGURE 2–13

Computer Data Elements

Name	*Size*
Bit...,............	One Binary Digit
Byte..............	Eight Bits
Word.............	Fixed Word-length Format: 4 Bytes (32 Bits)
	Variable Word-length Format: 1 to 256 Bytes
Page.............	2K or 4K Bytes
Segment...........	64K Bytes

be "packed" with two decimal digits. The byte is the basic unit of data in most modern computer systems. This is why the storage capacity of many computers and storage devices are now expressed in terms of bytes.

The next major computer data element is the *word,* whose size depends on whether the computer is operating in a "fixed word-length" or a "variable word-length" format. Computers operate in a fixed word-length format when each word consists of a fixed number of bits or bytes, while in the variable word-length format, the size of a word varies with the size of the data fields that are being processed. For many current computers, a word consists of four bytes (32 bits) in a fixed word-length format and can vary from one byte to 256 bytes in a variable word-length format. Fixed word-length formats may also permit the use of a "halfword" consisting of two bytes or a "doubleword" which consists of eight bytes. A word may consist of other arrangements of bytes or characters, but, for most computer systems, a word consists of one or more consecutive characters and frequently includes the contents of an entire data field.

Computer data elements that have been created due to the development of "multiprogramming" and "virtual memory" systems include the "page" and the "segment." We will discuss these developments in the next chapter. For many computers, the *page* consists of 2 K or 4 K bytes and represents a specific portion of a program or data, while a *segment* consists of 64 K bytes. Thus, the size of virtual memory systems is usually expressed in terms of a maximum number of segments, the number of pages in a segment, and the page size in bytes. Other computer data elements, such as the "book" and the "volume" have been created to assist in the management of data files and program "libraries." The size and use of these and other computer data elements varies among computer manufacturers and need not be discussed any further in this book.

Other Data Organization Concepts

Logical and physical data elements. A distinction should be made between "logical" and "physical" data elements. The common data elements previously discussed are *logical* data elements. *Physical* data elements are the individual physical data media or devices on which logical data elements are recorded. For example, a single punched card is a widely used "physical record," while a single reel of magnetic tape is frequently used as a "physical file." However, *logical* data elements are independent of the data media on which they are recorded. Thus, a punched card can contain several logical records, while several reels of magnetic tape may be utilized to store a single logical file. For example, a punched card may contain payroll data concerning two different employees (two logical records), while several reels of magnetic tape may be needed to store the payroll data file (one logical file), of a large business firm.

Keys, pointers, and indexes. Each record in a file contains one or more identification fields or *"keys"* which are utilized when searching or sorting a file. For example, a social security number might be used as the *record key* for each record in a payroll file. Records may contain other identifying fields which help in cross-referencing the contents of a file. An example would be a *"pointer"* field which contains the address of a related record in the file. A file or data base may contain an *"index"* or *"directory."* This is an ordered reference listing of record keys and associated addresses which helps locate individual records in the file or data base.

File organization.   The records in a file can be organized in two basic ways: in a predetermined sequence (*"sequential"* file organization) or in a random manner (*"random"* or *"nonsequential"* file organization. For example, payroll records in a payroll file could be organized in a *sequential* manner according to an alphabetical order based on employees' last names. Or, the same records could be placed in a file in a *random* manner, that is, in no particular order. However, in the latter case, the computer must keep track of the location of each record in the file so that they can be retrieved when needed.

Variations of the basic organizations include the *"indexed sequential"* method in which records are organized sequentially and also referenced by an index, and the *"list"* file organization, which uses indexes and pointers to locate records stored in a nonsequential manner. In the next chapter we will discuss several types of files that utilize one or more of these methods of file organization.

SUMMARY

The electronic, digital, stored program, general purpose computer is an electronic device that can accept data internally, store and execute a program of instructions, perform mathematical and logical operations on data and report the results. Computers can process data at fantastic speeds because their electronic circuitry is designed to provide them with internal storage, stored program, arithmetic and logic, and program modification capabilities. Computers can be classified by type (digital, analog, and hybrid), purpose (general purpose, special purpose, business, and scientific), size (mini, small, medium, large, and supercomputers), and generation (first, second, third, and fourth). A computer system performs input, storage, arithmetic-logic, control, and output functions. The hardware components of a system include input devices, a central processing unit, storage devices, and output devices. The execution of a computer instruction can be subdivided into an instruction cycle (when the computer prepares to execute an instruction) and an execution cycle (when it actually executes the instruction).

Data is represented in a computer in a binary form because of the two-state nature of the electronic and magnetic components of the computer. Most computers utilize special codes based on the binary, octal or hexidecimal number systems, such as the Extended Binary Coded Decimal Interchange Code (EBCDIC). Once data is effectively represented by a meaningful coding system it must then be organized in some logical manner so that it can be efficiently processed. Thus, data is commonly organized into characters, fields, records, and files. Within the computer, data is usually organized into bits, bytes, words, and other categories such as pages and segments. Common data elements can be described as either physical or logical elements, while data files can be organized in either a sequential or random manner.

KEY TERMS AND CONCEPTS

Computer, 27
Storage cycle time, 28
Internal storage, 28
Computer program, 30
Stored program, 30
Program modification, 30
Analog vs. digital computer, 31
Special purpose versus general
   purpose computers, 32–33
Computer sizes, 33–35
Computer system, 37–38
Input devices, 38
Central processing unit, 39
Primary storage unit, 39
Secondary storage devices, 38–39

Arithmetic-logic unit, 39
Control unit, 39–40
Output devices, 38, 40
Binary representation, 43–44
Binary number system, 44
Executing computer instructions, 40–42
Computer codes, 45–48
Common data elements:
   character, field, record, file, data
   base, 49
Computer data elements:
   bit, byte, word, 50–51
Logical and physical data elements, 51
Keys, pointers and indexes, 51
File organization methods, 52

ASSIGNMENTS

1. Test your understanding of the chapter material by reviewing the *purpose, outline, summary,* and *key terms and concepts* of this chapter. Are you confident that you have attained a basic understanding of the major concepts of the chapter? If not, reread the appropriate material as indicated by the page numbers after each key term and concept.

2. Discuss the differences and similarities between the following terms:
   a. Electronic computers versus electronic calculators
   b. Analog versus digital computers
   c. Special purpose versus general purpose computers
   d. Scientific versus business computers

3. Describe the major differences between the various sizes of computers.

4. Discuss the functions and components of a computer system.

5. Describe how a computer executes an instruction.

6. Explain why data representation in computers is based on the binary number system.

7. Provide examples to illustrate each of the common data elements.

8. Differentiate between a bit, byte, and word.

9. Discuss the concept of physical and logical data elements using examples to reenforce your answer.

10. Briefly describe the functions of keys, pointers, and indexes.

11. Identify and explain several methods of file organization.

Chapter Outline

Purpose of the Chapter

Development of Computers and EDP
The Pioneers, The First Generation, The Second Generation, The Third Generation, The Fourth Generation

The Electronic Data Processing System
Hardware, Software, Personnel, Types of EDP Systems

Batch Processing Systems
Definition, Sequential Access Files, Direct Access Files, Remote Access Batch Processing

Real-time Processing Systems
Inquiry Systems, Posting Systems, File Processing Systems, Full Capability Systems, Process Control Systems

Other EDP System Concepts
Data Communication Systems, Time-sharing Systems, Overlapped Processing, Multiprogramming, Multiprocessing, Virtual Memory, Virtual Computer Systems, Multisystem EDP

Summary

Key Terms and Concepts

Assignments

3

Fundamentals of
Electronic Data
Processing

Purpose of the Chapter

To promote a basic understanding of electronic data processing by analyzing:

1. The development of computers and electronic data processing,
2. The components and types of electronic data processing systems.

DEVELOPMENT OF COMPUTERS AND EDP

The development of computers and electronic data processing has been acclaimed as the most important technological development of the 20th century, a development that has caused an *information revolution* that rivals the Industrial Revolution of the 19th century. This sweeping claim is supported by evidence that the computer has significantly magnified man's ability to analyse, compute, and communicate, thereby greatly accelerating human technological progress. The electronic computer sprang from many origins, some well known, some lost in antiquity. The abacus and the slide rule were previously mentioned as early computing devices. The use of machinery to perform arithmetic operations through the development of the adding machine and the calculator was an important advancement. However, these and other devices are not computers, though they are important contributions to the development of machine computation.

The Pioneers

Charles Babbage is generally recognized as the first person to propose the concept of the modern computer. In 1833, this English mathematician outlined in detail his plans for an "Analytical Engine," a mechanical steam-driven computing machine that would accept punched card input, automatically perform any arithmetic operation in any sequence under the direction of a stored program of instructions, and produce either punched card or printed output. He produced thousands of detailed drawings before his death in 1871, but the machine was never built. Babbage had designed the world's first general purpose stored program digital computer, but his ideas were too advanced for the technology of his time.

Almost a hundred years passed before the ideas outlined by Babbage in 1833 began to be developed. Dr. Vannevar Bush of MIT built a large-scale electromechanical analog computer in 1925. The first large-scale electromechanical digital computer was developed by Dr. Howard Aiken of Harvard with the support of IBM in 1944. Aiken's Automatic Sequence Controlled Calculator, nicknamed Mark I, embodied many of the concepts of Charles Babbage and relied heavily on the concepts of IBM's punched card calculator developed in the 1930s. The first electronic digital computer, the ENIAC (Electronic Numerical Integrater and Calculator), was developed by John Mauchly and J. P. Eckert of the University of Pennsylvania in 1946. The ENIAC was electronic since it utilized over 18,000 vacuum tubes instead of the electromechanical relays of the Mark I. The ENIAC was built to compute artillery ballistic tables for the U.S. Army; it could complete in 15 seconds a trajectory computation that would take a skilled person with a desk calculator about ten hours to complete. However, the ENIAC was not a "stored program" computer and utilized the decimal system. Its processing was controlled externally by switches and control panels that had to be changed for each new series of computations.

The first stored program electronic computer was EDSAC (Electronic Delayed Storage Automatic Computer) developed under the direction of M. V. Wilkes at the University of Cambridge in England in 1949. The EDSAC and the first American stored program computer, the EDVAC (Electronic Discrete Variable Automatic Computer), which was completed in 1952, were based on the concepts advanced in 1945 by Dr. John von Neumann of the Institute for Advanced Study in Princeton, New Jersey. He proposed that the operating instructions or *program* of the computer be stored in a high-speed internal storage unit or *memory* and that both data and instructions be represented internally by the binary number system rather than the decimal system. These and other computer design concepts form the basis for much of the design of present computers. Several other early computers and many individuals could be mentioned in a discussion of the pioneering period of computer development. However, the high points previously discussed should illustrate that many men and many ideas were responsible for the birth of the electronic digital computer.

The First Generation

The UNIVAC I (Universal Automatic Computer), the first general purpose electronic digital computer to be commercially available, marks the beginning of the first generation of electronic computers. Computers developed before this time were special purpose one-of-a kind machines, whereas 48 UNIVAC I's were built. The first of these computers was installed at the Bureau of Census in 1951, and in 1954 a UNIVAC I became the first computer to process business applications when it was installed at a General Electric manufacturing plant in Louisville, Kentucky. An innovation of the UNIVAC I was the use of magnetic tape as an input and output medium. The most popular first generation computer was the IBM 650 which had a magnetic drum memory and utilized punched cards for input and output. The IBM 650 was an intermediate-size computer designed for both business and scientific applications. The first of these computers was installed in December, 1954, and almost 2,000 of them were produced. First generation computers were quite large and produced enormous amounts of heat because of their use of vacuum tubes. They had large electric power, air conditioning, maintenance, and space requirements.

The Second Generation

The replacement of vacuum tubes by transistors and other solid state devices marked the introduction of the second generation of computers in 1959. Transistorized circuits were a lot smaller, generated little heat, were less expensive, and required less power than vacuum tube circuits. Second generation computers were significantly smaller and faster and more reliable than first generation machines.

The use of magnetic cores as the primary internal storage medium and the introduction of removable magnetic disk packs were other major developments of the second generation. The most popular second generation computer was the IBM 1401, which along with the other models in the 1400 series claimed over 17,000 installations. The most popular scientific-type computers were the small-scale IBM 1620 and the large-scale IBM 7090.

The second generation also resulted in the displacement of punched card machines by electronic computers in business data processing. Almost all large and medium-sized punched card machine installations were converted to electronic data processing. The second generation also saw the emergence of magnetic tape as the primary input/output secondary storage medium for major computer installations, though punched cards and the new magnetic disk were also used.

The Third Generation

The introduction of the IBM System/360 series of computers in 1964 signaled the arrival of the third generation of computers. This generation featured the replacement of transistorized circuitry by integrated circuits in which all the elements of an electronic circuit are contained on a tiny silicon wafer or chip. These solid state microelectronic circuits are smaller and more reliable than transistorized circuits and significantly increased the speed and reduced the size of third generation computers. The third generation also featured improvements in the speed, capacity, and types of computer storage and input/output devices and the widespread use of magnetic disk units. The "family" or "series" concept, which stresses the standardization and compatibility that exist between the different models in a computer series, was also developed. Manufacturers sought to produce computers that could handle both business and scientific applications and process programs written for smaller models without major modifications.

Other features of the third generation were the emergence of "timesharing" and "data communications" applications, the ability to process several programs simultaneously through "multiprogramming," and the growth in importance of "software" as a means of efficiently using computers. "Operating systems" of computer programs were developed to supervise computer processing, and high-level programming languages such as FORTRAN and COBOL greatly simplified computer programming. The increased popularity of minicomputers and the introduction of small computers like the IBM System/3 were later developments of the third generation.

The Fourth Generation

In the latter part of 1970, several computer manufacturers announced the introduction of new computer systems. Since these computer systems, such as the IBM System/370, exhibited evolutionary rather than revolutionary changes in hardware and software, there has been some disagreement as to whether the fourth generation of computers has arrived or whether they represent the "3½ generation." However, developments announced since 1970 reflect changes of sufficient significance to merit the fourth generation designation for several computer systems introduced in the early 1970s.

Hardware developments include microscopic integrated circuits including MST circuits (Monolithic Systems Technology), LSI circuits (Large-Scale Integration), and MOSFET circuits (metal oxide silicon field effect transistor). The tiny silicon chips of the System/370 contain eight to 16 times the number of circuits of those used in the System/360 series. Several models of the System/370 became the first electronic computers with their main memories composed entirely of MST or MOSFET circuits. The use of such *"semiconductor memories"* is a dramatic change from the magnetic core memories used in the second and third generation computers.

Once again the trend toward increased microminiaturization significantly reduced the size and power requirements of the fourth generation computers, thus greatly increasing their processing speed compared to third generation computers. For example, the IBM System/370 Model 168, introduced in late 1972, has a semiconductor memory of MOSFET circuits. It requires about 40 percent less floor space and executes instructions ten to 30 percent faster than the System/370 Model 165, which has a magnetic core memory. The Model 165 had been introduced in late 1970 with significant reductions in space, power, and memory cycle times compared to the third generation System/360 Model 65 that it replaced.

Other impressive fourth generation advancements are "microprogramming" and "virtual memory." Though first developed in some earlier computers, these developments are being used extensively in fourth generation computer systems. *Microprogramming* involves the use of "microprograms" in a "read-only storage" (ROS) or "reloadable control storage" (RCS) module of the control unit of a

FIGURE 3–1

Computer Generations (selected major characteristics)

Characteristics	First generation	Second generation	Third generation	Fourth generation
Electronic circuitry.........	Vacuum tubes	Transistors	Integrated circuits	Large-scale integration
Primary storage.........	Magnetic drum	Magnetic core	Magnetic core	Semi-conductor storage
Secondary storage.........	Magnetic tape Magnetic drum	Magnetic tape Magnetic disk	Magnetic disk Magnetic tape Magnetic strip	Magnetic disk Magnetic tape Magnetic strip
Software.........	User-written programs Machine language	Canned programs Symbolic languages	Operating systems Higher-level languages	Data management systems
Other characteristics.........	Batch processing	Overlapped processing Real-time processing Data communication	Timesharing Multiprogramming Multiprocessing	Microprogramming Virtual memory Virtual computers

CPU. Microprograms are small, frequently used sets of elementary control instructions (called "microinstructions"), which were formerly "hardwired" into the circuitry of the CPU. *Virtual memory* is a development that allows secondary storage devices to be treated as an extension of the primary storage of the computer, thus giving the "virtual" appearance of a larger "real" memory than actually exists. These developments have greatly increased the speed, versatility, and capacity of fourth generation computers and will be analysed later in this chapter. The fourth generation also marks the extinction of punched card machine data processing installations in the United States. Since small computer systems like the IBM System/3 could be leased for about the same price as punched card accounting machines, electromechanical punched card machines are now relegated to the role of supporting the input/output functions of card-oriented computer systems. Figure 3–1 summarizes the major characteristics of the four computer generations.

THE ELECTRONIC DATA PROCESSING SYSTEM

Electronic data processing, or EDP, has previously been defined as the use of computers to process data automatically. An *electronic data processing system* can be defined as a combination of hardware, software, and personnel that processes data into information. See Figure 3–2. *Hardware* can be defined as all of the equipment and devices that make up a computer system. *Software* is a term used to describe all of the various types of programs or sets of instructions which direct the hardware to perform its data processing functions. Software refers not only to the *application software* which directs the processing of a particular application, such as a "payroll program," but also refers to *system software,* such as "control programs" which are supplied by the computer manufacturer and others to direct and control the operations of a computer system. It can be said that software "gives life" to computer hardware.

The meaning of hardware can be expanded to include all tangible EDP materials, especially input, output, and storage media such as punched cards, paper tape, magnetic tape, etc. Similarly, the meaning of software can be expanded to include all nontangible EDP requirements such as the policies and procedures required to manage and control an EDP system.

The final important component of an electronic data processing system is the *personnel* required for its operation. The categories of

FIGURE 3–2

The Electronic Data Processing System

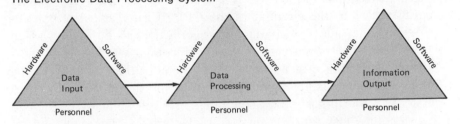

personnel that are required consist of "systems analysts," "programmers," "computer operators," and other managerial, technical, and clerical personnel. Basically, *systems analysts* design information systems and data processing systems based on the information requirements of an organization; *programmers* prepare computer programs based on the specifications of the systems analyst, and *computer operators* operate the computer. Such computer personnel or "computer professionals" should be differentiated from "computer users." A *computer user* is anyone who uses the output of a computer system, whether he or she be an accountant, salesman, engineer, clerk, or manager. We will discuss in detail the components and functions of hardware, software, and personnel in subsequent chapters.

Types of EDP Systems

There are two basic types of EDP systems: *"batch" processing systems* and *"real-time" processing systems.* All EDP systems in use today may be grouped into these two classifications, though many other terms may be used to describe them. For instance, batch processing systems are also known as "sequential," "serial," or "off-line" processing systems, while real-time systems may also be called "on-line," "in-line," "direct access," "random access," or even "on-line, real-time" systems! "Time-sharing" and "data communications" systems can possess the characteristics of either batch processing or real-time systems and are terms that also arise in discussions concerning the basic types of EDP systems. Though even experts disagree on the usage of such terms, in this book, *batch processing systems are those in which data is accumulated and processed periodically, while real-time systems process data immediately.*

BATCH PROCESSING SYSTEMS

Definition

Batch processing systems are the major type of EDP systems in use today, though real-time systems are rapidly gaining ground. In a batch processing system, data is accumulated over a period of time in batches and then processed periodically. Not only is the data for a particular application or job accumulated into batches, but a number of different jobs are accumulated into batches and "run" (processed) periodically. The rationale for batch processing is that data and jobs should be grouped into batches and processed periodically according to a planned schedule in order to efficiently use a computer system, rather than allowing data and jobs to be processed in an unorganized, random manner. Of course this efficiency, economy, and control is accomplished by sacrificing the immediate processing of data for computer users.

Figure 3–3 illustrates a batch processing system where batches of

FIGURE 3–3

A Batch Processing System

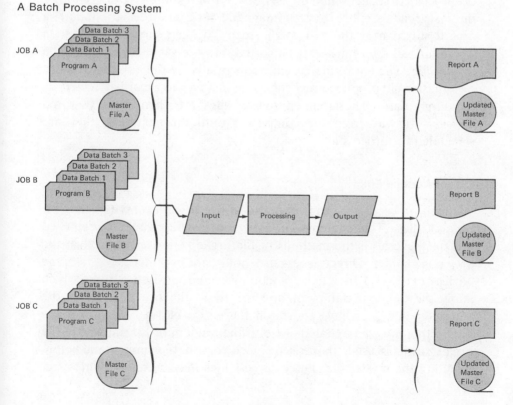

data, computer programs, and master files for several different jobs are processed periodically according to a schedule set up by the computer operations department of an organization. Output takes the form of required reports and updated master files. The reports produced could be reports required by management such as sales analysis reports, income and expense reports, or production status reports. The master files are updated by making any necessary changes to the records in the files based on the contents of the batches of input data. The data could be in the form of batches of sales transactions, income and expense figures or units of production.

Sequential Access Files

Batch processing systems may utilize either sequential access files or direct access files. *Sequential access files* are files which utilize the sequential method of file organization to store data in a predetermined sequence on secondary storage media such as punched cards, paper tape, or magnetic tape. When data is stored in such media, it must be processed sequentially or "serially." For example, the computer must search an entire reel of magnetic tape in order to update a record stored near the end of the reel. To keep such searches to a minimum, all data must first be sorted into the same sequence as the master file. The entire file is read sequentially by the computer and a new master file produced incorporating changes to records affected by the input data. The updated master files are then usually stored *"off-line"* (away from the computer) until the next time they are scheduled for processing.

Direct Access Files

Batch processing systems can also utilize *direct access (or random access)* files. The contents of direct access files can be organized utilizing several of the methods of file organization mentioned in the previous chapter. Direct access files hold data in direct access storage devices (DASDs) such as magnetic disks and magnetic drums which allow the direct updating of any record in the file. Therefore, the computer does not have to search the entire file in order to find a record that must be updated. Also, if the random or list method of file organization is used, there is no need to sort the input data before updating the master file. Direct access files may take the form of removable magnetic disk packs or magnetic strip cartridges that can be stored off-line until the next time the files are needed. However, direct access storage equipment such as magnetic disk or magnetic drum units are usually *"on-line"* devices, that is, they are electronically connected to the central processor of a computer system so that they can respond instantly to either batch processing or real-time processing assignments.

Remote Access Batch Processing

Batch processing systems can have a *remote access* capability, frequently called "remote job entry" (RJE). Batches of data can be collected and converted into an input medium at "remote" locations that are far away from the computer. Input/output devices at these locations (called *remote terminals*) are then used to transmit data over communications circuits to a distant computer. The batches of data are then processed, thus producing updated master files as well as information that is transmitted back to the remote terminal. Remote access batch processing can also involve "remote off-line input/output." For example, data can be transmitted from the keyboard of a terminal to an off-line magnetic tape unit where they are accumulated for subsequent batch processing. The use of communications circuits to transmit data between a computer and remote terminals is called *data communications* and will be analyzed in a later section.

REAL-TIME PROCESSING SYSTEMS

In full-fledged real-time processing systems, data is processed as soon as it is originated or recorded without waiting to accumulate batches of data. Data is fed directly into the computer system from on-line terminals without having to be sorted and is always stored on-line in direct access files. The master files are always up-to-date since they are up-dated whenever data is originated, regardless of its frequency, and information in the files can be retrieved almost instantaneously. A real-time processing system is illustrated in Figure 3–4.

Real-time processing is frequently called on-line, direct access, or random access processing, since all of these capabilities are required of the real-time processing system. However, use of such terms can be misleading because we have seen that batch processing systems can

FIGURE 3–4

A Real-Time Processing System

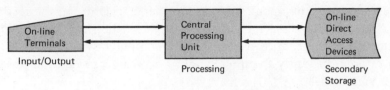

utilize on-line direct access or random access files in the processing of batches of data. As a compromise, experts may use the term "on-line real-time" (OLRT) processing. Some of the semantic confusion arises from the fact that there can be different levels of real-time processing systems depending on the data processing functions to be performed.

Real-time processing systems can be subdivided into the five levels shown below and illustrated in Figure 3–5.

1. Inquiry systems.
2. Posting systems.
3. File processing systems.
4. Full capability systems.
5. Process control systems.

The main function of an *inquiry system* is information retrieval. The user of the real-time inquiry system wishes a quick response to a request for information; for example, the current balance in a particular bank checking account. The main function of a *posting system* is the immediate but temporary collection and recording (posting) of data until it can be processed at a later date. Thus, the real-time posting system is designed to perform only the collection, conversion, and storage functions of data processing, leaving the manipulation function to a batch processing system. For example, some retail stores utilize on-line "point-of-sale" terminals to capture and record sales data on magnetic tape or disk during the day for subsequent remote batch processing at night.

File processing real-time systems perform all of the functions of data processing except the communication function. Thus, data is collected, converted, manipulated, and then stored, resulting in an immediate and continual updating of files. The communication function is performed by subsequent batch processing which produces

FIGURE 3–5

Examples of the Levels of Real-Time Processing Systems

Level of real-time processing	*Business examples*
Inquiry....................	Request customer balance in bank checking accounts utilizing on-line audio-response terminals. Request number of parts on hand in inventory utilizing on-line visual display terminals.
Posting....................	Collect sales data with on-line terminals and record on magnetic tape for later processing. Capture checking account transactions handled by bank tellers and record on temporary file for control purposes.
File processing..............	Update customer files due to sales transaction data captured by on-line terminals. Update work-in-process inventory files due to production data captured by data recording terminals on the factory floor.
Full capability..............	Process airline reservations utilizing on-line terminals and update on-line flight reservation files. Process data arising from the purchase or sale of securities utilizing on-line terminals and update on-line securities transaction files.
Process control..............	Control petroleum refinery process with on-line sensing and control devices. Control of electric power generation and transmission.

reports and other output, or by a real-time inquiry system which interrogates the files.

The full capability real-time processing system provides immediate and continuous performance of all of the functions of data processing. It can perform the services of any of the other levels of real-time systems, along with the immediate processing of assignments that require only data manipulation and communication of results. The reservation systems of the major airlines are a familiar example of full capability systems, they process passenger reservations in real-time utilizing on-line terminals at airline offices and airports. Real-time processing systems with a full data processing capability are being installed or developed by almost all users of large or medium-scale computers. A particular type of full capability real-time processing system is the *process control system,* which not only performs all of the data processing functions but, in addition, uses its information output to control an ongoing physical process, such as industrial production processes in the steel, petroleum, and chemical industries.

OTHER EDP SYSTEMS CONCEPTS

Data Communication Systems

Data communication systems are electronic data processing systems that combine the capabilities of the computer with high-speed electrical and electronic communications. Remote batch processing systems utilize data communication systems. All real-time processing systems (except when the input/output device used is near the computer) utilize data communication systems. All time-sharing systems, which will be explored in the next section, utilize data communication systems. Data communication systems (also called data transmission, telecommunication, or teleprocessing) provide for the transmitting of data over electronic communication links between a computer system and a number of terminals at some physical distance away from the computer.

A *terminal* can be defined as a device that uses communications channels to transmit or receive data. Terminal units exist which can accept data from such media as punched cards, paper tape, magnetic tape, magnetic disk, or data entered manually into a keyboard. The data is then converted into a form suitable for transmission over telephone, telegraph, and microwave circuits. Data received at a terminal unit can be punched into cards or paper tape, written on

FIGURE 3–6

A Data Communications System

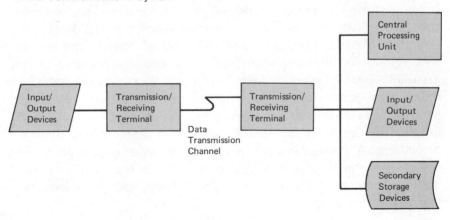

magnetic tape or disks, printed on paper, or directly entered into a computer. Direct communication between computers is a growing form of data communications and includes the use of small "satellite" computer systems at remote locations. Figure 3–6 illustrates a data communication system. Data received at the receiving terminal can be entered directly into input/output or secondary storage devices or into the central processing unit for further processing.

Time-sharing Systems

Time-sharing systems are electronic data processing systems in which many users in different locations share a computer system at the same time through the use of on-line input/output terminals. Time-sharing systems "interleave" the data processing assignments of many users by giving each user a small, frequently repeated "slice" of time. Time-sharing systems operate at such fast speeds that each user has the illusion that he alone is using the computer because of the seemingly instantaneous response. The ability of time-sharing systems to service many users simultaneously is sometimes hard to comprehend. However, one must remember that a computer operating in nanoseconds speeds can process several million instructions per second. Supercomputers capable of executing a billion instructions per second are expected by the mid-1970s.

Remote batch processing and real-time processing can be accomplished utilizing time-sharing systems. A time-sharing user could accumulate batches of data and periodically process them utilizing a time-sharing service. He could use input/output devices ranging from small terminals, to larger batch processing stations, to small satellite computer systems. However, time-sharing systems are currently used primarily for real-time processing applications. Time-sharing systems can easily handle the inquiry, posting, and file processing types of real-time processing assignments. Time-sharing is widely used for full-fledged real-time processing of the "short problem" type, where the solution of short problems or small segments of larger problems is sought by users such as students, scientists, engineers, systems analysts, and other staff specialists. These types of time-sharing applications allow users at on-line terminals to interact with the computer on a real-time basis as the solution to a problem is explored and finally accomplished. This type of frequent man-machine interaction is called *"interactive"* or *"conversational"* computing or processing.

Special purpose time-sharing systems exist which have been designed for a specific application such as an airline reservation system. More prevalent, however, are general purpose time-sharing systems which can be used internally within an organization such as a large business firm or university, where many remote time-sharing terminals allow simultaneous use of the computer by many users throughout the organization. The other major form of general purpose time-sharing is the time-sharing service offered by data processing service centers and other firms. Time-sharing services are provided to many subscribers representing various business firms and organizations. Subscribers pay for time-sharing services by paying an initial installation charge, basic monthly charges, and transaction charges which vary according to the amount of computer resources used. Firms which offer such time-sharing services are sometimes referred to as computer or information "utilities."

Time-sharing systems rely heavily on data communication systems and direct access storage devices in order to provide instantaneous responses to many users using remote terminals. Time-sharing systems are also heavily dependent on hardware and software capabilities developed to support remote batch processing systems and real-time processing systems. Five of these important developments in electronic data processing are overlapped processing, multiprogramming, multiprocessing, virtual memory, and virtual computer systems.

Overlapped Processing

A computer system with an *"overlapped processing"* capability can increase the utilization of its central processing unit by overlapping input/output and processing operations. *Input/output interface hardware (buffers, I/O control units, and channels)* and special software *(input/output control systems)* make such processing possible.[1] Overlapped processing is the opposite of serial processing, where the processing function cannot take place until the input function is completed, and the output function must wait until the processing function is completed. Thus, the input, processing, and output equipment of a computer system are idle for large portions of the time necessary to complete a data processing assignment. A computer system is "input/output-bound" if its CPU must wait while its

---

[1] Input/output interface hardware is discussed in Chapter Four and input/output control systems (IOCS) are discussed in Chapter Five.

FIGURE 3-7

Serial and Overlapped Processing

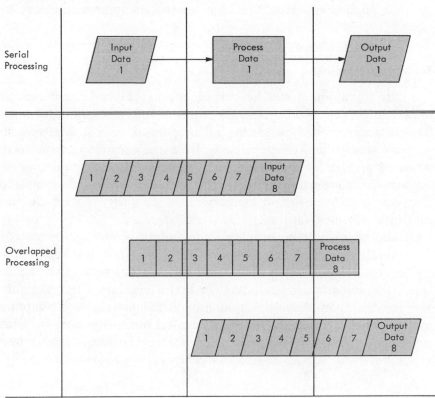

input/output equipment carries out their functions and is "process-bound" (or CPU-bound) if the input/output devices have to wait while the CPU is involved in computations and other operations. See Figure 3–7.

Overlapped processing (and multiprogramming and multiprocessing) was developed to help solve these problems and thereby to increase the *"throughput"* of a computer system. Throughput can be defined as the total amount of fully completed data processing occurring during a specific period of time. Thus, the efficiency of a computer system is gauged not by the speed of its input, processing, or output equipment, but by its throughput, that is, the amount of data processing completed during a period of time. The time it takes to complete a data processing assignment is called *"turnaround"* time.

Overlapped processing greatly increased the throughput of most business computer systems and reduced turnaround time because many business applications require a large amount of input/output operations.

Multiprogramming

Multiprogramming can be defined as the ability of a computer system to process two or more programs in the same period of time. This is accomplished by storing all or part of several programs in primary storage and then switching from the execution of one program to another in an interleaving process. The computer system does this by transferring entire programs or segments of programs and data into and out of main memory from secondary storage devices and by performing arithmetic or logic operations for one program while simultaneously performing input/output or storage operations for several other programs. Only one instruction at a time is executed by the central processing unit. However, the computer switches so quickly from one program to another that it gives the effect of simultaneous operation. A multiprogramming capability allows a computer system to better utilize the time of its central processing unit. In batch processing systems that do not use multiprogramming, a large part of a CPU's time can be wasted as it waits between jobs.

Multiprocessing

Multiprocessing can be defined as the ability of a computer system to process several instructions simultaneously. Multiprocessing occurs when two or more computers are interconnected and share each other's input, output, and storage units. In some cases, a large "master" computer utilizes smaller "slave" computers to handle "housekeeping" chores such as input/output operations. In other cases, several computers are interconnected in order to handle large processing assignments and to provide a backup capability that would not be present if only one large computer were used.

Some large, specially designed computer systems also have a multiprocessing capability because they have CPU configurations consisting of multiple arithmetic-logic and control units which share the same primary storage unit. This "multiprocessor" design gives the computer system a multiprocessing capability, since it can operate as if it has several central processing units.

Virtual Memory

Virtual memory has been defined as the ability to treat secondary storage devices as an extension of the primary storage of the computer, thus giving the "virtual" appearance of a larger ("virtually" unlimited) main memory than actually exists. This technique greatly increases the ability of the computer to handle large and multiple data processing assignments and simplifies programming by freeing programmers from the complex programming caused by primary storage limitations. Data and programs are subdivided into segments and pages which are transferred between main memory and secondary storage devices in such a way that it appears that the computer has a larger "real" memory than it actually does.

Computers with virtual memory capabilities utilize a "paging" process which automatically and continually transfers pages between primary storage and direct access storage devices such as magnetic disk or drum units. This technique places in primary storage only those pages that are actually needed for processing. This is contrasted to nonvirtual storage systems which require that entire programs or subprograms be present in main memory. Thus, the computer system can be utilized as if it had "virtually" unlimited storage. For example, one particular computer model with a "real" memory capacity of 512,000 bytes can act as though it has a memory size of 16 million bytes.

Virtual Computer Systems

The concept of virtual memory has grown to include the concept of virtual computer systems. Through a combination of "microprogramming" and other hardware and software developments, several different configurations of computers can be simulated by a single computer system. These simulated computers, or "virtual machines," provide one or more computer users not only with a virtual memory but with an entire virtual computer system, including "virtual software!"

The virtual machine concept relies heavily on the concept of *microprogramming*. We have defined "microprograms" as small sets of elementary control instructions called "microinstructions" or "microcodes." Such microprograms (also called "firmware" or "stored-logic") are a development that allows software (microprograms) to perform the functions of hardware (electronic circuitry). Microprograms stored in a read-only storage (ROS) module of the control unit interpret the machine-language instructions of a computer program and decode them into elementary microinstructions which are then executed. Thus, elementary microfunctions of the CPU that had formerly been executed by the "hardwired" circuitry of the control unit are now executed by the microprograms of the ROS.

Microprogramming increases the versatility of a computer system since it allows various degrees of "customizing" of the "instruction set" of a computer, including the creation of "virtual machines." With microprogramming, smaller computers can process programs written for larger computers, newer computers can process programs written for older models, and various control functions formerly performed by hardwiring can be performed by easily changed microprograms. Thus, microprogramming is vital to the creation of virtual computer systems.

Virtual machine control programs have been developed for time-sharing computer systems which allow time-sharing users to create and operate their own virtual computers. The virtual machines may differ with each other and with the "host" machine in their hardware and software capabilities. Each user can operate as though he were operating a single "real" machine. Time-sharing systems with a virtual machine capability can provide great flexibility to their users by allowing a wide variety of acceptable hardware and software specifications to be used.

Multisystem EDP

We shall conclude this chapter by stressing the concept of *"multisystem" electronic data processing*. We have discussed many different types of computer systems and many different types and levels of electronic data processing systems. This diversity is the cause of much confusion and misunderstanding concerning the use of computers. However, such diversity is really the key to the amazing versatility of the computer and the wide range of problems that can be handled by electronic data processing systems. Therefore, electronic data processing must be understood in a "multisystem" context, that is, that several types of EDP systems may be required to handle the data processing requirements of an information system. Just as the simplified marketing information system in Chapter One (see Figure 1–2) required several types of data processing systems, many types of EDP systems may be required by the various information systems of an organization.

Figure 3–8 illustrates the concept of multisystem EDP. Although it does not show software and people components, Figure 3–5 reveals an electronic data processing system composed of several EDP subsystems, including batch processing, remote processing, real-time

FIGURE 3–8

Multisystem Electronic Data Processing

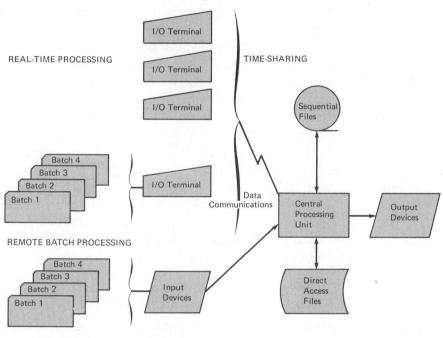

processing, time-sharing, and data communication systems. An EDP system with all of these subsystems would require a computer system with multiprogramming or multiprocessing capabilities. Such a system might require scheduling levels of priority for the different subsystems. High priority applications would be processed immediately, while low priority jobs would be processed on a "background" basis, i.e., whenever the CPU could spare a few milliseconds! Multisystem EDP is a concept that is being implemented in the electronic data processing systems of most large and medium-scale computer users.

SUMMARY

The development of computers and electronic data processing is a revolutionary technological development of the 20th century. The ideas and inventions of many men were responsible for the development of the electronic digital computer. First generation computers were first produced in 1951 and were large devices that utilized vacuum tubes in their circuitries. Transistors and other solid state devices were utilized in the second generation of computers which were introduced in 1959 and were smaller, faster, and cheaper than first generation machines. Magnetic cores were the primary internal storage medium, while magnetic tapes were widely used for input/output and secondary storage. Third generation computers were introduced in 1964 and replaced transistorized circuitry with integrated circuits. The third generation also featured improvements in the speed, capacity, and types of computer input/output and storage devices including the widespread use of magnetic disk units. Time-sharing, data communications, operating systems, and high-level programming languages were other developments of the third generation. The fourth generation began in 1970 with the introduction of computers which utilize such developments as microscopic integrated circuits, microprogramming, virtual memory, and the replacement of magnetic cores with integrated circuitry for primary storage.

An electronic data processing system is a combination of hardware, software, and personnel that processes data into information. Hardware is the equipment and devices of a computer system as well as all tangible EDP materials. Software consists of computer programs as well as EDP policies and procedures. EDP personnel include systems analysts, programmers, computer operators, and other managerial, technical, and clerical personnel. The two basic types of EDP systems are batch processing systems, in which data is accumulated and processed periodically, and real-time systems which process data immediately. Batch processing systems may utilize sequential access files or direct access files and can have a remote access capability. Real-time processing systems can be subdivided into the following levels: inquiry systems, posting systems, file processing systems, full capability systems, and process control systems.

Data communication systems are EDP systems that provide for the transmitting of data between a computer system and one or more remote terminals or stations. Time-sharing systems are EDP systems in which many users in different locations share a computer system at the same time through the use of on-line input/output terminals. Five of the most important developments which support modern electronic data processing are overlapped processing, multiprogramming, multiprocessing, virtual memory and virtual computer systems.

The different types, levels, and capabilities of electronic data processing systems must be understood in a multisystem context. Many different types of EDP systems may be required to handle the data processing requirements of an information system. Thus, a modern electronic data processing system may be composed of several EDP subsystems, including batch processing, real-time processing, time-sharing, and data communications systems.

KEY TERMS AND CONCEPTS

Computer generations, 59–62
Electronic data processing, 63–64
Hardware, 63
Software, 63
Systems analysts, 64
Programmers, 64
Computer operators, 64
Computer user, 64
Batch processing systems, 65–66
Sequential access files, 66
Direct access files, 66
Off-line, 66
On-line, 66
Real-time processing systems, 67–68

Levels of real-time processing, 68–69
Data communications, 70
Terminal, 70
Time-sharing, 71
Conversational computing, 71
Overlapped processing, 72–73
Throughput, 73
Turnaround time, 73
Multiprogramming, 74
Multiprocessing, 74
Virtual memory, 75
Virtual computers, 75–76
Microprogramming, 75–76
Multisystem EDP, 76–77

ASSIGNMENTS

1. Test your understanding of the chapter material by reviewing the *purpose, outline, summary,* and *key terms and concepts* of this chapter. Are you confident that you have attained a basic understanding of the major concepts of the chapter? If not, reread the appropriate material as indicated by the page numbers after each key term and concept.

2. Discuss the major characteristics of each generation of computers.

3. Discuss the functions and components of an electronic data processing system.

4. Differentiate between the following terms:
   a. Hardware vs. software
   b. Batch processing vs. real-time processing
   c. Sequential access vs. direct access
   d. Off-line vs. on-line

    e.   Data communications vs. time-sharing

    f.   Microprogramming vs. multiprogramming

    g.   Overlapped processing vs. multiprocessing

    h.   Virtual memory vs. virtual machines

5.   Utilize examples to illustrate five levels of real-time processing systems.

6.   "Electronic data processing must be understood in a multisystem context, i.e., that several types of EDP systems may be required to handle the data processing requirements of an information system." Explain this statement and give an example to illustrate your answer.

part two

Computer Hardware, Software, and Programming

Chapter Outline

Purpose of the Chapter

Introduction

The Central Processing Unit
    Arithmetic-Logic and Control Subunits, Primary Storage
    Classifications, Primary Storage Devices: Magnetic
    Core, Magnetic Thin Film, Semiconductor Storage,
    Primary Storage Developments.

Basic Peripherals and Media
    The Computer Console, Punched Card Hardware,
    Magnetic Tape Hardware, Magnetic Disk Hardware,
    Printers

Other Peripherals and Media
    Paper Tape Hardware, Magnetic Drum Hardware, Magnetic
    Cards and Strips, MICR Hardware, OCR Hardware,
    Visual Input/Output Hardware, Voice Input/Output
    Hardware, Microfilm Input/Output Hardware, Laser Strip
    and Film Storage, Other Input/Output Hardware.

Input/Output Interface Hardware
    Buffers, Channels, Input/Output Control Units, Data
    Communications Interface Units

Auxiliary Hardware
    Punched Card Equipment, Keyboard-to-Magnetic Tape
    Hardware, Keyboard-to-Magnetic Disk Hardware, Other
    Input Preparation Hardware, Off-line Output and Storage
    Hardware, Data Processing Materials.

Summary

Key Terms and Concepts

Assignments

4

Computer Hardware

Purpose of the Chapter

To promote a basic understanding of computer
hardware by analyzing:

1. The physical and performance characteristics of computer hardware devices,
2. The functions, benefits, and limitations of
   computer hardware.

INTRODUCTION

Computer hardware has previously been defined as the equipment
and devices that make up a computer system, as well as tangible EDP
materials such as input/output and storage media. Chapter Two
introduced the basic hardware components of a computer system
(refer back to Figure 2–6). This chapter does not explore the technical details of hardware. Instead, it provides information about hardware which is needed to manage the computer resources of a business
firm. Performance characteristics and other facts that describe each
hardware device are included, as well as an analysis of the benefits
and limitations of major types of equipment and media. Such information should help computer users begin the difficult task of
evaluating the proposals of computer professionals and manufacturers.

Computer hardware can be subdivided into four major categories:
the *central processing unit, peripheral equipment, auxiliary equipment,* and *media and materials.* These categories may be further subdivided to emphasize several major types of hardware.

1. Central Processing Unit
    Control Unit
    Arithmetic-Logic Unit
    Primary Storage Unit
    Other Subunits
2. Peripheral Equipment
    Input/Output and Secondary Storage Units
    Input/Output Interface Units
3. Auxiliary Equipment
    Input Preparation Equipment
    Off-line Output and Storage Equipment
4. Media and Materials
    Input/Output and Storage Media
    Data Processing Materials

The central processing unit is composed of arithmetic-logic, control, and primary storage units, as well as several subunits which will be explained shortly. *Peripheral equipment* is the second major category of computer hardware and refers to all devices that are separate from, but are under the control of, the central processing unit. The term "peripherals" covers a wide variety of input/output (I/O) and secondary storage equipment, as well as several types of input/output and data communications "interface" units. The third hardware category of *auxiliary equipment* consists of equipment that is "off-line," that is, equipment that is separate from and *not* under the control of the central processing unit. Auxiliary equipment assists and supports the input, output, and storage functions of a computer system. Major types of auxiliary equipment are "input preparation" (or "data entry") equipment, which prepares input media for entry into the computer system, and off-line output and storage equipment, which assists in the output and storage functions. *Media and materials,* the last hardware category, consists of input/output and storage media and data processing materials used in computer operations and programming.

THE CENTRAL PROCESSING UNIT

The internal architecture of the CPU is exceedingly complex. A detailed knowledge of the circuitry and scientific principles involved is beyond the scope of this book. In this text, we confine our discussion to a nondetailed analysis of the functions of major components of the

CPU. The basic functions of the arithmetic-logic, control, and primary storage units of the central processing unit were described in Chapter Two. We will now discuss several special purpose components of these units and explore how they help carry out the main functions of the CPU.

Arithmetic-Logic and Control Subunits

The arithmetic-logic and control units of the CPU include several types of subunits and special purpose circuitry such as registers, counters, adders, etc. *Registers* are areas of high-speed storage circuitry used as "work areas" for the temporary storage of instructions and data during the operation of the control and arithmetic-logic units. The number, function, and capacity of the registers and other subunits in a CPU depends on the internal architecture of each particular computer. For instance, the IBM System/360 and System/370 computers contain 16 general purpose registers which can carry out several functions and which have a capacity of 32 bits plus a sign bit. Besides general purpose or general registers, there may be other registers named according to their functions. A "storage" register temporarily holds data or instructions taken from or being sent to primary storage. An "address" register may hold the address of the storage location of data, or the address of an input/output device, or a control function. An "instruction" register contains the instruction being executed by the CPU. The "accumulator" is a register which accumulates the results of arithmetic or logic operations; the "multiplier-quotient" register holds either a multiplier or a quotient, while the "floating-point register" is used for floating-point arithmetic operations.

There are other subunits of the central processing unit besides registers. The *counter,* closely related to the register, is a device whose contents can be increased or decreased by a specific amount. The "instruction counter" is also called the "instruction address register" or the "sequence register" and contains the storage location address of the computer instruction being executed. The "index register" is a counter specifically set aside for modifying the portion of an instruction that indicates the address of data to be manipulated. This results in an operation known as "indexing" in which the CPU automatically repeats the performance of the same instruction until all of the data covered by the instruction is processed.

Adders are subunits that perform the arithmetic operations of the arithmetic-logic unit. They receive data from two or more sources, perform the specific arithmetic operation desired, and then convey the result to a receiving register such as the accumulator. *Comparators,* also called "comparers," are subunits of electronic circuitry which can indicate whether the contents of two registers are equal or unequal. Such comparisons are the key to the logic capability of the computer, for a change from one set of instructions to another is based on the results of such comparisons. The *encoder* translates data from decimal form into the coding system used by the computer. The *decoder* analyses the instruction code of the computer program and instigates the execution of instructions. Other decoders translate the internal code of the computer into decimal form for output purposes.

The CPU of most computers contains an *electronic clock* (sometimes called the "master clock"), which emits regular pulses at frequencies that range from several million to over a billion per second. These pulses are used to insure the exact timing necessary for proper operation of the CPU. For instance, most computers are "synchronous," that is, they utilize a fixed number of pulses to determine when to initiate the next machine operation. A few computers are "asynchronous," that is, the completion of a current operation signals the start of the next operation. In either case, exact timing is necessary to accomplish the machine operations that are required to execute a computer instruction.

The locations of the registers and other subunits described in the preceding paragraphs varies with different makes and models of computers. In general, registers and other subunits that perform arithmetic and logic operations, such as the accumulator and adder, are part of the arithmetic-logic unit, while subunits such as the instruction register and the decoder are part of the control unit. However, the physical location of these subunits is not important. What is important is the understanding that registers and counters are temporary work areas and that other subunits, such as adders and decoders, consist of electronic circuitry that analyze instructions and perform required arithmetic and logical operations.

Primary Storage Classifications

Chapter Two analyzed the internal storage characteristic of the modern computer and briefly described the function of the primary storage unit of the CPU. We learned that all data and instructions must be placed in primary storage before they can be used by the computer system. The primary storage unit can also hold data and instructions between processing steps and after processing is completed. We can therefore identify several types of primary storage depending on the particular storage function performed. Figure 4–1 summarizes the various primary storage classifications, though it is merely an illustration; the actual size and types of storage areas would vary with the computer program being processed and the computer system being used.

The major type of primary storage is sometimes called *"main data storage,"* "main memory," or "real storage" and is sometimes further subdivided into input storage, output storage, program storage, and "working" storage. *Working storage* is sometimes called "scratch pad

FIGURE 4–1

Primary Storage Classifications

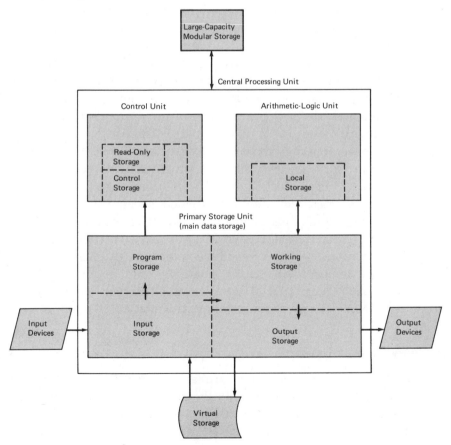

memory" because it may be a small high-speed storage area used to temporarily store data, instructions, and intermediate results during processing. Another type of primary storage results from the development of *large-capacity magnetic core modular storage,* known as "extended core," "mass core," or "bulk core." This type of primary storage is slower but cheaper than main data storage. Multiples of these modular units can be added to some computer systems thereby greatly increasing the storage capacity of the CPU. (In some systems, these units are used for high-speed secondary storage.) See Figure 4–2.

Other classifications of primary storage used by some computer designers are *"local storage,"* which consists of the high-speed registers of the arithmetic-logic unit, and *"control storage,"* which consists of the registers of the control unit as well as a recent development known as "read-only storage." Read-only storage (ROS), also known as "reloadable control storage" (RCS), is used to store "microprograms" which as previously mentioned are small, frequently used sets of elementary computer instructions called "microinstructions."

The term "read-only storage" is used to describe this unit because its contents cannot be altered during processing, since it will not accept input of data or instructions. Special procedures must be utilized to load microprograms into the ROS unit from "microcode" punched cards or magnetic disks. Some versions of microprogramming utilize special memory circuit cards that are plugged into place in the ROS unit. Microprograms can be changed by replacing these circuit cards.

A final primary storage classification is *virtual memory* (also called virtual storage) which has previously been defined as the ability of secondary storage devices to be treated as an extension of the primary storage unit, thus giving the "virtual" appearance of more "real storage" than actually exists. Data and instructions are transferred between primary storage and secondary storage devices in such a way that it appears that the computer has a larger main memory than it actually does. Special software and hardware has been developed to carry out the virtual storage concept.

Primary Storage Devices

Magnetic core.   A widely used primary storage device is magnetic core. Magnetic cores were previously described as tiny doughnut-shaped rings composed of iron oxide and other materials that are strung on wires which provide an electrical current that magnetizes the cores. A string of several cores represents one storage position (eight cores plus one for a check bit for all computers using the EBCDIC code). Thousands of cores strung on wires make up a core "plane" and several core planes make up a core "stack." Since the primary storage unit in many computers is composed of magnetic cores, primary storage is frequently referred to as "core storage." See Figure 4–3.

Magnetic core became the most widely used primary storage device for several reasons. Magnetic cores are a binary or two-state device since they can be magnetized in a clockwise or counter-clockwise direction producing the binary "on" or "off" state which is used to represent the binary digits 0 and 1. The direction of electric current in the wires running through the center of the cores determines their magnetic direction.

This magnetic direction can easily be changed, though the magnetic core can retain its magnetism indefinitely if so desired. The magnetic direction of each core can be individually sensed or changed, thus allowing the contents of each storage position to be sensed or changed at speeds in the nanosecond range. Magnetic core storage is therefore an extremely fast "direct access" storage medium. Four wires are used to control the magnetic core memories of most computer systems; however, two and three-wire systems are also used.

Magnetic thin film. Although magnetic cores are still the most common form of primary storage, other devices have recently been developed. Magnetic "thin film" devices consist of tiny spots of metallic alloy only a few millionths of an inch thick that are deposited on glass, plastic or metal plates, or on metal rods or wires. The spots can be magnetized like magnetic core but are a lot smaller, have a faster access time, and are more temperature and shock resistant than magnetic core memories. Since many thin film devices do not require as much production effort as magnetic core circuitry, they are potentially less expensive to manufacture. However, at the present time magnetic core storage is still generally less costly. Magnetic thin film storage is currently being used in several UNIVAC and NCR computers. See Figure 4–4.

Semiconductor storage. Semiconductor storage devices consisting of microscopic integrated circuits such as MST (Monolithic Systems Technology), LSI (Large-Scale Integration), or MOSFET (metal oxide silicon field effect transistor) circuits are the most recently developed primary storage devices. The entire primary storage unit of several models of the fourth generation IBM system/370 computers

FIGURE 4–2

Large-capacity Modular Storage Unit

Courtesy International Business Machines Corporation.

FIGURE 4–3

Magnetic Core Plane

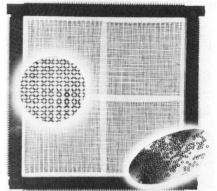

Courtesy International Business Machines Corporation.

FIGURE 4–4

Magnetic Thin Film Plane

Courtesy NCR.

FIGURE 4–5

Semiconductor Memory Module

Courtesy International Business Machines Corporation.

consists of MST or MOSFET circuits. Semiconductor storage circuitry was first used for extremely high-speed special purpose storage required in such primary storage elements as scratch pad memory, read-only storage, registers, and high-speed "buffer" memory. The primary storage semiconductor memory of some system/370 models consists of MOSFET chips less than an eighth of an inch square. Each chip contains several thousand circuit elements (such as transistors, resistors, diodes, capacitors, and connecting circuitry), and provides 128 positions (bytes) of storage. The chips are organized on storage "cards" which are utilized to form storage "modules" as shown in Figure 4–5.

Some of the major attractions of microscopic semiconductor storage devices are their small size, great speed, shock and temperature resistance, and potential for low-cost mass production. Access times for semiconductor memories are below 50 nanoseconds and into the picosecond range. Their cost had been greater than most other primary storage devices, but significant reductions in manufacturing costs have greatly increased their use.

Primary storage developments. Semiconductor storage devices will continue to replace magnetic cores and thin film as primary storage devices. However, research is currently underway which indicates the development of other primary storage devices. *"Cryogenic"* storage devices are being developed which will be much faster and smaller than semiconductor storage. Cryogenic devices consist of materials which become superconductors at extremely low temperatures. *Laser* storage devices which utilize crystalline material to change the polarization of light are being developed. Changes in the polarity of light captured by these crystals would provide a binary storage device operating at the speed of light. *"Magnetic bubble"* storage devices have been developed which utilize thin slices of magnetizable crystals on which tiny magnetized areas known as magnetic bubbles or "domains" can be generated. The data is represented by groupings of these magnetic bubbles which can be moved across the surface of the crystal slices by electrical currents or magnetic fields. Speeds exceeding 3 million bits per second have been demonstrated by such devices.

BASIC PERIPHERALS AND MEDIA

Many types of computer peripherals and media can be used for both input and output or for all three functions of input, output and secondary storage. For example, magnetic disk equipment and the magnetic disks they utilize as a data medium perform all three of the functions of input, output, and secondary storage. Also, some devices do not utilize data media for input or output. For example, devices such as a keyboard terminal enter data directly into a computer system, and cathode ray terminals directly display its output. Since there are so many types of computer peripherals and media, we shall first briefly describe and analyze the basic devices that are utilized by most computer systems. Other computer peripherals and media will then be covered.

The Computer Console

The computer console is frequently the only input/output device for minicomputers and some small computers. In these and other computer systems, it is the input/output device which enables the computer operator to monitor and control the operations of the computer. The computer console usually consists of a control panel and a console typewriter, though several recent computers are replacing one or both of these units with a CRT unit consisting of a television-like *"cathode ray tube"* plus a keyboard. The computer console is attached to the central processing unit in many computer systems, though in larger systems it is a separate unit. See Figure 4–6.

The switches and buttons on the console control panel and the keyboard of the console typewriter or CRT device allow the computer operator to enter data and instructions directly into the CPU. The console typewriter or CRT device and small lights on the console control panel are direct output devices that allow the computer operator to monitor the performance of the computer system. The small lights on the computer console display the contents of important registers and counters and the status of other important internal circuitry. The computer console allows the computer operator to start, stop, or change the operation of all or part of the computer system, and to correct some equipment malfunctions. The console typewriter or CRT unit prints or displays messages to the computer operator concerning error conditions, the beginning or end of various stages of processing, intermediate or final results of processing, or operating instructions. The computer console is therefore the input/output unit which allows the computer and the computer operator to communicate with each other concerning the operations of the computer.

Punched Card Hardware

Punched card hardware has historically been the most widely used type of equipment and media in electronic data processing because of the prior use of the punched card in electromechanical data processing systems. Punched card peripheral equipment for computer systems include the card reader, card punch, card read-punch, and the multifunction card unit. See Figure 4–7. These units use photoelectric cells to sense the holes in the punched cards and convert the data into electric pulses which are then converted into the internal code of the computer. Cards are read by two different reading stations in card reader units as a check on the accuracy of the operation. Card punch machines punch output data into cards under the control of the computer, and include a reading station to check on the accuracy of the punching process. The card read-punch combines the functions of reading and punching into a single unit. The multifunction card unit is a versatile input/output device which can perform most of the functions of the electromechanical punched card equipment described in Chapter One. This unit can read, punch, sort, collate, reproduce, and interpret cards. The reading speed of card reading devices varies from 100 to 2,000 cards per minute, while card punching speed varies from 60 to 500 cards per minute.

Benefits and limitations. Punched cards are a familiar, inexpensive, and simple input/output and secondary storage medium. Data in a file of cards can easily be changed by adding, deleting, or repunching a card. Punch card output can be in the form of a human-readable document which can later be used as input to an electronic data processing system. Punched card paychecks and utility bills are familiar examples. However, cards are bulky, can hold only a limited amount of data, and provide a very slow method of computer input/output compared to other widely used media. For instance, an inch of high-density magnetic tape can hold as many characters of data as 20 punched cards, while magnetic tape input speeds range up to 350,000 characters per second compared to a maximum of about 2,500 characters per second with punched cards. Another major limitation of punched cards is the keypunching, verifying, and other input preparation activities that are required before data can be utilized by the computer system.

Magnetic Tape Hardware — 2400 feet

Magnetic tape is a widely used input/output and secondary storage medium, especially for large-volume computer applications. Data is recorded in the form of magnetized spots on the iron oxide coating of a plastic tape somewhat similar to that used in home tape recorders. Magnetic tape is subdivided into seven or nine horizontal tracks or channels in order to accommodate a check bit and either the six-bit BDC Code or the eight-bit EBCDIC Code. Blank spaces known as "gaps" are used to separate individual data records or blocks of grouped records. Most magnetic tapes are ½ inch wide and 2400 feet long and are wound on plastic reels 10½ inches in diameter. The density of the data that can be recorded on such tape is frequently either 800 or 1600 bytes per inch. Thus, a reel of magnetic tape could contain over 45 million bytes which is the equivalent of over 500,000 punched cards.

Hypertape is a special high-density tape that is one inch wide, 1800 feet long, and records data in ten tracks at densities of over 3,000 bytes per inch. Hypertape is enclosed in a sealed cartridge containing a full tape reel and an empty take-up reel which protects the tape and minimizes tape loading and unloading effort. Magnetic tape also comes in the form of small cartridges and cassettes which are produced by magnetic tape typewriters and other devices that record data directly from a keyboard to magnetic tape. The small cartridge has a capacity equivalent to about 275 punched cards, while cassettes can store up to 2 million characters.

Devices that can read and write data on magnetic tapes are called *magnetic tape units, drives, or transports.* (See Figure 4–8). Electro-magnet read-write heads record data on each channel in the form of magnetic spots on the tape during writing operations. The read-write heads are also used in the reading operation to sense the magnetized spots on the tape and convert them into electronic impulses that are transmitted to the CPU. Reading and writing speeds range from 15,000 to 180,000 bytes per second using standard magnetic tape and up to 340,000 bytes per second for hypertape units. A small magnetic tape cartridge reader can read data at the rate of 900 characters per second while a magnetic tape cassette "deck" can read or write data at speeds ranging from 300 to 5,000 characters per second. Magnetic tape cassette decks are being used as low-cost input/output units for small computer systems and remote terminals.

Benefits and limitations.   Magnetic tape is a high-speed input/output medium as well as a high-density secondary storage medium. In comparison to punched cards, magnetic tape is less expensive because one reel of tape can replace hundreds of thousands of cards, occupy a lot less storage space, and can be reused many times because data can be easily erased and new data recorded. The limitations of magnetic tape include the fact that it is not human-readable, that it is a sequential access file medium, and that it is vulnerable to dust particles and stray magnetic fields. As was explained in the previous chapter, sequential access files may require the reading of an entire file in order to find one particular record in the file. Since dust particles and stray magnetic fields can alter the data contents of magnetic tape, environmental controls become necessary.

Magnetic Disk Hardware

Magnetic disks are the most widely used direct access medium for secondary storage and have even displaced punched cards and magnetic tape as a common input/output medium in many computer systems. Magnetic disks are thin metal disks which resemble large phonograph records and are coated on both sides with an iron oxide recording material. Several disks are mounted together on a vertical shaft which rotates the disks at speeds approaching 2,000 rpm. Read-write heads move between the slightly separated disks to read or write data on concentric circular "tracks." Data is recorded in the form of small magnetized spots arranged in serial order in a code such as EBCDIC. There are between 100 to 500 data tracks on each disk surface. See Figure 4–9.

There are several types of magnetic disk arrangements, but the most popular utilizes removable and interchangeable *"disk packs,"* which typically consists of six or 11 disks. Magnetic disk packs can be used interchangably in *magnetic disk units* and stored off-line when not in use. Disk packs are easy to handle; for example, the widely used IBM 2316 disk pack which contains 11 disks, is 14 inches in diameter, 6 inches high, and weighs 14 pounds. However, some magnetic disk units utilize nonremovable magnetic disk assemblies. A recent development is the "data module" which combines several magnetic disks and read-write heads into a removable "cartridge." These magnetic disk cartridges are designed to be faster, more reliable, and hold more data than magnetic disk packs.

The speed of magnetic disk units is expressed by their "average access time" and "data transfer rate." The average access time refers to the time it takes the read-write head to reach a specific data location on a magnetic disk. Each byte of data can have a specific address indicating the disk number, "cylinder," surface, and "sector."[1] The data transfer rate refers to the speed at which data can be transferred between the disk unit and the CPU. The average access time for most disks ranges from ten to 700 milliseconds and data transfer rates vary from 100,000 to 800,000 bytes per second. The speed of magnetic disk units depend on the number of access arms and the number of read-write heads as well as the speed of the revolving disks.

Storage capacity of magnetic disk units vary depending on the type, number, and arrangement of magnetic disks in a unit. Magnetic

---

[1] A "cylinder" is an imaginary vertical cylinder formed by the vertical alignment of one track from each surface of the disks in a disk unit. A "sector" is a section of a track.

FIGURE 4–6

Computer Console

FIGURE 4–7

Card Read-Punch

FIGURE 4–8

Magnetic Tape Drive

FIGURE 4–9

Magnetic Disk Unit

FIGURE 4–10

High-speed Printer

*Photos courtesy International Business
Machines Corporation*

disk units may contain one or more disk "drives," each of which can accommodate one disk pack. Other magnetic disk units contain non-removable groupings of magnetic disks and utilize fixed read-write heads for each track on a disk. Several thousand bytes of data can be recorded on each track of a disk. The storage capacity of a single disk pack ranges from about one million bytes to over 100 million bytes, while magnetic disk units may exceed a billion bytes of on-line storage.

Benefits and limitations.   The major attraction of magnetic disks is that they are superb direct access input/output and secondary storage devices. They are thus superior to magnetic tape for applications which require direct access files, such as real-time processing, time-sharing, and virtual memory systems. Thus, the magnetic disk provides the benefits of direct access files described in Chapter Three. One of the limitations of magnetic disks is their higher cost compared to magnetic tape. Also, updating a magnetic disk file results in the loss of old data, whereas magnetic file updating results in a new tape file, with the old tape file still available as a "backup" file. Magnetic disks are also slower and more expensive than magnetic tape for many batch processing applications where sequential access files are satisfactory.

Printers

Most computer systems utilize printing devices to produce permanent (*hard copy*) output in human-readable form. The most common printing devices are the high-speed *impact printer* and the electric typewriter, both of which print by pressing a printing element and an inked ribbon against the face of a continuous paper form. Multiple copies are produced by using carbon paper and other multiple copy forms. High-speed impact printers print from 120 to 132 characters per line, at speeds up to 2,000 lines per minute. Higher speeds can be attained by reducing the number of characters used. Most high-speed impact printers utilize either a metal chain or cylinder of characters as their printing element. Typewriter printer speeds vary from 600 to 900 characters per minute. See Figure 4–10.

Another type of high-speed printer is the nonimpact printer which prints by means of electrostatic or electrochemical processes. Such printers can print over 5,000 lines per minute but cannot produce multiple copies or high-quality printing. Other printing devices include small slow-speed nonimpact printing terminals, and off-line electromechanical printers formally used as punched card equipment.

Benefits and limitations.   Printing devices provide a computer system with the ability to produce printed reports and forms of all kinds. Printing of excellent quality can be done at high speeds. However, the speed factor is the cause of two contradictory problems. Computers can now produce printed reports so quickly that managers can be "buried" in mountains of paper. The ability of managers to use the information in computer printed reports to assist their decision making is diminished by the rapid flow of volumes of paper. On the other hand, high-speed printers are not fast enough output devices for most computer systems, thus causing an "output-bound" condition. The data transfer rate of high-speed printers is over 4,000 characters per second, which is quite slow compared to over 300,000 characters per second for magnetic tape output. This problem is being solved by the use of visual display terminals, off-line magnetic tape to printer operations, and microfilm output devices.

OTHER PERIPHERALS AND MEDIA

Most computer systems include a computer console, card reader-punch, magnetic tape or disk units, and printing devices. However, many other peripherals and media may be used by modern computer systems, and their number continues to grow as new devices are developed. We shall describe and analyze the more important devices in the following pages.

Paper Tape Hardware

Prior to its use as an input/output and secondary storage medium for computer systems, punched paper tape was utilized by teletype, automatic typewriter, and other electromechanical data processing systems. Data is recorded on strips of paper tape in the form of small round holes in a variety of codes. See Figure 4–11. Paper tape readers, punches, and reader-punch units perform their functions in a manner that is comparable to card punch equipment. In addition, punched paper tape is frequently produced as a by-product of cash registers, bookkeeping machines, and other data processing machines. The punched paper tape is then sent to a computer center for processing. Paper tape is also a popular data medium for low-volume scientific and time-sharing applications.

Benefits and limitations.   Paper tape is cheaper and does not have the data capacity limitations of punched cards. Paper tape equipment is simpler and less expensive than punched card machines, especially when it can be produced as a by-product of other business machines. However, paper tape is a slower input/output data medium than punched cards. Paper tape can be read at speeds ranging from 10 to 2,000 characters per second, and punched at speeds ranging from 10 to 300 characters per second. The accuracy of tape punching is harder to verify, and the addition, deletion, and correction of data requires splicing or repunching the tape. Paper tape cannot be used as a human-readable document, nor can the data it contains be easily sorted and collated like the data in punched cards.

Magnetic Drum Hardware

Magnetic drums were used for primary storage in first generation computers but are now used as on-line direct access secondary storage media. These devices are faster than most magnetic disk units but have a smaller storage capacity. Magnetic drum devices are similar to magnetic disk units except that the magnetic drum is a cylinder instead of a group of disks and drums have fixed read-write heads for every track or "band" on the surface of the drum. A typical drum might rotate at 3,500 r.p.m., have 800 data tracks on which over 4 million bytes can be stored, and have an access time of less than 10 milliseconds and a data transfer rate of 1,200,000 bytes per second. However, smaller and faster magnetic drum units and large slow-speed drums containing over 100 million bytes of storage are also available. See Figure 4–12.

Benefits and limitations. Magnetic drums are slower but cheaper than magnetic core storage and usually faster but more expensive than magnetic disk units. They are typically used as high-speed direct access storage devices to store data and instructions which are frequently referred to during processing, such as mathematical tables and special purpose programs. However, magnetic disks with fixed read-write heads for each data track are seriously competing with magnetic drums.

Magnetic Cards and Strips

Magnetic cards and strips combine the inexpensive high-capacity benefits of magnetic tape with the direct access advantages of magnetic disks and drums. These advantages are offset to some extent by a slower access time. Magnetic cards and strips are similar to magnetic tape but can be about 3 inches wide and up to 14 inches long.

FIGURE 4–11

Paper Tape Punch and Coding

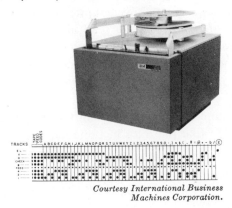

Courtesy International Business Machines Corporation.

FIGURE 4–12

Magnetic Drum Unit

FIGURE 4–13

Magnetic Strip Unit

Courtesy International Business Machines Corporation.

Courtesy International Business Machines Corporation.

Several hundred cards or strips are mounted in removable cartridges or "cells" which can be stored off-line. The magnetic card or strip unit allows the computer to select an individual card or strip, move it under a read-write head, and return it to its cartridge. The NCR magnetic card device is called a CRAM unit (Card Random Access Memory) while the IBM magnetic strip device is called a "data cell drive." Such units may store between 100 million to 600 million bytes of data with access times ranging from 200 milliseconds to 500 milliseconds and data transfer rates that vary between 25,000 to 55,000 characters per second. See Figure 4–13.

Benefits and limitations. Magnetic card and strip units offer large-capacity random access storage at a lower cost than magnetic disks and drums. They are used for applications that do not require fast access times, such as for a large inventory file in a batch processing system.

MICR Hardware

Magnetic ink character recognition (MICR) allows the computer systems of the banking industry and the Federal Reserve System to magnetically "read" checks and deposit slips and thus sort, tabulate, and post them to the proper checking accounts. Such processing is possible because the identification numbers of the bank and the customer's account number are now preprinted on the bottom of most checks with an iron-oxide based ink. The first bank receiving a check after it has been written must encode the amount of the check in "magnetic ink" on its lower right hand corner. The MICR system utilizes 14 characters (the ten decimal digits and four special symbols) of a unique design called "type font E-13B." See Figure 4–14. MICR characters can be preprinted on documents or can be encoded on documents utilizing a keyboard-operated machine called a "proof-inscriber," which also segregates checks into batches and accumulates batch totals. Equipment known as MICR *reader-sorters* "read" a check by first magnetizing the magnetic ink characters and then sensing the signal induced by each character as it passes by a reading head. The check is then sorted by directing it into one of the pockets of the reader-sorter while the data is electronically captured by the computer system. Reader-sorters can read over 2,000 checks per minute with a data transfer rate of over 3,000 characters per second. See Figure 4–15.

Benefits and limitations. MICR processing has been tremendously beneficial to the banking industry. Banks would be hard pressed to handle the processing of checks (23 billion checks were written in 1973) without MICR and computer technology. MICR documents are human-readable as well as machine-readable. MICR has proven to be a highly accurate and reliable method for the direct entry of data on a source document. Major limitations of MICR is the lack of alphabetic and other characters and the necessity to encode the amount of the check in a separate manual processing step.

OCR Hardware

Optical character recognition (OCR) equipment can read alphabetic, numeric, and special characters that are printed, typed or handwritten on ordinary paper. OCR is an attempt to provide a method of direct input of data from source documents into a computer system. The conversion of data into punched card, paper tape, or magnetic tape form is not necessary when OCR is used. However, OCR devices such as *optical readers* and *optical reader-sorters* can only read certain types of printing or handwriting, though progress is continually being made in increasing the reading ability of OCR equipment. A widely used character design for OCR is shown in Figure 4–16. Typical speeds of optical readers vary from 100 to 3,000 characters per second and up to several thousand documents per minute. There are many types of optical readers, but they all employ photoelectric devices to scan the characters being read and convert reflected light patterns of the data into electronic impulses which are accepted as input into the computer system. Documents which contain characters which do not meet the character design standards of the optical reader are rejected. See Figure 4–17.

Optical character recognition devices can not only read preprinted characters but also characters produced by typewriters, cash registers, adding machines, credit card imprinters and handwriting, providing the characters meet OCR standards. OCR equipment can also read pencil marks made in specific positions of a form. This is a variation of "mark-sensing" in which marks made by special pencils can be electrically sensed by special punched card equipment. OCR devices can also read documents that contain "bar coding" which is a code that utilizes bars to represent characters. Bar coding on packages of food items and other products has become common-place since it is required for the POS (Point-of-sale) systems being developed for the supermarket industry. A variation of this method involves scanning strips of flourescent tape on the side of railroad cars with a special camera and transmitting the number, location, and direction of the cars in a moving train to a computer.

Benefits and limitations. The major benefit of OCR is that it provides a method of direct input of data from a source document into a computer system. It thus eliminates much costly input preparation activity and increases the accuracy and speed of an electronic data processing system. OCR is extensively used in the credit card billing

FIGURE 4–14

A Check with MICR Encoding

Courtesy International Business Machines Corporation.

FIGURE 4–15

MICR Reader-Sorter

Courtesy International Business Machines Corporation.

FIGURE 4–16

USASCSOCR (USA Standard Character Set for Optical Character Recognition)

ABCDEFGHIJKLMNOPQRS
TUVWXYZ0123456789·¬
'-{}%?♩ΨH:¦=+/≑*"&

FIGURE 4–17

Optical Character Reader

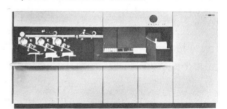

Courtesy International Business Machines Corporation.

operations of credit card companies, banks, and oil companies. It is also used to process utility bills, insurance premiums, airline tickets, and cash register and adding machine tapes. OCR is used to automatically sort mail, score tests, and process a wide variety of forms in business and government. The major limitations of OCR are the stringent character design requirements and the high cost of many optical reading units. Another major limitation for some applications is a document rejection rate that ranges between one and ten percent and an error rate of approximately one percent.

Visual Input/Output Hardware

Visual input/output devices use a *cathode ray tube* (CRT) which is similar to a television tube for the display of data output and, in some cases, the direct input of data. Most *CRT terminals* (also called visual display units) combine a typewriter-like keyboard for input, with a CRT screen for visual display of output. Keyed-in data can be displayed and corrected before entry into the computer system. Output is quickly and silently flashed onto the screen whenever requested. Many CRT units display a point of light called a "cursor" to assist the user in the input of data. The cursor may be a circle or other shape that indicates the position of data that is to be entered or changed. See Figure 4–18.

A more advanced (and more expensive) CRT terminal does not only display alphanumeric information but also displays drawings and graphs. Such "graphic" CRT terminals allow the results of scientific, engineering, and business analysis to be converted into graphs, curves, drawings, and other forms of graphic output. See Figure 4–19.

Another type of advanced CRT terminal can accept visual input through the use of a "light pen" or "data tablet." The light pen is a pen-shaped device which utilizes photoelectric circuitry to enter data into the computer through the CRT terminal. A user can "write" on the CRT screen because the light-sensitive pen enables the computer to calculate the coordinates of the points on the screen being touched by the light pen, even though a CRT screen may contain over one million points of light. The data tablet is a small electronic tablet utilizing a stylus to trace drawings which appear simultaneously on the CRT screen. Thus, graphic or alphanumeric data can be entered directly into the computer system and later changed, or deleted, though substantial software support is required. Visual input (sometimes called graphic input) is being used in military applications, mathematical analysis, engineering and architectural design, and other applications. See Figure 4–20.

Other visual input/output hardware includes large screen display devices, hard copy devices for CRT terminals, and "tactile input" CRT devices. *Large screen display units* project a CRT-like image on a large screen. Hard copy reproductions of CRT images can be provided by optional equipment such as typewriters, high-speed printers, copying machines, or photographic devices. *Tactile input devices* utilize the sense of touch to enter data into a computer system

FIGURE 4–18

CRT Terminal

Courtesy Bunker Ramo Corporation.

FIGURE 4–19

Graphic CRT Terminal with
Hard Copy Unit

Courtesy Tektronix, Inc.

FIGURE 4–20

Using a Light Pen

*Courtesy International Business Machines
Corporation.*

FIGURE 4–21

Audio-response Unit

*Courtesy International Business
Machines Corporation.*

by touching the surface of a special "sensitized" CRT screen with a finger or pointer.

Benefits and limitations. CRT units are faster and quieter than printing devices and do not flood users with rivers of paper. A specific piece of information or an entire data record can be displayed instantly in either alphanumeric or graphic form. The ability to correct and edit input data displayed by a CRT before entry into a computer system is a major benefit. The light pen and data tablet provide a valuable method of visual input especially for engineering and architectural design.

Visual input/output units are a major advance in man-computer communications, but they do have several limitations. Special hardware or software is needed to "refresh" the image of most CRT units or the data being displayed will fade away. The cost of graphic display and visual input CRT units is higher than less advanced forms of input/output. This cost limitation becomes more pronounced if other equipment is required to produce the hard copy that CRT units do not provide. These limitations have prompted much research to discover methods other than a CRT to generate an image electronically. Electroluminescent, laser, and "plasma" display technologies seem most promising.

Voice Input/Output Hardware

Voice input/output devices are limited in their current applications but should be widely used in the future. Most devices of this type utilize a keyboard for input and have a voice output (usually called "audio-response") capability. The simplest such device is the common push-button (Touch-Tone) telephone. Input of data is accomplished by depressing the buttons of the telephone while output is in the form of a voice produced by the *audio-response unit* of the computer and transmitted to the telephone receiver. An audio-response unit is a peripheral device which has a vocabulary of words, phrases, or syllables that have been prerecorded by human voice and are stored on a magnetic disk or drum. The computer prepares the required output information and then directs the audio-response unit to assemble and transmit a verbal answer. Audio-response units have a limited vocabulary (32 to 128 words, for example) based on the most frequently used words for a specific application. See Figure 4–21.

Voice input of data into a computer system is at the frontier of man-computer interaction. Complex combinations of hardware and software have been developed which can convert sound waves into an electronic digital form for entry into a computer system. Much of this development is still experimental, though operational use of voice input does exist on a limited basis. The two main types of voice input are "word recognition" and "speaker recognition." IBM has an operational *word recognition*/audio-response system which allows its field engineers throughout the nation to test data communication terminals by conversing with a computer at a test center in Raleigh, N.C. The computer is programmed to ask a series of diagnostic questions (through its audio-response unit) which the engineer answers in a normal tone of voice. Though the computer understands only 13 words, this is enough for it to select the correct testing procedure for the terminal.

Several firms have operational *speaker recognition* systems in which voice input to a computer is analyzed to verify the identification of a speaker. A speaker's voice is compared to a file of previously recorded voices (sometimes called "voiceprints") in order to establish the identification of the speaker. Widespread use of this type of voice input is expected as the basis of identification and security measures required by a future "cashless-checkless society" where *electronic funds transfer systems* (EFTS) replace cash and checks as the primary method of payment.

Benefits and limitations. Voice input/output devices provide the quickest and easiest method of man-computer communications, since every telephone becomes a potential computer terminal. Push-button telephones and audio-response units are widely used by many large banks to verify a customer's checking account balance. Other applications currently using audio-response systems include insurance policy analysis, inventory status reports, telephone company messages, and stock trading information. The major limitations of voice input/output devices are the high cost of audio-response units (over $60,000 each) and the infant status of voice input technology.[2]

Microfilm Input/Ouput Hardware

The use of microfilm as an input medium is known as CIM (*computer input microfilm*), while the use of microfilm as an output medium is known as COM (*computer output microfilm*). COM is widely used to replace computer printing devices which are too slow and produce too much paper. COM hardware can have a data transfer rate up to 500,000 characters per second and "print" up to 60,000 lines per minute which is 30 to 50 times faster than most high-speed printers and equals or exceeds the output rate of magnetic tape or

---

[2] Even more "far out" on this frontier are computers which "read human minds!" Experiments are being conducted in which a computer reads the brain waves of subjects fitted with electronic sensors and then executes their simple commands.

disk units. Microfilm output also takes up only two percent of the space of paper output. COM hardware includes a microfilm recorder, developer and duplicator, a hard copy printer, and microfilm readers or reader-printers.

Microfilm recorders can capture computer output directly when connected on-line to a computer or indirectly when connected to an off-line magnetic tape unit. Most microfilm recorders project alphanumeric or graphic data onto the screen of a cathode ray tube and capture the data on microfilm rolls or "microfiche" through the use of a high-speed microfilm camera. Once the microfilm is developed by a microfilm developer unit, it can be viewed directly by microfilm readers or viewers. Microfilm copies can be reproduced by a microfilm duplicator, while a microfilm printer can produce paper copies when necessary. Another type of microfilm output is the "electron beam recorder," which does not take microfilm pictures of a CRT display but instead aims an electron beam directly at dry-silver microfilm. No film developing is necessary in this process. Microfilm recording with laser beams has also been developed. See Figure 4–22.

Some microfilm storage and retrieval systems mount microfilm on a punched card, known as an "aperture card" so that individual microfilm records can be easily stored and retrieved by punched card equipment. Other systems utilize a computer to automate the retrieval of any desired microfilm frame from a large microfilm file.

The use of microfilm as a computer input medium (CIM) is still in the early stages of development, though a few CIM systems are being marketed. CIM systems utilize an OCR (Optical Character Recognition) device to scan microfilm, thus resulting in high-speed input of data.

Benefits and limitations. Microfilm output is a lot faster and takes up much less space than paper output. The storage, handling, and retrieval of microfilm files is substantially easier and cheaper than paper documents. COM requires less CPU time than printing devices. COM is used to sharply reduce the volume of computer printed paper even though some COM users record *all* transaction data instead of merely producing printed "exception reports." Such users claim that they can provide better customer service and better information for management because the computer provides them with up-to-date microfilm records of all transactions, recording only exception items on paper. Some firms have replaced magnetic strip-CRT information retrieval systems with COM systems because the COM system proved to be substantially cheaper, could provide microfilm or paper copies more quickly, and was more reliable and flexible. The major limitation of COM is the high cost of hardware. COM is thus limited to high-volume applications or the COM facilities of a data processing service bureau. The microfilm recorders, developers, duplicators, printers, and viewers required by COM cannot be economically justified for small-scale computer systems.

Laser Strip and Film Storage

Laser strip storage is a recently developed method for large capacity direct access secondary storage. Large-capacity storage devices such as laser strip units, magnetic card and strip units, and large-capacity magnetic core units, are also known as "mass" or "bulk" storage devices. The laser strip storage system utilizes a laser beam to record data by burning microscopic holes in the metallic coating of a plastic strip. Thus, data is recorded in a binary code pattern by the presence or absence of these tiny spots. A four by 32-inch strip can store millions of bits, and a laser strip unit can store trillions of bits in an on-line direct access file containing hundreds of strips. Data is read by scanning a selected strip with a low-power light beam to detect the reflected pattern of bits.

Laser film storage is a sequential access storage medium utilizing lasers to record binary data on 8mm microfilm. One type of "laser optical recorder/reproducer" unit has a data transfer rate of ten million bits per second and can store over four billion bits on one reel of film.

Benefits and limitations.   The major benefit of laser strip storage is its ability to permanently store large masses of data in a compact, low-cost direct access file. Laser film storage offers low-cost sequential access storage since one reel of laser film can store as much data as 40 standard magnetic tape reels. The laser recording method is also less subject to loss of data than magnetic recording methods. Major limitations are the slow access times of laser strip storage and the inability to reuse strips or film since recorded data can not be erased.

Other Input/Output Hardware

It would take volumes to describe and analyze the multitude of devices that can be connected to a computer for the purposes of input and output. Therefore, we shall conclude this section with a brief description of additional input/output hardware.

Data communications hardware. Any input/output device we have discussed can become a data communications *terminal,* and a grouping of input/output devices (which may include a small computer) can become a data communications *station* or *satellite* computer system. *Intelligent terminals* which are really minicomputers with input/output and data communications capabilities are another type of data communications hardware. See Figure 4–23. However, all of these devices must be modified to include or be attached to special *data communications interface hardware* (discussed in a following section) in order to have data communications capabilities. Most traditional input/output devices are available in specially modified data communications versions including some unique small and portable devices. See Figure 4–24.

Keyboard devices. The wide-spread use of devices which utilize a keyboard for data input should be emphasized. Typewriter terminals, CRT units, and push-button telephones are widely used examples, though many other specialized devices also use keyboards for input. Some terminals do not have an output capability but utilize a keyboard as a simple input device. On-line keyboard devices allow direct entry into a computer system without the use of data media.

Transaction recorders. One class of data communication terminals is commonly called *"transaction recorders."* The purpose of these terminals is to bypass the input preparation function and enter data directly into a computer system utilizing a variety of input media. Transaction recorders are frequently described as "point-of-origin," "point-of-use," or "point-of-sale" terminals and are also known as "data collection" or "data acquisition" devices. Many transaction recorders include a slot into which badges, plastic cards, inventory tags, or prepunched cards can be inserted. Data from these input media is automatically read by the recorder, and additional information is usually entered through a keyboard or by manipulating keys or levers. For example, a *data recorder* in a factory could utilize an employee's plastic badge, prepunched cards, and a keyboard to enter data directly into a manufacturing control system. Similarly, on-line *"teller terminals"* are used by banks and other savings institutions to update directly a customer's savings account balance in the files of the computer and record it on his bank book. Cash registers connected on-line to a computer are known as *POS terminals* (point-of-sale terminals) and allow instant credit verification and direct entry of sales data into the computer system. See Figure 4–25.

FIGURE 4–22

Microfilm Recorder

Courtesy Quantor Corporation.

FIGURE 4–23

Intelligent Terminal with CRT screen
and Dual Cassette Decks

Courtesy Datapoint Corporation.

FIGURE 4–24

Portable Data Communications Terminal

*Courtesy Computer Transceiver
Systems, Inc.*

Plastic card hardware. Plastic cards are a widely used input medium in the form of embossed credit cards issued by oil companies, banks, and credit card companies, and department stores. A simple *"imprinter"* device uses a customer's credit card to imprint his account number on a sales invoice in OCR characters which can then be read by OCR equipment. A card-dialing telephone which uses punched plastic cards for automatic dialing is sometimes used as a data communications terminal. Data can be punched into the plastic cards which are inserted into a reading slot of the phone which then transmits the data. See Figure 4–26. Plastic badges of factory employees are also used as input media by transaction recorders which "read" the employee's number and other information from the badge.

Plastic credit cards with a strip of magnetic tape attached to the back of the card have been used as a computer input/output medium. The *"mag stripe" card,* as it is called, has already been used in several communities in pilot projects sponsored by the banking industry. Special computer terminals read the magnetic stripes in order to authorize credit, transfer funds, and reduce the "cash" balance recorded on the stripe.[3] Other plastic "money cards" using different technologies are being developed.

Plotters.   Computer output devices called *"plotters"* produce graphic data on paper using a pen and ink process, electrical inscribing, or electrochemical nonimpact techniques. The mechanical arm of the plotter draws lines on the paper under the direction of the computer. Plotters can operate on-line, or be operated off-line by special magnetic tape units. See Figure 4–27.

Magnetic ledger cards.   Magnetic ledger cards were described in Chapter One as an input/output medium for electronic bookkeeping machines. However, *magnetic ledger card units* can be attached to some small computer systems, such as the IBM System/3. Magnetic ink or tape stripes on the back of a paper ledger card allow a computer to electronically read and write data such as account numbers and account balances. Current transactions and balances can also be typed by a typewriter device on the front of the card. Some magnetic ledger card readers can automatically feed and read-write data on the cards at a speed of 50 cards per minute.

Copying machines.   The use of CRT display devices which do not produce hard copy output, COM devices which do not produce paper output, and nonimpact printers which do not produce multiple copies has spawned a variety of *copying machines* to produce multiple paper copies of computer reports. The copying machines can be directly connected to an output device such as a high-speed printer or they can operate as an off-line copying device. Many of these devices can reduce computer output to an 8½x11-inch size and

---

[3] Students at California Institute of Technology won a $5,000 first prize and a $1,500 second prize in a contest sponsored by First National City Bank of New York to see how easily the mag stripe card could be defrauded. Several simple and ingenious methods of cheating the mag stripe card were discovered. Citibank sponsored the contest because a subsidiary is developing a computer-readable credit card utilizing a different type of technology.

FIGURE 4–25

Point-of-Sale Terminal with OCR Device

Courtesy NCR.

FIGURE 4–26

Plastic Card Telephone Terminal

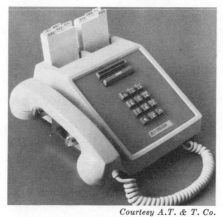

Courtesy A.T. & T. Co.

FIGURE 4–27

Graph Plotter

*Courtesy of California Computer Products, Inc.,
Anaheim, California.*

also produce xerox or multilith masters. Xerox, IBM, and many other firms manufacture a variety of these computer output copying machines.

Process and machine control hardware.   *Process control* applications of computers involve the processing of data arising from an ongoing physical process such as scientific or engineering experiments and various manufacturing processes. Process control requires the use of special input devices that measure physical phenomena such as temperature or pressure changes. If a digital computer is being used, the measurements must be converted into digital form before they can be processed. Process control also involves the use of unique output devices that will convert output data into physical movements which adjust thermostats, valves, or other control devices.

An extension of process control is the *numerical control* of machines by a computer. Numerical control involves the direction of the actions of a machine by commands from a computer. Thus, machines such as machine tools, typesetting machines, weaving machines, and other industrial "robots" become automated work-producing output devices. Numerical control can be accomplished off-line by using special paper tape or magnetic tape units which utilize the output of a computer to direct a machine. "Direct numerical control" is the term used to describe an on-line numerical control system where a computer is in direct communication with one or more machines. See Figure 4–28.

INPUT/OUTPUT INTERFACE HARDWARE

Several computer system subunits exist which are difficult to classify since they can be physically part of the CPU, a separate peripheral unit, or can be built into an input/output or storage unit. The main purpose of subunits such as "buffers," "channels," "input/output control units," and "data communication interface units," is to assist the CPU in its input/output assignments, thus making possible advanced EDP systems. These subunits have been developed to provide a uniform, flexible, and efficient *"standard interface"* between the CPU and its input/output units. (*An interface is a connection or boundary between systems or parts of systems.*) They provide modern computer systems with the ability to carry out many input and output functions simultaneously, while at the same time allowing the CPU to carry out other processing functions since it no longer must directly control I/O devices. See Figure 4–29.

FIGURE 4–28

Computer Controlled Machine Tool

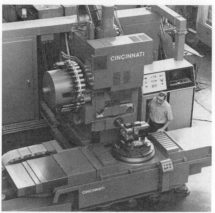

Courtesy Cincinnati Milacron, Inc.

FIGURE 4–29

Input/Output Interface Hardware

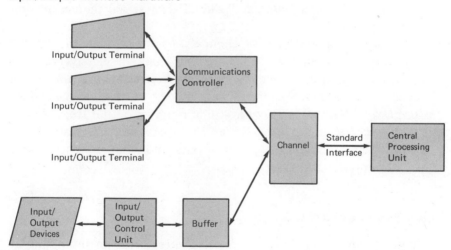

Buffers

Buffers are high-speed storage units which are used for the temporary storage of input or output data in order to reduce the demands of input/output operations on the CPU. Buffers (also known as "synchronizers") are sometimes built into the CPU or into the input/output device or may be housed separately in a peripheral unit. When buffers are used, the CPU does not have to wait for the input or the output of data but can initiate an input or output command and then return to other processing. Data can then move from the input device into the buffer or from the buffer into an output device without tying up the CPU. High-speed transfer of data occurs when an input buffer transfers data to a CPU or when a CPU can transfer data into an output buffer. However, buffers alone cannot provide the *overlapped processing* capability required when many input/output devices are operated concurrently.

Channels

Channels are like special purpose minicomputers which control the movement of data between the CPU and input or output devices. Channels are housed within the CPU or can be separate peripheral units and may contain buffer storage. Once the channel receives an input or output command from the CPU, it can control the operations of several input/output units simultaneously without disturbing the CPU. Only when the input or output operation is completed will the channel "interrupt" the CPU to signal the completion of its assignment.

There are two main types of channels, each of which can handle several input or output units. The *"selector channel"* selectively allows each input or output device temporarily to monopolize the entire channel in what is called the "burst mode" of data transmission. *"Multiplexor" channels* can control data input or output from several slower devices simultaneously in a "multiplex mode." Most multiplexor channels can also operate in a burst mode in order to service high-speed input/output devices.

Input/Output Control Units

Channels are normally not connected directly to an input/output device but to an *input/output control unit*. A control unit can be built into an input/output device or housed as a separate unit (frequently called a *"controller"*) that controls several input/output devices. The job of the control unit is to decode the input/output commands from the CPU or the channel and to control the operation of the appropriate input/output device, including the coding, decoding and checking of data transmitted from the CPU. Buffer storage units are part of the control units of some input/output devices.

Data Communications Interface Units

Examination of the data communications system illustrated in Figure 3–6 of the previous chapter reveals transmission and receiving terminals connected by a data transmission channel. Several types of data communication interface units are required at transmission and receiving terminals to enable data to be transmitted between remote terminals and computers. Most data transmission channels currently in use (telephone, telegraph and microwave radio) were designed primarily for voice communications. These public communications networks were designed to handle continuous analog signals, such as the human voice. However, since data from computers is in digital form, devices are necessary to convert the digital signals into appropriate transmission frequencies and vice versa. The only other alternative is the construction of special digital communications channels. Several private channels have been built and nationwide digital networks were completed in 1974.

"Modems" (also called data sets) are devices used to convert the digital signals from input/output devices into appropriate frequencies at a transmission terminal and convert them back into digital signals at a receiving terminal. This process is called modulation and demodulation. The word modem is a combined abbreviation of the two words. A simple and widely used modem is the *"data phone"* (see Figure 4–30), which is used to convert several types of input/output devices into data communications terminals. The data phone

FIGURE 4–30

Data-phone

Courtesy A.T. & T. Co.

and other telephone type modems are frequently used as *"accoustic couplers."* These are modems used to connect portable or movable devices to a telephone line by cradling the telephone receiver in a special holder.

Other interface devices are needed to code and decode the data, to control the data communications equipment, and to allow many data communications terminals to use the same data transmission channel. A *"data communications control unit"* (sometimes called a *"communications controller"* or *"datanet"*) is also required in data communications systems. These units usually include temporary buffer storage, error detection, and synchronization capabilities. Both the modem and the data communication control unit may be separate units or may be housed in the input/output terminal device. However, communications controllers that manage data communications systems containing many terminals are frequently special purpose small computers or minicomputers. The internally stored programs of these controllers relieve the central computer of its data communications control functions.

Other data communication interface devices are the "multiplexor" and the "concentrator" which allow a single communications channel to carry simultaneously data transmissions from many terminals. The multiplexor is a complex hardware device, while the concentrator is similar to a small special purpose computer since it utilizes an internally stored program to carry out its functions.

AUXILIARY HARDWARE

Our analysis of computer hardware concludes with a brief look at off-line equipment and materials that support the input, output, and storage functions of a computer system. Such *"auxiliary hardware"* includes *input preparation equipment, off-line output and storage equipment,* and *data processing materials.*

Punched Card Equipment

Most of the *punched card machines* discussed in Chapter One are now used as input preparation equipment or off-line output and storage equipment for computer systems which use punched cards as a primary data medium. For example, data is usually recorded on punched cards by keypunch machines and checked for accuracy through the use of verifiers. Versatile machines known as "card data recorders" which can punch, verify, and interpret cards can also be used. The cards are then sorted, organized, imprinted, and reproduced utilizing sorters, collators, interpreters, and reproducers. Even the electromechanical accounting machine is used by some computer installations as an off-line printing device that lists the data contents of punched cards on a printed paper form. These operations take place before the cards are used as input into a computer system, or after they have been produced as output, but before they are placed in off-line storage. (Refer back to Figure 1–11).

Keyboard-to-Magnetic Tape Hardware

Keyboard-to-magnetic tape devices enter data directly from a keyboard onto a magnetic tape. The aim of such input preparation devices is to bypass the process of first recording data into punched cards or punched paper tape and then converting these media into magnetic tape utilizing *"data converter"* equipment. Keyboard-to-magnetic tape devices are known as "key-tape" machines, "magnetic data recorders," magnetic data inscribers," and "magnetic tape typewriters." These devices produce magnetic tape in the form of standard-size magnetic tape reels, small cartridges, and cassettes. See Figure 4–31.

Data recorded on standard-size magnetic tape reels can be used by the magnetic tape units of a computer system, while small magnetic cartridges and cassettes require special computer peripheral equipment such as tape cartridge readers and cassette decks. However, keyboard-to-cassette or cartridge devices are small, portable, and less expensive than keyboard-to-standard magnetic tape reel devices. Automatic electric typewriters that utilize magnetic tape

FIGURE 4–31

Keyboard-to-Magnetic Tape Device

Courtesy Honeywell, Inc.

cartridges, such as the IBM Magnetic Tape Selectric Typewriter (MTST), can also be used as keyboard-to-magnetic tape input devices.

Keyboard-to-Magnetic Disk Hardware

Input preparation systems utilizing many keyboard "stations," all of which input data simultaneously to a central magnetic disk unit, are a recent development. Such systems can be connected on-line to a main computer or can be off-line, though the assistance of a mini-computer is usually required. These expensive systems can only be justified for applications requiring large volumes of data from many sources where real-time processing is not required. The major advantage of such *key-to-disk* systems over key-to-tape methods is that they do not require the merging and sorting of magnetic tapes from many different keyboard-to-magnetic tape devices.

A more recent input preparation development is the magnetic *"diskette,"* or *"floppy disk,"* which is a small flexible, magnetic disk that resembles a small phonograph record. Each eight-inch diameter diskette can hold as much data at 3000 80-column punched cards. The reusable diskette is packaged in plastic and is easily filed or mailed. The diskette is inserted into a slot of a keyboard and CRT equipped "data station." Data is entered via the keyboard, visually verified through display on the CRT, and recorded on the diskette. Data on the diskettes can be transferred to magnetic tape by a "data converter," or read directly into a computer.

Other Input Preparation Hardware

Many other types of *input preparation devices* have been developed. We have previously mentioned devices which print MICR or OCR characters on various input documents. Even computer peripherals may perform an input preparation function. High-speed printers and computer card punch units can produce output in the form of punched cards or documents printed in OCR or MICR characters. Cards or forms produced in this manner are known as *"turnaround" documents,* since they are designed to be returned to the sender. For example, many computer printed invoices consist of a turnaround portion which is returned by a customer along with his payment. The turnaround document can then be automatically processed by OCR or MICR equipment. Thus, the high-speed printer has performed an input preparation function.

CRT/keyboard terminals also perform an input preparation function since keyed-in data can be displayed and corrected before input into the computer system. The computer may be programmed to display a report format on the CRT. A user "fills out" this electronic form by using the keyboard, guided in some models, by the small point of light called the cursor. When both the computer and the user agree that the form is properly filled out, the data is entered into the computer system.

Equipment previously described as transaction recorders or data collection devices can also perform an input preparation function that is sometimes called *"source data automation"* (SDA). Off-line transaction recorders such as credit card imprinters, cash registers, adding machines, bookkeeping machines, and other devices, are frequently used to convert data into OCR documents, punched paper tape, or punched cards. This process usually occurs as a by-product of the operation of the machine. Thus, many cash registers and bookkeeping machines perform an auxiliary input preparation function by producing punched paper tape or OCR paper tape during their normal operation.

Off-line Output and Storage Hardware

Most computer systems require a variety of off-line devices that support the *output* and *storage* functions. We have previously mentioned the role that microfilm systems, copying machines, and punched card equipment can play in providing such a support function. Microfilm systems produce microfilm output and provide a compact and easily retrievable storage medium. Copying machines provide multiple copies of computer output. Punched card equipment can organize and produce printed lists of punched card output.

Off-line magnetic tape units, card punch units, paper tape units and high-speed printers also fall into the category of *off-line output/ storage equipment*. They are widely used to convert data from one medium to another. In many cases, the computer will use magnetic tape as a high-speed output medium to avoid an "output-bound" condition. Output is then converted into printed documents or punched cards by off-line equipment. A similar process can be used to avoid an "input-bound" condition. Punched card or paper tape input can be converted off-line into magnetic tape form for later high-speed input. Devices used for such activities are known as *"off-line data conversion equipment."*

The multiple copy output of high-speed printers requires a variety of *output support equipment* such as form detachers, separators, "bursters," sorters, and imprinters. These devices are used to separate and assemble computer produced reports and documents. Filing equipment of various types is also required for the off-line storage of punched cards, magnetic tapes, magnetic disk packs, and computer-printed reports or "printouts."

Data Processing Materials

Data processing materials include forms, manuals, and supplies used in computer operations and programming. The operation of a computer system requires *input/output control forms* such as data "batch tickets" and data transmittal sheets whose purpose is to assure the proper processing of input and transmittal of output. *Operations control forms,* such as job transmittal documents, run setup sheets, and computer operations logs, are used to organize and control the flow of work in a computer installation. Other data processing supplies include *programming forms* and aids which facilitate the programming process.

SUMMARY

Figure 4–32 summarizes the types of computer hardware which have been discussed in this chapter. Computer hardware includes the central processing unit, peripheral equipment, auxiliary equipment, and media and materials. The central processing unit includes arithmetic-logic, control, and primary storage units. It also includes sub-units such as registers and counters, which are temporary work areas, and adders and decoders, which consist of electronic circuitry that analyzes instructions and performs required arithmetic and logical operations. Primary storage can be subdivided into several classifications because of the variety of primary storage functions that must be performed. Main data storage is sometimes subdivided into input storage, output storage, program storage and working storage. Other classifications include local storage, control storage, read-only storage, and virtual storage. The most commonly used primary storage devices are magnetic cores, magnetic thin film, and semiconductor storage, though other devices are being developed.

FIGURE 4–32

Computer Hardware Summary

CENTRAL PROCESSING UNIT

Control Unit, Arithmetic-logic Unit, Primary Storage Unit, Other Subunits (Registers, Counters, etc.)

Primary Storage Media
  Magnetic Core, Magnetic Thin Film, Semiconductor Storage

PERIPHERAL EQUIPMENT

Secondary Storage Devices
  Magnetic Tape, Magnetic Disk, Magnetic Drum, Magnetic Card and Strip, and Laser Strip and Film Units

Input/Output Devices
  Secondary Storage Devices, Punched Card, Paper Tape, MICR, OCR, Microfilm, Plastic Card, and Magnetic Ledger Card Units, Printers, Plotters

Direct Input/Output Devices
  Keyboard Devices, Light Pen, CRT Display Units, Audio-response Units, Voice Input, Console Keys, Switches and Lights, Process and Machine Control Devices

Input/Output Interface Devices
  Buffers, Channels, Input/Output Control Units, Data Communications Controllers, Concentrators, and Other Interface Units

AUXILIARY EQUIPMENT

Punched Card Equipment, Keyboard-to-Magnetic Tape, Keyboard-to-Magnetic Disk, Off-line Paper Tape, OCR and MICR Input Preparation Equipment, Off-line Data Conversion Equipment, Copying Machines, Filing Equipment

MEDIA AND MATERIALS

Input/Output and Secondary Storage Media (used in devices shown above), Data Processing Materials: Forms and Other Supplies

The basic peripherals and media used by most computer systems include a computer console, card read-punch, magnetic tape or disk units, and printing devices. However, many other hardware devices are used by modern computer systems and their number continues to grow as new devices are developed. The physical and performance characteristics, and the functions, benefits, and limitations of many types of input/output and secondary storage hardware have been discussed. Input/output interface hardware, such as buffers, channels, input/output control units, and data communications interface units have become important hardware devices because many current computer systems utilize multiple input/output devices, including data communications terminals. Computer hardware includes off-line auxiliary hardware which supports the input/output, processing, and storage functions of the computer system. Input preparation hardware, off-line output and storage hardware, and data processing materials are included in this category.

KEY TERMS AND CONCEPTS

Peripheral equipment, 84
Auxiliary equipment, 84
Registers and other CPU subunits, 85
Classifications of primary storage, 87
Primary storage devices, 88–90
Computer console, 92
Punched card hardware, 92–93
Magnetic tape hardware, 93–94
Magnetic disk hardware, 95
Printers, 97
Paper tape hardware, 98
Magnetic cards and strips, 99–100
MICR hardware, 101
OCR hardware, 102
CRT units, 104–105
Audio-response, 106
COM hardware, 107–108

Laser hardware, 109
Transaction recorders, 110
POS terminals, 110
Plotters, 112
Process control, 114
Numerical control, 114
Interface, 114
Buffers, 116
Channels, 116
I/O control units, 117
Modem, 118
Communications controller, 118
Input preparation devices, 84, 119–121
Off-line output and storage hardware, 121
Data processing materials, 122

ASSIGNMENTS

1. Test your understanding of the chapter material by reviewing the *purpose, outline, summary,* and *key terms and concepts* of this chapter. Are you confident that you have attained a basic understanding of the major concepts of the chapter? If not, reread the appropriate material as indicated by the page numbers after each key term and concept.

2. Discuss the functions, benefits, and limitations of several hardware devices selected from each of the following hardware categories:
    a. Central processing unit
    b. Secondary storage hardware
    c. Input/output hardware
    d. Input/output interface hardware
    e. Auxiliary hardware

3. Visit the computer center of your school or business. Identify and classify the various types of computer hardware being utilized. Determine the physical and performance characteristics of the major components of your computer system.

Chapter Outline

Purpose of the Chapter

Introduction

System Software

Programming Languages
Machine Languages, Assembler Languages, Macro
Instructions, Subroutines, Compiler Languages:
Advantages of Compiler Languages, Types of Compiler
Languages

Operating Systems
Types of Operating Systems, Stacked Job Processing,
Dynamic Job Processing: Swapping, Partitioning,
Paging, Spooling

Control Programs
The Supervisor, Input/Output Control Systems, Data
Communications Control Programs, Other Control
Programs

Processing Programs
Language Translators, Simulators, Emulators, and
Conversion Programs, Service Programs, Data
Management Systems

Application Software
Computer Applications, Canned Programs

EDP Policies and Procedures
Documentation

Summary

Key Terms and Concepts

Assignments

5

Computer Software

Purpose of the Chapter

To promote a basic understanding of computer software by analyzing the functions, benefits and limitations of major software components.

INTRODUCTION

Computer software includes all types of programs which direct and control *computer hardware* in the performance of data processing functions. Software also includes all nontangible EDP requirements such as the policies and procedures required to manage and control an EDP system and the detailed description of computer programs and EDP procedures which is known as *"documentation."* Computer software can be subdivided into three major categories: *system software, application software,* and *EDP policies and procedures.* These categories may be further subdivided as shown below.

1. System Software
    Programming Languages
        Machine, Assembler, and Compiler Languages
    Operating Systems
        Control Programs
            Supervisor, Input/Output Control System, and Other Control Programs
        Processing Programs
            Language Translators, Service Programs, and Data Management Systems
2. Application Software
    Business, Scientific, and Other Application Programs

3.   EDP Policies and Procedures
     Policies and Procedures for EDP Systems Development,
     Programming, and Operations.

SYSTEM SOFTWARE

System software consists of computer programs which control and support the computer system and its data processing activities. One major category of system software is *"programming languages,"* like COBOL and FORTRAN, for example, which allow computer instructions to be written in a language that is mutually understandable to both people and computers. The other major category of system software is *"operating systems,"* which is further subdivided into *"control programs"* and *"processing programs."* An operating system is an integrated system of programs which supervises the processing operations of the CPU, controls the input/output functions of the computer system, translates programming languages into machine languages, and provides various support services. The functions of each of the components of system software will be discussed in the sections that follow.

PROGRAMMING LANGUAGES

Machine Languages

Programming languages can be subdivided into three levels: "machine" languages, "assembler" languages, and "compiler" languages. *Machine languages* are the most basic level of programming languages. In the early stages of computer development, instructions were written utilizing the internal binary code of the computer. This type of programming involves the extremely difficult task of writing instructions in the form of coded strings of binary digits. Programmers had to have a detailed knowledge of the internal operations of the specific CPU they were using and had to write long series of detailed instructions in order to accomplish even simple data processing tasks.

Programming in machine language requires specifying the storage locations for every instruction and item of data used. Instructions must be included for every register, counter, switch, and indicator that is used by the program. These requirements made machine language programming a slow, difficult, and error-prone task. Depending on the internal code used by the particular computer being programmed, machine language instructions could be expressed in pure binary form, binary, octal, or hexadecimal codes, or even codes which utilize decimal numbers and/or alphabetical characters (which were then decoded by the circuitry of the CPU into pure binary form.) For example, a machine language program that would add two numbers together in the accumulator and store the result $(X = Y + Z)$ might take the form shown below. Like many computer instructions, these instructions consist of an "operation code" that specifies what is to be done and an "operand" which specifies the address of the data or device to be operated upon.

Operation Code	Operand	
1010	11001	(Replace the current value in the accumulator with the value (Y) at location 11001).
1011	11010	(Add the value (Z) at location 11010 to the value (Y) in the accumulator.)
1100	11011	(Store the value (X) in the accumulator at location 11011.)

The three machine language instructions shown above merely compute the sum of two one digit numbers and store the results in a single storage location. Many more instructions would be needed in order to complete a computer program which would accept data from an input device, perform the addition operation, and transmit the results to an output device.

Assembler Languages

Assembler languages are the next level of programming languages and were developed in order to reduce the difficulties in writing machine language programs. The use of assembler languages (and compiler languages) requires the use of a program called a *"language translator"* or a "language processor," which allows a computer to convert the instructions of such languages into machine instructions. The language translator is called an *"assembler"* for an assembler language and a *"compiler"* for a compiler language. We will analyze these translators in an upcoming section of this chapter.

Assembler languages are frequently called *"symbolic"* languages because symbols are used to represent operation codes and storage locations. Convenient alphabetic abbreviations called *"mnemonics"* (memory aids) and other symbols are used to represent operation codes, storage locations, and data elements. For example, the computation $(X = Y + Z)$ in an assembler language program might take the following form:

Operation Code	Operand	
LDA	Y	(Load Y into the accumulator)
ADA	Z	(Add Z to the accumulator)
STA	X	(Store the result X)

Notice how alphabetical abbreviations that are easier to remember are used in place of the actual numeric addresses of the data. This greatly simplifies programming, since the programmer does not need to know or remember the exact storage locations of data and instructions. However, it must be noted that an assembler language is still "machine-oriented" since assembler language instructions correspond closely to the machine language instructions of the particular computer model being used. Also, notice that each assembler instruction corresponds to a single machine instruction so that the same number of instructions are required in both illustrations. This "one-for-one" correspondence between assembler instructions and machine instructions is a major limitation of many assembler languages.

Assembler languages are widely used by professional programmers as a method of programming a computer in a machine-oriented language. Most computer manufacturers provide an assembler language which reflects the unique machine language *"instruction set"* of a particular line of computers. This characteristic is particularly desirable to *"systems programmers"* who program systems software (as opposed to *"applications programmers"* who program applications software) since it provides them with greater control and flexibility in designing a program for a particular computer. They can then produce more *"efficient" software,* ie., programs that require a minimum of instructions, storage, and CPU time to perform a specific data processing assignment.

Macro Instructions

Many assembler languages have been improved by the development of a *"macro instruction"* capability which is also a basic concept in the design of compiler languages. A macro instruction is a single instruction which generates one or more machine instructions when it is translated into machine language. Macro instructions are provided by the software supplier or written by a programmer for such standard operations as arithmetic computations and input/output operations. The format and sequence of instructions that will be generated by the *"macro"* must first be defined, but from then on a single macro can be written each time the desired sequence of instructions are required in a program. The development of a macro instruction capability for modern assembler languages reduces the number of instructions required in an assembly language program, thereby reducing programming time and effort and the potential for programming errors.

For example, an assembler language with a macro instruction capability would probably include a macro for the process of addition. The computation of $(X = Y + Z)$ might then take the form of a single macro instruction which would later be translated into the three machine instructions required for addition. The macro instruction might take the form:

ADD   Y, Z, X

Subroutines

Assembler languages were further improved by the development of the *"subroutine"* concept which is also used by all compiler languages. A "routine" is a sequence of instructions in a program that performs a particular data processing activity, such as an "input" routine, and "addition" routine, "sort" routine, etc. The term "subroutine" is used to describe a special purpose routine or small program which can be made part of a larger "main" program in order to perform a standard data processing task. Subroutines eliminate the necessity of programming a particular data processing operation each time it is required in a computer program. For example, many input/output activities and mathematical and statistical calculations can be performed by using standard "preprogrammed" subroutines. Subroutines that check input data for errors or compute the square root of numbers are examples of the many types of subroutines that are frequently used.

A subroutine can be defined at the beginning of a program and then used whenever needed in the program by the use of a specific macro instruction which causes the program temporarily to *"branch"* to the subroutine, perform necessary operations, and then return to the regular sequence of the program. A more widely used method of using subroutines involves storing many standard subroutines in an on-line *"subroutine library"* that is available to all computer users. In this method, the main program of a computer user would *"call"* a subroutine by the use of a particular macro instruction whenever the subroutine was needed. The computer would then branch to the specific subroutine in the subroutine library, perform necessary operations, and then return to the main program. The subroutine is therefore a powerful tool which minimizes programming effort and errors and provides different computer users with an efficient method of performing common but special purpose data processing operations.

Compiler Languages

Compiler languages are also known as "high-level" or "human-oriented" languages. The instructions of compiler languages are called *"statements"* and closely resemble human language or the standard notation of mathematics. Individual compiler language statements are really macro instructions since each individual statement generates several machine instructions when translated by a compiler program. Most compiler languages are designed to be *machine-independent,* ie., a compiler language program can usually be processed by computers of different sizes or manufacturers. Compiler language statements do not resemble machine or assembler language instructions. Instead they resemble the English language or mathematical expressions required to express the substance of the problem or procedure being programmed. The *"syntax"* (vocabulary, punctuation, and grammatical rules) and the *"semantics"* (meaning) of compiler language statements do not reflect the internal code of any particular computer but instead are designed to resemble English or mathematical expressions as closely as possible. For example, the computation $(X = Y + Z)$ would be programmed in the compiler languages of FORTRAN and COBOL as:

$$\text{FORTRAN:} \quad X = Y + Z$$
$$\text{COBOL:} \quad \text{COMPUTE } X = Y + Z$$

If we defined X as GROSSPAY, Y as SALARY, and Z as COMMISSIONS we could illustrate how close to the English language a compiler language statement can be with the FORTRAN and COBOL statements:

FORTRAN: GROSSPAY = SALARY + COMMISSIONS
COBOL: ADD SALARY TO COMMISSIONS GIVING
          GROSSPAY

Advantages of compiler languages. A compiler language is obviously easier to learn and understand. It takes less time and effort to write an error-free computer program or to make corrections and revisions that may be required. However, compiler language programs are usually less efficient than assembler language programs and require a significantly greater amount of computer time for translation into machine instructions. These characteristics were considered serious limitations when compiler languages were first developed. However, the savings in programmer time and training, the increased speed and storage capacity of third and fourth generation computer hardware, and the efficiency and versatility of modern computer software have made compiler languages the most widely used programming languages for business, scientific, and other applications.

Since compiler languages are machine-independent, programs written in a compiler language can be processed by different models and makes of computers without major modifications. This means that computer programs do not have to be reprogrammed when a new computer is installed and that a computer programmer does not have to learn a new language for each computer he programs. Compiler languages have less ridged rules, form and syntax, thus reducing the potential for errors. Compiler language translators (compilers) include extensive diagnostic capabilities that assist the programmer by recognizing and identifying programming errors.

Types of compiler languages. Compiler languages are frequently subdivided into "procedure-oriented" languages and "problem-oriented" languages. *Procedure-oriented languages* are general purpose languages that are designed to express the "procedure" or logic of a data processing problem. The programmer does not have to concern himself with the details of how the computer will process his program. Popular procedure-oriented languages are FORTRAN, COBOL, PL/1, and BASIC.

Problem-oriented languages are designed to provide an efficient programming language for specialized types of data processing problems. The programmer does not even specify the procedure to be followed in solving the problem but merely specifies the input/output requirements and other parameters of the problem to be solved. Such programming simplicity is possible because the specialized nature of the language allows the problem solving procedure to be "preprogrammed." Some examples of problem-oriented languages are: RPG, which is used to produce reports and update files, GPSS, which is used for simulation applications, LISP, which is used to process lists of symbolic data, and COGO, which is used for the solution of civil engineering problems.

Hundreds of other programming languages have been developed, many of them with humorous names ranging from FRED and LOLITA to STRUDL and SYNFUL. However, five of the most widely used compiler languages in business data processing, FORTRAN, COBOL, PL/1, BASIC and RPG, are briefly described in the next chapter. The last four chapters of this book present the fundamentals of these languages.

OPERATING SYSTEMS

Operating systems are also known as "executive systems," "monitor systems," "control systems," and "system control software." We have defined an *operating system* as *an integrated system of programs which supervises the operations of the CPU, controls the input/output functions of the computer system, translates programming languages into machine languages, and provides various support services.* The primary goal of an operating system is to maximize the throughput of a computer system by operating it in the most efficient manner possible. An operating system minimizes the amount of human intervention required during processing by performing many functions that were formerly the responsibility of the computer operator. An operating system also simplifies the job of the computer programmer, since it includes control programs and processing programs which greatly simplify the programming of input/output operations and many other standard data processing functions. Operating systems have become indispensible for medium and large computer users in order to handle the overlapped processing and multiprogramming requirements of large-volume batch processing, and the time-sharing and data communications characteristics of real-time processing systems.

Of course, it must be emphasized that some small computer systems do not utilize an operating system but instead use only a few simple control and processing programs. Such small computers do not employ complete operating systems but instead are provided with several control programs, language translators, and service programs by the computer manufacturer, with other programs usually available at additional cost. Also, most operating systems are designed as a collection of program *"modules"* which can be organized in several combinations to form operating systems with various capabilities. Such operating systems can therefore be tailored to the requirements of a particular computer system.

Types of Operating Systems

The components of two widely used IBM operating systems are shown in Figure 5–1 to illustrate the variety of program modules found in many operating systems. IBM has several operating systems available for its System/360, System/370, and other computer systems. However, the two major types are DOS (Disk Operating System) and OS (Operating System). DOS is designed for small to medium-scale computers and is available in a virtual storage version, DOS/VS. OS is utilized by medium to large-scale computers and is available in two virtual storage versions, OS/VS1 and OS/VS2.

Stacked Job Processing

Operating systems allow computers to perform *"stacked job processing"* in which a series of batch processing jobs are executed continuously without operator intervention being required between each job. Necessary information must be communicated to the operating system through the use of a *job control language* (JCL) consisting of several job control statements or "commands" that frequently are recorded on punched cards called *"control cards."* Control cards provide the operating system with such information as the sequence in which jobs are to be processed and the input/output devices required for each job. Since most batch processing jobs consist of one or more "job steps," information on the requirements of each job step is also necessary. A description of segments or "overlays" of programs too large for main memory may also be furnished. It should be

FIGURE 5–1

Two IBM Operating Systems

DISK OPERATING SYSTEM (DOS)

DISK OPERATING SYSTEM (DOS)
    Control Programs: Supervisor, IOCS, Job Control, IPL
    Processing Programs
        Language Translators: Assembler, COBOL, FORTRAN, PL/1, RPG
        Service Programs: Linkage Editor, Librarian, Sort-merge, Utilities, Autotest

OPERATING SYSTEM (OS)
    Control Programs: Data Management, Job Management, Task Management, IPL
    Processing Programs
        Language Translators: Assembler, ALGOL, COBOL, FORTRAN, PL/1, RPG
        Service Programs: Linkage Editor, Sort-merge, Utilities, TESTRAN, Loader

Source: *Introduction to IBM Data Processing Systems*, IBM Corporation (Poughkeepsie, N.Y.), pp. 90–93.

apparent that instead of communicating directly with the computer or through the computer operator as a middleman, the computer user and the computer operator must communicate with the computer through the operating system.

Dynamic Job Processing

Dynamic job processing is a term used to describe the constantly changing computer operations required by modern multisystem electronic data processing. We described *multisystem EDP* in Chapter Three (refer back to Figure 3–8) as an electronic data processing system composed of several EDP subsystems which might include batch processing, remote processing, real-time processing, time-sharing and data communications systems. The operating system for a computer that must operate in such a multisystem environment must provide dynamic job processing, as opposed to stacked job processing. Jobs are not processed sequentially in stacks but are processed according to a constantly changing *"priority interrupt system."* A system of priorities is established for jobs, job steps, and various operational situations which indicate when the CPU can be "interrupted" in its processing and diverted to another task. For example, an error indication or a signal from the computer operator would have a higher priority than a batch processing computation.

Swapping

A priority interrupt system usually requires "time slicing" in which each job is allocated a specified "slice" of CPU time (frequently a fraction of a second) as measured by the electronic clock of the computer. Jobs are interrupted if they exceed their allocated time slice, are replaced with a waiting job, and are assigned another priority for later processing. A priority interrupt system usually results in a waiting line or *"queue"* of jobs that may be stored in primary storage or in direct access storage devices called "swapping" storage. Thus, dynamic job processing involves the continual *swapping* of jobs and job steps between the primary storage and the swapping storage on the basis of a continually revised queueing and priority interrupt schedule.

Partitioning

When dynamic job processing involves *multiprogramming* a more complex operating system is needed. Multiprogramming requires the allocation of portions of primary storage among various jobs and job segments. The operating system subdivides primary storage into several fixed or variable "partitions," or into a large number of "pages." This allows several programs to be processed during the same period of time. Figure 5–2 shows the allocation of primary storage into three *fixed partitions:* one for the operating system, a "foreground" partition for high priority programs, and a "background" partition for low priority programs. Typically, high priority programs have extensive input/output requirements but require only small amounts of CPU processing time. Low priority jobs usually have extensive CPU processing requirements or are routine jobs which do not require immediate processing. For example, a real-time interactive system with many remote terminals may utilize the foreground partition, while batch processing might take place in the background partition.

Figure 5–2 shows how application programs and parts of the operating system are stored on direct access storage devices such as magnetic disk units, so that they can be shuttled back and forth between primary storage and secondary storage devices. Notice that only part of the operating system "resides" continually in the "resident area" of primary storage. Other programs of the operating system are transferred to a "transient area" of primary storage from a magnetic disk "systems residence device" whenever they are needed.

FIGURE 5–2

Multiprogramming with Fixed Partitions

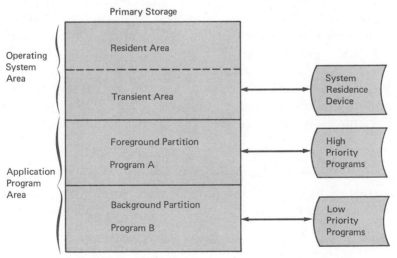

Subdividing storage into *variable partitions* requires a more complex operating system. Several jobs of various sizes are "squeezed" into primary storage so that it can be more efficiently utilized. A *"dynamic relocation"* procedure is utilized when necessary to relocate programs within primary storage. Therefore, the number of programs and their locations in storage is subject to continual revision.

Paging

Another form of dynamic relocation is *"paging"* which is the basis for *virtual memory* (virtual storage) systems. Primary storage is segmented into a large number of *pages* whose contents and location are automatically controlled by the operating system and the use of special hardware registers. A programmer may subdivide his program into pages or this may be done automatically by the operating system. *Segments* consisting of many pages are moved to and from secondary storage devices and retrieved as needed. This paging and segmentation is hidden from the computer user. His program may appear to be stored and processed in a single section of primary storage, when in reality it is subdivided into pages which are scattered throughout primary and secondary storage.

Paging and virtual memory systems require a sophisticated operating system (see Figure 5–3), as well as hardware features such as special registers and direct access secondary storage devices. Paging allows a computer to appear as if it had virtually unlimited primary storage, which is another basis for the term "virtual memory."

With virtual memory, large programs can be easily processed since programs do not have to reside entirely in main memory and subdividing large programs into segments or overlays is no longer necessary. Efficient use is made of primary storage since pages of programs can be placed wherever space is available. Many more programs can be run simultaneously when paging is used. For example, the third generation multiprogramming operating systems of one computer manufacturer allowed from six to 14 user programs to run concurrently, while its virtual memory operating system has a theoretical maximum of 250 concurrent users. This difference is primarily due to the fact that virtual memory systems require that only a few pages of a program being processed be in primary storage. Only those parts of a program containing the specific instructions and data actually being processed are required.

FIGURE 5–3

UNIVAC Virtual Memory Operating System (VMOS)

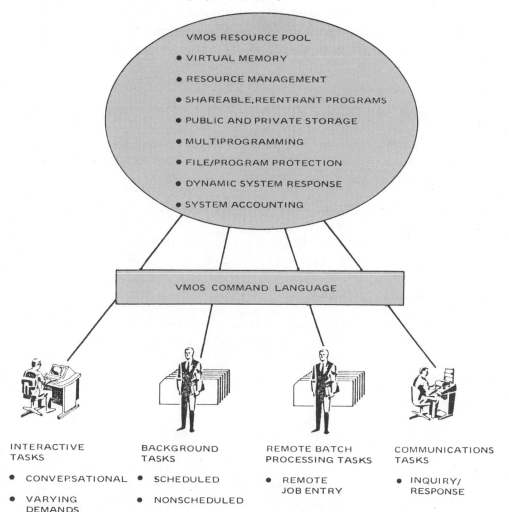

Source: *VMOS Programming System Information Manual*, UNIVAC Division of the Sperry Rand Corporation (Cinnaminson, N.J., 1972), p. 1-6.

Spooling

Dynamic job processing frequently involves a multiprogramming activity known as *"spooling"* (Simultaneous Peripheral Operation On-Line) which allows input and output operations to occur simultaneously with processing operations. Input data from low-speed devices is stored temporarily on high-speed secondary storage units to form a queue which can be quickly accessed by the CPU. Output data is also written at high speeds onto tape or disk units and form another queue waiting to use slow-speed devices such as a printer or a card punch. The operating system supplies a special utility program to control the spooling process.

CONTROL PROGRAMS

Operating systems are composed of control programs and processing programs. *Control programs* perform three major functions which can be described as shown below.

1. *Task management.*   Supervising the execution of processing programs.
2. *Data management.*   Controlling the input/output of data as well as its location, storage, and retrieval.
3. *Job management.*   The preparation and scheduling of jobs for continuous processing.

Control programs usually include a supervisor, an input/output control system, data communications control programs, a job control program, and an initial program loader.

The Supervisor

The most important component of an operating system is the control program called the *"supervisor,"* also known as the "executive," the "monitor," the "controller," or "the master control program." The supervisor directs the operations of the entire computer system by controlling and coordinating the other components of the operating system, as well as the activities of all of the hardware components of the computer system. Portions of the supervisor "reside" in primary storage whenever the computer is operating, while other supervisor routines are transferred back and forth between a transient area of primary storage and the system residence device. The supervisor monitors input/output activities and handles interrupt conditions, job scheduling and queueing, program fetching, and primary storage allocation. The supervisor also communicates with the computer operator through the computer console concerning the status of computer system operations and records important information required for proper job accounting, such as the amount of CPU time utilized by each job being processed.

Input/Output Control Systems

The "input/output control system" (IOCS) is a collection of subroutines which performs all of the functions required for the input and output of data. Input/output control systems can be subdivided into "physical" IOCS and "logical" IOCS. *Physical* IOCS subroutines are usually considered part of the supervisor and deal with the actual physical location and format of data in channels, buffers, and input/output and storage devices. *Logical* IOCS subroutines are generated by input/output macro instructions contained in an application program. The logical IOCS subroutines are stored in the system residence device and are concerned with the "logical" organization of data into input/output and storage records, files, and other data elements.

The input/output control system handles input/output scheduling, input/output error corrections, and performs various data management functions which create and maintain data files. Many writers estimate that approximately 40 percent of business application programs consist of input/output instructions. Given the complexity of modern EDP systems, the use of IOCS greatly simplifies the job of programming business applications. The programmer merely uses several standard input/output macro instructions to direct the IOCS to perform complex input/output and data management operations.

Data Communications Control Programs

Input/output control programs for data communications systems are usually considered separately from IOCS. *Data communications control programs* perform such functions as data collection, message switching, and remote inquiry and transaction processing. Data communications terminals may be automatically checked for input/output activity (this is called "polling"), and automatic queueing of input and output transactions is usually provided.

Other Control Programs

The *"initial program loader"* (IPL) is a small control program whose function is to load the supervisor from the system residence device into primary storage when the computer system begins operation. The *"job control program"* is a control program that is called into primary storage by the supervisor between jobs. Its function is to prepare the computer system for the start of the next job by executing job control language statements.

PROCESSING PROGRAMS

The *processing programs* of an operating system consist of language translators and service programs. *Application programs* are sometimes considered as part of the processing programs of system software; however, we will consider them as the separate major software category of *applications software.*

Language Translators

We have previously defined *language translators* (also called language processors) as programs which convert assembler language instructions and compiler language statements into machine language instructions. The language translator is called an *assembler* for an

FIGURE 5–4

The Language Translation Process

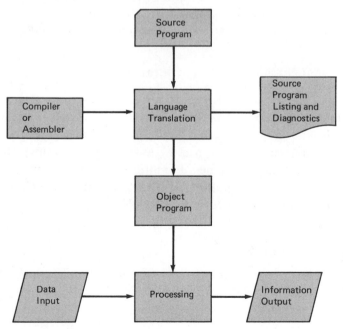

assembler language and a *compiler* for a compiler language. A program written in an assembler or compiler language is called a *source program*. When the source program is translated into machine language it is called the *object program*. The computer then processes the object program.

The language translation process is called "compiling" when a compiler is used and "assembling" when an assembler is used. Figure 5–4 illustrates the typical language translation process. Other types of language translators exist, such as *"interpreters,"* which translate and execute each source program statement one at a time, instead of first producing a complete object program. Besides the object program, most compilers and assemblers also produce a listing of the source program and a listing of error messages, called *"diagnostics,"* which identify programming errors recognized by the translator.

Simulators, Emulators and Conversion Programs

Special software and hardware have been developed which enable a computer to process programs originally written for an older computer or the computer of another manufacturer. "Simulation" is a software approach which utilizes a program called a *"simulator"* to perform this function, while "emulation" is a combination of software and hardware features. The hardware portion of emulation requires a *read-only storage device* within the CPU and the use of special *microprograms* stored in the ROS. The software portion of emulation consists of a program called an *"emulator"* which performs functions which cannot be handled by the microprograms. The purpose of such software and hardware is to enable a computer user to avoid the costly and time-consuming process of rewriting programs that have become obsolete because of the development of new generations of computer hardware and software.

Simulation and emulation are temporary approaches that ease the transition between computers of different generations or different manufacturers, since they do not make efficient use of the full capabilities of a new computer. The only permanent solution is the modification of obsolete programs. This is accomplished by reprogramming or the use of special "conversion programs." *Language conversion programs* (LCPs) can translate some obsolete programs into programs that are acceptable to new computer systems. Other conversion programs assist in the conversion of data files to new methods of data organization.

Service Programs

Service programs are specialized programs which perform common routine and repetitive functions and are made available to all of the users of a computer system. Service programs, language translators, specialized subroutines, and most control programs and applications programs are usually maintained in *"program libraries."* A subroutine library consisting of frequently used subroutines is a vital component of the service programs provided by most operating systems. An important service program is the *"librarian"* which catalogs, manages, and maintains a directory of the programs, subroutines, and macro instruction definitions that are stored in the various libraries of the computer system. Another important service program is the *"linkage editor"* which edits an object program by defining the specific storage locations it requires and linking together parts of the object program with required subroutines. *"Sort-merge"* programs are important service programs which perform the sorting and merging operations on magnetic tape or magnetic disk units which are required in many data processing applications.

Many operating systems provide special service programs for automatic program testing and *"debugging,"* which is the process of correcting errors (bugs) in a program. Finally, a major category of service programs are *"utility" programs* or "utilities," which are a group of miscellaneous programs that perform various "housekeeping" and file conversion functions. Utility programs clear primary storage, load programs, record the contents of primary storage, ("memory dumping") and convert a file of data from one storage medium to another, such as card-to-tape, tape-to-disk, etc.

Data Management Systems

A *"data management system"* (DMS) is a generalized set of computer programs which control the creation, maintenance, and utilization of the data bases and data files of a computer-using organization. Such systems are also called "data base management systems" (DBMS). Early forms of such software were known as "file maintenance systems" or "file management systems." Advanced data management systems automatically perform the following tasks for computer users:

1. *Data Base Creation.* Defining and organizing the data needed to support an information system.

2. *Data Base Maintenance.* Adding, deleting, updating, correcting, and protecting the data in a data base.
3. *Data Base Processing.* Utilizing the data in a data base to support various data processing assignments such as information retrieval and report generation.

A data management system is controlled by the operating system of a computer system. A DMS can be viewed as a generalized group of service programs which control all use of a data base. It works in conjunction with the "data management" control programs (such as IOCS) of the operating system which are primarily concerned with the physical input, output, and storage of data during processing. Data management systems have been developed by major computer manufacturers and several independent software companies. Some examples are MARK IV by Informatics, IMS by IBM, and IDS by Honeywell.

A DMS removes the data base from the control of individual programmers and computer users. This improves the integrity and security of the data base and facilitates its use by programmers and users. For example, programmers do not have to design the format of data files and records each time they write a program. Instead, they can include several simple macroinstructions in their programs which direct the DMS to perform necessary data base creation, maintenance, and/or processing activities.

Computer users do not have to write complete computer programs in order to retrieve information they seek from a data base. Instead, they may merely fill out a simple information request form or key in a few instructions on a computer terminal using a simple, English-like *"data manipulation language"* (DML). For example, a request by a sales manager for the amount of sales made by a particular salesman could take the following form:

> FILE IS SALES
> SALESMAN IS 024
> PRINT CURRENT SALES

A real-time data management system would respond almost instantly to such an "ad hoc" inquiry by providing the sales manager with the requested information.

APPLICATION SOFTWARE

Application software consists of computer programs which direct a computer system to perform specific data processing activities required for the solution of business, scientific, and other problems of computer users. Thus, application software is also known as "problem programs" or "user programs" and is frequently subdivided into "business application programs" and "scientific application programs."

Computer Applications

A *"computer application" is the use of a computer to solve a specific problem or to accomplish a particular operation.* Computer applications are frequently subdivided into business, scientific, and other applications categories. In Chapter Two, we described business applications as involving the processing of business and administrative data while scientific applications involved complex mathematical calculations and problem solving. Thus, a computer program that directs a computer to process a payroll or update an inventory is called a *business application program* whether it is used by a business firm, a government agency, or an educational institution. Likewise, a computer program that involves complex statistical analysis might be called a *scientific application program,* even though it is used by business analysts as well as by scientists and engineers. The *"other applications programs"* category covers a wide variety of applications in such areas as education, law enforcement, art, medicine, etc. We will analyze important applications of the computer in greater detail in subsequent chapters of this book.

Canned Programs

Applications software can be subdivided into *"user-written programs"* which are written by the computer programmers of a computer user, and *"canned programs"* (also known as "proprietary software," "applications packages," "software packages," or "packaged programs") which are supplied by computer manufacturers, independent software companies, or other computer users. Figure 5–5 provides an example of canned application programs supplied by a computer manufacturer.

The distinction between user-written programs and canned programs can also be applied to *system software.* Though control programs and service programs can be developed by a computer user, they are usually procured from a computer manufacturer or a software company. Figure 5–6 provides a description of a simple canned service program offered by a software company.

FIGURE 5–5

Business Application Canned Programs

Assignment. Determines how to assign jobs to machines or how to assign people to jobs at minimal cost.

Automatically Programmed Tools. Develops numerical control programs for a wide variety of manufacturing equipment.

Bond Pricing. Computes the price and accrued interest for a bond.

Bond Yield. Computes the before and after tax yield to maturity of a bond.

Cash Flow Analysis. Calculates the present values of up to four cash flows for a given cost of capital.

Critical Path Scheduling. Solves critical path or PERT networks of project activities.

Depreciation Analysis Program. Computes the monthly depreciation of an asset over its depreciable life using: 1. straight line, 2. double declining balance, 3. sum-of-the-year digits, and 4. 150 percent declining balance. Identifies the depreciation method that best maximizes the present value of cash flows.

Investment Analysis. Evaluates capital investments by projecting cash flows and determining expected rates of return for a proposed investment.

Lease-Purchased Analysis. Compares leasing versus purchase of equipment.

Loan-Interest Rate Analysis. Determines the true annual interest rate being paid on a loan.

Loan Repayment. Determines the amount of money to be paid back at each installment period to pay off a loan.

Mortgage Fact-Finder. Determines the interest rate, life, amount to be borrowed, or the monthly payment for a mortgage.

Proforma Statement Analysis. Projects up to five years of financial statements (balance sheet and income statement) for a firm.

Return on Investment. Computes returns for an investment in a common stock.

Transportation Linear Program. Determines the least cost schedule for transporting goods from several sources to several destinations.

Source: *VMOS Applications Abstracts,* Series 70 Publications, UNIVAC Division of The Sperry Rand Corporation (Cinnaminson, N.J., 1972).

A computer user is usually provided with an operating system or control programs by his computer manufacturer, who also makes available a variety of application software. Additional canned software must usually be purchased or leased from computer manufacturers, software companies, or other computer users. Time-sharing service companies provide a variety of canned programs to users of their time-sharing services and are therefore an additional source of canned programs.

Canned programs have several advantages for computer users. They reduce the need for the expensive and time-consuming effort required to develop user-written programs. The number of computer programmers required by a computer-using organization can be minimized. Computer manufacturers and software companies can frequently develop more efficient programs than a computer user because they are specialists in software development. Of course, canned pro-

FIGURE 5–6

Canned Service Program

COBOL-EZE is an inexpensive way to stretch your programming dollar, according to its developer. It allows users—for $100 plus a $2 handling charge—to define their own shorthand expressions for words and phrases in their COBOL programs. Instead of the statement "APPLY PAGE-END TO FORM-OVERFLOW ON PRINT" the user might write "APP FOP." The real names are substituted for the abbreviations at object time, and a new sequence and labeled source deck with the expansions can be requested.

A source deck, sample substitution cards, DOS, JCL, and operating instructions are included in the price. The only other investment required is 13,000 bytes of memory. General Systems Corp., Seattle, Wash.

Source: *Bank Automation Newsletter*, Management Reports, Inc. (Boston, Mass., November, 1972), p. 6.

grams do have their limitations. Some "ready-made" programs may be too generalized and have to be tailored to the needs of a specific user through extensive programming effort. Other canned programs may have been written for specific users and require reprogramming before they can be utilized by other users.

Canned programs usually come in the form of decks of punched cards or reels of magnetic tape along with manuals and other printed material that describes and documents the programs. Time-sharing service subscribers can utilize canned programs by merely requesting that a specific program be made available to their time-sharing terminal. (See Conversational Computing in Chapter Six.) As Figure 5–6 indicates, the amount of storage capacity required by a canned program is an important consideration. Information about canned programs is available from computer manufacturers, time-sharing service companies, software firms, and several publications which provide listings and abstracts of canned programs available in the U.S.

EDP POLICIES AND PROCEDURES

We have included in our definition of computer software, a major category that includes nontangible EDP requirements such as the *policies and procedures* required to manage and control an EDP system. This category of software also includes the detailed *documentation* of such policies and procedures, as well as the programs, operational procedures, and systems design of each computer application. We will discuss the policies and procedures required for effective management of an EDP system in a subsequent chapter devoted to the management of the computer.

Documentation

Operations, program, and systems *documentation* is a vital component of computer software. EDP documentation is the detailed description of a computer application utilizing words, flow diagrams, and other illustrative methods. *Operations documentation* enables a computer operator to properly carry out each step required in processing a specific computer job. *Program documentation* provides a detailed description of the design and instruction content of a computer program. This documentation is extremely important in diagnosing program errors, making programming changes, or reassembling a lost program, especially if its original programmer is no longer available. *Systems documentation* is similar to program documentation but provides a description of the information requirements and the systems design of a computer application. We will discuss such documentation in the following three chapters, which cover computer programming and information systems development.

SUMMARY

Computer software includes all programs which direct and control computer hardware in the performance of data processing functions, as well as all nontangible EDP requirements such as the policies and procedures required to manage an EDP system. Computer software can be subdivided into the three categories of system software, application software, and EDP policies and procedures. System software consists of computer programs which control and support the computer system and its data processing activities. A major category of system software includes programming languages which allow computer instructions to be written in a language that is understandable to both people and computers. The three major levels of programming languages are machine languages, assembler languages, and compiler languages. Compiler languages such as FORTRAN and COBOL are the most widely used programming languages for business, scientific, and other applications.

The other major category of system software is operating systems. An operating system is an integrated system of control and processing programs which supervises the processing operations of the CPU, controls the input/output of the computer system, translates programming languages into machine languages, and provides various support services. In modern computer systems, the computer user and the computer operator communicate with the computer through the operating system. Operating systems have become indispensible for medium and large computer users in order to handle the stacked job processing and dynamic job processing required by large-volume batch processing and real-time processing systems. Dynamic job processing requires techniques such as swapping, partitioning, paging, and spooling which allow the computer to process jobs according to a constantly changing priority interrupt system.

The control programs of an operating system include the supervisor, input/output control system, data communications control programs, and other control programs. Control programs perform the three major functions of task management, data management, and job management. The processing programs of an operating system consist of language translators and service programs. Language translators such as compilers and assemblers convert programming language instructions into machine language instructions. Service programs are specialized programs which perform common support functions for the users of a computer system. Data management systems which control the creation, maintenance, and utilization of data bases and files are an important major category of service programs.

The other major categories of computer software are application software and EDP policies and procedures. Application software consists of computer programs which direct a computer system to perform specific data processing activities required for the solution of business, scientific, and other problems of computer users. Application software can be subdivided into business application programs and scientific application programs. Both applications software and system software can be subdivided into user-written programs and canned programs. Policies and procedures required to manage and control an EDP system, and operations, program, and systems documentation are other important components of computer software.

KEY TERMS AND CONCEPTS

System software, 128
Programming languages, 128
Machine languages, 128
Assembler languages, 129
Macro instructions, 130
Subroutines, 131
Compiler languages, 132
Operating systems, 134
Stacked job processing, 135

Dynamic job processing, 136
Swapping, 136
Partitioning, 137
Paging, 138
Spooling, 139
Control programs, 140
Task management, 140
Data management, 140
Job management, 140

ASSIGNMENTS

1. Test your understanding of the chapter material by reviewing the *purpose, outline, summary,* and *key terms and concepts* of this chapter. Are you confident that you have attained a basic understanding of the major concepts of the chapter? If not, reread the appropriate material as indicated by the page numbers after each key term and concept.

2. Differentiate between the following terms:
    a. System software vs. applications software
    b. Assembler languages vs. compiler languages
    c. Macro instructions vs. subroutines
    d. Control programs vs. service programs
    e. Stacked job processing vs. dynamic job processing
    f. Business application vs. scientific application

3. Discuss the functions and components of an operating system.

4. Discuss the functions and benefits of data management systems.

5. Discuss the benefits and limitations of canned programs and user-written programs.

6. Discuss the importance of EDP documentation.

7. Determine the various types of system and application software used by your computer center. For example, determine the type of operating systems, programming languages translators, service programs, and canned programs that are utilized.

Chapter Outline

Purpose of the Chapter

Introduction

Programming Analysis

Program Design
Layout Forms, Flowcharts, System Flowcharts, Program Flowcharts, Using Flowcharts, Decision Tables, Using Decision Tables

Program Coding
Types of Instructions, Popular Programming Languages: FORTRAN, COBOL, PL/1, BASIC, RPG

Program Verification
Programming Errors, Checking, Testing

Program Documentation

Program Maintenance

Conversational Computing
Interactive Programming, Conversational Computing Example: Activating the Terminal, the Conversation, the Program

Summary

Key Terms and Concepts

Assignments

6

Computer Programming

PURPOSE OF THE CHAPTER

To promote a basic understanding of computer programming by analyzing:

1. The functions of the six stages of computer programming,
2. The construction and use of flowcharts and decision tables,
3. The use of an interactive program for conversational computing.

INTRODUCTION

Computer programming is a process which results in the development of a *computer program,* which we have defined as a set of detailed instructions which outline the data processing activities to be performed by a computer. Computer programming is just one of several steps in the development of *computer-based information systems.* (We will discuss *information systems development* in the next chapter.) However, a knowledge of the fundamentals of computer programming is necessary before a systems analyst can analyze and design a computer-based information system. Business managers and other computer users must also be aware of the steps involved in computer programming if they are to communicate effectively with programmers concerning computerized solutions to business problems. Finally, the development of time-sharing terminals, minicomputers, and high-level computer languages make it possible for "every computer user to be his own computer programmer." Thus, a basic knowledge of computer programming is desirable for all present and potential computer users.

Computer programming is a process that involves more than the writing of instructions in a programming language. Computer programming may be subdivided into six separate stages, each of which is summarized below.

1. *Programming analysis.*   Analyzing a proposed computer application to determine what the computer program is expected to accomplish.
2. *Program design.*   Planning and designing the input/output characteristics and the processing procedures required by the proposed application. Flowcharts, decision tables, and layout forms are frequently used during this stage.
3. *Program coding.*   Writing the computer program that converts the program design into a detailed set of programming language statements.
4. *Program verification.*   Checking, testing, and correcting a newly written computer program. Commonly called "debugging."
5. *Program documentation.*   Recording a detailed description of the design and instruction content of a computer program.
6. *Program maintenance.*   Revising an established computer program that requires improvement such as updating, expansion, or correction.

PROGRAMMING ANALYSIS

Programming analysis is the important first step in computer programming in which the computer programmer seeks the answer to the question: "What is the program supposed to do?" The amount of work involved in answering this question is directly related to the type of application being programmed and the amount of *"systems analysis and design"* that has previously been accomplished by a systems analyst. If the application to be programmed is viewed as a *problem* that requires a solution, then programming analysis can be considered to be a process of "problem definition," and "problem specification." If the application to be programmed is considered a *system,* then programming analysis involves the determination of "systems objectives," "systems requirements," and "systems specifications."

Programming analysis may be relatively simple for short problems or for complex mathematical problems whose arithmetic form clearly

FIGURE 6–1

Systems Specifications for Programming Analysis

PROGRAM/PROJECT SPECIFICATIONS

Number	Assigned by Programming Date When written
Title	Assigned by Systems
Purpose	This should be a concise statement (one paragraph) of what is to be accomplished by the program/project.
Scope	This should describe in one sentence the extent of the program/project.
General Description	
Input	This should describe the types of data to be processed, in detail. Included should be the *source, format, volume, codes*, etc. The actual layout should be made by the programmer.
Output	This should describe all information produced, in detail. Included should be *type, format, volume, codes, forms, sizes, copies, distribution. . . .* Actual layouts should be made by the programmer.
Exceptions	This should describe any input or output to be handled but not processed by the program. An example of this would be where all records are read from a tape, but certain types or codes are to be ignored completely in the actual manipulation of data.
Process	This should describe the actual steps to be followed to achieve the results required of the program/project. Normally this should be the largest section in the specifications, but every attempt should be made to make this area as clear and concise as possible. Included in this section should be all of the manipulations to be made on the input/output.
Formulae	This should describe as clearly as possible the actual calculations to be performed in the processing. It should be shown separately so that examples can be included but should be referenced by the Process section.
Decision Tables	This should show complex editing and control situations in an easily understandable way. The intention of the decision table would be to eliminate large amounts of writing in the process section by referencing the process to the decision table.
Controls	This should describe the internal and external controls to be incorporated into the program/project. Also included in this section would be any error messages to be generated by the programmer.
Comments	This should include any information that the systems analyst feels will clarify or make the programming easier.
Schedule	This should specify the normal frequency and running time of the program/project. Also, it should include the retention cycle of the tape or disks used in the operation.
Samples, Forms, Examples	This should include source documents, printer layouts, test data generated by the systems analyst.
Approval	To be signed and dated on the completion of the program project once it has become operational. Should include the date of final review.

Source: From *Automatic Data Processing and Management* by Nathan Berkowitz and Robertson Munro, p. 245. Copyright c 1969 by Dickenson Publishing Company, Inc., Belmont, California—reprinted by permission of the publisher.

defines the problem to be solved. Even complex problems and systems may not require extensive programming analysis if a thorough job of systems analysis and design has been accomplished by a systems analyst *before* the proposed computer application is turned over to the computer programmer. If this is the case, then programming analysis will consist of an analysis of the objectives, requirements, and specifications of the proposed program as outlined by the systems analyst. See Figure 6–1.

Whether the application to be programmed is simple or complex, and whether the proposed application has been subjected to an extensive systems analysis and design effort, the programming analysis stage requires the programmer to determine exactly what the program is supposed to accomplish. The programmer must determine: (1) the *output* required, (2) the *input* available, and (3) the *processing* (mathematical, logical, and other procedures) that will probably be required. Once these preliminary determinations have been made, the final step of programming analysis is to determine whether the proposed application "can" or "should" be programmed. The computer programmer must determine whether programming the proposed application is possible and practical. He may request more information about the proposed application or recommend that the proposal be redesigned or abandoned.

PROGRAM DESIGN

The program design stage of computer programming involves the planning and design of the specific input/output characteristics and processing procedures required by the proposed application. As in the case of the programming analysis stage, the amount of effort required in the program design stage depends on the complexity of the application and the amount of systems analysis and design work that has previously been performed. Program design requires the development of a logical set of rules and instructions that specify the operations required to accomplish the proposed data processing application. This aspect of program design is known in computer science as the development of an *"algorithm,"* which can be loosely defined as a set of rules or instructions that specify the operations required in the solution of a problem or the accomplishment of a task.

The computer programmer must determine:

1. The *input* available—its source, format, media, organization, volume, and frequency.
2. The *output* required—its format, media, organization, volume, frequency and destination.
3. The *processing* needed—the mathematical, logical, and other procedures required to transform input into output.

In the program design stage the programmer first develops the general organization of the program as it relates to the main functions to be performed. The program is usually divided into several main subdivisions, such as a beginning "initialization" section, input, processing, and output sections, as well as an ending "termination" section. Most programs also have sections that deal with the testing and control of exceptional conditions such as errors or other deviations from normal processing requirements. The use of common subroutines that are available to perform operations required by any section of the program must also be considered during the design stage.

Program design for large programs may require that programs be segmented into a series of subprograms or *"program modules."* Some program modules are independent subprograms called "overlays" since they replace each other in main storage after performing their part of a program. Dividing a lengthy program into program modules may facilitate efficient program design, coding, testing, and documentation. However, the development of *virtual memory* has made it unnecessary for programmers to segment a program because of limitations in primary storage capacity. The virtual memory software automatically segments a program into segments and pages which are moved between secondary storage devices and primary storage as needed. This significantly simplifies the programming of applications with large memory requirements.

The computer programmer frequently utilizes "flowcharts," "decision tables," and input/output and storage "layout forms" to assist him in the program design stage. We will now discuss these analytical tools with the understanding that they are used by systems analysts as well as computer programmers. In fact, if a thorough job of systems analysis and design has been performed, the computer programmer will be furnished with input/output and storage layout forms, systems flowcharts, and decision tables which describe the general design and requirements (system specifications) of the proposed application. If this is the case, the job of the computer programmer in the program design stage consists of formulating the specific detailed steps (the algorithm) which accomplish the data processing task required by the system specifications.

Layout Forms

Layout forms are used to design the form of input, output, and storage media. They usually consist of preprinted forms on which the form and placement of data and information can be "laid out." Layout forms are used to design source documents, input/output and storage records and files, and output reports. Layout forms for punched cards, magnetic tape, magnetic disks, and printed reports are widely used. See Figure 6–2.

Flowcharts

The *flowchart* is an important tool of the computer programmer and systems analyst. A flowchart (also called a "flow diagram" or "block diagram") is a graphic representation of the steps necessary to solve a problem, accomplish a task, complete a process, or it may be used to illustrate the components of a system. There are two basic types of flowcharts, "system flowcharts" and "program flowcharts." A system flowchart is a representation of the components and flows of a system. A program flowchart represents the data processing steps (algorithm) to be performed within a computer program. Commonly used system and program flowcharting symbols are illustrated and described in Figure 6–3.

System Flowcharts

The *system flowcharts* used in information systems development show the flow of data between the components of a data processing system or information system. System flowcharts were used several times in the preceding chapters of this book to illustrate components and flows of data in various systems. The system flowchart emphasizes how data moves in various forms through the stages of input, processing, output, and storage. It does not show the details of the processing that takes place in the computer program. System flowcharts can vary in their degree of complexity. For example, Figure 6–4 is a "general" systems flowchart which illustrates a payroll system, utilizing the three basic flowcharting symbols that indicate input/

FIGURE 6–2

Card Layout Form

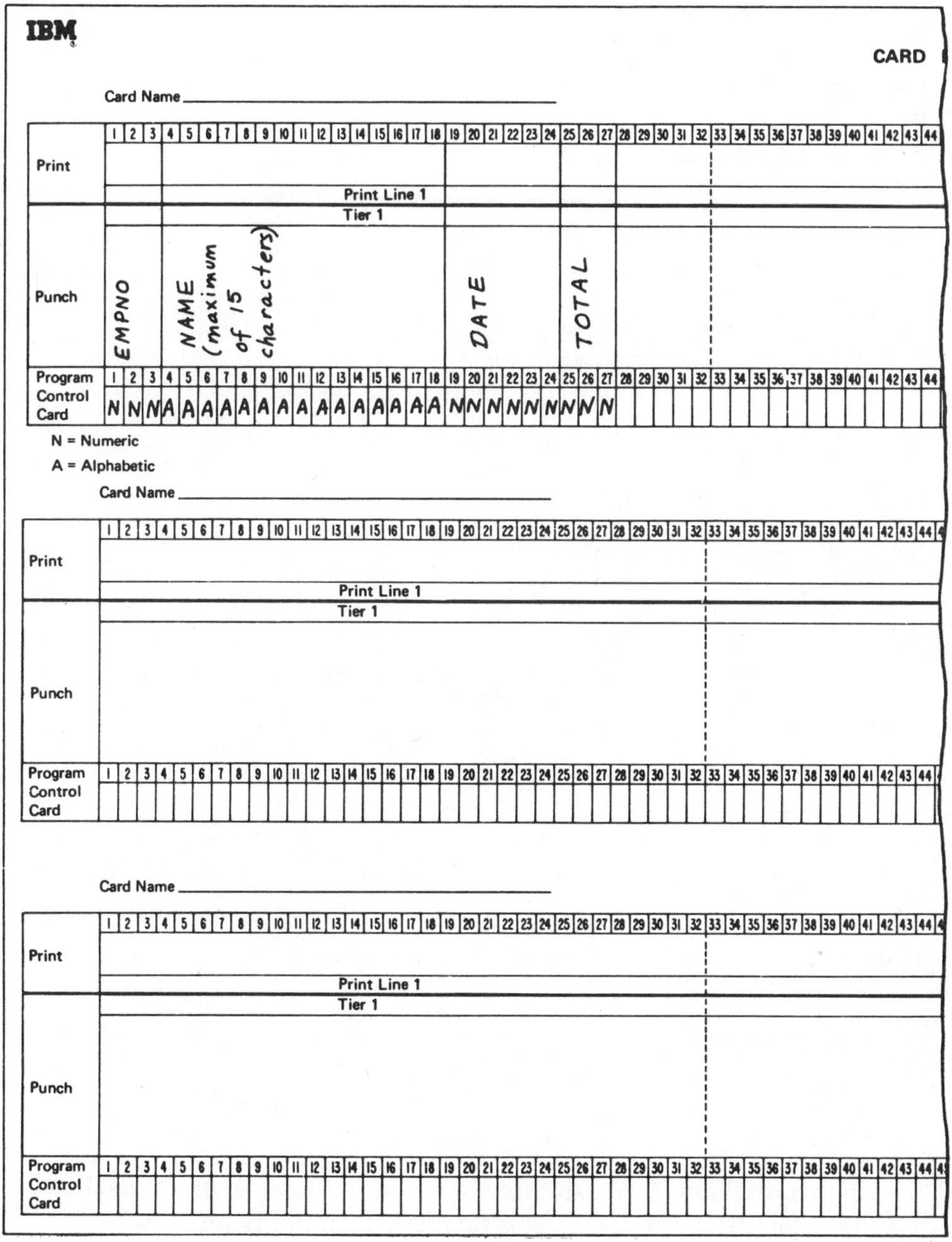

IBM

CARD

Card Name _____

	1	2	3	4	5	6	7	8	9	10	11	12	13	14	15	16	17	18	19	20	21	22	23	24	25	26	27	28	29	30	31	32	33	34	35	36	37	38	39	40	41	42	43	44
Print																																												

Print Line 1

Tier 1

Punch: EMPNO   NAME (maximum of 15 characters)   DATE   TOTAL

Program Control Card:

1	2	3	4	5	6	7	8	9	10	11	12	13	14	15	16	17	18	19	20	21	22	23	24	25	26	27	28	29	30	31	32
N	N	N	A	A	A	A	A	A	A	A	A	A	A	A	A	A	A	A	N	N	N	N	N	N	N	N	N	N			

N = Numeric

A = Alphabetic

Card Name _____

Print / Print Line 1 / Tier 1 / Punch / Program Control Card

Card Name _____

Print / Print Line 1 / Tier 1 / Punch / Program Control Card

FIGURE 6–3

Flowchart Symbols

PROGRAM FLOWCHART SYMBOLS

SYMBOL	REPRESENTS
	PROCESSING A group of program instructions which perform a processing function of the program.
	INPUT/OUTPUT Any function of an input/output device (making information available for processing, recording processing information, tape positioning, etc.).
	DECISION The decision function used to document points in the program where a branch to alternate paths is possible based upon variable conditions.
	PREPARATION An instruction or group of instructions which changes the program.
	PREDEFINED PROCESS A group of operations not detailed in the particular set of flowcharts.
	TERMINAL The beginning, end, or a point of interruption in a program.
	CONNECTOR An entry from, or an exit to, another part of the program flowchart.
	OFFPAGE CONNECTOR A connector used instead of the connector symbol to designate entry to or exit from a page.
∧∨<>	**FLOW DIRECTION** The direction of processing or data flow.

SUPPLEMENTARY SYMBOL
FOR SYSTEM AND PROGRAM FLOWCHARTS

	ANNOTATION The addition of descriptive comments or explanatory notes as clarification.

SYSTEM FLOWCHART SYMBOLS

PROCESSING		INPUT/OUTPUT	
PROCESSING A major processing function.		**INPUT/OUTPUT** Any type of medium or data.	
PUNCHED CARD All varieties of punched cards including stubs.		**PUNCHED TAPE** Paper or plastic, chad or chadless.	
DOCUMENT Paper documents and reports of all varieties.		**TRANSMITTAL TAPE** A proof or adding-machine tape or similar batch-control information.	
MAGNETIC TAPE		**ONLINE STORAGE**	
OFFLINE STORAGE Offline storage of either paper, cards, magnetic or perforated tape.		**DISPLAY** Information displayed by plotters or video devices.	
COLLATE Forming two or more sets of items from two or more other sets.		**SORTING** An operation on sorting or collating equipment.	
MANUAL INPUT Information supplied to or by a computer utilizing an online device.		**MERGE** Combining two or more sets of items into one set.	
MANUAL OPERATION A manual offline operation not requiring mechanical aid.		**AUXILIARY OPERATION** A machine operation supplementing the main processing function.	
KEYING OPERATION An operation utilizing a key-driven device.		**COMMUNICATION LINK** The automatic transmission of information from one location to another via communication lines.	
FLOW	<>∨∧	The direction of processing or data flow.	

output, processing, and the direction of data flow. A more detailed system flowchart of the payroll system is shown in Figure 6–5. Notice that the flowchart illustrates the flow of data in the system and the input/output and storage media that are utilized and does not present the details of computer programs that will be required.

FIGURE 6–4

General System Flowchart—Payroll

FIGURE 6–5

Detailed System Flowchart—Payroll

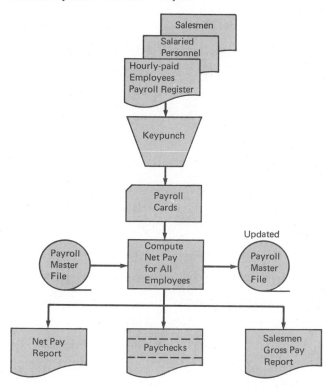

Program Flowcharts

A *program flowchart* illustrates the detailed sequence of steps required by a computer program. Program flowcharts also vary in their complexity, ranging from "general" flowcharts to "detailed" program flowcharts. Figure 6–6 is a general program flowchart of the "salesmen gross pay program," which is one of the computer programs required by the payroll system. Notice the various program flowcharting symbols used, especially the function of the "decision" symbol. Figure 6–7 shows a portion of a detailed program flowchart that could be

FIGURE 6–6

General Program Flowchart—Salesmen Gross Pay

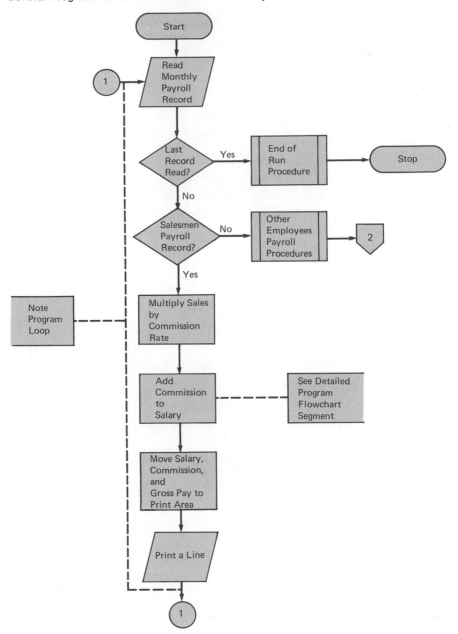

FIGURE 6–7

Detailed Program Flowchart Segment

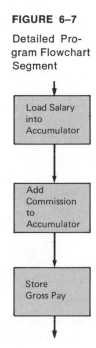

drawn for the salesmen gross pay program. The three processing symbols shown replace the single "add commission to salary" processing symbol on the general program flowchart. Such detailed program flowcharting is used when programming in an assembler language but is usually unnecessary when programming in a compiler language since a single compiler statement accomplishes many detailed computer operations.

The general program flowchart in Figure 6–6 outlines the steps that result in the printing of the salesmen gross pay report. This process would ordinarily be just a segment of a larger payroll program but has been modified so that the use of more program flowcharting symbols can be shown. A salesman's monthly payroll data record is read and his commission and gross pay calculated and included in a printed report. The data record could be in the form of a punched card or could have been converted into magnetic tape or magnetic disk form. An "offpage connector" symbol reveals that payroll procedures for other employees are displayed on another page of flowcharts.

The flowchart shows the use of a simple *program loop* which allows any computer program automatically to repeat a series of operations. In this example, the input, processing, and output operations are repeated until the last payroll record is read. The *looping* process is then ended by the *program modification* feature which allows computer programs automatically to modify themselves by *branching* to another routine. In this example, when the last record is read, the program *branches* to an "end of run" procedure and stops. The looping process is shown in general program flowcharts by an arrow that connects the flowchart symbols that are part of the loop or by the use of two connector symbols containing the same label. The main loop of the program shown in Figure 6–6 is identified by the connector symbols containing the number "1" which identifies the entry and exit points of the loop. (The dotted arrow that also reveals the loop is therefore not necessary but is used for purposes of illustration only.)

You should notice that the processing symbol entitled "add commission to salary" in the general program flowchart (Figure 6–6) can be expressed by the FORTRAN and COBOL language statements used in Chapter Five as examples of compiler language statements. The detailed program flowchart segment (Figure 6–7) illustrates the three assembler language instructions also used as examples in Chapter Five. These instructions direct the computer to perform the "add commission to salary" processing step of the general program flowchart.

Using Flowcharts

We have briefly described the different uses of system and program flowcharts and general and detailed flowcharts. You should be able to follow the flow of data processing activities or instruction logic of the various flowcharts illustrated. Usually, the flow is from top to bottom and from left to right unless arrow or connector symbols indicate otherwise. The shape of the symbol and the notation within it explain the data processing media, device, and activity that is involved. The combination of symbols and words that constitute a flowchart reveals the relationships and sequences of a data processing alogrithm or system much more clearly than a detailed written description.

A flowchart is a graphic model or blueprint of a system or program and is an indispensible tool of the systems analyst and computer programmer. Flowcharts are used in the programming analysis and program design stages to analyze a data processing problem and plan a program for its solution. Programmers usually start the program design stage by drawing a general program flowchart (also called a "macro" or "overall" flowchart) and then draw one or more supplementary detailed flowcharts (also called "micro" flowcharts) when more detail is needed to facilitate the coding of specific sections or modules of the program. This process is similar to the drawing of a set of maps, each one a more detailed "blowup" of a section of the preceding map. A flowchart should be used to: (1) visualize the logic and sequence of steps in an operation, (2) experiment with various programming approaches, and (3) keep track of all processing steps, including procedures for alternatives and exceptions. Once final versions of the general and detailed flowcharts for a program are completed, they serve as an important guide during the program coding, testing, documentation, and maintenance stages of computer programming.

Most programmers use a metal or a plastic *"flowcharting template"* on which the flowcharting symbols appear as cutout forms. The template allows the programmer to draw the flowcharting symbols easily. *"Flowcharting worksheets"* may also be used to assist the flowcharting process. The flowcharts can also be drawn with the aid of a computer through the use of special flowcharting programs that enable the computer to printout a flowchart. Computer flowcharting programs are primarily utilized by large computer users to update the flowcharts of complex programs that have been modified.

Decision Tables

Decision tables are another important tool of the systems analyst and computer programmer and are used in conjunction with or in place of flowcharts. Using flowcharts for the analysis and design of complex systems and programs involving many specified conditions and decision paths becomes an extremely difficult process. The flow of data and the logical sequence of the program or system become hard to follow, and errors or omissions may result. Decision tables are used in such cases as a powerful tool for the analysis and design of programs and systems involving complex conditional decision logic.

A decision table is a tabular presentation of system or program logic. The general format of a decision table is shown in Figure 6–8. It shows that there are four basic parts to the decision table:

1. The "condition stub" which lists conditions or questions similar to those contained in a flowchart decision symbol.
2. The "action stub" which lists statements describing all actions that can be taken.

FIGURE 6–8

General Format of a Decision Table

Table Heading	*Decision Rule Heading*
Condition Statements	Condition Entries
Action Statements	Action Entries

3. The "condition entry" which indicates which conditions are being met or answers the questions in the condition stub.
4. The "action entry" which indicates the actions to be taken.

Most decision tables also include a table heading and decision rule headings or numbers. The columns in the condition entry and action entry section of the table (called the "body" of the table) illustrate various *"decision rules"* since they specify that *if* certain conditions exist, *then* certain actions must be taken. Depending on the complexity of the decision logic, condition entries are indicated by a Y (yes), or a N (no), comparison symbols such as $<\leq=\geq>$, quantities, codes or are left blank to show that the condition does not apply. Action entries are usually indicated by an X. When a decision table is completed, each rule indicates a different set of conditions and actions.

A simple example should help clarify the construction and use of a decision table. Figure 6–9 illustrates a decision table based on the payroll system and program examples flowcharted in the preceding pages. The decision logic has been made more complex than in the previous example in order to illustrate the usefulness of decision tables for the analysis of decision logic. Examine Figure 6–9 to see what actions are taken when various possible conditions occur. For example, decision rule number six concerns the case of a salesman who has made sales for the month but has not exceeded his sales quota. Given these conditions, the payroll processing actions that must be taken are to compute his salary and commission (but not a bonus), perform other salesmen payroll processing, perform net pay processing common to all employees, and print the salesmen gross pay and commission report. The information in column six of the decision table can therefore be expressed in words by the following

FIGURE 6–9

Payroll Decision Table

DECISION RULE NUMBERS

PAYROLL TABLE NO. 1		1	2	3	4	5	6	7
CONDITIONS	Hourly-paid Employee	Y						
	Salaried Employee		Y					
	Executive Employee			Y				
	Unclassified Employee				Y			
	Salesman					Y	Y	Y
	Made Sales?					N	Y	Y
	Exceeded Quota?					N	N	Y
ACTIONS	Compute Wages	X						
	Compute Salary		X					
	Compute Sales Salary					X	X	X
	Compute Commission						X	X
	Compute Bonus							X
	Salesmen Gross Pay Processing					X	X	X
	Net Pay Processing	X	X			X	X	X
	Go to Payroll Table Number:			2	3			

decision rule statement: "*If* an employee is a salesman who has had sales for the month but has not exceeded his quota, *then* compute his salary and commissions, complete salesmen payroll processing and all-employee net pay processing, and include him in the salesmen gross pay and commission report."

Using Decision Tables

Decision tables should be used by systems analysts and programmers for the representation of complex procedures. However, flowcharts are much more widely used than decision tables primarily because they are a more familiar analytical tool. Also, since many data processing applications have only a few branches to different routines, a flowchart can adequately represent the total sequence of events involved. The use of decision tables is increasing, however, especially for the systems analysis and design effort required by complex scientific, engineering, and business data processing problems. Decision tables prepared by systems analysts can be supplied to a computer programmer, who can then prepare program flowcharts before coding the program. The use of decision tables by programmers should increase, especially since special translator programs like FORTAB or DETAB are available which allow a computer to translate decision tables directly into FORTRAN or COBOL language programs.

The benefits of decision tables are the basis for many forecasts that predict their future widespread acceptance in the area of business data processing. Since they cannot be prepared as arbitrarily as flowcharts, they impose the discipline required to prepare a complete and accurate description of a data processing system or computer program. Decision tables are a more simple and concise form of analysis than the use of words or flowcharts. They are thus easier to construct and to change and easier to understand. Decision tables are therefore a valuable method of system and program documentation and communication, since systems analysts, computer programmers, and computer users can easily verify the decision logic expressed in the tables.

PROGRAM CODING

Program coding is the process that converts the logic designed during the program design stage (as outlined in program flowcharts or decision tables) into a set of programming language statements that constitute a computer program. The term "programming" is frequently used to refer only to the program coding stage, but, as we have seen, five other important steps are also necessary. Most application programs are written in a high-level compiler programming language, while systems programmers utilize assembler languages to code the instructions of systems software. Coding in machine language is rarely performed.

Depending on the programming language used, coding involves a rigorous process which requires the computer programmer to strictly follow specific rules concerning format and syntax (vocabulary, punctuation, and grammatical rules). *Language specification manuals* and *coding forms* are used for most languages to help computer programmers comply with the rules of the language they are using. When coding of a program is completed, one card is usually keypunched for each line on a coding sheet. The resulting "deck" of punched cards represents the source program and is called the *"source deck."* Figure 6–10 shows a FORTRAN coding form with the statements and flow-chart of a simple FORTRAN program. The program reads values of Y and Z from an undetermined number of data cards, computes $X = Y + Z$, and prints the resulting values of X.

It must be emphasized that there is no "one way" of program coding, just as there are many ways to design a program to accomplish a data processing application. Different programmers will develop different sequences of instructions to perform a given operation, just as they would probably develop different flowcharts in designing a computer program. These differences arise because there are usually several ways to arrange the logical sequences of instructions required by a program, as well as a choice of instructions or statements that can be used to perform an operation.

FIGURE 6–10

Coding Form with the Statements and Flowchart of a Simple FORTRAN Program

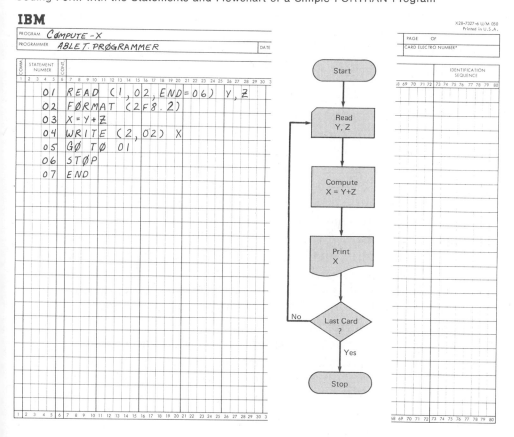

Of course, some programming differences can also develop because an expert programmer will usually design and code more efficient programs than less expert programmers. We have defined *efficient software* as programs that require a minimum of instructions, storage, and computer time to perform a specific data processing assignment. Expert programmers try to develop the most simple sequence of instructions that performs an operation as fast as possible, using a minimum of main storage. The goal of professional programmers is to develop programs which possess an optimum combination of simplicity, speed, and minimum storage space requirements. Much expertise and experience is needed because these characteristics are frequently in conflict.

Types of Instructions

The types of instructions available to a computer programmer for program coding depends on the program language used and the *"command repertoire"* or *"instruction set"* of the computer CPU. However, computer instructions can usually be subdivided into six categories: (1) specification, (2) input/output, (3) data movement, (4) arithmetic, (5) logical, and (6) control.

1. *Specification instructions* are descriptive instructions which describe the data media to be used, the size and format of data records and files, the constants to be used, and the allocation of storage. Many of these instructions are based on the input/output and storage layout sheets completed during the program design stage. The "FORMAT" statement of FORTRAN or the "PICTURE" statement of COBOL are examples of specification instruction statements.
2. *Input/Output instructions* transfer data and instructions between the CPU and input/output devices. "READ" or "PRINT" statements are examples of such instructions.
3. *Data movement instructions* involve rearranging and reproducing data within primary storage. "MOVE," "SHIFT," or "STORE" instructions are examples.
4. *Arithmetic instructions* are instructions which accomplish mathematical operations, such as "ADD," "SUBTRACT," etc.
5. *Logical instructions* perform comparisons and test conditions as illustrated in the decision symbol of program flowcharts. Examples are "IF, THEN" or "COMPARE" statements.

6. *Control instructions* are used to stop and start a program, change the sequence of a program through a branching process, and control the use of subroutines. "GO TO," and "BRANCH" statements are examples of control instructions.

Popular Programming Languages

The five compiler languages most widely used for the coding of business application programs are FORTRAN, COBOL, PL/1, BASIC, and RPG. A brief description of each language is presented in this section. The fundamentals of each of these languages (including sample computer programs) are contained in the last four chapters of this book. These chapters discuss how to code simple computer programs in each language.

FORTRAN. FORTRAN (FORmula TRANslation), developed in 1957, is the oldest of the popular compiler languages. As its name indicates, FORTRAN was designed primarily for solving the mathematical problems of scientists, engineers, and mathematicians. Therefore, FORTRAN programs use many mathematical statements utilizing words, symbols, and numbers in algebraic types of expressions, as was shown by the examples in Chapter 5, and Figure 6–10. Refer to Chapter 15 for other examples of FORTRAN programs.

FORTRAN is also used in business data processing since many business problems can be expressed as a series of mathematical calculations. However, since FORTRAN cannot express certain input/output and nonnumeric operations, it is not suitable for many business data processing applications which require extensive processing of alphanumeric data files stored on many secondary storage devices. FORTRAN IV, the latest version of FORTRAN, is the most widely used programming language for scientific and engineering data processing. (In Europe, however, ALGOL, ALGOrithmic Language, is the most widely used scientific-mathematical programming language.)

COBOL. COBOL (COmmon Business Oriented Language) was designed by a committee called CODASYL (Conference on Data Systems Languages) consisting of representatives of computer manufacturers, computer users, and government agencies. The committee was formed in 1960 at the request of the U.S. Department of Defense in order to devise a common language for business data processing. The Department of Defense is a major user of computers and subsequently announced that it would not lease or purchase computers for which COBOL software was not available. COBOL has since become the most widely used language for business data processing. It is an English-like language specifically designed to handle the input, processing, and output of large volumes of alphanumeric data from many data files that is characteristic of business data processing. The examples in Chapter Five showed how close to the English language a COBOL statement can be. Refer to Chapter 16 for examples of several complete programs in COBOL.

A COBOL program consists of four divisions:

1. *The identification division* identifies the program by listing such information as the name of the programmer, the date the program was written, and other comments which identify the purpose of the program.
2. *The environment division* specifies the type of computer and peripheral equipment that will be used to process the program.
3. *The data division* describes the organization of the data to be processed by the program.
4. *The procedure division* contains the COBOL statements describing the procedure to be followed by the computer in accomplishing the data processing assignments.

PL/1. PL/1 (Programming Language 1) was developed by IBM in 1965 in an attempt to devise a general purpose language which could be used for both business and scientific applications. PL/1 was designed to include the best features of FORTRAN and COBOL as well as some of the capabilities of assembler languages and ALGOL. PL/1 is supposed to be a "general purpose" language that is designed to take full advantage of the characteristics of new generations of general purpose computers.

A PL/1 statement to compute $(X = Y + Z)$ would resemble the FORTRAN statements shown in the examples in Chapter Five except that a semicolon is used to end each PL/1 statement. Refer to Chapter 18 for an example of a PL/1 program. PL/1 has been criticized as being difficult to learn and inefficient to program, though even its critics agree it is a highly flexible general purpose language. PL/1 is not as widely used as COBOL and FORTRAN, primarily because only a few software suppliers besides IBM have developed PL/1 software.

BASIC. BASIC (Beginner's All-purpose Symbolic Instruction Code) was developed in the early 1960s at Dartmouth College as a simple easily learned language that would allow students to engage in interactive (conversational) computing, utilizing a time-sharing computer system. At first, BASIC resembled a shortened and simplified version of FORTRAN. With only a few hours of instruction, a student could solve small problems by "conversing" with a computer utilizing a time-sharing terminal. BASIC proved so easy to learn and utilize that it quickly became a widely used time-sharing language. Several versions of BASIC have been developed, including a batch processing version developed at the University of Washington. These versions of BASIC have transformed it into a more powerful language which can handle a wide variety of data processing assignments utilizing either batch processing or real-time processing systems. A complete BASIC program that would add Y to Z and print the result X is shown below:

```
10 INPUT Y, Z
20 LET X = Y + Z
30 PRINT X
40 END
```

RPG. RPG (Report Program Generator) is a simple problem-oriented language which was originally designed to generate programs that produced printed reports. However, several versions of RPG have been developed which have made RPG a widely used language for report preparation, file maintenance, and other business data processing applications of small computer users. RPG cannot handle large complex applications which require a *procedure-oriented language* and a large computer system. However, RPG can easily handle many types of straightforward business applications and can be used with small computer systems that do not have the storage capacity required by procedure-oriented languages.

Since it is a *problem-oriented language,* RPG does not require the use of statements which outline the procedure to be followed by the computer. Instead, a person using RPG fills out a few simple *"specification sheets"* which are used to describe the form of the input data, the input/output devices and data files to be used, the format of output reports, and the calculations that are required. Given these specifications, the RPG translator program generates a machine language program that performs the necessary data processing operations and produces the required reports.

RPG is comparatively easy to learn and simple to use, which adds to its popularity with small computer users. Refer to Chapter 18 for an example of a complete RPG program. The computation ($X = Y + Z$) might take the following form on a RPG calculations specification sheet:

Factor 1	Operation	Factor 2	Result Field
Y	ADD	Z	X

PROGRAM VERIFICATION

Program verification, more commonly known as *"debugging,"* is a stage of programming that involves checking, testing, and correction processes. Program verification is a necessary stage of computer programming because newly coded programs usually contain errors (bugs) which must be identified and corrected by a debugging process.

Programming Errors

Programming errors are of three major types: (1) clerical errors, (2) logic errors, and (3) systems design errors. *Clerical errors* (also called syntax errors) are caused by violating the rules of the programming language in which the program is coded or by making mistakes in the organization and format of data. These are called clerical errors because they can be as simple as a misplaced decimal point or comma and can be made by the programmer or be the result of an error made in the keypunching of the source program.

Logic errors are errors that occur because of mistakes in the logical structure of a program. Necessary procedures may have been omitted or incorrect procedures included in a program. For example, a payroll program that did not distinguish between hourly paid employees and salaried employees or which used an incorrect commission for salesmen would produce logic errors. *Systems design errors* are errors caused by a lack of communication between the computer programmer and the systems analyst or computer user. A program may be free of clerical and logic errors and still not meet all of the requirements of a proposed data processing application. Such errors are caused by failures in communication between the programmer and the systems analyst or computer user.

Clerical errors are easier to detect than logic errors because they are usually identified during the compiling or assembling process by the diagnostic listings produced. Clerical errors may also cause the computer to "reject" a program during compiling or processing. Logic errors are harder to detect, since they will not be identified by the translator diagnostics, and the complete program may be processed by the computer without being rejected. The output of such a program, however, will be incorrect. The incorrect and sometimes nonsensical results caused by program and input errors are humorously referred to as "garbage." This is the basis for the phrase "garbage in, garbage out" (GIGO) which is well-known to members of computer-related professions. It emphasizes that the computer will blindly process incorrect data and instructions and will willingly produce volumes of incorrect and useless results. Therefore, much checking, testing, and control procedures must be built into all EDP systems and computer programs.

Checking

Program checking must take place during the program design, program coding, and program verification stages. Checking should take place after flowcharts and decision tables are developed to verify that all program requirements have been met and to determine that the flowchart or decision table correctly represents the logic developed by the program. Checking should take place at the completion of the program coding stage by inspecting the program coding sheets to insure that the instructions correctly translate the logic of the flowcharts and decision tables and that any clerical errors have been identified. This "desk-checking" process continues after the coding sheets are keypunched by inspecting the contents of the source deck to insure that no keypunching errors were made. This is done by examining the printing at the top of the source cards or by inspecting a printed listing of the contents of the cards.

The final checking process involves attempting to compile or assemble the *source program* into an *object program*. During or after such a translation process *diagnostic messages* will be printed identifying mistakes in the source program. The programmer makes necessary corrections to the source program and then makes another attempt to compile or assemble the program. This final checking process is repeated until an error-free "pass" is accomplished and the resulting object program is ready for a test period.

Testing

A properly checked object program is tested to demonstrate whether it can produce correct results utilizing "test data." This *testing* must attempt to simulate all conditions that may arise during processing. Therefore, test data must include unusual and incorrect data as well as the typical types of data which will usually occur. Such test data is required to test the ability of the program to handle exceptions and errors as well as more normal forms of data. The programmer must have previously prepared the test data by manually (and carefully) calculating and determining the correct results. After the object program has processed the test data, the output is compared to the expected results. If correct results are produced, the program is considered properly tested and ready for use.

Complex computer programs may require many testing "runs" because the actual and expected output does not agree. When this occurs, a very difficult type of debugging is required, which is considered by many programmers as the most difficult stage of programming. Some programs may consist of thousands of instructions and may require several months to debug. Each time a test run yields incorrect results, errors must be found and corrected, and the source program reassembled or recompiled, unless corrections can be made directly to the object program by "patching" the object deck. During this phase of debugging, programmers may request a "memory dump" which produces a printed listing of the contents of primary storage, registers, and counters at the specific point in the program where error conditions seem to be occurring.

The final phase of program verification is a temporary period in which actual data is used to test a computer program. If the program has been designed to replace an older data processing method, this procedure is known as *"parallel processing."* The parallel run allows the results of the new program to be compared to the results produced by the system it is to replace. If the results agree over a specified period of time the old operation is then phased out. At this point, errors may still remain undetected in a complex new computer program. Some of them may remain undetected for years, only to surface when unusual conditions occur that bring them to light. Such errors are the cause of many publicized computer "mistakes" which periodically appear in news reports. Other errors are never detected, which is why many experts agree that a complex computer program can never be completely debugged.

PROGRAM DOCUMENTATION

Program documentation is a process that should occur throughout all of the other stages of computer programming. We have previously defined program documentation as the detailed description of the design and the instruction content of a computer program. Program documentation is extremely important in diagnosing program errors, making programming changes, or reassembling a lost program, especially if its original programmer is no longer available. Descriptive material produced in the previous stages of computer programming should be collected and refined, and new material developed. A "program manual" should be assembled which includes:

1. The *program specifications* that describe what the program is supposed to do.
2. The *program description* which consists of input/output and storage layout sheets, program flowcharts, decision tables, object program listing, and a narrative description of what the program does.
3. The *verification documentation* which includes listings of test data and results, memory dumps, and other test documents.
4. The *operations documentation* which consists of operating instructions which describe the actions required of the computer operator during the processing of the computer program.
5. The *maintenance documentation* which is a detailed description of all changes made to the program after it was accepted as an operational "production program" and used to perform the data processing job for which it was designed.

PROGRAM MAINTENANCE

The final stage of computer programming begins after a computer program has been accepted as a production program. *Program maintenance* refers to the continual revision of computer programs that is required if they are to be improved, updated, expanded, or corrected. The requirements of business data processing applications are subject to continual changes and revisions due to changes in company policies, business operations, government regulations, etc. Program maintenance is therefore an important stage of computer programming, involving the analysis, design, coding, verification, and documentation of changes to operational computer programs.

Large computer users frequently have a separate category of application programmers, called *maintenance programmers,* whose sole responsibility is program maintenance. Theirs is a difficult assignment, since they must revise programs they did not develop. This should emphasize the importance of the program documentation stage, since good documentation is essential for proper program maintenance. Inadequate documentation may make program maintenance impossible and require the rewriting of an entire program.

CONVERSATIONAL COMPUTING

Conversational computing (also known as interactive processing) has been previously described as a type of real-time processing involving frequent man-machine interaction. A remote time-sharing terminal may be used to explore and accomplish the solution to a problem with the real-time assistance of a central computer. Conversational computing requires extensive hardware and software support. This frequently includes the use of "interactive programs" which are canned application programs specifically designed for interactive processing.

Interactive Programming

"Interactive programming" and "conversational computing" are *not* synonymous terms. No actual programming is necessary when canned interactive programs are used for conversational computing. The computer user does not have to perform the activities of the six stages of computer programming; they have all been accomplished by the systems analysts and programmers who developed the program.

Conversational computing involves *interactive programming* only when a computer user or programmer actually designs and codes the processing and decision logic of a computer program with the real-time assistance of a computer. Thus, computers have been programmed to (1) assist a programmer by translating decision table logic into programming language statements, (2) automatically produce flowcharts, (3) develop alternative versions of a computer program, (4) compile, test and debug a program, and (5) assist in the documentation and maintenance of a program—all in real-time! In more common situations, however, interactive programming involves the use of a terminal to code, test, debug, and develop alternatives for a new program in a real-time environment.

Conversational Computing Example

The *Loan-Interest Rate Analysis* program mentioned in Figure 5–5 of the previous chapter can be used as a brief example of conversational computing with an interactive program. Such programs illustrate how simple the use of a computer can be for many computer users. No *programming is necessary;* only a few simple entries and responses are required. The interactive program is designed to direct the computer system to request and wait for input from the user, who must only choose among alternatives offered by the computer and provide it with data. Computer and user "converse" briefly and simply and the problem is solved. The systems design and programming effort, the complex hardware devices, and the advanced operating system required are all hidden from the eyes of the user. All the user sees are the questions, comments, and responses that appear on the terminal as the solution to the problem is accomplished.

The Loan-Interest Rate Analysis program (EFFRATE) is a simple interactive canned program which determines the true annual interest rate (the *effective* interest rate) being paid on a loan. Directions for using a terminal, questions, comments, and responses of the computer and the user (underlined), and the author's comments in parenthesis, are shown in the following example.[1]

Activating the Terminal

1. Depress the TALK button on the data set and listen for the dial tone.
2. Dial the time-sharing service number and wait for a shrill tone.
3. Depress the DATA button and hang up the receiver.

The Conversation

The computer terminal will now begin to type or display (CRT) messages and the user will respond using the keyboard of the terminal. The resulting conversation is shown below:

PLEASE LOGON	(The computer wants you to "log on" to the system with your identification code.)
LOGON USER-JAO	(You key in your identification code. In this example, USER-JAO is the code used.)

---

[1] Based on material in *VMOS Application Abstracts,* UNIVAC Division of the Sperry Rand Corporation (Cinnaminson, N.J.), p. 107, and an actual "conversation" with a computer using a time-sharing terminal.

LOGON ACCEPTED FROM LINE #021 AT 1310 ON 07/31/74

(Your LOGON is accepted from your terminal which is on data communications line 21 at the time and date shown.)

EXEC BASIC

(You ask the computer to execute the program you are going to select using the BASIC compiler since the program is written in the BASIC language.)

BASIC, NEW OR OLD

(The computer wants to know if you want to use a previously written program in BASIC or to write a new one.)

OLD

(You want to use a canned program.)

OLD PROGRAM NAME

(What is the name of the program you want to use, asks the computer?)

EFFRATE

(You key in the program name.)

READY

(The computer is ready to process the EFFRATE program.)

RUN

(You tell the computer to begin.)

EFFECTIVE INTEREST RATE FINDER

(The program title.)

DO YOU WANT INSTRUCTIONS (ANSWER YES OR NO)?

(Do you want instructions on how to use the program?)

YES

(Yes, you do.)

THIS PROGRAM IS USED TO CALCULATE THE EFFECTIVE INTEREST RATE (TRUE ANNUAL INTEREST). IT MUST BE SUPPLIED WITH THE FOLLOWING INFORMATION:

(The computer describes the program and how it should be used.)

    AMT—   THE ORIGINAL LOAN IN DOLLARS
    PMT—   EACH PAYMENT IN DOLLARS
    NOPMT—TOTAL NUMBER OF PAYMENTS
    YRPMT—NUMBER OF PAYMENTS PER YEAR.

AFTER THE EFFECTIVE INTEREST RATE IS PRINTED
THE PROGRAM WILL REQUEST NEW VALUES. YOU
MAY TYPE IN THE NEW VALUES, OR, IF YOU ARE
FINISHED, TYPE IN 0, 0, 0, 0.

AMT, PMT, NOPMT, YRPMT?	(What is the amount of the loan, the monthly payment, the total number of payments, and the number of payments in a year?)
1000, 50, 24, 12	(You ask the computer to calculate the effective interest rate for a loan of $1,000, assuming payments of $50 per month for 24 months.)
THE EFFECTIVE INTEREST RATE IS 18.16 %	(You receive your answer.)
AMT, PMT, NOPMT, YRPMT?	(Do you want to try again?)
0, 0, 0, 0.	(No, you are finished.)
BYE	(Say goodbye to the EFFRATE program.)
LOGOFF	(You terminate your conversation with the computer.)
LOGOFF AT 1315 ON 07/31/74 CPU TIME USED: 2.4447 SECONDS	(The computer notes the time you finished your conversation and the amount of CPU time you used.)

The Program

The program used in this example is written in the BASIC programming language and is shown in Figure 6–11. You should notice that many of the program statements are concerned with input/output, error, and exception routines. The calculation of (i) the effective interest rate (beginning on line 2220) is accomplished by solving the formula

$$X = \frac{ip}{1 - \dfrac{1}{(1 + i)^m}}$$

where (X) is the monthly payment (p) is the amount of the loan, and (m) is the number of payments. As you have just seen, none of these "details" were needed by the computer user for the solution of his problem. The details of writing simple programs in three widely

FIGURE 6-11

The EFFRATE Program

```
1000 PRINT
1010 PRINT
1020 PRINT "     *****EFFECTIVE INTEREST RATE FINDER*****"
1030 PRINT
1040 PRINT "DO YOU WANT INSTRUCTIONS (ANSWER YES OR NO)";
1050 INPUT Z$
1060 IF Z$="NO" THEN 2000
1070 PRINT
1080 PRINT
1090 PRINT "THIS PROGRAM IS USED TO CALCULATE THE EFFECTIVE"
1100 PRINT "INTEREST RATE (TRUE ANNUAL INTEREST).  IT MUST BE"
1110 PRINT "SUPPLIED WITH THE FOLLOWING INFORMATION:"
1120 PRINT "    AMT --   THE ORIGINAL LOAN IN DOLLARS"
1130 PRINT "    PMT --   EACH PAYMENT IN DOLLARS"
1140 PRINT "    NOPMT -- TOTAL NUMBER OF PAYMENTS"
1150 PRINT "    YRPMT -- NUMBER OF PAYMENTS PER YEAR."
1160 PRINT
1170 PRINT "AFTER THE EFFECTIVE INTEREST RATE IS PRINTED THE"
1180 PRINT "PROGRAM WILL REQUEST NEW VALUES.  YOU MAY TYPE IN"
1190 PRINT "THE NEW VALUES; OR, IF YOU ARE FINISHED, TYPE "
1200 PRINT "IN 0,0,0,0."
1210 GOTO 2000
2000 PRINT
2010 PRINT
2020 PRINT "AMT,PMT,NOPMT,YRPMT";
2030 INPUT P0,P,N,Y
2040 IF P0=0 THEN 3000
2050 IF N*P>P0 THEN 2220
2060 IF N*P<P0 THEN 2090
2070 LET I=0
2080 GOTO 2270
2090 PRINT "ERROR: THE AMOUNT TO BE PAID BACK IS LESS THAN THE"
2100 PRINT "ORIGINAL AMOUNT."
2110 GOTO 2000
2220 D=.1/Y
2230 LET X=-D
2240 LET X=X+D
2250 IF X<19.5*D THEN 2330
2260 IF X>20.5*D THEN 2330
2270 PRINT "THE CALCULATED INTEREST RATE EXCEEDS 200%."
2280 PRINT "DO YOU WISH TO CONTINUE (ANSWER YES OR NO)";
2290 INPUT Z$
2300 IF Z$="NO" THEN 2000
2330 LET I=X+D
2340 LET M=I*P0/(1-(1/(1+I))^N)
2350 IF M<P THEN 2240
2360 IF M>P THEN 2500
2370 PRINT
2380 PRINT
2390 PRINT "THE EFFECTIVE INTEREST RATE IS ";
2400 PRINT INT(10000*Y*I+.5)/100;"%"
2410 GOTO 2000
2430 GOTO 2000
2500 LET D=D/2
2510 IF D<.000001 THEN 2370
2520 LET I=I-D
2530 M=I*P0/(1-(1/(1+I))^N)
2540 IF M>P THEN 2500
2550 IF M=P THEN 2270
2560 LET D=D/2
2570 IF D<.000001 THEN 2370
2580 LET I=I+D
2590 GOTO 2530
3000 END
```

used programming languages (FORTRAN, COBOL, and BASIC) are described in Chapters 15, 16, and 17.

SUMMARY

Computer programming is a process which results in the development of a detailed set of instructions which outline the data processing activities to be performed by a computer. Computer programming may be subdivided into the six stages shown below.

1. *Programming analysis.* Analyzing a proposed computer application to determine what the computer program is expected to accomplish.
2. *Program design.* Planning and designing the input/output characteristics and the processing procedures required by the proposed application. Flow charts, decision tables, and layout forms are frequently used during this stage.
3. *Program coding.* Writing the computer program that converts the program design into a detailed set of programming language statements.
4. *Program verification.* Checking, testing, and correcting a newly written computer program. Commonly called "debugging."
5. *Program documentation.* Recording a detailed description of the design and instruction content of a computer program.
6. *Program maintenance.* Revising an established computer program that requires improvement such as updating, expansion, or correction.

Flowcharts and decision tables are important techniques which are used during the program design stage. Program coding of business application programs usually involve the use of FORTRAN, COBOL, PL/1, BASIC, or RPG, since they are the most widely used programming languages for business data processing. Once a computer program has been written in one of these languages, it may be verified by a debugging process, documented with suitable program documentation, and revised when necessary by the program maintenance activity.

Conversational computing involves the real-time solution of a problem by a process of man-computer interaction. This results in interactive programming if a programmer designs and codes the processing and decision logic of a computer program with the real-time assistance of a computer. However, programming is *not* necessary if an interactive canned program is utilized. The computer user merely chooses among alternatives offered by the computer and provides it with data.

KEY TERMS AND CONCEPTS

Computer programming, 154
Programming analysis, 154
Programming specifications, 155
Program design, 156
Algorithm, 156
Layout forms, 158, 159
System flowcharts, 158, 161
Program flowcharts, 161–163
Program loops, 163–164
Branching, 164
Decision tables, 165–167
Program coding, 168
Types of computer instructions, 170
FORTRAN, 171
COBOL, 171–172

PL/1, 172
BASIC, 172–173
RPG, 173–174
Program verification, 174
Debugging, 174
Clerical errors, 174
Logic errors, 174
System design errors, 174
Garbage in, garbage out, 175
Program checking, 175
Program testing, 175–176
Program documentation, 176–177
Program maintenance, 177
Conversational computing, 178
Interactive programs, 178
Interactive programming, 178

ASSIGNMENTS

1. Test your understanding of the chapter material by reviewing the *purpose, outline, summary,* and *key terms and concepts* of this chapter. Are you confident that you have attained a basic understanding of the major concepts of the chapter? If not, reread the appropriate material as indicated by the page numbers after each key term and concept.

2. Briefly describe the functions of each of the six stages of computer programming.

3. Discuss the effect of systems analysis and design on the programming analysis and program design stages.

4. Describe the purpose of layout forms, system flowcharts, program flowcharts, and decision tables.

5. Prepare a detailed system flowchart (see Figure 6–5) for one of the following systems. Use your imagination to furnish the details. However, do not allow yourself to get bogged down in excessive detail.
   a. A payroll system for hourly paid employees
   b. A customer credit verification system for a retail store
   c. A student grade recording and reporting system
   d. A system of your choice

6. Prepare a general program flowchart (see Figure 6–6) that outlines the steps that might be required to accomplish some of the data

processing activities shown in the system flowchart you prepared in assignment 5.

7. Prepare a decision table (see Figure 6–9) that outlines the decision logic used in the program flowchart you prepared in assignment 6.

8. Discuss the reasons for the following statement: "It must be emphasized that there is no 'one way' of program coding, just as there are many ways to design a program to accomplish a data processing application."

9. Briefly describe the six basic types of computer instructions.

10. Discuss the basic purpose and features of FORTRAN, COBOL, PL/1, BASIC, and RPG.

11. Differentiate between clerical, logic, and systems design errors.

12. Explain what is meant by the phrase: "garbage in, garbage out."

13. Discuss the checking, testing, and correcting activities that should occur during program debugging.

14. Discuss the purpose and content of program documentation and program maintenance.

15. Differentiate between conversational computing and interactive programming.

16. Are computer terminals and interactive canned programs available for your use? If so, utilize a terminal and a simple canned program to solve a short problem similar to the conversational computing example at the end of the chapter.

part three

Developing Business Information Systems

Chapter Outline

Purpose of the Chapter

Introduction

The Stages of Systems Development

Systems Investigation
Selecting a System for Development, Defining Problems and
Opportunities, Determining Information Needs,
Determining System Objectives, Identifying Systems
Constraints and Criteria, System Feasibility,
Economic Feasibility, System Costs, System Benefits,
Cost/Benefit Analysis, The Feasibility Study Report

Systems Analysis

Systems Design

Programming

Systems Implementation
Acquisition, Training, Testing, Documentation, Operation

Systems Maintenance

Summary

Key Terms and Concepts

Assignments

7

Information Systems Development

Purpose of the Chapter

To promote a basic understanding of how information systems should be developed by analyzing:

1. The functions of the six stages of information systems development,
2. The activities required to investigate and select a system for development, conduct system feasibility studies, implement a newly developed system, and maintain established systems.

INTRODUCTION

Computer-based information systems do not just happen. They must be conceived, designed, and implemented. This process is known as *information systems development*. Developing an information system requires the steps of (1) investigation, (2) analysis, (3) design, (4) programming, (5) implementation, and (6) maintenance. It is important to understand that activities such as computer programming or systems analysis are only *two* of the activities required for the development of computer-based information systems.

It is imperative that computer users become familiar with the stages of information systems development. Inadequate performance of many computer-based business information systems is frequently attributed to an inadequate job of systems development. Business managers must accept the responsibility for the effective management of systems development projects. They must become active participants in the development of information systems which support their decision-making responsibilities.

Computer users must become familiar with the stages of information systems development discussed in this chapter and with the fundamentals of *systems analysis and design* which are explained in the following chapter. However, the analysis and design of even simple computer-based information systems requires a fundamental understanding of the concepts in two additional areas. First, computer users must learn to apply the systems concept to the operations, management, and information systems of a business firm. This is the purpose of Chapter 9 which discusses *"management information systems."* Secondly, computer users must then understand the many ways computers are used in business. This topic will be covered in the remaining chapters of Part Four which deal with *computer applications in business.*

THE STAGES OF SYSTEMS DEVELOPMENT

Information systems development may be subdivided into six stages, each of which is summarized below.

1. *Systems investigation.*   Surveying, defining, and selecting the system to be developed. Making a preliminary determination of the information needs of prospective users, and the objectives, constraints, basic resource requirements, cost/benefits, and feasibility of the proposed system. Frequently called a "feasibility study," "systems survey," or "preliminary system study."
2. *Systems analysis.*   Analyzing in detail the information needs of prospective users and developing the *"system requirements"* of the proposed system. Requires detailed analysis of (1) the organization that will use the system, (2) the system presently used, if any, and (3) the input/output and processing requirements of the proposed system. Sometimes called "information analysis," a "systems study," or "functional requirements analysis."
3. *Systems design.*   Designing an information system that meets the system requirements of the analysis stage. Input documents, output reports, storage files, and processing procedures are designed, and hardware, software, and personnel *"system specifications"* are developed for the proposed system.
4. *Programming.*   Developing computer programs that meet the programming specifications of the design stage.
5. *Systems implementation.*   Acquiring and installing new hard-

ware and software, testing and documenting the new system, and training personnel to operate and use the system.
6. *Systems maintenance.*   Monitoring, evaluating, and modifying an established system.

Information systems development should be viewed as a continuous process that "recycles" through each stage until a system is discarded. It is thus frequently referred to as the *"systems life cycle."* See Figure 7–1. Another important point to remember is that most of the stages overlap each other during the actual development of a system. In fact, the activities we have described as occurring in the systems analysis and systems design stages occur to some extent in each of the other stages of systems development. Therefore, the term "systems

FIGURE 7–1

The Life Cycle of
Information Systems
Development

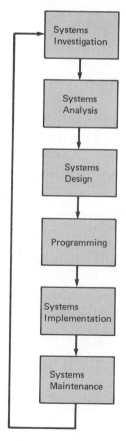

analysis and design" is frequently used to describe most of the activities of information systems development.

The fundamentals of the computer programming stage of systems development were discussed in Chapter Six. This chapter will concentrate on the systems investigation, systems implementation, and systems maintenance stages. Systems analysis and systems design will be covered in detail in the next chapter.

SYSTEMS INVESTIGATION

The information systems development process begins with the *systems investigation phase* which results in the selection and definition of the particular system that will be developed. Systems investigation is the stage which answers the question: "Should we develop new or improved systems?" Because the process of developing a new or improved system can be a costly one, the systems investigation stage requires that a preliminary study called a *feasibility study* be made. The systems investigation stage is also known as "needs research," "preliminary analysis," and "the preproposal stage." Systems investigation should include the following steps. (See Figure 7–2.)

1. *Systems survey.* Determine whether new or improved information systems are required or desired.
2. *System selection.* Select one or more systems for preliminary study.

FIGURE 7–2

The Systems Investigation
Stage

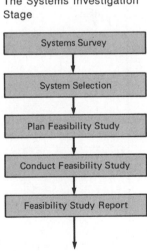

Systems Survey

System Selection

Plan Feasibility Study

Conduct Feasibility Study

Feasibility Study Report

To Systems Analysis Stage
(with management approval)

3. *Plan feasibility study.* Organize for the feasibility study by establishing the objectives, methodology, time and cost constraints, and the personnel that will conduct the study.
4. *Conduct feasibility study.* Conduct a feasibility study to determine whether the proposed information system can achieve technological, economic, and operational feasibility.
5. *Feasibility study report.* Report to management on the results of the feasibility study.

Selecting a System for Development

Requests for information systems development projects may come from present and potential computer-using departments of an organization or may be proposed by the computer services department of the firm. Proposed information systems development projects should also be identified by continually surveying the information needs of the organization in order to identify the need for possible new information systems. Projects should also be identified by a formal *systems maintenance* activity which involves the monitoring and evaluating of established information systems in order to identify the need for modifying or replacing systems. In any case, most business firms will have more proposed systems projects than it is possible for them to develop. Limitations of money, manpower, time, and technology require that the systems investigation phase result in the selection of information systems development projects which best utilize the resources of the firm.

The systems investigation phase should, therefore, include a survey of possible information systems development projects, and the selection of projects for further investigation. A *feasibility study* is then made to determine the information needs of a prospective user and the objectives, constraints, basic resource requirements, cost/benefits and feasibility of a proposed project. The findings of such a feasibility study are usually formalized into a written report called a *"feasibility study report"* or a "systems development proposal," which is submitted to the management of the firm for approval. If management approves the proposal, the other stages of information systems development can then begin. Projects approved by management for immediate or future development are usually included in an information system development *"master plan"* which outlines the timing and resources required by each stage of information systems development for all approved projects.

Defining Problems and Opportunities

The problems and opportunities of information systems must be identified and defined in the systems investigation stage. *Symptoms* must be separated from *problems*. For example, the fact that "sales are declining" is not a properly defined problem. A statement that "salesmen are losing orders because they cannot get current information on product prices and availability" gets closer to the facts of the problem. *Opportunities* are indicated by statements such as: "We could increase sales 20 percent if salesmen could receive instant response to requests for price quotations and product availability."

Determining Information Needs

The systems development stage requires the preliminary determination of the *information needs* of prospective users. The types of information needed by users in order to obtain the objectives of the system must be determined. *Who* wants *what* information and *when, where,* and *why* they want it are the basic questions that must be answered. The users may express their information needs by describing a problem that has developed, such as: "We are not receiving production information early enough in our shipping department." The systems analyst must treat such statements as symptoms of an underlying information system problem which he must identify and define with the help of all related system users. Information needs should also be stated specifically. "Get me all the facts" or "Give me the same information I am getting now" are not specific statements of information needs. A request for "immediate notification on any products that have fallen below the minimum inventory level" is a better statement of information needs.

Determining System Objectives

The systems investigation stage should determine the *objectives* of the system. Objectives should not be stated in vague terms such as "improve efficiency" but in more specific statements, such as, "Pay all invoices before the due date." Another example of the objective of a proposed system could be: "Provide production status information to the shipping department within one hour of the end of each shift but without disturbing the production process." Such specific system objectives bring "the real world" into the system development process since they emphasize that the purpose of an information system is to improve the effectiveness of the users of the system in the performance of their business activities. Thus, systems objectives which stress the *effectiveness* of a proposed system should be given a stronger emphasis than those which stress the *efficiency* of the system.

Identifying Systems Constraints and Criteria

The systems investigation stage must identify the *"constraints"* of the proposed system, also known as the "restrictions" or "boundaries" of a system. Constraints are restrictions which limit the form and content of the systems design. Constraints can be internal or external to the business organization. For example, an external constraint, also called an "environmental" constraint, might restrict the format and size of a source document or output document to specifications required by law or industry agreement. The checks of the banking industry and the "W-2" forms of the Internal Revenue Service are specific examples. Internal constraints may arise due to a scarcity of organizational resources or due to the conflicting information needs and objectives of departments and personnel within an organization. For example, the objective of providing timely production status information to the shipping department may be restricted by constraints that specify: "Don't impose new duties on production personnel," or "Operating costs of any new system must not exceed the costs of the present system."

An important step in systems investigation is defining the *"criteria"* to be used in evaluating the feasibility of the alternative systems being proposed. Criteria must also be ranked in order of their importance because a criterion such as "low cost" may conflict with a criterion such as "instant response." Figure 7–3 summarizes many of the cri-

FIGURE 7–3

System Performance Criteria Categories

1. Cost—operating, maintenance, unit
2. Time—response (input, operations), access, elapsed, cycle, process, turnover
3. Accuracy—frequency and number of errors, significance of errors
4. Reliability—stability, durability, life
5. Security—legal, safety, secrecy
6. Quality—appearance, tolerance
7. Flexibility—variability, sensitivity
8. Capacity—average load, low load, peak load
9. Efficiency—performance ratios
10. Acceptance—customer, employee, management, stockholder

Source: From *Management Systems* by Thomas B. Glans, Burton Grad, David Holstein, William E. Meyers and Richard N. Schmidt. Copyright (c) 1968 by Holt, Rinehart and Winston, Inc. Reprinted by permission of Holt, Rinehart and Winston, Inc.

teria which can be used to specify the performance required of a system.

System Feasibility

Systems investigation includes the evaluation of alternative systems through cost/benefit analysis and other methods of evaluation so that the most feasible and desirable system can be selected for development. The "feasibility" of a proposed system can be evaluated in terms of economic, technological, and operational feasibility. The *economic feasibility* of a proposed system depends on whether expected cost savings, increased profits, and other benefits exceed the costs of developing and operating the system. The *technological feasibility* of a proposed system depends on whether reliable hardware and software required by a proposed system is available or can be acquired by the business firm. *Operational feasibility* focuses on the willingness and ability of the management, employees, customers, suppliers, etc., of an organization to operate, use, and support a proposed system. In this section, we will concern ourselves with economic feasibility. Technological and operational feasibility will be explored in other sections and chapters of the text.

Economic Feasibility

Feasibility studies should include a *cost/benefit analysis* of the proposed system. Costs must include the costs of computer hardware and software, CPU time, systems analysis and design, programming, personnel, training, installation, and operating costs. Costs are comparatively easy to quantify compared to the analysis of benefits. Some benefits are easy to estimate, such as the decrease in payroll costs caused by a reduction in personnel or a decrease in inventory carrying costs caused by a reduction in inventory of the proposed system. Other benefits are much harder to estimate and are frequently called "intangible" benefits. Such benefits as "better customer service" or "faster and more accurate information for management" fall in this category. In any event a determined effort must be made to detail the costs and benefits that are expected from a proposed system.

The economic feasibility of computerizing an information system frequently depends on the amount of information activity supported by the system. For example, computerizing an inventory information system would require that a minimum amount of sales orders and purchase orders be processed per day and a minimum amount of items be normally carried in inventory in order for the system to "pay its own way." Therefore, many feasibility studies attempt to determine the number and frequency of transactions, inquiries, and computations that will be supported by a proposed information system. Systems that support a low volume of information activity may not be economically feasible.

System Costs

System costs can be subdivided into development, operational, and intangible costs. *Development costs* for a computer-based information system includes the costs of the systems development process such as (1) the salaries of systems analysts and computer programmers who design and program the system, (2) the cost of converting and preparing data files, documents and other media, (3) the costs of preparing new or expanded computer facilities, and (4) the costs of testing and documenting the system, training employees, and other *startup* costs.

The operating costs of a computer-based information system include (1) hardware and software rental or depreciation charges, (2) the salaries of computer operators and other data processing personnel who will operate the new system, (3) the salaries of systems analysts and computer programmers who perform the systems maintenance and programming maintenance functions, (4) the cost of data preparation and control, (5) the cost of data processing supplies, (6) the cost of maintaining the proper physical facilities including power, light, heat, air conditioning, building rental or other facility charges, and equipment and building maintenance charges, and (7) overhead charges of the business firm. The costs of developing and operating EDP systems are discussed in greater detail in Chapter 12.

Intangible costs are costs that cannot be easily measured. For example, the development of a new system may disrupt the activities of an organization and cause a loss of employee productivity or morale. Customer sales and goodwill may be lost by errors made during the installation of a new system. Such "costs" are difficult to measure in dollars but are directly related to the introduction and operation of an information system.

System Benefits

The benefits which result from developing new or improved information systems that utilize EDP can be subdivided into "tangible" and "intangible" benefits. *Tangible benefits* are those that can be accurately measured and directly related to the introduction of a new system, such as a decrease in data processing costs. *Intangible benefits* such as "an improved business image" are harder to measure and define. Intangible benefits frequently include the accuracy, flexibility, and expandability of the new system. "Better customer service" is a frequently mentioned intangible benefit which usually means that customers will receive a product or a service in a more attractive and timely manner. Presumably better customer service would result in retaining and increasing sales to present customers and generating sales from new customers.

Benefits (with examples) that could result from the development of computer-based information systems are summarized in Figure 7–4.

FIGURE 7–4

Benefits of Computer-based Information Systems

1. Increase in Sales or Profits. (Improvement in product or service quality)
2. Decrease in Data Processing Costs. (Elimination of unnecessary procedures and documents)
3. Decrease in Operating Costs. (Reduction in inventory carrying costs)
4. Decrease in Required Investment. (Decrease in inventory investment required.)
5. Increased Operational Ability and Efficiency. (Improvement in production ability and efficiency; for example, less spoilage, waste, and idle time.)
6. New or Improved Information Availability. (More timely and accurate information, and new types and forms of information.)
7. Improved Abilities in Computation and Analysis. (Mathematical simulation.)
8. Improved Customer Service. (More timely service.)
9. Improved Employee Morale. (Elimination of burdensome and boring job tasks.)
10. Improved Management Decision Making. (Better information and decision analysis.)
11. Improved Competitive Position. (Faster and better response to actions of competitors.)
12. Improved Business and Community Image. ("Progressive" image as perceived by customers, investors, other businesses, government, and the public.)

Cost/Benefit Analysis

It is not a simple task to determine whether the dollar value of benefits exceeds the dollar value of development and operating costs. It may be difficult to answer the question of management: "Will investing in a new or improved system produce a satisfactory rate of return?" This question must be answered, though many times it can never be adequately answered by numbers alone. The cost/benefit framework of a feasibility study is frequently expressed in terms of the *rate of return on an investment* as summarized below.

$$\frac{\text{INCREASED PROFITS DUE TO COST SAVINGS AND/OR INCREASED REVENUE}}{\text{NEW INVESTMENT REQUIRED LESS REDUCTIONS IN INVESTMENT}} = \begin{array}{c} \text{RETURN} \\ \text{ON} \\ \text{INVESTMENT} \end{array}$$

The return on investment (ROI) concept emphasizes three potential methods of achieving economic feasibility:

1. Cost reduction (such as lower operating costs)
2. Increased revenue (such as an increase in sales)
3. Decreased investment (such as a decrease in inventory requirements).

Many firms do attempt to compute a percentage rate of return on investment for new and improved systems.

Some firms utilize various forms of "present value analysis" which takes the time value of money into account in analyzing the invest-

FIGURE 7–5

Present Value Analysis of a Proposed System

Year	Increase in net cash flow due to the proposed system	Ten percent discount factors*	Present value of net cash flows
1.........	$(10,000) (Loss)	.909	$ (9,090)
2.........	10,000	.826	8,260
3.........	20,000	.751	15,020
4.........	50,000	.683	34,150
5.........	100,000	.621	62,100
Total Present Value........................			$110,440
Less Required Investment†....................			100,000
Net Present Value‡			$ 10,440

* The average cost of financing this business firm is ten percent.
† The proposed system requires a net initial investment of $100,000.
‡ The project should be accepted since the net present value is positive.
  Note: Alternate analysis: The "time adjusted" rate of return of the project could be calculated. It is the rate at which the present value of the net cash flows equals the present value of the required investment. In this example, the rate is 12.5 percent. Since this exceeds the average cost of financing of the business firm (ten percent), the project is acceptable.

ment and costs required and the benefits to be produced. A smaller number of firms utilize methods which try to take into account the uncertainty of the estimated costs and benefits by using various forms of probability analysis. However, a detailed discussion of these types of analyses is beyond the scope of this book. Figure 7–5 illustrates several methods of present value analysis.

The Feasibility Study Report

The results of the systems investigation stage must be recorded in written form in a feasibility study report.

The feasibility study report should include:

1. Preliminary specifications of the proposed new or improved system,
2. An evaluation of the economic, technical and operational feasibility of the proposed system, and
3. A plan for the development of the proposed system. See Figure 7–6.

This report serves two purposes. First of all, it documents the stated information needs of users and the objectives, constraints, resource requirements, and cost benefits of the proposed system. Such documentation helps keep the systems development project "on target" in achieving its objectives. Secondly, the feasibility study report is a communications device which describes the proposed system for

FIGURE 7–6

Feasibility Study Report Outline

Introduction
1. Statement of the problem or opportunity
2. Objectives of the proposed information system
3. Estimates of the benefits, limitations, life, and cost of the proposed system
4. Constraints and priorities

Systems Description
1. The present system
2. Information requirements, present and future
3. Estimate of hardware, software, and personnel required
4. Cost/benefit analysis of alternatives

Development Plan
1. Budget and schedule estimates for the project
2. Techniques of data gathering and analysis
3. Personnel assignments
4. Project control reports

Conclusion
1. Summary of proposal
2. Request for management action

management and other systems users. Management utilizes the information in the feasibility study report as the basis for a decision to approve or disapprove the proposed systems development project. The feasibility study report also serves as the source document when an oral presentation describing the proposed project is made to management.

SYSTEMS ANALYSIS

The second stage of information systems development is the *systems analysis stage.* The goal of the systems analysis stage is to produce the *system requirements* of the proposed information system (also called "general system specifications," "functional requirements," or the "gross design concepts"). The system requirements describe the data processing and information requirements of the proposed information system and is developed by a detailed analysis of (1) the organization that will use the system, (2) the information requirements of the user organization, and (3) the information system presently used, if any.

The systems analysis stage includes the steps summarized below and illustrated in Figure 7–7. The steps of systems analysis will be discussed in greater detail in the next chapter.

FIGURE 7–7

The Systems Analysis Stage

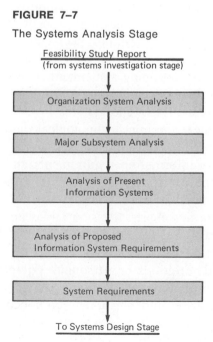

1. *Analysis of the organization system.* Analyze the background of the organization and define its major management, operating, and information systems.
2. *Major subsystem analysis.* Analyze the components and relationships of specific major subsystems that will be affected by the proposed information system. Identify subsystem activities and their requirements.
3. *Present information systems analysis.* Analyze the components and functions of the information systems presently used that will be affected by the proposed system. Identify the components and operations of all data processing subsystems.
4. *Proposed information system requirements analysis.* Analyze the input, processing, output, storage, and control requirements of the proposed information system and its subsystems.
5. *System requirements.* Develop the "system requirements" report which documents the objectives, constraints, and requirements of the proposed information system.

SYSTEMS DESIGN

The *systems design stage* involves the design of an information system that meets the system requirements developed in the analysis stage. This involves the detailed design of input documents, output reports, storage files, and processing procedures. Personnel, data media, equipment, and programming specifications are also developed for the proposed system. Designing an efficient, economical, and effective system is a challenging assignment. However, the success of the systems design stage depends on a thorough job of systems investigation and systems analysis. The systems investigation stage should have determined the economic, technological, and operational feasibility of the proposed system, and the systems analysis stage should have developed the information requirements and the input/output, storage, control, and processing requirements of the proposed system.

The systems analyst designs the new system by developing general and detailed system flowcharts, decision tables and input/output and storage layout forms that describe how available data will be transformed into required information by the new information system. Detailed written descriptions of personnel, equipment, manual procedures, and programming specifications are developed that outline the hardware, software, and personnel components of the proposed system. The systems design stage can be segmented into the four major steps outlined below and illustrated in Figure 7–8. The steps of systems design will be discussed in greater detail in the next chapter.

1. *Basic system design.*   Develop and finalize the basic system design by a thorough analysis of alternative "gross design concepts."
2. *Detailed system design.*   Design in detail the specific input, processing, output, storage, and control media, methods, and procedures of the proposed system.
3. *System implementation planning.*   Plan for the implementation of the new system including procedures and schedules for training, testing, acquisition, and installation.
4. *System specifications.*   Develop the "system specifications" report which documents the detailed systems design and specifies the hardware, software, and personnel to be used by the system.

FIGURE 7–8

The Systems Design Stage

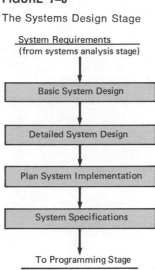

PROGRAMMING

The *programming stage* which involves the development of a computer program that meets the programming specifications of the design stage has been described in Chapter Six. However, it must be emphasized in this chapter that the programming stage requires continual interaction between the systems analysts, programmers, and the computer users who may be part of a "systems development project team." This is true especially during the program analysis and program design stages, as well as during program verification, implementation, and maintenance. The systems specifications and systems design developed by the project team can be considered as a model of the "real world" which must be continually refined and revised during the programming, implementation, and maintenance stages of systems development. Programmers may have to confer frequently with the other members of the project team as they dig deeper into the processing procedures and logic required by the programming specifications and when they attempt to debug and test the program.

SYSTEMS IMPLEMENTATION

We have described the activities of the *systems implementation stage* as involving the testing, documenting, acquiring, installing, and operating of a newly designed system, and the training of personnel to operate and use the system. The steps required to implement a new system should have been scheduled and defined in the planning of the systems development project. These steps are summarized below and illustrated in Figure 7–9.

1. *Acquisition.* Evaluate, acquire, and install necessary hardware and software, create or convert the data base and data files, and prepare required physical facilities.
2. *Training.* Select, train, educate, and communicate with all personnel who will operate or use the system.

FIGURE 7–9

The Systems Implementation Stage

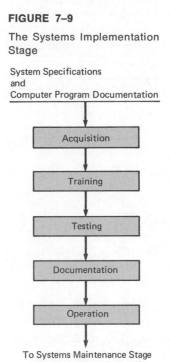

System Specifications
and
Computer Program Documentation

Acquisition

Training

Testing

Documentation

Operation

To Systems Maintenance Stage

3. *Testing.*   Test, evaluate, and debug the system.
4. *Documentation.*   Complete the documentation for the new system including system, programming, operations, and user documentation.
5. *Operation.*   Operate the system. This may involve a process of "conversion" from the old system, if any, to the new.

Acquisition

The first step of the *acquisition* process is an evaluation of the proposals of manufacturers and other suppliers to furnish the hardware and software components of the system. (The software components to be furnished are those that will not be developed by the computer user's own programmers.) The hardware and software requirements of the system should have been described in detail in the system specifications. Various methods of evaluation are used to analyze the hardware and software being proposed by competing suppliers. The physical and performance characteristics of hardware, for example, can be evaluated by test conditions which simulate the operation of the hardware in the new system.

Evaluation is an important part of the acquisition process because the computer user must choose from among many different models and suppliers of hardware and software components. The material discussed in Chapters Four and Five should have given you a basic idea of the functions and physical and performance characteristics of various hardware and software components. The objective is *not* to select the "cheapest" or the "fastest" component. Rather, it is to select the hardware and software components that best meet the requirements of the system specifications. The evaluation and acquisition of computer resources is discussed in detail in Chapter 12.

The acquisition process includes other important activities. The hardware or software components must be purchased or leased from computer manufacturers or other suppliers and installed. Physical facilities (building space, electricity, air conditioning, etc.) must be prepared. The data base and data files to be used by the new system must be created or converted from the previous information system, if any. Data processing supplies must also be acquired.

Training

Implementation of a new system involves personnel and organizational considerations that require *orientation* and *training* of management, users, and operating personnel and the "selling" of the new system to each of these groups. Of course, if an adequate job of management and user *involvement* in systems development has been accomplished, the "shock effect" of transferring to a new system should be minimized. It is at this point that the benefits of involving users in the development of the new system should become evident. If user representatives participated in the development of the system as members of a "project team," the problems of installation, conversion, and training should be minimized. User resistance should be minimal if user representatives were involved in every stage of the systems development effort. (User involvement and resistance is discussed further in Chapters 8 and 14.)

Management, users, and operating personnel should be generally familiar with (1) why the systems development project was authorized, (2) what the benefits of the new system are, and (3) what changes are involved in the new system. Besides a general orientation, users and operating personnel must develop specific skills in order to operate and use the system. This is the function of a training program which involves training techniques and activities that are tailored to the specific system being implemented. Training materials and a training program must be developed utilizing user documentation and other methods such as group meetings, individual instruction, training films, etc.

Testing

Systems implementation requires the *testing* of the newly designed and programmed system. This involves not only the testing and debugging of all computer programs but the testing of all other data processing procedures, including the production of test copies of reports and other output which should be reviewed by the users of the proposed system for possible errors. We have previously described the testing procedures required in the development of a computer program. Such tests are part of the systems development process as well as other methods which test all or part of the system before it begins normal operations. Systems can be tested by testing a model of a new system or by testing the real system with a "dry run" or "dress rehearsal" type of test. Testing does not only occur during the systems implementation stage but should occur throughout the systems development process by "desk checking" parts of the system as it is being developed. For example, input documents and procedures can be tested before their final form is determined by allowing them to be examined and critiqued by users and operators of the proposed system.

Documentation

Systems documentation has been defined as a detailed description of the information requirements and the systems design of an information system, utilizing words, system flowcharts, decision tables, layout sheets and other forms. Chapter 6 illustrated several of these documentation techniques. Chapter 8 will provide more examples of such documentation. Systems documentation is an important process that should record the activities and results of each stage of information system development. Systems documentation is important because it both *records* and *communicates* information about the progress of information systems development. Proper documentation allows management to monitor the progress of the information systems development project and reduces the problems that arise when changes are made in the systems design.

Documentation serves as a method of communication between systems analysts and other personnel that are responsible for a project. Documentation not only helps to eliminate duplication and redundancy of effort but serves to stimulate the systems development process. Documenting a proposed system "in black and white" for the first time frequently reveals the "holes" in the system caused by incorrect or missing procedures. Documentation is also vital to the systems implementation and systems maintenance stages of information systems development. Installing and operating a newly designed system or modifying an established system requires a detailed record of the systems design.

Information systems documentation must describe *who* is to do *what, when, where, how,* and *why.* As has previously been pointed out, systems documentation usually includes many tools used in the analysis and design of the system. Systems documentation should be produced in each stage of information systems development. We have previously described the program documentation produced by the computer programmer and the operations documentation which provides operating instructions for computer operators. The systems specifications developed during the systems design stage can be considered as the first formal collection of documentation for a new system. The process of documenting a new system is frequently completed during the systems implementation stage by collecting all previous systems documentation and organizing it into *manuals* such as "program manuals," "operations manuals," "systems manuals" or "user manuals." Figure 7–10 summarizes the contents of a system manual and a user manual.

FIGURE 7–10

Outlines of Systems Documentation Manuals

System manual	*User manual*
System Summary	System Summary
Organizational Requirements	Operating Schedule
Hardware and Software Requirements	Operating Procedures
Input Data Definition	Input/Output Descriptions
Output Data Definition	Job Descriptions
Data Base Definition	System Controls
Data Processing Logic	Sample Forms and Reports
Index of Computer Programs	
Computer Operations Summary	
Manual Processing Procedures	
Sample Forms and Reports	

Operation

Systems implementation also involves the *operation* of the new information system. The initial operation of a new computer-based information system can be a very difficult task, especially when it involves replacing an information system that did not utilize EDP. Such an operation becomes a *"conversion process"* in which the personnel, procedures, equipment, input/output forms, and data files of the old system must be converted to the requirements of the new system. However, conversion problems should be minimized if an adequate job of systems analysis and design has been performed.

Conversion can be done on a "parallel" basis, whereby both the old and the new system are operated until the project development team and user management agree to switch completely over to the new system. It is during this time that the operations and results of both systems are compared and evaluated. Errors can be identified and corrected, and operating problems can be solved before the old system is abandoned. Installation can also be accomplished by a direct "cut over" to the newly developed system or on a "phased" basis where only one department, branch office, or plant location at a time is converted to a new system. A phased conversion allows a gradual systems implementation process to take place within an organization.

SYSTEMS MAINTENANCE

Systems maintenance is the monitoring, evaluating, and modifying of an established system in order to make desirable or necessary improvements. For example, errors in the operation or use of the system must be corrected by the systems maintenance activity. Installation of a new system usually results in the phenomenon known as the "learning curve." Personnel who operate and use the system will make mistakes simply because they are not familiar with the new system. However, such errors diminish as experience is gained with the new system. Systems maintenance is also necessary for unexpected failures and problems that arise during the operation of the system. Systems maintenance personnel must then perform a "troubleshooting" function to determine the causes and solutions to a particular problem.

The systems maintenance activity requires a periodic review or "audit" of the system to ensure that it is operating properly and meeting its objectives. This activity is in addition to a continual monitoring of the new system. Systems maintenance also includes the improvement of the system due to changes within the business organization or in the business environment.

Systems maintenance also includes the concept of "compliance analysis." Systems analysts must determine whether personnel are using or operating the system according to the procedures outlined in the system documentation. The reasons for noncompliance must be determined since changes in systems design or training programs may be indicated. Finally, systems maintenance should include an evaluation of the systems development project that developed the new system. The head of the systems development team should analyze the reasons for any deviations from the schedules and budgets for the project as well as the original objectives and constraints of the system. The efficiency and effectiveness of the information systems development process must be evaluated so that improvements can be made in the development process of other systems.

SUMMARY

Information systems development is a process that results in the creation of computer-based information systems. Information systems development, also known as the "systems life cycle," can be subdivided into the six stages shown below.

1. *Systems investigation.*   Surveying, defining, selecting, and determining the feasibility of the system to be developed.
2. *Systems analysis.*   Analyzing in detail the information needs of prospective users and developing the "system requirements" of the proposed system.
3. *Systems design.*   Designing an information system that meets the system requirements developed in the analysis stage. Developing the "system specifications" for the proposed system.
4. *Programming.*   Developing computer programs that meet the programming specifications of the design stage.
5. *Systems implementation.*   Acquiring and installing new hardware and software, testing and documenting the new system, and training personnel to operate and use the system.
6. *Systems maintenance.*   Monitoring, evaluating, and modifying an established system.

In this chapter we concentrated much of our attention on the systems investigation and systems implementation stages of systems development. A major activity of the systems investigation stage is the planning and conducting of a "feasibility study" to determine the economic, technological, and operational feasibility of a proposed information system. The determination of economic feasibility requires a cost/benefit analysis of a proposed system which focuses on the tangible and intangible costs and benefits that would result from the implementation of the system. The conclusions of a feasibility study are reported to management and serves as the basis for a decision to approve or disapprove a proposed systems development project.

Once the development of a proposed information system has been approved by management, the steps of system analysis, systems design, and programming can be performed. When these stages are accomplished, the system can be implemented by such activities as (1) evaluating, acquiring, and installing necessary hardware and software (2) selecting and training required personnel, (3) testing the new system, (4) completing the documentation for the new system, and (5) operating the new system, which may include converting from a previous system to the new system. The final major stage of systems development is the systems maintenance activity which requires the continual monitoring, evaluating, and improvement of an established system.

KEY TERMS AND CONCEPTS

Information systems development, 190
Systems investigation, 190, 192
Systems analysis, 190, 201–202
Systems design, 190, 202–203
Systems implementation, 190, 204–205
Systems maintenance, 190, 209
Systems life cycle, 191
Feasibility study, 192–193
System objectives, 194
System constraints, 195

System criteria, 195
Economic feasibility, 196
Technological feasibility, 196
Operational feasibility, 196
Tangible and intangible costs, 197
Tangible and intangible benefits, 198
Return on investment, 199
Cost/benefit analysis, 196, 199
Systems documentation, 207–208
Systems conversion, 208

ASSIGNMENTS

1. Test your understanding of the chapter material by reviewing the *purpose, outline, summary,* and *key terms and concepts* of this chapter. Are you confident that you have attained a basic understanding of the major concepts of the chapter? If not, reread the appropriate material as indicated by the page numbers after each key term and concept.

2. Briefly describe the functions of each of the six stages of information systems development.

3. Explain why the process of information systems development can be called "the systems life cycle."

4. Describe the purpose and content of a feasibility study.

5. Provide an example to illustrate each of the following:
   a. Systems problems or opportunities
   b. Information needs
   c. System objectives
   d. System constraints
   e. System criteria

6. Distinguish between economic, technological, and operational feasibility.

7. Discuss some of the potential costs and benefits of a computer-based information system.

8. Explain how the return on investment concept can indicate the economic feasibility of a proposed system.

9. Describe two major purposes of the feasibility study report.

10. Briefly describe the specific activities that should take place during each of the five steps of systems implementation.

11. Describe several methods of systems conversion.

12. Discuss the purpose and content of systems documentation and systems maintenance.

Chapter Outline

Purpose of the Chapter

Introduction

Origins of Systems Analysis and Design
Methods and Procedures, Systematic Analysis,
   Operations Research, The Systems Approach,
   The Systems Development Cycle

Systems Analysis
Analysis of the Organization System, Major Subsystem
   Analysis, Present Information Systems Analysis,
   Proposed Information System Requirements Analysis,
   System Requirements Development

Systems Design
Basic System Design, Detailed System Design,
   System Implementation Planning, System Specifications
   Development

Systems Analysis and Design: Additional Topics
Techniques of Systems Analysis and Design,
   The Human Factor in Systems Analysis and Design,
   Mathematical Models in Systems Analysis and Design,
   System Simulation, Forms Design and Control

Checklist for Systems Analysis and Design
Input, Processing, Output, Storage, and Control
   Considerations

Summary

Key Terms and Concepts

Assignments

8

Systems Analysis and Design

```
Purpose of the Chapter

To promote a basic understanding of the analysis
and design of information systems by analyzing
the origins, activities, techniques, and require-
ments of systems analysis and design.
```

INTRODUCTION

Systems analysis and design describes the process used by systems analysts who design information systems and data processing systems based on the information requirements of an organization. Systems analysis and systems design can be considered the most important stages in the development of computer-based information systems, since ineffective and inefficient use of computers in business is frequently attributed to a failure to understand and apply the *systems concept* to the information requirements of the business organization. To a great extent, therefore, successful use of the computer in business requires that "every computer user should learn to be his own systems analyst."

Computer users should therefore have a basic understanding of the process of systems analysis and design. The previous chapter emphasized that systems analysis and systems design are two of the major stages of information systems development. In this chapter, we will explore the origins, activities, techniques and requirements of effective systems analysis and design. This should provide you with several important systems concepts that will facilitate a proper under-

213

standing of the management information systems concepts of Chapter 9, and the business computer applications described in Chapters 10 and 11.

ORIGINS OF SYSTEMS ANALYSIS AND DESIGN

Methods and Procedures

The systems analysis and design function in many business firms originated in "methods and procedures" groups and may still exist in "systems and procedures" departments. *Methods and procedures* departments applied the techniques of "scientific management" to the data processing and communications functions of a business. Thus, systems analysis is related to scientific management and industrial engineering. The founder of scientific management was Frederick W. Taylor (1856–1915) who proved that industrial processes could be significantly improved if (1) production was segmented into individual tasks, (2) alternative ways of accomplishing these tasks were developed, and (3) the best sequence of operations was adapted as a standard for all workers. Though Taylor concentrated on factory operations, he maintained that *all* work could be improved if the techniques of scientific management were utilized. By the early 1900s, scientific management techniques spread from the factory to the office. For example, techniques such as time and motion studies, which had been used to improve the efficiency of "blue collar" manufacturing personnel, were used to improve the efficiency of "white collar" office personnel.

The increase in paperwork and shortage of clerical employees during World War II encouraged the development of specialists in "office procedures" or "methods and procedures" in government agencies and large business firms. These specialists engaged in such activities as *forms design, forms control, work simplification, time and motion studies, work sampling, office layout design, procedure writing,* etc. Methods and procedures departments composed of specialists such as "methods analysts," "procedures analysts," and "forms designers" began to emerge. Some of these specialists are still utilized today by large organizations.

Methods analysts are responsible for analyzing in detail how an activity is or should be accomplished. They may utilize time and motion studies, including the use of stop watches to measure the time taken to perform segments of an activity. *Forms designers* are responsible for the design and control of forms used in the organization. *Procedures analysts* are responsible for analyzing the procedures, forms, and equipment used to perform clerical tasks and work to improve efficiency by developing new procedures. They are responsible for developing and maintaining manuals of "standard operating procedures" (SOPs) which described in detail the standard procedures for an activity. They may also prepare and maintain "job descriptions" which describe the responsibilities and activities of each position in the firm.

Systematic Analysis

The term "systems analysis" is frequently used to describe a type of systematic analysis of problems which was popularized by the U.S. Department of Defense during the 1960s. This type of systems analysis is really a modification of the "scientific method" which has long been used by scientists and scholars to analyze problems and develop alternative solutions. The scientific method was modified to apply more specifically to the solution of management problems. Figure 8–1

FIGURE 8–1

The Scientific Method and Systematic Analysis

The scientific method	*Systematic analysis**
1. Recognize a problem.	1. Define the problem.
2. Develop a hypothesis.	2. Define the objectives.
3. Gather data.	3. Define the alternatives.
4. Test the hypothesis through experimentation.	4. Make assumptions concerning the system.
5. Reach conclusions about the hypothesis.	5. Define the constraints.
	6. Define the criteria.
	7. Collect the data.
	8. Build the model.
	9. Evaluate the alternatives.

* Source: Richard L. Shell and David F. Steltzer, "Systems Analysis: Aid to Decision Making," *Business Horizons* (December 1971), p. 68.

compares the steps of the scientific method with the steps of *"systematic analysis,"* which is a term that better describes the Department of Defense version of systems analysis.

Operations Research

Systems analysis is sometimes considered as one of the tools of "operations research," which is also known as "management science," or "decision science." *Operations research* can be defined as the application of scientific techniques to organizational problems utilizing a methodology based on the concepts and techniques of mathematics and the natural, physical, and social sciences. This definition can also be applied to management science and decision science, though these terms emphasize the decision making and scientific orientation of the theories and techniques that are utilized. Operations research (O.R.) stresses the systems approach since it looks at an organization "as a whole" before analyzing the problems of organizational components. O.R. stresses the "team approach" by utilizing teams of specialists with expertise in different scientific and technical fields to develop *feasible* (not optimal) solutions to complex organizational problems. Operations research strives to provide management with "decision aids" or *"decision rules"* to help managers make better decisions. Finally, O.R. places great emphasis on the development of *"models"* of the problem being investigated. We will discuss the use of "mathematical models" in systems development in a later section of this chapter. Figure 8–2 summarizes the steps in the operations research approach to problem solving.

FIGURE 8–2

The Operations Research Approach

1. Define the problem.
2. State the criteria.
3. Construct the model.
4. Manipulate the model.
5. Evaluate and modify the model.
6. Test the solution in the real world.
7. Implement the solution.
8. Periodically review the solution.

Source: Kalman J. Cohen and Frederick S. Hammer, *Analytical Methods in Banking* (Homewood, Ill., 1966), Richard D. Irwin, Inc., pages 5–14.

The Systems Approach

The *"systems approach"* is a term which describes the use of the systems concept in studying a problem and formulating a solution. We defined the concept of a *system* as a group of interrelated components that seeks the attainment of a common goal by accepting inputs and producing outputs in an organized process. The systems approach has two basic characteristics. *First,* the process by which we study a problem and formulate a solution is organized as a system of activities. Therefore, studying a problem and formulating a solution can be considered as a system (frequently called the "systems development cycle") composed of investigation, analysis, design, programmining, implementation, and maintenance activities. *Secondly,* "using the systems approach" means trying to find systems, subsystems, and components of systems in the phenomena we are studying so that all important factors and their interrelationships are considered. Therefore, the systems approach encourages us to look for the components and relationships of a *system* as we analyze a specific problem and formulate its solution.

> The Systems Approach is an orderly way of appraising a human need of a complex nature, in a let's-stand-back-and-look-at-this-situation-from-all-angles frame of mind, asking oneself: How many distinguishable elements are there in this seeming problem? What cause-and-effect relationships exist among these elements? What functions need to be performed in each case? What trade-offs may be required among resources once they are defined?[1]

The Systems Development Cycle

Figure 8–3 illustrates the systems approach as a "recycling" process of systems development. This model summarizes the stages of the *systems development cycle* and can be applied to *all systems,* not just information systems. It incorporates concepts of systems theory, operations research, and scientific management. Notice that the systems development cycle consists of two distinct cycles. The "testing cycle" involves testing the model or system and performing any necessary redesign, reprogramming, and retesting activities. The maintenance cycle involves performing the systems development activities required to improve an established system.

We have briefly analyzed the fundamental activities of the scientific method, systematic analysis, operations research, and the systems development cycle. Did you notice the similarities and differences among these methods? (Refer back to Figures 8–1, 8–2, and 8–3 if necessary.) All of these concepts have contributed to the formulation of the modern concept of systems analysis and design. We should now be better able to understand the basic activities required to analyze and design computer-based information systems.

---

[1] P. G. Thome and R. G. Willard, "The Systems Approach, A Useful Concept of Planning," *Aerospace Management* (Fall/Winter 1966), p. 25.

FIGURE 8–3

The Systems Approach as a Systems Development Cycle

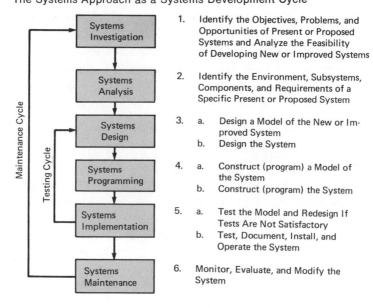

1.	Identify the Objectives, Problems, and Opportunities of Present or Proposed Systems and Analyze the Feasibility of Developing New or Improved Systems
2.	Identify the Environment, Subsystems, Components, and Requirements of a Specific Present or Proposed System
3. a.	Design a Model of the New or Improved System
b.	Design the System
4. a.	Construct (program) a Model of the System
b.	Construct (program) the System
5. a.	Test the Model and Redesign If Tests Are Not Satisfactory
b.	Test, Document, Install, and Operate the System
6.	Monitor, Evaluate, and Modify the System

SYSTEMS ANALYSIS

In the previous chapter, we stated that *systems analysis* involved analyzing in detail the information needs of prospective users and developing the *system requirements* of a proposed system. The systems analysis stage follows the stage of systems investigation in which a feasibility study for a proposed system was accomplished. Assuming a "go-ahead" decision by management, the stage of systems analysis can begin. Systems analysis consists of five major activities which were summarized in the previous chapter but which will now be explored in greater detail. See Figure 8–4. These five activities are:

1. Analysis of the organization system.
2. Major subsystem analysis.
3. Present information system analysis.
4. Proposed information system requirements analysis.
5. System requirements development.

Analysis of the Organization System

The development of a major information system requires an extensive study of the organization if an efficient and effective infor-

FIGURE 8–4

The Systems Analysis Stage

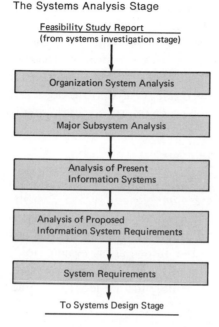

Feasibility Study Report
(from systems investigation stage)

Organization System Analysis

Major Subsystem Analysis

Analysis of Present
Information Systems

Analysis of Proposed
Information System Requirements

System Requirements

To Systems Design Stage

mation system is to result. *Organization system analysis* views a business organization as a system and requires that a broad "background study" of the business firm be undertaken to analyze factors and characteristics such as those outlined in Figure 8–5.

Why is such a background study important to information systems development? The answer is obvious. Information systems must be tailored to the organizational background of a business. The information systems of business firms differ because business firms are different. Each business may have its own unique objectives, organization, management style, products, technology, financial status, customers, employees, and suppliers.

FIGURE 8–5

Factors in Organization System Analysis

1. History of the organization, its performance and prospects
2. Background of the industry and competition
3. Government regulation and other environmental factors
4. Goals, objectives, and strategies
5. Policies and practices
6. Resources, products, and services
7. Organizational structure and management systems
8. Major operational systems
9. Present information systems

Let us examine the importance of knowing the "goals, objectives and strategies" as an example. If we wished to develop an information system to support the sales activity of a business, we would surely discover that business objectives and marketing strategy would significantly affect the design of the proposed system. For example, a decision by a business firm to enter the consumer goods market utilizing a marketing strategy of door-to-door selling would greatly affect the design of a new or improved marketing information system.

Major Subsystem Analysis

We can view a business organization as a *"business system"* whose major subsystems are *management systems, operational systems,* and *information systems.* (We will analyze these systems in detail in Chapter 9.) Specific major subsystems of the business organization will be affected by the information system to be developed. The components and relationships of these subsystems, including their activities and requirements, must be identified. Each major subsystem should be identified and documented with system flowcharts and other descriptive material. The *interface* or connection between subsystems must also be determined.

Analyzing the activities that make up specific major subsystems of the organization is sometimes referred to as *"activity analysis."* Activity analysis is the study of the activities and the requirements of the specific major subsystems that will be supported by the new information system. Each activity is analyzed as an individual subsystem which has specific "requirements" in the form of required inputs, operations, outputs, and resources. See Figure 8–6.

Present Information Systems Analysis

Systems analysis includes an evaluation of the data media and data processing procedures utilized in the *present system.* In many cases, systems analysis consists primarily of the analyis of an existing information system. The present system may be computer-based or it may be a combination of manual and mechanical methods. It may be a highly structured formalized system or be informal and unorganized. Of course, if a system is to be developed for a new organization or for an activity which has never been undertaken by the organization, the systems analysis stage will not include an analysis of an existing system. Instead, forecasts of the expected informa-

FIGURE 8–6

Requirements of a Custom-Order Processing System

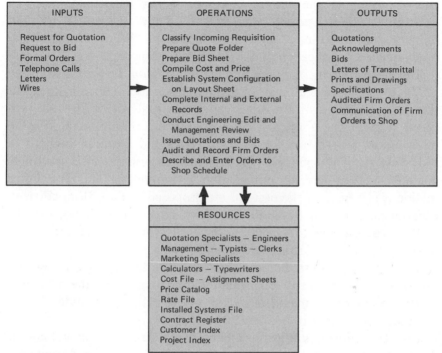

INPUTS	OPERATIONS	OUTPUTS

Request for Quotation
Request to Bid
Formal Orders
Telephone Calls
Letters
Wires
	Classify Incoming Requisition
	Prepare Quote Folder
	Prepare Bid Sheet
	Compile Cost and Price
	Establish System Configuration
	  on Layout Sheet
	Complete Internal and External
	  Records
	Conduct Engineering Edit and
	  Management Review
	Issue Quotations and Bids
	Audit and Record Firm Orders
	Describe and Enter Orders to
	  Shop Schedule
		Quotations
		Acknowledgments
		Bids
		Letters of Transmittal
		Prints and Drawings
		Specifications
		Audited Firm Orders
		Communication of Firm
		  Orders to Shop

RESOURCES

Quotation Specialists – Engineers
Management – Typists – Clerks
Marketing Specialists
Calculators – Typewriters
Cost File – Assignment Sheets
Price Catalog
Rate File
Installed Systems File
Contract Register
Customer Index
Project Index

Source: From *Management Systems* by Thomas B. Glans, Burton Grad, David Holstein, William E. Meyers and Richard N. Schmidt. Copyright (c) 1968 by Holt, Rinehart and Winston, Inc. Reprinted by permission of Holt, Rinehart and Winston, Inc.

tion requirements of the new organization or activity will have to be developed.

System characteristics are determined by collecting and analyzing data and information about the activities of an organization. Several methods—meetings, interviews, questionnaires, review of internal and external documents, and direct observation—can be used. Input/output charts, flowcharts, decision tables, and other specialized forms are used to record and analyze the activities of the organization in order to determine its information requirements. Techniques of systems analysis are discussed and illustrated later in the chapter.

Proposed Information System Requirements Analysis

The previous steps of systems analysis should have defined the major operational, management, and information systems that will be affected by the proposed system. This step focuses on what the information system components *should be,* rather than what they *are* at present. The systems analyst must therefore determine the *required* characteristics of the system components. In particular, he must determine the *information requirements* of the prospective users of the new system. He must answer the question: "What information is *really needed* for decision-making or other purposes?"

The development of *management information systems* (discussed in Chapter 9) requires that systems analysis focus on the decisions that must be made within the organization that will utilize the proposed system. The emphasis should be on determining exactly what information is necessary for such decisions and the best methods of providing such information. The systems analyst must be careful to distinguish between the information *requirements* and the information *preferences* of the users of the proposed system. If an efficient, economical, and effective information system is to be developed, the systems analyst must differentiate between essential information and unwanted and unnecessary information.

The systems analyst should also attempt to determine whether certain decisions could be performed automatically by the proposed system. Such *programmed decisions* would then be included in the computer program to be developed for the proposed system. Of course, the information requirements of an organization cannot be limited to a decision-making focus. Organizations require information for historical, legal, and operational purposes. For example, payroll tax information must be supplied to government agencies, financial information to stockholders, and sales information to customers.

Whether analyzing the information requirements of the organization, the data processing activities of the present information system, or the requirements of the proposed system, the systems analyst must determine the important characteristics of the (1) input, (2) output, (3) processing, (4) storage, and (5) control components of the information system. Figure 8–7 summarizes some of the important characteristics of information system components. A more detailed outline of the input, output, processing, storage, and control considerations of systems analysis and design is found at the end of the chapter in a section entitled: "Checklist for Systems Analysis and Design."

The analysis of system requirements must not be confined to *information requirements*. It must focus on *all* major categories of system requirements, such as required inputs, outputs, operations, and resources. Much information about systems requirements should

FIGURE 8-7

Important Characteristics of Information System Components

1. *Input.* Source, format, media, organization, volume (average and peak), frequency, codes, and conversion requirements.

2. *Output.* Format, media, organization, volume (average and peak), frequency, copies, destination, codes, and conversion required.

3. *Processing.* The data processing hardware, software, and people utilized, and the basic types of data manipulation (sorting, calculating, comparing, summarizing) used to transform input and output.

4. *Storage.* Organization, content, and size of the data base and files, types, and frequency of updating and inquiries, and the length and rationale for record retention or deletion.

5. *Control.* Control methods for system input, output, processing, and storage which promote the accuracy, validity, safety, and adaptability of the system.

have been generated by the feasibility study and during the activity analysis accomplished when the major subsystems of the organization were analyzed. (Refer back to Figure 8–6 and 8–7.) However, the analysis of system requirements must continue to be focused on what the components of the proposed information system *should be,* rather than what they *are* at present.

System Requirements Development

Development of the *system requirements* report is the final step of the systems analysis stage. See Figure 8–8. The system requirements must provide a detailed description of the input/output, processing, and storage requirements of the proposed system utilizing written descriptions, general systems flowcharts, input/output and storage descriptions, and other documents. The kinds of input data available, the contents of present or proposed data bases or files, the control considerations required, the types of information required,

FIGURE 8-8

Outline of the System Requirements Report

System Summary
System Objectives
System Constraints
General System Flowchart
Related Subsystems
Input Requirements
Output Requirements
Data Base Requirements
Processing Requirements
Control Requirements
Other Required Capabilities

and processing considerations such as volumes, frequencies, and turnaround times must be described in detail. The purpose of the system requirements is to provide all the information necessary to design a new or improved information system. The systems requirements are then transformed into the *systems specifications* in the systems design stage.

SYSTEMS DESIGN

The systems design stage involves the design of an information system that meets the system requirements developed during the analysis stage. *System specifications* for the proposed system are the final product of this stage. The major activities of systems design (illustrated in Figure 8–9) are:

1. Basic system design.
2. Detailed system design.
3. System implementation planning.
4. System specifications development.

Basic System Design

Early in the systems investigation stage, the systems analyst developed the "gross systems concepts" which is a *rough* or *general* idea of the basic components and flows of the proposed information sys-

FIGURE 8–9

The Systems Design Stage

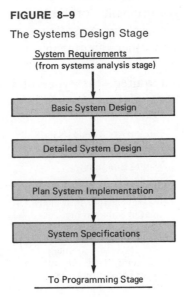

tem. Several alternative "gross design concepts" may have been developed before a single basic concept was tentatively selected. This is the point at which "general systems flowcharts" are frequently used to picture a gross design in rough form. It is also at this stage that a presentation is made to management to obtain approval of the gross design concepts and permission to continue with the systems development project.

In the systems design stage the gross design concepts are refined and finalized by a thorough analysis of alternative design concepts and their effect on the systems requirements. Trade-offs may have to be made between various system criteria. For example, management may demand that inventory stock outs never occur, which would override the criterion of minimizing inventory costs. Some criteria, on the other hand, can be adjusted to accommodate the requirements of other criteria. For instance, the criterion of low fuel costs may be adjusted to accommodate the criterion of a low level of environmental pollution.

Basic systems design should also include the consideration of the "ideal system." This is the systems design concept which would best meet the information requirements of the organization and which ignores economic, technological, and operational considerations. Once the basic specifications of the ideal system are developed, alternative "realistic systems" which take into account the resource limitations of the organization should then be considered. Developing the general specifications of the ideal system encourages the systems analyst to be creative and comprehensive and emphasizes that meeting the information requirements of the organization is the primary goal of information systems development. The development of alternative realistic systems encourages the systems analyst to be flexible and realistic and emphasizes that several ways must be found to meet the information requirements of the organization while taking into account the limited financial, personnel, and other resources of most organizations.

It is important to try to develop alternative designs that meet the objectives of the system. This encourages creative and flexible systems design and avoids spending too much effort on a system design that may later have to be rejected. General system flowcharts that illustrate the components, relationships, and flows of each alternative system are developed. Though each alternative gross design concept has advantages and disadvantages, a single design concept for the proposed system must be selected so that the "detailed design" stage can begin. Which concept seems to provide the most effective, efficient, and economical method of achieving the objectives of the system? Answering this question may be simple or it may require methods of cost analysis and selection similar to those used in the systems investigation stage.

Detailed System Design

The systems designer must utilize his knowledge of data processing and computer hardware and software to develop the *detailed design* of an information system that meets the systems requirements developed during the systems analysis stage. He must decide whether manual, mechanical, or electronic data processing systems can be utilized by the information system. He must decide what types of input/output and storage media and equipment are required and the processing procedures and hardware that are necessary. If electronic data processing systems are to be used, he must decide the requirements of batch processing and real-time processing systems, including the use of sequential access or direct access files, direct data entry devices, remote data communications terminals, and time-sharing capabilities. The systems analyst must also decide whether to modify certain system requirements in order to design an economical, efficient, and effective system. For example, he may have to reduce the number of characters per record and the number of records which were desired in a particular data file. This decision may be based on the type of storage media required and the number of "keys" to the file that he must include in his design in order to meet the processing requirements of the system.

Just as in the systems analysis stage, the systems analyst must relate the detailed systems design to the input, processing, output, storage, and control components of the proposed information system. Since these considerations are so numerous, they are summarized at the end of the chapter in a section entitled "Checklist for Systems Analysis and Design."

System Implementation Planning

This activity of systems design involves the development of plans for the *systems implementation* stage of systems development. Procedures and schedules for training, testing, acquisition, and installation must be devised. Such planning is usually part of a "project management" effort which plans and controls the progress of information systems development projects. Project management will be discussed in Chapter 13.

System Specifications Development

The final step of the systems design stage is the development of a document called the *system specifications* or the "systems definition." It provides a final description of the objectives and scope of the proposed system and a detailed description of the systems design. It includes specifications for source documents, files, and output, procedures for data preparation and collection, and data processing procedures both manual and electronic. It should include a plan for the implementation of the new system including training, testing, documenting, and installation procedures. It includes specifications for the hardware and software that will be utilized by the new system, including programming specifications which outline the computer programming requirements of the new system.

The major sections of a *system specifications* report are summarized in Figure 8–10.

FIGURE 8–10

Contents of the System Specifications Report

1. *Systems Description.* The objectives, constraints, costs, and functions of the system, utilizing written descriptions, system flowcharts, and other documentation methods.
2. *Software Specifications.* The required software components and the computer programming specifications of the proposed system.
3. *Data Media Specifications.* The content, organization, and format of input/output and storage media such as forms, documents, reports, and the data base.
4. *Hardware and Facilities Specifications.* The physical and performance characteristics of the equipment and facilities required by the proposed system.
5. *Personnel Specifications.* "Job descriptions" of persons who will operate the system.
6. *Procedures Manuals.* Specific instructions for the personnel who will operate or use the proposed system.
7. *Implementation Plans.* Plans for training personnel and testing, acquisition, and installation of the new system.

SYSTEMS ANALYSIS AND DESIGN: ADDITIONAL TOPICS

Any discussion of systems analysis and design would be incomplete without the consideration of several additional important topics. The sections of this chapter that follow will discuss:

1. Techniques of systems analysis and design.
2. The human factor in systems development.

3. Mathematical models in systems development.
4. System simulation.
5. Forms design and control.

Techniques of Systems Analysis and Design

We have discussed *what* systems analysis and design is, but we have not emphasized *how* it is accomplished. Information about the present and proposed system must be collected and analyzed, and a new or improved system must be designed. How is this accomplished? First of all, information must be gathered from present and prospective users and operators of the system to be developed. This information is collected by:

1. Personal interviews.
2. Questionnaires.
3. Personal observation of the system.
4. Examination of documents, reports, data media, procedures manuals, and other methods of systems documentation.
5. Inspecting accounting and management reports to collect operating statistics and cost data of data processing operations.

The types of information that should be collected for systems analysis and design describe the characteristics of the input, processing, output, storage, and control components of the system being studied. We have mentioned these characteristics in previous sections and describe them in more detail in the final section of this chapter. In collecting such information the members of the systems development team must be careful to control their own biases and not antagonize management and operating personnel. However, neither should they "believe everything they hear." For example, the systems analyst must give first priority to the objectives, constraints, and requirements specified for the system in determining whether or not additional output will be useful to a particular recipient. Computers have been known to overwhelm users with unnecessary information, while some users have been known to demand nonessential information.

Once the required information for the systems study has been collected, it must be "analyzed and synthesized," utilizing several tools and techniques of systems analysis and design which are summarized below.

1. *System flowcharts.* Graphically portrays the flow of data media and the data processing procedures that take place in an information system. See Figures 6–4 and 6–5 of Chapter Six.

2. *Decision tables.* Identifies the conditional decision logic of the information system. See Figure 6–9 of Chapter Six.

3. *Layout forms.* Shows the content and format of input/output and storage media. See Figure 6–2 of Chapter Six.

4. *Grid charts.* Identifies each type of data element and information in the system and whether it is present in the form of input, output, and/or storage media. It is often utilized to identify redundant data elements and can result in the consolidation and elimination of forms, files, and reports. See Figure 8–11.

5. *Activity analysis forms.* Analyzes a specific activity of a user's operations and summarizes the data processing system components that support this activity. See Figure 8–12.

6. *Information requirements tables.* Describes all data processing activities present in an information system or subsystem and the contents of input/output and storage media used. See Figure 8–13.

7. *Mathematical models.* Represents in mathematical form the components, constraints, relationships, and decision rules of an information system or subsystem. Techniques of simulation and mathematical analysis can then be used to provide valuable information for systems analysis and design. Refer ahead to Figure 8–16.

FIGURE 8–11

A Grid Chart

Reports, Documents, and Files / Data Items	Order Acknowledgment	Shipping Papers	Invoice	Sales by Customer Report	Customer Credit Report	Customer Master File	Etc.
Customer Number	✓	✓	✓	✓	✓	✓	
Customer Name	✓	✓	✓	✓	✓	✓	
Customer Address	✓	✓	✓			✓	
Discount Code			✓			✓	
Credit Code				✓	✓	✓	
Salesman Name	✓			✓		✓	
Etc.							

FIGURE 8–12

Activity Analysis Form

Activity (transaction)		Network Diagram Activity Number
Purpose and Description		
Inputs	Media	
Outputs	Media	
Sequence of Elements	Performer	Decision Rule

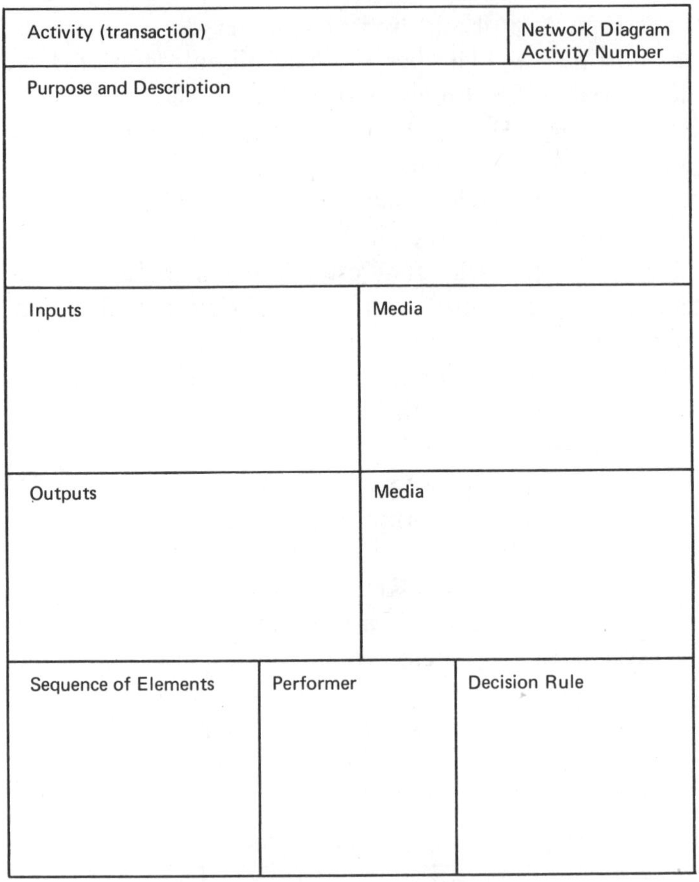

Source: Robert Murdick and Joel Ross, *Information Systems for Modern Management* (Englewood Cliffs, N.J.: Prentice-Hall, 1971), p. 479.

8. *Statistical analysis.* The systems development team may collect *samples* of data concerning important characteristics and components of a system instead of trying to analyze *all* of the information about a system. Statistical techniques such as probability distribution analysis, regression analysis, and tests of statistical significance and confidence are then used to analyze the relationships within the system.

9. *Other tools and techniques.* Many other types of graphic and written analysis can be used such as organization charts, position descriptions, financial statements and reports, work distribution charts, activity analysis forms, and forms which describe the content and

FIGURE 8–13

Information Requirements Form

Subsystem name	Activity name	Output	Data base		Input
			File name	Data element	
Order processing	Edit, credit check, and book	Open-order file, unaccepted orders.	Customer master	Cust # Cust name Cust addr. Credit code	Customer orders
	Check inventory avail., price and print acknowledgement	Customer acknowledgements	Part number and inv. master	P/N Avail. bal. Description Qty. reserved List price Xfer price Discount code	Open-order file
			Customer master	Cust # Cust name (Bill to) Cust addr. (Bill to) Cust name (Ship to) Cust addr. (Ship to) Date last trans.	
	Print product shippers and invoices	Picking lists, packing lists, invoices	Part number and invoice master	P/N Desc Loc code Pieces/pkg Package type Package # List price Xfer price Discount code	Open-order file (ack. date)
			Customer master	Cust # Cust name (Bill to) Cust addr. (Bill to) Cust name (Ship to) Cust addr. (Ship to) Tax code Ins. limit Ship inst. Hold code	

Source: Jerome Kanter, *Management Guide to Computer Selection and Use* (Englewood Cliffs, N.J.; Prentice-Hall, 1970), p. 79.

format of data records, data files, documents, and reports. See Figure 8–14.

The tools and techniques of systems analysis and design are used in every stage of systems development as analytical tools, design tools, and as documentation methods. For example, a flowchart can be used to analyze an existing system, express the design of a new system, and provide the documentation method for a newly developed system.

FIGURE 8–14

Data Element Analysis Form

```
┌─────────────────────────────────────────────────────────────────┐
│                 DATA ELEMENT DESCRIPTION                          │
│                                                                   │
│   File Name_____       │
│                                                                   │
│   File Number _____    Date _____       │
│                                                                   │
│   Data Element_____         │
│                                                                   │
│   Field Element _____ Group Label_____      │
│                                                                   │
│   Form _____ Source _____       │
│                                                                   │
│   Maximum Length (Characters/Item Group) _____      │
│                                                                   │
│   Storage Medium_____         │
│                                                                   │
│   Retention Characteristics _____      │
│                                                                   │
│   _____         │
│                                                                   │
│   Update Procedure _____      │
│                                                                   │
│   _____         │
│                                                                   │
│   _____         │
│                                                                   │
│   Initial Value _____       │
│                                                                   │
│   Units _____                             │
│                                                                   │
└─────────────────────────────────────────────────────────────────┘
```

Source: Robert Murdick and Joel Ross, *Information Systems for Modern Management* (Englewood Cliffs, N.J.: Prentice-Hall, 1971), p. 519.

The Human Factor in Systems Analysis and Design

The human factor in systems analysis and design should be considered in three different contexts:

1. *People* will use the product of the information system.
2. *People* will help process the information.
3. *People* will be involved in information systems development.

The focus of information systems development must be *people-oriented* or *user-oriented* rather than *hardware-oriented* or *software-*

oriented. The analysis of the information requirements of an organization and the design of an information system to meet those requirements must take into account the needs and capabilities of the users of the information produced. The designers of an information system must take into account the fact that people are an integral component of most information systems. Many information systems include manual and mechanical data processing subsystems which require significant amounts of human involvement. Even electronic data processing systems require significant amounts of human effort, especially in the input preparation activity.

The fact that people are both *producers* and *users* of information makes it essential that persons representing the people that will be affected by a proposed system be included in the information systems development effort. The formation of information systems development "project teams" composed of systems analysts, computer programmers, and affected computer users is recommended for all but the smallest projects. This approach is contrasted to the "us versus them" approach, where a team of systems analysts and computer programmers meet periodically with affected computer users.

The participatory approach results in a more people-oriented and user-oriented information system which has several distinct advantages. First, the systems analysts responsible for the development of the proposed system should be able to do a better job of determining the true information requirements of the organization and the true capabilities of the people who will help operate the new system. Secondly, *user involvement* helps insure the acceptability of the new system since it is a result of a joint effort rather than a system developed by a group of "outsiders." This involvement is also vital in the systems implementation and systems maintenance stages since it insures that users will cooperate in the solution of problems that arise when any new system is installed and operated. Figure 8–15 is a tongue-in-cheek illustration of what happens to a systems development project when users are not involved.

User involvement in systems development is also important in reducing the threat that new systems, especially computer systems, may pose to the affected members of an organization. The users on the systems development project team can help plan and carry out programs of *consultation, orientation, education,* and *training* which may be required in the system implementation phase. User involvement also helps identify organizational conflicts which might otherwise escape the notice of an outside systems analyst. Conflicts between groups of

FIGURE 8-15

Systems Development Without User Involvement

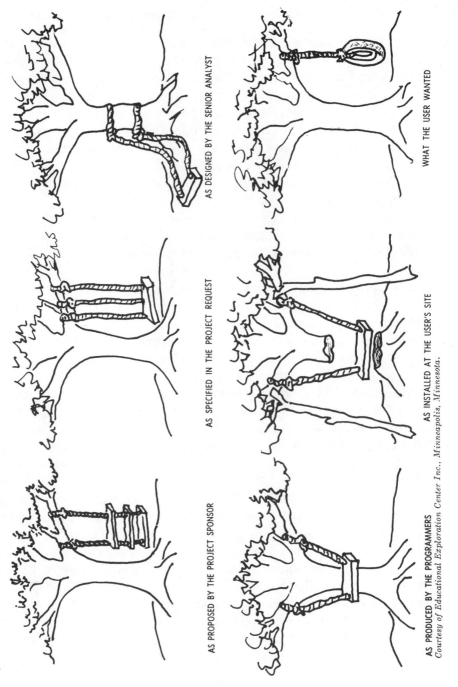

AS PROPOSED BY THE PROJECT SPONSOR

AS SPECIFIED IN THE PROJECT REQUEST

AS DESIGNED BY THE SENIOR ANALYST

AS PRODUCED BY THE PROGRAMMERS

AS INSTALLED AT THE USER'S SITE

WHAT THE USER WANTED

Courtesy of Educational Exploration Center Inc., Minneapolis, Minnesota.

people, such as the departments of an organization, can have a major effect on the design and implementation of a new system.

Other aspects of the human factor in systems analysis and design is the necessity for a "human relations" approach in accomplishing each stage of information systems development. This approach requires stressing and showing that the systems development effort is a *joint effort* of systems analysts and the users and operators of the proposed system. The fact that the people who will use and operate the system can provide valuable and essential information that is essential for the development of a good system must also be stressed.

Finally, the systems analyst must make it clear that he considers himself as a *consultant* to the people who will use and operate the system. He should approach his assignment with an open mind and be eager to learn about the information requirements of the organization and suggestions for its improvement. The systems analyst should stress that he has expertise in systems development but that the users and operators of the proposed system are the experts in the operations that will be affected by the new system. The systems analyst should also display his concern for the impact of the proposed system on the people in the organization.

Mathematical Models in Systems Analysis and Design

We have mentioned that "mathematical models" are an important tool in systems analysis and design. A *model* can be defined as a simplified abstraction of reality which illustrates the fundamental components and relationships of a system or other phenomenon. Models can be "physical models" such as a model airplane, "verbal models" such as a written description of a system, "graphic models" such as the flowchart of a computer program, and "mathematical models" which represent a system by means of mathematical equations and expressions.

Engineers and scientists have long used mathematical models as an economical and practical method of analyzing and testing a physical system. Mathematical models have been developed to analyze the performance of electronic circuits, highway systems, spacecraft, biological systems, etc. Mathematical models have been widely used in operations research because they have proven to be the most concise, simple, and flexible type of model to use in analyzing complex organizational problems. Mathematical models of large, complex business and scientific systems consisting of hundreds of mathematical equations and statements have been developed.

Mathematical models are frequently used to express the "decision rules" utilized by business information systems.[2] For example, in an inventory control system the decision to order more inventory is based on a decision rule which specifies the best number of items to order to maintain the proper inventory of a specific product while minimizing inventory costs. This decision rule can be expressed by the mathematical model shown in Figure 8–16. Solving the economic order quantity (EOQ) model determines the optimal quantity of inventory units that a business firm should order. In the example in Figure 8–16, this is 100 units.

FIGURE 8–16
The EOQ Model

THE MODEL: $EOQ = \sqrt{\dfrac{2FS}{C}}$

Where: EOQ = Economic Order Quantity
F = Fixed Cost of Ordering
S = Number of Units to Be Sold
C = Carrying Cost per Unit

EXAMPLE
If: F = \$10, S = 100 units, and C = 20¢ per unit

Then: $EOQ = \sqrt{\dfrac{2 \times 10 \times 100}{.2}} = 100$ units.

Just as the graphic model of the systems flowchart is a widely used technique in systems analysis and design, the mathematical model can be a powerful tool in information systems development. System models are utilized for many reasons. First of all, designing and testing a model is usually cheaper, more practical, and less dangerous than designing or testing the real system. Attempting to develop a model can provide valuable assistance to the systems analysis and design process because it forces us to think about the most basic components and relationships of a system. A model can also be a good communications and training tool. Of course, models have their limitations. They can become either so simple or so complex that they do not adequately represent the *real world* system. Also, it is still difficult to communicate with the average business man or computer user by

---

[2] Several business computer applications which utilize mathematical models are discussed in Chapter 11.

using mathematical models of systems. However, the benefits of utilizing models in systems analysis and design far outweigh their limitations.

The use of mathematical models begins with the development of a model that represents the components and activities of a system with mathematical equations and expressions. The mathematical model can describe the essential system components and relationships precisely and concisely while providing the flexibility needed for testing and changing the systems design. This is analogous to the use of physical models in research and development projects, such as testing a scale model of an airplane in a wind tunnel. Mathematical models can be tested by making changes to specific values and relationships and analyzing their effect on the values of the components of the system represented by the mathematical model. We can thus experiment with a proposed system before it is completely designed and implemented and experiment with an existing system without damaging the system or disrupting its functions. Thus, systems analysis and design may involve the analysis and design of a mathematical model of a system and a process of experimentation with the resulting mathematical model.

System Simulation

Mathematical models can be used for systems analysis and design utilizing two distinct approaches: *mathematical analysis* and *mathematical simulation*. Traditional mathematical analysis involves the solution of the equations in a mathematical model in order to derive the *best possible* (optimum) values for certain components of a system. For example, we have seen that the mathematical model of an inventory control system usually includes an EOQ (economic order quantity) model which can be solved to provide information on the *best* quantity of goods to order to avoid excessive inventory carrying costs or the possibility of running out of a specific item. Mathematical analysis can also yield *predictions* of *probable* values for certain system components. This requires the use of a mathematical model that incorporates statistical probability in the relationships described by the model.

System simulation is the experimental use of a model to analyze the behavior of a system over time. Simulation allows the systems analyst to explore the subsystems, components, and interrelationships of a system so that he can do a better job of defining the systems requirements. He can then use simulation to explore alternative system components and procedures and to evaluate alternative system designs. Traditional mathematical analysis of mathematical models usually yields "optimal" solutions and assumes a set of unchanging conditions and relationships. Simulation, on the other hand, yields tentative solutions and assumes that conditions and relationships will change dynamically over time as repeated experiments are conducted. In mathematical simulation, the computer manipulates a dynamic mathematical model by changing the values of specific variables and performing repeated solutions of the equations in the model. This simulates the operation of the system over several time periods. The results of the operation of the model in "simulated time" are then recorded and analyzed to provide valuable information about the operations of the "real world" system.

Forms Design and Control

An important responsibility of the systems analyst (or a forms design specialist) is the design and control of the incredible variety of forms used by modern business organizations. Almost any information systems development project will result in changes in the forms used by an organization. New forms will have to be designed and old forms modified or eliminated. Forms design specialists try to develop forms which are easy to read, use, and fill out, but must also consider such factors as cost, size, color, multiple copies, and ease of duplicating and filing. The number of entries, the amount of preprinted data and instructions, and the spacing and position of entries are other major considerations.

Besides the *design* of efficient forms, the major concern of the systems analyst is the *control* of the types and numbers of forms used in the information systems of the organization. Systems development projects have resulted in significant cost savings through forms simplification and elimination. Eliminating forms eliminates not only the cost of obtaining the forms but the cost of completing, processing, filing, and retrieving them. Many systems development projects are started because of complaints concerning the cost or use of forms in an organization.

One of the goals of the systems maintenance activity is to monitor the use of forms in an information system in order to eliminate unused or outmoded forms. However, it should be emphasized that it may be difficult to convince some members of an organization that certain forms should be eliminated. The importance of forms control has increased with the emergence of electronic data processing, since the computer can produce all types of forms and reports in great quantities at tremendous speed. Forms and report control measures are required to diminish the "paper blizzard" which has been spawned by some computer-based information systems. Of course, EDP systems utilizing "paperless" input and output methods such as on-line point-of-sale terminals and CRT units can significantly reduce the paper flow of information systems.

CHECKLIST FOR SYSTEMS ANALYSIS AND DESIGN

Information systems development should focus on the analysis and design of the *input, processing, output, storage,* and *control* components of the proposed information system. The systems analyst must determine what data processing functions and activities are being accomplished by the present system and should be accomplished by the proposed system. (Refer back to Figure 1–3.) He must also determine the types of data processing systems, methods, and devices that are being utilized by the existing information system and that should be incorporated into the proposed system. (Refer back to Figure 1–4.) He must consider the physical and performance characteristics and the benefits and limitations of the various types of EDP systems and their hardware and software components as described in the previous chapters.

The following checklist describes and explains in more detail some of the typical input, processing, output, storage, and control considerations of systems analysis and design.

Input Considerations:
1. How is data captured? Will the input be in the form of source documents, turnaround documents, or is it entered directly into the computer system by a keyboard or other device?
2. Will the source documents be in machine-readable form (MICR, OCR, punched card) or must they be converted into another data medium such as punched cards or magnetic tape?
3. Will input data be accumulated into batches or will it be processed in real-time?
4. Is sorting of input data required?
5. What effect will variations in volume of input data, speed of data entry, and size of input data elements have on the system?

6. Are input preparation procedures and input media designed to facilitate correct data entry by the people who will operate and use the system?
7. Will coding, classifying, and editing procedures be necessary?
8. What control procedures will be used to insure accurate input?
9. Have input format and procedures been designed to accommodate changes due to growth, organizational policy, or environmental demands?

Processing Considerations:
1. What types of processing activities (sorting, calculating, comparing, summarizing, etc.) are required?
2. Should any processing activities be performed manually or mechanically instead of by the electronic computer?
3. Is a batch processing or real-time processing system required?
4. What types of EDP subsystems (batch, remote batch, time-sharing, real-time: inquiry, posting, file processing, full capability, process control) will be required to process input into output?
5. Can the processing procedures and methods produce accurate and timely output given the types and volumes of input and output that are required and the financial, hardware, software, and personnel resources of the organization?
6. Are processing procedures designed to achieve the turnaround time, response time, and throughput requirements expected of the system even if growth and changes occur?
7. How much human intervention will be required during processing?
8. Are processing procedures designed and documented to facilitate the operation of the system by its users?
9. What controls are built into the processing procedures?

Output Considerations:
1. Will output be in the form of printed documents and reports or is information to be displayed on devices such as CRT terminal?
2. Should output be in a machine-readable form such as punched cards or magnetic tape which require off-line conversion to a human-readable document?
3. Will output of the system become the input to another system? (Such as turnaround documents)
4. Will output be accumulated in batches or is real-time output required?

5. Does output have to report every transaction or activity, or should only exceptional items be reported (exception reporting), or is summarized information acceptable?
6. Must output be generated on demand, on schedule, or on exception?
7. Are output support procedures such as editing, copying, microfilming, sorting, and distributing required?
8. Is output for external users (such as invoices, statements, and reports for customers, suppliers, or government agencies) or for internal users such as reports for operating and management personnel?
9. Are output support procedures and output media formats designed to insure accurate, timely, and useable information to the users of the system?
10. Can certain output reports and documents be standardized, consolidated, or eliminated?
11. What control procedures are necessary to insure the accuracy and timeliness of output?
12. Have output format and procedures been designed to accommodate growth or possible changes in organizational policy or the environment?

Storage Considerations:
1. Can the information system utilize an integrated data base (central information file) instead of several separate data files?
2. If multiple files are to be used, are procedures designed to update all files that are affected by a particular item of data or information?
3. Will data and information be stored in sequential access files or direct access files?
4. Will the data base be used to support real-time or batch processing?
5. How should the data base or data files be organized? What should be the design of the data elements (characters, fields, records) that will be included?
6. Can multiple keys, pointers, and directories be provided for direct access files so that data and information can be easily retrieved and updated?
7. Are the files or data base designed to facilitate interactive processing by users of the system? Will data management software be utilized in this regard?

8. What are the criteria for retention or deletion of data records?
9. Are controls built into file processing and inquiry procedures in order to limit the possibility of unauthorized entry into the files, loss of data and information, or incorrect recording or transmittal of data or information?
10. Is storage design flexible? Does it take into account possible changes in the type, size, volume, and frequency of data elements, inquiries, and file processing due to growth, organizational changes, or external environmental developments?

Control Considerations:
1. Are input/output control methods which detect invalid and inaccurate input data or output information included in this system? (Examples are batch control totals, check digits, and reasonableness checks.)
2. Are processing control procedures which detect invalid and incorrect processing of data included in the system? (For example, checkpoints can be designed into the computer program.)
3. What procedures have been devised to monitor input, output, processing, and storage files so that the computer system will provide instant notification of unusual conditions or results which require investigation or action by the computer user?
4. Are storage control procedures which protect the accuracy and confidentiality of the data base or data files included in the system? (For example, identification codes which limit file updating and inquiries to authorized personnel and programs.)
5. Are "backup" file procedures which limit the loss of data caused by physical breakdowns or incorrect processing included in this system? ("Dumping" the contents of direct access files onto magnetic tape is an example.)
6. Are data processing control forms required for this system? (Input batch tickets and output transmittal sheets are examples.)
7. Are feedback-control procedures included in the systems design so that fraudulent use of the system can be detected or prevented?
8. Are "audit trails" which allow the flow of an item of data or a document to be traced through the entire information system included in the system design?
9. Have the control procedures of the system been designed to avoid "over control"? (This condition may be caused by conflicting control procedures.)

10. Have control procedures been provided which facilitate and control the systems maintenance activity? (The system is monitored, evaluated, and modified when corrections and changes are necessary.)

SUMMARY

Systems analysis and design is a process utilized by systems analysts who design information systems and data processing systems based on the information requirements of an organization. In this chapter, we explored the origins, activities, techniques, and requirements of effective systems analysis and design. Systems analysis and design embodies some of the principles and techniques of scientific management, systematic analysis, and operations research. Systems analysis and design requires the use of the "systems approach" which encourages us to look for the components and relationships of a system as we analyze a specific problem and formulate its solution.

Systems analysis is the second major stage of information systems development and begins after a feasibility study for a proposed system has been completed and a "go ahead" decision has been made by management. The objective of systems analysis is to determine the information requirements and other "system requirements" of a proposed information system. Systems analysis includes the following major activities.

1. *Analysis of the organization system.* Analyze the background of the organization and define its major management, operating, and information systems.
2. *Major subsystem analysis.* Analyze the components and relationships of specific major subsystems that will be affected by the proposed information system. Identify subsystem activities and their requirements.
3. *Present information systems analysis.* Analyze the components and functions of the information systems presently used that will be affected by the proposed system. Identify the components and operations of all data processing subsystems.
4. *Proposed information system requirements analysis.* Analyze the input, processing, output, storage, and control requirements of the proposed information system and its subsystems.
5. *System requirements.* Develop the "system requirements" report which documents the objectives, constraints, and requirements of the proposed information system.

Systems design is a stage of information systems development which involves the design of an information system that meets the systems requirements developed in the systems analysis stage. Systems design requires the completion of the four major steps outlined below.

1. *Basic system design.* Develop and finalize the basic system design by a thorough analysis of alternative "gross design concepts."
2. *Detailed system design.* Design in detail the specific input, processing, output, storage, and control media, methods, and procedures of the proposed system.
3. *System implementation planning.* Plan for the implementation of the new system including procedures and schedules for training, testing, acquisition, and installation.
4. *System specifications.* Develop the "system specifications" report which documents the detailed systems design and specifies the hardware, software, and personnel to be used by the system.

Several important topics related to systems analysis and design were discussed in this chapter. Information about present and proposed information systems is collected by personal interviews, questionnaires, personal observations, and examination of documents and reports. This information is then "analyzed and synthesized," utilizing various tools and techniques of systems analysis and design such as system flowcharts, decision tables, layout forms, grid charts, etc. This includes the use of mathematical models to represent the components and relationships of an information system. Techniques of system simulation and mathematical analysis can then be used to provide valuable information for systems analysis and design.

A major consideration in systems analysis and design is the "human factor." This aspect of systems analysis and design must be stressed because people (1) utilize the product of information systems, (2) help process data into information, and (3) are involved in information systems development. Thus, the focus of information systems development must be "user-oriented" rather than hardware-oriented or software-oriented. A final major consideration in systems analysis and design is the design and control of the wide variety of forms and reports utilized by modern business organizations.

KEY TERMS AND CONCEPTS

Methods and procedures, 214
Scientific management, 214
Systematic analysis, 215
Scientific method, 215
Operations research, 216
Systems approach, 216–217
Systems development cycle, 217–218
Organization system analysis, 218–219

Activity analysis, 220
System requirements, 222–223
System specifications, 227
Project teams, 233
User involvement, 233
Mathematical models, 235–236
System simulation, 237
Forms design and control, 238

ASSIGNMENTS

1. Test your understanding of the chapter material by reviewing, the *purpose, outline, summary,* and *key terms and concepts* of this chapter. Are you confident that you have attained a basic understanding of the major concepts of the chapter? If not, reread the appropriate material as indicated by the page numbers after each key term and concept.

2. Discuss how the following concepts are related to systems analysis and design:
   a. Methods and procedures
   b. Scientific management
   c. Systematic analysis
   d. The scientific method
   e. Operations research
   f. The systems approach
   g. The systems development cycle

3. Discuss two ways you could utilize "the systems approach" in solving a problem.

4. Explain why an analysis of the organization system is important to information systems development.

5. Discuss the purpose and content of the system requirement and the system specifications.

6. Explain why basic systems design should include consideration of the ideal system and alternative realistic systems.

7. Describe several methods of collecting information for systems analysis and design.

8. "The tools and techniques of systems analysis and design are used in every stage of systems development as analytical tools, design tools and documentation methods." Describe several tools and techniques which substantiate this statement.

9. Explain why the human factor should be considered in systems analysis and design.

10. Describe how user involvement can take place in systems analysis and design. Discuss the benefits of such involvement.

11. Discuss the use and benefits of mathematical models in systems analysis and design.

12. Explain how forms design and control is related to systems analysis and design.

13. "Information systems development should focus on the analysis and design of the input, processing, output, storage, and control components of the proposed information system." Discuss the rationale for such a statement.

14. Discuss several input, processing, output, storage and control considerations of systems analysis and design. Illustrate your answer with appropriate examples based on one of the systems for which you drew a detailed system flowchart in assignment 5 of Chapter 6. The systems were:
   a. A payroll system for hourly paid employees
   b. A customer credit verification system for a retail store
   c. A student grade recording and reporting system
   d. A system of your choice

15. Describe several input, processing, output, storage, and control considerations of one of the many business computer applications discussed in Chapters 10 and 11.

part four

Applying the Computer to Business Management

Chapter Outline

Purpose of the Chapter

Introduction

The Cybernetic Systems Concept
Feedback and Control, Adaptive Systems, Cybernetic Systems

The Business System
Operational Systems, Management Systems, Operational Information Systems, Management Information Systems, The Business Environment

Information Requirements of Operational Systems
Information Requirements of Environmental Systems
Customer Systems, Competitor Systems, Supplier Systems, Labor Union Systems, Stockholder Systems, Financial Institution Systems, Governmental Systems, Community Systems.

Information Requirements of Management Systems
The Functions of Management, The Management System, Management Information Requirements: Organizations as Decision Systems, Programmed Decisions, Management by Exception, Management Subsystems.

Management Information Systems
The Management Information System, MIS Information Output: Internal Information from an MIS, External Information from an MIS.

Business Information Systems
Production/Operations, Marketing, Financial, Accounting, Personnel, and Other Information Systems.

Integrated Information Systems
Common Data Flows, The Common Data Base, The Total Information System.

Summary

Key Terms and Concepts

Assignments

9

Management
Information Systems

Purpose of the Chapter

To promote a basic understanding of the role of management information systems in business by analyzing:

1. The cybernetic systems concept,
2. The business firm as a system,
3. The information requirements of the business system,
4. The information requirements of management,
5. The concepts of management information systems, business information systems, and integrated information systems.

INTRODUCTION

The concept of *management information systems* (MIS) originated in the 1960s and became the byword (and the "buzzword") of almost all attempts to relate computer technology and systems theory to data processing in business. During the early 1960s, it became evident that the computer was being applied to the solution of business problems in a piecemeal fashion, focusing almost entirely on the computerization of clerical and recordkeeping tasks. The concept of management information systems was developed to serve as a systematic framework for organizing business computer applications and to emphasize the management orientation of electronic data processing in business. Therefore, business applications of computers should be viewed as *computer-based subsystems* of the major information systems in a business firm; subsystems whose primary goal is the support of *management decision-making.*

Effective management information systems are needed by all business organizations because of the increased complexity and rate of change that are characteristics of our present civilization. Management information systems must help management cope with the "future shock" caused by the accelerated pace of social and technological changes which has drastically shortened the "life cycle" of products, production methods, personnel practices, organizational relationships, and "proven facts," to name a few. These changes have triggered an "information explosion." Management needs effective information systems that can cope with the rapidly expanding production and accumulation of information and knowledge and provide selective and strategic information to support decision-making responsibilities.

We can define a management information system as *"an information system that provides the information required to support management decision-making."* However, we cannot really understand this definition until we explore several other basic concepts which underlie the concept of a management information system. We must understand concepts such as *cybernetic systems, business systems,* and *management systems* before we can appreciate the revolutionary impact that the MIS concept is having on the effective use of computers in business.

THE CYBERNETIC SYSTEMS CONCEPT

We have defined the systems concept several times in this text, primarily in the context of information and data processing systems. We should not forget, however, that a system can be very simply defined as a group of interrelated or interacting elements. Many examples of systems can be found in the physical and biological sciences, in modern technology, and in human society. Thus, we can talk of the physical system of the sun and its planets, the biological system of the human body, the technological system of an oil refinery, and the socio-economic system of a business organization.

Feedback and Control

We have defined the three basic components of a system as *input, processing,* and *output.* We should enlarge our understanding of the systems concept by including two additional components: *feedback* and *control*. Figure 9–1 illustrates a system with feedback and control components. Such a system is called a *"cybernetic system,"* that is, a self-monitoring and self-regulating system. *Feedback* is information concerning the components and operations of a system. *Control* is the systems component that evaluates feedback to determine whether the system is moving toward the achievement of its goal and then makes any necessary adjustments to the input and processing components of the system to insure that proper output is produced. The components of feedback and control are frequently combined into the single systems characteristic of "feedback-control" (or simply "control") since feedback can be considered as an essential part of the self-monitoring and self-controlling activities of the control function.

FIGURE 9–1

A Cybernetic System Model

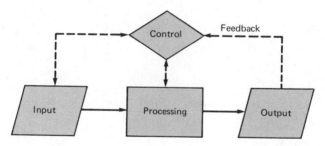

Adaptive Systems

The feedback-control concept can be extended to include the characteristic of "adaptiveness." Many cybernetic systems are "closed systems" because they are completely self-contained. *Adaptive cybernetic systems* are "open systems" which possess the feedback-control characteristic of cybernetic systems but also interchange input and output and receive feedback from their *environment*. Adaptive cybernetic systems therefore have the ability to adjust themselves to their environment as well as to adjust themselves to an internally established goal. Thus, the feedback-control concept not only allows a system to regulate its operations to achieve a predetermined goal but can enable a system to *change itself, including its goals,* in order to survive in a changing environment. See Figure 9–2.

FIGURE 9–2

An Adaptive Cybernetic System

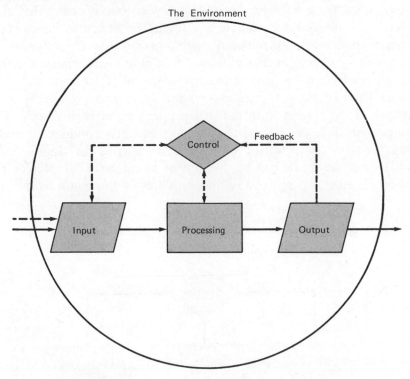

Cybernetic Systems

The concepts of feedback-control and adaptiveness are vital to the development of many types of systems, including information systems. A familiar example of a closed cybernetic system is the thermostatically controlled heating system found in many homes, which automatically monitors and regulates itself to produce a desired temperature. Another familiar example is the human body, which can be considered as an adaptive cybernetic system. Such cybernetic systems display a characteristic, called "homeostasis," which is a tendency to maintain a state of "equilibrium" or stability by operating between certain upper and lower limits. A cybernetic system may not be able to achieve such stability under certain extreme conditions. It will then "go out of control" and "explode" or "extinguish" itself because its adaptive and self-regulating mechanisms can not properly regulate the operations of the system.

FIGURE 9–3

A Data Processing System

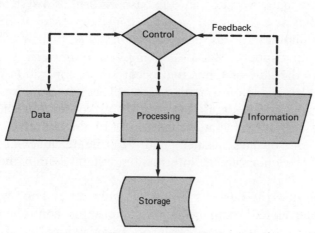

Feedback-control in adaptive cybernetic systems is an important concept in *information systems development* because the purpose and function of most information systems is to support the feedback-control function in an organization. For example, management information systems support the feedback-control function required for the management of an organization, while process control information systems support the feedback-control function required to control a physical process. Thus, *information systems can be viewed as the feedback-control subsystems of a business system.* (We will discuss this subject in more detail in the next section.

The cybernetic systems concept can also be applied to all types of data processing systems and computer systems. *Computer systems* are "closed-loop" self-regulating systems. Feedback circuitry is built into all hardware components of the computer system while the control function is performed by the control unit of the CPU. *Data processing systems* can also be viewed as cybernetic systems. Figure 9–3 is a modification of the cybernetic systems model to include the storage function of all data processing systems. Thus, any data processing system, whether it be manual, mechanical, or electronic, should possess input, processing, output, storage, and control components. This is why the previous chapter stressed the use of the cybernetic system concept in the analysis and design of information systems and data processing systems.

THE BUSINESS SYSTEM

There are many ways to view the business firm as a system. We can view the business firm as a *social system* composed of people and their interrelationships, as an *information system* which relies on information to support decision-making, as a *financial system* that emphasizes the flow of funds that occurs in the operation of a business, or as an *economic system* which utilizes economic resources to produce economic welfare. However, let us concentrate on a model of the business system that emphasizes: (1) the adaptive cybernetic nature of the business system, and (2) the feedback-control role played by the management information systems within the business system.

We can view the business firm as a *"business system"* which consists of interrelated components which must be controlled and coordinated toward the attainment of organizational goals such as

FIGURE 9–4

The Business System

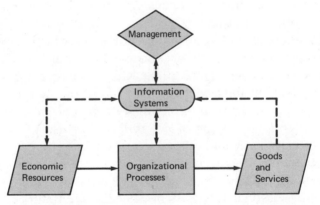

profitability and social responsibility. Figure 9–4 is an illustration of the basic business system. In this simple model of the business system, economic resources (input) are transformed by various organizational processes (processing) into goods and services (output). Information systems provide information on the operations of the system (feedback) to management for the direction and maintenance of the system (control).

We should also view the business firm as an *adaptive subsystem of society* and as a system composed of several basic *subsystems*. Figure 9–5 illustrates these attributes of the business system. Let us analyze this important systems concept.

FIGURE 9–5

The Business System: Basic Subsystems and Components

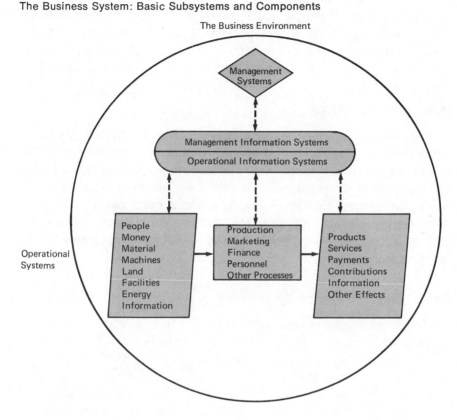

Operational Systems

The most basic subsystems of the business system are its *operational systems* (also called "operating systems" or "physical systems"). They constitute the input, processing, and output components of the business system as summarized below:

1. *Input.* Employs people, money, material, machines, land, facilities, energy, and information.
2. *Processing.* Utilizes various kinds of organizational processes including production, marketing, finance, personnel, etc., known as the *"functions of business,"* and other processes that help transform input into output (such as engineering, research and development, legal services, etc.).
3. *Output.* Produces products, services, payments (such as employee benefits, dividends, interest, taxes, payments to suppliers, etc), contributions, information, and other effects.

The types of input, processing, and output utilized by operational systems depends on the particular business activities of each business firm. For example, one of the operational systems of an oil company would include the physical system of oil fields, pipe lines, tankers, and refineries that transforms oil into various petroleum products.

Management Systems

The *management systems* of a business firm constitute the control component of the business system. The management of an organization can be viewed as an integrated group of subsystems composed of managers at all organizational levels and divisions. The management systems can also be viewed as an integrated network of planning, organizing, staffing, directing, and controlling activities (called the *"functions of management"*) that direct the operations of the business system.

Operational Information Systems

Operational information systems (OIS) are a basic category of business subsystems which perform information feedback functions for the business system, as well as producing information that is required as an output of the business system. An *operational information system* is an information system that collects, processes, and stores data generated by the operational systems of the business and produces data and information for input into a management information system or for the control of an operational system. Operational information systems process data that is generated by business operations (sales transactions, production results, employee payroll, etc.) but do not produce the kind of information that can best be used by management. Further processing by a management information system is usually required.

Management Information Systems

Management information systems (MIS) constitute another major group of subsystems of the business system. Management information systems play a vital feedback role in support of the management of the business firm by processing the data generated by the other subsystems of the business system into information for management decision-making. Information produced by the management information systems may also constitute part of the output of the business system. Management information systems can be viewed as an information network within the business system which supports the decision-making responsibilities of management.

The Business Environment

The business firm is a subsystem of society and is surrounded by the other systems of the *"business environment."* Therefore, the business firm must maintain proper interrelationships with the other economic, political, and social subsystems in its environment, such as other business firms, labor unions, government agencies, etc.

INFORMATION REQUIREMENTS OF OPERATIONAL SYSTEMS

Once we can visualize the business firm as a business *system,* we can then identify the major systems in the business environment and the major subsystems of the business system. If our purpose is to develop new or improved *information systems,* we can then begin the process of information systems development discussed in Chapter 7. This "systems approach" is vital to the development of effective management information systems and operational information systems. For example, the development of *information systems* for a manufacturing firm should begin with a definition of the manufacturing *operational system.* See Figure 9–6. An integrated series of information subsystems can then be developed to meet the information requirements of this operational system.

Figure 9–7 illustrates several possible information systems for a manufacturing firm as an integrated series of nine subsystems built

FIGURE 9–6

The Basic Operational System of a Manufacturing Firm

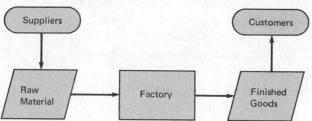

FIGURE 9–7

Selected Information Systems of a Manufacturing Firm

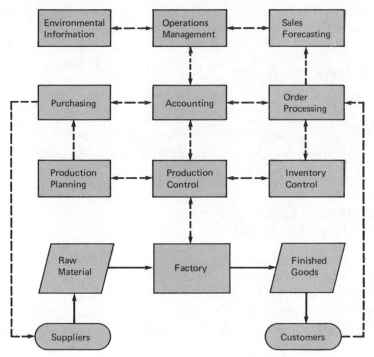

upon a manufacturing operational system. These information sub-systems are summarized below.

1. *The order processing subsystem.* Processes orders received from customers and produces invoices for customers and data needed for sales forecasts, inventory control, and accounting.

2. *The sales forecasting subsystem.* Receives data concerning customer orders and the business environment. Produces sales forecasts for inventory control and operations management.

3. *Inventory control subsystem.* Receives information concerning customer orders, sales forecasts, production control, receipts of raw material, and produces shipping documents. Issues reports on products moving through each stage of production and provides data needed for production requirements generation and the filling of customer orders.

4. *The production planning subsystem.* Receives data concerning finished goods requirements from the inventory control subsystem and determines manufacturing process, material, and labor requirements.

Produces purchase requisitions for required material and a production schedule for the factory.

5. *The production control subsystem.* Receives the production schedule and data from the factory concerning completed jobs, work-in-process, the amount of labor and material utilized, and the expenses incurred in production. Produces job orders for the factory and production variance reports for the accounting and operations management subsystems.

6. *The purchasing subsystem.* Receives purchase requisitions from the production planning system and produces purchase orders for suppliers and accounts payable data for the accounting subsystem.

7. *The accounting subsystem.* Receives data from many other information subsystems and provides financial and operating data to the operations management subsystem. The accounting subsystem is composed of many specialized subsystems. For example, information from the order processing subsystem is processed by an "accounts receivable" subsystem, and data from the purchasing subsystem is processed by an "accounts payable" subsystem.

8. *The operations management subsystem.* Receives financial and operating data and information from the accounting subsystem and environmental data from the environmental subsystem. Produces management directives, plans, and budgets.

9. *The environmental information subsystem.* Receives information from the environmental systems surrounding the business system and provides environmental data (such as economic or market trends) to the operational management and sales forecasting subsystems.

INFORMATION REQUIREMENTS OF ENVIRONMENTAL SYSTEMS

The systems in the environment surrounding the business firm include customers, suppliers, competitors, stockholders, labor unions, financial institutions, governmental agencies, and the community. See Figure 9–8. Let us summarize briefly how *information systems* must be developed to help the business firm shape its relationships to each of these *environmental systems*.

Customer Systems

Information systems should help the business firm understand what consumers want and why they want it, so *consumers* can be converted

FIGURE 9–8

Systems in the Business Environment

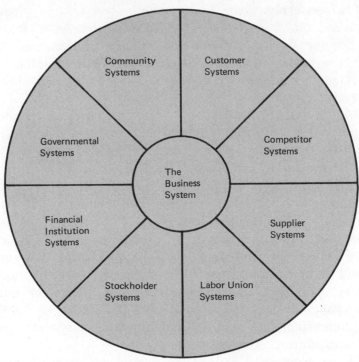

into *customers*. These systems process data and provide information concerning the sales activity that is required by customers, management, and the accounting subsystem. Such "marketing information systems" support marketing activities such as advertising, selling, pricing, distribution, product development, and market research.

Competitor Systems

Information systems must provide management and all functions of the business with information on present and potential *competitors,* why they are competitors, and what their competitive activities are and will be. Such information helps management shape its competitive strategy. Information on trends in the industry as a whole is also important.

Supplier Systems

Suppliers provide a business firm with goods and services in exchange for money. The goods may be in the form of raw material, components, supplies, and equipment while various services are provided by management and technical consultants, subcontractors, and others. Information systems must provide information to support the purchasing function so that the business firm can minimize its purchasing cost and maximize the value of goods and services that it procures. Management needs such information as purchasing trends, alternative sources of supply, and inventory and transportation arrangements. Information systems must support the accounts payable subsystem of the accounting system which provides management and suppliers with proper information and documents of financial transactions with suppliers.

Labor Union Systems

Though employees are a vital component of the business system, they are frequently represented by an environmental system—the *labor union*. Labor unions negotiate the provision of labor to the firm in return for wages and other economic benefits to the employees. Information systems must provide management, employees, and labor unions with information on employee compensation and labor productivity within the firm and competing business systems.

Stockholder Systems

Though *stockholders* are the owners of business firms that are organized as corporations, they can be considered as an environmental system because many business firms are owned by many different and distant stockholders. Stockholders invest in the firm in return for a share of ownership which provides them with dividends, potential growth in the value of their stock, and voting rights in the management of the firm. Information systems must provide information concerning dividends and financial and operating performance to management and stockholders. Information is needed to support the efforts of management to convert private and institutional investors into stockholders of the business firm.

Financial Institution Systems

Financial institutions provide the business system with money, credit and various financial services. Commercial banks are the primary financial institution in the environment of a business firm. Information systems must provide management and financial institutions with information on the financial and operating performance of a firm. Management needs information about the state of the financial markets in order to plan and control the flow of funds between the business firm and various financial institutions.

Governmental Systems

Business firms are governed by laws and regulations of *government agencies* at the city, county, state, federal, and foreign government levels. Governments also provide many services to the business system, such as police and fire protection, transportation networks and facilities, education, and monetary services. Businesses also provide goods and services to government customers and pay taxes in return for government services. The information systems of a business firm must supply many types of information and documents to various governmental agencies concerning many aspects of the operations of a firm. Information concerning financial performance and employee compensation requires much data processing activity, as does new information requirements such as hiring practice reports and environmental impact statements. Management also needs information on political, legal, and legislative developments so that it can effectively deal with changes in laws and regulations.

Community Systems

The business firm resides in local, regional, national, and world *communities*. The business firm is expected to be a "good citizen" of each of these communities and to maintain good relationships with the members of each community. Information systems must provide the management of business firms with information concerning how well they are meeting their community responsibilities.

INFORMATION REQUIREMENTS OF MANAGEMENT SYSTEMS

The Functions of Management

Before we discuss the information requirements of management systems, we should define what the term *"management"* means. Management is traditionally described as a process of leadership involving the functions of planning, organizing, staffing, directing, and controlling. These traditional functions can be used in response to the question, "What docs a manager do?" A manager should *plan* the activities of his organization, *staff* it with required personnel, *organize* its personnel and their activities, *direct* the operations of the organization, and *control* the direction of the organization by evaluating feedback and making necessary adjustments.

Planning involves the development of long and short-range plans which requires the formulation of goals, objectives, strategies, policies, procedures, and standards. It also involves the perception and analysis of opportunities, problems, and alternative courses of action, and the design of programs to achieve selected objectives. *Organizing* involves the development of a structure which groups, assigns, and coordinates activities by delegating authority, offering responsibility, and requiring accountability. *Staffing* involves the selecting, training, and assignment of personnel to specific organizational activities. *Directing* is the leadership of the organization through communication and motivation of organizational personnel. *Controlling* involves observing and measuring organizational performance and environmental activities and modifying the plans and activities of the organization when necessary.

The Management System

Figure 9–9 illustrates a management system. Information from management information systems is the *input* to this system. Information is subjected to *analysis and synthesis,* utilizing data and techniques from the MIS data base. Alternative decisions are evaluated in the light of the *goals and objectives* of the firm. *Output* of the system is in the form of planning, organizing, staffing, directing, and controlling *decisions.* The management decision output is then transmitted to the appropriate subsystems of the business system or to the business environment.

Management Information Requirements

Figure 9–9 emphasizes why information is an indispensable ingredient in the management system. Each of the management functions requires *the analysis and synthesis of information* before a specific decision can be made. This information must be accurate, timely, complete, concise, and relevant or the quality of the decisions being

FIGURE 9–9

The Management System

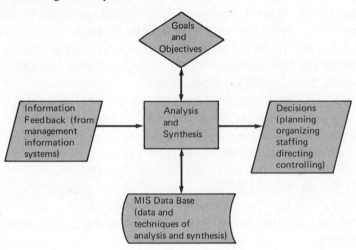

made will suffer. Of course, even the best information cannot guarantee good decisions if managers do not have the ability to use it effectively. This is why information must be presented in a form which is easy to understand and use. Figure 9–9 also emphasizes the importance of information systems since they supply management with the *feedback* and *data base* required for decision-making.

It must be emphasized that management cannot possibly absorb all of the information that can be produced by an information system. Therefore, systems developers must determine not only what information management *wants,* but what information management *needs.* Several concepts which guide the determination of the information requirements of management are outlined below.

Organizations as decision systems. The analysis of management information requirements must begin with an analysis of management decisions. Developers of information systems which support management systems must focus on the flow of decision information between "decision centers" where decisions are made to "action points" where decisions are implemented. It must be emphasized that the decision system of an organization may not be identical to the formal organizational structure of the firm. Thus, the "organization chart" of a firm may differ with a "decision network" that outlines the decision centers and action points of the organization.

The factors that are important in making each decision must be identified. *What* decisions must be made, *who* should make them, and *when, where,* and *how* they should be made in the organization must be determined. Only then can we identify the types of information required to support each decision.

Programmed decisions.   Another important consideration is the presence or potential for *"programmed decisions."* Programmed decisions are decisions that can be automated (programmed) by basing them on a "decision rule" which outlines the steps to take when confronted with the need for a specific decision. A programmed decision does not have to be part of a computer program, though this is usually the case since the computer is the usual method for automating information systems. Therefore, a study of the management system should be made to determine if any decisions can be "programmed."

Management by exception.   "Exception reporting" or *"management by exception"* is another important concept which is utilized by system designers to avoid "drowning managers in a sea of information." Information is provided to managers only when exceptional conditions occur which require management decision-making. For example, a credit manager might only be notified of the account status of delinquent customers, rather than giving him a report listing the account balances of all customers of his firm.

Management subsystems.   The information requirements of management depends on the management subsystem or management level involved. Figure 9–10 illustrates how a management system can be subdivided into three major subsystems: (1) strategic management, (2) tactical management, and (3) operational management. These subsystems are related to the traditional management levels of top management, middle management, and operating management. The activities and results of each management subsystem are summarized, as well as the types of information required by each subsystem. Figure 9–10 emphasizes that *the information requirements of the management system are directly related to the types of activities that predominate in each management subsystem.* For example, the strategic management subsystem requires more special one-time reports and forecasts to support its heavy planning and policymaking responsibilities. The operational management subsystem, on the other hand, may require more regular internal reports emphasizing current and historical data comparisons which support its control of day-to-day operations.

FIGURE 9–10

Management Subsystems: Activities and Information Requirements

Management subsystem	*Primary activities*	*Activity results*	*Activity examples*	*Information requirements*
Strategic management	Long-range planning	Goals Objectives Policies	Policy on diversification	Forecasts Simulations Inquiries
	Determine organizational resource requirements and allocations	Long-range plans and other strategic decisions	Social responsibility policy Major capital expenditure policy	External reports One-time reports Condensed internal reports
Tactical management	Allocate assigned resources to specific tasks Make rules Measure performance Exert control	Budgets Procedures Rules and other tactical decisions	Personnel practices Capital budgeting Marketing mix	Forecasts and historical data Regular internal reports Exception reports Simulations Inquiries
Operational management	Direct the utilization of resources and the performance of tasks in conformance with established rules	Directions Commands Actions and other operational decisions	Production scheduling Inventory control Credit management	Regular internal reports Detailed transaction reports Procedures manuals Current and historical data Programmed decisions

Based in part on: Sherman C. Blumenthal, *Management Information Systems: A Framework for Planning and Development* (Englewood Cliffs, N.J.: Prentice-Hall, 1969), p. 29.

MANAGEMENT INFORMATION SYSTEMS

A management information system is an information system which provides the information required to support management decision-making. Like other information systems, a management information system may utilize several kinds of data processing systems (manual, mechanical, electronic) in order to collect and process data and disseminate information to management. Many business firms have *"computer-based management information systems"* which make extensive use of computer hardware, software, and personnel in attempting to provide management with better information for more effective decision-making. The term "management information systems" is frequently used in a plural form because most organizations utilize several information subsystems to furnish information to management. Thus, we could talk of financial, production, marketing, and personnel management information systems.

The Management Information System

Before analyzing the many possible categories of management information systems, let us first examine the basic systems model of a management information system. Figure 9–11 illustrates that a management information system consists of the system components summarized below.

1. *Input.* Collects data generated by the other subsystems of the business system and the business environment.
2. *Processing.* Utilizes data processing systems to transform data into information, or to process information into a more suitable form for decision-making.
3. *Storage.* Maintains a data base containing data and information in the form of historical records, forecasts, plans, standards, decision rules, models, and other managerial and analytical techniques.
4. *Output.* Provides information on demand, according to a sched-

FIGURE 9–11

The Management Information System

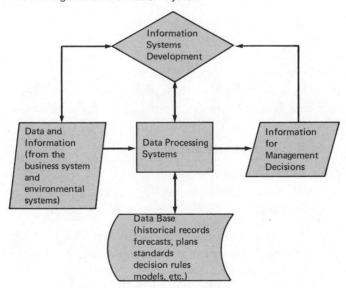

ule, or on an exception basis which is needed to support the decision-making activities of a management system.

5. *Control.* Utilizes a continual process of information systems development to control the performance of the MIS.

The goal of a management information system is to assist managers in making the decisions required for the effective management of an organization, i.e., planning, organizing, staffing, directing, and controlling decisions. Therefore, management information systems are sometimes called *"information-decision systems"* since they can provide "decision assistance" or actually make certain "programmed decisions." A management information system helps management produce decisions in the following forms: (1) statements of goals and strategy, (2) long-range master plans, (3) short-range plans (sales forecasts, financial budgets, and operating budgets), (4) policies, procedures, and directives, and (5) programmed decisions.

MIS Information Output

An MIS should provide management with information (1) *on demand,* (2) *according to a predetermined schedule,* or (3) *when exceptional conditions occur.*

Advanced EDP systems have greatly improved the ability of an MIS to respond to the information needs of management. See Figure 9–12. Management can "converse" directly with a computer without the delays and distortions that would arise when batch processing EDP systems were utilized. Systems analysts and programmers do not have to translate and modify each information request of management. Instead, they can spend their time developing a software interface (such as data management, business analysis, and simulation programs) and a common data base that allows managers to receive information in a form that best supports their decision-making needs.

Internal Information from an MIS

An MIS should provide management with information (and *information analysis techniques*) about the internal operations of the business system. Several types of information can be identified.

1. *Activity information.* Information techniques that summarize, analyze, and evaluate information concerning the activities taking place in the operation of the business system.
2. *Status information.* Information on the performance status of

FIGURE 9–12

From Batch Processing to Real-Time MIS

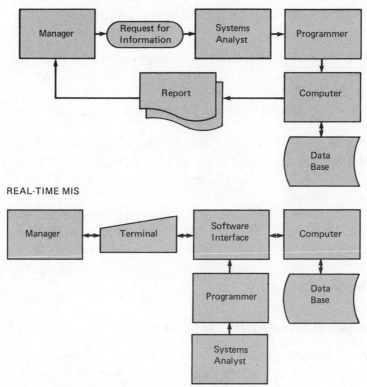

Adapted from Robert V. Head, *Managers Guide to Management Information Systems* (Englewood Cliffs, N.J.: Prentice-Hall, 1972), pp. 80–81.

various aspects of the business system, such as customer accounts, work in process, or project completion reports.

3. *Resources information.* Information about the resources of the business system, such as personnel, material, and facilities.

4. *Resource allocation information.* Information and techniques for cost/benefit analysis which allow management to make "tradeoffs" between competing proposals and thus allocate scarce resources among the competing needs of the business system.

5. *Planning and control information.* Information and techniques required to produce plans, budgets, schedules, project specifications, forecasts, and standards. Mathematical models can help provide such planning and control information. Simulation techniques allow managers to ask "what if" questions and receive answers needed for planning and control decisions.

External Information from an MIS

Management information systems should also provide management with information from the business environment. Information should be provided concerning the present status and expected developments and trends in areas such as:

1. *Politics and government.* Information on political, legal, and legislative developments, laws and regulations, monetary and fiscal policies, etc.
2. *Society.* Information on demographic, cultural, and social trends.
3. *The economy.* Information on the components of the Gross National Product and other economic indicators.
4. *Technology.* Information on the development of new products and processes.
5. *Competition.* Information on past and present operations and possible trends in the industry as a whole and in competing firms.
6. *Resources.* Information on the present status and expected trends in the supply of necessary resources such as labor, materials, financing, energy, etc.

BUSINESS INFORMATION SYSTEMS

Figure 9–13 illustrates the basic functional categories of information systems and subsystems that exist in most business firms. The

FIGURE 9–13

Basic Categories of Business Information Systems

Production/Operations	*Marketing*	*Finance*
Production/Operations Planning	Sales Forecasting	Cash Management
Production/Operations Control	Sales Analysis	Capital Budgeting
Inventory Control	Order Processing	Portfolio Management
Purchasing	Advertising and Promotion	Credit Management
Transportation and Physical	Analysis	Financing Analysis
Distribution	Marketing Channels Analysis	Investment Analysis
Process Control	Pricing Analysis	Financial Forecasting
Facilities Planning	Market Research	

Accounting	*Personnel*	*Other*
Accounts Receivable	Payroll	Strategic Planning
Accounts Payable	Labor Analysis	Research and Develop-
General Accounting	Compensation Analysis	ment
Property Accounting	Personnel Recordkeeping	Operations Research
Cost Accounting	Employee Skills Inventory	Project Control
Tax Accounting	Training and Development	Engineering
Budgeting	Analysis	Legal
	Personnel Requirements	Environmental
	Forecasting	

basic systems are (1) production/operations, (2) marketing, (3) finance, (4) accounting, (5) personnel, and (6) other systems. We speak of *business* information systems because each category supports one of the traditional *"functions of business,"* such as marketing, finance, production, etc. Also, each category consists of many subsystems and includes both *operational* and *management* information systems. For example, sales order processing is typically considered to be an operational information subsystem, while sales analysis is considered a management information subsystem. However, both are subsystems of the marketing information system. The sales order processing subsystem collects and records sales transaction data and provides input to the sales analysis subsystem which produces management reports concerning sales generated by each salesman, sales territory, customer, product, etc.

It is important to understand several basic concepts about the information systems and subsystems of the business firm.

1. *Business computer applications.* Computer applications in business should be viewed as "computerized" or "computer-based" information subsystems of a business firm and *not* as unrelated applications of computers to individual business problems. For example, sales analysis is not an isolated computer application but is a subsystem of the marketing MIS. This concept must be kept in mind in evaluating the many applications of the computer described in the next two chapters of the text.

2. *Interrelated information systems.* Each information system relies on data and information supplied by other management information systems and operational information systems. For example, production and sales activity data generated by operational information systems are utilized by the marketing MIS for sales forecasts, which are then used by the production MIS for production scheduling.

3. *Integrated information systems.* The long-term goal of many information systems developers is to tie together or "integrate" all of the management information systems and operational information systems of a business firm into a single, integrated, "total" information system. We will discuss this concept in a later section of this chapter.

Production/Operations Information Systems

Production/operations information systems include subsystems such as production/operations planning, production/operations control, inventory control, purchasing, transportation and process control. They support the *production function,* which can be broadly defined to include all activities concerned with the planning, monitoring, and control of the processes that produce goods or services. Thus, production systems are also known as *"operations management"* systems since they are concerned with the management of all types of operational systems, not just manufacturing operations. They are not only utilized by manufacturing companies but also by all other firms which must plan, monitor, and control inventories, purchases, and the flow of goods and services. Therefore, firms such as transportation companies, wholesalers, retailers, financial institutions, and service companies must utilize production/operations information systems to plan and control their operations.

Marketing Information Systems

Marketing information systems include subsystems such as sales forecasting, sales analysis, sales order processing, advertising and sales promotion analysis, marketing channels analysis, and market research. Marketing information systems provide information for the planning and control of the marketing function. *Marketing planning information* assists marketing management in product planning, pricing decisions, planning advertising and sales promotion strategy and expenditures, forecasting the market potential for new and present products, and determining channels of distribution. *Marketing control information* supports the efforts of management to control the efficiency and effectiveness of the selling and distribution of products and services.

Financial Information Systems

Financial information systems consist of subsystems which support management in decisions concerning the *financing* of the business and the *allocation and control of financial resources* within the business firm. Accounting information systems are frequently included as financial subsystems but will be treated as a separate category of business information systems. Some financial information subsystems are cash management, capital budgeting, portfolio management, credit management, financing analysis, and investment analysis. Financial information systems provide information on present or proposed sources of financing for the operations of the business firm. They also support the financial analysis of present business operations and proposed projects in terms of costs, risks, cash needs, and, most importantly, profitability.

Accounting Information Systems

Accounting information systems are the oldest and most widely used business information systems. They record and report business transactions and other economic events. Accounting information systems are based on the double-entry bookkeeping concept, which is hundreds of years old, and other more recent accounting concepts such as responsibility accounting and profitability accounting. The accounting systems record and report the flow of funds through the organization on a historical basis and produce financial statements such as the balance sheet and income statement. Accounting systems also produce forecasts of future conditions such as projected financial statements and financial budgets. *Operational accounting systems* emphasize legal recordkeeping, while *management accounting systems* focus on the planning and control of business operations. Accounts receivable, accounts payable, general accounting, property accounting, cost accounting, tax accounting, and budgeting are examples of accounting information subsystems.

Personnel Information Systems

Personnel information systems are used by many business firms (1) to produce paychecks and payroll reports, (2) to maintain personnel records, and (3) to analyze the amounts, types, and costs of labor utilized in business operations. Many firms have gone beyond these traditional functions and have developed personnel information systems which support (1) recruitment, selection, and hiring, (2) job placement, (3) performance appraisals, (4) employee benefits analysis, (5) training and development, and (6) health, safety, and security. Personnel information systems support the concept of *"manpower management,"* which emphasizes *planning* to meet the manpower needs of the business and the *control* of all personnel policies and programs, so that effective and efficient use is made of the *personnel resources* of the company. Personnel information subsystems include payroll, labor analysis, compensation analysis, personnel recordkeeping, employee skills inventory, and training and development analysis.

Other Information Systems

A wide variety of information systems may be used by a business firm besides the basic categories of production, marketing, finance, accounting, and personnel. Their use depends on the size of the business firm and the particular business activities in which it engages. We will not describe each possible category at this time. However, their names provide a substantial clue to their functions. Some of these information systems are *strategic planning, research and development, operations research, project control, engineering, legal,* and *environmental.* In some business firms, these systems are subsystems of the basic categories described above. For example, engineering and research and development may be subsystems of the production information system, while strategic planning and operations research subsystems may be found in the marketing and financial information systems.

INTEGRATED INFORMATION SYSTEMS

Frequent references are made in the computer industry to the concept of a single management information system for an entire organization. This *integrated management information system* is a "super-system" that is the long-term goal of many information system designers. The various management and operational information systems of an organization would become integrated subsystems of a single *"total system."* For most business firms, a single integrated information system remains a distant goal because of limited financial and personnel resources and the limitations of present computer technology. However, most business firms agree that integration and coordination should exist between the various information systems of the organization and are working toward that goal in their information systems development. Integrated management information systems promise many benefits such as economy, efficiency, effectiveness, and control.

Of course, many current information systems are combinations of management information subsystems and operational information subsystems. For example, a payroll system that processes employee time cards and produces employee paychecks should be classified as an *operational* information system. An information system which utilizes payroll data to produce labor analysis reports, which show variances and trends in labor cost and utilization, should be classified as a *man-*

agement information system. However, in most cases, a composite *management-operational information system* includes a payroll subsystem that not only processes employee time cards and produces paychecks but also furnishes management with labor analysis information.

Common Data Flows

An important feature of integrated information systems is *"common data flows,"* which is the use of common input, processing, and output procedures and media whenever possible or desirable. Systems analysts try to design systems which capture data only once and as close to its original source as possible. They then try to utilize a minimum of data processing procedures and subsystems to process the data and strive to minimize the number of output documents and reports produced by the system. For example, many payroll systems try to capture as much data as possible from an employee's time card while sales, accounts receivable, and inventory systems try to capture as much data as possible at the time and place a sales order is received. This eliminates much duplication in data collection documents and procedures.

This kind of integration can avoid duplication, simplify operations, and produce an *efficient* information system. However, some duplication is necessary in order to insure *effective* information systems. For example, duplicate copies of reports may be required if several users require "hard copy" output, or duplicate storage files may be necessary if a "back-up" capability is required. *Carrying systems integration to an extreme* could result in systems that are costly, cumbersome, or unreliable and which do not effectively meet the information needs of users. Therefore, some duplication and "redundancy" is usually required in systems design.

The Common Data Base

A major characteristic of integrated information systems is a *common data base* which avoids duplication in the storage and retrieval of data and information. A data base has been defined as a "superfile" which consolidates and integrates data records formerly stored in many separate data files. The term data base is also used in a "generic" sense to describe the data and information upon which a system is "based." For example, the term is sometimes used to describe *all* of the data and information that *could* be used to support an organization or function, such as the "management data base" or the "marketing data base." Sometimes the term is used to describe the data that has been collected and organized to support a particular information subsystem, such as the "personnel management data base" or the "production planning and control data base." A statement such as: "The data base for the payroll system is the personnel file" is another example of the generic use of the term.

To clarify this situation, we will further define a data base as *an integrated collection of data and information which is utilized by several information subsystems of an organization.* See Figure 9–14. A data base can be organized as a integrated collection of data records into a single "superfile," or it can be organized as an integrated collection of several data files. However, a group of data files does not constitute a data base unless the files are *integrated* by placing them under the control of a central computer system and eliminating duplication in the types of data records stored in the files. The organization of a data base allows it to be accessed by several information subsystems and eliminates the necessity of duplication in data storage, updating, deletion, and protection. In order to emphasize the cen-

FIGURE 9–14

The Common Data Base

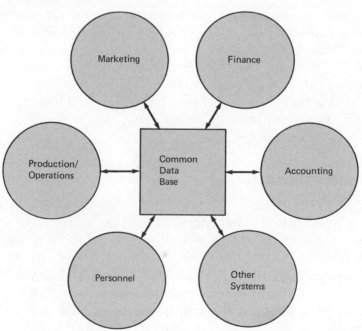

tralized and integrated nature of a common data base, it is frequently called a "central data base," "central information file" (CIF), or *"data bank."*

The Total Information System

A *total information system* is a systems concept in which all the information systems and subsystems of an organization are combined into a single system. A total information system would have the important characteristics summarized below.

1. *Common data processing.* Common source documents, common input media, and a common data base are utilized so that unnecessary processing activities, storage files, input data, and output information are eliminated.

2. *Immediate data entry.* Data created from transactions and operations are entered directly into the computer system from the point of origin, which may be a local or remote terminal.

3. *Real-time processing.* Data is processed in real-time.

4. *Central data bank.* Current and historical data, forecasts, plans, standards, decision rules, mathematical models, and other analytical techniques are stored in a direct access data base for use by all subsystems.

5. *Integrated information subsystems.* The major categories of business information systems are integrated into a single information system which provides an efficient and effective flow of information to management.

6. *Decision orientation.* The computer system utilizes decision rules, mathematical models, and other tools and techniques to evaluate the data being processed, the information produced, and the contents of storage files. As a result, the computer may make programmed decisions, specify decisions that must be made, specify actions to be taken, notify users of unusual conditions requiring decision-making, or may request more information or further instructions.

7. *Conversational computing.* Data communications terminals, data management software, and other computer system capabilities encourage conversational computing. Computer users can simply and instantly direct the computer to solve problems, answer questions, process data, update files, and produce output in any format desired.

A completely integrated total information system does not exist. However, such information systems are the goal of many systems analysts, computer professionals, and business executives. Many considerations may make such systems unfeasible for particular organizations. For example, a single data base for an entire organization may be economically unfeasible if the organization is a large business firm that has offices and plants throughout a nation and various foreign countries. The cost of controls to prevent errors, loss or destruction of data, and unauthorized use, while providing instant response capabilities may be prohibitive. However, the concept of a total integrated information system must be understood by computer users since it indicates the direction being taken and the goal being sought by many developers of computer-based information systems.

SUMMARY

A management information system is an information system that provides the information required to support management decision-making. In order to understand the vital role of management information systems, we must also gain a basic understanding of the feedback-control function of adaptive cybernetic systems and the concept of the business firm as a "business system" whose major subsystems include operational systems, management systems, and information systems.

Our understanding of the systems concept is not complete until we add the components of feedback and control to the previously introduced components of input, processing and output. Feedback is information concerning the components and operations of a system. Control is the component of a system that evaluates feedback to determine whether the system is moving toward the achievement of its goal, and then makes necessary adjustments to the input and processing components of the system to insure that proper output is produced. Feedback and control are essential for self-monitoring and self-regulating systems known as "cybernetic systems." "Adaptive" cybernetic systems interchange input and output with their environment and therefore have the ability to adjust themselves to their environment as well as to adjust themselves to an internally established goal.

The business firm should be viewed as a business system in which economic resources (input) are transformed by various organizational processes (processing) into goods and services (output). Information systems provide information on the operation of the system (feedback) to management for the direction and maintenance of the system (control). Business systems should be viewed as being composed of "operational systems" which perform the input, processing, and output functions, "management systems" which constitute the control component of the business system, and "information systems" which perform the feedback function.

The two basic categories of information systems are "operational information systems" and "management information systems." Operational information systems (OIS) collect, process, and store data generated by operational systems and produce data and information for input into a management information system or for the control of an operational system. Management information systems (MIS) can be viewed as an information network within the business system which provides information to support the decision-making responsibilities of management.

We must also realize that the business firm is a subsystem of society and is surrounded by other systems of the "business environment." Therefore, business firms must maintain proper interrelationships with the other economic, political, and social subsystems in their environment. These include customers, competitors, suppliers, labor unions, stockholders, financial institutions, government agencies, and the community.

Management systems receive information from management information systems as input and rely on the data and techniques from the MIS data base to support the process of analysis and synthesis in which alternative decisions are evaluated in the light of the goals and objectives of the organization. Output of a management system is in the form of planning, organizing, staffing, directing, and controlling decisions. In order to provide management with information that is accurate, timely, complete, concise and relevant, the developers of management information systems must view an organization as a "decision network." They must be aware that the information needs of management differ since management decisions can be subdivided into three major subsystems: (1) strategic management, (2) tactical management, (3) operational management. "Programmed decisions" and "management by exception" are other important concepts which help increase the quality of information provided to management.

The major components of a management information system are summarized below.

1. *Input.* Collects data generated by the other subsystems of the business system and the business environment.
2. *Processing.* Utilizes data processing systems to transform data

into information or to process information into a more suitable form for decision-making.

3. *Storage*. Maintains a data base containing data and information in the form of historical records, forecasts, plans, standards, decision rules, models, and other managerial and analytical techniques.

4. *Output*. Provides information on demand, according to a schedule or on an exception basis which is needed to support the decision-making activities of a management system.

5. *Control*. Utilizes a continual process of information systems development to control the performance of the MIS.

The information systems of a business firm consist of many interrelated subsystems which include both operational and management information systems. Thus, the term "business information system" is utilized to describe an information system which provides information required for both the operations and management of a business firm. Basic categories of business information systems include (1) production/operations, (2) marketing, (3) finance, (4) accounting, (5) personnel, and (6) other systems. Each of these systems support the operations and management of specific business functions.

A final major concept of modern management information systems is the concept of "integrated information systems." In its most advanced form, this concept would involve combining the various management and operational information systems of an organization and transforming them into integrated subsystems of a single "total system." For most business firms, however, the concept of integrated information systems is a goal which emphasizes that integration and coordination should exist between the various information systems of the organization. Such systems include the use of common input, processing, and output procedures and media whenever possible. It also involves the use of a "common data base" which avoids duplication in the storage and retrieval of data and information. The major characteristics of future integrated information systems include (1) common data processing, (2) immediate data entry, (3) real-time processing, (4) central data bank, (5) integrated information subsystems, (6) decision orientation, and (7) conversational computing.

KEY TERMS AND CONCEPTS

Management information systems, 250, 267
Cybernetic systems, 251–253
Feedback, 251
Control, 251
Adaptive systems, 251
The business system, 254–255
Operational systems, 255
Functions of business, 255
Management systems, 256, 263–264
Operational Information systems, 256

Environmental systems, 259–262
Functions of management, 263
Decision systems, 264
Programmed decisions, 265
Management by exception, 265
Management subsystems, 265–266
Business information systems, 270–274
Integrated information systems, 274
Common data flows, 275
Common data base, 275–276
Total information systems, 277

ASSIGNMENTS

1. Test your understanding of the chapter material by reviewing the *purpose, outline, summary,* and *key terms and concepts* of this chapter. Are you confident that you have attained a basic understanding of the major concepts of the chapter? If not, reread the appropriate material as indicated by the page numbers after each key term and concept.

2. Discuss the potential benefits of the application of the management information systems concept to computer use in business.

3. Discuss the role played by feedback and control in closed cybernetic systems and adaptive cybernetic systems. Utilize examples to illustrate your answer.

4. Identify the basic subsystems of the business system and explain their functions as components of the business system.

5. Figure 9–7 illustrates some of the information systems that provide information needed by the operational system of a manufacturing firm. Draw a similar systems flowchart that illustrates the information systems that might be required to support the operational system of a merchandising or distribution firm.

6. Discuss the information requirements generated by several systems in the business environment.

7. Discuss how the information requirements of management systems are affected by the concepts of:
   a. The functions of management
   b. The organization as a decision system
   c. Programmed decisions
   d. Management by exception
   e. Management subsystems or levels

8. Discuss the functions of each component of the basic systems model of a management information system.

9. "An MIS should provide management with information on demand, according to a predetermined schedule, or when exceptional conditions occur." Utilize examples to illustrate how this might occur in a business firm.

10. Describe several types of information that an MIS should provide to management concerning internal operations and external developments. Utilize examples to illustrate your answer.

11. Identify the basic functional categories of business information systems. Give an example of an information system for each category.

12. Identify several usages of the term "data base."

13. Summarize the important characteristics of a total information system.

14. Discuss how the concept of integrated information systems is related to:
    a. Composite management-operational information systems
    b. Common data flows and a common data base
    c. A total information system

15. "Carrying systems integration to an extreme could result in systems that are costly, cumbersome, or unreliable and which do not effectively meet the information needs of users." Discuss the rationale for this statement.

Chapter Outline

Purpose of the Chapter

Introduction

Types of Computer Applications

Trends in Computer Applications

The General Form of Business Computer Applications

The Common Business Applications

The Sales Order Processing Application
Objectives, Input, Data Base, Output

The Inventory Control Application
Objectives, Input, Data Base, Output

The Billing and Sales Analysis Application
Objectives, Input, Data Base, Output

The Accounts Receivable Application
Objectives, Input, Data Base, Output

The Accounts Payable Application
Objectives, Input, Data Base, Output

The Payroll and Labor Analysis Application
Objectives, Input, Data Base, Output

The General Accounting Application
Objectives, Input, Data Base, Output

Summary

Key Terms and Concepts

Assignments

10

Computer Applications in Business I

Purpose of the Chapter

To promote a basic understanding of how the computer is used in business by analyzing:

1. Trends in computer applications in business,
2. The general form of business computer applications,
3. The objectives, input, data base, and output of seven common computer applications in business.

INTRODUCTION

This chapter will attempt to answer questions concerning specific uses of the computer in business. What do computers do in business? How are computers used in business operations? How is the computer applied to business management? This chapter and the one that follows will explore the answers to such questions by focusing on specific applications of the computer in business firms and other computer-using organizations.

In this chapter we shall briefly describe each of the common business applications, with particular attention paid to the input data required and the output information produced by each system. More specialized and advanced business computer applications will be analyzed in the next chapter. This coverage should provide you with a basic understanding of how the computer is utilized by business firms. Such an understanding is vital to the effective present and future use of computers by business management.

TYPES OF COMPUTER APPLICATIONS

We defined a "computer application" in Chapter 5 as the use of a computer to solve a specific problem or to accomplish a particular operation. We also mentioned that computer applications are frequently subdivided into (1) *business applications* involving the processing of business and administrative data, (2) *scientific applications* involving complex mathematical calculations and problem solving, and (3) *other applications* covering a wide variety of applications in such areas as education, law enforcement, art, medicine, etc.

Other ways of classifying various types of applications may also be used. For example, *process control applications* are frequently considered a separate category of computer applications. Process control applications involve the measuring and processing of data arising from an on-going physical process and utilize information output to control the on-going process; for example, a scientific experiment, a manufacturing process, or a spacecraft control system. Of course, there can never be a completely satisfactory method of classifying computer applications, since applications can always be found which seem to fit more than one category or which seem to require the creation of additional categories.

No matter how computer applications are classified, it is important to view them as "information subsystems" of a computer-using organization. The previous chapter stressed the viewpoint that computer applications are usually not isolated and unrelated applications of computers to individual business problems but are *computer-based information systems* of the business firm. In particular, computer applications which support management decision-making must be considered as subsystems of the computer-based management information systems of a business firm. Figure 9–13 of the previous chapter summarized the basic categories of business information systems.

TRENDS IN COMPUTER APPLICATIONS

We mentioned in the previous chapter that the computer was first applied to the solution of business problems in a piecemeal fashion and that most computer applications consisted of the computerization of clerical and recordkeeping tasks. The trend of computer applications since that time has been away from such *operational informa-tion systems* and toward the concept of *management information systems.* Systems of integrated computer applications whose main purpose is to provide information to support management decision-making are being developed. Figure 10–1 illustrates that the trend in

FIGURE 10–1

The Trend in Business Computer Applications

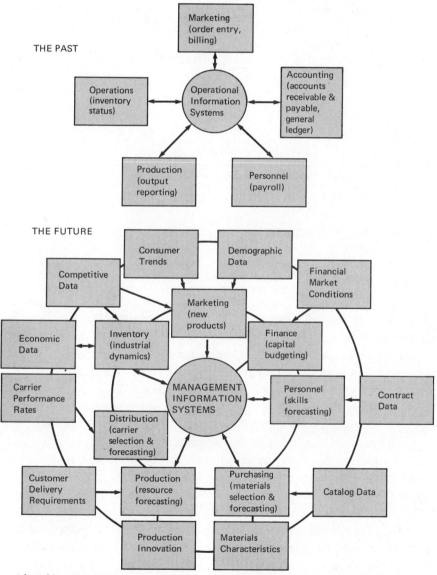

Adapted from John Diebold, "Bad Decisions on Computer Use," *Harvard Business Review* (January/February, 1969), pp. 14–28.

FIGURE 10–2

Three Stages of Computer Applications in Business

Stage	Function involved	Benefits	Payoff
1	Recordkeeping	Reduced clerical cost Reduced marginal cost of increased volume Improved speed Improved accuracy	Immediate upon introduction of effective, working system
2	Operations	Improved service Improved product design Improved production scheduling Improved production control Reduced inventory Reduced cost of product	One to three years after intro- duction of system
3	Strategic Planning	Improved information Improved prediction Improved decisions by top management	Five to ten years after intro- duction of system

Source: John E. Cooke and Ted Kuchta, *Cost and Management* (September–October, 1970), p. 12. *Cost and Management* is the official journal of the Society of Industrial Accountants of Canada.

computer applications can be viewed as a change from the *clerical recordkeeping* functions of operational information systems to the *decision-making support* functions of management information systems.

There are many reasons to explain why computer applications are shifting from recordkeeping functions to the managerial functions of planning and control. First of all, in many businesses, the computer replaced punched card electromechanical data processing systems which had been used primarily for clerical types of applications. Secondly, computerizing recordkeeping applications is a lot easier and cheaper than developing computer-based management information systems. Recordkeeping applications are simpler, more familiar, and more formalized than managerial applications, thus making it easier and cheaper to develop (or purchase) the systems design and computer programs that are required. The third major reason for the application of the computer to recordkeeping functions was that direct and immediate cost reductions could usually be shown when the cost of EDP was compared against the cost of the clerical personnel and data processing equipment that would be replaced by the computerized system. Therefore, many business firms begin their use of computers by computerizing recordkeeping applications.

Figure 10–2 illustrates the stages of computer applications in computer-using business firms. Computers are first applied to *recordkeeping* functions where the payoff is frequently an immediate reduction in costs; then the computer is applied to *operational* functions which have a less immediate payoff and whose benefits are less tangible. Larger firms with many years of computer experience move to a third stage where computers are used to support the *strategic planning* functions of top management but whose payoff may take many years to occur. Thus, as the use of the computer moves from "paper work automation" to "operations control" and then to "strategic planning" applications, the benefits of computer usage change from tangible *cost reductions* to less tangible benefits such as operating improvements and improved decision-making which are frequently described as *profit producing* benefits.

THE GENERAL FORM OF BUSINESS COMPUTER APPLICATIONS

Before discussing any specific business computer application, we should first study the "general form" of most business applications. The common business applications are frequently referred to as "business data processing applications" or "business information systems." Figure 10–3 illustrates the general form of a typical business information system.

Input into the system consists of (1) transactions data, (2) data base adjustments, (3) inquiries, and (4) the output of other systems. Input is frequently collected from "source documents" and converted to machine-sensible data by a "data preparation" process such as keypunching, key-to-tape, etc. Other input data may be generated by on-line terminals. Additional data or information is supplied from the records and/or files contained in the *data base* of the information system. Computer system hardware and software and EDP personnel *process* the data, resulting in an updated data base and the *output* of information in the form of (1) reports, (2) documents, (3) responses and displays, (4) control listings, and (5) input to other systems.

Figure 10–3 is called a "general systems flowchart" of a business information system. Such general systems flowcharts summarize the

FIGURE 10–3

General Form of Business Computer Applications

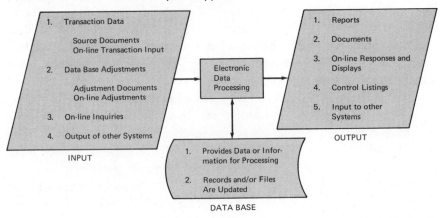

input and output media and the data base that is required by a particular computer application. This is the kind of information *computer users* need; details of the *hardware, software,* and *personnel* required for the *electronic data processing* utilized in this application can be left to *computer professionals.* This is why the processing component of each information subsystem described in this chapter is portrayed in the general systems flowchart by a processing rectangle labeled simply "electronic data processing."

THE COMMON BUSINESS APPLICATIONS

Out of all of the possible applications of the computer in business, several basic applications stand out because they are common to most business computer users. Most of these applications exist in both large and small computer-using business firms, whether they are experienced computer users or are utilizing the computer for the first time. These *common business applications* are summarized below and illustrated in Figure 10–4.

1. *Sales order processing.*   Processes orders received from customers and produces invoices for customers and data needed for sales analysis and inventory control.
2. *Inventory control.*   Receives data concerning customer orders, prepares shipping documents if the ordered items are available, and records all changes in inventory.
3. *Billing and sales analysis.*   Receives filled orders data from the

FIGURE 10-4

How the Common Computer Applications in Business Are Related

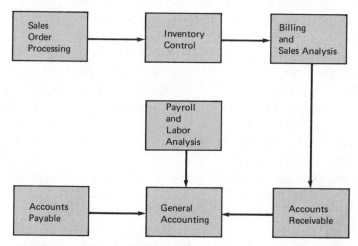

inventory control system and produces customer invoices and management reports analyzing the sales generated by each sales-man, customer, product, etc.

4. *Accounts receivable.* Receives data concerning customer invoices and payments and produces monthly customer statements and credit management reports.

5. *Accounts payable.* Receives data concerning purchases from suppliers and produces checks in payment of outstanding invoices and cash management reports.

6. *Payroll and labor analysis.* Receives data from employee time cards and other records and produces paychecks, payroll reports, and labor analysis reports.

7. *General accounting.* Receives data from accounts receivable, accounts payable, payroll and labor analysis, and many other business information subsystems. Produces the general ledger trial balance, the income statement and balance sheet of the firm, and various income and expense reports for management.

The common business computer applications are a mixture of *operational information subsystems* and *management information subsystems.* For example, the billing and payroll applications are operational information subsystems while the sales analysis and labor analysis applications can be considered management information subsystems. However, we have previously mentioned that many operational and management information subsystems are interrelated, with the output of one subsystem becoming the input of another. Thus, billing and sales analysis are frequently combined into one application, as is the case for payroll and labor analysis.

The description of each common computer application has been simplified since our purpose is to understand computer applications from the viewpoint of a *business computer user* rather than that of *computer professional*. Therefore, no attempt is made to describe all of the variations that are possible for each common computer application, since the particular form of an application will vary depending upon the type of business firm involved. For example, the sales order processing system that will be described is most often utilized by business firms whose customers are other business firms rather than consumers. Another example is the inventory control system which we will describe. It is most widely used to control the inventory of wholesale or retail firms or the finished goods inventory of manufacturing firms. However, in all cases the applications we describe represent the basic form of the computer applications most widely utilized by business computer users.

THE SALES ORDER PROCESSING APPLICATION

Objectives

The objectives of the *sales order processing* application are:

1. To provide a fast, accurate, and efficient method of recording and screening customer orders.
2. To provide the inventory control system with information on accepted orders so that they can be filled as quickly as possible.

Figure 10–5 is a general systems flowchart that summarizes the components of the sales order processing system that should be understood by computer users.

Input

Sales orders from customers or salesmen are received by mail, telephone or telegraph, or are made in person. They are usually recorded on a standard "sales order" form by clerical personnel in the sales office of the business firm. See Figure 10–6.

Sales order source documents must be converted into punched

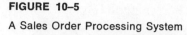

FIGURE 10–5

A Sales Order Processing System

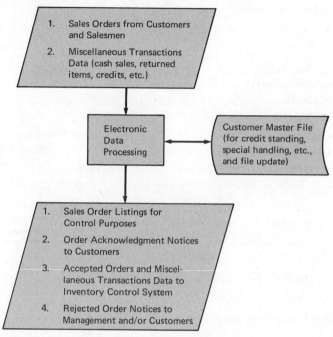

cards, paper tape, or magnetic tape form unless OCR documents are utilized. Of course, advanced sales order processing systems utilize *point-of-sale terminals* and other types of remote terminals to enter sales order data directly into the computer system. Though sales order data is the primary form of input into the sales order processing system, other types of input data must also be captured. Data from "miscellaneous transactions" such as cash sales, returned items, credits for damaged goods, etc., are also entered into the system.

Data Base

The sales order processing system utilizes a "customer master file" as its data base. The customer master file contains data on each customer such as (1) name, number, address, and phone number, (2) codes indicating sales tax liability, eligibility for discounts, etc., and (3) other information such as location, line of business, credit limits, assigned salesmen, etc. This file provides information on the credit standing of customers, special handling requirements, and other in-

FIGURE 10–6

A Sales Order Form

			OFFICE USE ONLY
			CREDIT DEPT. OK

Sold To *Seaview Home Supply Co.*
14 Oceanside Ave.
Richards Reef
New Hampshire

Ship To *Same*

Date To Be Shipped *4-15-*
Via *Freight*

Date *3-1-*   Cust. Order No. *311*   Salesman *G. Henry*   No. *86*   Inv. No. _____

Please Show Commodity Number

Quantity	Description	Commodity Number	Price	
3 dz.	Koldflo Elec Fan 12 in.	19941		
6 dz.	Koldflo Elec Fan 8 in.	19939		
3	Korn king Corn Poppers	42641		
3 oz.	Vacu-Tok Vacumm Bottles 1 Pt.	66488		
1 oz.	Luxury Heat Pads.	12996		
				Customer's Authorization

ALL PRICES SUBJECT TO CHANGE WITHOUT NOTICE DELIVERIES WILL BE MADE FROM NEAREST BRANCH	DZ – DOZEN GR – GROSS C – HUNDRED M – THOUSAND CS – CASE CT – CARTON	SALES OFFICES ARE LOCATED IN ALL PRINCIPAL CITIES

Source: *Guide to Order Writing, Billing, Inventory, Accounts Receivable and Sales Analysis* (White Plains, N.Y.: IBM Corporation, 1969), p. 16.

formation which is utilized to decide which orders should be accepted. The file can also be updated to reflect changes in credit standing, new customers, address changes, etc.

Output

Like most business computer applications, the output of the sales order processing system includes listings (also called logs or registers)

FIGURE 10–7

Punched Card Transaction Record

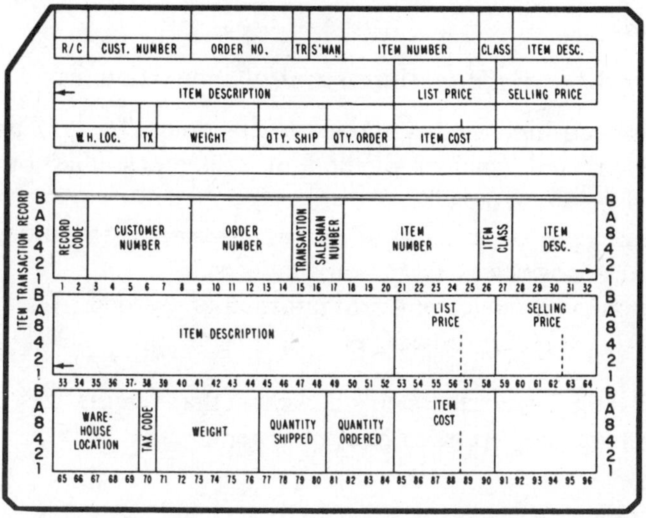

Source: *Guide to Order Writing, Billing, Inventory, Accounts Receivable and Sales Analysis* (White Plains, N.Y.: IBM Corporation, 1969), p. 13.

of each sales order transaction which allow control totals and other types of data processing controls to be accomplished. The purpose of such controls is to guard against errors or fraud in the input or processing of the data and to provide an "audit trail" to facilitate the auditing of the system. Electronic data processing controls are discussed in detail in Chapter 13.

The primary output of the sales order processing system consists of data describing sales orders which have been accepted because they meet the criteria for accuracy and credit standing of the system. This data may be recorded on punched cards, magnetic tape, or magnetic disk and becomes the input into the inventory control system. Figure 10–7 illustrates the types of output data required to describe a single item on a sales order in the form of a punched card.

The output of some sales order processing systems includes notices to customers acknowledging receipt of their orders. Orders not accepted by the system because of inaccurate information are corrected by EDP personnel after consultation with salesmen or customers and reentered into the system. Orders rejected for exceeding credit limits or other reasons are usually referred to operating management (such as credit managers or sales managers) for corrective action or may be returned to the customer.

THE INVENTORY CONTROL APPLICATION

Objectives

The objectives of the *inventory control* application are:

1. To provide high-quality service to customers by utilizing a fast, accurate, and efficient method of filling customer orders and avoiding "stock outs."
2. To minimize the amount of money invested in inventory and required to cover inventory "carrying costs."
3. To provide management with information needed to help achieve the two preceding objectives.

Figure 10–8 is a general systems flowchart that summarizes the major components of the inventory control system.

FIGURE 10–8

An Inventory Control System

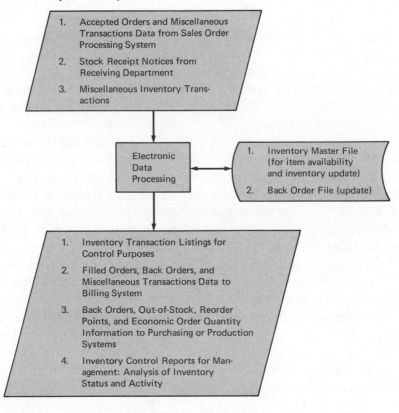

1. Accepted Orders and Miscellaneous Transactions Data from Sales Order Processing System
2. Stock Receipt Notices from Receiving Department
3. Miscellaneous Inventory Transactions

Electronic Data Processing

1. Inventory Master File (for item availability and inventory update)
2. Back Order File (update)

1. Inventory Transaction Listings for Control Purposes
2. Filled Orders, Back Orders, and Miscellaneous Transactions Data to Billing System
3. Back Orders, Out-of-Stock, Reorder Points, and Economic Order Quantity Information to Purchasing or Production Systems
4. Inventory Control Reports for Management: Analysis of Inventory Status and Activity

Input

Input into the inventory control system consists of accepted order data from the sales order processing system, as well as data describing stock received by the receiving department of the business firm. Input may also include "miscellaneous inventory transactions" such as adjustments for lost or damaged stock. The stock receipt notices from the receiving department must be converted into machine-sensible form and entered into the computer system.

Data Base

The data base of this application consists of an "inventory master file" which is checked for item availability and updated to reflect changes in inventory caused by filling sales orders or receipt of new stock. A "back order file" is also updated for sales orders that cannot be filled because of stock outs. Some customers are willing to wait until new stock is received. The back order file provides data on outstanding back orders that must be filled when stock receipt notices are received for back-ordered items.

Output

The output of the inventory control system includes inventory transactions listings for control purposes. Data describing filled orders, back orders and miscellaneous sales order transactions is a major system output and becomes the primary input into the billing and sales analysis system. Information concerning back orders, out-of-stock items, reorder points, and economic order quantities is sent to the purchasing or production departments for entry into their information subsystems. The purchasing department will utilize such information to procure more inventory, while a manufacturing firm would utilize this information to schedule the production of additional finished goods inventory.

A final major category of output consists of inventory control reports for management. These reports analyze inventory status and activity in order to help management meet the objectives of inventory control. Management must determine (1) whether the items being reordered and the amounts being reordered require adjustment, (2) the amount of unfilled orders that are occurring, (3) whether any items are becoming obsolete, (4) unusual variations in inventory activity, and (5) the items which account for the majority of the sales of the business. Figure 10–9 illustrates several inventory control reports.

Fixed order points and order quantities may be arbitrarily set by management and utilized by the inventory control system. However, the computer can be programmed to utilize mathematical techniques

FIGURE 10–9

Inventory Control Reports for Management

DATE 2/14/--				STOCK STATUS REPORT				PAGE 17			
ITEM NO.	DESCRIPTION	QUANTITY ON HAND	QUANTITY ON ORDER	TRANSACTION QUANTITY	QUANTITY B/O	AVERAGE UNIT COST	EXTENDED COST	LAST RECEIPT	LAST ISSUE	MIN. BAL.	MAX. BAL.
411116	B500 TWINLITE SOCKET BLUE	458	500			.35	160.30			800	1600
	ADJUSTMENT			42		.35	14.70				
	RECEIPT			500		.37	185.00				
	ISSUE			50-		.36	18.00-				
		950*				.36	342.00	2/11/--	2/14/--		
411122	B506 SOCKET ADAPTER BROWN	325				.19	61.75			300	800
	ISSUE			20-		.19	3.80-				
	ISSUE			38-		.19	7.22-				
	ISSUE			10-		.19	1.90-				
		257*				.19	48.83	12/19/--	2/11/--	UNDER	
411173	C151C SILENT SWITCH IVORY	50	150			1.16	58.00			100	200
	RECEIPT			150		1.20	180.00				
		200*				1.19	238.00	2/10/--	2/03/--		
411254	A210 PULL CORD GOLD	62	75			2.25	139.50			80	165
	ISSUE			16		2.25	36.00				
	ISSUE			30		2.25	67.50				
		16*	75			2.25	36.00	11/17/--	2/09/--		
	FINAL TOTALS	BEG. INV.		48295.26							
		CHANGE		700.08							
		NEW VALUE		48995.34							

							PLANNING			
Stock No.	Description	Opening Balance	+ Receipts	- Issue	= On Hand	+ On Order	= Available	Order Point	OP	
11398	TRANSFORMER	210			210	300	510	400		
11402	MOTOR ASM 50	1205	500		1705	1500	3205	2000		
11610	CAM	10341		1423	8918		8918	9000	*	
11682	LEVER	433	3500	1255	2678	500	3178	2750		

	Cumulative Count		Annual	Unit	Annual	Cumulative Sales	
Item No.	Number	%	Units	Cost	$ Sales	$	%
T 7061	1	.01	51,553	3.077	158,629	158,629	.5
-	-	-	-	-	-	-	-
S 6832	13	.12	243,224	.317	77,102	1,652,385	5.0
K 5322	110	1.0	8,680	3.286	28,522	5,882,489	17.8
S 5678	549	5.0	244,690	.045	11,011	13,252,124	40.1
S 6121	2,198	20.0	7,239	.490	3,547	23,662,146	71.6
-	-	-	-	-	-	-	-
-	-	-	-	-	-	-	-
-	-	-	-	-	-	-	-
S 6219	6,593	60.0	15,360	.050	768	31,395,306	95.0
-	-	-	-	-	-	-	-
-	-	-	-	-	-	-	-
-	-	-	-	-	-	-	-
M 3742	10,988	100.0	0	.073	0	33,047,690	100.0

FIGURE 10–9—*Continued*

INVT. CLASS	PART NUMBER	DESCRIPTION	12 MONTH USAGE	AVERAGE INVENTORY	TURN-OVER	UNIT COST	
140	2345	BASE CASTING 203	1,235	325	3.8	$ 45.50	
140	2988	BASE CASTING 308	540	230	2.3	37.75	
140	3075	FRAME	1,235	164	7.5	28.80	
140	3146	DRIVE SHAFT	753	80	9.4	32.40	
140	3234	CAM	3,705	208	17.8	12.20	
140	3289	GEAR	4,994	305	16.4	3.38	

INVENTORY ANALYSIS
DATE 7/1/--

Source: *Guide to Inventory and Material Accounting* (White Plains, N.Y.: IBM Corporation, 1969), pp. 4, 11, 45–46.

to calculate optimum order points and economic order quantities for use by the inventory control system. Such calculations take into account the cost of an item, its carrying cost, its annual sales, the cost of placing an order, and the length of time it takes to process, procure, and receive an item. (Refer back to Figure 8–16 for an illustration of an EOQ calculation).

Too little stock may mean lost sales or excessive rush orders for stock replenishment. Too much stock may mean increased carrying costs, higher interest on invested capital, additional warehousing expenses, and greater loss to obsolescence. In many cases, carrying costs can run as high as 25 percent.[1]

THE BILLING AND SALES ANALYSIS APPLICATION

Objectives

The objectives of the *billing and sales analysis* application are:

1. To prepare customer invoices (bills) quickly and accurately and thus maintain customer satisfaction and improved cash flow into the business.
2. To provide management with sales analysis reports which provide information concerning sales activity and trends which is required for effective marketing management.

[1] *Management Reports in Today's Business* (White Plains, N.Y.: IBM Corporation, 1973), p. 12.

FIGURE 10–10

A Billing and Sales Analysis System

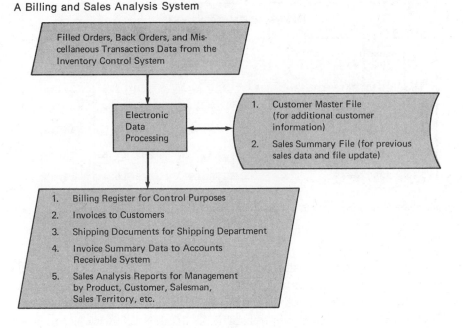

Figure 10–10 summarizes the important components of the billing and sales analysis system.

Input

The input into the billing and sales analysis system consists of data from the inventory control system which describes the filled orders, back orders, and miscellaneous transactions. (This is sometimes called the "billing file.")

Data Base

The data base for this system consists of the "customer master file" which is utilized to provide additional information about a customer that is required by a billing operation. Examples are customer "ship to" addresses, shipping instructions, special handling, etc. A "sales summary file" is updated with current sales order data and provides information concerning previous sales for the sales analysis reports.

Output

The output of the billing and sales analysis system includes a "billing register" which is a summary listing of all invoices that is utilized for control purposes. A major output of the system is customer invoices such as that shown in Figure 10–11. (The computer calculates all required invoice amounts.) Other output of the system includes shipping documents such as "picking slips," shipping labels, "bills of lading," delivery receipts, etc. The computer frequently lists the items on the invoice in a warehouse-location sequence so that a copy of the invoice can be used as a "picking slip" by warehouse personnel when assembling an order for shipment. Summarized data for each invoice is recorded on cards, tape, or disk to provide the major category of input to the accounts receivable system.

The final major output of the billing and sales analysis system is sales analysis reports for management such as those shown in Figure 10–12. Sales analysis reports can analyze sales by product, product line, customer, type of customer, salesman, sales territory, etc. Such reports help marketing management determine the sales performance of products, customers, and salesmen. They can determine whether a firm is expending too much sales effort on low-volume customers or low-profit products.

FIGURE 10–11

Customer Invoice

LAURENTIAN INDUSTRIES, INC.

SOLD TO	SHIP TO	CUSTOMER NO.
S. W. STAPLES 498 RIVERVIEW STREET SAN JOSE, CALIF. 94067	RODRIGUEZ DESIGN HOMES DIVISION OF S. W. STAPLES 8363 OLIVE STREET SUNNYVALE, CALIF. 95117	430875

DATE 09/15/--	INV. NO. 138265	ORDER NO. 717690	SHIPPING INSTRUCTIONS VIA SMITH TRANSPORT	STATED TERMS 2% 15 DAYS NET 30	SALESMAN G. PEREZ

QUANTITY ORDERED	QUANTITY SHIPPED	QUANTITY B/O	DESCRIPTION	UNIT PRICE	EXTENDED AMOUNT	DISCOUNT AMOUNT	NET AMOUNT	TAX-ABLE
40	40		B500 TWINLITE SOCKET B	.60	24.00	1.20	22.80	
350	100	250	B506 SOCKET ADAPTER BRN	.32	32.00	3.20	28.80	
200	150	50	C151C SILENT SWITCH IVORY	1.20	180.00	9.00	171.00	•
175	175		A210 PULL CORD GOLD	.42	73.50		73.50	•
60		60	1436 LAMP ENTRANCE	.50				
175	105	70	A200 FIXTURE 5 LIGHT	20.13	2113.65	211.37	1,902.28	
			FREIGHT CHARGE					
			PACKING CHARGE				18.95	
							45.00	

TAXABLE 244.50	TAX 12.23	FREIGHT 18.95	MISC. SPECIAL CHARGE 45.00		INVOICE AMOUNT 2,274.56

Source: *Management Reports in Today's Business* (White Plains, N.Y.: IBM Corporation, 1973), p. 6.

FIGURE 10–12

Sales Analysis Reports for Management

LAURENTIAN INDUSTRIES, INC.

COMPARATIVE ANALYSIS OF SALES BY ITEM

PERIOD ENDING 10/31/--   PAGE

ITEM NO.	DESCRIPTION	CURR. PERIOD QUAN. THIS YR	LAST YR	PCT CHG	YTD QUANTITY THIS YR	LAST YR	PCT CHG
624634	D20068 OVERHAUL GASKET	10	14	29-	90	98	8-
624832	17D0011 BELT DYNAMIC FAN	190	150	27	1,820	1,905	4-
624901	DMK6448 HUB ASSEMBLY J2	1-	5	120-	18	18	0

LAURENTIAN INDUSTRIES, INC.

SALES BY ITEM CLASS

MONTH ENDING 03/31/--

ITEM CLASS	CLASS DESCRIPTION	SOLD THIS MONTH	GROSS PROFIT	PROFIT PERCENT	SOLD THIS YEAR	GROSS PROFIT	PROFIT PERCENT
1	ABRASIVES	2,720.19	271.36	10	9,900.17	907.60	9
2	ACIDS AND CHEMICALS	1,216.27	170.27	14	3,139.68	408.07	13
3	BRASS	6,220.83	435.45	7	16,341.47	1,143.87	7

LAURENTIAN INDUSTRIES, INC.

COMPARATIVE SALES ANALYSIS

BY ITEM CLASS FOR EACH CUSTOMER

MONTH ENDING 05/31/--   PAGE

CUST NO	ITEM CLASS	CUSTOMER/ITEM CLASS NAME	MONTHLY SALES THIS YEAR	LAST YEAR	PRCNT CHG	YEAR TO DATE SALES THIS YEAR	LAST YEAR	PRCNT CHG
3310		TARDELL HARDWARE						
	11	BUILDER HARDWARE	103.19	91.31	13	515.92	729.43	29-
	12	ELECTRICAL SUPPLIES	87.58	85.02	2	435.57	375.29	16
	13	GIFTS AND SUNDRIES	63.01	.00		315.09	490.36	35-
	14	HOUSEWARES	198.05	150.23	32	990.32	1,123.19	12-

LAURENTIAN INDUSTRIES, INC.

COMPARATIVE SALES ANALYSIS BY CUSTOMER

FOR EACH SALESMAN

PERIOD ENDING 07/31/--   PAGE

SLMN NO.	CUST. NO.	SALESMAN/CUSTOMER NAME	THIS PERIOD THIS YEAR	THIS PERIOD LAST YEAR	YEAR-TO-DATE THIS YEAR	YEAR-TO-DATE LAST YEAR
10		A R WESTON				
	1426	HYDRO CYCLES INC	3,210.26	4,312.06	10,010.28	9,000.92
	2632	RUPP AQUA CYCLES	7,800.02	2,301.98	20,322.60	11,020.16
	3217	SEA PORT WEST CO	90.00CR	421.06	900.00	593.10
		SALESMAN TOTALS	10,920.28	7,035.10	31,732.88	20,614.18
12		H T BRAVEMAN				
	0301	BOLLINGER ASSOCIATES	100.96	0.00	100.96	0.00

Source: *Management Reports in Today's Business* (White Plains, N.Y.: IBM Corporation, 1973), p. 11.

. . . one distributor discovered he had 1300 accounts, representing 32 percent of all customers, who purchased less than 1 percent of his total volume. Looking at the other end of the report, he found that he had more than 1700 accounts who bought at least $1,000 annually and accounted for 95 percent of the volume.[2]

THE ACCOUNTS RECEIVABLE APPLICATION

Objectives

"Accounts receivable" represents the amounts of money owed to a company by its customers (accounts). The objectives of the *accounts receivable* application are:

1. To stimulate prompt customer payments by preparing accurate and timely monthly statements to credit customers.
2. To provide management with the information required to control the amount of credit extended and the collection of money owed, in order to maximize profitable credit sales while minimizing losses from bad debts.

Figure 10–13 illustrates a typical accounts receivable system.

Input

Input into the system consists of invoice summary data from the billing system and source documents showing payments received from customers. The usual customer payment document is the return portion of an invoice or statement which the customer returns by mail along with a check in payment of his account. Another type of input into this system is "miscellaneous adjustments" which are prepared by the accounting department to adjust customer accounts for mistakes in billing, the return of goods, bad debt write-offs, etc.

Data Base

The data base for the accounts receivable application includes the "accounts receivable file" which provides current balances for each customer account and which is also updated by the new billing, payments, and adjustments input data. The "customer master file" is

---

[2] *Management Reports in Today's Business* (White Plains, N.Y.: IBM Corporation, 1973), p. 10.

FIGURE 10–13

An Accounts Receivable System

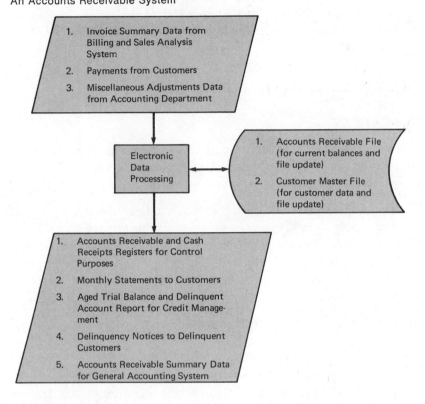

utilized to provide data needed for customer statement preparation. The customer credit standing information in this file is also updated as a result of changes in accounts receivable balances.

Output

Proper data processing control requires that listings and control totals be prepared for all cash received and for each customer account in the accounts receivable file. Thus, the output of the accounts receivable system includes an accounts receivable register and a cash receipts register. Monthly statements are also prepared for each customer which show recent charges and credits as well as the present balance owed. See Figure 10–14. Notice that this customer statement also indicates amounts that are overdue.

The accounts receivable system can also be programmed to automatically produce delinquency notices which are sent to customers

FIGURE 10-14

Customer Monthly Statement

LANG COMPANY

STATEMENT

DATE 9/30/--

CUSTOMER NO.
554386

HITTON CORPORATION
138 MARSHALL DR.
PO BOX 851
LONG PORT   CALIF   94134

DATE		INVOICE	REFERENCE	DESCRIPTION	AMOUNT
MO	DY	YR	NUMBER	NUMBER		
09	06	--			PRIOR BALANCE	$2,565.46
09	10	--	185163		INVOICE	1,685.91
09	15	--	075126	091531	PAYMENT	1,856.00CR
09	30	--			LC ADJUSTMENT	13.00CR
					LATE CHARGES	8.00

CURRENT AMOUNT	30 DAYS	60 DAYS & OVER	BALANCE DUE
$1,693.91	$696.46		$2,390.37

RETAIN THIS PORTION FOR YOUR RECORDS

LANG COMPANY

STATEMENT

DATE 9/30/--

CUSTOMER NO.
554386

HITTON CORPORATION
138 MARSHALL DR
PO BOX 851
LONG PORT   CALIF   94134

DATE		INVOICE	REFERENCE	DESCRIPTION	AMOUNT
MO	DY	YR	NUMBER	NUMBER		
09	08	--			PRIOR BALANCE	$2,565.46
09	10	--	185163		INVOICE	1,685.91
09	15	--	075126	091531	PAYMENT	1,856.00CR
09	30	--			LC ADJUSTMENT	13.00CR
					LATE CHARGES	0.00

CURRENT AMOUNT	30 DAYS	60 DAYS & OVER	BALANCE DUE
$1,693.91	$696.46		$2,390.37

Source: *Guide to Order Writing, Billing, Inventory, Accounts Receivable and Sales Analysis* (White Plains, N.Y.: IBM Corporation, 1969), p. 53.

FIGURE 10-15

Accounts Receivable Aged Trial Balance

ACCOUNTS RECEIVABLE AGED TRIAL BALANCE

DATE 6/30/1

CUSTOMER NUMBER	CUSTOMER NAME	SALESMAN'S NUMBER	BALANCE	CURRENT	OVER 30 DAYS	OVER 60 DAYS	90 DAYS & OVER	CREDIT LIMIT	EXCEEDS CREDIT LIMIT
13985	ANDERSON CORP.	27	1324 35	1200 00	121 50		2 85	3500 00	
14007	ARMSTRONG INTL.	27	3896 68	439 61	1911 25	499 00	1046 82	3000 00	-
37243	CONTI RENTAL	27	379 80	379 80				500 00	
48277	DELTA LIGHTING	27	241 28	65 98	175 30			500 00	
63365	FOXBORO CORP.	27	222 18	222 18				2000 00	
72466	HINDS ELECTRIC	27	2767 15	1632 09	1135 06			15000 00	
78144	INNSBRUCK ELEC.	27	861 70	27 50	54 40	127 23	652 57	1000 00	
85433	MILLER SUPPLY	27	457 90	202 60	50 70	120 70	83 90	500 00	
87542	PALMER APPL.	27	40 24	40 24				500 00	
93421	SMYTHE CO.	27	336 05	260 40		75 65		1500 00	
95642	WELLS HARDWARE	27	3195 98	469 76	325 01	151 63	2249 58	3000 00	-
	FINAL TOTALS		13723 31	4940 16	3773 22	974 21	4035 72		

Source: *Management Memorandum: The Business Information System* (White Plains, N.Y.: IBM Corporation), p. 9.

whose accounts are seriously overdue. Management reports produced by the system include a delinquent account report and an "aged trial balance" report (also called an "aged accounts receivable report"). Figure 10–15 illustrates an aged trial balance which helps the credit manager identify accounts which are seriously overdue and require special collection efforts. The final output of the accounts receivable system consists of accounts receivable summary data which is utilized as input by the general accounting system.

THE ACCOUNTS PAYABLE APPLICATION

Objectives

"Accounts payable" refers to the amounts of money that a business firm owes to its suppliers. The primary objectives of the *accounts payable* application are:

1. Prompt and accurate payment of suppliers in order to maintain good relationships with suppliers, insure a good credit standing, and secure any discounts offered for prompt payment.
2. Provide tight financial control over all cash disbursements of the business.
3. Provide management with information needed for the analysis of payments, expenses, purchases, and cash requirements.

Figure 10–16 illustrates the accounts payable application.

Input

Input into the accounts payable system consists of invoices (bills) from suppliers and others who have furnished goods or services to the business firm. Input may also be in the form of expense "vouchers" for various business expenses and miscellaneous payments and adjustments from the accounting department. (A *voucher* is an accounting form which records the details of a transaction and authorizes its entry into the accounting system of a firm.) For example, expense vouchers may be prepared to reimburse employees for authorized expenditures. Typically salesmen and managerial personnel request reimbursement by completing an "expense account" statement and submitting it to the accounting department.

Payments from "petty cash" or adjustments from suppliers for billing errors are other types of miscellaneous input. Receiving reports from the receiving department acknowledge the receipt of goods from suppliers and are required before payment can be authorized. A copy of purchase orders from the purchasing department provides data describing purchase orders that have been sent to suppliers. This data is utilized to record "pending payables" and to help determine whether the business firm has been accurately billed by its suppliers.

FIGURE 10–16

An Accounts Payable System

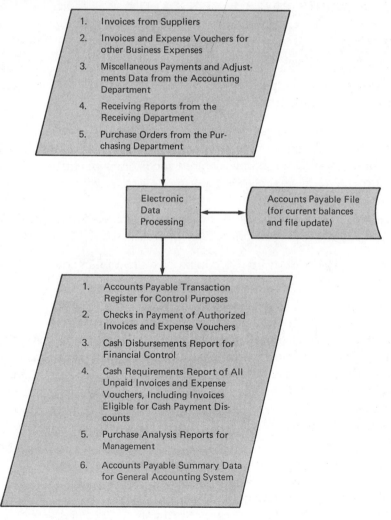

Data Base

The data base for the accounts payable application is the "accounts payable file" which provides current balances for all accounts and is updated by the new input data.

Output

As in previous applications, data processing control requires that an "accounts payable transaction register" be produced. This output document lists all system transactions and computes various control totals. A major form of output of the system are checks in payment of authorized invoices and expense vouchers. See Figure 10–17. A "cash disbursements report" provides a detailed record of all checks written and contributes to proper financial control of the cash disbursements of the firm.

An important output of the system for management is the "cash

FIGURE 10–17

Check and Remittance Statement

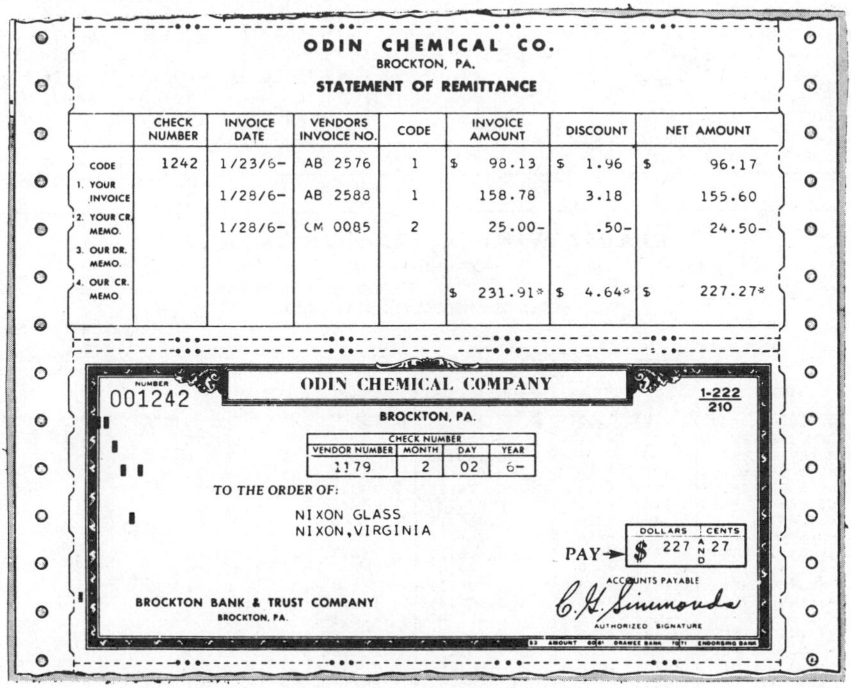
ODIN CHEMICAL CO.
BROCKTON, PA.
STATEMENT OF REMITTANCE

	CHECK NUMBER	INVOICE DATE	VENDORS INVOICE NO.	CODE	INVOICE AMOUNT	DISCOUNT	NET AMOUNT
CODE	1242	1/23/6–	AB 2576	1	$ 98.13	$ 1.96	$ 96.17
1. YOUR INVOICE		1/28/6–	AB 2588	1	158.78	3.18	155.60
2. YOUR CR. MEMO.		1/28/6–	CM 0085	2	25.00–	.50–	24.50–
3. OUR DR. MEMO.							
4. OUR CR. MEMO					$ 231.91*	$ 4.64*	$ 227.27*

ODIN CHEMICAL COMPANY
NUMBER 001242
1-222
210
BROCKTON, PA.

CHECK NUMBER			
VENDOR NUMBER	MONTH	DAY	YEAR
1179	2	02	6–

TO THE ORDER OF:
NIXON GLASS
NIXON, VIRGINIA

PAY → DOLLARS $ 227 AND CENTS 27

ACCOUNTS PAYABLE
C. G. Simmonds
AUTHORIZED SIGNATURE

BROCKTON BANK & TRUST COMPANY
BROCKTON, PA

Source: *Accounts Payable* (White Plains, N.Y.: IBM Corporation, 1967), p. 17.

requirements report" which lists and/or summarizes all unpaid invoices and expense vouchers and identifies all invoices eligible for cash payment discounts during the current period. The computer can also be programmed to analyze unpaid invoices and expense vouchers so that forecasts of the cash requirements for several future periods can be included in the cash requirements report. See Figure 10–18. The accounts payable system can also produce "purchase analysis reports" for management which summarize the purchases and payments made to each supplier of the firm. (This report is sometimes produced by a separate *purchasing* system.) The final category of output consists of summarized accounts payable transaction data which is recorded on cards, tape, or disk and becomes input data for the general accounting system.

FIGURE 10–18

Purchase Analysis and Cash Requirements Reports

PURCHASE ANALYSIS BY VENDOR

VENDOR'S NO.	VENDOR'S NAME	AMOUNT THIS MONTH	RETURNS YEAR TO DATE	NET AMOUNT YEAR TO DATE	NET AMOUNT LAST YEAR TO DATE	INCREASE OR DECREASE
27	ABBOT MACHINE CO	1286 44		3194 26	3010 42	183 84
58	ACE TOOL CO			1975 15	1859 76	115 39
66	ACME ABRASIVE CO	342 86		1505 93	1482 50	23 43
324	ALLAN ALLOYS CO		95 10	4675 22	4410 15	265 07
367	AMERICAN TOOL CO			986 74	1293 84	307 10 CR
425	ANGUS METAL WORKS			842 89	795 22	47 67
475	APEX CORPORATION	2316 84	245 73	10476 79	9473 65	1003 14
502	ARCO STATIONERY CO			319 42	445 93	126 51 CR
					1902 64	43 19

KRAUSZ MANUFACTURING COMPANY
ACCOUNTS PAYABLE

CASH REQUIREMENTS STATEMENT

DATE APR 1 2 196-

ROUTE: *Mr. J. R. Crossin - Dept 100*

SHEET *1* OF *2*

VENDOR	VENDOR NUMBER	DUE DATE	INVOICE AMOUNT	DISCOUNT	CHECK AMOUNT
SOLVAY GEN SUP	1016	4/16	$ 773.30	$ 15.47	$ 757.83
ROCHESTER PR CO	1021	4/16	1,620.18	32.40	1,587.78
CALABRIA CONT	1049	4/16	143.65	2.87	140.78
ONONDAGA STL CO	1077	4/16	5,982.82	119.66	5,863.16
BLACK & NICHOLS	1103	4/16	14.25	.71	13.54
AUSTERHOLZ INC	1240	4/16	624.77	12.50	612.27
AUSTERHOLZ INC	1240	4/16	1,833.19	36.66	1,796.53
CHRISTIE & CO	1366	4/16	745.54		745.54
WILSON & WILSON	2231	4/16	2,936.12	58.72	2,877.40
CLAR. HIGGINS	2590	4/16	1,000.00		1,000.00
HONOUR BROS	3101	4/16	97.36	1.95	95.41
BASTIANI & SON	3112	4/16	3,580.85	71.62	3,509.23
DRJ WIRE CO	3164	4/16	256.90	5.14	251.76
HASTING-WHITE	3258	4/16	1,144.42	22.89	1,121.53
DARONO ART MET	3427	4/16	32.75	.66	32.09
DARONO ART MET	3427	4/16	127.52	2.55	124.97
DARONO ART MET	3427	4/16	96.60	1.93	94.67

Source: *Accounts Payable* (White Plains, N.Y.: IBM Corporation, 1967), pp. 16, 22.

THE PAYROLL AND LABOR ANALYSIS APPLICATION

Objectives

The primary objectives of the *payroll and labor analysis* application are:

1. Prompt and accurate payment of employees.
2. Prompt and accurate reporting to management, employees, and appropriate agencies concerning earnings, taxes, and other deductions.
3. Providing management with reports analyzing labor costs and productivity.

The payroll and labor analysis application is widely computerized because it involves many complex calculations and the production of

FIGURE 10–19

A Payroll and Labor Analysis System

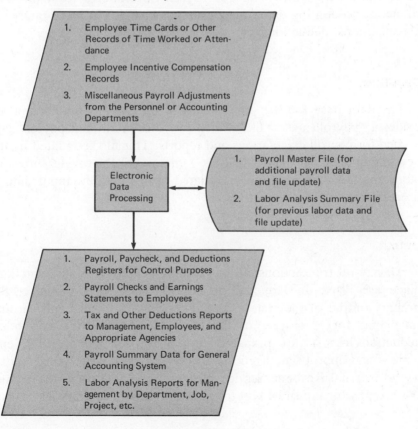

many types of reports and documents, many of which are required by government agencies. Besides earnings calculations, many types of taxes and fringe benefit deductions must be calculated. Payroll processing is also complicated because many business firms employ hourly paid employees and salaried personnel and may have several kinds of incentive compensation plans. Figure 10–19 illustrates the payroll and labor analysis application.

Input

The input into the payroll and labor analysis system consists of employee time cards or other records of time worked or attendance. Time cards are normally utilized by hourly paid employees while some type of attendance record is usually kept for salaried personnel. An additional input are records of employee incentive compensation such as factory piecework or salesmen's commissions. Input may also be in the form of miscellaneous payroll adjustments from the personnel or accounting departments such as changes in wage rates, job classifications, deductions, etc.

Data Base

The data base for the payroll and labor analysis application includes a "payroll master file" which provides additional payroll data needed for payroll calculations and reports. This file is updated by the new input data. A "labor analysis summary file" provides previous labor analysis data and is also updated each time new input data is processed.

Output

All payroll transactions, all pay checks written, and all deductions made are listed and totalled on control registers. Of course, the primary output of the system consists of payroll checks and earning statements for employees of the firm. In addition, tax and other deductions reports are prepared periodically for management, employees and appropriate agencies. These include quarterly tax reports to the Internal Revenue Service such as Form 941a and the annual W–2 form which must be sent to employees before January 31 of each

FIGURE 10–20

Paycheck and Earnings Statement

CHECK DATE 4/30/69					90–1211 0519		

J.R.SMITH & CO.

CHECK NUMBER
1303

PAY *136 DOLLARS AND 35 CENTS   **136.35

TO THE ORDER OF   A H ANKSTER

SPECIMEN

COMMERCIAL TRUST BANK

⑆0 2⑈0⑈098 7⑇ ⑉12⑉ 0036 0⑈

EMPLOYEE NUMBER	EMPLOYEE NAME		DEPT.	PAY PERIOD	PAY PERIOD ENDED	CHECK NO.	CHECK DATE
0123	A H ANKSTER		03	8	4/30/69	1303	4/30/69

EARNINGS AND STATUTORY DEDUCTIONS

HOURS	RATE	REGULAR PAY	OVERTIME PAY	OTHER PAY	GROSS PAY	FED.W/TAX	F.I.C.A. TAX	STATE TAX
5C.0	2.75	137.50	11.25	12.80	161.55	7.75	8.70	1.62

VOLUNTARY DEDUCTIONS

MEDICAL INS.	LIFE INS.	CREDIT UNION	UNION DUES	CHARITY	SAVINGS BONDS	ALL OTHERS	NET PAY
2.00		4.13	1.00				136.35

SOCIAL SECURITY AND W–2 INFORMATION

SOCIAL SECURITY NO.	EXEMPT	Y.T.D. GROSS	Y.T.D. FED. W/TAX	Y.T.D. F.I.C.A.	Y.T.D. STATE TAX	
312–32–1337	X	2,105.92	222.98	101.08	21.06	NOT NEGOTIABLE

Source: *Guide to Payroll* (White Plains, N.Y.: IBM Corporation, 1969), p. 20.

year. See Figure 10–20. Reports listing and summarizing other tax and deduction information are prepared for management and agencies such as school districts, city, county, and state agencies, labor unions, insurance companies, charitable organizations, credit unions, etc. See Figure 10–21.

"Labor analysis reports" for management are another major form of output of the payroll and labor analysis system. See Figure 10–22. These reports analyze the time, cost, and personnel required by departments of the firm or by jobs and projects being undertaken. They assist management in planning labor requirements and controlling the labor cost and productivity of on-going projects. The final output of the payroll and labor analysis system is "payroll summary data" which is utilized as input by the general accounting system.

FIGURE 10–21

W–2 and 941a Forms

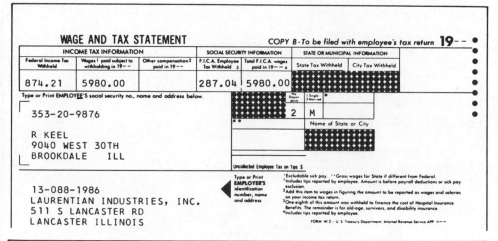

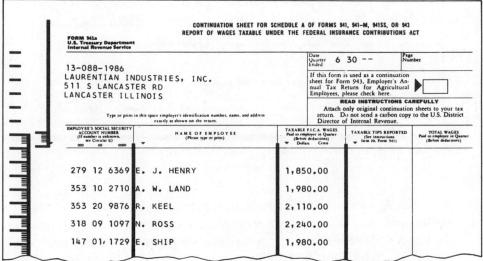

Source: *Management Reports in Today's Business* (White Plains, N.Y.: IBM Corporation, 1973), pp. 19–20.

THE GENERAL ACCOUNTING APPLICATION

The general accounting application (frequently called the "general ledger" application) consolidates financial data from all of the other accounting subsystems and produces the monthly and annual financial statements of the firm. The many financial transactions of a business are first recorded in chronological order in "journals," then transferred

FIGURE 10–22

Labor Analysis Reports

```
DATE  8/08/--            PAYROLL DISTRIBUTION FOR PERIOD ENDING  7/31/--          PAGE    3

  GENERAL LEDGER    EMP.  PAY   TIME  OVT  SHIFT  PAYROLL    PAYROLL
  ACCOUNT NUMBER    NO    PER    CD   CD   CODE   COST       HOURS     EMPLOYEE  NAME

  9111-0006-0021  70723   30     1          1    135.00     40.0 G  SAMPSON
  9111-0006-0021  12921   30     1          1    165.00     35.5 H  ADAMS
  9111-0006-0021  59705   30     1          1    235.00     40.0 F  MULLIN
  9111-0006-0021  51680   30     1          1     60.00     10.0 M  MALONE
  9111-0006-0021  49105   30     1          1    285.00     40.0 M  JONESON
  9111-0006-0021  36158   30     1          1    200.00     40.0 J  HATCHFORD

                   ACCOUNT TOTALS               1,080.00    205.5

  9121-4085-7801  15120   30     2    3     3     52.50     10.5 B  BROWN
  9121-4085-7801  19364   30     2    3     3     24.80      6.2 C  CARLSON
  9121-4085-7801  20662   30     2    3     3     49.20     12.0 D  DONALDSON

                   ACCOUNT TOTALS                126.00     28.7


                   GRAND TOTALS               7,590.00    1,780.0   DETAIL RECORDS      507
```

```
DATE  8/08/--                      WORK IN PROGRESS REPORT                        PAGE    3
                                      FOR JULY 19--

JOBNO  FINISH    PROGRESS  WORK  EMPNO  EST JOB  ACT JOB  % HRS  EST JOB   ACT JOB   % $
       DATE      DATE      DEPT         HOURS    HOURS    USED   DOLLARS   DOLLARS   USED
11111  10/30/70  6/30/--                120.0    30.0     25.0   635.00    190.00-   30.0
                 7/05/--   360  00508             8.0                        40.00
                 7/10/--   360  00508             8.0                        40.00
                 7/11/--   360  00604             6.0                        24.00
                 7/30/--   360  00501            10.0                        60.00

TOTAL JOB 11111 TO DATE STATUS          120.0    62.0     51.7   635.00    354.00    55.7

23468  9/30/70   4/30/--                100.0    80.0     80.0  1000.00    700.00    70.0
                 7/06/--   400  10105             8.0                        80.00
                 7/28/--   506  36350             4.0                        80.00
                 7/29/--   506  36350             4.0                        80.00
                 7/30/--   506  36350             5.0                       100.00

TOTAL JOB 23468 TO DATE STATUS          100.0   101.0    101.0  1000.00   1040.00   104.0

33335  7/15/70   6/30/--                 40.0    42.0    105.0   160.00    200.00   125.0
                 7/14/--   500  40608             4.0                         8.00
                 7/18/--   360  00508             8.0                        40.00

TOTAL JOb 33335 TO DATE STATUS           40.0    54.0    135.0   160.00    248.00   155.0

40608  11/30/70  4/30/--                200.0   120.0     60.0  1600.00    960.00    60.0

TOTAL JOB 40608 NO CURRENT ACTIVITY

FINAL TOTALS  JOBS IN PROGRESS   25   2700.0  1507.0    55.8  16200.00   8250.00    50.9
```

Source: *Management Reports in Today's Business* (White Plains, N.Y.: IBM Corporation, 1973), p. 35.

("posted") to "subsidiary ledgers" where they are organized into "accounts" such as cash, accounts receivable, inventory, etc. The summary of all accounts and their balances is known as the "general ledger."

At the end of each accounting period (at the end of each month or fiscal year) the balance of each account in the general ledger must be computed, the profit or loss of the firm during the period must be calculated, and the financial statements of the firm (the balance sheet and income statement) must be prepared. This is known as "closing the books" of the business. The income statement of the firm presents its income, expenses, and profit or loss for a period, while the balance sheet shows the assets, liabilities, and net worth of the business as of the end of the accounting period.

Objectives

The primary objective of the *general accounting* application is to utilize the power of the computer to accomplish the many accounting tasks mentioned in the preceding paragraph in an accurate and timely manner. Utilizing the computer for general accounting can result in greater accuracy, earlier closings, and more timely and meaningful financial reports for management. The computer can frequently accomplish this with less manpower and at a lower cost than manual bookkeeping and accounting methods. Figure 10–23 is a general systems flowchart of the general accounting application.

FIGURE 10–23

A General Accounting System

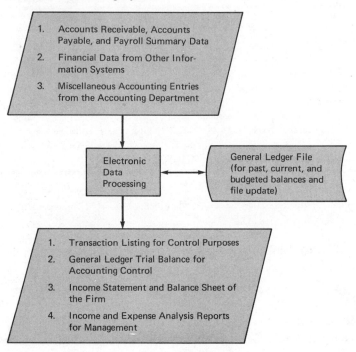

Input

Input into the general accounting system consists of summary data from the accounts receivable, accounts payable, and payroll systems, as well as financial data from other information systems (such as production control, purchasing, engineering, etc.) that we have not described in this chapter. Another form of input is "miscellaneous accounting entries" from the accounting department that record changes to accounts such as cash, marketable securities, plant and equipment, etc.

Data Base

The data base of the general accounting application is the "general ledger file" which is updated by the new input data and provides information on past, current, and budgeted balances for each general ledger account.

Output

The output of the general accounting system includes a listing of all transactions for control purposes and a general ledger "trial balance" report which provides accounting control by summarizing and balancing all general ledger accounts. See Figure 10–24. The income

FIGURE 10–24

General Ledger Summary Report

```
                              A B C COMPANY

                           SUMMARY LEDGER REPORT

                               03/31/69                          PAGE 01

      ACCOUNT NO.        ACCOUNT DESCRIPTION          ACCOUNT BALANCES YEAR TO DATE
      MAJ. MIN.                                       THIS YEAR        LAST YEAR
      111  000    CASH ON HAND AND IN BANKS                36,710.23       25,893.26
      112  000    ACCOUNTS RECEIVABLE - NET              122,273.47      117,762.80
      114  000    NOTES RECEIVABLE                         8,000.00        4,000.00
      116  000    INVENTORIES                            703,402.65      590,808.40
      121  000    LAND                                   500,000.00      500,000.00
      122  000    BUILDINGS                            1,850,000.00    1,800,000.00
      123  000    ACCUMULATED DEPRECIATION ON BUILDINGS    49,000.00       48,000.00
      124  000    EQUIPMENT AND MACHINERY                450,850.00      425,465.00
      125  000    DEPREC RESERVE FOR EQUIP AND MACH        79,456.00       76,305.00
      221  000    NOTES PAYABLE                           40,000.00       35,000.00
      321  000    SURPLUS                                 75,203.76       50,397.73
      411  000    SALES                                1,075,113.85      950,675.33
      412  000    COST OF GOODS SOLD                     375,819.10      255,839.19
      421  000    SELLING EXPENSE                        185,615.25      195,267.48
```

Source: *Guide to General Ledger on the IBM System/3 Model 10* (White Plains, N.Y.: IBM Corporation, 1969), p. 14.

statement and balance sheet of the firm for an accounting period is a major output of the system and is of primary importance to financial management and the top management of the firm. See Figure 10–25. A final important output of the general accounting system is "income and expense analysis reports" which can be produced for all levels of management. Such reports analyze the financial performance of a

FIGURE 10–25

Comparative Income Statement and Balance Sheet

HASTING-WHITE TOOL COMPANY
COMPARATIVE BALANCE SHEET

PERIOD ENDING JUNE 30. 19—

MAJOR ACCOUNT	DESCRIPTION	PREVIOUS PERIOD THIS YEAR	CURRENT PERIOD		OVER* OR UNDER-	% OVER* OR UNDER-
			THIS YEAR	LAST YEAR		
	ASSETS					
	CASH AND RECEIVABLES					
111	CASH	$ 15,673.38	$ 16,739.73	$ 15,248.61	$ 1,491.12 *	9.8 *
112	ACCOUNTS RECEIVABLE	32,967.21	33,291.18	32,968.32	322.86 *	.9 *
113	RESERVE FOR BAD DEBTS	329.67-	332.91-	329.68-	3.23 *	.9 *
114	NOTES RECEIVABLE	1,000.00		1,500.00	1,500.00 -	100.0 -
115	MARKETABLE SECURITIES	2,164.30	5,898.13	3,673.21	2,224.92 *	60.6 *
	TOT	$ 51,475.22*	$ 55,596.13*	$ 53,060.46*	$ 2.535.67***	
	INVENTORIES					
116	INVENTORIES	$ 183,621.83	$ 161,298.67	$ 149,238.61	$ 12,060.06 *	8.1 *
	TOT	$ 183,621.83*	$ 161,298.67*	$ 149,238.61*	$ 12,060.06***	
	LAND AND BUILDINGS					
121	LAND		$ 50,238.96		$ 50,238.96 *	*
122	BUILDINGS					
123	RES. FOR DEPREC.	$ 2,116.45-	2,363.74-	$ 1,767.88-	595.36 *	33.7 *
	TOT	$ 2,116.45-	$ 47,875.22*	$ 1,767.88-	$ 49,643.10***	
	EQUIP. AND MACHINERY					
124	EQUIP. AND MACHINERY	$ 10,873.98	$ 8,339.61	$ 16,298.38	$ 7,958.77 -	48.8 -
125	RES. FOR DEPREC.	3,245.67-	3,469.22-	2,975.12-	494.10 *	16.6 *
	TOT	$ 7,628.31*	$ 4,870.39*	$ 13,323.26*	$ 8,452.87*-*	

SOUTH LAKE SAND COMPANY
COMPARATIVE INCOME STATEMENT

Routing
☐ President's Office
☑ Treasurer
☐ Comptroller
☐ Accounting
☐ Sales Manager
☐ Plant Superintendent

PERIOD ENDING MAY 31. 19—

ACCOUNT NUMBER	DESCRIPTION	CURRENT PERIOD		YEAR-TO-DATE		INCREASE* OR DECREASE-
		THIS YEAR	LAST YEAR	THIS YEAR	LAST YEAR	
411	SALES					
411-100	GROSS SALES	$ 1,223,195.85	$ 1,083,474.02	$ 4,739,999.14	$ 3,415,174.67	$ 1,324,824.47 *
411-200	LESS RETURNS & ALLOW	1,726.40	1,912.71	3,245.97	3,464.22	218.25 -
412-100	NET SALES	$ 1,221,469.45	$ 1,081,561.51	$ 4,736,753.17	$ 3,411,710.45	$ 1,325,042.72 *
	LESS COST OF SALES	581,786.15	541,950.16	2,852,146.73	2,008,762.23	843,384.50 *
	GROSS PROFIT	$ 639,683.30*	$ 539,611.15*	$ 1,884,606.44*	$ 1,402,948.22*	$ 481,658.22 *
421	SELLING EXPENSES					
421-100	SALARIES & COMMISSIONS	$ 184,373.27	179,264.48	$ 705,623.06	541,579.46	$ 164,043.60 *
421-200	TRAVELING EXPENSE	14,425.15	13,790.80	53,726.92	42,968.21	10,758.71 *
421-300	DELIVERY EXPENSE	6,140.20	5,956.00	28,364.15	16,428.19	11,935.96 *
421-400	ADVERTISING EXPENSE	1,582.00	1,450.25	18,250.00	5,225.75	13,024.25 *
421-500	OFFICE SALARIES	27,684.35	25,829.15	94,342.18	79,415.14	14,927.04 *
421-600	STATIONERY & SUPPLIES	1,380.60	1,295.00	4,982.76	3,576.82	1,405.94 *
421-700	TELEPHONE	1,315.85	1,305.62	4,148.15	3,381.26	766.89 *
421-800	BUILDING	6,725.00	6,215.10	25,175.00	18,634.55	6,540.45 *
421-900	MISCELLANEOUS	1,460.38	1,385.75	4,965.48	3,519.47	1,446.01 *
	TOTAL SELLING EXPENSE	$ 245,086.80*	$ 236,492.15*	$ 939,577.70*	$ 714,728.85*	$ 224,848.85 *

Source: *Guide to General Ledger* (White Plains, N.Y.: IBM Corporation, 1969), pp. 16–17.

FIGURE 10–26

Income and Expense Analysis Reports for Management

MANAGEMENT INFORMATION SYSTEM

PRESIDENTIAL LEVEL

EARNINGS SUMMARY

AUGUST 2, 196—

4 WEEKS ENDED

	ACTUAL	PLANNED	VARIANCE
SALES	2,475.0	2,300.0	+ 7.6%
GROSS MARGIN	993.0	900.0	EVEN
CONTROLLABLE EXPENSE	388.0	350.0	OK
OPERATING PROFIT	605.0	550.0	+10.0%
FIXED EXPENSE	310.0	300.0	+ 3.3%
NET PROFIT	295.0	250.0	
PROVISION FOR TAX	129.8	110.0	
NET PROFIT AFTER TAXES	165.2	140.0	+18.0%

COMMENTS: EACH STORE MET PLANNED GOALS WITHIN PRESCRIBED TOLERANCES.

YEAR TO DATE:	SALES	17.5 MILLION	+5.1 OVER PLAN
	NET AFTER TAXES:	1.1 MILLION	+9.7 OVER PLAN

Source: *Management Information System for Retailers* (White Plains, N.Y.: IBM Corporation, 1970), p. 13.

FIGURE 10–26—Continued

EXPENSE BUDGET STATEMENT

DEPT NAME: TYPEMAKING
DEPT MANAGER: W J GROTHAUS 20
PROJECT MANAGER: W E RAYHER 35
PROJECT NO 20 NO 80 210
MONTH ENDING FEB 19

ACCOUNT NAME	ACCT NO	DEPT NO	CURRENT MONTH — WORKING DAYS 20	BUDGET AMOUNT	ACTUAL EXPENSE	DIRECT HOURS 3006	OVER(=) OR UNDER BUDGET	YEAR TO DATE — WORKING DAYS TO DATE 35	ORIGINAL BUDGET AMOUNT	AUTHORIZED (+ OR −) CHANGES	ACTUAL EXPENSE	WORKING DAYS REMAINING	DIRECT HOURS 5395	OVER(=) OR UNDER BUDGET	PERCENT
DIRECT LABOR															
DIRECT LABOR	100	090	20	6272	6386		114−	35	10976		11406			430−	3.9−
SERVICE SALARIES & WAGE															
TECHNICIAN	217	090		420	388		32		735		670			65	8.8
PARTS IN PROCESS INSP	242	090		44			44		77					77	100.0
MACHINE & EQUIP MAINT	252	090		48	122		74−		84		213			129−	153.6−
TOOL MAINTENANCE	258	090		200	80		120		350		129			221	63.1
CLEANER & GARDENER	260	090		4	6		6−				8			8−	−0−
GENERAL LABORER	262	090					4		7					4−	100.0
STOCK ROOM & REC	268	090		100	102		2−		175		179			4−	2.3
REWORK LABOR PRODUCT	280	090		40			40		70		1			69	98.6
OTHER INDIRECT LABOR	281	090		32	49		17−		56		202			146−	260.7−
SERVICE FEES ETC															
MACHINE & EQUIP MAINT	513	090		20			20		35					35	100.0
TOOL MAINTENANCE	514	090		40			40		70					70	100.0
MANUFACTURING	516	090		4			4		7					7	100.0
TRAVELING & SUBSIST	588	090			16		16−				16			16−	−0−
RECOVERIES & ADJUSTMENT															
SERVICE OVERHEAD RED	895	090		32	3		29		56		3			53	94.6
TOTAL				2340	2164		176		4095		4148			53−	

Source: General Ledger and Financial Control (White Plains, N.Y.: IBM Corporation, 1971), p. 23.

department or the business firm by comparing current performance to past and forecasted (budgeted) figures. The difference ("variance") between actual and budgeted amounts shows managers in what area their performance is falling short or surpassing their financial objectives for a period. See Figure 10–26.

SUMMARY

A basic understanding of how the computer is utilized by business firms is vital to the effective present and future use of computers by business management. Computer applications are not isolated and unrelated applications of computers to individual business problems but are "computer-based information systems." The trend of business computer applications has been away from the clerical recordkeeping functions of operational information systems to the decision-making support functions of management information systems.

In most business computer applications, input consists of (1) transactions data, (2) data base adjustments, (3) inquiries, and (4) the output of other systems. Additional data or information is usually supplied from the records and files contained in the data base of the information system. EDP hardware, software, and personnel then process the data, resulting in an updated data base and the production of information in the form of (1) reports, (2) documents, (3) responses and displays, (4) control listings, and (5) input to other systems.

Several common business applications exist in both large and small computer-using business firms, whether they are experienced computer users or are utilizing the computer for the first time. The objectives, input, data base, and output of seven common business applications were described in this chapter. These common business applications are summarized below.

1. *Sales order processing.* Processes orders received from customers and produces invoices for customers and data needed for sales analysis and inventory control.
2. *Inventory control.* Receives data concerning customer orders, prepares shipping documents if the ordered items are available, and records all changes in inventory.
3. *Billing and sales analysis.* Receives filled orders data from the inventory control system and produces customer invoices and management reports analyzing the sales generated by each salesman, customer, product, etc.

4. *Accounts receivable.* Receives data concerning customer invoices and payments and produces monthly customer statements and credit management reports.

5. *Accounts payable.* Receives data concerning purchases from suppliers and produces checks in payment of outstanding invoices and cash management reports.

6. *Payroll and labor analysis.* Receives data from employee time cards and other records and produces paychecks, payroll reports, and labor analysis reports.

7. *General accounting.* Receives data from accounts receivable, accounts payable, payroll and labor analysis, and many other business information subsystems. Produces the general ledger trial balance, the income statement and balance sheet of the firm, and various income and expense reports for management.

KEY TERMS AND CONCEPTS

Trend in computer applications, 287–288
General form of business computer
 applications, 289–290
Common business applications, 290–291
Sales order processing, 292–295
Inventory control, 296–299

Billing and sales analysis, 299–302
Accounts receivable, 303–306
Accounts payable, 307–310
Payroll labor analysis, 311–313
General accounting, 314–319

ASSIGNMENTS

1. Test your understanding of the chapter material by reviewing the *purpose, outline, summary,* and *key terms and concepts* of this chapter. Are you confident that you have attained a basic understanding of the major concepts of the chapter? If not, reread the appropriate material as indicated by the page numbers after each key term and concept.

2. Discuss why and how computer applications should be viewed as computer-based information systems of a computer-using organization.

3. Discuss the trend in computer applications in business. Identify several reasons for such trends.

4. Describe the general form of a business computer application by identifying the basic systems components of business information systems.

5. Briefly describe each of the seven common computer applications in business.

6. Discuss the objectives, input, data base, and output of one of the common business applications. Explain how such a system might handle the information requirements of specific types of business firms or industries, such as manufacturing firms, retail stores, financial institutions, wholesalers, construction firms, etc.

7. Prepare a "Computer Application Analysis Report" which describes and evaluates how a specific type of business firm or industry utilizes one of the common business applications. Do the research for your report by contacting a computer-using business firm, the local office of a computer manufacturer, or by reviewing books and articles on specific computer applications in your library.

Chapter Outline

Purpose of the Chapter

Introduction

Business Application Categories

Computer Applications in Marketing
  Marketing Information Systems, Computer Applications in
    Retailing, The Point-of-Sale Revolution, Other
    Marketing Applications

Computer Applications in Production/Operations
  Manufacturing Information Systems, Benefits of
    Computer-based Manufacturing Systems, Plant
    Communications, Process Control, Numerical Control,
    Computer-aided Design, Physical Distribution
    Information Systems, Purchasing and Receiving,
    Other Production/Operations Applications

Computer Applications in Finance
  Financial Information Systems, Financial Performance
    Models, Accounting Information Systems,
    Applications in Banking, Applications in Investments

Other Computer Applications in Business
  Personnel Information Systems, Operations Research
    Applications, Information Retrieval, Other Business
    Applications: Airlines, Agribusiness, Construction,
    Insurance and Real Estate, Nonbusiness Computer
    Applications: Government, Education, and Medicine.

Summary

Key Terms and Concepts

Assignments

11

Computer Applications in Business II

```
+--------------------------------------------------+
|              Purpose of the Chapter              |
|                                                  |
|  To promote a basic understanding of how com-    |
|  puters are utilized to support specific business|
|  functions and selected industries by analyzing: |
|                                                  |
|  1. Computer applications in marketing, pro-     |
|     duction/operations, finance, and personnel,  |
|  2. Other business and nonbusiness applications  |
|     of the computer.                             |
+--------------------------------------------------+
```

INTRODUCTION

There are as many computer applications in business as there are business activities to be performed, business problems to be solved, and business opportunities to be pursued. It is therefore impossible to acquire a complete understanding of all computer applications in business. However, a business computer user should not have a *vague, unorganized* idea of business computer applications. As a present or future computer user, you should have a *basic* but *organized* understanding of the major ways the computer is used in business. You should have a *basic,* but *specific* understanding of how computers affect a *particular business function* (marketing, for example), or a *particular industry* (banking, for example), that is directly related to *your career objectives.* Thus, someone whose career objective is a *marketing* position in *banking* should acquire a basic understanding of how computers are used in banking and how computers support the marketing activities of banks and other business firms.

The purpose of this chapter is to begin to provide a basic understanding of computer applications in several major industries and functional areas of business. This chapter (and the preceding one) cannot provide more than a good start at achieving such understanding. Additional understanding must be achieved by learning more about a particular industry and business function through continued study and experience. However, this chapter should provide a valuable introduction to major business computer applications for computer users in business.

BUSINESS APPLICATION CATEGORIES

In the previous chapter, we analyzed the basic characteristics of seven common business computer applications. In this chapter, we will briefly describe many other important computer applications in business.

These applications will be discussed according to the business function they support (marketing, production/operations, finance, accounting, and personnel) or according to the industry in which they are utilized (retailing, banking, insurance, etc.). This should help you acquire a *basic, organized* and *specific* understanding of how computers support the management and operation of modern business firms.

Figure 11–1 illustrates how major computer applications can be grouped into functional and industry categories. You will note that the functional application categories are similar to the major categories of business information systems discussed in Chapter 9. Also note that the common computer applications discussed in the previous chapter are included in several functional application categories.

COMPUTER APPLICATIONS IN MARKETING

The business function of *marketing* is concerned with the planning, promotion, and sale of existing products in existing markets and the development of new products and new markets to better serve present and potential customers. Thus, marketing performs a vital function in the operation of a business enterprise. Performing the marketing function in the businesses of today has become a much

FIGURE 11–1

Major Business Applications by Functional and Industry Categories

Marketing
  Sales Order Processing
  Marketing Planning
  Sales Forecasting
  Sales Management
  Product Management
  Advertising Analysis
  Pricing Analysis
  Market Research
  Point-of-Sale Systems
  Promotional Distribution Systems

Production/Operations
  Production Planning
  Production Scheduling
  Production Control
  Process and Numerical Control
  Plant Maintenance Analysis
  Purchasing and Receiving
  Inventory Management
  Physical Distribution Planning
  Distribution Center Management
  Traffic Management

Finance
  Cash Management
  Portfolio Management
  Credit Management
  Capital Budgeting
  Financial Forecasting
  Financing Requirements Analysis
  Financial Performance Analysis

Accounting
  Accounts Receivable
  Accounts Payable
  General Accounting
  Property Accounting
  Cost Accounting
  Tax Accounting
  Budgeting

Personnel
  Payroll
  Labor Analysis
  Personnel Recordkeeping
  Employee Skills Inventory
  Training and Development Analysis
  Compensation Analysis
  Personnel Performance Analysis
  Personnel Requirements Forecasting

Industry categories
  Retailing
  Banking
  Investments
  Airlines
  Agribusiness
  Construction
  Insurance
  Real Estate, etc.

more difficult assignment because of the dynamic environment of today which includes:

1. Rapidly changing market demands.
2. Steadily increasing consumer pressures.
3. Shortened product life spans.
4. Proliferation of new products.
5. Intensified competition.
6. Growing government regulations.[1]

Business firms have increasingly turned to the computer to help them perform the vital marketing function in the face of the rapid changes of today's environment. The computer has been the catalyst

---

[1] Some of the material in this section has been adapted from *Consumer Goods Information System—Marketing* (White Plains, N.Y.: IBM Corporation, 1973), pp. 8–9.

in the development of a *"marketing information system"* which integrates the information flows required by many marketing activities. The subsystems of the marketing information system utilize the computer in a variety of ways. We shall now briefly analyze the major subsystems of the marketing information system and several computer applications in marketing. This should provide you with a basic understanding of how computers help business firms perform their marketing activities.

Marketing Information Systems

The marketing information system consists of the following major subsystems:

1. Sales order processing.
2. Marketing planning.
3. Sales forecasting.
4. Sales management.
5. Product management.
6. Advertising and promotion.
7. Market research.

The sales order processing subsystem is primarily an operational information system, while the other six subsystems are management information systems. Each of these subsystems is summarized below. The information flows in a marketing information system are illustrated in Figure 11–2.

1. Sales order processing. A basic form of this subsystem was described in the previous chapter. It captures and processes customer orders and produces invoices for customers and data needed for sales analysis and inventory control. In many firms, it also keeps track of the status of customer orders until goods are delivered.

2. Marketing planning. This information subsystem assists marketing management in developing short and long-range plans outlining product sales, profit, and growth objectives. It also provides information feedback and analysis concerning performance-versus-plan for each area of marketing. Mathematical marketing models may be utilized to investigate the effects of various alternative plans.

3. Sales forecasting. Figure 11–3 illustrates the flows of data and information in the sales forecasting subsystem. The basic functions of the sales forecasting system can be grouped into the two categories of "short-range forecasting" and "long-range forecasting." Short-range

FIGURE 11–2

Information and Decision Flows in Marketing Management

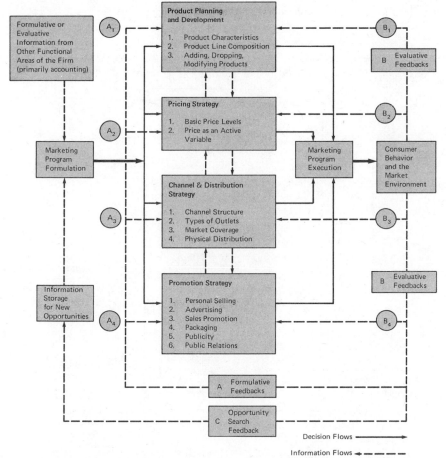

Source: Smith, Brien, and Stanford, *Readings in Marketing Information Systems* (Boston: Houghton Mifflin Company, 1968), p. 3.

forecasting deals with forecasts of sales for periods up to one year, while long-range forecasting is concerned with sales forecasts for a year or more into the future.

4. Sales management. This system provides information to help sales management plan and monitor the performance of the sales organization. The *sales analysis* application described in the previous chapter is a basic form of this system.

5. Product management. This information subsystem provides information to help management plan and control the performance of specific products, product lines, or brands. Revenue, cost, and

FIGURE 11–3

Information Flows in the Sales Forecasting System

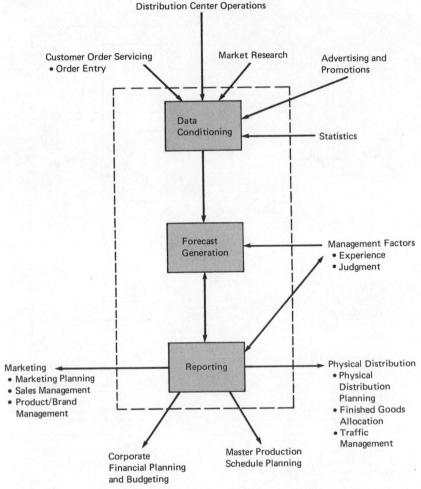

Source: *Consumer Goods Information System—Marketing* (White Plains, N.Y.: IBM Corporation, 1973), p. 18.

growth information is required for existing products and new product development.

6. Advertising and promotions. The objective of this system is to provide management with information to achieve sales objectives at the lowest possible costs for advertising and promotion. Information and analytical techniques are utilized to select media and promotional methods, allocate financial resources, and control and evaluate results.

FIGURE 11–4

A Market Research Information System

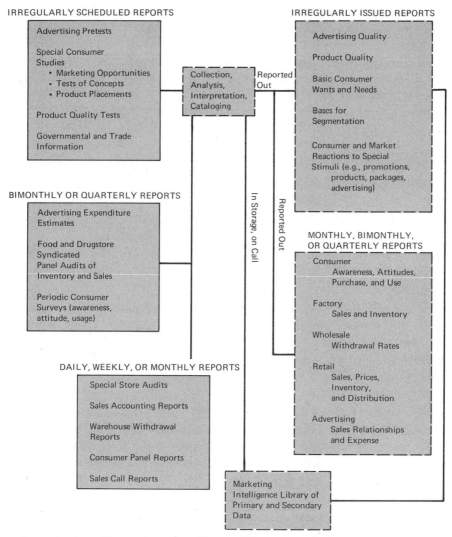

IRREGULARLY SCHEDULED REPORTS

- Advertising Pretests
- Special Consumer Studies
  - Marketing Opportunities
  - Tests of Concepts
  - Product Placements
- Product Quality Tests
- Governmental and Trade Information

Collection, Analysis, Interpretation, Cataloging

Reported Out

IRREGULARLY ISSUED REPORTS

- Advertising Quality
- Product Quality
- Basic Consumer Wants and Needs
- Bases for Segmentation
- Consumer and Market Reactions to Special Stimuli (e.g., promotions, products, packages, advertising)

BIMONTHLY OR QUARTERLY REPORTS

- Advertising Expenditure Estimates
- Food and Drugstore Syndicated Panel Audits of Inventory and Sales
- Periodic Consumer Surveys (awareness, attitude, usage)

In Storage, on Call

Reported Out

MONTHLY, BIMONTHLY, OR QUARTERLY REPORTS

- Consumer Awareness, Attitudes, Purchase, and Use
- Factory Sales and Inventory
- Wholesale Withdrawal Rates
- Retail Sales, Prices, Inventory, and Distribution
- Advertising Sales Relationships and Expense

DAILY, WEEKLY, OR MONTHLY REPORTS

- Special Store Audits
- Sales Accounting Reports
- Warehouse Withdrawal Reports
- Consumer Panel Reports
- Sales Call Reports

Marketing Intelligence Library of Primary and Secondary Data

Source: Lee Adler, "Systems Approach to Marketing," *Harvard Business Review,* vol. 45, no. 3, 1967, p. 111.

7. Market research.   The market research information subsystem provides "marketing intelligence" to help management make more effective marketing decisions. It also provides marketing management with information to help plan and control all of the research projects of the market research department of the business firm. The computer helps the market research activity provide marketing intelligence in an efficient, economical, and effective manner. The market research information subsystem utilizes the computer to collect, analyze, and maintain an enormous amount of information on a wide variety of market variables which are subject to continual change. Marketing intelligence is provided in the form of standard or "customized" reports and analyses which are generated periodically, on demand, or on an exception basis. The information input and output of the market research information system for a large corporation is shown in Figure 11–4.

Computer Applications in Retailing

The computer has traditionally been utilized by many retailers for one or more of the basic applications such as customer billing, accounts receivable, inventory control, general accounting, and payroll. The basic form of such applications have been discussed in the previous chapter and will not be repeated here. However, the computer is being utilized for more advanced applications in retailing which are based on several recent developments.

1. Point-of-sale terminals. Point-of-sale terminals are being utilized to provide one-time capture and recording of information as it becomes available throughout the retail organization. This substantially eliminates copying information, reduces transcription errors, and speeds the flow of information to management.

2. Scientific inventory management. Inventory management programs utilizing mathematical inventory models can increase the availability of merchandise while maintaining a minimum inventory.

3. Sales forecasting. Some retailers are using advanced methods of trend detection utilizing mathematical and statistical techniques which are tempered by management selected and weighted factors.

4. Management information systems. Retailers are developing information systems whose primary purpose is to provide management with better information for decision-making. Such systems feature "selective reporting" which provides the information analysis and the information needed at the required level of detail. Standard and customized reports are produced periodically, on demand, or when exceptional conditions occur. Figure 11–5 illustrates the basic components of a retail management information system. Figure 11–6 depicts a standard retail management report which analyzes the expenses and profit contribution for various product lines and retail

FIGURE 11–5

A Retail MIS

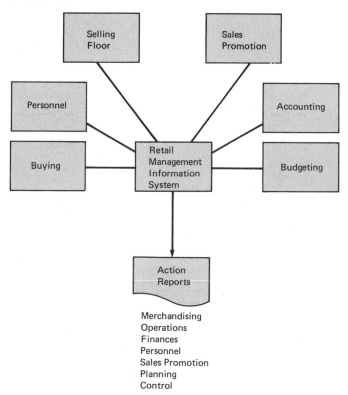

Source: *MIS for Retailers* (White Plains, N.Y.: IBM Corporation, 1970), p. 2.

FIGURE 11–6

A Retail Management Report Format

Dept.	Category	Line	Sales	Gross Margin		Com-mission Expense	Adver-tising Expense	Floor Space Expense	Direct Contribution	
				%	$				%	$

Source: Arthur M. Kramer and Lewis M. Weinstein, "How Computers can Help the Retail Merchandiser," *Management Services* (June 1966), p. 27.

FIGURE 11–7

A Customized Retail Management Report

```
EXPENSE CONTROL
PERFORMANCE                12 WEEKS ENDED 4/30/19-

    SALES PROMOTION
        NEWSPAPER LINAGE UP 21.0%
        DOLLAR COST UP 14.0%
    INITIAL ADVERTISING SCHEDULE CREATED 60% OF
    FORECASTED DEMAND IN PERIOD ENDED 2/28.
    REINSERTED DURING PERIOD ENDED 3/28. DEMAND
    WAS 115% OF REVISED FORECAST.

OPERATIONS
    RECEIVING EXPENSE UP 12.7%
    RECEIPTS 48% OF FORECAST DURING PERIOD ENDED
    2/28.
    OVERTIME EXPENSE $40,000 REQUIRED TO HANDLE
    INCREASED RECEIPTS DURING 6 WEEKS ENDED 4/16.
```

Source: *MIS for Retailers* (White Plains, N.Y.: IBM Corporation, 1970), p. 8.

departments. Figure 11–7 depicts the kind of "customized" management report that could be provided on demand to the on-line terminals of retail executives.

The Point-of-Sale Revolution

Computer-based retail information systems with on-line *point-of-sale terminals* in retail outlets is a major new computer application in retailing. Figure 11–8 illustrates a retail POS (Point-of-Sale) system. Most POS systems consist of several cash register-like terminals which are on-line to a data controller or data concentrator located somewhere in the store. The data controller could be a minicomputer with peripherals, or it can merely be a unit for storing transactions from the POS registers on magnetic tape and transmitting data over communication lines to a regional computer center.

In many POS systems, the "cash register" is an *intelligent terminal* which can guide the operator through each transaction, step by step. These terminals can also perform necessary arithmetic operations, such as tax, discount and total calculations. Some terminals permit on-line credit verification for credit transactions.

FIGURE 11–8

A Retail POS System

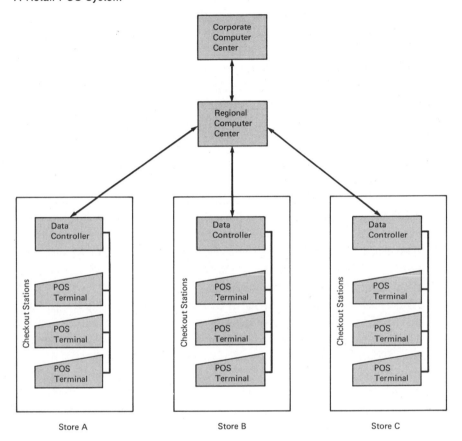

Most **POS** terminals can automatically read information from perforated tags or merchandise labels. Data on perforated tags is captured by inserting the tag into a reader. Hand-held "wands" or other optical reading devices are utilized by some terminals to scan the merchandise label and capture price and stock data. Data may be printed on the merchandise labels and tags in OCR or MICR characters or may utilize various optical, bar-coding methods. Several large retail chains are utilizing color bar-coded merchandise tags and labels which are read by optical wand readers. The grocery industry has agreed on a "universal product code" utilizing bar-coding on merchandise labels which will be scanned by optical reading devices in automated checkout counters, (see Figure 4–25 of Chapter 4).

As transactions are processed, they are usually recorded simultaneously on magnetic tape by an in-store data collector. Each night (or whenever desired) a central computer can "poll" the data collectors in the system. All transaction data for the day can be transmitted to the central computer in a matter of minutes and is then available for processing.

Benefits of POS systems. What are the benefits of retail POS systems? Obviously, POS terminals, data controllers, and other data communications hardware are expensive devices. However, tests by one large retail chain resulted in the following comparisons between a POS system and the previously used cash register system.[2]

1. The POS terminals cost 20 percent more than the cash registers they replaced.
2. It took only 40 seconds to complete a sales transaction on a POS terminal as opposed to 160 seconds on a conventional cash register.
3. The number of checkout registers could be reduced by 20 percent to 25 percent with a POS system. Checkout personnel requirements can also be reduced.
4. The POS terminal can perform functions either impossible or uneconomical on the conventional cash register (such as credit verification). It is estimated that more than 80 percent of the input data required by retail information systems can be captured by POS terminals.
5. Large retail stores which utilized a minicomputer as a communications controller allowed store managers to make on-line inquiries concerning merchandise availability and customer credit and to receive must faster reports on sales activity, merchandise replenishment, customer billing, clerk productivity, and store traffic.
6. POS terminals demonstrated greater accuracy, increased customer service, and a 50 percent reduction in personnel training time.

Large manufacturers of consumer products (such as food products, household products, and appliances) are counting on information systems utilizing POS terminals and on-line management terminals to reduce costs, increase efficiency, and improve management decisions. Figure 11–9 shows the computer-based management information system of a large consumer products manufacturer. One of the major benefits of such systems is their ability to produce advanced

---

[2] "The Terminal Takeover," *Infosystems* (March 1972), pp. 22–28.

FIGURE 11–9

An MIS for a Consumer Products Manufacturer-Retailer

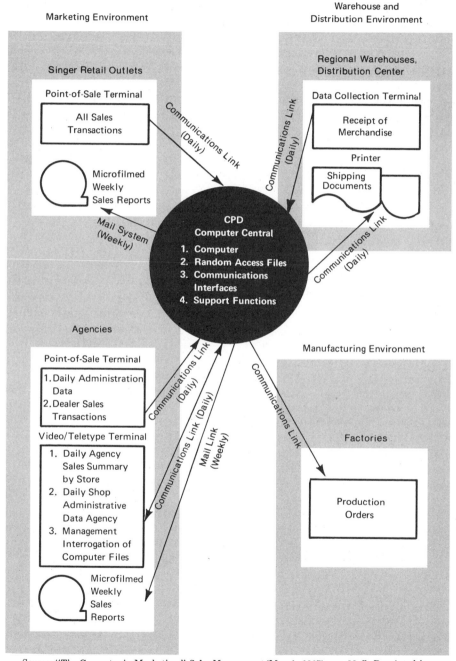

Source: "The Computer in Marketing," *Sales Management* (May 1, 1967), pp. 33 ff. Reprinted by permission from *Sales Management, The Marketing Magazine.*

types of *sales and advertising impact analysis* by quickly providing a detailed analysis of sales by store and product, as well as such vital merchandising facts as shelf life, shelf position, displays, and the promotions and displays of competitors.

Other Marketing Applications

There are many other applications of the computer in marketing. They are too numerous to discuss in much detail in this text. They range from complex pricing analysis applications to the more mundane production of promotional mailing lists. Other applications include product test marketing, advertising budget determination, advertising media determination, and the use of CRT terminals for on-line sales order processing, inventory control, and sales analysis. Many advanced computer applications utilize mathematical marketing models and operations research techniques. We will discuss computer applications in operations research in a later section of this chapter. Figure 11–10 summarizes several typical marketing applications and provides examples of the benefits which can result when the computer is applied to marketing.

FIGURE 11–10

Benefits of Computer-based Marketing Information Systems

	Typical applications	*Benefits*	*Examples*
Control Systems	1. Control of marketing costs.	1. More timely computerized reports.	1. Undesirable cost trends are spotted more quickly so that corrective action may be taken sooner.
	2. Diagnosis of poor sales performance	2. Flexible on-line retrieval of data.	2. Executives can ask supplementary questions of the computer to help pinpoint reasons for a sales decline and reach an action decision more quickly.
	3. Management of fashion goods.	3. Automatic spotting of problems and opportunities	3. Fast-moving fashion items are reported daily for quick reorder, and slow-moving items are also reported for fast price reductions.
	4. Flexible promotion strategy	4. Cheaper, more detailed, and more frequent reports.	4. On-going evaluation of a promotional campaign permits reallocation of funds to areas behind target.

	Typical applications		*Benefits*		*Examples*
Planning systems	1.	Forecasting	1.	Automatic translation of terms and classifications between departments.	1.	Survey-based forecasts of demand for complex industrial goods can be automatically translated into parts requirements and production schedules.
	2.	Promotional planning and corporate long-range planning.	2.	Systematic testing of alternative promotional plans and compatibility testing of various divisional plans.	2.	Complex simulation models both developed and operated with the help of data bank information can be used for promotional planning by product managers and for strategic planning by top management.
	3.	Credit management.	3.	Programmed executive decision rules can operate on data bank information.	3.	Credit decisions are automatically made as each order is processed.
	4.	Purchasing	4.	Detailed sales reporting permits automation of management decisions.	4.	Computer automatically repurchases standard items on the basis of correlation of sales data with programmed decision rules.
Research Systems	1.	Advertising strategy.	1.	Additional manipulation of data is possible when stored for computers in an unaggregated file.	1.	Sales analysis is possible by new market segment breakdowns.
	2.	Pricing strategy.	2.	Improved storage and retrieval capability allows new types of data to be collected and used.	2.	Systematic recording of information about past R &D contract bidding situations allows improved bidding strategies.
	3.	Evaluation of advertising expenditures.	3.	Well-designed data banks permit integration and comparison of different sets of data.	3.	Advertising expenditures are compared to shipments by county to provide information about advertising effectiveness.
	4.	Continuous experiments.	4.	Comprehensive monitoring of input and performance variables yields information when changes are made.	4.	Changes in promotional strategy by type of customer are matched against sales results on a continuous basis.

Source: Donald Cox and Robert Good, "How to Build a Marketing Information System," *Harvard Business Review*, vol. 45, no. 3, 1967, p. 146.

COMPUTER APPLICATIONS IN PRODUCTION/OPERATIONS

We have previously defined the *production/operations* function as a vital business function which includes all activities concerned with the planning, monitoring, and control of the processes that produce goods or services. Thus, the production/operations function is concerned with the management of the operational subsystems of all business firms, whether they are manufacturing companies or transportation, merchandising, or service companies. However, we will concentrate on manufacturing and physical distribution to illustrate the application of the computer to the production/operations function. A few examples of such applications should spotlight the dramatic impact of computer applications on the production/operations function.

Manufacturing Information Systems

Production/operations information systems in manufacturing companies can be called *"manufacturing information systems."* A manufacturing information system consists of both operational and management information systems. *Management information systems* in manufacturing are concerned with (1) production planning, (2) production control, (3) production inventory control, (4) purchasing, (5) physical distribution management, (6) production engineering management, and (7) facilities planning. These and other activities are frequently known as "production management" or "operations management."

Operational information systems in manufacturing include such subsystems as plant floor operations, plant communications, and process monitoring and control. Figure 11–11 illustrates some of the activities of several subsystems of a manufacturing information system. Figure 11–12 emphasizes the concept of "computer-aided manufacturing" (CAM) in which a central computer and several "subhost" minicomputers are utilized to automate the operational systems of a manufacturing plant.

A manufacturing information system can be subdivided into five major subsystems, such as[3]:

---

[3] Some of the material in this section has been adapted from *Consumer Goods Business Information System—Manufacturing* (White Plains, N.Y.: IBM Corporation, 1973), pp. 8–13.

FIGURE 11–11

Subsystems of a Manufacturing Information System

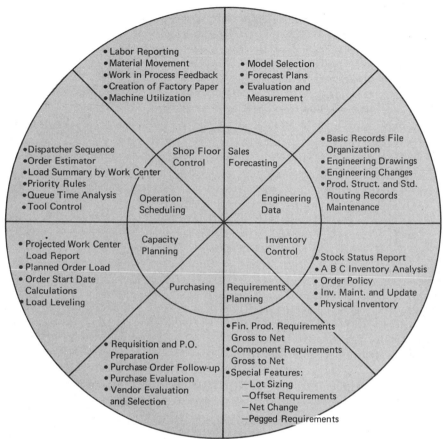

Source: *The Production Control and Information System* (White Plains, N.Y.: IBM Corporation, 1968), p. 14.

1. Production planning. This information subsystem assists in the development of a master production schedule and in the determination of long-range resource requirements such as cash, plant capacity, and material requirements. The master production schedule is based on many factors including long-range forecasts of sales and required production resources. Some of the subsystems of the production planning system are facilities planning, manpower planning, and resource requirements planning.

2. Production inventory management. This information subsystem "explodes" the master production schedule to determine specific material requirements. This system also coordinates the purchasing,

FIGURE 11-12

A Computer-aided Manufacturing (CAM) System

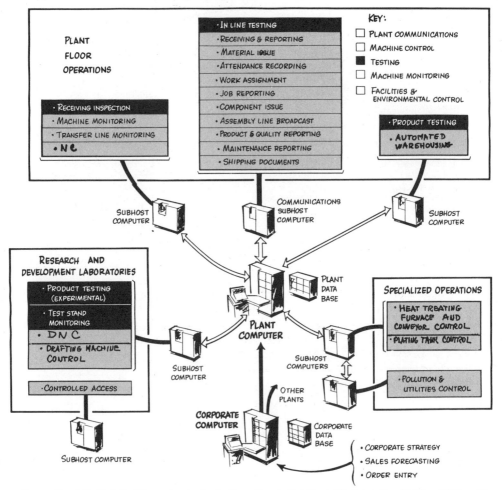

Source: Frank L. Stadulis, "Computers in Production—How to Get Started," *Automation* (October 1973), p. 24.

receiving, accounting, and storage activities required for proper production inventories.

3. Production scheduling. This subsystem provides the information required for the detailed scheduling of production which consists of assigning production starting dates, making short-range capacity adjustments, allocating materials from production inventories, and "releasing" production orders to the plant floor.

4. Production control. This information subsystem provides continuous information feedback to production management concerning labor, production, and maintenance by such reporting activities as labor reporting, machine-down time reporting, and production counts. Production control also includes the information subsystems required for "process control" which involves the direct monitoring and control of an on-going production process. Production control information subsystems also provide information for the "quality control" activity which involves the detection and analysis of deviations from production standards.

5. *Plant maintenance.* This subsystem provides management with information for maintenance planning, work order dispatching, maintenance costing, and preventive maintenance scheduling.

Benefits of Computer-based Manufacturing Systems

Some of the benefits of computer-based manufacturing information systems are listed below.

1. Increased efficiency due to better production schedule planning and better balancing of production workload to production capacity.
2. Improved utilization of production facilities, higher productivity, and better quality control resulting from continuous monitoring, feedback and control of plant operations.
3. Reduced investment in production inventories through better planning and control of production and finished goods requirements.
4. Improved customer service by reducing out-of-stock situations and producing products that better meet customer requirements.

Plant Communications

The *plant communications* information subsystem is a rapidly developing computer application that utilizes in-plant RDC (Remote Data Collection) terminals to capture the data generated by all production activities in a manufacturing plant. See Figure 11–13. RDC terminals are the manufacturing equivalent of the POS terminals utilized in retailing. (Refer back to Chapter 4 for more information on remote transaction recording terminals.) The plant communications subsystem provides management with strategic production information such as absent employees, variances in production yields, critical machine availability, and material shortages.

FIGURE 11–13

A Plant Communications Information System

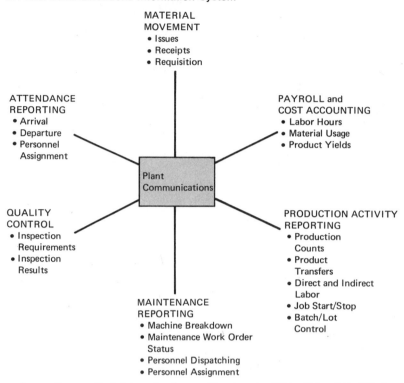

Source: *Consumer Goods Information System—Manufacturing* (White Plains, N.Y.: IBM Corporation, 1973), p. 36.

A computerized plant communications information subsystem can perform the following functions:

1. Controls access to the plant through badge identification.
2. Reports attendance and absences.
3. Reports production activity data such as job start, job stop, lot or badge identification, interruptions, personnel job assignments, and production counts.
4. Provides machine status reporting for plant maintenance such as machine breakdown, maintenance work order status and maintenance personnel assignments.
5. Provides material requisition notices to the production inventory subsystem.
6. Allows quality control personnel to quickly notify production

management of changes needed to correct substandard production conditions.

7. Allows plant management to receive instant responses to inquiries concerning production status.
8. When the remote terminals have a printing or CRT output capability, plant management can send instructions to foremen and supervisors on the production floor.

Process Control

We have previously described *process control* as the use of computers to control an on-going physical process. Process control can be considered as a subsystem of the production control system which controls a manufacturing or other industrial process. Process control computers are utilized to control physical processes in petroleum refineries, cement plants, steel mills, chemical plants, food product manufacturing plants, pulp and paper mills, electric power plants,

FIGURE 11–14

A Process Control Computer System

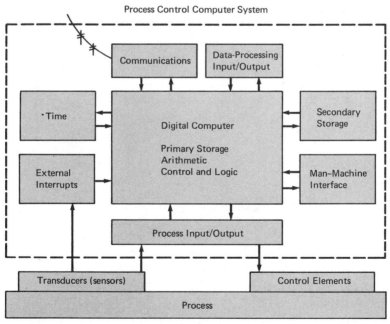

Source: Thomas Harrison, *Handbook of Industrial Control Computers* (New York: Wiley-Interscience, 1972), p. 12.

FIGURE 11–15

Process Plant Information System

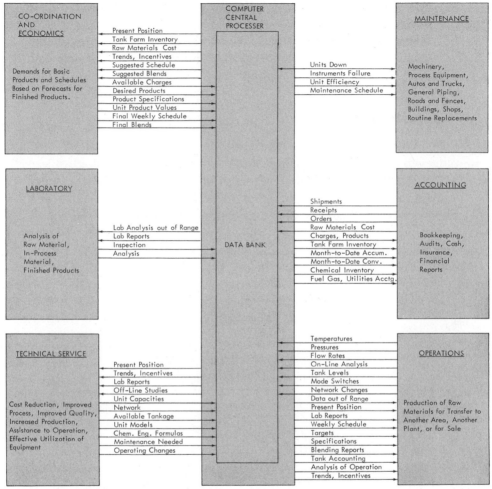

Source: Thomas Harrison, *Handbook of Industrial Control Computers* (New York: Wiley-Interscience, 1972), pp. 38–39.

etc. A process control computer system requires the use of special sensing devices that measure physical phenomena such as temperature or pressure changes. These continuous physical measurements are converted to digital form by analog-to-digital converters and relayed to the computer for processing. Process control computer programs utilize mathematical models to analyze the data generated by the on-going process and compare it to standards or forecasts of required results. Output of a process control system can take three forms:

1. Periodic reports analyzing the performance of the production process.
2. Messages and instructions which allow a human operator to control the process.
3. Direct control of the process by the use of control devices which control the process by adjusting thermostats, valves, switches, etc. See Figure 11–14.

Of course, the control of the physical process is just one subsystem of the information system utilized by industrial plants whose production involves continuous physical processes. Information subsystems must provide data for planning, scheduling, laboratory analysis, engineering support, maintenance, and accounting. Figure 11–15 illustrates the information flows of an information system for a "process plant."

Numerical Control

We have defined *numerical control* as the use of a computer to control the actions of a machine. (Refer back to Figure 4–28 which pictures a computer-controlled machine tool.) The control of machine tools in factories is a typical numerical control application,

FIGURE 11–16

A Numerical Control System

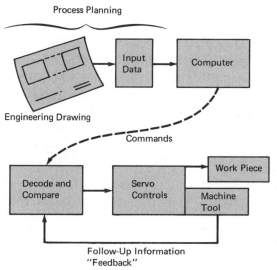

Source: From *Digital Computer Principles and Applications* by A. Favret © 1972 by Litton Educational Publishing, Inc.

though numerical control can also be used for typesetting machines, weaving machines, and other industrial "robots." Numerical control computer programs for machine tools convert geometric data from engineering drawings and machining instructions from process planning into a numerical code of commands which controls the actions of a machine tool. See Figure 11–16. Numerical control is usually accomplished off-line by using special paper tape or magnetic tape units which utilize the output of a computer to direct a machine. "Direct numerical control" is a type of numerical control involving the on-line control of machines by a computer.

Computer-aided Design

The geometric equations describing a part that requires machining may have been stored in the computer as the result of another type of computer application called *"computer-aided design."* Engineers and designers can utilize graphic CRT terminals and light pens to design parts, products, or structures with the computer furnishing previously stored specifications data and special design programs. The computer translates such "rough drawings" into updated design specifications and displays the resulting "finished drawing" on the CRT. (Refer back to Figure 4–20 in Chapter 4.)

Physical Distribution Information Systems

A major activity of the production/operations function is known as *"physical distribution."* Physical distribution is concerned with moving raw materials to the factory and moving products from the production floor to the ultimate consumer. Physical distribution involves a "distribution network" which connects raw material sources, manufacturing plants, warehouses, middle men, wholesale and retail outlets, and customers. It also involves the storage, transfer, and transportation of goods from manufacturer to customer.

Physical distribution information systems which support various physical distribution activities are frequently computerized. The major subsystems of a physical distribution information system are summarized below.[4]

---

[4] Part of this section is adapted from *Consumer Goods Business Information System—Physical Distribution* (White Plains, N.Y.: IBM Corporation, 1973), pp. 11–13.

FIGURE 11–17 An Advanced Inventory Control Information System

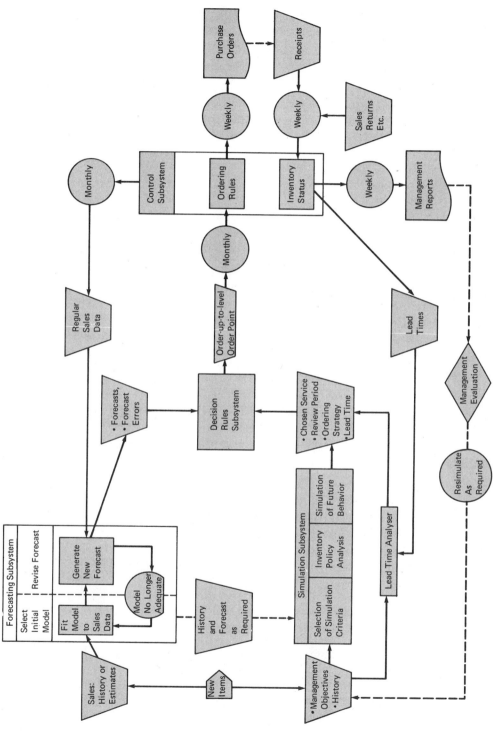

Source: *Retail IMPACT—Inventory Management and Control Techniques* (White Plains, N.Y.: IBM Corporation, 1970), p. 8.

1.   Physical distribution planning.   This information subsystem provides information for the planning of the physical distribution system of a business firm. Short and long-range plans must be developed which specify the structure and operations of the distribution network of a firm. Mathematical models may be used to analyze alternative distribution networks by considering such factors as customer characteristics, manufacturing locations and capabilities, the number and location of warehouses, processing and inventory management policies, and alternative transportation arrangements.

2.   Finished goods inventory control.   A basic model of this system was described in the previous chapter. It must process inventory data and provide information to assist management in minimizing inventory costs and improving customer service. Figure 11–17 illustrates an advanced inventory control information system for large retail firms. This system utilizes mathematical decision rules, forecasting models, and simulation techniques to generate inventory replenishment decisions and various management reports.

3.   Distribution center management.   This information subsystem supports the management and operations of "distribution centers" which consist of warehouses, shipping and receiving terminals, and other distribution support facilities. The objective of this system is to process data and provide information to assist management in the effective utilization of warehousing, shipping, and receiving personnel, facilities, and equipment, while maintaining a high level of customer service.

4.   Traffic management.   This information subsystem supports the daily planning and control of the movement of the products within the distribution network of a firm. It must provide information required for the scheduling of transportation requirements, the tracking of freight movement, the audit of freight bills, and the determination of efficient and economical methods of transportation.

Purchasing and Receiving

Purchasing and receiving is a traditional production/operations activity which has been computerized in large business firms. The purchasing and receiving information subsystem provides information to insure availability of the correct quantity and quality of the required materials at the lowest possible price. The purchasing subsystem assists in the selection of suppliers, placement of orders, and the follow-up activities to insure on-time delivery of materials. The

FIGURE 11–18

A Purchasing Information System

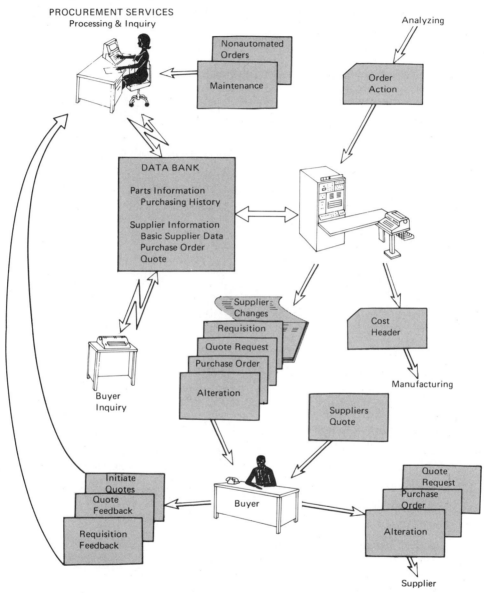

Source: Joseph F. Kelley, *Computerized Management Information Systems* (New York: The Macmillan Company, 1970), p. 155.

receiving subsystem identifies and validates the receipt of materials and routes the received material to its proper destination in storage or on the production floor. Figure 11–18 illustrates a computerized purchasing information system.

Other Production/Operations Applications

The computer has been applied to many of the activities and information subsystems of production/operations in addition to those previously mentioned in this section. Information systems which support the activities of engineers and scientists in production/operations planning and control or the research and development function are frequently considered to be production/operations subsystems and are frequently computerized. For example, computers are utilized for engineering design and specifications development, bill of materials preparation, research and development project control, process control of research experiments, quality control measurement and reporting, etc. Some operations research applications and scientific applications could also be categorized as production/operations application. For example, computerized scheduling and queueing applications are frequently utilized for production/operations problems.

COMPUTER APPLICATIONS IN FINANCE

Computer applications in *finance* involve the use of computers in financial information systems, accounting information systems, and in industries which perform a financial function in our economy. For example, computers are utilized in financial subsystems such as cash management and capital budgeting, accounting subsystems such as accounts receivable and accounts payable, and in the banking and securities industries.

Financial Information Systems

We have defined *financial information systems* as information systems which support management in decisions concerning the financing of the business and the allocation and control of financial resources within the business firm. Major financial information systems include cash management, portfolio management, credit management, capital budgeting, financial forecasting, financing requirements analysis, and financial performance analysis. Accounting information systems are also frequently included as a major group of financial information subsystems. Figure 11–19 illustrates that the financial performance analysis subsystem ties together the other financial information subsystems to produce financial planning and control information. The major financial information subsystems are summarized below.

1. Cash management. This subsystem collects information on all cash receipts and disbursements throughout a company on a real-time or periodic basis. Such information allows business firms to deposit or invest excess funds more quickly and thus increase the income generated by deposited or invested funds. This subsystem also produces daily, weekly, or monthly forecasts of cash receipts or disbursements (cash flow forecasts) which are utilized to spot future cash deficits or cash surpluses. Mathematical models may be utilized to determine optimum cash collection programs and to determine alternative financing or investment strategies for dealing with forecasted cash deficits or surpluses.

2. Portfolio management. Many business firms invest their excess cash in short-term marketable securities (such as U.S. Treasury bills, commercial paper, or certificates of deposit) so that investment income may be earned until the funds are required. The "portfolio" of such securities must be managed by buying, selling, or holding each

FIGURE 11–19

Financial Information Systems

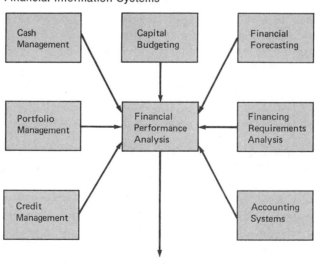

FINANCIAL
PLANNING and CONTROL
INFORMATION

type of security so that an optimum "mix" of securities is developed which minimizes risk and maximizes investment income. Computerized portfolio management involving stocks, bonds, and other marketable securities will be discussed in a later section.

3. *Credit management.* Computerized credit management information systems utilize data generated by the accounts receivable subsystem and additional data stored in a master customer data file to plan and control the extension of credit to the customers of a firm. The subsystem provides information which is utilized to control credit operations and evaluate proposed credit policies in order to minimize bad debt losses and investment in accounts receivable while maximizing sales and profitability. Advanced information systems of this type utilize the computer to automate the "screening" of credit applications and the decision to accept or reject a credit application.

4. *Capital budgeting.* This subsystem provides information utilized to evaluate the profitability and financial impact of proposed capital expenditures. Large, long-term expenditure proposals can be analyzed utilizing a variety of computer-based analytical techniques such as present value analysis and probability analysis.

5. *Financial forecasting.* This subsystem provides information and analytical techniques which result in economic or financial forecasts such as national and local economic conditions, wage levels, price levels, interest rates, etc. This information subsystem is obviously heavily dependent on data gathered from the external environment and the utilization of various mathematical models and forecasting techniques.

6. *Financing requirements analysis.* This information system supports the analysis of alternative methods of financing the business. Information concerning the economic situation, business operations, the types of financing available, interest rates, and stock and bond prices are utilized to develop an optimum financing plan for the business.

7. *Accounting systems.* Several types of accounting systems have been discussed in the previous chapter and will be discussed further in an upcoming section.

8. *Financial performance analysis.* This major information subsystem utilizes data provided by accounting systems and other financial information systems to evaluate and control present financial performance and to formulate short and long-range plans based upon their effect on projected financial performance. Advanced systems utilize "financial performance models" which allow management to evaluate the effect of various proposals on the revenues, cost, and

profitability of the business firm. This subsystem will be covered in more detail in the next section.

Financial Performance Models

Advanced computer applications in finance utilize mathematical techniques and models for such applications as cash management, portfolio management, and capital budgeting. A more recent develop-

FIGURE 11–20

A Financial Performance Model

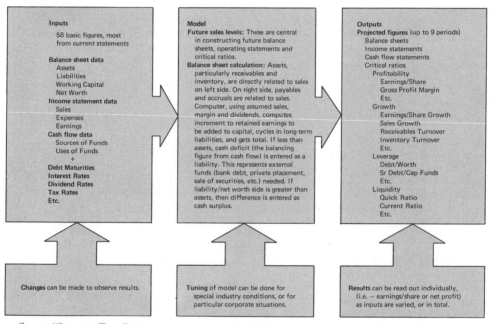

Source: "Successes Turn Detractors to Computer-Methods Converts," *Computer Decisions* (January 1972), p. 40.

ment is the use of computerized financial models which analyze the financial performance of the entire business firm or one of its divisions or subsidiaries. Figure 11–20 illustrates the components of a *financial performance model* of a business firm while Figure 11–21 illustrates how the financial model fits into the decision-making processes of business management. Computerized financial performance models are utilized for the following purposes:

1. To control the present performance by analyzing and evaluating current operations in comparison to budgeted objectives.
2. To plan the short and long-range operations of the firm by

evaluating the effect of alternative proposals on the financial performance of the firm.

3. To determine the future financing requirements and the optimum types of financing required to finance alternative proposals.

The model shown in Figure 11–20 is utilized by a large bank to evaluate the financial performance and financing needs of business firms who are prospective borrowers of bank funds. The model

FIGURE 11–21

Management Decision Making with a Financial Performance Model

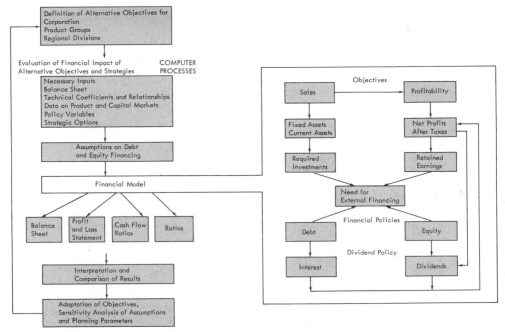

Source: "A New Breed of Financial Systems Is Coming," Reprinted from *Computer Decisions*, January, 1972, p. 27, © 1972, Hayden Publishing Company.

utilizes 58 basic financial figures as input and can produce major financial statements and critical financial ratios as output. Adjustments can be made to input or to the model itself to take into account the characteristics of particular situations, business firms, or industries. Even more advanced computerized financial performance models are now being utilized by a few firms. A large oil company has utilized a financial performance model that consists of about 2,000 mathematical equations and requires 1500 input items while producing 5,200 output figures in 61 reports.[5]

---

[5] George Gershefski, "Building a Corporate Financial Model," *Harvard Business Review* (July–August 1969), pp. 47–53.

Accounting Information Systems

We have previously mentioned that *accounting information systems* are the oldest and most widely used business information systems. *Operational accounting systems* emphasize legal and historical record-keeping and the production of accurate financial statements. *Management accounting systems* focus on the planning and control of business operations through the development of financial budgets and projected financial statements. In the previous chapter, we described the major accounting information systems of accounts receivable, accounts payable, and general accounting. Other accounting information systems are summarized below.

1. *Property accounting* is concerned with the physical control and the financial recordkeeping caused by the use and depreciation of fixed assets.
2. *Cost accounting* is concerned with the accumulation and apportionment of costs within a business firm. For example, costs must be grouped into specific cost categories and attributed to specific products, projects, departments, etc.
3. *Tax accounting* is concerned with the recording and payment of business taxes such as income taxes, sales taxes, inventory taxes, etc.
4. *Budgeting* is concerned with the development of forecasts of expected performance for future time periods for each department or division of the firm. Budgets are short-term planning and control devices which contain revenue and expense projections and other estimates of expected performance for the firm or its subdivisions.

Figure 11–22 provides an overview of the relationships of various accounting information systems.

Applications in Banking

Computers have had a major impact on the *banking industry*. The computer has not only affected the accounting and reporting operations required by traditional bank services but has influenced the form and extent of all such services and made possible a variety of new "computer services." The computer is playing an even more decisive role in the operation of many banks through its use in financial models and other management science applications.

Traditional and new bank services that are computerized include:

FIGURE 11–22 Accounting Information Systems

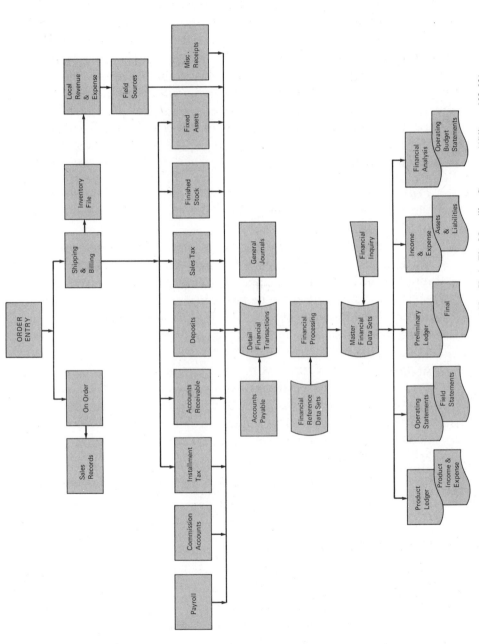

Source: Joseph F. Kelly, *Computerized Management Information Systems* (New York: The Macmillan Company, 1970), pp. 200–201.

1. Demand deposit accounting. This application concerns the automation of checking account processing. This was the first and most widely utilized computer application in banking. It depends heavily on the use of MICR coded checks and deposit slips and the use of MICR reader-sorters to automate the capture of input data. Output of this system includes control transactions listings, master accounts listings, special reports concerning such items as new accounts, closed accounts, overdrawn accounts, etc., and monthly customer statements. See Figure 11–23.

2. Savings. Most banks have some form of computerized savings account processing. Some banks still use batch processing systems to process deposits and withdrawals and post them to their proper ac-

FIGURE 11–23

The Demand Deposit Accounting Application

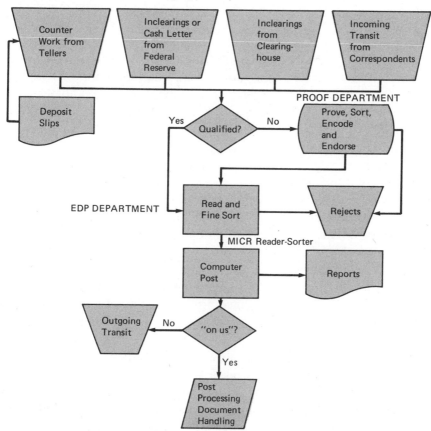

Source: James A. O'Brien, *The Impact of Computers on Banking* (Boston: Bankers Publishing Co. 1968), p. 42.

counts on a daily basis. Other banks utilize a real-time savings application which utilizes data communications terminals at the teller's windows which are electronically linked to the computers in the bank. Such systems automatically update a customer's balance on the computer while it is updating his passbook or other transaction document. Mutual savings banks and savings and loan associations are other major users of computers for real-time savings applications.

3. *Consumer, commercial, and mortgage loans.* Banks have computerized many aspects of the data processing required by their lending activities to consumers and business firms. The widespread development of bank credit card plans has greatly increased the use of computers to process the multitude of transactions generated by millions of bank credit card holders. Banks also lend money on a long-term basis for real estate mortgages and are the major source of short-term credit for many business firms. Most banks utilize punched card, MICR, or OCR source documents to automate the capture of input transaction data into their computerized loan systems. Output of this application includes transaction lists, trial balances of loan accounts, monthly customer statements, delinquency notices, interest and tax reports, and various loan analysis reports.

4. *Trust applications.* The trust function of banks involves the management of corporate trusts, personal trusts, pension funds, and health and welfare funds. The computer is utilized to handle a wide variety of accounting chores and produce management reports and legal documents. Advanced trust applications involve the use of computerized security analysis and portfolio selection applications which will be discussed in a following section.

5. *Computer services.* Many banks are offering computer services to their customers that are quite different from the traditional banking services. Through the use of computers, banks are offering a wide variety of services to other banks and financial institutions, business and professional firms, government and public organizations, and individuals. Some banks have "spun-off" their EDP departments into separate EDP service subsidiaries that compete with independent computer service bureaus. Banks offering computer services must operate within specific legal restrictions but still manage to offer a wide variety of services. See Figure 11–24.

6. *Advanced applications.* Many large banks are utilizing computerized financial performance models for internal planning and control and to evaluate the financial condition and financing requirements of bank customers. Banks are utilizing many other tools of

FIGURE 11–24

Bank Computer Services

Financial Institution Services
   Savings bank and savings and loan association accounting
      Savings
      Mortgage loan
   Credit union accounting
      Share accounting
      Installment loan
      Mortgage loan
   Mortgage company accounting
   Insurance company accounting
   Finance company accounting
   Mutual fund accounting
   Securities broker accounting
Services to Business and Professional Firms
   Account reconciliation
   Payroll accounting
   Billing service
   Accounts receivable accounting
   Accounts payable accounting
   Freight plans
   Lock box plans including the preparation of input for the customer's
      computer system
   Bill collection for utilities, insurance companies, and other businesses
   General accounting for small businesses
   Cost accounting
   General ledger
   Sales analysis
   Expense analysis
   Inventory control
   Integrated systems for particular industry groups
   Property management accounting
   Computer time rental
   Computer program "packages"
   EDP systems analysts and programmer services
Services to Government and Public Organizations
   County and municipal governments
      Real property tax billing and collection
      Municipal services billing
   Public schools
      Class scheduling
      General accounting

Source: James A. O'Brien, *Managing and Marketing Bank Computer Services* (Boston: Warren, Gorham, & Lamont, Inc., 1971), pp. 15–16.

operations research that require the computational power of the computer. The computer will also be the primary component of a future "cashless-checkless society" where *electronic funds transfer systems* (EFTS) replace cash and checks as the primary method of payment. The banking industry is in the forefront of efforts to develop the hardware, software, and procedures required by EFTS systems.

Applications in Investments

Computers have been used by firms in the *investment industry* for many years to perform "back office operations," that is, recording transactions, billing customers, preparing monthly statements, etc. More recent applications of the computer in the investment industry are summarized below.[6]

1. Stock exchange automation.   The stock exchanges and other organizations in the investment industry are moving towards the automation of the stock exchange function. Stock sale transactions completed on the floor of a stock exchange are now recorded on OCR documents and read by optical scanners at each "trading post." The transaction data (stock symbol, number of shares, and price) are transmitted to the computer center of the exchange which records the transaction and transmits the information to stock tickers and visual display terminals throughout the country. Transactions in 100 share lots ("round lots") between stock exchange member firms and stock exchange "specialists" can be automatically executed by the computer.

Real-time computer-based information networks have been developed to facilitate the exchange of information between securities brokers, dealers, and large institutional investors. The National Association of Securities Dealers (NASD) operates a nationwide real-time computer-based information network for over-the-counter (OTC) stocks called NASDAQ. See Figure 11–25. Establishment of a central depository for stock certificates and a common number code for securities (CUSIP) are enabling New York clearinghouse banks and brokerage firms to deliver securities by automated bookkeeping entries, rather than through actual physical delivery. These and other developments are moving us towards the day of a centralized nationwide computerized central market for all securities trading.

2. Financial information retrieval.   Investment advisory service companies now provide the investment industry with computerized data banks, computer developed reports, and specialized time-sharing services. A major source of computerized investment data is "Compustat" which was developed by Standard and Poor's and is now maintained by a subsidiary, Investor's Management Sciences Incorporated. Compustat data is available in the form of magnetic tapes or through a number of time-sharing services. See Figure 11–26.

---

[6] Some of the material in this section is adapted from Jerome B. Cohen, Edward D. Zinbarg, and Arthur Zeikel, *Investment Analysis and Portfolio Management,* (Homewood, Ill.: Richard D. Irwin, Inc., 1973), pp. 66–67, 106–108, 134–38, 837–41.

FIGURE 11–25 The NASDAQ Stock Quotation System

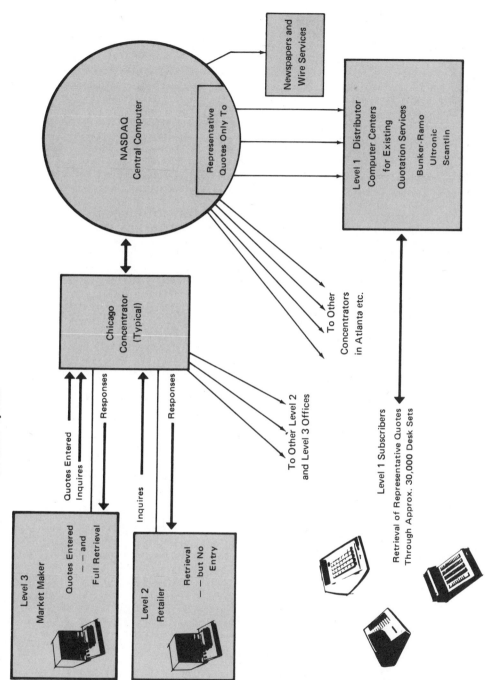

Source: Information Services Division, Bunker-Ramo Corporation.

FIGURE 11–26

Contents of the Compustat Data Files

Annual Industrial Files

— Balance Sheet —	— Income Statement —	— Other Data —
Cash and Equivalent	*Net Sales	*Stock Price – High
Receivables	Unconsolidated Subsidiaries Remitted Earns.	*Stock Price – Low
Inventories	Cost of Goods Sold	*Stock Price – Close
Total Current Assets	Labor & Related Costs	*Dividends Per Share
Investments & Advances to Subsidiaries	Pension & Retirement Expenses	*Adjustment Factor
Investments & Advances to Others	Incentive Compensation Expenses	Number of Common Shares Traded
Gross Plant	Selling & Advertising Expenses	Amount of Convertible Debt & Preferred Stock
Net Plant	Research & Development Expenses	Number of Common Shares
*Intangibles	Rental Expenses	Reserved for Conversion
Total Assets/Liabilities	Operating Income	Number of Common Shares
Debt in Current Liabilities	*Depreciation and Amortization	Purchased/Sold—Net
Total Current Liabilities	*Fixed Charges	Total Future Tax Credits
*Long-Term Debt	*Minority Interest	Unconsolidated Subsidiaries—Excess Equity
*Deferred Taxes & Investment Credit	*Deferred Taxes	Unconsolidated Subsidiaries—
*Minority Interest	Investment Credit (U.S. Files Only)	Unremitted Earnings
*Preferred Stock (Involuntary)	*Income Taxes	Diluted Earnings Per Share—
Preferred Stock at Redemption Value	Non-Recurring Income or Expenses	Excluding Extra. Items
*Common Equity	(Not Net of Taxes)	*Earnings Per Share—Excluding Extra. Items
*Total Invested Capital	*Net Income	Capital Expenditures
*Number of Common Shares Outstanding	*Preferred Dividends	Inventory Valuation
	*Available for Common	Inventory Cost
	*Common Dividends	Number of Employees
	Non-Recurring Income or Expenses	Exchange Rate (Canadian File Only)
	(Net of Taxes)	

*Included in OTC File (1960 through 1967).

Quarterly Industrial File

— Income Statement —	— Other Data —	
Net Sales	Monthly Closing Price	12 Month Moving EPS—
Operating Income Before Depreciation	(1st, 2nd & 3rd of Quarter)	Excluding Extra. Items
Depreciation and Amortization	Dividends Per Share	Number of Shares Used to Calculate
Fixed Charges	Indicated Annual Dividend	Quarterly EPS
Pretax Income	Adjustment Factor	Number of Shares Used to Calculate
Income Taxes	EPS—Including Extra. Items	12 Month Moving EPS
Net Income	EPS—Excluding Extra. Items	Number of Common Shares Traded
Preferred Dividends	Diluted EPS—Including Extra. Items	Report Date of Quarterly EPS
Available for Common Before Adjustments	Diluted EPS—Excluding Extra. Items	
for Common Stock Equivalents		
Available for Common		
Extra. Items		

Annual Utility File

— Balance Sheet —	— Income Statement —	— Other Data —
Gross Plant	Operating Revenues	Electric Sales—KWH
Total Assets	Cost of Gas Purchased	Residential
Common Stock & Surplus	Maintenance Expense	Commercial
Preferred Stock	Total Operating Expense	Total
Mortgage Debt	Depreciation, Depletion and Amortization	Average Residential Usage—KWH
Long-Term Debt	Federal Income Taxes	Gas Sales—MMCF
Short-Term Debt	Deferred Income Taxes	Residential
Reserve for Depreciation	Net Operating Income	Commercial
and Amortization	Gross Income	Total
Reserve for Deferred Taxes	Charges in Lieu of Income Taxes	Average Residential Usage—MCF
Common Equity	Available for Fixed Charges	Customers
Total Invested Capital	Interest Charges	Electric Residential
Number of Shares Outstanding	Interest Credits	Gas Residential
	Total Fixed Charges	Residential Gas Space Heating
	Net Income	Construction Expenditures
	Preferred Dividends	Plant Retirements
	Available for Common	Total Generating Capability
	Common Dividends	Peak Load
	Flow-Through Tax Savings	Stock Price
	Restricted Surplus re Deferred Taxes	High
	Electric Revenues	Low
	Residential	Close
	Commercial	Dividends per Share
	Total	Adjustment Factor
	Gas Revenues	Number of Shares Traded
	Residential	Total Convertible Debt & Preferred
	Commercial	No. of Shares Reserved for Conversion
	Total	

Source: Compustat: Investors Management Sciences, Inc.

FIGURE 11–27   Financial Data Bases for Investment Analysis

CAPABILITIES

ON-LINE DATA BASES & SYSTEMS

Interactive specializes in providing its subscribers with large-scale, on-line data bases and proprietary processing programs to enable them to monitor, access, and display this information.

The on-line data bases and processing programs are oriented primarily to the financial and economic communities. They are used by Finance, Acquisition, and Treasury Departments within Banks, Brokerage Houses, Insurance Companies, and other financial institutions; and by Economists and Economic Business Forecasting Departments — to assist them in making better business decisions and in reducing related costs.

An *Interactive Account Representative* will be pleased to discuss these data bases and processing programs in more detail.

DATA BASES

The Securities' Price Data Base

- Daily since January 1968; price and volume data for all New York and American Stock Exchange Common Stocks and 1800 Over-the-Counter Stocks; Split factors resulting from capitalization changes are also indicated
- Daily market indexes on
  — New York Stock Exchange
  — American Stock Exchange
  — Dow Jones Industrial, Transportation & Utilities
  — Standard & Poor's 425 and 500

The Corporate Financial Data Base [1]

- Sixty annual items from balance sheets, income statements and company ratios for the past twenty years on 1800 key industrial companies and utilities
- Sixteen quarterly financial items plus monthly price information for the past ten years for 1800 key industrial companies.

The Financial XSPERT™ Data Bases

- all daily stock return from the New York and American Stock Exchanges for the past eight years
- monthly returns for 230 mutual funds for the past ten years

The XTICK [2] Data Base

Provide data on trading throughout the day with summary and transaction data for the current trading day for every security listed on the New York and American Stock Exchange tickers (15 minutes delayed per Exchange regulations). Closing prices are available shortly after 4:00 PM each day.

The Bond Data Base

- Daily price and volume information on over 1800 bonds traded on the New York and American Stock Exchanges.

The Split and Dividend Data Base

- Daily information on all New York and American Stock Exchange stocks and 1800 Over-the-Counter stocks.
- Accessible by stock symbol or ex-date
- Ex-date, record date, payable date and type of distribution available

The Economic Data Base [3]

- Weekly, monthly, quarterly, and annual time-series describing more than six thousand separate economic variables. This data, which highlights a wide variety of U.S. economic indicators, is grouped as follows:

  — National Income and Product Accounts
  — Gross National Product and Components by Industry
  — U.S. Balance of International Payments Accounts
  — New Plant and Equipment Expenditures
  — Retail and Wholesale Trade and Inventory by Type of Store
  — Manufacturers' Shipments, Inventories, and Orders
  — Profit and Loss Statements and Balance Sheet Data for Manufacturing Corporations
  — Measures of Economic Activity in 425 Manufacturing Sectors
  — Selected Business Indicators and Product Line Statistics
  — Federal Reserve Board Production Indexes
  — Population; Labor Force: Employment, Hours, and Earnings by Industry
  — Consumer and Wholesale Prices Indexes
  — Monetary Statistics
  — Weekly Statistics

Private Data Bases

- Subscribers may create their own private data bases containing any information which they wish to enter. This data can then be analyzed independently or in conjunction with data maintained in the above data bases.

Interactive Data Corporation
486 Totten Pond Road
Waltham, Massachusetts 02154

THE PROCESSING SYSTEMS

Interactive's Processing Systems access the above data bases and analyze and prepare reports in a wide variety of formats. The processing systems are easy to learn and use and generally require no previous computer experience.

ANALYSTICS® II [4]

Information in the Securities' Price, Corporate Financial, Economic, and Private Data Bases may be analyzed and displayed by the following Analytics II Processing Systems:

- First Financial Language screens and displays financial information
- RGR/360[5] performs a variety of statistical functions
- XSTAT[6] computes statistical and other functions

XPORT II [7]

XPORT II is a time shared, on-line portfolio appraisal system which allows subscribers immediate access to up-to-date portfolio reports and portfolio management information. In addition, it conveniently produces appraisals, transaction journals, Schedule D information, performance reports, and security inventory lists. Portfolios can be valuated based on data from either the Securities' Price or XTICK Data Bases.

The Portfolio Performance Monitor gives the Portfolio Manager the ability to monitor the performance of his portfolios and to compare the performance of his managed portfolios with unmanaged index portfolios.

XTICK

Accessing the XTICK Data Base, XTICK provides traders and money managers with the ability to monitor and analyze stock market transactions as they occur. XTICK displays information on past transactions and continuously updated summary statistics.

XSPERT

Reading the financial XSPERT Data Bases, XSPERT measures the risk and return of adding additional securities to a portfolio. It also assists to evaluate buy and sell recommendations and to compare portfolio performance to the monthly returns of over 200 mutual funds.

IAL [8] (Investment Analysis Language)

IAL is a set of computer routines which translate financial, statistical, and computer science concepts into a set of interlocking commands. The language assists a FORTRAN programmer in preparing a wide variety of financial analysis programs.

Special Accessing Routines

Interactive also provides special accessing routines which can be incorporated in conventional FORTRAN, COBOL, and Assembly Language programs to access the above data bases. This means that subscribers are not restricted to *Interactive's* proprietary processing systems in order to analyze financial and economic data.

OTHER INTERACTIVE SERVICES

Interactive Data Corporation offers other specialized services as well as general time sharing services. The Capabilities Sheet "SUMMARY OF INTERACTIVE SERVICES" describes these services, *Interactive's* computer system, and system software.

– – – – – –

[1] Interactive obtains data for the Corporate Financial Data Base from the Compustat® Service of Investors Management Sciences, Inc., a subsidiary of Standard & Poor's Corporation, New York, New York.

[2] XTICK is a servicemark of Interactive Data Corporation.

[3] The Economic Data Base is owned by its creator, Lionel D. Edie & Company, Incorporated, New York, New York, which distributes it exclusively on Interactive's computers.

[4] ANALYSTICS is a registered servicemark of Interactive Data Corporation.

[5] Both the program and the servicemark RGR are owned by the Boston Company Investment Research and Technology, Inc., Boston, Massachusetts.

[6] XSTAT was developed for Interactive by Dynamics Associates, Inc., Cambridge, Massachusetts.

[7] XPORT is a servicemark of Interactive Data Corporation.

[8] IAL and its programs are provided by the American Bankers Association, New York, New York.

Source: Interactive Data Corporation.

FIGURE 11–28

Output of a Security Analysis Application

```
MINNESOTA MINING AND MANUFACTURING       OFFICE EQUIPMENT
YEAR     HIGH      LOW        EPS      DIVIDEND
 57     33.000    19.000    0.780      0.400
 58     38.000    24.000    0.860      0.400
 59     60.000    37.000    1.250      0.500
 60     88.000    53.000    1.380      0.580
 61     87.000    66.000    1.460      0.650      A
 62     70.000    41.000    1.610      0.800
 63     73.000    52.000    1.730      0.900
 64     70.000    54.000    1.920      1.000
 65     71.000    54.000    2.180      1.100
 66     86.000    61.000    2.590      1.200
 67            83.880 (CURRENT)  2.750(EST)  1.450(EST)
MINNESOTA MINING AND MANUFACTURING       OFFICE EQUIPMEN 10 YEARS OF DATA
PROJECTED AND CURRENT PRICE                       EARNINGS GROWTH RATES
   1-10        108.08                        1-4       23.19
   6-1          90.10    B                    4-7        8.07    C
   8-10         88.82                         7-10      14.31
   CURRENT      83.88

PROJECTED 5 YEAR PRICE                          EARNING GROWTH RATES
   1-10        176.52                           1-10      13.05
   6-10        144.57    D                       6-10      12.55    E
   8-10        161.62                            8-10      16.14

AVERAGE AND CURRENT PRICE-EARNINGS RATIO     PROJECTED CURRENT EARNINGS AND ESTIMATED CURRENT EARNINGS
  10 YEAR      37.16                            1-10       2.91
   5 YEAR      31.97                            6-10       2.82
   3 YEAR      29.75    F                       8-10       2.99    G
  CURRENT      30.50                         ESTIMATED      2.75

5 YEAR HIGH AND LOW PRICE-EARNINGS RATIO
AVERAGE HIGH AND LOW PRICE-EARNINGS RATIO       PROJECTED LAST YEARS EARNINGS AND ACTUAL EARNINGS
  HIGH           59.59                            10 YEARS      2.57
  LOW            23.55                             5 YEARS      2.50
  HIGH AVERAGE   41.25    H                        3 YEARS      2.57    I
  LOW AVERAGE    29.53                             ACTUAL       2.59
                                                                       K
AVERAGE YIELD AND CURRENT YIELD               GROWTH RATE STABILITY=        92.10
  10 YEAR     1.34                             MAXIMUM EARNINGS DEVIATION=           1.15
   5 YEAR     1.69                                                                        L
   3 YEAR     1.67    J                        MINIMUM EARNINGS DEVIATION=           0.89
  CURRENT     1.73

                     10 YEAR PRICE
            EARNINGS      EARNINGS                          CURRENT   YIELD TO
            GROWTH        RATIO        EARNINGS  PRICE     YIELD     MATURITY
10 YEAR                                                                        M
  RATE  13.05            37.16           4.75    176.52    1.28      21.00
 3 YEAR
  RATE  16.14            37.16           5.43    201.88    1.28      25.07    N
                    CURRENT PRICE
            EARNINGS      EARNINGS
            GROWTH        RATIO
 3 YEAR
  RATE  16.14            30.50           5.43    165.70    1.56      19.15    O

10 YEAR
  RATE  13.05            30.50           4.75    144.89    1.56      15.29
                                                                            P
```

Source: Frederick Amling, *Investments: An Introduction to Analysis and Management* (New York: Prentice-Hall, 1970), p. 216.

A major source of on-line time-sharing investment information is provided by specialized time-sharing services such as Interactive Data Corporation. IDC maintains a number of large-scale financial data bases and a variety of software packages which provide valuable information and analytical techniques for security analysis. See Figure 11–27.

FIGURE 11–29

Integrated Portfolio Management System

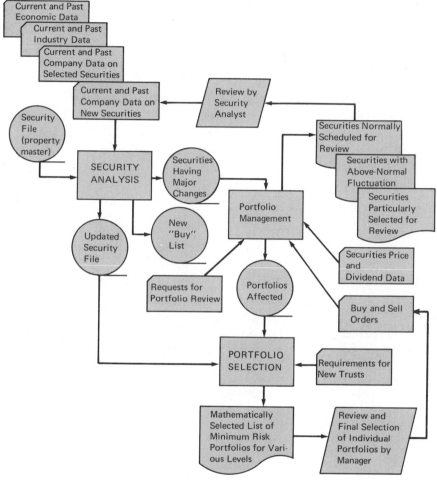

Source: *Personal Trust Accounting on the IBM System/360* (White Plains, N.Y.: IBM Corporation, 1967), p. 13.

3. Security analysis.   Security analysis involves the analysis and evaluation of the value of an individual security. This type of analysis focuses on the financial position and prospects of a corporation in order to forecast the market price of its securities. Computerized security analysis utilizes data on selected corporations provided by financial advisory services and time-sharing companies. Various types of financial, economic, and market analyses are then made in order to forecast alternative values for the security being analyzed. See Figure 11–28.

4. Portfolio management. Portfolio management involves the management of a combination of securities by holding, selling, or buying selected securities in order to minimize the risk and maximize the return of the entire "portfolio" of investments. Computerized portfolio management utilizes a computer program that contains mathematical models which can select one or more portfolios which minimize risk for specific levels of investment return and which also satisfy various investment constraints. In most cases the portfolio selection process produces a list of acceptable portfolios which are reviewed by a "portfolio manager" who then makes the final hold, buy, and sell decisions for each portfolio he manages. Figure 11–29 illustrates an integrated portfolio management system.

OTHER COMPUTER APPLICATIONS IN BUSINESS

We said at the opening of this chapter that there are as many computer applications in business as there are business activities to be performed, business problems to be solved, and business opportunities to be pursued. It is therefore impossible to cover all the computer applications in business that we have not yet discussed. In this section we will explore several major computer applications that should contribute to a basic, but well-rounded understanding of the use of computers in business.

Personnel Information Systems

The *personnel* function involves the recruitment, placement, evaluation, compensation, and development of the employees of an organization. The goal of the personnel function can be described by the term "people management" which emphasizes that planning is needed to meet the personnel needs of the business and that all personnel policies and programs should be controlled so that effective and efficient use is made of the "human resources" of the company. It is generally accepted that the personnel function is one of the least computerized of all of the major business functions. Automated systems may not be necessary for small firms, but larger business firms are finding that computer-based personnel information systems are becoming necessary for the proper performance of the personnel function.

The man in charge of inventories can say exactly how many machine tools he has on hand, but can personnel say, for example, how many people in the company have more than three years of experience on a certain machine tool? The financial expert can plot meticulously the rate of return on his investments, but can personnel know what the effect of lowering retirement age would be on salary costs or on the makeup of the work force? The purchasing agent can state exactly what he is getting and how much it costs, but does personnel know what it costs to hire and train a man?[7]

The major personnel information subsystems are summarized below.

1. Payroll and labor analysis. This subsystem was discussed in the previous chapter. It involves processing data concerning employee compensation and work activity and producing paychecks, payroll reports, and labor analysis reports.

2. Personnel recordkeeping. This subsystem is concerned with additions, deletions, and other changes to the records in the personnel data base. Changes in job assignments and compensation, or hirings and terminations are examples of information that would be utilized to update the personnel data base.

3. Employee skills inventory. This subsystem is utilized to locate specific human resources within a company and to maximize their use. The employee skills inventory system utilizes the employee skills data from the personnel data base to locate employees within a company who have the skills required for specific assignment and projects.

4. Training and development analysis. This subsystem allows personnel management to plan and control employee recruitment, training, and development programs by analyzing the success history of present programs. It also analyzes the career development status of each employee to determine whether development methods such as training programs or performance appraisals should be recommended.

5. Compensation analysis. This subsystem analyzes the range and distribution of employee compensation (wages, salaries, incentive payments, and fringe benefits) within a company and makes comparisons with compensation paid by similar firms or with various economic indicators. This subsystem provides information which is useful for planning changes in compensation, especially if negotiations with a

---

[7] John J. Bricker, "The Personnel Systems Concept," *The Systems Approach to Personnel Management,* AMA Report No. 62 (New York: AMA, 1965), p. 16.

FIGURE 11–30

Skills Inventory Profile Report

```
                                    Confidential              Skills Inventory Profile-T

  NAME                                  DEPT OFFICE NO      DATE          PAGE          EMPLOYEE SERIAL
   JAMESON        JAMES L                  626           05/65            1               342971
     LAST          FIRST & INITIAL
                                                                                              CHANGE
            SKILL                    NO OF  LAST        COMMENTS          SKILL      A   B   C
                                     YEARS  YEAR                          CODE     NO OF LAST DEL
                                                                                  YEARS YEAR LETE

  MANAGEMENT/PROJECT LDR EXPERIENCE
        MANAGER                       3.0 65                                       AC105
        MANAGER                                    FIRST PREFERENCE      96 AC105

  ENGINEERING/SCIENTIFIC/TECH FIELDS
        ELECTRICAL-ELECTRONICS ENGINEER 10+ 65                              BC001
        CIRCUIT DESIGN-GENERAL         8.0 62                                BC145
        CIRCUIT DESIGN-GENERAL                    FIRST SPECIALTY        91 BC145
        CIRCUIT DESIGN-SOLID STATE    *5.5 64                                BC150
        INTEGRATED CIRCUITS           3.5 63                                BC280

  COMPONENTS EXPERIENCE - EE
        CORE CIRCUITS                          63 DESIGN                 08 CL090
        DDTL                                   62 QUALITY ENGR           28 CL160

  INSTRUMENTS EXPERIENCE
        ELECTROMETERS                 4.0 62                                CU140

  IBM PRODUCTS EXPERIENCE
        UNIT RECORD EQUIPMENT                  61 RESEARCH OR DEV ENGR 21 TB100
        IBM 360/20                             65 RESEARCH OR DEV ENGR 21 TD060
        IBM 360/40                             65 RESEARCH OR DEV ENGR 21 TD070
        IBM 1401                               63 PRODUCT TEST ENGR     26 TD220
        DISK FILES                             64 RESEARCH OR DEV ENGR 21 TG140
        IBM 1311                               64 RESEARCH OR DEV ENGR 21 TG160

  FOREIGN LANGUAGE PROFICIENCY
        GERMAN                                    INTERPRET             87 VE260
        RUSSIAN                                    SUMMARIZE IN ENGLISH 88 VE510
```

Source: *Personnel Data System* (White Plains, N.Y.: IBM Corporation, 1968), p. 5.

labor union are involved. It helps keep the compensation of a company competitive and equitable, while controlling compensation costs.

6. Personnel requirements forecasting. Short and long-range planning is required to assure a business firm of an adequate supply of high-quality human resources. This subsystem provides information required for forecasts of personnel requirements in each major employment category for various company departments or for new projects and other ventures being planned by management. Such long-range "manpower planning" may utilize a computer-based simulation model to evaluate alternative plans for recruitment, reassignment, or retraining programs.[8]

The personnel data base utilized by the systems described above may include the following major categories of data:

_____

[8] Some of the material in this section is adapted from Joseph F. Kelly, *Computerized Management Information Systems* (New York: The MacMillan Company, 1970), p. 198.

1. *Employee profile data.*   Personal data about the employee such as name, address, marital status, number of dependents, etc.
2. *Employment history.*   Details the job assignments the employee has held within the company, salary changes, and performance appraisals.
3. *Professional data.*   Includes previous employment, professional assignments, patents held, publications, etc.
4. *Educational data.*   Describes all types and levels of education achieved.
5. *Employee skills inventory.*   Includes the career-oriented skills of each employee such as electronic circuit design, accounting expertise, computer programming ability, foreign language proficiency, etc.

Figure 11–30 illustrates a printed report produced by a skills inventory system.

Operations Research Applications

Operations research (or management science) represents a major area of computer use that has been applied to many of the functions and activities of both business and nonbusiness organizations. In Chapter 8, we defined operations research as the application of scientific techniques to organizational problems, utilizing a methodology based on the concepts and techniques of mathematics and the natural, physical, and social sciences. We discussed how operations research techniques usually involve the formulation of "mathematical models" of the system being investigated. We then discussed how mathematical models could be utilized for problem solving, utilizing either "mathematical analysis" or "mathematical simulation." Therefore, most computer applications in operations research involve the use of computer programs containing mathematical models which are then solved or "manipulated," utilizing various types of mathematical analysis or simulation. Figure 11–31 outlines the function, effect, and software requirements of several operations research techniques.

The wide variety of computer applications in operations research is illustrated in Figure 11–32, which illustrates some of the applications of simulation, which is just one of the many techniques of operations research. A more detailed look at a computer application in operations research is shown in Figure 11–33. Operations research techniques such as linear programming and simulation and the processing power of the computer are utilized by a shipping company for

FIGURE 11–31 Analysis of Selected Operations Research Applications

Operations research technique	Function	Effect	Software tools available
Mathematical analysis	Utilize complex mathematics for solving engineering/research problems.	Computational processing is performed at electronic speeds. Special languages and subroutines facilitate expression and solution of problems.	Math library-precoded routines e.g., numerical analysis, interpolation, exponential and log functions and matrix analysis.
Statistical analysis	Analysis of quantitative and statistical data for such applications as market research, sales forecasting, inventory control, research, and quality control.	Improves accuracy and validity of decision making by providing more sophisticated analysis.	Statistics library e.g., variance, T-ratio, standard deviation, binomial distribution, random number generator, regression analysis, etc.
Linear programming	Mathematical technique for solving problems of competing demands for limited resources where there are a great number of interacting variables.	Resolves complex problems that can only be approximated or guesstimated by conventional means. Increases accuracy and improves decision making in broad class of decisions.	Linear programming (LP) packages assist in problem structuring and formulation and then provide high-speed computing power to efficiently produce solutions based on alternate decision rules.
Network analysis	Scheduling, costing and status reporting of major projects.	Improves planning, scheduling and implementing of complex projects comprised of multiple events and activities. Permits continuous evaluation of projects' progress to increase probabilities of on-time, on-cost performance.	PERT (program evaluation and review technique) and CPM (critical path method) software systems for processing large networks of events and activities producing a variety of computer reports to pinpoint schedule slippages, critical events, and action needed to get back on schedule.
Queueing Theory	Solving problems where it is desirable to minimize the costs and/or time associated with waiting lines or queues.	Improves management ability to improve operations like checkout counters, receiving docks, machine centers or turntoll stations.	General purpose simulators aid the construction and development of complex simulation models. The simulator has the ability to produce random numbers to test various activity patterns and optimize the use of resources.
Simulation	Determines the impact of decisions using hypothetical or historical data in lieu of incurring the expense and risk of trying out decisions in actual operations	Business managers can test and project the effects of decisions on a wide variety of operational areas thus ensuring optimal results when the decisions and policies are put into practice.	General purpose simulators as above.

Source: Adapted from: Jerome Kanter, *Management-Oriented Management Information Systems* (Englewood Cliffs, N. J.: Prentice-Hall, 1973), p. 168.

FIGURE 11–32

Computer Applications of Simulation

Air traffic control queueing
Aircraft maintenance scheduling
Airport design
Ambulance location and dispatching
Assembly line scheduling
Bank teller scheduling
Bus (city) scheduling
Circuit design
Clerical processing system design
Communication system design
  Computer time-sharing
  Telephone traffic routing
  Message system
  Mobile communications
Computer memory-fabrication test-facility
  design
Consumer behavior prediction
  Brand selection
  Promotion decisions
  Advertising allocation
Court system resource allocation
Distribution system design
  Warehouse location
  Mail (post office)
  Soft drink bottling
  Bank courier
  Intrahospital material flow
Enterprise models
  Steel production
  Hospital
  Shipping line
  Railroad operations
  School district
Equipment scheduling
  Aircraft
Facility layout
  Pharmaceutical center
Financial forecasting
  Insurance
  Schools
  Computer leasing
Insurance manpower hiring decisions
Grain terminal operation
Harbor design

Industry models
  Textile
  Petroleum (financial aspects)
Information system design
Intergroup communication (sociological
  studies)
Inventory reorder rule design
  Aerospace
  Manufacturing
  Military logistics
  Hospitals
Job shop scheduling
  Aircraft parts
  Metals forming
  Work-in-process control
  Shipyard
Library operations design
Maintenance scheduling
  Airlines
  Glass furnaces
  Steel furnaces
  Computer field service
National manpower adjustment system
Natural resource (mine) scheduling
  Iron ore
  Strip mining
Parking facility design
Numerically controlled production facility
  design
Personnel scheduling
  Inspection department
  Spacecraft trips
Petrochemical process design
  Solvent recovery
Police response system design
Political voting prediction
Rail freight car dispatching
Railroad traffic scheduling
Steel mill scheduling
Taxi dispatching
Traffic light timing
Truck dispatching and loading
University financial and operational
  forecasting
Urban traffic system design
Water resources development

Source: James R. Emshoff and Roger L. Sisson, *Design and Use of Computer Simulation Models* (New York: The Macmillan Company, 1970), p. 264.

the scheduling of tankers. This "ship scheduling information system" provides management with alternative feasible monthly schedules which outline the effects of each alternative. Such information dramatically increases the effectiveness of management decisions.

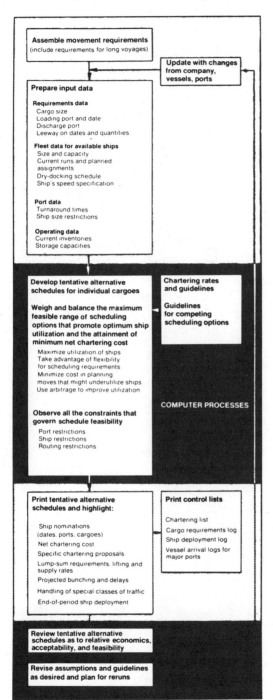

FIGURE 11–33

Scheduling Ships: A Computer Application of OR

Source: "The Management Sciences Are Ready for Business," Reprinted from *Computer Decisions*, January, 1972, p. 34, © 1972, Hayden Publishing Company.

Information Retrieval

Information retrieval (also called information storage and retrieval) is a major category of computer applications which concentrates on the storage and retrieval of information needed by an organization. Computer-based information retrieval systems are frequently considered a scientific application of the computer because they are utilized by the research departments of government agencies, universities, and large business firms. Information retrieval harnesses the power of the computer to cope with the "information explosion" of modern times. Computer-based information retrieval systems are necessary to cope with the rapidly expanding production and accumulation of information and knowledge. They provide researchers with selective and appropriate information and can drastically minimize the time formerly spent in searching for necessary information or in duplicating research which had already been accomplished.

Information retrieval systems may utilize electronic media (such as magnetic strip files) or copies of documents may be stored (such as microfiche files). Much research and development work has been done and is continuing in this area as business firms and other organizations seek to develop a common data base and information storage facility that can handle all of their information needs. Information retrieval systems are being utilized to store data concerning legal precedents, medical developments, military intelligence, scientific and technological research, and business and economic data. For example, subsystems could be utilized to obtain all articles written about a particular topic such as the symptoms associated with a specific disease, or the court rulings concerning a particular point of law, or the different uses of a particular product.

Some of the major factors being studied and developed in information retrieval systems are listed below.

1. Identifying strategic information users and their information needs.
2. Selecting the data, and/or documents from both internal and external sources which are to be stored.
3. Maintaining up-to-date "interest profiles" of the information needs of users.
4. Designing methods for classifying and indexing data and information.

5. Developing procedures for retrieval and dissemination of information to appropriate users.
6. Determining the type of storage media and devices (e.g., magnetic strip vs. microfiche).
7. Determining the media and format of information output (e.g., CRT display or hard copy).
8. Maintaining the data base and information storage facility through updating, deletion, and protection procedures.

Other Business Applications

A quick glance at how the computer is utilized in several industries should be sufficient to emphasize the amazing versatility of the computer and the variety of its applications in business.

1. Airlines. Airline reservation systems were the earliest major real-time application of computers in business. Real-time computer systems are on-line to terminals in airline offices both nationwide and overseas. Besides such real-time passenger reservation systems and traditional business applications, computers provide information for (1) flight plan preparation, (2) fuel loading, (3) meal catering, (4) air cargo routing, and (5) freight, supplies, and spare parts inventory control.

2. Agribusiness. Agriculture has become a big business—"Agribusiness." Many corporate and family farms and ranches are now utilizing the power of the computer. Major applications include (1) farm and crop recordkeeping and analysis, (2) financial and tax accounting, and (3) optimal feed-blending, fertilizing, and crop-rotation programs. Computer services are provided by government agricultural extension agencies, commercial banks, EDP service bureaus, and farm cooperatives.

3. Construction. Large construction companies have been utilizing computers for many years for traditional business applications such as payroll and general accounting. Scientific applications requiring mathematical computations for design engineering analysis have also been utilized. The most recent major application, however, is the use of network analysis techniques like PERT (Program Evaluation and Review Technique) and CPM (Critical Path Method) for construction planning and scheduling. The computer can utilize such techniques to produce plans and schedules (in terms of time, men, money, and materials) for each stage of complex construction projects.

4. Insurance. Like the banking industry, the insurance industry was an early user of computers. Insurance companies have a huge data processing job because of the large number of insurance policies, claims, premium notices, and dividends that must continually be processed. Large numbers of customers and complex insurance policy provisions require the maintenance of a large data base. Complex actuarial computations (such as life expectancy statistics) must also be performed. A major recent application is the use of real-time inquiry systems that allow branch offices and salesmen to interrogate the central data base for customer policy information. Another application is the use of the computer to perform part of the "underwriting" function by preparing detailed insurance coverage proposals for presentation to prospective customers.

5. Real estate. Real estate applications fall into several major categories. "Real estate investment" applications analyze financial, tax, marketing, and physical requirements data to compute rate-of-return alternatives for proposed real estate projects. "Property management" applications assist the management of rental property by processing rental statements, rental payments, and maintenance and utility disbursements and by providing various management reports, such as income and expense analysis. "Property listing applications" (also called a "multiple listing service") maintain up-to-date listings of all properties registered for sale with participating realtors. "Mortgage loan accounting" and "property title accounting" are other applications in the real estate category that are usually performed by banks and title companies, respectively.

Nonbusiness Computer Applications

We should not leave the subject of computer applications in business without at least a brief mention of computer usage for *nonbusiness applications*. It must be emphasized that the computer has become a powerful and indispensable tool for many nonbusiness organizations. A detailed treatment of such applications is beyond the scope of this book. However, we will briefly describe the use of computers in three major application categories. In addition, several brief examples of how computers help solve human and social problems are discussed in the "social applications" section of Chapter 14.

1. Government. Many applications of the computer in government can be classified as "business applications," since government agencies utilize computers in various types of financial, accounting, operational, and personnel information systems. In addition, computers are utilized for many scientific and engineering applications such as those having to do with space exploration, military projects, flood control, agricultural research, pollution control, medical research, highway design, etc. More unique types of governmental applications include law enforcement information systems, traffic control systems, and legislative and judicial information retrieval systems.

2. *Education.* The two major uses of the computer in education are (1) educational administration and (2) instruction. Applications in educational administration include computerized class scheduling, registration, and grade reporting, as well as more traditional "business applications" such as student fee accounting, payroll, budgeting, etc. Instructional applications include student use of the computer to solve assigned problems or assist in research projects. Many colleges are now able to provide computer problem solving facilities through the use of remote time-sharing terminals throughout a campus.

A major development in instructional applications is "computer-assisted instruction" (CAI) in which a computer engages in a teaching-learning dialogue with a student through the use of an on-line terminal. CAI programs allows the pace and form of instruction to be tailored to each student. CAI systems can provide "drill-and-practice sessions," "tutorial sessions" on a particular concept, or "research sessions" which explore a topic in depth.

3. *Medicine.* Computer applications in medicine were formerly relegated to accounting applications in large hospitals and to the medical research programs of government agencies and pharmaceutical companies. However, progressive hospitals are now developing computer-based "hospital information systems" (HIS) which perform the following functions: (1) patient admission and billing, (2) surgical scheduling and reporting, (3) laboratory scheduling and reporting, (4) pharmaceuticals prescription and administration, and (5) medical records maintenance.

Various operational and administrative applications are also utilized, such as hospital payroll and inventory systems, insurance company and government agency reporting, and other accounting and financial analysis subsystems. Advanced medical computer applications include (1) "patient care systems" which monitor and report the medical condition of patients, (2) "medical diagnosis systems" which assist in the diagnosis of health conditions, and (3) "medical testing systems," which can automatically perform many complex medical laboratory tests with impressive time and cost savings.

SUMMARY

Business management should have a basic and organized under-standing of the major ways the computer is utilized to support the basic functions of a business firm. Individual business computer users should have a basic and specific understanding of how computers affect a particular business function or a particular industry that is directly related to their career objectives. Thus, in this chapter, we briefly described many important computer applications in business according to the business function they support (marketing, produc-tion/operations, finance, accounting, and personnel) and according to the industry in which they are utilized (retailing, banking, invest-ments, airlines, agribusiness, construction, insurance, and real estate). We also described computer applications in operations research and information retrieval which are utilized to support many business functions in many different industries. Finally, we concluded with a look at several major nonbusiness computer applications in govern-ment, education, and medicine. Refer back to Figure 11–1 for a summary of major business computer applications by functional and industry categories.

KEY TERMS AND CONCEPTS

Marketing information systems, 328–331
Computer applications in retailing, 332–334
The point-of-sale revolution, 334–336
Manufacturing information systems, 340–343
Physical distribution information systems, 348, 350
Financial information systems, 352–354
Financial performance models, 355–356

Accounting information systems, 357
Computer applications in banking, 359–361
Computer applications in investments, 362–367
Personnel information systems, 368–371
Operations research applications, 371–374
Information retrieval, 375–376

ASSIGNMENTS

1. Test your understanding of the chapter material by reviewing the *purpose, outline, summary,* and *key terms and concepts* of this chapter. Are you confident that you have attained a basic understanding of the major concepts of the chapter? If not, reread the appropriate material as indicated by the page numbers after each key term and concept.

2. "As a present or future computer user in business you should have a basic, organized, and specific understanding of how computers affect

a particular business function or a particular industry that is directly related to your career objectives." Explain the rationale for this statement.

3. Briefly describe several ways that the computer is used to support one of the functions of business (marketing, production/operations, finance, accounting, and personnel), or a particular industry (such as retailing, banking, investments, airlines, agribusiness, construction, insurance, real estate, etc.) Explain the benefits and limitations of such computer use.

4. Discuss the use of computers for operations research and information retrieval.

5. Prepare a "Computer Application Analysis Report" which describes and evaluates how a specific computer application (a computer-based information system) is used by a specific type of business firm or industry. Do the research for your report by contacting a computer-using business firm, the local office of a computer manufacturer, or by reviewing books and articles on specific computer applications in your library.

6. Prepare a "Computer Applications Report" which summarizes several of the computer applications being utilized by a specific type of business firm or industry. Conduct the research for this report as recommended in assignment five.

part five

Managing the Computer

Chapter Outline

Purpose of the Chapter

The Computer-Based Business Environment

The Computer Industry
Scope of the Industry, Harware Suppliers,
Software Suppliers, EDP Service Suppliers

Utilizing External EDP Services
Benefits and Limitations

Evaluating Computer Acquisitions
Hardware Evaluation Factors, Software Evaluation Factors,
Evaluation of Vendor Support

Financing Computer Acquisitions
Rental, Purchase, Leasing

The Cost of Computer Resources
Systems Development Costs, Operations Costs,
Administrative Costs, Controlling Computer Costs

Summary

Key Terms and Concepts

Assignments

12

Acquiring Computer Resources

Purpose of the Chapter

To promote a basic understanding of how computer resources should be acquired by business firms by analyzing:

1. The scope and role of the computer industry,
2. The use of external EDP services,
3. The evaluation of computer acquisitions,
4. The financing of computer resources,
5. The cost of computer resources.

The computer-using business firm must acquire computer resources from many sources in the computer industry. In addition, business computer users must interact effectively with external computer users in society. Therefore, business management must have a basic understanding and appreciation of the role of the computer industry and the impact of computers on society. The computer industry is a major new industry in the United States and offers a variety of essential services to computer-using business firms. Computers have also had a major impact on society and thus impose serious responsibilities upon the management of computer-using business firms. In this chapter we shall explore the important segments and services of the computer industry and discuss how computer users should evaluate the acquisition of computer resources. The major economic and social effects of the use of computers by business firms will be analyzed in Chapter 14.

THE COMPUTER-BASED BUSINESS ENVIRONMENT

The use of computers in business does not take place in a vacuum. The business firm should be viewed as a system that interacts with many other systems in its environment. The computer operations of a business firm should thus be viewed as taking place in a "computer-based business environment." See Figure 12–1.

From an organizational standpoint, the electronic data processing services of a business firm are provided by the hardware, software, and personnel of a *"computer services department."* This department consists of EDP personnel (also called "computer professionals") who perform the functions of systems analysis, programming, and computer operations. The computer services department provides computer services to *"internal computer users,"* that is, the other departments in the firm that require electronic data processing. Outside of the business firm is the *"computer industry"* which includes computer manufacturers, other hardware and software companies, and the suppliers of other computer-related services such as EDP service bureaus and time-sharing service companies. The computer services

FIGURE 12–1

The Computer-Based Business Environment

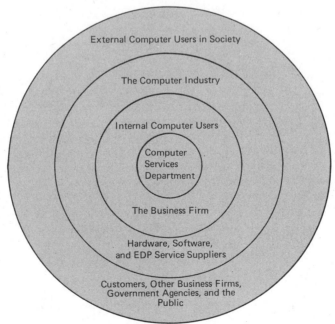

department of a business firm relies heavily on the hardware, software, and services supplied by the computer industry. Beyond this ring of computer support organizations are *"external computer users in society"* such as customers, other business firms, governmental units, and the general public. These external groups provide input or utilize output produced by the computer-based information systems of the business firm or are affected in some way by the business uses of the computer.

THE COMPUTER INDUSTRY

Business management cannot effectively utilize their computer resources unless they have a basic understanding of the computer industry. Business computer users should view the computer industry as a vital source of computer hardware, software, and EDP services. Effective and efficient use of the computer by computer users requires the continual support of firms within the computer industry. Figure 12–2 groups the major types of firms within the computer industry into the three major categories of hardware suppliers, software suppliers, and EDP service suppliers. Figure 12–3 lists some of the major firms in the computer industry.

FIGURE 12–2

The Computer Industry

Hardware suppliers

Computer manufacturers
Independent peripheral manufacturers
Data processing supplies companies
Computer leasing companies
Used computer equipment companies

Software suppliers

Computer manufacturers
Independent software companies
User developed software suppliers

EDP service suppliers

Computer manufacturers
EDP service bureaus
Time-sharing service companies
Facilities management companies
Other EDP service suppliers
    Computer time rental, Systems design services
    Contract programming, EDP consulting,
    EDP education, Hardware maintenance

FIGURE 12-3 Major Firms in the Computer Industry

Computerworld Stock Trading Summary

TRADE★QUOTES

All statistics compiled,
computed and formatted by
TRADE★QUOTES, INC.
Cambridge, Mass. 02139

COMPUTER SYSTEMS

EXCH		1973-74 RANGE (1)	CLOSE AUG 15 1974	WEEK NET CHNGE	WEEK PCT CHNGE
N	BURROUGHS CORP	49-126	81 3/8	-10	-10.9
N	COLLINS RADIO	16- 26	24 3/4		0.0
O	COMMINS DATA AUTOMATION	16- 20	17	-2 1/4	-9.8
N	CONTROL DATA CORP	20- 62	20 5/8	-2 3/4	-11.2
N	DATA GENERAL CORP	20- 49	21 3/4		0.0
N	DATAPOINT CORP	9- 21	10 1/4		0.0
O	DIGITAL COMP CONTROL	2- 6	2 1/4	- 1/8	-5.2
N	DIGITAL EQUIPMENT	73-121	86	-6 1/8	-6.6
N	ELECTRONIC ASSOC.	2- 6	2 7/8		0.0
O	ELECTRONIC ENGINEFR.	23- 48	26 1/2	-7/8	-3.1
O	FOXBORO	22- 55	25 1/4	-2 1/4	-8.1
N	GENERAL AUTOMATION	5- 7	5 5/8	-R 1/8	-10.6
N	GRI COMPUTER CORP	68- 99	68 3/4		-10.2
N	HEWLETT-PACKARD CO	38-139	38 1/4		-10.2
N	HONEYWELL INC	134-140	200	-8	0.0
N	INTERDATA INC	12- 19			0.0
O	MICRODATA CORP	2- 10	3 7/8	- 1/4	-6.0
N	NCR	27- 46	29 1/4	-1 5/8	-5.2
N	RAYTHFON CO	27- 39	29 1/4		-3.3
N	SINGER CO	24- 74	25 1/2	-2 3/8	-8.5
N	SPERRY RAND	31- 56	31 1/4	-2 3/4	-8.0
O	SYSTEMS ENG. LARS	1- 8	1 3/4		0.0
N	TEXAS INSTRUMENTS	73-138	75	-5 1/4	-6.5
N	ULTIMACC SYSTEMS INC	1- 11	1 1/2		0.0
N	VARIAN ASSOCIATES	10- 20	12 3/4	-1 1/8	-12.6
N	XEROX CORP	86-169	85 7/8	-9 3/8	-9.8

LEASING COMPANIES

EXCH		1973-74 RANGE	CLOSE AUG 15 1974	WEEK NET CHNGE	WEEK PCT CHNGE
A	BOOTHE COMPUTER	1- 5	1 1/8	0	0.0
O	BRESNAHAN COMP.	1- 7	2 1/8	0	0.0
A	COMDISCO INC	2- 17	5 5/8	- 3/8	-18.7
O	COMPUTER EQUIP CORP	3- 4			0.0
O	COMPUTER EXCHANGE	1- 2	1		0.0
O	COMPUTER INVSTRS GRP	1- 4	1 3/8	+ 1/8	+10.0
O	COMP. INSTALLATIONS	1- 2	1/4		0.0
O	DATRONIC RENTAL	1- 3	3/4		0.0
N	DCL INC	0- 9	3/4		0.0
A	EPP RESOURCES	2- 9	3 1/4	- 3/8	-20.0
A	GRANITE MGT	1- 6	1 1/2		0.0
A	GREYHOUND COMPUTER	3- 6	4 1/2	- 3/8	-8.5
A	ITEL	4- 12	6		-3.7
O	LEASCO CORP	5- 18	6 7/8	+ 1/4	-16.6
O	LEASPAC CORP	4- 8	5 7/8	+ 1/8	0.0
N	NPG INC	1- 7	2 1/4		0.0
O	PIONEER TEX CORP	2- 10	2 1/2	- 1/4	-9.0
O	ROCKWOOD COMPUTER	1- 3	3/4		-7.0
N	U.S. LEASING	R- 36	7 5/8	- 1/8	-1.6

SOFTWARE & EDP SERVICES

EXCH		1973-74 RANGE (1)	CLOSE AUG 15 1974	WEEK NET CHNGE	WEEK PCT CHNGE
O	ADVANCED COMP TECH	1- 2	1		0.0
O	APPLIED DATA RES.	2- 4	1 3/4	0	-12.5
O	APPLIED LOGIC	1- 3	1 1/8	- 1/4	-8.2
N	AUTOMATIC DATA PROC	21- 94	25	-2 1/4	-8.2
O	BRANDON APPLIED SYST	1- 6	3/8		0.0
O	CENTURY DATA SYSTEMS	1- 6	1 1/2		0.0
O	COMPUTER DIMENSIONS	1- 4	1 1/2		0.0
O	COMPUTER HORIZONS	1- 6	1 3/4	+ 1/8	+10.0
O	COMPUTER NETWORK	2- 6	2 5/8		0.0
O	COMPUTER SCIENCES	2- 5	1		0.0
O	COMPUTER TASK GROUP	1- 3	1 1/2	+ 1/8	+100.0
O	COMPUTER USAGE	2- 9	1		0.0
O	COMPRESS	2- 4	2 1/4		0.0
O	COMSHARE	2- 15	2 1/2		0.0
O	CORDURA CORP	2- 15	1 5/8		0.0
O	DATATAB	1- 2	5/8		0.0
O	ELECTRONIC DATA SYS.	15- 52	15 1/2	-1 3/4	-10.1
O	INFORMATIONL INC	5- 2	1 1/2		0.0
N	I.R.A. DATA CORP	1- 1	3/4		0.0
O	IPS COMPUTER MARKET.	1- 5	3/4		0.0
O	KEANE ASSOCIATES	2- 17	3 1/4	- 3/8	-70.2
N	KEYDATA CORP	2- 8	2 1/8	+ 1/8	0.0
O	LOGICON	2- 7	3 1/4		0.0
O	MANAGEMENT DATA	1- 6	1 1/4	- 1/8	-9.0
O	NATIONAL CSS INC	10- 42	11 1/2	-2	-14.8
O	NATIONAL INFO SRVCS	1- 2	1/8		0.0
O	NATIONAL INFO SRVCS	2- 37	23	+ 1/2	-2.1
O	PLANNING RESEARCH	2- 7	2 7/8	+ 1/4	+10.0
O	PROGRAMMING METHODS	1- 25	17	+ 3/4	0.0
O	PROGRAMMING & SYS	1- 4	3/4		0.0
O	RAPIDATA INC	2- 24	2 7/8	- 1/8	-5.8
O	SCIENTIFIC COMPUTERS	1- 1	7/8	0	0.0
O	SCIENTIFIC COMPUTER	2- 13	3/4		0.0
N	TCC INC	4- 13	8 1/4	-1 1/8	-13.3
O	TYMSHARE INC	3- 14	3 1/4	- 1/4	-7.6
O	UPS SYSTEMS	2- 8	2 1/2	+ 1/8	+5.2
N	WYLY CORP	3- 11	2 1/2	- 1/8	+4.7

PERIPHERALS & SUBSYSTEMS

EXCH		1973-74 RANGE	CLOSE AUG 15 1974	WEEK NET CHNGE	WEEK PCT CHNGE
N	ADDRESSOGRAPH-MULT	5- 34	5 3/4	- 5/8	-9.8
O	ADVANCED MEMORY SYS	3- 23	3 1/4	- 1/4	-10.5
N	AMPEX CORP	2- 6	2 1/4	- 1/4	-7.1
O	ANDERSON JACOBSON	2- 6	2 1/4		0.0
N	BEEHIVE MEDICAL ELEC	6- 12	6	- 1/4	-10.0
O	BOLT-BERANEK & NEW	5- 18	5	-1 1/4	-17.2
N	BUNKER-RAMO	1- 7	1 1/4	- 1/4	-9.0
O	CAMBRIDGE MEMORIES	1- 5	1 1/2	- 1/2	-5.7
N	CENTRONICS DATA COMP	12- 38	12 1/4	+ 1/2	-7.5
A	CODEX CORP	8- 19	13 1/4	-1 1/4	-8.4
O	COGNITRONICS	1- 3	7/8		0.0

Scope of the Industry

Though the computer industry consists of over 5,000 companies, only eight firms are "major computer manufacturers." These computer manufacturers (sometimes called "the big eight" or "IBM and the seven dwarfs") consists of the International Business Machines Corporation (IBM), which has about 65 to 70 percent of the market for computers (defined as the dollar value of computers installed in the U.S.); Honeywell Information Systems; and the Univac division of the Sperry Rand Corporation, each having about eight to ten percent of the computer market; Control Data Corporation (CDC); National Cash Register (NCR); and Burroughs Corporation, each having between three to seven percent of the market; and Xerox Data Systems (XDS); and Digital Equipment Corporation (DEC), each having about one percent of the computer market.

IBM's dominant position in the computer industry has kept it in "hot water" over the years due to antitrust actions taken by the Justice Department and court suits brought by competitors alleging monopolistic practices. However, IBM continues to be the leading firm in the computer industry in terms of profitably supplying the major share of computer systems manufactured and marketed in this country.

Many companies have unsuccessfully attempted to manufacture and market computer systems. Two major firms that withdrew after many years of trying were General Electric, which sold its computer business to Honeywell in 1970, and RCA, which withdrew as a computer manufacturer in 1971, selling a major part of its computer business to Univac. Both firms lost hundreds of millions of dollars before deciding to give up the manufacture of computers.

Figure 12–4 outlines the number and value of computers and peripheral equipment installed in the United States at the end of 1971

FIGURE 12–4

Computer Hardware Installed in the U.S.

	1971 Estimate		Range of 1976 Estimates
	Number	*Dollar value*	*Dollar value*
General purpose computer systems	54,500	$26.5 Billion	$33–$48 Billion
Mini and special purpose systems	33,500	$ 1.6 Billion	$ 2–$3.5 Billion
Peripheral equipment	553,500	$ 2.8 Billion	$ 5–$6 Billion
Total		$30.9 Billion	$40–$57.5 Billion

Source: *The State of the Computer Industry in the United States* (Montvale, N.J.: American Federation of Information Processing Societies, 1973), p. 9.

and provides a range of estimates of dollar value for 1976. The number of computers in use in the United States exceeded 100,000 during the early 1970s with an estimated value approaching 50 billion dollars by 1976.

The computer industry is international in scope. Britain, France, Holland, West Germany, Japan, and Russia are major producers of computers. However, U.S. computer manufacturers have supplied a majority of the computers in use in foreign countries. In recent years from one-third to one-half of computers produced by U.S. manufacturers have been "overseas" shipments to foreign computer users. Figure 12–5 illustrates the dominance of U.S. computer manufacturers in the international market. IBM's share of the European market is estimated at 50 percent, while Honeywell, Univac, NCR, and Burroughs together hold about 30 percent of the European market. However, Japan has become a major competitor in the international markets, and several major European computer manufacturers have merged their computer operations in order to compete more effectively with the U.S.

FIGURE 12–5

Computers Installed Outside the U.S. by Country of Manufacturer
(at the end of 1971)

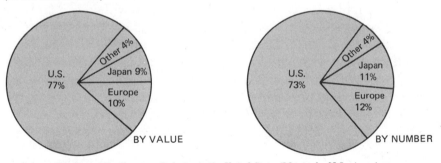

Source: *The State of the Computer Industry in the United States* (Montvale, N.J.: American Federation of Information Processing Societies, 1973), p. 22.

Hardware Suppliers

The primary sources of *computer hardware* are the major computer manufacturers who manufacture computer systems, peripheral equipment, and data processing supplies. Smaller computer manufacturers may produce minicomputers, small computer systems, special purpose computers, and a few types of peripheral devices. Other hardware suppliers can be classified as "independent peripheral manufacturers" since they do not manufacture central processing units (CPU's).

These firms confine themselves to the production of peripheral computer equipment such as input, output, storage, and data preparation devices. Independent peripheral equipment manufacturers have had significant success in convincing many computer users to purchase or lease their equipment rather than the peripheral devices available from computer manufacturers. This has also been true of data processing supplies companies which manufacture data processing media and materials such as punched cards, magnetic tape and disks, and paper forms.

An important supplier of computer hardware is computer leasing companies who purchase computers from computer manufacturers and lease them to computer users at rates that may be 10 to 20 percent lower than the manufacturer's rental price. Leasing companies are able to offer lower prices because they are willing to gamble that they can recover their costs and make a profit at the lower rates before their computers become obsolete. A final source of computer hardware is used computer equipment companies which purchase used computers from computer users and sell them at substantial discounts.

Software Suppliers

System software and *application software* can be obtained from several sources if a computer user does not wish to develop his own software. Computer manufacturers are the largest source of software in the computer industry. They supply most of the system software (such as operating systems and other control programs and service programs) for computer users and are the major source of canned application programs. However, independent software companies which specialize in the development of software packages have become major software suppliers. Software can also be obtained from other computer users. These "user-developed software suppliers" are computer users who have developed application programs or service programs that can be utilized by other computer users. Such programs are available free of charge in some cases or may have to be purchased or leased.

EDP Service Suppliers

The four major sources of external EDP services are computer manufacturers, EDP service bureaus, time-sharing companies, and facilities management companies. They and other types of firms in the computer industry offer a variety *EDP services* such as off-premise computer processing of customer jobs, time-sharing services, computer time rental, systems design services, contract programming, EDP consulting, EDP education, and hardware maintenance. Many companies, especially computer manufacturers, supply several or almost all of these services.

An *EDP service bureau* (also called a computer service center) is a company that processes the jobs of many customers who are too small to acquire their own computer systems. Larger computer users also utilize service bureaus to handle specialized applications (such as computer-output-microfilm) or when problem situations occur, such as peak volume periods or during periods of computer "down time." *Time-sharing service companies* provide real-time processing services to many subscribers utilizing remote terminals and a central computer system. Time-sharing service companies are utilized by many computer users who have specialized data processing needs which require real-time processing and a large computer system. *Facilities management companies* are firms which take over complete responsibility for a computer user's EDP operation. Thus, a business firm may "subcontract" all of his EDP service needs to an outside contractor. The facilities management firm might take over all computer facilities at the user's site, utilizing its own hardware, software, and EDP personnel.

Firms in the computer industry and computer users frequently rent computer time to computer users who wish to run a specific job on a computer that cannot be handled by their own computer system. This is called *"computer time rental."* Many computer industry firms provide systems design, computer programming, and certain consulting services to computer users on a fee basis. *"Contract programming,"* for example, is utilized by computer users who do not have the time or the computer programmers required to develop the computer programs for a particular application. *EDP education* is a critical need of many computer users and is a service offered by many computer industry firms. For example, IBM operates over 25 education centers which offer more than 50 classroom courses and 40 private study courses in electronic data processing. Management, operating personnel, and EDP personnel frequently require educational programs in order to better operate or utilize computer-based systems. A final EDP service is *hardware maintenance* which is usually provided by computer manufacturers but can be obtained from other firms in the computer industry.

UTILIZING EXTERNAL EDP SERVICES

Information systems development and data processing services can be acquired from sources outside the organization rather than developing such capabilities within the firm. In the preceding section, we discussed the many types of services that are available from suppliers of EDP services. For example, many small and new business firms utilize the computers, programs, and personnel of EDP service bureaus for specific applications such as payroll or customer billing. Such firms do not have the volume of applications or the financial and personnel resources to acquire and operate their own computer systems. Other firms may have their own data processing personnel and computer programs but rent or lease computer time on an "off-premise" computer that is owned by another firm. Many firms rent their excess computer time to such users. Of course, a major source of external services are time-sharing service companies which provide "computer power" to the remote computer users. Time-sharing service users lease or purchase their remote terminals and pay installation, and monthly and usage fees to the time-sharing company for its services.

A major form of external services that is being used by some medium-scale and large-scale computer users is "facilities management" in which a data processing service company takes over the entire data processing operation of an organization. The data processing services company manages and operates the computer facilities of the organization for a negotiated fee. Another major external service is the employment of data processing consultants to perform one or more of the stages of information systems development. The business firm may feel that it does not have the time or expertise to develop a computer-based information system for a specific application, so it hires an outside firm to provide the systems analysts and computer programmers that are required. Of course, the purchase of canned applications and service programs represents a use of external services since the computer user is acquiring a "ready-made" software package instead of developing it internally.

Benefits and Limitations

The major benefit of using external sources is that the computer user pays only for the information systems development and data processing services that he needs. Purchasing or leasing computer hardware or software and employing a staff of data processing professionals creates fixed costs, such as minimum machine rental payments, depreciation charges, and the salaries of professional and managerial data processing personnel. The use of external services also eliminates the personnel and management problems caused by the employment of a group of highly paid technical professionals in a rapidly changing and highly technical field such as computers and electronic data processing. The managements of many organizations utilize external sources to avoid such problems. In some cases the cost of external services may be lower than if the computer-using firm performed its own data processing services. This may be due to "economies of scale" since a large data processing service company may utilize larger and more efficient computer hardware and software to serve its many customers.

External services do have several limitations. The loss of control over data processing procedures and confidential information is one limitation. Off-premise computer processing may be inconvenient. The cost of external services may be significantly higher in some cases because the data processing service company must not only meet expenses but must include a profit in its fee to computer users. Many firms are unwilling to depend on an outsider to provide vital data processing services. They want to have more control over data processing procedures, report deadlines, and changes in computer programming, hardware and software, and processing schedules.

External services are widely used by small firms and firms which are using computer processing for the first time. The use of time-sharing services is another popular external service which offers smaller computer users a convenient way of using the computer power of a large time-sharing computer. However, the majority of computers in the United States are purchased or leased by organizations for their own use.

EVALUATING COMPUTER ACQUISITIONS

The evaluation and selection of computer resources should be a formal process that requires manufacturers and suppliers to present bids and proposals based on *systems specifications* developed during the design stage of systems development. Minimum acceptable physical and performance characteristics for all hardware and software requirements should have been established during this stage. A formal evaluation process reduces the possibility of buying unnecessary computer hardware or software. This sometimes happens because computer users and computer professionals want to keep up with their competitors and with the latest developments in computing. Badly organized computer operations, inadequate systems development, and poor purchasing practices may also cause unnecessary acquisitions.

The cost of each component of hardware and software required by the system must be determined. The prices quoted by various hardware manufacturers and software suppliers must be compared to each other and to the performance characteristics and support services promised by each vendor. The reliability and control features built into hardware and software is another important consideration. The ability to improve the performance characteristics of hardware and software by adding on additional hardware or software "modules" must be determined. For instance, the primary storage capacity of some computer systems can be increased without replacing the computer with a larger model. "Modularity" is the name for this important characteristic.

Whatever the claims of hardware manufacturers and software suppliers, the *performance* of hardware and software must be demonstrated and evaluated. Hardware and software should be demonstrated and evaluated either on the premises of the computer user or by visiting the operations of other computer users who utilize similar type of hardware or software. Other users are frequently the best source of information needed to evaluate the claims of manufacturers and suppliers. Large computer users frequently evaluate proposed hardware and software by requiring the processing of special "benchmark" test programs and test data. Users can then evaluate test results to determine which hardware device or software package displayed the best performance characteristics. Special simulators have also been developed which simulate the processing of typical jobs on several computers and evaluates their performances.

Large computer users may utilize a "scoring" system of evaluation when there are several competing proposals for a hardware or software acquisition. Each evaluation factor is given a certain number of maximum possible points. Then each competing proposal is assigned part or all of the possible points for each factor, depending on how well it meets the specifications of the computer user. Scoring each evaluation factor for several proposals helps organize and document the evaluation process and spotlights the strengths and weaknesses of each proposal. See Figure 12–6.

FIGURE 12–6

Scoring System of Evaluation

Factor/CPU	*A*	*B*	*C*	*D*	*E*	*F*	*G*	*H*
Computer								
Word	40	20	0	0	40	40	0	40
Cycle time	6	12	18	6	12	12	0	24
Instruction	15	0	10	10	15	15	15	15
Arithmetic	4	2	0	2	4	4	0	4
Addressing	12	8	16	16	8	12	4	16
Registers	12	0	24	18	18	12	0	18
Interrupts	28	7	21	7	21	14	28	28
Input/output	32	24	8	16	24	24	8	8
Physical size	4	4	4	4	4	3	4	2
Console	6	6	9	6	9	6	6	9
Subtotal	159	83	110	85	155	142	65	164
Vendor								
Delivery time	14	21	28	28	28	0	28	21
Past performance	12	12	8	8	16	4	8	8
Maintenance	9	6	3	12	9	6	9	9
Location	4	0	8	8	8	0	8	8
Alternative	2	4	2	2	2	4	2	2
Number installed	12	16	4	16	16	8	4	8
Training	20	15	5	10	15	15	10	10
Subtotal	73	74	58	84	94	37	79	76
Total	232	157	168	169	249	179	144	240

Source: Robin T. Oliver, "A Technique for Selecting Small Computers," Reprinted with permission of *Datamation*, ® copyright 1970 by Technical Publishing Company, Greenwich, Connecticut 06830

Hardware Evaluation Factors

The evaluation of computer *hardware* includes a technical analysis of specific physical and performance characteristics for each hardware component to be acquired. Many of these characteristics were discussed in Chapter Four. For example, some of the factors that should be considered in the evaluation of the central processing unit of a computer system are listed in Figure 12–7.

Evaluating hardware acquisitions should also involve the analysis of several general categories of hardware performance. These hardware evaluation factors are summarized below.

1. *Performance.* What is its speed, capacity, and throughput?
2. *Cost.* What is its lease or purchase price? What will be its cost of operation and maintenance?
3. *Reliability.* What is the risk of malfunction and maintenance requirements?

FIGURE 12–7

CPU Evaluation Factors

1. Cycle time
2. Word size
3. Instruction set
4. Arithmetic
5. Addressing
6. Registers
7. Interrupts
8. Primary storage capacity
9. Secondary storage capability
10. Input/Output capability and interface
11. Communications capability
12. Microprogramming options
13. Multiprogramming capability
14. Virtual storage capability
15. Physical size and environmental requirements
16. Console capabilities

4. *Availability*.   When is the firm delivery date?
5. *Compatibility*.   Is it compatible with existing hardware and software?
6. *Modularity*.   Can it be expanded and upgraded by acquiring modular "add-on" units?
7. *Technology*.   Is it "ahead of its time" or does it run the risk of obsolescence?
8. *Usability*.   Is it easy to use?
9. *Software*.   Is system and application software available that can best utilize this hardware? (See below)
10. *Support*.   Are the services required to support and maintain it available? (See below)

Software Evaluation Factors

Software should be evaluated according to many factors that are similar to those used for hardware evaluation. Thus, the factors of performance, cost, reliability, availability, compatibility, modularity, technology, usability, and support mentioned above should also be used to evaluate the acceptability of proposed software acquisitions. In addition, however, the following factors must also be evaluated.

1. *Efficiency*.   Is the software a well-written system of computer instructions that does not utilize much storage space or CPU time?

2. *Flexibility.* Can it handle its data processing assignment easily without major modification?
3. *Language.* Is it written in a programming language that is used by our computer programmers?
4. *Documentation.* Is the software well-documented?
5. *Hardware.* Does existing hardware have the features required to best utilize this software?

Evaluation of Vendor Support

Vendor support services which assist the computer user during the installation and operation of hardware and software must be evaluated. Assistance during installation or conversion of hardware and software, employee training, and hardware maintenance are examples of such services. Some of these services are provided without cost by hardware manufacturers and software suppliers. Other types of services can be contracted for at a negotiated price. Evaluation factors for vendor support services are summarized below.

1. *Performance.* What has been their past performance in terms of their past promises?
2. *Systems development.* Are systems analysts and programming consultants available? What are their quality and cost?
3. *Maintenance.* Is equipment maintenance provided? What is its quality and cost?
4. *Conversion.* What systems development, programming, and hardware installation services will they provide during the conversion period?
5. *Training.* Is the necessary training of personnel provided? What is its quality and cost?
6. *Documentation.* Are the necessary hardware, software, and applications manuals available?
7. *Backup.* Are several similar computer facilities available for emergency backup purposes?
8. *Proximity.* Does the vendor have a local office? Are sales, systems development, programming, and hardware maintenance services provided from this office?
9. *Hardware.* Do they have a wide selection of compatible hardware and accessories?
10. *Software.* Do they have a wide variety of useful system software and application programs?

FINANCING COMPUTER ACQUISITIONS

Computer hardware can be rented, purchased, or leased, while software is usually purchased, leased, or is sometimes made available without charge by the hardware manufacturer. Computer manufacturers offer all three methods of financing, while peripheral equipment manufacturers usually offer purchase or lease arrangements. Independent computer-leasing companies utilize long-term lease arrangements, while used computer equipment companies offer used equipment for purchase. The benefits and limitations of each method of financing computer acquisitions are analyzed in the following paragraphs.

Rental

The majority of all computer systems are *rented* from the computer manufacturer. However, the percentage of rented computers is declining as more computer users have turned to purchasing or leasing their equipment. Computer users have favored the rental arrangement for several reasons. For example, the rental price includes the cost of maintenance, and the rental agreement can be cancelled without penalty by the user with only a few months' notice. Thus, the computer user does not have to arrange for the maintenance of the equipment and does not have to commit himself to a long series of lease payments or to the financing of a large purchase price. Renting computer hardware provides greater flexibility in changing equipment configurations and greatly reduces the risk of technological obsolescence since users are not "locked in" to a purchased computer that has become obsolete due to a few technological developments. The monthly rental price is commonly based on 176 hours of use per month (8 hours per day for 22 working days in an average month). Use of rented computers for second and third shifts results in additional charges which are much lower than the rate for the first 176 hours. The major disadvantages of equipment rental is the higher total cost incurred if equipment is rented for more than four or five years. Hardware manufacturers base their rental prices on a four or five-year life, during which they will recover the cost of the equipment as well as a substantial profit. Therefore, if computer hardware is going to be used for a longer period (especially if it is going to be used for more than 176 hours per month) the cost of rental is higher than the cost of purchase.

Purchase

The number of computer users *purchasing* their equipment has grown in recent years for several reasons. First of all, computer users feel that third and fourth generation computer equipment will not become technologically obsolete as quickly as previous computer generations. Therefore, computer users can plan to keep their equipment for a longer period of time, thus making purchase substantially cheaper than rental. This is especially true for computer users who utilize their computers for more than one shift per working day, since they do not have to pay additional charges for such "overtime" use. Purchase also has a tax advantage since buying a computer is considered a capital investment and thus allows the computer user to qualify for an investment tax credit which reduces his income tax liability. One of the major disadvantages of the purchasing arrangement is that equipment maintenance is not included in the purchase price and therefore must be arranged separately with the computer manufacturer, an independent computer maintenance company, or be maintained by the computer user's own personnel. Two other major disadvantages have been previously mentioned: (1) the risk of technological obsolescence and (2) the necessity to finance a large purchase price.

Leasing

Leasing computer hardware from independent computer-leasing companies was a major development of the third generation of electronic data processing. So successful did such "third-party" leasing become that computer manufacturers themselves now offer long-term lease arrangements. Leasing companies typically purchase specific equipment desired by a user and then lease it to the user for a long-term period such as five years. Leasing arrangements include a maintenance contract, purchase and trade-in options, no charges for extra shift operation, and a reduction in lease charges after a minimum period of time. However, a cancellation charge is assessed if a lease is terminated before the end of the minimum lease period.

The leasing method combines some of the advantages and disadvantages of rental and purchase. Leasing does not require the financing of a large purchase price and is less expensive than renting equipment for the same period of time. The decline of lease charges after a minimum period, the inclusion of maintenance in the lease charges, and the absence of additional charges for overtime usage are other benefits. The major disadvantage is the long-term period of the lease contract which cannot be terminated without the payment of a substantial cancellation charge.

THE COST OF COMPUTER RESOURCES

Acquiring computer resources may involve substantial expenditures. See Figure 12–8. The percentage of business operating costs attributed to data processing has continued to increase each year. A recent study of several hundred of the largest corporations in the United States showed that the most profitable companies allocated over one percent of total revenues to EDP. Another study estimated that total EDP spending in 1973 exceeded $23 billion. This amount was spent in the percentages shown below.

	Percent
Personnel Compensation	44
Hardware Acquisition	39
EDP Services	9
Supplies	6
Software Acquisition	2
	100

It should be noted that *equipment costs* were once the largest part of EDP costs but have been steadily decreasing so that *personnel costs* are now the major cost category in providing computer services. Another way to analyze the cost of providing computer services is to group costs into the functional categories of (1) "systems development," (2) "operations," and (3) "administration." A summary of costs based on these categories is shown in Figure 12–9. A further breakdown of the cost of providing computer services is illustrated in Figure 12–10 which details some of the typical costs of a medium-scale computer installation. Note that the costs of systems development are frequently amortized (spread out) over a period of five or six years instead of charging total development costs against income during the year that they were incurred.

Systems Development Costs

Systems development costs arise primarily from salaries and other compensation for the systems analysts and programmers en-

The cost of a typical system.

Even if your computer system is efficiently used, the cost of computing can get out of hand. For it's not just the cost of the computers you have to contend with. It's the expense of the vast amount of peripheral equipment you must lease to run your computers efficiently.

For example, a popular new computer for large data base applications rents for $36,900 per month. Just the computer.

In addition, you need at least 16 tape drives at $11,375 per month. Plus at least 5 high-speed discs at $10,900 per month.

You'll need two printers and a controller at $2,190 per month and two card I/O units at $1,750 per month.

So each month you write a check for $63,115 for hardware alone, but that's only the beginning.

For efficient, 24-hour operation, you'll need 12 operators at about $12,000 a month in salaries. Plus a systems programmer at about $1,600 a month. Plus 10 or so key punch operators and their machines at about $8,000 a month.

You'll also need at least 10 application programmers at $12,000 a month and a D.P. manager at $2,000 per month. So D.P. salaries can total more than $35,000 a month—without overtime.

Add the rent allocation for your data center, perhaps $50,000 a year, plus whatever you'll spend for forms and miscellaneous costs and the typical computer installation can easily cost nearly a million and a quarter dollars a year.

And these figures represent the computing costs of a medium-size company. Large companies may spend $30 million a year for computing.

FIGURE 12–8

Computer Cost Considerations

Source: *A Helpful Guide on How to Keep Your Computers from Putting You in the Poorhouse* (Bethpage, N.Y.: Grumman Data Systems), pp. 9–10.

FIGURE 12–9

Computer Cost Categories

Systems Development Costs

Systems Development Personnel
Computer Program Testing
Systems Development Supplies
Facilities Preparation and Furnishing
Personnel Training
Other Installation and Conversion Costs

Operations Costs

Equipment
Supplies
Software
Program Maintenance
Operations Personnel
Occupancy and Utilities
Other Costs

Administrative Costs

Management Personnel
Administrative Staff
Secretarial and Clerical Personnel
Miscellaneous Costs
Organizational Overhead

gaged in the development of new or improved computer applications. Installation and conversion costs include the cost of (1) training employees to operate and use a newly developed system, (2) preparing and furnishing facilities needed by a new system, and (3) testing the new system, file conversion, parallel operations, etc. Other costs may also be included under the systems development category such as the cost of financing the development of a new system. The facilities preparation and furnishing cost may be substantial for a new system. Most computers require environmental considerations such as air conditioning, humidity control, and dust control. Computers require electrical power and false flooring under which interconnecting electric cables can be laid. Emergency equipment such as fire prevention systems and auxiliary generating equipment may also be required.

Operations Costs

A major *operating cost* is equipment rental or lease charges. If equipment is purchased, then the cost of financing the purchase and the depreciation and maintenance costs of the equipment must be included. The cost of supplies, purchased or leased software, and the

FIGURE 12–10

Examples of Computer Costs

Development costs		Annual equipment costs	
Site	$ 35,000	4 tape drives	
Training (direct)	10,000	2 disks	$9,000/month
Initial Supplies	10,000	20,000 characters	= $108,000
Facilities and Furniture	15,000	of storage	
Test Time	5,000		
Systems Design (10 man-years @ $12,000 inclusive of training & fringe)	120,000	Printer	$500/month
		Card Reader Punch	= 6,000
		Total	$114,000
Programming (15 man-years @ $10,000 inclusive)	150,000		
Conversion	40,000		
Installation (4 months duplex	92,000	*Annual personnel costs*	
(Subtotal)	477,000	*(operating)*	
Money Cost (6%, 5 years, straight line = 15% of $477,000)	72,000	DP Manager (½)	8,000
		Operations Mgr.	11,000
		Analyst	13,000
Total	$549,000	Programmer	11,000
		Secretary	6,000
		4 Operators	24,000
		6 Keypunch Operators	27,000
		2 Peripheral Operators	12,000
		1 Schedulor	8,000
		(Subtotal)	120,000
		20% Fringe	24,000
		Total	$144,000

Summary of costs

Equipment	$114,000
Personnel	144,000
Supplies	20,000
Development (÷5)	110,000
Total Annual Cost	$388,000

Source: From Brandon, Dick H., *Management Planning for Data Processing* (New York), © Mason/Charter Publishers, Inc., 1970, p. 147. Reprinted by permission of Mason/Charter.

cost of office space and building utilities are other operating costs. Another major operations cost category is salaries and other compensation for operations personnel and maintenance programmers. Other costs include charges for custodial, building maintenance, and security personnel or services.

Administrative Costs

Salary and other compensation expense for management personnel, administrative staff, and secretarial and clerical personnel is the major category of *administrative costs*. Organizational overhead is a major cost category for business firms who insist that the computer services department bear its share of administrative and general expenses of the company. Miscellaneous costs may include such items as employee travel and training that cannot be attributed to specific systems development projects.

Controlling Computer Costs

The cost of providing computer services has become a major operating expense of computer-using business firms. Therefore, an extensive cost control program is necessary if computer costs are to be controlled. Some of the major *cost control techniques* that are utilized by computer users are summarized below.

Systems development. The costs of systems development must be controlled by a formal *project management* program in which a combination of plans, budgets, schedules, and reporting techniques are utilized to control the cost and direction of a systems development project. Some computer users also find it cheaper to utilize contract programming or systems design services from external sources rather than hire the additional personnel required for such systems development effort. Other firms find that buying or leasing software packages provide a cheaper method of systems development for some applications.

Computer Operations. Several techniques are used to control computer operations costs. A formal *cost accounting* system is a major cost control technique. All costs incurred must be recorded, reported, allocated, and charged to specific computer users. Under this arrangement the computer services department becomes a "service center" whose costs are charged directly to computer users rather than being lumped together with other administrative and service costs and treated as an overhead cost.

The use of *financial budgets* is another method of managing computer costs. Budgets can be defined as detailed, short-term plans (one year or less) which forecast the resources required and the results expected during a period. Budgets are a short-range planning device as well as a widely used method of control. Financial budgets should be required for computer operations as well as for systems development. Cost control is exercised by identifying and investigating the reasons for deviations from the budget.

External EDP services such as facilities management and EDP service bureaus have been found to be a cheaper method of computer operations for some computer-using firms. Many computer users have found such services to be a decisive method of identifying and reducing the cost of computer operations.

Hardware. Computer hardware costs can be controlled by a formal *evaluation and selection* process as was described in the previous section of this chapter. Computer hardware costs can sometimes be reduced by replacing peripheral equipment supplied by the computer manufacturer with those offered by independent peripheral equipment companies. Some computer users have a policy of purchasing the CPU and renting the peripheral equipment of a computer system. In this way they can obtain some of the cost advantages of equipment purchase, while providing themselves with the flexibility and protection from obsolescence of equipment rental. Hardware costs can also be reduced by leasing equipment from independent computer leasing companies or by purchasing a "second-hand" computer from a used computer dealer. The major disadvantage of these approaches is the possibility of inferior service and support that may arise.

SUMMARY

The computer-using business firm must acquire computer resources from many sources in the computer industry. Therefore, business computer users should acquire a basic understanding of the computer industry since it is a vital source of computer hardware, software, and EDP services. The computer industry is international in scope, though U.S. firms are the major source of computers utilized throughout the world. The U.S. computer industry consists of a few major computer manufacturers and many smaller suppliers of hardware, software, and EDP services. Effective and efficient use of the computer by business firms requires the continual support of many firms within the computer industry.

Information systems development and data processing services can be acquired from sources outside the business firm instead of developing such capabilities within the organization. Many business firms utilize the "external EDP services" provided by EDP service bureaus, time-sharing companies, facilities management companies, etc. The major benefit of using external EDP services is that the computer user pays only for the specific services he needs and does not have to acquire or manage EDP hardware, software, and personnel. Some loss of control over the data processing function, inconvenience, and higher costs are limitations that are attributed to some forms of external EDP services.

Computer users should have a basic understanding of how to evaluate the acquisition of computer resources. The evaluation and selection of computer resources should be a formal process that requires manufacturers and suppliers to present bids and proposals based on systems specifications developed during the design stage of systems development. A formal evaluation process reduces the possibility of incorrect or unnecessary purchases of computer hardware or software. Several major "evaluation factors" such as performance, cost, reliability, etc. should be utilized to evaluate computer hardware, software and vendor support. The use of rental, purchase, or lease arrangements in financing computer acquisitions must also be evaluated.

A major concern of computer users is the control of the cost of computer resources. Acquiring computer resources usually involves substantial expenditures for hardware, software, EDP services, supplies, and EDP personnel compensation. Major cost control programs are necessary in order to control the cost of systems development, computer operations, and EDP administration.

KEY TERMS AND CONCEPTS

Computer-based business environment, 384
Computer industry, 385–390
EDP service bureau, 390
Facilities management, 390
External EDP services, 391–392
Hardware evaluation factors, 394–395

Software evaluation factors, 395–396
Evaluation of vendor support, 396
Financing computer acquisitions, 397–398
Computer cost categories, 399–402
Computer cost control, 403–404

ASSIGNMENTS

1. Test your understanding of the chapter material by reviewing the *purpose, outline, summary,* and *key terms and concepts* of this chapter. Are you confident that you have attained a basic understanding of the major concepts of the chapter? If not, reread the appropriate material as indicated by the page numbers after each key term and concept.

2. Discuss the relationship of the various elements of the computer-based business environment to the computer services department of a business firm.

3. Identify several types of firms in the computer industry in each of the following categories:
    a. hardware suppliers,
    b. software suppliers, and
    c. EDP service suppliers.
    Describe the specific products or services each firm supplies to computer users.

4. Discuss the domestic and international composition of the computer industry and its effect on computer-using organizations.

5. Discuss the benefits and limitations of utilizing external EDP services.

6. Discuss several of the evaluation factors that should be considered in evaluating:

a. hardware,

b. software, and

c. vendor support

Which of these factors do you consider most important? Why?

7. Discuss the benefits and limitations of the rental, leasing, and purchase of computer resources.

8. Describe several major categories of EDP costs. Identify several specific costs in each category.

9. Discuss several methods of controlling the cost of systems development, computer operations, and computer hardware.

Chapter Outline

Purpose of the Chapter

Introduction

Organizing Computer Resources
Organizational Functions, Systems Development, Operations, Administration, Organizational Location, Organizational Structure, Other Organizational Arrangements

Staffing for Computer Services
Systems Development Personnel, Programming Personnel, Operations Personnel, Administrative Personnel, Personnel Management

Managing Systems Development
Long-Range Planning, Project Identification, Project Teams, Project Management

Managing Computer Operations
Operations Management, Production Planning and Control

Controlling Electronic Data Processing
Data Processing Controls, Input Controls, Processing Controls, Output Controls, Storage Controls, Organizational Controls, Facility Controls, Auditing EDP

Summary

Key Terms and Concepts

Assignments

13

Managing Computer Resources

Purpose of the Chapter

To promote a basic understanding of how business firms must manage their computer resources by analyzing:

1. The organization and staffing of a computer services department,
2. The management of systems development and computer operations,
3. The control of electronic data processing.

INTRODUCTION

Managing the computer resources of a business firm has become a major new responsibility of business management. Inadequate management of computer performance by many business firms is well-documented and will be discussed in the next chapter. In this chapter, we will first analyze the basic functions performed by the computer services department of a computer-using firm. We will then discuss methods of managing these functions, with special emphasis given to the *planning, organizing, staffing, and controlling* activities that are required.

ORGANIZING COMPUTER RESOURCES

Organizational Functions

The computer services organization is usually given departmental or divisional status. We will use the name *"computer services depart-*

ment," though other names such as "information systems," information processing," "management information systems," "data processing," or "EDP" department are also used. However, no matter what name is utilized, the computer services organization performs several basic functions and activities which we will now explore. The major activities which must be performed can be grouped into three basic functional categories: (1) *systems development,* (2) *operations,* and (3) *administration.* Figure 13–1 illustrates this grouping of computer service functions and activities.[1]

FIGURE 13–1

Major Functions and Activities of a Computer Services Organization

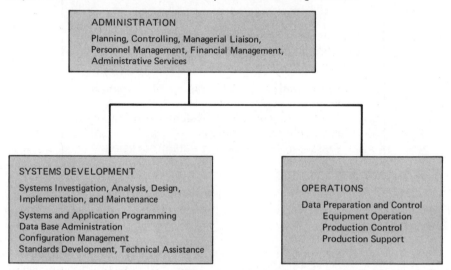

Systems Development

Systems development activities include the investigation, analysis, design, programming, implementation, and maintenance of information systems within the computer-using organization. These activities were discussed in detail in Chapter 8. In addition, the systems development function frequently includes the activities of system programming, data base administration, configuration management, development of data processing standards, and technical assistance. These additional systems development activities are summarized below.

------

[1] Some of the material in this section has been adapted from *Organizing the Data Processing Activity* (White Plains, N.Y.: IBM Corporation, 1973), pp. 12–28.

1. Systems programming. Design and maintenance of system software such as operating systems and other control programs and service programs.

2. Data base administration. Design and maintenance of data bases and data management software.

3. Configuration management. Planning and evaluating present and proposed hardware and software systems, i.e., "configurations." Results in recommendations for hardware and software modifications or acquisitions.

4. Development of data processing standards. Development, publication, distribution, and maintenance of standards and procedures that govern the performance of all data processing activities.

5. Technical assistance. Assist computer users and computer personnel by providing information, consulting assistance, training programs, and other technical resources such as a library of system and program documentation and a technical library of EDP publication such as books, periodicals, and manuals.

Operations

The *operations* function of the computer services department is concerned with the processing of data into information through the use of hardware, software, and EDP personnel. The operations function includes the major activities of data preparation, equipment operation, production control, and production support. The content of these activities are summarized below.

1. Data preparation and control. Includes converting input source documents into machine-sensible form by keypunching, key-to-tape or key-to-disk operations, utilizing a variety of data entry equipment. The data control aspect of this activity refers to the continual checking and monitoring of input data and output reports to insure their accuracy, completeness, and timeliness.

2. Equipment operation. Includes the operation of the computer system including the computer console, on-line peripheral equipment, and data communications terminals and control equipment. It also includes the operation of off-line equipment such as off-line magnetic tape units and printers, and other types of off-line data conversion or output support equipment.

3. Production control. Includes the scheduling, monitoring, and control of facilities and data processing jobs. It includes the scheduling of equipment, data files, and necessary data processing supplies, scheduling and logging job input and output, and communicating with users on scheduling requirements and the status of specific jobs.

4. Production support.   Activities which support data processing operations include acquisition and maintenance of data processing supplies, maintaining a library of data files on magnetic tape, magnetic disk, or punched cards, maintaining a library of operations documentation, providing for the physical security of the computer facilities, and distribution of computer output.

Administration

The *administration* of computer services requires the performance of several specific managerial activities. These activities include planning, controlling, managerial liaison, personnel management, financial management, and administrative services. The content of these activities is summarized below.

1. Planning.   Includes long and short-range planning of computer operations, systems development projects, hardware, software, and facilities acquisition.

2. Controlling.   Includes the monitoring and evaluating of computer operations, systems development projects, and hardware, software, facilities, and personnel utilization. Reporting systems are developed to compare performance with plans. The controlling activity also includes the development and maintenance of a program of security procedures designed to protect the security of the personnel, programs, data, equipment, and facilities of the computer services department.

3. Managerial liaison.   This activity involves communicating and reporting to computer users and top management concerning the plans and performance of the computer services department. Managerial liaison also includes meeting and maintaining proper relationships with hardware and software vendors and suppliers.

4. Personnel management.   Includes defining personnel requirements, recruiting and selection of personnel, employee training and development, performance evaluation, and personnel recordkeeping.

5. Financial management.   Includes developing and maintaining methods of financial recordkeeping and financial analysis so that the cost of computer operations and systems development projects can be analyzed and controlled. This activity also includes billing computer users for EDP costs, providing cost estimates for planning purposes, and purchasing required hardware, software, and services.

6. Administrative services. Includes the supply of services such as secretarial and clerical assistance, hardware maintenance scheduling, and custodial services.

Organizational Location

The *location* of the computer services department within the structure of the business firm depends on the size of the computer operation and the emphasis given to computer services by top management. It also depends on the historical development of data processing in the organization. For example, many computer services departments are located within a finance or accounting division because many of the first applications which utilized punched card equipment and computers were developed for accounting purposes. Small-scale computer operations are usually located within a functional department of the firm such as manufacturing or finance. Large-scale operations usually become independent departments or divisions whose managers may have vice-presidential status in the firm.

Another aspect of the organizational location of computer services concerns the centralization or decentralization of data processing within the firm. In the next chapter we will discuss how computers can support either centralization or decentralization within an organization. The development of large computers with centralized data files utilizing remote data communications terminals has supported the *centralization* of computer services within one department of many organizations. However, the development of minicomputers, improved small computers, data communications, and time-sharing can support *decentralization* of computer services within an organization. Business firms can establish divisional or regional computer service departments throughout the organization, thus decentralizing data processing.

The extent to which business firms should centralize or decentralize computer services depends on many factors. *Centralized* computer facilities are usually more economical and efficient in terms of hardware, software, and personnel cost and utilization. This is especially true for firms with a high volume of repetitive business data processing. In addition, centralization fosters integration and standardization of information systems within an organization. However, *decentralized* computer services are usually more responsive to user needs, encourage greater utilization of the computer, and reduce the risks of computer errors and malfunctions. A compromise utilized by several large firms is to centralize computer services by establishing a few regional computer centers while providing organizational units with remote terminals and allowing them to employ their own systems analysts. Smaller firms have of necessity tended toward centralization of the computer services within a single department.

Organizational Structure

The internal *organizational structure* of a computer services organization must reflect its major functions and activities. However, the particular structure utilized depends on many factors, including organizational location, centralization or decentralization of data processing, and the size of the computer services organization. For example, if a business firm utilizes a minicomputer or very small computer, the responsibility for computer services may be assigned to one individual. However, in most computer-using firms, the responsi-

FIGURE 13–2

A Functional Organizational Structure for a Computer Services Department

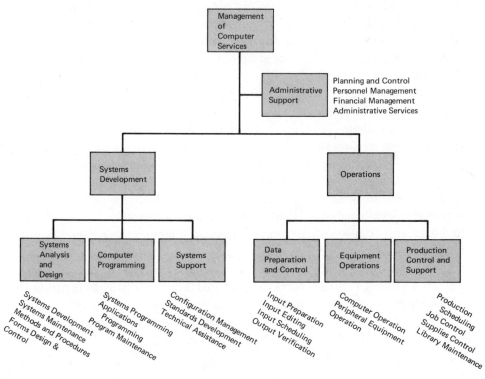

bility for performing computer service functions and activities is distributed among several groups of EDP personnel. The resulting organizational structure is a grouping of functions and activities that best fits the management philosophy, business environment, computer operations, and EDP personnel of each particular computer-using business firm. Figure 13–2 illustrates a basic organizational structure that reflects the functions and activities of many computer service organizations. However, this is only a general model, with many variations being utilized by computer-using organizations.

The organizational structure for a *small-scale* computer operation may reflect the fact that only three or four people are involved: a data processing manager (who often doubles as a systems analyst), a computer programmer, a computer operator, and a data preparation clerk (many times a keypunch operator). See Figure 13–3. The organizational structure of a *medium-scale* or *large-scale* computer operation is more complex because many more people are involved in the performance of necessary functions and activities. The managers of systems development, programming, and operations are frequently supported by supervisory personnel known as project leaders, lead programmers, shift supervisors, and lead computer operators. The organizational structure of the computer operations section of large computer users usually reflects the fact that the computer is operated on a "round-the-clock" basis. Supervisory positions such as "shift supervisor" are usually created to supervise the operations of the computer during each shift. See Figure 13–4.

Other Organizational Arrangements

Computer services departments utilize several organizational arrangements which may not be revealed by the organization charts of

FIGURE 13–3

Small-Scale Organization Structure

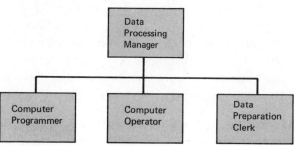

FIGURE 13–4

Medium-Scale Organization Structure

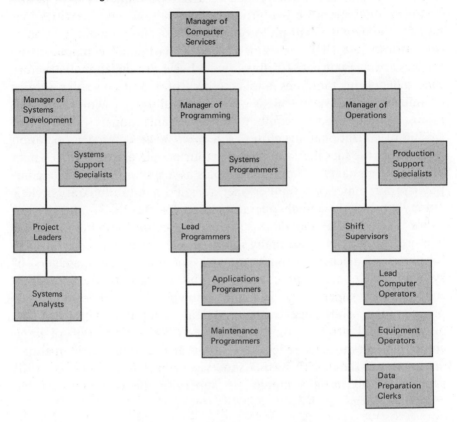

computer-using business firms. Many firms utilize a *project management* type of organizational structure for systems development projects. Systems analysts and computer programmers are frequently assigned to *"project teams"* for the development of specific information systems. Thus, a systems analyst or computer programmer is supervised by the "project leader" of the project team to which he is assigned, as well as by the manager of the systems development or programming departments. Many project teams also include representatives of the computer users for whom an information system is being developed. The establishment of systems development project teams with user representation provides the "user involvement" that is necessary for the development of "user-oriented" information systems.

Management of computer services involves the organization of information systems efforts throughout the company as well as in the computer services department. Many firms utilize a top level *"executive EDP committee"* which acts as a steering committee for the EDP activities of the organization. The committee consists of several members of top management and includes the heads of user departments and the computer services department. The function of this committee is to coordinate and control the information systems of the firm. Long-range plans which establish goals, set priorities, allocate resources, and schedule projects are developed by this committee. The progress of information systems development and the success of existing information systems is monitored and evaluated by the committee. The activities of the executive EDP committee provide the top management involvement and support that is vital to successful information systems.

STAFFING FOR COMPUTER SERVICES

The success or failure of a computer services organization rests primarily on the quality of its personnel. Many computer users consider recruiting, training, and retaining qualified personnel as their greatest single EDP problem. There are over a million persons employed in the computer services organizations of computer users. National employment surveys continually forecast shortages of qualified services personnel (especially programmers and systems analysts) that range into the hundreds of thousands. Employment opportunities in the computer field are excellent since the need for systems analysts, programmers, and managerial personnel is expected to expand significantly as business firms continue to expand their use of computers. Therefore, it is important to analyze the types of jobs and the managerial problems associated with computer services personnel.

Figure 13–5 presents an organization chart which illustrates the wide variety of job types that are possible in a computer services organization. However, the positions available in a computer services department can be grouped into four occupational categories: (1) *systems development,* (2) *programming,* (3) *operations,* and (4) *administration.* The types of jobs and the number of persons required for each job type depends on the size of the computer services organization. Large-scale computer operations allow more specialization of job assignments and thus create more types of jobs.

FIGURE 13–5

Job Titles in a Large-Scale Computer Services Organization

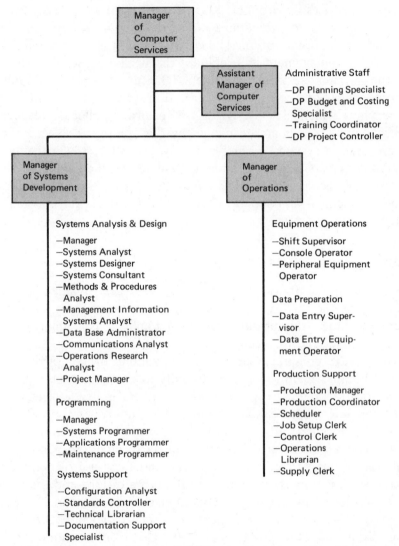

Source: This chart and the job descriptions in this section are based in part on *Organizing the Data Processing Activity* (White Plains, N.Y.: IBM Corporation, 1973), pp. 29–38.

Systems Development Personnel

The most common type of job in this category is the job of *"systems analyst."* Larger computer service operations expand this job operation into several specialized job types. Job descriptions for several jobs in this category are summarized below.

1. Systems analyst.   Gathers and analyzes information needed for the development or modification of information systems. Develops a statement of system requirements and prepares detailed system specifications on which computer programs will be based. Supervises installation of new systems and evaluates existing systems for possible improvements.

2. Systems designer.   Translates systems requirements prepared by the systems analyst into alternative systems designs. Develops detailed systems specifications for the system being developed.

3. Management information systems analyst.   Plans, designs, and installs information systems which utilize integrated data bases and advanced processing systems to provide management with information for decision-making.

4. Data base administrator.   Designs and maintains the data bases of the organization. Prepares and enforces standards for the use and security of information in the data bases.

5. Communications analyst.   Plans, designs and installs data communications networks including the specification and selection of software, terminals, and communications control equipment.

6. Operations research analyst.   Applies mathematical techniques to the solution of difficult problems in systems analysis and design as well as in other areas of the business.

7. Methods and procedures analyst.   Develops and installs improved clerical methods, procedures, and forms as part of the development of new or improved systems.

8. Systems consultant.   Assists computer users in the development and installation of new computer systems and the maintenance of existing systems. Frequently serves as a liaison between computer users and the computer services department.

Other systems development job categories are frequently classified as "systems support" occupations. These include: (1) a *configuration analyst* who is responsible for evaluating and improving hardware and software performance, (2) a *standards controller* who develops and maintains data processing standards and procedures for the organization, (3) a *technical librarian* who develops and maintains a library of system documentation and technical information, and (4) a *documentation support specialist* who assists systems analysts and programmers in developing detailed system, programming, and operations documentation.

Programming Personnel

Programming personnel are responsible for the development of computer programs. The most common job title is *"programmer,"* but several other job titles are also used that reflect the specialization in particular types of programming effort.

1. Programmer. Develops program logic and codes, tests and documents computer programs.

2. Applications programmer. Develops programs required for specific applications of computer users.

3. Maintenance programmer. Modifies and improves existing programs.

4. Systems programmer. Develops, modifies and maintains the operating system and other system software utilized by a computer services organization.

5. Analyst programmer. A systems analyst who does his own application programming, or visa versa, an applications programmer who does his own systems analysis and design.

Operations Personnel

Operations personnel are responsible for operating or controlling the operation of electronic data processing equipment. Operations personnel job types can be grouped into the categories of (1) *equipment operations,* (2) *data preparation,* and (3) *production support.*

1. Computer operator. Monitors and controls the computer by operating the central console. Adjusts the configuration of the computer system in response to messages from the operating system or instructions contained in the operations documentation. Operates peripheral equipment in smaller installations.

2. Peripheral equipment operator. Assists the computer operator by setting up and operating tape drives, magnetic disk drives, printers, etc. Also operates off-line input/output equipment.

3. Data entry equipment operator. Converts data on source documents into machine-sensible form by use of a keyboard-driven machine, such as a keypunch, key-to-tape, CRT terminal, etc.

4. Production coordinator. Coordinates and controls the mix of data processing jobs to achieve optimum equipment utilization and service to users.

5. Scheduler. Prepares and maintains schedules for data processing jobs by working with users and the production coordinator. Maintains records of job and equipment performance.

6. Control clerk. Maintains controls on inputs and jobs for computer processing. Reviews outputs to see that they satisfy job requirements and distributes them to users.

7. Job setup clerk. Assembles the files and data processing materials for individual jobs in accordance with processing schedules and instructions contained in operations documentation.

8. Operations librarian. Maintains and issues magnetic tape and disk files.

9. Supply clerk. Maintains and issues data processing supplies.

Administrative Personnel

Administrative personnel manage and supervise the activities of the computer services organization. They include administrative staff positions which support management in administrative planning and control.

1. Manager of computer services. Plans and directs the activities of the entire computer services organization.

2. Assistant manager of computer services. Assists the manager of computer services and acts for the manager in his absence.

3. Manager of systems development. Directs the activities of the systems development process.

4. Operations manager. Directs the operation of all data processing equipment and the production of all data processing jobs.

Other administrative positions include the managers of systems analysis and design, programming, systems support, production support, and "shift supervisors" who supervise equipment operations during each shift of a working day. Additional administrative job classifications exist in many computer services organizations due to the recognition of seniority and the assignment of supervisory responsibilities. Thus, titles such as "Lead Systems Analyst," "Lead Programmer," and "Lead Computer Operator" recognize the assignment of supervisory responsibilities to these positions. Titles such as "Senior Systems Analyst," "Junior Programmer," or "Senior Computer Operator" reflect the degree of seniority and expertise of the persons in those positions.

Besides managerial and supervisory positions, several administrative staff positions may also be present in a large computer services organization.

1. Data processing planning specialist. Prepares long and short-range plans for application selection, systems development, and acquisition of hardware, software and personnel resources.

2. Project controller.   Develops and administers a planning, control, and reporting system for systems development projects.

3. Training coordinator.   Develops and administers training programs for computer services personnel and computer users.

4. Budget and costing specialist.   Develops budgets for the computer services organization and evaluates performance against the budget. Develops and administers a system for allocating the costs of computer services to computer users.

Another widely used administrative job type is the position of *project manager* or *project leader.* This person is frequently a senior systems analyst who supervises the activities of a systems development project team composed of systems analysts, programmers, and user representatives.

Personnel Management

Management of computer services requires the management of computer personnel such as systems analysts, programmers, and other managerial, technical, and clerical personnel. One of the most important jobs of the manager of computer services is to recruit qualified personnel and to develop, organize, and direct the capabilities of the existing personnel. He may also have to select and direct the work of outside consultants that are hired on a temporary basis for the development of certain information systems. Employees must be continually trained to keep up with the latest developments in a fast-moving and highly technical field. Employee job performance must be continually evaluated, and outstanding performance rewarded with salary increases or promotions. Salary and wage levels must be set, and "career paths" must be designed so that individuals can move to new jobs through promotion and transfer as they gain in seniority and expertise.

The management and development of computer services personnel poses some unique problems for management. For example, systems analysts and computer programmers are creative, professional personnel who cannot be managed with traditional work rules or evaluated by traditional performance criteria. How do you measure how well a system analyst or programmer is doing? This question has plagued the management of many computer-using business firms. However, it should be emphasized that this question is not unique to computer professionals but is common to the management of many professional personnel, especially the scientists and engineers employed in the research and development activities of many organizations. Effective *project planning, controlling, and reporting* techniques are available which provide the information required for the evaluation of systems development and programming personnel.

Another personnel management problem area is the professional loyalty of computer services personnel. Like other professionals, computer services personnel may have a greater loyalty to the "data processing profession" than to the organization which employes them. Thus, a computer programmer considers himself a programmer *first,* and an employee, *second.* When this attitude is coupled with the shortages of many qualified EDP personnel, a serious problem in retaining qualified personnel may arise. This problem can be solved by effective personnel management. Providing computer services personnel with opportunities for merit salary increases, promotions, transfers, and attendance at professional meetings and seminars provides the flexible job environment needed to retain competent personnel. Challenging technological and intellectual assignments and a congenial atmosphere of fellow professionals are other major factors in retaining computer services personnel.

Figure 13–6 illustrates the desired qualifications for systems analysts, programmers, and computer operators. Notice the differences between the educational requirements and personal characteristics desired for each type of job, as well as the length of training period and types of training concepts that are desirable. It should be obvious that the position of systems analyst requires more education and training and distinctly different personal characteristics than the position of computer programmer or operator.

Figure 13–6 also points out that it is possible for systems analysts (and data processing managers) to achieve the professional designation of CDP (Certificate in Data Processing) which requires a Bachelor's Degree, a minimum of three years of experience in data processing, and passing the CDP examination. The examination consists of a five-hour, 300-question exam covering the five sections of (1) data processing equipment, (2) computer programming and software, (3) principles of management, (4) quantitative methods, and (5) systems analysis and design. Figure 13–6 also indicates that professional programmers can seek the RBP designation (Registered Business Programmer) which certifies that they have mastered the technical knowledge required to be effective business programmers at approximately the senior programmer level. The RBP exam consists of a 2½ hour, 150-question exam that covers the five categories of

FIGURE 13–6

Desired Qualifications for Selected EDP Personnel

	Systems analyst	*Programmer*	*Operator*
Educational requirement	Bachelor's degree in any applied or analytical science, e.g., business administration, economics, mathematics, etc.	High school diploma, or equivalent. (Scientific programmer will require 2 years of college math)	High school diploma, or equivalent.
Personal characteristics	Imagination and creativity Logical ability Organizational ability High degree of initiative Communicative skills Tact	Logical aptitude (As indicated by programming aptitude tests) Reasonable motivation or initiative Attention to detail Limited writing ability	Average intelligence Manual dexterity Ability to follow instructions
Formal train-needs	20 weeks	8–10 weeks	1 week
On-the-job training	12–15 months 12 months average	6–12 months 9 months average	4 weeks
Possible professional certification	CDP	RBP	None
Desirable training concepts	Basic business skills Data gathering techniques Documentation analysis File management concepts Data analysis Hardware Basic programming Computer applications Advanced concepts of systems technology	Logical analysis Language coding Testing techniques Documentation skills, and requirements	Normal operating procedures Exception procedures Emergency procedures Data file protection

Source: Based in part on Brandon, Dick H., *Management Planning for Data Processing* (New York), Mason / Charter Publishers, Inc., 1970, p. 174. Reprinted by permission of Mason / Charter.

(1) principles of programming, (2) programming language translators, (3) problem-oriented languages, (4) data processing systems design, and (5) computational topics. Both the CDP and the RBP programs are administered by the Data Processing Management Association (DPMA) which is an international organization for data processing managers and professionals.

Differences in the degree of skills required is reflected in the salary information contained in Figure 13–7. Notice the differences in salaries between computer operators, programmers, and systems analysts. Figure 13–7 also gives a valuable insight into the high salaries commanded by many computer services personnel. These weekly

FIGURE 13–7

Growth in Weekly Salaries for Computer Services Personnel

Job description	National average 1969	National average 1974	Percent of increase (5 years)
Manager of Data Processing............................	$303	$383	26.4
Asst. Manager of Data Processing..................	265	355	34.0
Mgr. or Sup. of Computer Systems Analysis..........	280	376	34.3
Lead Computer Systems Analyst....................	253	334	32.0
Senior Computer Systems Analyst..................	230	301	30.9
Junior Computer Systems Analyst..................	189	250	32.3
Manager or Supervisor of Programming..............	251	331	31.9
Lead Programmer.................................	217	293	35.0
Senior Programmer...............................	190	259	36.3
Junior Programmer...............................	152	211	38.8
Programmer Trainee..............................	—	172	—
Manager or Supervisor of Computer Operations.......	211	283	34.1
Lead Computer Operator..........................	160	209	30.6
Senior Computer Operator........................	139	182	30.9
Junior Computer Operator........................	119	158	32.8
Computer 1/0 Control Manager....................	161	186	15.5
Tape Librarian..................................	115	147	27.8
Keypunch Supervisor.............................	131	180	37.4
Lead Keypunch/Tape Operator....................	110	149	35.5
Senior Keypunch/Tape Operator..................	100	136	36.0
Junior Keypunch/Tape Operator..................	90	122	35.6

Source: Derived from *INFOSYSTEMS* (September 1974), p. 35.

figures translate into average annual salaries of approximately $20,-000 for data processing managers, $16,000 for senior systems analysts, and $13,000 for senior programmers. Of course, these figures are national averages, and actual salaries can range much higher and lower depending on such factors as the size and geographic location of the computer services organization.

MANAGING SYSTEMS DEVELOPMENT

Planning, organizing, and controlling the *systems development* function of a computer services department is a major managerial responsibility. Important methods utilized in the management of systems development include (1) long-range planning, (2) project identification, (3) project teams, and (4) project management.

Long-Range Planning

The *"master information systems development plan"* for managing the computer resources of a business firm is a description of the information systems development projects that the business firm intends to accomplish in the future, i.e., in the next two to five years. The plan indicates a tentative time table for the projects and provides "ball park" estimates of the resources required and the benefits to be obtained. The master information systems development plan should be developed in conjunction with the long-range planning being done by the organization. In some large firms, long-range planning groups at the corporate level or in the information systems division are given the responsibility for developing such long-range plans. Long-range planning specialists are employed to gather data and formulate the alternatives required in the planning process. These alternatives are presented to the top management *Executive EDP Committee* for review and final decision-making.

Project Identification

The systems development process may start with a request for new or improved information from operating personnel, management, or persons outside the business firm such as customers, suppliers, governmental agencies, or outside consultants. The computer services department itself may initiate the systems development process as part of the long-range plan for information systems development or because of the need for modifications revealed by the systems maintenance activity. Requests for information systems development should be formalized in written form and reviewed and approved by the management of the computer services department, the prospective user department, and the management EDP committee before a feasibility study is made. See Figure 13–8. If a feasibility study is approved, the report of the feasibility study results should be reviewed by the management EDP committee which makes the final decision on whether the information system should be developed.

Project Teams

Small systems development projects are handled in many business firms by single systems analyst whose duties may also include writing the necessary computer programs. However, we have previously mentioned that larger projects usually utilize a *project team* composed of systems analysts, computer programmers, and representatives of user departments which will be most directly affected by a new system. In some cases the project team may also include members from

FIGURE 13–8

MANAGEMENT INFORMATION SERVICES – PROJECT REQUEST

<u>FORM 835 – REV. 4/66 – (4GG39) – 50</u>

PROJECT NAME	PROJECT NO.
REQUESTING DEPARTMENT	REQUESTED COMP.

BRIEF DESCRIPTION

				FREQUENCY
COMPLETED BY REQUESTOR	COST REDUCTION	$ _____	PER _____	☐ MONTHLY
	PROFIT IMPROVEMENT	$ _____	PER _____	☐ ANNUALLY
				☐ ONE TIME
COMPLETED BY DATA PROCESSING	OPERATING COST	$ _____	PER _____	☐ OTHER (SPECIFY)
	NET BENEFIT	$ _____	PER _____	
	INSTALLATION COST	$ _____		

APPROVED BY:	REQUESTING DEPT. DIRECTOR	DATE

FOR DATA PROCESSING DEPARTMENT USE ONLY

SERVICES REQUIRED	ASSIGNED TO		ESTIMATED COMPLETION DATE	DATE COMPLETED
	NAME	DATE		
☐ COMPUTER SYSTEMS				
☐ COMMUNICATIONS				
☐ COMPUTER OPERATIONS				

NO. OF COPIES	SIZE PAPER OR FORM	DISTRIBUTION	REMOVE CARBON

REMARKS:

REQUEST WAS ☐ APPROVED ☐ RETURNED	SIGNATURE, DIRECTOR, DATA PROCESSING	DATE

Source: A. C. Throldahl, *Project Management—Computer System Projects* (Minneapolis: University of Minnesota, School of Business Administration, 1969), p. 21.

outside the organization such as computer manufacturer "systems engineers" and management consultants. The project team leader usually reports to the head of the computer services department who usually bears overall responsibility for all systems development projects. In many business firms, the manager of a user department is also involved directly or indirectly in the management of the project team.

The use of project teams is a major aspect of the "project management" approach which is discussed in the following section. Assigning systems analysts and programmers to specific projects headed by a project leader allows better control of the progress of systems development. The alternative is to assign personnel to work on projects on a "when available" basis. This method usually results in a lack of project control and a waste of human and financial resources.

Project Management

Project management is the term used to describe the management of the development work required by a proposed information system project. The concept of project management requires that each information system be developed by a project team according to a specific plan that is formulated during the systems investigation stage. Such a *project plan* will include descriptions of the tasks involved and the assignment of responsibility for each task. Estimated startup and completion dates for the entire project, as well as for major checkpoints or "milestones" in the development of the project must also be included. Specified amounts of time, money, and manpower should be allocated to each segment of the project.

The project plan should include provisions for handling suggested changes to the proposed system including a "design freeze" policy. Such a policy prohibits changes in systems design after specified project deadlines unless the change is formally approved by top management. Provisions must also be made for revision of the project schedule due to major unforeseen developments. Recordkeeping forms which report the progress of individual members of a systems development project are also used in many project management systems. Good project management also requires that each phase of systems development be properly documented before new stages are begun. This is especially important because there is usually some degree of personnel turnover among the members of the project team.

All information systems development projects should be planned and controlled by several types of project management techniques. Many firms utilize special reporting forms to insure that all systems development projects are properly authorized and controlled. See Figure 13–9. Several types of charts are used to plan and control projects such as the Gantt chart which specifies the times allowed for the various activities required in information systems development. See Figure 13–10. The PERT system (Program Evaluation and Review Technique) which involves the use of a network diagram of required events and activities is also used by some computer users. See Figure 13–11. The use of financial and operating budgets is another method of managing systems development projects. Budgets serve as a short-range planning device as well as a method of control. Deviations from budgeted amounts identify projects which need closer management attention.

FIGURE 13–9

Systems Development Progress Report Form

Date: __9/2/7__

Job Activity and Scheduling Report

Project: __Pilot - Phase II of Yield__

System: __002-003 Update__

System Analyst: __Systems Analyst 1__   Programmer: __Programmer 2__

	Est. Time	Act. Time	Date Started	Date Completed	Cause of Delay
Systems Development - Post Programming					
1. Alloted Time for Programming Assistance — Inc. Auto-Test	2	2	11/2/7-	11/5/7-	
2. Review accuracy of Output with Programmer	2	2	11/6/7-	11/9/7-	
3. Parallel Run	1	1	11/9/7-	11/9/7-	
a. Prepare input data					
b. Arrange for running time					
4. Have Parallel Run results approved	1	1	11/10/7-	11/10/7-	
a. Have Operating Mgr. approve results					
b. Have client approve results					
c. Make any necessary corrections					
5. Instruct Operational and Client Personnel	2	2	11/11/7-	11/12/7-	
6. Turn job over to Operation Manager	1	1	11/13/7-	11/13/7-	
7. Review System with Maintenance and Programming Manager	1	1	11/16/7-	11/16/7-	
8. Total Time	10	10	11/2/7-	11/16/7-	

Source: *PERT for Data Processing Systems Development* (White Plains, N.Y.: IBM Corporation), p. 4.

FIGURE 13–10

Gantt Chart Showing Progress of a Systems Development Project

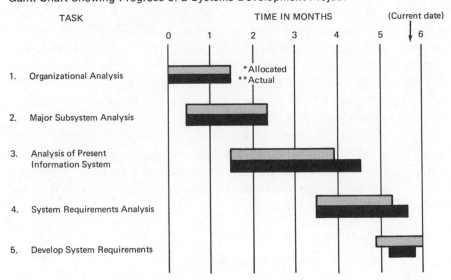

Note: Steps 3 and 4 have exceeded their allocated time, and therefore step 5 is behind schedule.

MANAGING COMPUTER OPERATIONS

Planning and controlling the operations of the computer services department is a major management responsibility. *"Operations management"* refers to the major areas of responsibility of the manager of computer operations that require planning and control activities such as those outlined below.

Operations Management

1. Operations planning.   Forecasting changes in the volume and type of computer applications and their effect on future hardware, software, and personnel requirements.

2. Production planning.   Formulating daily, weekly, and monthly forecasts which schedule specific systems and applications for computer processing.

3. Operating and financial budgets.   Developing budgets for EDP operations and comparing performance to budget.

4. Computer system utilization.   Analysis of computer system utilization by computer users and types of applications. Determination of any excess capacity or need for additional capacity.

FIGURE 13–11

PERT Network for a Systems Development Project

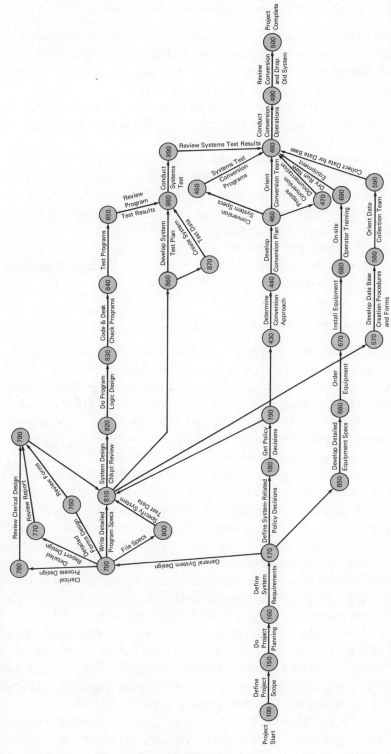

Source: From Brandon, Dick H., & Gray, Max, *Project Control Standards* (New York), © Mason / Charter Publishers, Inc., 1970. p. 111. Reprinted by permission of Mason / Charter.

5. Computer system performance. Analysis of computer "down time," aborted jobs, reruns, input/output errors, late reports, etc.

6. Computer operations costs. Analysis of the cost of computer hardware, software, and operating personnel.

7. Computer user service and assessments. Evaluating the quality of user service and assessing users for the costs of computer operations.

8. Computer systems acquisition. Evaluating plans and negotiations for hardware and software changes and their effect on EDP operations.

9. Systems implementation. Planning and supervising the effect on on-going operations of the installation and conversion of information systems or computer systems.

10. Controls and security. Control of data preparation, input, processing, and output. Control of storage files and computer facilities. Fraud control.

Production Planning and Control

Production planning and control methods are necessary for effective management of EDP operations. A production schedule of all data processing jobs must be prepared including the scheduling of all hardware, software, and operating personnel that will be required. The production schedule must take into account the requirements of data processing jobs that cannot be scheduled, such as program testing and real-time processing applications. The difficulty of production scheduling is compounded by unanticipated developments such as equipment malfunctions, unusual variations in volumes of data to be processed, processing errors, etc. However, the development of multiprogramming and virtual memory systems has significantly facilitated production scheduling. Many jobs can be processed at the same time since the computer has sufficient virtual storage to handle most small nonscheduled jobs that arise. Production planning of EDP operations obviously requires a thorough knowledge of computer operations and the data processing demands of the business firm.

Effective production planning and control requires that information be gathered to produce reports concerning the hardware, software, and personnel utilized by each data processing job. Information must be gathered concerning job-processing times, equipment utilization, time spent by operating personnel, and the production status of each job. Information is also needed on computer malfunctions, the number and type of reruns, processing delay and errors, and other evidences of unsatisfactory or unusual conditions. Such information is used to produce reports on computer system utilization, costs, and performance. These reports are then used as the basis for production planning, distribution of computer costs to users, control of computer system performance, and quality control of service to computer users.

Software packages are available which monitor the processing of computer jobs for several days and then develop a planned schedule of computer operations which is supposed to optimize the use of the computer system. Some advanced operating systems have the ability to monitor computer system performance and produce detailed statistics that are invaluable for effective production planning and control. For example, an advanced operating system could automatically generate the information shown in Figure 13–12.

FIGURE 13–12

Production Planning and Control Statistics
Generated by System Software

1. Applications program statistics:
   a. Applications executed
   b. CPU time used by each application
   c. Elapsed time for each (throughput)
   d. Control program services used by each
2. Operating system statistics:
   a. Control program functions executed
   b. Average time for each service
   c. CPU utilization by control services
   d. Frequency of use of each service program
3. Operations statistics:
   a. Overall CPU utilization
   b. Overall idle and input/output wait times
   c. Device utilization (by application program)

Source: John W. Sutherland, "Tackle System Selection Systematically." Reprinted from *Computer Decisions,* April, 1971. © 1971 Hayden Publishing Company.

CONTROLLING ELECTRONIC DATA PROCESSING

In Chapter 8 we described the concept of *control* as a vital component of any system which must be consciously included by systems analysts into the design of information systems. In Chapter 9 we described control as a vital function of management which must be supported by the data processing activities of management information systems. In the preceding chapter we discussed several methods of EDP cost control, and in this chapter we have outlined methods of systems development control and EDP production control. In this section, we shall describe *"EDP Controls"* as the methods utilized to insure the *accuracy, integrity,* and *safety* of the electronic data processing activities and resources of computer users.

Another way to describe EDP controls is that they are methods which attempt to minimize *errors, fraud,* and *destruction* in the computer services organization. Of course we mentioned in Chapter 8 that no amount of control methods can guarantee 100 percent accuracy, integrity, and safety. We also mentioned that requiring too many control methods and devices would lead to an "over-controlled" condition and result in information systems that are too costly, inflexible, and unresponsive. Therefore, a balance must be maintained between the accuracy, integrity, and safety required and the effect of controls in terms of cost, flexibility, and responsiveness.

Does electronic data processing increase or decrease the probability of errors, fraud, and destruction of data processing facilities? Computers have proven that they can process huge volumes of data and perform complex calculations more accurately than manual or mechanical data processing systems. However, we know that errors do occur in EDP systems, computers have been used for fraudulent purposes, and computers and their data files have been accidentally or maliciously destroyed. There is no question that computers have had some detrimental effect on the detection of errors and fraud. Manual and mechanical data processing systems involve data processing media that can be visually checked by data processing personnel. Several persons are usually involved in such systems and, therefore, cross-checking procedures are easily performed. These characteristics of manual and mechanical data processing systems facilitate the detection of errors and fraud.

Electronic data processing systems, on the other hand, utilize machine-sensible data processing media and accomplish data processing manipulations within the electronic circuitry of a computer system. The ability to check visually the progress of data processing activities and the contents of data processing files is significantly reduced. In addition, a relatively small number of EDP personnel may effectively control all of the data processing activities of the entire organization. Therefore, the ability to detect errors and fraud can be reduced by computerization.

However, the purpose of EDP controls is to develop methods and procedures which will result in effective detection of errors and fraud and protect the data processing resources of the organization. Effective EDP controls can make an electronic data processing system more free of errors and fraud than other types of data processing. The speed and accuracy of the computer can be put to work to monitor itself and all its data processing activities through *"data processing con-*

trols." "Organizational controls" can be developed for the computer services organization to maintain proper methods of systems development and computer operations. *"Facility controls"* can be developed to protect the facilities of the computer services department. We shall therefore group electronic data processing controls into three major categories: (1) data processing controls, (2) organizational controls, and (3) facility controls. See Figure 13–13.

FIGURE 13–13

Major Categories of EDP Controls

EDP Controls

Data processing controls
    Input controls, processing controls, output controls, storage controls

Organizational controls
    Production control, separation of duties, standard procedures, documentation, authorization requirements, conversion scheduling, EDP auditing

Facility controls
    File controls, computer failure controls, physical protection controls, insurance

Data Processing Controls

Data processing controls are methods and devices which attempt to insure the accuracy, validity, and propriety of data processing functions and activities. Controls must be developed to ensure that all proper input data is collected, converted into a form suitable for processing, and entered into the computer system. Thus, data processing controls can be organized according to the *input, processing output,* and *storage* components of any data processing system. See Figure 13–14.

FIGURE 13–14

Types of Data Processing Controls

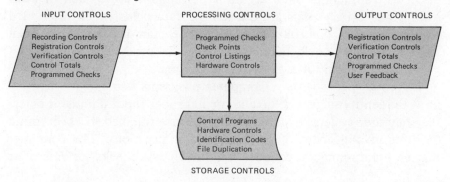

INPUT CONTROLS
Recording Controls
Registration Controls
Verification Controls
Control Totals
Programmed Checks

PROCESSING CONTROLS
Programmed Checks
Check Points
Control Listings
Hardware Controls

OUTPUT CONTROLS
Registration Controls
Verification Controls
Control Totals
Programmed Checks
User Feedback

STORAGE CONTROLS
Control Programs
Hardware Controls
Identification Codes
File Duplication

Input Controls

Input controls that are frequently utilized are summarized below.

1. Recording controls.   Prenumbered forms help identify missing input documents. Input recording aids help reduce the chance for error. Prepunched cards, templates over the keys of key-driven input devices, and source documents whose printed format assists proper data recording are other examples.

2. Registration controls.   Source documents are registered by recording them in a log book when they are received by data preparation personnel. Batches of data are usually logged by recording information that identifies the batch and when it was received. "Batch tickets" which identify the type of processing required and record the completion of processing steps usually accompany batches of data. External labels attached to the outside of magnetic tapes or disks are another method of registering the contents and disposition of input data.

Real-time systems that utilize direct access files frequently record all inputs into the system on magnetic tape "control logs." Such logs preserve evidence of all system inputs and are utilized to develop "control totals" which can be compared to control totals generated during processing.

3. Verification controls.   Visual verification of source documents or input media by clerical personnel and machine verification as performed by punched card verifier equipment are examples.

4. Control totals.   A "record count" is a control total which consists of counting the total of source documents or other input records and comparing this total to the number of records counted at other stages of input preparation. If the totals do not match a mistake has been made. "Batch totals" and "hash totals" are other forms of control totals. A batch total is the sum of a specific item of data within a batch of transactions such as the sales amount in a batch of sales transactions. Hash totals are the sum of data fields which are added together only for control comparisons. For example, employee social security numbers could be added together to produce a control total in the input preparation of payroll documents.

5. Programmed checks.   Computer programs can include instructions to identify incorrect, invalid, or improper input data as it enters the computer system. Computers can be programmed to check input data for invalid codes, data fields, and transactions. The computer may be programmed to conduct "reasonableness checks" to determine if input data exceeds certain specified limits. Input data that is out of sequence can also be identified.

Processing Controls

Processing controls are developed to identify errors in arithmetic calculations and logical operations. They are also used to insure that data is not lost or does not go unprocessed. Processing controls can be categorized as "programmed controls" and "hardware controls" and are summarized below.

Programmed controls. Validity checks, reasonableness checks, sequence checks, and control total checks similar to the programmed checks on input mentioned above are also utilized during the processing stage. The computer can also be programmed to check the "internal file labels" at the beginning and end of magnetic tape and disc files. These labels contain information identifying the file as well as providing control totals for the data in the file. These internal file labels allow the computer to insure that the proper storage file is being used and that the proper data in the file has been processed.

Another major programmed control is the establishment of *checkpoints* during the processing of a program. Checkpoints are intermediate points within a program being processed where intermediate totals, listings, or "dumps" of data are written on magnetic tape or disc or listed on a printer. Checkpoints minimize the effect of processing errors or failures since processing can be restarted from the last checkpoint rather than from the beginning of the program. They also help build an "audit trail" which allows transactions being processed to be traced through all of the steps of processing.

Hardware controls. Hardware controls are special checks built into the hardware to verify the accuracy of computer processing. Hardware checks include:

1. Multiple read-write heads on certain hardware devices.
2. Parity checks which were described in Chapter 2.
3. Duplicate circuitry within the computer.
4. Echo checks which require that a signal be returned from a device or circuit to verify that it was properly activated.
5. Switches and other devices. Switches can be set which prohibit writing on magnetic tapes or disks. This is more frequently accomplished on magnetic tape reels by a removable plastic or metal ring which can be removed to prevent writing on the tape.

6. Miscellaneous hardware controls. There are many other kinds of hardware controls such as duplicate arithmetic, load checks, overflow checks, sign checks, and CPU timing and voltage checks. These controls are important for proper hardware operations, but it is not necessary for the average computer user to understand the details of their use.

Output Controls

Output controls are developed to insure that output information is correct and complete and is transmitted to authorized users in a timely manner. Several types of output controls are similar to input control methods. For example, output is frequently logged, identified with route slips, and visually verified by input/output control personnel. Control totals on output are compared with control totals generated during the input and processing stages. Prenumbered output forms are utilized to control the loss of important output documents such as stock certificate or payroll check forms. Distribution lists help input/output control personnel insure that only authorized users receive output. Access to the output of real-time processing systems is controlled by hardware or software which identifies who can receive output and the type of output they are authorized to receive. Finally, persons who receive output should be contacted on a regular basis for feedback on the quality of output.

Storage Controls

Many data files are protected from unauthorized or accidental use by control programs which require proper identification before a file can be used. The primary storage of computers utilizing multiprogramming is protected by a combination of software and hardware controls. When two or more programs are in primary storage at the same time, controls are needed to prevent one program from accidentally destroying the data or instructions of another program. Each program must contain instructions which identify it with a particular block of primary storage.

Hardware devices and software routines are utilized to protect the data base of real-time processing systems from unauthorized use or processing accidents. "Lock words" (also called "pass words") and other identification codes are frequently used to restrict access to authorized users. Data is sometimes stored or transmitted in "scrambled" form and unscrambled by the computer system only for authorized users. A list or catalog of authorized users enables the computer system to identify eligible users and determine which types of information they are authorized to receive. The operating system of real-time computers supervises requests for file access from multiple remote terminals (as well as requests for input, processing, and output). The operating system assigns priorities and creates a waiting line of transactions to insure that only one transaction at a time can update a specific data file.

Organizational Controls

Organizational controls are methods of organizing and performing the functions of the computer services organization that facilitate the accuracy and integrity of computer operations and systems development activities. Some of these controls are discussed below.

1. Production control. We have previously mentioned that the computer services department should include a production control section whose job is to monitor the progress of data processing jobs, data preparation activities, and the quality of input/output data. The production control section has a major responsibility in maintaining the accuracy and integrity of computer operations.

2. Separation of duties. A basic principle of organizational control in EDP is to assign the duties of systems development, computer operations, and control of data and program files to separate groups of EDP personnel. For example, systems analysts and computer programmers are not allowed to operate the computer console and primary peripheral equipment, while computer programmers are not allowed to make changes to data or programs being processed. In addition, the responsibility for maintaining a library of data files and program files in the form of magnetic tape reels, disk packs, and decks of punched cards is assigned to a librarian who does not engage in systems development or equipment operations activities.

3. Standard procedures. Manuals of standard procedures for systems development, computer programming, and computer operations should be developed and maintained. Following standard procedures promotes uniformity and minimizes the chances of errors and fraud.

4. Documentation. Systems, program, and operations documentation must be developed and kept up-to-date to insure the correct processing and maintenance of each computer application.

5. Authorization requirements. Requests for systems development, program changes, or computer processing must be subject to a formal process of review before authorization is given. Several appropriate administrative personnel should review and approve such requests in order to insure that adequate steps are taken to minimize errors and fraud. For example, program changes generated by maintenance programmers should be approved by the manager of programming after consultation with the manager of computer operations and the manager of the affected user department.

6. Conversion scheduling. Conversion to new hardware and software, installation of newly developed information systems, and changes to existing programs should be subjected to a formal notification and scheduling procedure to minimize their detrimental effects on the accuracy and integrity of computer services. Many errors and accidents in electronic data processing can be traced to a lack of proper planning and organization of such changes.

7. Auditing of EDP. The computer services organization and its EDP activities must undergo periodic examinations or "audits" to determine the accuracy, integrity, and safety of all computer-based information systems. We'll discuss this important aspect of organizational control in a later section.

Facility Controls

Facility controls are methods utilized to protect the computer service facility and its contents from loss or destruction. Computer centers are subject to such hazards as accidents, natural disasters, sabotage, vandalism, industrial espionage, and theft. Therefore, physical safeguards and various control procedures are necessary to protect the hardware, software, and, most importantly, the vital information and records of computer-using organizations. Several important facility controls are described below.

1. File controls. Control over files of computer programs and data must be maintained. A librarian is responsible for storing files of magnetic tapes and disks and punched cards in a special section of the computer center. The librarian issues files to authorized personnel and receives files after processing has been completed. Many firms utilize "backup" files which are duplicate files of data or programs. Such files may be stored "off-premise," that is, in a location away from the computer center, sometimes in special storage vaults in remote locations. Many real-time processing sytems utilize duplicate files that are updated by data communication links. Files are also protected by "file retention" measures which involves storing copies of master files and transaction files from previous periods. If current files are destroyed, the files from previous periods are used to reconstruct new current files.

2. Computer failure controls.   A variety of controls are needed to prevent computer failure or minimize its effects.

Computers fail or "go down" for several reasons, such as power failure, electronic circuitry malfunctions, mechanical malfunctions of peripheral equipment, hidden programming errors, and computer operator errors.

> "If the lights in your office blink enough for you to notice, odds are that your computer has gone down. Once down, it can take anywhere from a half hour to four hours or more to get the computer back up. By that time a backlog has developed which can upset scheduling, and therefore performance, for days."[2]

Therefore, the computer services department must take steps to prevent equipment failures and to minimize their detrimental effects. A program of "preventive maintenance" of hardware must be developed. Adequate electrical supply, air conditioning, humidity control, and fire prevention standards must be set. A "backup" computer system capability should be arranged with other computer-using organizations. Major hardware or software changes should be carefully scheduled and implemented. Finally, computer operators must have adequate training and supervision.

3. Physical protection controls.   Providing maximum security and disaster protection for the computer installation requires many types of controls. Only authorized personnel are allowed access to the computer center through such techniques as identification badges for EDP personnel, electrical door locks, burglar alarms, security police, close circuit TV, and other detection systems. The computer center should be protected from disaster by such safeguards as fire detection and extinguishing systems, fireproof storage vaults for protection of files, emergency power systems, electromagnetic shielding, temperature, humidity, and dust-control, etc.

4. Insurance.   Adequate insurance coverage must be secured to protect the business firm from substantial financial losses in the event of accidents, disasters, fraud, and other risks. Several insurance companies offer special EDP policies which include insurance against fire, natural disasters, vandalism and theft, liability insurance for data processing errors or omissions, fidelity insurance for the bonding of

---

[2] *A Helpful Guide on How to Keep Your Computers from Putting You in the Poorhouse* (Bethpage, N.Y.: Grumman Data Systems), p. 19.

EDP personnel as a protection against fraud etc. The amount of such insurance should be large enough to replace computer equipment and facilities. Insurance is also available to cover the cost of reconstructing data and program files.

Auditing EDP

We have previously mentioned that the computer service organization should be periodically examined or *audited* by internal auditing personnel of the business firm or by external auditors from professional accounting firms. Such audits should review and evaluate whether proper and adequate data processing controls, organizational controls, and facility controls have been developed and implemented. The audit usually includes a test of the accuracy and integrity of the data processing of several important computer applications.

There are two basic approaches for testing the data processing activities of a computer application. They are known as (1) "auditing around the computer," and (2) "auditing through the computer." *Auditing around a computer* involves verifying the accuracy and propriety of computer input and output without evaluating the computer programs utilized to process the data. This is a simpler and easier method which does not require auditors with EDP or programming experience. However, since this auditing method does not trace a transaction through all of its stages of processing and does not test the accuracy and integrity of the computer program, it should not be the only method used for large-volume, sophisticated computer applications.

Auditing through the computer involves verifying the accuracy and integrity of the computer programs that process the data, as well as the input and output of the computer system. Auditing through the computer requires a knowledge of EDP operations and computer programming. Some firms employ special "EDP auditors" for this assignment. Special *test data* may be used to test processing accuracy and the control procedures built into the computer program. The auditor may develop a special *test program* or utilize a packaged *audit program* to process the data of the business firm. He then compares the results of processing, utilizing his audit program with the results generated by the computer users' own programs. One of the objectives of such testing is to detect the presence of unauthorized changes or "patches" to computer programs. Unauthorized program patches

FIGURE 13–15

Protecting Computer-Based Information Systems with Adequate EDP Controls

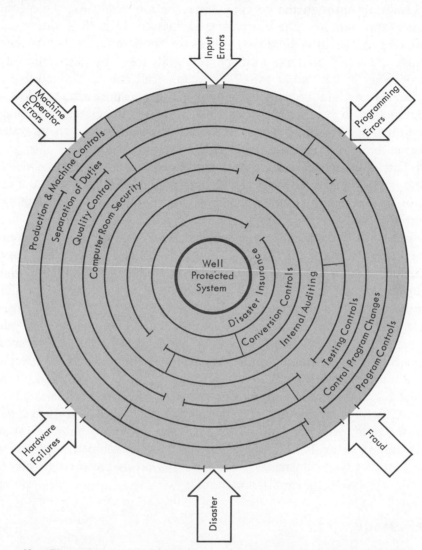

Note: The attack arrows have as their objectives destruction of the "Well-Protected System,"
If the system is properly controlled, each of the factors represented by an arrow will be interrupted
and negated by applicable control elements as it attempts to penetrate the control maze.

Source: Joseph J. Wasserman, "Plugging the Leaks in Computer Security," *Harvard Business Review* (September–October 1969), p. 124.

may be the cause of "unexplainable" errors or may be utilized by an unscrupulous programmer for fraudulant purposes.

Auditing through the computer may be too costly for some computer applications. Therefore, a combination of both auditing approaches is usually employed. However, both auditing approaches must effectively contend with the changes caused by electronic data processing to the *"audit trail."* The audit trail can be defined as the presence of data processing media and procedures which allow a transaction to be traced through all stages of processing, beginning with its appearance on a source document and ending with its transformation into information on a final output document.

The audit trail of manual data processing systems was quite visible and easy to trace. However, EDP has changed the form of the audit trail. Information formerly available to the auditor in the form of visual records is no longer available or is recorded on media which can be interpreted only by machines. Real-time processing systems have increased the "invisibility" of the traditional audit trail. Paper documents and historical record files are frequently eliminated when remote transaction recording terminals and direct access files are utilized. Such developments make the auditing of EDP systems a complex but vital assignment. Therefore, auditing personnel should be included on the project team of all major systems development projects and consulted before smaller systems projects are implemented. In addition, auditing personnel should be notified of all changes to computer programs caused by the program maintenance activity. Such procedures give the auditor the opportunity to suggest methods of preserving the audit trail and providing adequate data processing controls in systems that are being developed or modified.

Figure 13–15 illustrates the types of controls required to protect computer-based information systems.

SUMMARY

Managing the computer resources of a business firm has become a major new responsibility of business management. Business computer users must learn how to plan, organize, staff, and control the activities of their computer service departments. The major activities of a computer services department can be grouped into three basic functional categories: (1) systems development, (2) operations, and (3) administration.

The activities of systems development have been discussed in previous chapters. However, additional activities include systems programming, data base administration, configuration management, data processing standards development, and technical assistance. The operations function of a computer services department includes the major activities of data preparation, equipment operation, production control, and production support. The administrative function of a computer services department involves the performance of several managerial activities such as planning, controlling, managerial liason, personnel management, financial management, and administrative services. The organizational structure, location, and staffing of a computer services department must reflect these basic functions and activities. However, many variations exist, which reflect the attempts of business computer users to tailor their organizational and staffing arrangements to their particular business activities and management philosophy.

There is a wide variety of job types in many computer-using organizations. However, computer services personnel can be grouped into four occupational categories: systems development, programming, operations, and administration. The number of different types of jobs in a computer-using business firm depends on the size of its computer services department. Thus, large-scale computer operations allow more specialization of job assignments and thus create more types of jobs. Managing the wide variety of technical personnel in a computer services department is a major personnel management assignment of business computer users.

Another major managerial responsibility in computer-using business firms is the planning, organizing, and controlling of the systems development function. Management of systems development requires long-range planning, project identification, project teams, project management, and project communications techniques. Managing computer operations requires many applications of "operations management" including various production planning and control techniques.

One of the most important responsibilities of the management of computer-using business firms is the *control* of its EDP activities. "EDP controls" are methods utilized to insure the accuracy, integrity, and safety of the electronic data processing activities and resources of computer users. Such controls attempt to minimize errors, fraud, and destruction in the computer services department. EDP controls can be grouped into three major categories: (1) data processing controls, (2) organizational controls, and (3) facility controls. Data processing controls are methods which attempt to insure the accuracy, validity, and propriety of data processing functions and activities. They include various types of input, processing, output, and storage control. Organizational controls are methods of organizing and performing computer operations and development activities to insure their accuracy and integrity. Organizational controls include production control techniques, separation of duties, standard procedures, documentation, the auditing of EDP, etc. Facility controls are methods utilized to protect the computer service facility and its contents from loss or destruction from such hazards as accidents, natural disasters, vandalism, etc. Various physical safeguards and control procedures are utilized to protect the hardware, software, and vital information and records of computer-using organizations.

The computer services department should be periodically audited to review and evaluate whether proper and adequate data processing controls, organizational controls, and facility controls have been developed and implemented. EDP auditing, therefore, plays a vital role in insuring proper managerial control of computer resources and EDP activities.

KEY TERMS AND CONCEPTS

Organizational functions of computer services organizations, 410–412

Centralization or decentralization of computer services, 413

Organizational structure of computer services, 414–415

Executive EDP committee, 417

Job categories of computer services personnel, 417–422

Project management, 428–430

Operations management, 430–432

EDP controls, 434–435

Data processing controls, 435–438

Organizational controls, 439–440

Facility controls, 440–441

Auditing EDP, 442–443

Audit trail, 444

ASSIGNMENTS

1. Test your understanding of the chapter material by reviewing the *purpose, outline, summary,* and *key terms and concepts* of this chapter. Are you confident that you have attained a basic understanding of the major concepts of the chapter? If not, reread the appropriate material as indicated by the page numbers after each key term and concept.

2. Describe several activities that are involved in each of the three basic functions of a computer service organization, i.e., systems development, operations and administration.

3. Describe several factors that affect the organizational location of the computer services department, including the aspect of centralization or decentralization of computer services within a firm.

4. Identify the basic components in the organizational structure of a computer services organization.

5. Discuss the role of project teams and the executive EDP committee in computer-using organizations.

6. Describe the job responsibilities of several types of computer services personnel in each of the four basic occupational categories, i.e., (1) systems development, (2) programming, (3) operations, and (4) administration.

7. Explain why effective personnel management is a critical requirement for computer-using organizations.

8. Describe some of the desired qualifications for systems analysts, programmers, and computer operators.

9. Describe several methods for managing the systems development function, including the concept of project management.

10. Describe some of the planning and control activities of the operations management function.

11. Does electronic data processing increase or decrease the probability of errors, fraud, and destruction? Explain.

12. Describe several types of (1) data processing controls, (2) organizational controls, and (3) facility controls that can be utilized by a computer-using organization.

13. Explain the distinction between "auditing around the computer" and "auditing through the computer." Which method is preferable?

14. Discuss how the computer has affected the "audit trail." What steps can be taken to assist the auditing of EDP in this regard?

15. Interview the manager and/or other EDP personnel of a computer center. Discuss methods they utilize to plan, organize, staff, and control their EDP activities.

Chapter Outline

Purpose of the Chapter

The Challenge of Computer Performance
Poor Computer Performance, Management Involvement,
The User Generation, User Resistance, User Involvement,
Management Audit

The Challenge to Management Performance
The Impact of Computers on Management
Centralization versus Decentralization of Data Processing,
Centralization versus Decentralization of Management and
Operations, Computers and Middle Management
The Systems Approach to Management
The Computer as a Catalyst, Managing Organizational
Development, The Systems Approach to Management
Decision-Making
Enlarging the Job of Management
From Paper Shufflers to Managers, Managers as Systems
Analysts, Using Advanced Quantitative Techniques,
The Challenge of the Future MIS

The Social Challenge of the Computer
The Impact of Computers on Society, Impact on
Employment and Productivity, Impact on Competition,
Impact on Individuality, Impact on the Quality of Life,
Impact on Privacy, Other Social Effects, Social
Applications, Systems Design and Social Responsibility

Summary

Key Terms and Concepts

Assignments

14

Computers, Management, and Society

Purpose of the Chapter

To promote a basic understanding of the major challenges that computers present to business management by analyzing:

1. The challenge of computer performance,
2. The challenge to management performance,
3. The social challenge of the computer.

The preceding chapters of this text should have emphasized that the computer is a valuable and powerful resource that presents a major challenge to business management. In this chapter we will conclude our study of computers in business management by focusing on three major aspects of the management challenge of the computer:

1. The challenge of computer performance.
2. The challenge to management performance.
3. The social challenge of the computer.

THE CHALLENGE OF COMPUTER PERFORMANCE

Computers are utilized by business firms to reduce costs, increase profits, provide better service to customers, and provide better information to management. Computers should reduce the cost of doing business by automating the processing of data and the control of operations. Better customer service and improved management information is supposed to result from the speed and accuracy of the computer. Thus, computers should improve the competitive position and profit performance of business firms. However, this has not occurred in many documented cases. Studies by management consulting firms, computer-user groups, and others have shown that many business firms moved too far and too fast into computer processing without adequate personnel resources and management involvement, and that many computer users and computer professionals have not yet learned how to manage this vital but expensive business resource.[1]

Poor Computer Performance

There can be no doubt that the computer has become an indispensable tool for modern business management. Without computers, management could not plan, operate, and control the operations of most of the businesses of today. However, it is obvious that the management of many computer-using business firms have not yet learned to plan, organize, and control the operations of their own computers and computer service departments. For example, the computer is not being used *effectively* by companies which utilize the computer primarily for recordkeeping applications. Computers are not being used *efficiently* by computer service departments which provide inadequate service to users while failing to properly utilize their computing capacity. Many computer systems are also not being used *economically*. Data processing costs have risen faster than other costs in many business firms, even though the cost of processing each unit of data is decreasing due to improvements in hardware and software technology.[2] Thus, the valuable resource of the computer is not being effectively, efficiently, and economically utilized by such business firms.

Poor computer performance can take many forms, as illustrated by the list of "symptoms" of a "sick" computer services department shown in Figure 14–1. Further, poor computer performance is not limited to small business firms with limited financial and human resources. Many large business firms have openly admitted their failure to manage the computer effectively. For example, General Motors, the largest corporation in the world, had the following troubles with computer performance in its Chevrolet division:

---

[1] For example, see *Unlocking the Computer's Profit Potential* (N.Y.: McKinsey & Co., 1968).

[2] IBM reports that the average cost of doing 100,000 multiplications by a computer decreased from $1.26 in 1952 to *one cent* in 1974!

The division had twenty-five computers, and they had not been co-ordinated into an efficient system. When a new car was designed, its specifications had to be taken from the engineering department's computer and reprogrammed into the manufacturing department's computer. Things broke down altogether when the 1969 models were introduced; the computers failed to invoice hundreds of new cars.[3]

FIGURE 14–1

Symptoms of a Sick Computer Services Department

Computers not used, when applicable, in key business
   areas
Poor establishment of project priorities
Inability to provide management with information
   needed to make decisions
Dissatisfied users
Spiraling costs
Inability to establish or verify the payback on invest-
   ments in systems development
Low productivity of people or equipment
Schedules not being met
High turnover of personnel, including management
Low morale
Poor internal communications

    Source: "How to Spot the Ailing EDP Department," *Bank Automation Newsletter* (May 1972), p. 4.

What is the solution to the problem of poor computer perform-ance? Is more hardware, software, and sophisticated computer sys-tems the answer? Or does the solution lie in the emotional reaction of some business computer users who have "pulled the plug" and "disintegrated their integrated information systems" by "decomputer-izing"? The solution to poor computer performance does not lie in either extreme position. There are no "quick and easy" answers to this problem. Solutions such as "better management of computer re-sources and services" are obvious but much too vague. However, the experiences of successful computer users reveal that the basic in-gredient of high-quality computer performance is *extensive and mean-ingful management and user involvement* in the development and operation of computer-based information systems. This should be the key ingredient in shaping the response of management to the challenge of improving the quality of computer services.

Management Involvement

Proper management involvement requires the knowledgeable and active participation of management in the planning and control of

---

[3] "The Automobile Industry Has Lost Its Masculinity," *Fortune* (September 1973), p. 191.

computer-based information systems. Being an involved manager means more than knowing: (1) the make and model number of the computers of the company, (2) where they are located, (3) whether they are operating satisfactorily, (4) which person is responsible for computer operations, (5) what major information systems are being developed, and (6) whether the computer department is staying within its budget. Management must know a lot more about the development and use of computer-based information systems within the firm. Managers should know, for instance, the answers to questions such as:

1. How do our computer resources contribute to the short and long-term profitability of this company?
2. Have we invested too little or too much in computer resources?
3. Do we have realistic long-range plans for information systems development and acquisition of computer resources that will improve the efficiency of business operations and the quality of management decisions?
4. Are information systems development projects and our computer operations being properly managed?
5. To sum it all up, are computer resources being utilized efficiently, effectively, and economically in every part or activity of this organization?

Without a high degree of management involvement, managers will not know the answer to such questions and thus will not be able to control the quality of computer performance. Management can no longer claim that acquiring knowledge about computer fundamentals and computer use in business is too difficult or time-consuming. (Hopefully this book has shown that this is not the case.) Management can acquire a basic knowledge of the technology, development, and control of computer-based business information systems through a short series of training sessions or courses offered by their own computer services department, the computer industry, or educational institutions. Such information would be sufficient to allow managers to become active participants in the development and management of computer-based information systems. Such participation will provide a form of "on-the-job training" which would further reinforce the ability of management to manage the computer resource effectively.

Several studies have shown that companies which are successfully utilizing computers view the development and management of computer-based information systems as a responsibility of both top management and operating management. These companies have come to understand that systems analysts cannot design information systems that effectively support the decision needs of management without management involvement in the systems design process. Systems development projects will not "manage themselves." They need the planning and control activities of management personnel. The computer services department needs the active support of top management and user management to improve and maintain the quality of computer services. Figure 14–2 illustrates several levels of management involvement.

Top management can involve itself in the planning and development of a new information system by (1) defining its goals and ob-

FIGURE 14–2

Levels of
Management
Involvement

Executive
EDP
Committee

Management
Working
Committee

Management
Representation
on Systems
Development
Project Teams

Individual
Management
Input to
Systems
Development
Projects

Individual
Management
Feedback
Concerning
Computer
Performance

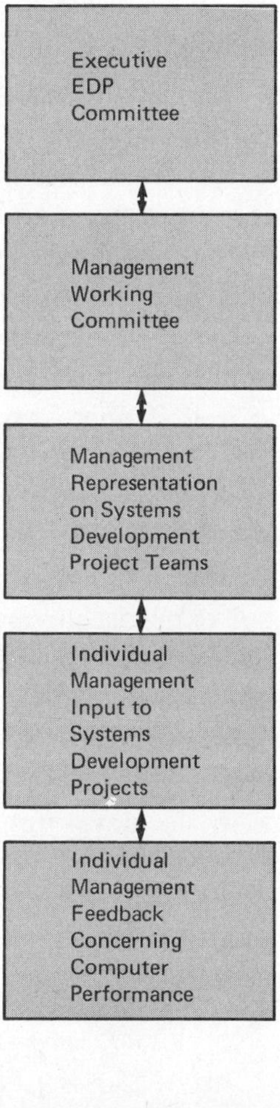

jectives, (2) approving the feasibility of systems development, (3) managing the progress of the project, and (4) resolving organizational conflicts that may arise when restructuring of organizational boundaries and functions arise as the result of a new system. Many business firms utilize an *"Executive EDP committee"* of top management to develop long-range plans and coordinate the development of information systems. We have previously mentioned that this committee includes the senior management of the major divisions of the firm, as well as the manager of the computer services organization. The executive EDP committee should meet regularly to (1) approve long-range plans for computer usage, (2) discuss the status of systems development projects, (3) select systems to be developed, and (4) monitor the success of existing systems.

In addition to top management involvement and support, each information systems development project should utilize the expertise of managerial personnel from departments that will be affected by the new systems. If a major strategic information system is being developed, management involvement may take the form of active participation in systems development as members of the systems development project team. Another form of participation by middle management and operating management personnel is the "working *committee.*" This involves the formation of a committee of middle managers and/or operating managers and management personnel from the computer services department which oversees the progress of one or more project teams. The committee meets on a regular basis during the existence of systems projects that affect the users represented on the working committee. It reviews progress made, settles disputes, and changes priorities if necessary.

The role of middle management and operating management personnel in the development and management of a new information system can be summarized as follows:

1. Furnish the operational expertise to insure that all revelant factors are included in the systems analysis and design, so that the new system really meets their decision-making information needs.
2. Provide correct data and information about the information requirements of the system.
3. Guide and participate in the development of the system.
4. Monitor and evaluate the quality of the information provided by the system.

The User Generation

As each succeeding generation of computer systems is developed, it becomes exceedingly difficult for management and computer professionals to pacify computer users with past excuses based on untried applications, inexperienced EDP personnel, or inadequate equipment. Most computer users rightly feel that the "experimental" stage of EDP has passed and that a "normal production" phase with high-quality service is expected from the computer services organization. Instead of debating the question of whether or not we are in the third or fourth generation of computer systems, business management and computer professionals must now realize that a *"user generation"* of computer usage has begun which will continue indefinitely into the future.

The attitudes of computer users in the user generation are accentuated by an increased awareness of the current state-of-the-art of the computer industry. The public news media, the space program, computer industry propaganda, and company publications have touted the speed, power, and sophistication of modern computer systems. Imagine the chagrin of a computer user who knows that though the computer of his firm can process many jobs at a time, due to multiprogramming and virtual storage capabilities, he may still have to wait several days for his particular job to be processed and may even receive output of questionable quality. One does not have to be a mind reader to understand the thoughts of top management who continue to receive complaints about poor quality computer service after years of spending huge sums on the computer resources of the business firm.

Thus, the use of computers in business is entering a new generation, "the user generation." Computer users are demanding economical, efficient, and effective computer-based information systems. They are becoming impatient with the rising costs of EDP, the inefficiencies and "down times" of computer operations, and the long lead times of information systems development. They want more consistent accuracy, flexibility, and timeliness in the information produced by current information systems. Management users want new information systems which provide information which more effectively supports their planning and decision-making functions. They want these new systems to integrate the information produced by the organization and disperse it wherever and whenever needed throughout the organization. Computer-using business firms want information systems which allow management and operating personnel without any technical sophistication to easily utilize an information system in carrying out their assignments. They want flexible well-planned information systems that can keep pace with the growth in volume and complexity of the business system without the disruptions of major systems conversions every few years. What the new generation of computer users want is a new generation of *"user-oriented information systems."*

User Resistance

The coming of the user generation has intensified the potential for resistance by computer users. Any "new way of doing things" generates some resistance by the people affected. However, computer-based information systems can generate a significant amount of fear and reluctance to change. There are many reasons for this state of affairs, some of which we will explore in a later discussion concerning the impact of computers on society. Whatever the reasons for user resistance, it is the responsibility of business management and computer professionals to find ways of reducing the conflict and resistance that arises with the use of computers. A brief discussion of several reasons for user resistance is outlined below:

1. Ignorance.   Computer users do not have a sufficient knowledge of EDP, while computer professionals do not have a sufficient knowledge of the operations and problems of the business.

2. Performance.   Poor computer performance as previously described, resulting in broken promises and inadequate service.

3. Participation.   Users have not been made active participants in systems development and systems maintenance.

4. Communication.   Computer users may not understand the technical jargon of computer professionals, and EDP personnel may not adequately understand the unique terminology of each group of computer users.

5. Personnel problems.   Some computer users resent the influence of computer professionals on their work activities. EDP personnel are viewed as "technical types" with different work assignment, different working conditions, and different promotion and other personnel policies.

6. Organizational conflict.   The computer services department is sometimes viewed as trying to gain too much influence and control within the organization, getting involved in too many operations of the company and receiving "special treatment" such as a disproportionate share of the financial and personnel resources of the company.

User Involvement

Solving the problems of *user resistance* requires meaningful *user involvement* based on formal methods of (1) *education,* (2) *communication,* and (3) *participation.* Like management, user personnel must be educated in the fundamentals of computer technology and their application to business information systems. This basic knowledge should be supplemented by specific programs of orientation, education, and training concerning computer-based information systems which affect specific groups of computer users. As was pointed out in Chapters 7 and 8, such programs are frequently part of the implementation stage of the development of new information systems. Another important aspect of the educational effort needed to reduce conflict between computer users and computer professionals are training programs and rotating work assignments which would acquaint computer professionals with the operations and problems of the user departments in the organization.

We have discussed several methods of increasing user participation and communication in previous chapters. We have emphasized, in particular, the necessity of including user representatives on project teams charged with the development of new information systems. We stressed that direct user participation should provide the type of user involvement required to improve the quality of computer services and reduce the potential for user resistance. Such user involvement helps assure that computer-based information systems are "user-oriented" in their design. Systems that tend to inconvenience or frustrate their users cannot be effective systems, no matter how efficiently they process data. *Systems must be designed to appear more responsive to the user, rather than appear to force users to be responsive to the system.*

Several methods of *"user liaison"* are utilized by successful computer users. The manager of the computer services department should meet frequently with the heads of user departments on an individual basis to discuss the status of new and existing systems. Also, many firms have created the position of "user liaison specialist." Each computer-user department is assigned a representative from the computer services department who is the original contact for all communications. User liaison specialists perform a vital role by "trouble shooting" the problems of computer users, gathering and communicating information from users required for systems maintenance, and coordinating educational efforts for computer user personnel. These activities improve communication and coordination between the user and the computer services department because all questions and problems that arise are referred to one individual. This avoids the "run-around" effect that can frustrate computer users and is an important reminder of the user orientation of the computer services department.

Management Audit

The management of business firms which have achieved successful computer performance periodically audit their utilization of computer resources and the quality of computer services. This self-examination should reveal how efficiently, economically, and effectively a business firm is developing and utilizing computer-based information systems. Such a formal examination and evaluation process is called a "management audit" and is performed by a committee of management and senior staff personnel or by an outside management consulting firm. The following questions summarize the categories examined by a leading management consulting firm in their audits of the information systems activity of business firms.[4]

1. Managerial involvement. How effectively is top management involved in the management of the information systems division?

2. Systems planning. Is there a formal master systems plan? How is it developed? Is it an adequate plan? Is it being utilized?

3. Project identification. Do systems development projects originate with operating managers or with the information systems division? Is there a backlog of projects? Have potential projects gone unrecognized? Is systems maintenance explicitly recognized?

4. Project selection. Who makes the final selection of projects and sets priorities? Has the firm become committed to information systems development projects without fully appreciating the major risks or ramifications?

5. Project management. How does management control information systems development projects once they get under way? Are

---

[4] Adapted from Donald F. Heany, *Development of Information Systems* (New York: The Ronald Press Company, 1968), pp. 297–301.

projects periodically reassessed when major changes occur within the organization or in the business environment? How often are projects abandoned or redefined? Do projects stay within their time tables and budgets, or are project plans even used?

6. *Performance of present systems.*   Are user managers and other personnel pleased with systems that have recently been developed? Can they give specific examples of the effectiveness or ineffectiveness of existing systems in reducing costs, increasing profits, or supporting management decision-making? Do users criticize the systems development process, i.e., took too long, cost too much, interferred with operations, etc.? How is the systems maintenance activity accomplished? Do users complain about the quality of computer services?

7. *Organization.*   What is the place of the information systems activity in the organizational structure of the business? Is the information systems division isolated from or involved in the other activities of the business? Has information systems development had a major impact on the organization, operations, or strategy of the business? Is the information systems division well-organized and managed?

8. *Personnel.*   Do computer personnel have a promotion path? Is the turn-over rate low, the salaries competitive, the morale high? Is there a formal training program?

9. *Hardware and software.*   Are computer systems adequate or excessive? Are provisions for expansion and backup adequate? Is there evidence that the computer is input/output-bound or process-bound?

10. *Operations.*   Are physical facilities adequate ·and well-organized? Is there adequate physical protection of computer facilities? Is there evidence that the computer is "always down" or "always behind schedule"? Are formal operations planning and control methods utilized? Has there been a recent in-depth audit of the activities and data processing controls of the computer operations department? Does the operating cost of the information systems division seem excessive when compared to the types and volumes of processing accomplished and the experiences of similar firms?

THE CHALLENGE TO MANAGEMENT PERFORMANCE

Much has been written on the impact of computers on management. The computer has affected the organizational structure of computer-using business firms as well as the activities of management. We will discuss these changes in the context of their present and potential effect on the improvement of managerial performance.

The Impact of Computers on Management

When computers were introduced into business, predictions were made that there would be significant changes in management because the data processing power and programmed decision-making capability of the computer would cause drastic reductions in employees, including middle management and supervisory personnel. A centralized computer system would process all of the data for the organization, control most of its operations, and make most of its decisions. This has not proven to be the case. Changes in organizational structure and types of personnel have occurred, but they have not been as dramatic as has been predicted. Naturally, highly automated systems do not require as many people as manual methods. Therefore, there has been significant reductions in the amount of people required to perform certain manual tasks in certain organizations. However, this has been countered to some extent by the need for increased data processing personnel and computer professionals to run the computer-based systems of the organization.

Centralization versus Decentralization of Data Processing

Organizational changes have occurred because of the change to electronic data processing. However, many of these changes are part of the consolidation of data processing activities into a single computer services department. Computers have caused the *centralization* of data processing activities within many firms. However, even this development is being modified by recent changes in electronic data processing. The development of remote terminals, time-sharing, data communications, and minicomputers has had a *decentralizing* effect on data processing activities within an organization. Such developments have encouraged operating employees and management to perform many of their own data processing tasks rather than relying completely on a central data processing organization. Therefore, though large computers with centralized data files have *centralized* data processing in many organizations, their remote time-sharing capabilities can also foster *decentralized* data processing activities.

Centralization versus Decentralization of Management and Operations

Computers have caused increased *centralization* of the management and operations of some firms but have resulted in *decentraliza-*

tion for other organizations. Real-time computer systems with centralized files can allow the top management of the firm to *centralize* decision-making formerly done at lower levels of the organization and reduce the number of branch offices, manufacturing plants, and warehouses needed by the firm. However, companies have also used the computer to foster *decentralization* of management and operations. Computers allow top management to delegate more responsibility to middle managers and to increase the number of branch offices or other company units while still providing top management with the ability to control the organization. Thus, whether the computer encourages centralization or decentralization depends on the philosophy of top management and the nature of the operations of the specific business firm.

Computers and Middle Management

The elimination of middle management by the computer was predicted by several business "prophets" when computers began to be extensively utilized by business firms. However, the computer has not eliminated middle management. While some middle management jobs have been eliminated, there has been an upgrading and enlargement of other middle management positions. While the computer has taken over the routine decisions and clerical activities that were formerly required of middle management, it now provides him with more information to plan and control the operations for which he is responsible. By freeing middle management from clerical tasks and routine decisions, the computer has allowed middle managers to enlarge the scope of their positions. For example, the middle manager can now spend more time on marketing, planning, and personnel matters. We will discuss the opportunities created by the computer for management at all levels in the section that follows.

The Systems Approach to Management:
The Computer as a Catalyst

The challenge of the computer to business management can be considered in a positive sense if the computer is viewed as a "catalyst" for applying the systems concept to business management. Computerizing information systems requires huge commitments of time, money, and personnel. It requires intensive studies of the various operations and information requirements of the business. It puts management "eyeball to eyeball" with the highly sophisticated technology of computer hardware, software, and personnel. It forces painful decisions that change "the way we always used to do things."

Faced with these pressures, management can take the easy way out by computerizing information systems in the traditional "piecemeal" approach, i.e., the information requirements of each department in the firm is computerized, one after the other, as resources permit. Instead, management should welcome the computer as a *catalyst* for *the systems approach*. If the business firm is a business "system" rather than just a series of departments which perform various functions, the piecemeal approach can be disastrous. Management must use the systems approach when confronted with the need to introduce computers into the business system.

In Chapters Eight and Nine, we saw that a thorough job of information systems development should result in a "systems study" of the business firm which identifies and analyzes the subsystems, components, flows, major decision-making points, interrelationships, environmental systems, and information requirements of the entire business system, *not* just the particular operations that will be computerized. This "study of the business" stage of information systems development can be used as a powerful tool to promote the use of the systems approach. Once we begin to study the business as a system composed of interrelated components and as a subsystem of society, we will begin to identify many problems and opportunities of the present business system. Important changes in organizational structure, activities, and goals may be identified as necessary or desirable.

Managing Organizational Development

Thus, the computer can challenge managers to use the systems approach in defining and accomplishing the functions of management. Managing a business firm becomes a form of systems development which we can call *"organizational development."* Managers can then look upon their assignment as the management of a systems development project. In this context, the job of management consists of the following basic tasks:[5]

1. Define the company as a specific business system.
2. Identify environmental systems.
3. Establish the goals and objectives of the business system.

---

[5] Adapted from Seymour Titles, "The Managers Job: A Systems Approach," *Harvard Business Review* (January–February 1962), p. 74.

4. Establish performance criteria.
5. Design the subsystems of the business system.
6. Utilize the systems development process to plan, organize, direct, control, and integrate the operations of the subsystems of the business firm so that the goals of the business system are achieved.

Sophisticated computer-based management information systems will not improve the performance of a business firm if they are superimposed on a business system that needs to reorganize and redirect its management and operations. The challenge of the computer to management is to use the computer as a catalyst for the systems approach to organizational development. If management does not accept this challenge, the instant response of real-time management information systems will be providing "instant bad news" about the poor performance of the business firm.

The Systems Approach to Management Decision-Making

The systems approach should also be applied to the decision-making process. One way to illustrate this is to convert the stages of *information systems development* into stages of *management decision-making* as illustrated below:

1. Systems investigation. Survey the subsystems of the business system and the business environment for problems and opportunities. Separate symptoms from problems. Select the most urgent and most feasible problems to be solved or opportunities to be pursued.

2. Systems analysis. Gather and analyze information about the selected problem or opportunity in terms of the systems and subsystems that are involved.

3. Systems design. Develop alternative courses of action by designing and testing models of the systems and subsystems that affect the problem or opportunity.

4. Programming. Choose a single course of action and develop plans, programs, budgets, policies, and necessary procedures.

5. Systems implementation. Put the decision into effect by implementing the plans developed in the programming stage.

6. Systems maintenance. Monitor and evaluate the results of the decision since the subsystems of the business system and the business environment are subject to continual change. Modify the decision as necessary.

Enlarging the Job of Management: From Paper Shufflers to Managers

A major challenge to management arises from the ability of the computer to handle clerical details and simple decisions which can be programmed, thus freeing management from these routine tasks. Many managers can no longer use the excuse that "I'm too tied up with details and paper work," or "I can't get the right information at the right time in the right form in the right place." Management must develop new and creative activities including the use of the computer to support high-level decisions.

Letting the computer take over routine decisions should not be viewed as a threat by management but as an opportunity to engage in more activities that are beneficial to the business firm. Many managers have reported that the computer has finally given them the time to "get out of the office and into the field." They can finally spend enough time pursuing their *marketing responsibilities* with customers and salesmen, their *personnel management responsibilities* with subordinates, and their *social responsibilities* with various public and governmental groups. Managers can spend more time on *planning* activities instead of spending much of their time "putting out fires." Thus, the computer can enable many managers finally to become "managers" rather than "paper shufflers."

Managers as Systems Analysts

Another challenge of the computer to business management arises from the potential ability of computer-based management information systems to provide decision-makers at all management levels with the information required to support their decision-making activities. Though this ability does not exist in many firms, the capability of providing the information required by certain types of decisions is present in many computer-based information systems. When such a capability exists, the challenge to management is to *use* this information.

Management involvement in the information systems development process will help insure that information needed for decision-making is actually produced by an information system. In some firms, such information may already be produced but is being ignored by management. In either case, the challenge to top management is to invest time, money, and personnel in programs to educate management personnel on how to request and use information for decision-making. In effect, *managers must become their own systems analysts* so they can educate computer professionals to their information requirements and then properly use the information provided by modern management information systems.

Using Advanced Quantitative Techniques

Another aspect of the management challenge lies in the ability of the computer to help management make strategic planning and control decisions. The use of the computer must rise above the "paper shuffling" level to a higher level which utilizes simulation and other mathematical and statistical techniques to analyze the important factors that must be considered in management decisions and to test the possible results of proposed decisions. Before the computer, such techniques would require teams of mathematicians, scientists and other personnel who were highly skilled in the technical and mathematical aspects of such techniques. However, the computer requires only a few seconds to process business data using many of these techniques. Software packages that utilize such techniques can be acquired if systems analysts and programmers who can develop such software are not available. Managers themselves do not have to know the mathematical and technical *details* of such techniques. The challenge to management is to become acquainted with the *basic concepts* that underlie methods of quantitative business analysis so that they can intelligently use these techniques in planning and control decisions.

The Challenge of the Future MIS

The management information system of the future will be an interactive real-time system. It will collect and process data and update files in real-time. It will provide management with real-time analysis of data upon request. It will provide management with powerful analytical tools, utilizing statistical and mathematical techniques and simulation. Models of various aspects of the operations of the firm and of the firm itself will be provided so that the manager can test the effect of proposed decisions on an interactive real-time basis. Such an ultimate management information system will provide a manager with up-to-date information on all aspects of the operations of his firm and its environment, provide him with instant analysis of such data, allow him to test the results of his decisions before they are made, and provide him with instant feedback on the performance of his organization. The ultimate MIS will provide management with a real-time capability which will greatly increase effectiveness in solving the problems and capitalizing on the opportunities facing a business firm in a rapidly changing world. Thus, the managers of tomorrow must prepare *today* to accept the challenges posed by future management information systems.

THE SOCIAL CHALLENGE OF THE COMPUTER

We are in the midst of a "computer revolution" that experts expect to continue for many years. There can be no doubt that the computer has significantly magnified man's ability to analyze, compute, and communicate, thereby greatly improving his ability to plan and control many varieties of human endeavor. However, several social commentators have become alarmed at the "ubiquitous" nature of the computer. They note that computers seem to be present everywhere in all the activities of daily life in our present society. Such commentators worry about our continually increasing dependence on the computer and have identified many adverse social effects of computer usage. What should our attitude be towards the widespread use of the computer in business and society? In order to answer this question, we shall analyze some of the major social and economic effects of computers and the computer industry.

The Impact of Computers on Society

The impact of computers on society can be analyzed in terms of "social applications" and "social-economic effects." The *social applications* of the computer include its use to solve human and social problems such as crime and pollution. *Social-economic effects* of the computer refers to the impact on society of the use of computers. For example, computerizing a production process may have the *adverse* effect of a decrease in employment opportunities and the *beneficial* effect of providing consumers with products of better quality at lower cost. Business managers must understand the beneficial and adverse effects of computer usage on society. Such an understanding will help them plan and control the development and operation of computer-based information systems within their organizations. We will therefore analyze the following aspects of the impact of the computer on society:

1. Employment and productivity.
2. Business competition.
3. Individuality.
4. Quality of life.
5. Privacy.
6. Other social effects.
7. Social computer applications.

Impact on Employment and Productivity

The Industrial Revolution of the 18th century saw the development of *"mechanization"* in which machines replaced muscle power. The term *"automation"* began to be used around the middle of this century and refers to the automatic transfer and positioning of work by machines or the automatic operation and control of a production process by machines. The assembly line operations of an automobile manufacturer or the petroleum refinery operations of an oil company are examples of automation. Thus, automation is the use of machines to control other machines and physical processes and replaces some of the human "brain power" and manual dexterity formerly required. The term *"cybernation"* then came into use to emphasize the automatic control aspect of automation, especially automatic self-regulating "process control" systems. Automation and cybernation can occur without electronic computers. However, the increasing use of computers to control automatically all types of production processes as well as traditional clerical tasks ("office automation") are major developments of the second half of the 20th century.

The impact of computers on employment and productivity is therefore directly related to the use of computers to achieve automation and cybernation. There can be no doubt that the use of computers has created new jobs and increased productivity, while also causing a significant reduction in some types of job opportunities. Computers utilized for office data processing or the numerical control of machine tools are accomplishing tasks formerly performed by many clerks and machinists. Also, jobs created by the computer within a computer-using organization require different types of skills and education than the jobs eliminated by the computer. Therefore, specific individuals within an organization may become unemployed unless they can be retrained for new positions or new responsibilities.

However, the productivity of an individual worker is significantly increased by computerization. One worker can now do the work of several, and the length of time required to perform certain tasks has been drastically shortened. Increased productivity may lead to lower costs and lower prices which may increase demand for a product and thus generate increased employment. The higher profits caused by increases in productivity may also stimulate more investment to expand productive facilities, resulting in increased employment. These positive effects on employment have been characteristic of the *"mass production"* of goods and services in our economy.

Another point to remember is that the higher standard of living caused by increased productivity generates *more* rather than *less* demand for more types and amounts of goods and services. "Yesterday's luxuries become today's necessities" is a statement which emphasizes the almost limitless demands for goods and services that our society seems to exhibit. This phenomena should be related to the impact of computers on employment since an increased standard of living seems to lead to expansion of demand for goods and services which must result in an increase in employment opportunities.

There can be no doubt that the computer industry has created a host of new job opportunities for the manufacture, sale, and maintenance of computer hardware, software, and other services. Many new jobs such as systems analysts, computer programmers, and computer operators have been created in computer-using organizations. Many new jobs have been created in service industries which provide services to the computer industry and computer-using firms and the people that work for them. Additional jobs have been created because the computer makes possible the production of complex industrial and technical goods and services which would otherwise be impossible to produce. Thus, jobs have been created by activities that are heavily dependent upon the computer in such fields as space exploration, microelectronic technology, and scientific research.

The controversy over the effect of computers on employment will continue as long as activities formerly performed by people are computerized. *Unemployment is more than a statistic;* office and factory workers whose jobs have been eliminated by computerization are real people with real employment needs. Such persons will take little comfort in the fact that computers have many beneficial effects upon employment. Business firms and other computer-using organizations, labor unions, and government agencies must continue to provide job opportunities for people displaced by computers. This includes transfers to other positions, relocation to other facilities, or training for new responsibilities. Only if society continues to take positive steps to provide jobs for people displaced by computers can we take pride in the increase in employment caused by computer usage. The effect of computers on employment can be a positive one if new job opportunities and incentives are provided that offset specific instances of unemployment caused by the computer.

Impact on Competition

The impact of computers on *competition* concerns the effect that computer systems have on the size of business organizations. Computers allow large firms to become more efficient. This can have several anticompetitive effects. Small business firms that could exist because of the inefficiencies of large firms are now driven out of business or absorbed by the larger firms. The efficiency of the larger firms allows them to continue to grow and combine with other business firms and thus create the large corporations that exist today. The previously high cost of most computer systems (which only larger firms could afford) accentuated this trend toward bigness. This is also true of new computerized production systems which can produce goods at lower cost than many less automated systems. Small firms which cannot afford complex cybernetic systems will not be able to survive.

It is undoubtedly true that computers allow large organizations to grow larger and become more efficient. Organizations grow in terms of people, productive facilities, and geographic locations such as branch offices and plants. Only a computer-based information system is capable of controlling the complex activities and relationships that occur. However, it should be noted that the cost and size of the computer systems continues to *decrease* and the availability of computer services continues to *increase* due to the activities of computer service bureaus and time-sharing companies. Therefore, even the small firm can take advantage of the productivity and efficiency generated by computer-based systems.

It should also be noted that the computer is changing the *nature* of competition as well as the size of the competing units. As business firms possess better information on their own internal position and their business environment and as they utilize new analytical techniques such as mathematical stimulation, the competition between business firms will become very keen and their response to each other's competitive moves will become more accurate and more rapid. Thus, only firms with effective computer-based information systems will be able to survive this type of dynamic competition.

Impact on Individuality

A frequent criticism of computers concerns their negative effect on the *"individuality"* of people. Computer-based systems are criticized as impersonal systems which dehumanize and depersonalize activities which have been computerized since they eliminate the human relationships present in noncomputer systems. Because it is more efficient for a data processing system to deal with an individual as a number than as a name, many people feel the loss of identity that seems inherent in systems where they seem to be "just another number."

Another aspect of the loss of individuality is the regimentation of the individual that seems to be required by some computer-based systems. These systems do not seem to possess any flexibility. They demand strict adherence to detailed procedures if the system is to work. "Do not fold, spindle, or mutilate" is the statement on punched card documents that has become a popular symbol of the regimentation and inflexibility of computer-based systems. The negative impact of computers on individuality is reinforced by "horror stories" which describe how inflexible and uncaring computer-based systems are when it comes to rectifying their own mistakes. Many of us are familiar with stories of how computerized customer billing and accounting systems have continued to demand payment and send warning notices to a customer whose account has already been paid despite repeated attempts by the customer to have the error corrected.

Is there any rational arguments against the charges that the computer robs people of their individuality? One major fact that must be considered is summed up by the statement "computers don't make mistakes, people do." That is to say that the errors and inflexibility of computer-based systems are primarily caused by poor systems design or mistakes in computer programming or operations. Thus, the computer can be blamed only for occasional hardware malfunctions. Systems analysts, computer programmers, and other EDP personnel must accept the responsibility for errors in systems design, computer programming, and data processing operations.

Another point to emphasize is that computer-based systems can be designed to minimize depersonalization and regimentation. *"People-oriented"* and *"user-oriented" information systems* can be developed. The computer hardware, software, and systems design capabilities that make such systems possible are increasing rather than decreasing. Many of the errors and inflexibility of past and present computer-based systems can be attributed to the "pioneering" nature of the hardware, software, and systems design utilized by such systems.

The computer is frequently blamed for the "bigness" of business firms and other institutions in which the individual is treated as no more than a statistic. However, it must be remembered that though computers may help make bigness possible, computers alone are not responsible for the growth in size and complexity of our institutions. We live in a society which is attempting to provide *all people,* rather than a small elite, with food, clothing, shelter, employment, education, medical care, and other "necessities" of life while continuing to protect the freedom of the individual. This is an awesome task, accomplished by no previous civilization. Much of the bigness and complexity of modern institutions is caused by our attempt to provide the necessities and amenities of life to vast numbers of people in an efficient and effective manner, rather than reserving them for a small aristocracy. In this regard, the computer is *helping* rather than *hindering* our attempts to provide the "good life" to each individual.

It can also be argued that computers can help promote greater personalization and attention to the individual than would otherwise be possible, given the large size of organizational units, the complexity of individual and organizational relationships, and the volume of individual activities. Computer systems can easily handle large masses of routine transactions, thus allowing *more personal attention* to important transactions. Computer systems can provide information and analytical techniques that allow individuals a *diversity* of choice so that the *individual preferences* of the users of the system can be accommodated in the operation of the system. This is what is meant by *people-oriented* or *user-oriented* systems.

Impact on the Quality of Life

The impact of the computer on the quality of life is directly related to its impact upon employment and productivity. For example, computerized business systems increase productivity and allow the production of better quality goods and services at lower costs. Thus, the computer is partially responsible for the high standard of living we enjoy. In addition, the computer has eliminated monotonous or obnoxious tasks in the office and the factory that formerly had to be performed by people. In many instances, this allows people to concentrate on more challenging and interesting assignments, has upgraded the skill level of the work to be performed, and created challenging jobs requiring highly developed skills in the computer industry and within computer-using organizations. Thus, computers can be said to upgrade the quality of life because they can upgrade the quality of working conditions and the content of work activities.

Of course, it must be remembered that some jobs created by the computer, keypunching, for example, are quite repetitive and routine. Also, to the extent that computers are utilized in some types of automation, they must take some responsibility for the criticism of assembly line operations which require the continual repetition of elementary tasks, thus forcing a worker to "work like a machine" instead of like a skilled "craftsman." Many automated operations are also criticized for relegating people to a "do nothing" standby role where a worker spends most of his time waiting for infrequent opportunities to "push some buttons." Such effects do have a detrimental effect on the quality of life, but they are more than offset by the less burdensome and more creative jobs created by the computer.

Computers have contributed to the increased availability of leisure time. The increase in productivity provided by computer usage has helped allow the American worker to produce more goods and services in less time. We have gone from the six-day week to the five-day week to the four-day week in some industries. The working day has decreased from 12 hours to 8 hours or less. The number of holidays and the length of vacations have increased, as well as the types and length of personal and professional leaves. Young people tend to stay in school longer before seeking permanent employment, while workers now retire at an earlier age. Thus, the quality of life is improved because people have more time for recreation, entertainment, education, and creative activities. This development in itself has created more employment since many new jobs have been created in the "leisure industry" to serve the leisure time activities of people.

Impact on Privacy

Modern computer systems make it technically and economically feasible to collect, store, integrate, interchange and retrieve data and information quickly and easily. This characteristic has an important beneficial effect on the efficiency and effectiveness of computer-based information systems. However, the power of the computer to store and retrieve information can have a negative effect on *the right to privacy* of every individual. Confidential information on individuals contained in centralized computer data files by credit bureaus, government agencies, and private business firms could be misused and result in the invasion of privacy and other injustices. Unauthorized use of such information would seriously invade the privacy of individuals, while errors in such data files could seriously hurt the credit standing or reputation of an individual. Such developments were possible before the advent of the computer. However, the speed and power of a large computer with centralized direct access information files and remote terminals greatly increases the potential for such injustices. The trend towards nationwide integrated information systems with integrated data bases by business firms and government agencies substantially increases *the potential* for misuse of computer-stored information.

Business firms, government agencies, and other organizations have good reasons for maintaining files of information concerning their customers, suppliers, stockholders, taxpayers, and other groups of citizens. Such information is necessary if we are to expect effective, efficient, and fair methods for providing business products and services such as insurance coverage and credit extension, as well as governmental services such as social security and police protection. However, society has recognized the seriousness of past abuses and the increased potential for invasion of privacy generated by computerized "data banks." Legislation has been enacted and is being considered which defines the responsibilities of organizations which store data on individuals. The Fair Credit Reporting Act, for example, restricts the use of negative information about an individual without his knowledge and limits the time that personal information can be maintained in files utilized for credit reporting purposes.

A proposed Federal Privacy Act is under consideration by Congress which would strictly regulate the collection and use of personal data by governmental agencies and other organizations engaging in interstate commerce. This legislation would require that: (1) an individual be notified when a record of information about him exists, (2) an individual be notified of any transfer of such information, (3) an individual would have the right to inspect such records, make copies, add to the information, and correct or remove erroneous or misleading information, (4) individuals must be notified before such information is disclosed to anyone unless legally required, and (5) a record of all persons inspecting personal files would have to be maintained. Such legislation should emphasize and accelerate the efforts of systems designers to utilize hardware, software, and procedural controls to maintain the accuracy and confidentiality of computerized files.

Other Social Effects

Computer usage creates the *potential* for several other *negative social effects* which have not been previously mentioned. The potential for fraud and embezzlement by "electronic criminals" has been proven by several widely publicized instances of "computerized crime." Incriminating personal information in computerized files can be used to blackmail individuals. Fraud or errors in election vote counting systems can occur. Integrated information systems which allow greater centralization in the control of an organization may give some individuals too much power over other people. In the political sphere, this centralization of power is viewed as a potential threat to democracy if centralized government planning and control robs people of their individual freedoms. Computers can also be misused to distort information about candidates in political campaigns.

Our great and increasing dependence upon computers in the operations of our economy and society is seen as a potential threat by some social observers. Such observers worry about "computers taking over" since we have become so dependent upon their use. They also worry that computer malfunctions might have disastrous consequences if military weapons systems, industrial control systems, and financial information systems are involved. Such potential negative effects pose serious challenges to the *control* aspects of systems design.

Social Applications

Computers can have many direct *beneficial effects* on society when they are used to solve human and social problems through *"social applications"* such as medical diagnosis, computer-assisted instruction, governmental program planning, environmental quality control, and law enforcement. Computers can be used to help diagnose an illness, prescribe necessary treatment, and monitor the progress of hospital patients. Computer-assisted instruction (CAI) allows a computer to serve as a "tutor" since it utilizes conversational computing on remote terminals to tailor instruction to the needs of a particular student. This is a tremendous benefit to students, especially those with learning disabilities.

Computers can be used for crime control through various law enforcement applications which allow police to identify and respond quickly to evidences of criminal activity. Computers have been used to monitor the level of pollution in the air and in bodies of water in order to detect the sources of pollution and to issue early warnings when dangerous levels are reached. Computers are also utilized for the program planning of many government agencies in such areas as urban planning, population density and land use studies, highway planning, urban transit studies, etc. Computers are being used in the development of a nationwide job placement system by the Department of Labor to help match unemployed persons with available jobs. These and other applications illustrate that the computer can be used to help solve the problems of society.

Systems Design and Social Responsibility

It should be obvious that management must insist that the social and economic effects of computer usage be considered when a computer-based system is being developed. A major management objective should be to develop systems which can be easily and effectively utilized by the individual system user. The objectives of the system must also include the protection of the privacy of the individuals, and the defense of the system against fraudulent use. Control hardware, software, and procedures must be included in the systems design. The potential for misuse and malfunction of a proposed system must be analyzed with respect to the impact on computer-using organizations, individuals, and society as a whole.

Many of the potential negative effects of computer usage mentioned previously have or would result from errors in systems design and programming. Increased emphasis on the control capabilities of computer-based systems would protect us from many of these potential effects. Computer-based systems can be designed to prevent their own misuse and remedy their own malfunctions. Computers make it possible for us to monitor the activities of computer-based systems and thus prevent computerized crime and correct systems malfunctions. Management must recognize that the *design and maintenance of systems controls* is the key to minimizing the negative effects of computer misuse and malfunction.

However, the elimination of some adverse effects of computer usage may require *government regulation* or *a greater evidence of social responsibility* on the part of the management of computer-using organizations. For example, many business firms have been able to assure their employees that no person would be laid off because of a conversion to computer systems, though some employees have had to accept changes in assignments. Business firms are frequently able to make such a guarantee (and stay in business) because their long-term employment needs have continued to increase due to the growth of the business and the normal attrition of other employees. Such a policy also improves employee morale and productivity and enhances the long-run position of the business firm in society.

It should be obvious that many detrimental effects of the computer on society are caused by improperly designed systems or by individuals and organizations who are not willing to accept the social responsibility for their actions. Like other powerful tools, the computer possesses the potential for great good or evil. Managers, computer users, and computer professionals must accept the responsibility for its proper and beneficial use.

SUMMARY

The computer is a valuable and powerful resource that presents a major challenge to business management. In this chapter, we analyzed three major aspects of the management challenge of the computer:

1.   The challenge of computer performance.
2.   The challenge to management performance.
3.   The social challenge of the computer.

Poor computer performance in many business firms is well-documented and reveals that many computer users and computer professionals have not learned how to manage this vital but expensive business resource. The computer is not being used effectively, efficiently, and economically by many business firms. However, the experiences of successful computer users reveal that the basic ingredient of high-quality computer performance is extensive and meaningful management and user involvement in the development and operation of computer-based information systems. This should be the key ingredient in shaping the response of management to the challenge of improving the quality of computer services. Effective methods of management and user involvement can be utilized to improve computer performance in the present "user generation" of computer usage in business.

The challenge of the computer to management performance is based on its role as a catalyst for a systems approach to management. The benefits of computer-based information systems should challenge management to utilize systems concepts of organizational development and decision-making. The power of the computer can enlarge the job of management by freeing managers from routine tasks and allowing them more time for marketing, personnel, and planning activities. Computers can also allow management to easily utilize simulation and other mathematical and statistical techniques, to analyze the important factors that must be considered in management decisions, and to test the possible results of proposed decisions.

The third major challenge of the computer to management concerns the impact that computers can have on society. Computers have had a major impact on society and thus impose serious responsibilities upon the management of computer-using business firms. Computers have had a major effect on employment, productivity, and competition in the business world. Computers have had both beneficial and detrimental effects on individuality, the quality of life, and privacy. Social applications of computers provide a direct beneficial effect to society when they are used to solve human and social problems. Business management must accept the responsibility for the proper and beneficial use of computers in business. They must insist that effective measures be utilized to insure that the social and economic effects of computer usage are considered during the development and operation of computer-based information systems.

KEY TERMS AND CONCEPTS

Poor computer performance, 450
Management involvement, 451–454
The user generation, 455
User resistance, 456
User involvement, 457
Management audit, 458–459
Centralization vs. decentralization, 460
The computer as a catalyst, 461–462
Computers and organizational development, 462

Systems approach to decision-making, 463
Computers and management job enlargement, 464–465
Social-economic effects of computers, 467–474
Social applications of computers, 474–475
Systems design and social responsibility, 475–476

ASSIGNMENTS

1. Test your understanding of the chapter material by reviewing the *purpose, outline, summary,* and *key terms and concepts* of this chapter. Are you confident that you have attained a basic understanding of the major concepts of the chapter? If not, reread the appropriate material as indicated by the page numbers after each key term and concept.

2. Describe what is meant by "poor computer performance." What is the cause? What is its solution?

3. "Proper management involvement requires the knowledgeable and active participation of management in the planning and control of computer-based information systems." Explain how this policy can be implemented.

4. Discuss the concept of the "user generation."

5. Identify several reasons for user resistance to computerization.

6. "Solving the problems of user resistance requires meaningful user involvement based on formal methods of (1) education, (2) communication, and (3) participation." Explain how this policy can be implemented.

7. Discuss the role and content of a management audit of an organization's computer effort.

8. Discuss how the computer can support either the centralization or decentralization of:
   a. Data processing
   b. Management
   c. Operations

9. Discuss how the computer can be a "catalyst" for the systems approach to business management in each of the following areas:
   a. Information systems development
   b. Organizational development
   c. Management decision-making

10. Identify several ways that the computer can enlarge and enrich the job of management, both now and in the future.

11. Discuss the impact of computers on society in terms of one or more of the following:
    a. Employment and productivity
    b. Competition
    c. Individuality
    d. Quality of life
    e. Privacy
    f. Potential for misuse
    g. Excessive dependency

12. Describe several social applications of the computer which have helped to solve human and social problems.

13. "Management must insist that the social and economic effects of computer usage be considered when a computer-based system is being developed." Explain how this policy can be implemented.

14. "The elimination of some adverse effects of computer usage may require government regulation or greater evidence of social responsibility on the part of the management of computer-using organizations." Explain the rationale behind this statement.

part six

Fundamentals of Computer Programming Languages

Chapter Outline

Purpose of the Chapter

Introduction

A Fundamental FORTRAN Vocabulary
Arithmetic Statements, Input/Output Statements,
Specification Statements, Control Statements,
Subprogram Statements

Fundamental Rules of FORTRAN
Rules For Using Arithmetic Statements: Constants and
Variables, General Form of the Arithmetic Statement,
Priority of Arithmetic Operations, Mathematical
Functions; Rules For Using Input/Output Statements:
The READ Statement, the WRITE Statement; Rules
For Using Specification Statements: The FORMAT
Statement, FORMAT Specifications, Other FORMAT
Rules, the DIMENSION Statement, Arrays and
Subscripts; Rules for Using Control Statements: The
GO TO Statement, the IF Statement, the DO Statement,
CONTINUE, STOP, and END Statements

Sample FORTRAN Programs
Sample Program One, the END Option, Sample Program
Two, Sample Program Three, Analysis of the Program,
Programming Alternatives

Preparing FORTRAN Programs
The FORTRAN Coding Form, Executing the Program,
Interactive FORTRAN Programming

Key Terms and Concepts

Assignments

15

Fundamentals of FORTRAN Programming

Purpose of the Chapter

To promote a basic understanding of FORTRAN programming by:

1. Reviewing the basic vocabulary and rules of FORTRAN,
2. Analyzing several FORTRAN programs,.
3. Writing simple programs in FORTRAN.

INTRODUCTION

FORTRAN is one of the most widely used programming languages. It is a high-order (compiler) language that can be used by the computer systems of most manufacturers. As we mentioned in Chapter 6, FORTRAN (FORmula TRANslation) was originally designed for solving the mathematical problems of scientists, engineers, and mathematicians. However, FORTRAN is also utilized to program business computer applications which involve many mathematical calculations. For example, FORTRAN is frequently utilized to program quantitative business applications in operations research and management science that require such techniques as statistical analysis, mathematical models, network analysis, linear programming, etc. However, we do not have to program complex mathematical applications in order to appreciate the power and simplicity of FORTRAN. In this chapter, we will learn how to program a few simple business problems in the FORTRAN programming language.

Many versions of FORTRAN have been developed by computer

manufacturers, and large computer users have added special features to their FORTRAN compilers. For example, several versions of FORTRAN have been developed to simplify the teaching of FORTRAN in schools or to facilitate interactive programming in FORTRAN. One of the most noticeable features of some versions (such as WATFOR, WATFIV, XTRAN, and FASTRAN) is that they allow "free-form" input/output statements similar to the BASIC programming language described in Chapter 17. We will briefly discuss interactive FORTRAN programming in the last section of this chapter.

FORTRAN IV, the latest version of FORTRAN, now exists in two standard forms: FORTRAN and Basic FORTRAN. These standard versions were developed by the American National Standards Institute in cooperation with the computer industry. Basic FORTRAN is a shorter and simpler version of standard FORTRAN and is probably the most widely used form of the FORTRAN language. The full standard version of FORTRAN IV is really an extension of Basic FORTRAN with advanced features and a greater variety of instructions.

In this chapter we will concentrate on fundamentals and will not attempt to cover the advanced features of the various versions of FORTRAN. This should enable us to quickly learn to write several simple FORTRAN programs which can be run on a wide variety of computer systems. *This kind of programming knowledge is sufficient for most computer users.* Persons wishing to become professional programmers should build on this foundation by additional study and practice utilizing programming texts or manuals that provide an in-depth coverage of the advanced features and statements of FORTRAN.

We can begin our study of FORTRAN by analyzing it as we would any language, i.e., by analyzing its "vocabulary" and its "grammar." FORTRAN has a vocabulary of words and symbols and a grammar of rules for writing computer instructions. It is essential that we learn the fundamental vocabulary and grammatical rules of FORTRAN if we wish the computer to properly accomplish specific data processing tasks. Therefore, in this chapter we will organize our study of FORTRAN in the manner shown below.

1. *Fundamental FORTRAN vocabulary.* We first take a brief look at the basic words and symbols utilized in FORTRAN programming.

2. *Fundamental rules of FORTRAN.* We then summarize the basic rules for writing FORTRAN statements.
3. *Sample FORTRAN programs.* Several examples of simple FORTRAN programs are presented and discussed.
4. *Preparing FORTRAN programs.* Instructions on the mechanics of writing and processing FORTRAN programs are presented.
5. *FORTRAN programming assignments.* The only way to really learn a language is to use it. Therefore, you are asked to write several simple FORTRAN programs at the end of the chapter.

A FUNDAMENTAL FORTRAN VOCABULARY

A fundamental vocabulary of "key words and symbols" in the FORTRAN language is discussed in this section. This "limited instruction set" is sufficient for the purposes of this chapter. Like other high-level compiler languages, FORTRAN has "reserved words" and symbols which are utilized to write computer instructions called "statements" that are translated by the FORTRAN compiler into machine-language instructions and executed by the computer.

There are five major categories of FORTRAN statements: (1) *arithmetic,* (2) *input/output,* (3) *specification,* (4) *control,* and (5) *subprogram* statements. We shall organize our fundamental vocabulary by grouping the key words and symbols into these five categories. Figure 15–1 illustrates several types of statements in a simple FORTRAN program which reads the values of Y and Z and computes and prints the result X.

FIGURE 15–1

Types of Statements in an Actual FORTRAN Program

```
      READ (1, 10) Y, Z          Input/Output statement
  10  FORMAT (2F8.2)             Specification statement
      X = Y + Z                  Arithmetic statement
      WRITE (2, 10) X            Input/Output statement
      STOP                       Control statement
      END                        Control statement
```

Arithmetic Statements

Arithmetic statements specify the arithmetic operations to be performed. The mathematical symbols utilized to perform arithmetic operations are shown below.

Symbol	*Operation*
+	Addition
−	Subtraction
*	Multiplication
/	Division
**	Exponentiation

Input/Output Statements

Input/output statements direct the computer to transfer data between the CPU and input/output devices. Fundamental input/output words are READ and WRITE.

1. READ statements read the contents of specific data fields from the input unit specified. (Card-reader, magnetic tape unit, etc.)
2. WRITE statements write output data of specific data fields on the output unit specified. (Printer, card punch, magnetic tape unit, etc.)

Specification Statements

Specification statements describe the size and format of input/output or storage media to be used, the allocation of storage, and the use of constants. The fundamental specification words are FORMAT and DIMENSION.

1. FORMAT statements specify the "format" (size, type, number, etc.) of input or output data fields and records.
2. DIMENSION statements specify the dimensions (rows, columns, levels) of "arrays" of data items, and reserve the memory locations required to store each element in an array.

Control Statements

Control statements control the order in which a program is executed, perform comparisons and test conditions, change the sequence of a program through a branching process, or stop a program. Fundamental control words are GO TO, IF, DO, CONTINUE, STOP and END.

1. GO TO and IF statements alter the sequential execution of program statements by transferring control to another statement.
2. DO statements command the computer to repeatedly execute a series of statements (a "program loop" or "DO loop") that are part of the computer program.

3. CONTINUE statements are frequently used at the end of a DO loop.
4. STOP statements stop a program without a provision for re-starting.
5. END statements inform the compiler the program is completed.

Subprogram Statements

Subprogram statements define functions and subroutines and direct the computer to utilize them in a program. Subprogram statements include CALL, RETURN, FUNCTION, and SUBROUTINE statements. Such statements allow programmers to develop and utilize many complex "preprogrammed" functions and subroutines that are stored in the "subroutine library" of the computer system. The use of such statements will not be covered in this text.

FUNDAMENTAL RULES OF FORTRAN

Like any programming language, FORTRAN has specific grammatical rules which must be followed if the computer is to process a program correctly. If these rules are not followed, clerical errors will result which will cause the computer to do one or more of the following:

1. Reject the program without compiling or processing it,
2. Print diagnostic error messages,
3. Produce incorrect or invalid results.

We will confine our discussion in this chapter to fundamental rules of FORTRAN that are sufficient for the programs which we will illustrate and which you will be asked to write. We shall organize these fundamental rules into categories that are related to the basic categories of FORTRAN statements. In order to make the task of programming easier for beginners, we will simplify our presentation by omitting some of the details concerning the forms and restrictions governing the use of various FORTRAN statements. Persons wishing to make full use of all of the features of FORTRAN in their programming should consult the many FORTRAN texts and manuals that are available.

RULES FOR USING ARITHMETIC STATEMENTS

The rules for using arithmetic statements will be described first because they affect the rules governing the other types of statements. The rules may appear quite complicated, but experience in programming a few short FORTRAN programs should assure you that they are comparatively easy to follow.

Constants and Variables

1. Constants. Constants are known quantities written in numerical form. A minus sign identifies a negative constant. An unsigned constant is treated as positive; therefore, the use of a plus sign is optional. The allowable size of constants is restricted according to the specific FORTRAN compiler used and the "mode" of the constant.

2. Constant modes. Constants (and variables) can be written in either the "integer" or "real" modes. An *integer* is a number *without* a decimal point. (It is also called a "whole number" or "fixed-point" number.) A *real number* is a number *with* a decimal point. (It is also called a "floating-point" or "double-precision" number.) Real numbers are usually written in decimal form unless they exceed the maximum limit of the particular FORTRAN compiler being used. Then they are written in an exponent form (also known as floating-point or double-precision format.) This form uses a real number in decimal form followed by the letter E and an integer exponent. The exponent is the power of ten by which the real number is to be multiplied. Examples of each of these modes are shown below.

Integer Constant: 463

Real Constant
Decimal form: 463.0
Exponent form: 4.63E2

Most FORTRAN compilers accept integers with up to five digits and real numbers (decimal form) with up to eight digits. Real numbers in exponent form can usually range between 10^{-38} and 10^{38}. Many compilers accept numbers of much greater size.

3. Variables. A variable is an unknown quantity or a quantity that can possess varying values. Variables are identified by names which consist of from one to six alphabetic or numeric characters (five character limit in Basic FORTRAN). The first character *must* be alphabetic and no special characters are allowed. Also, no FORTRAN "reserved word" can be used as a variable name.

4. Variable modes. Variables can be expressed in the integer or real modes. Integer variables must use either I,J,K,L,M, or N as the first character of the variable name. Real variables must start with one of the other letters of the alphabet.

> *Examples:* Integer Variable: JACK
>
> Real Variable: TOTAL

General Form of the Arithmetic Statement

The general form of an arithmetic statement is:

$$v = e$$

1. The *"v"* is a variable name and *"e"* is an arithmetic expression. The equal sign is *not* a symbol of mathematical equality. The statement $v = e$ means that *"the variable v is assigned the value of the arithmetic expression e."* Thus, arithmetic statements in FORTRAN are frequently called "arithmetic assignment statements." For example, the arithmetic statement $X = Y + Z$ means that the current value of X is replaced by the result of adding Y and Z.

2. Only a single variable name may be on the left of the equal sign, while the right-hand side must be an arithmetic expression that consists of one or more constants, variables, and appropriate symbols. However, all elements of the arithmetic expression must be of the same mode, integer or real.

3. If *v* and *e* are of different modes (in the arithmetic statement $v = e$) the result of the execution of *e* will be converted into the mode of *v*. If *v* is an integer expression and *e* is a real expression, then the fractional part of the result of *e* will be dropped. (This is called "truncation.") Truncation also occurs whenever the division of integers produces fractional results.

> *Examples:* J = 2.5   (J will have a value of 2)
>
> A = 5/2   (A will have a value of 2)

4. Exponentiation can be accomplished by utilizing an integer expression with an integer exponent or a real expression with either a real exponent or an integer exponent.

> *Examples:* J**2 or A**2.0 or A**2

5. Arithmetic operation symbols must *not* be next to each other but must be separated by a parenthesis or other valid character. Spaces are ignored by the computer.

Priority of Arithmetic Operations

1. Arithmetic operations in a statement are executed from left to right according to the following order of priority (hierarchy):

> First priority—exponentation
> Second priority—multiplication and division
> Third priority—addition and subtraction

2. Parenthesis must be used in pairs and overrule the normal order of priority. Thus, operations in parenthesis are performed first. When a statement contains parenthesis inside another parenthesis, the operations in the innermost parenthesis are executed first.

3. *Examples:*

The FORTRAN arithmetic statement:
$$X = Y + Z * A/B ** 2 - C$$
is executed like the mathematical equation

$$X = Y + \left(\frac{ZA}{B^2}\right) - C$$

The FORTRAN arithmetic statement:
$$X = (Y + Z) * (A/B)**2 - C$$
is executed like the mathematical equation:
$$X = (Y + Z)(A/B)^2 - C$$

Mathematical Functions

Most FORTRAN compilers provide several mathematical functions for use in arithmetic statements. Some examples are square root (SQRT), logarithmic (ALOG), and trigonometric (SIN,COS) functions. An example of the use of such "built-in" functions in an arithmetic statement is shown below.

> *Example:* $X = SQRT(Y + Z)$
> *Explanation:* $X = \sqrt{Y + Z}$

RULES FOR USING INPUT/OUTPUT STATEMENTS

The READ Statement

The general form of the READ statement is:

$$READ\ (a, b)\ list$$

1. The "a" is a number (an unsigned integer) for an input device. The type of input unit referred to depends on the compiler used.

2. The *"b"* is the statement number of a specific FORMAT statement which specifies the format of the data media being utilized.

3. The "list" is a list of variable names separated by commas that are in the order they are to be read.

Example: READ (5, 21) A, B, C

Explanation: Read the values of *A, B* and *C* from a punched card in card reader No. 5 using the format of statement 21.

The WRITE Statement

The general form of the WRITE statement is similar to the READ statement. It is:

WRITE (a, b) list

Example: WRITE (8, 3) X, Y, Z

Explanation: Print the current value of the variables *X, Y,* and *Z* on printer No. 8 using the format of statement 3.

RULES FOR USING SPECIFICATION STATEMENTS

The FORMAT Statement

The general form of the FORMAT statement is:

nFORMAT   (specifications)

1. The *"n"* is the statement number of this FORMAT statement.

2. "Specifications" is a list of input/output data specifications separated by commas that are in the order they are to be utilized.

Example: 21   FORMAT (3F5.2, I8)

Explanation: FORMAT statement 21 specifies the format of a data record containing three *real variables* (each of which has five characters with two positions after the decimal point) and an *integer variable* containing eight characters.

FORMAT Specifications

The general form of several fundamental FORMAT specifications is summarized below.

rFw.d   Specifies a *real variable* having *w* characters with *d* digits to the right of the decimal point that is to be repeated *r* times. (*r* is optional if only one variable is specified.)

Example: (2F5.2)

Explanation: Two data fields for real variables having five characters. Each variable has two places after the decimal point.

rEw.d   Specifies the *exponent* form of a real variable. Its form is similar to the *F* specification above.

rIw   Specifies an *integer variable* having *w* characters which is to be repeated *r* times. (*r* is also optional as above.)

Example: (2I3)

Explanation: Two data fields for real integers containing three characters each.

rAw   Specifies an "*alphameric*" (alphabetic, numeric, and special characters) field having *w* character positions that is to be repeated *r* times. It allows the manipulation of alphameric data by the computer, as well as its input/output. The length of an alphameric field is limited to four, five, or six characters in many computers.

Example: (3A5)

Explanation: Three alphameric data fields having five character positions each.

wHc   Specifies that we wish to read or write *w* characters "exactly as is." The "*c*" represents a "carriage control" character which directs a printer according to the following rules:

blank   single space before printing
0   double space before printing
1   skip to the top of the next page
+   do not space

This "*Holerith*" or "*literal*" specification allows the printing of titles and headings and the reading of alphameric data fields such as an employee's name on a punched card payroll record.

Example: (21H0 SALES ANALYSIS REPORT)

Explanation: Doublespace and print (with a WRITE statement) the 21 characters including blank spaces of the title: SALES ANALYSIS REPORT

'   '   Quotation marks can also be used as a Holerith or literal specification.

Example: ('SALES ANALYSIS REPORT')

wX   Specifies that *w* character positions in the input/ output media are to be skipped over.

Example: (6X)

Explanation: Skip six character positions.

n/   Slashes specify how many *n* physical records (punched cards, lines of printing, etc.) should be skipped during input or output.

Example: (F5.2//I3)

Explanation: Read or write a real variable field, skip two physical records, then read or write an integer field.

Other FORMAT Rules

Other important FORMAT rules are:

1. Data is "justified to the right" of a data field when read into storage or written on an output data media. This means that the *right-most* positions of a data field are filled with characters first.

2. Sufficient positions must be allowed for decimal points and arithmetic signs. Lack of sufficient positions will cause an *overflow* error condition or *truncation*. (Some FORTRAN compilers do not require that a position be specified for the arithmetic sign of a positive value.)

Example: The number (-743.85) requires a FORMAT specification of (F7.2).

3. FORMAT statements referred to by WRITE statements that utilize a printer for output must not specify printing in the first (leftmost) print position, or an error condition will result. This position is needed for carriage control and must be left blank by specifying a larger output data field than necessary, or by specifying at least one blank space with the X, H, or literal specifications.

The DIMENSION Statement

The general form of the DIMENSION statement is:

DIMENSION   (array dimensions)

"Array dimensions" is a list of the maximum number of rows, columns, and/or levels for each "array" specified by the DIMENSION statement.

Example: DIMENSION   A(10), B(10,5), C(5,5,5)

> *Explanation:*   The dimensions of three arrays (named *A, B* and *C*) are specified, and the computer is directed to reserve the memory locations required to store each item in the arrays. *A* is a single list of ten items, *B* is a "matrix" of ten rows and five columns, and *C* is a "cube" consisting of five rows, columns and levels.

Note: Statement numbers cannot be used in front of DIMENSION statements.

Arrays and Subscripts

An *"array"* can be defined as an arrangement of items. A *list* of items is "one-dimensional array." A *table* or *"matrix"* of items arranged in rows and columns is a "two-dimensional" array. A three-dimensional arrangement of items in rows, columns, and levels is a "three-dimensional array." See Figure 15–2.

The dimensions of an array are specified by stating the maximum number of rows, columns, and levels in the array. For example, array B in the DIMENSION statement above is a "ten-by-five" array or matrix since it has ten rows and five columns. (*Rows are mentioned first, then columns, then levels.*)

Any item in an array is identified by integer numbers called *"subscripts"* which indicate the position of the item in an array, i.e., the number of its row, column, and/or level. For example, an item in the *seventh row* and the *third column* of a matrix called "ALPHA" would be identified as ALPHA $_{7,3}$ in mathematical notation and ALPHA (7,3) in FORTRAN notation. Subscripts can be integer variables as well as integer constants in FORTRAN, such as ALPHA (K,L). However, only integer constants can be used as subscripts in DIMENSION statements.

FIGURE 15–2

Arrays

XXXXXXXXXX
XXXXXXXXXX
XXXXXXXXXX
XXXXXXXXXX
XXXXXXXXXX
XXXXXXXXXX
XXXXXXXXXX
XXXXXXXXXX

XXXXX	XXXXX	XXXXX
XXXXX	XXXXX	XXXXX
XXXXX	XXXXX	XXXXX
XXXXX	XXXXX	XXXXX
XXXXX	XXXXX	XXXXX
XXXXX	XXXXX	XXXXX
XXXXX	XXXXX	XXXXX
XXXXX	XXXXX	XXXXX

One-Dimensional Array   Two-Dimensional Array

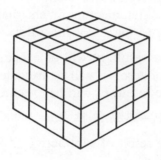

Three-Dimensional Array

RULES FOR USING CONTROL STATEMENTS

The GO TO Statement

The general form of the *"unconditional* GO TO statement is:

GO TO n

where *n* is a statement number which will be executed next.

> *Example:* GO TO 45

> *Explanation:* Execute statement 45 next.

The general form of the *"conditional"* GO TO statement is:

$$GO\ TO\ (n,n_2,\ .\ .\ .\ ,n_m),i$$

1. The *"$n,n_2\ .\ .\ .\ ,n_m$"* are statement numbers that are eligible to be executed next.

2. The *"i"* is an integer variable whose value determines which statement number will be executed next. Thus, if the value of *i* is two, statement n_2 will be executed next.

Example: GO TO (9, 47, 28), J

Explanation: Execute statement nine if *J* is one, statement 47 if *J* is two, and statement 28 if *J* is three.

The IF Statement

The general form of the *"arithmetic"* IF statement is:

$$IF\ (e)\ n_1,n_2,n_3$$

1. The *"e"* is an arithmetic expression.

2. The *"n_1,n_2,n_3"* are statement numbers that are eligible to be executed next according to the following rule:

a.   If *e* has a negative result, n_1 will be executed.
b.   If *e* has a value of zero, n_2 will be executed.
c.   If *e* has a positive result, n_3 will be executed.

Example: IF (AGE $-$ 18.0) 9, 47, 28

Explanation: If the result of subtracting 18.0 from the value of the variable AGE is:

> *negative* : execute statement 9 next,
> *zero*   : execute statement 47 next,
> *positive* : execute statement 28 next.

The general form of the *"relational"* IF statement is:

$$IF\ (e)\ s$$

1. The *"s"* is a FORTRAN statement which will be executed next if the "relational expression" *e* is *true*. If not, the computer will execute the next sequential statement. The *"s"* can be any FORTRAN statement other than another *relational* IF statement or a DO statement.

2. A *relational expression* is constructed utilizing the following "relational operators."

.LT.   Less than
.LE.   Less than or equal to
.EQ.   Equal to
.NE.   Not equal to
.GT.   Greater than
.GE.   Greater than or equal to

Example: IF (AGE .GE. 18.0) LEGAL=LEGAL + 1
Explanation: If the variable AGE is greater than or equal to 18.0, add one to the value of the variable LEGAL.

The *"logical operators"* .AND. and .OR. can be used to link two or more relational expressions.

Example: IF (AGE.GE.18.0.AND.SCHOOL.LT.12.0) GO
             TO 44.

Explanation: If the variable AGE is greater than or equal to 18.0, and the variable SCHOOL is less than 12.0, execute statement 44 next.

The DO Statement

The general form of the DO Statement is:

$$DO \ n \ i = m_1, m_2, m_3$$

1. The *"n"* is the statement number of the last statement in the "program loop."
2. The *"i"* is an integer variable called the "loop variable" or "counter" that controls the execution of the program loop.
3. The *"m"* is the initial value of the loop variable.
4. The *"m_2"* is the maximum value that the loop variable can attain.
5. The *"m_3"* is the incremental value by which the counter is to be modified for each trip through the program loop. If m_3 is not specified, the FORTRAN compiler will assume an m_3 value of one.
6. The *"m_1, m_2, and m_3"* can be unsigned integer variables or unsigned integer constants.
7. A program loop that utilizes a DO statement is called a "DO loop." A DO loop *cannot* end with a GO TO, IF, DO, PAUSE, RETURN, or STOP statement.
8. The first statement after the DO statement *cannot* be a "nonexecutable" statement such as FORMAT and other specification statements.

9. A DO loop may contain a conditional control statement (such as IF or GO TO) that allows a transfer out of a DO loop before the full loop is executed.

Example: DO 85 J $= 1,10,1$

Explanation: All statements following this DO statement will be executed up to and including statement 85. This process will be repeated ten times. The initial value of *J* is set to one and is increased by an increment of one each time the program loop is executed, until *J* reaches a value of ten. Then the computer "exits from the loop" and executes the statements that follow statement 85.

CONTINUE, STOP, and END Statements

The general form of the CONTINUE statement is:

CONTINUE

It is a "dummy" statement used at the end of a DO loop to satisfy rule seven above.

The general form of the STOP statement is:

STOP

It must be used before the END statement.

The general form of the END statement is:

END

It must be the last statement of a FORTRAN program.

SAMPLE FORTRAN PROGRAMS

No one expects a programmer (much less a beginning programmer) to remember all of the rules of FORTRAN. With practice, many of the rules become "second nature," but most programmers still have to refer occasionally to "language specification manuals" to assist their programming efforts. Even then, the presence of "bugs" in many programs when they are first written is evidence that a programmer may have inadvertently violated some of the rules of FORTRAN. Therefore, be sure to consult the FORTRAN rules in the previous section to assist you in correctly writing the programs that are assigned at the end of this chapter.

Sample Program One

Let us now analyze a few examples of FORTRAN programs before you "take the plunge" and attempt your first program. We will begin with the very simple problem of adding two quantities together $(X = Y + Z)$ that we have used as an example several times in Chapters Five and Six. Let us assume that the values of Y and Z that we wish to add are on punched cards and that we will print each resulting sum of X on the printer of the computer.

Figure 15–1 illustrated a FORTRAN program which can perform these simple data processing tasks. However, the program of Figure 15–1 can read the data on only *one* punched card. Since in most cases, data is punched into *several* "data cards," sample program one has been developed. Figure 15–3 illustrates the program statements and flowchart of a computer program that can compute values of X

FIGURE 15–3

Program and Flowchart of Sample
Program One

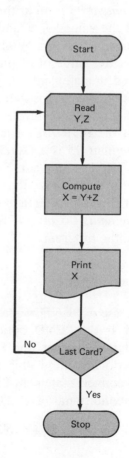

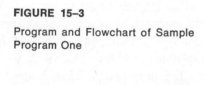

```
01   READ (1, 02, END = 06) Y, Z
02   FORMAT (2F8.2)
03   X = Y + Z
04   WRITE (2, 02) X
05   GO TO 01
06   STOP
07   END
```

when values of Y and Z are punched into an undetermined number of data cards.

Let us closely examine the flowchart and statements of this program. You should notice that the only change from the program illustrated in Figure 15–1 is that the READ statement has been modified and a GO TO statement added to enable more than one data card to be processed.

Statement 01 is a READ statement which directs the computer to read the variables Y and Z (as specified by FORMAT statement 02) from a punched card using card reader No. 1. The use of "END $=$ 06" in the READ statement tells the computer to transfer control to statement 06 and execute the statements which terminate the program when it senses that there are no more data cards to read.

Statement 02 is a FORMAT statement which specifies that there are two input/output data fields for real variables, each having a field size of eight positions and two places after the decimal point.

Statement 03 is an arithmetic statement which directs the computer to add the values of Y and Z and assign the result to the variable X.

Statement 04 is a WRITE statement which directs the computer to print the value of X on printer No. 2 using the data field format specified in statement 02. This assumes that no value of X will need more than seven positions, since the leftmost position is needed for printer carriage control. (The computer ignores the second data field of the FORMAT statement.)

Statement 05 is a GO TO statement which transfers control back to the READ statement. This statement causes the computer to repeat the entire "program loop" from statement 01 through statement 05 until it runs out of data cards.

Statements 06 and 07 are STOP and END statements which terminate the program.

The END Option

The use of "END $=$ statement number" in the READ statement is known as the "END option" and is provided by most FORTRAN compilers. However, the FORTRAN compilers of some small computers do not allow this feature. In that case, many programmers would convert statement 05 to a "relational" IF statement containing an "unconditional" GO TO operand such as:

$$\text{IF (Y .NE. } - 9999.99) \text{ GO TO 01}$$

This method requires that a special "last card" or "trailer card" be added to the deck of data cards which contains a Y value of −9999.99. (Blanks, zeros, or any other symbols that would not be a possible value for Y could also be used.) The IF statement would test the Y field of each card read. When Y *is not* equal to −9999.99, the GO TO portion of the statement directs the computer to go back to statement 01 and read another card. The computer repeats the execution of this program loop until it senses the "last card" signal that occurs when Y = −9999.99. The computer would then execute the STOP and END statements that terminate the program.

Sample Program Two

The second sample program modifies Program One by adding the following features:

1. The computed values of *X* are accumulated in the computer as well as printed.

2. After all the data cards are read, the total of all the *X* values and the average value (arithmetic mean) of *X* are computed and printed.

Figure 15–4 illustrates the program and flowchart of Program Two. Notice that the number of statements has *doubled* just because we added a few additional tasks to the job of the computer! Let us briefly analyze the statements of this program.

Statements 01 and 02 "clear" the contents of a counter (COUNTR) and an accumulator (TOTAL) that we are reserving for later use. We accomplish this "initializing" routine by setting COUNTR and TOTAL to zero.

Statements 03 and 04 are similar to the READ and FORMAT statements of program one. (We could have increased the size of the data fields of the FORMAT statement from eight to ten positions. This might be done in order to use the same FORMAT statement for both input and output, since the total X values we are going to compute and print may require up to nine positions, plus one position for printer carriage control. This would reduce the number of FORMAT statements in the program. Of course, it would require that we use a "field size" of ten positions for both Y and Z on our data cards.) Be sure to note that the "END option" used in statement 03 will transfer control to statement 10 when there are no more data cards to read.

Statement 05 increments a "counter" by 1.0 each time new values

FIGURE 15–4

Program and Flowchart of Sample
Program Two

```
01   COUNTR = 0.0
02   TOTAL = 0.0
03   READ (1, 04, END = 10) Y, Z
04   FORMAT (2F8.2)
05   COUNTR = COUNTR + 1.0
06   X = Y + Z
07   TOTAL = TOTAL + X
08   WRITE (2, 12) X
09   GO TO 03
10   AVRAGE = TOTAL / COUNTR
11   WRITE (2, 12) TOTAL, AVRAGE
12   FORMAT (1X, 2F10.2)
13   STOP
14   END
```

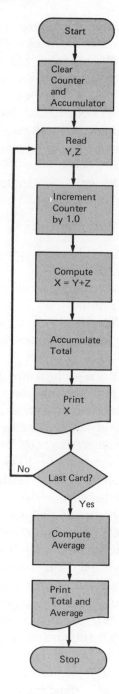

of Y and Z are read. This keeps track of the number of X values that are computed (COUNTR) and will be used to calculate an average value for X.

Statement 06 computes values for X and *Statement 07* accumulates the total value of all X values (TOTAL). *Statement 08* prints each value of X that is computed, using the format of statement 12. *Statement 09* transfers control back to the READ statement.

Statement 10 computes the average value of X (AVRAGE) by dividing TOTAL by COUNTR. This occurs after the last data card has been read. *Statement 11* prints TOTAL and AVRAGE using the format specified in statement 12. (The first print position is for printer control.) *Statements 13 and 14* terminate the program.

Sample Program Three

Our final sample program demonstrates some features of FORTRAN that we have not utilized in the two previous programs. This makes the program more complex, but it also makes it more "powerful, flexible, and user-oriented."

1. Powerful. The program can efficiently perform more data processing tasks. For example, DO loops, IF statements, and a DIMENSION statement are used to perform a greater variety of operations.

2. Flexible. The program can handle changes in input/output volume, size, format, etc., without major modifications being required. For example, the DO loop and DIMENSION statement allow the program to handle changes in the volume of data categories or the number of counters required.

3. User-oriented. The program can produce output that is more attractive and usable for persons who will utilize its results. For example, the program reads and prints the names of people and provides appropriate descriptive titles and headings for the output report.

The sample program is based on the examples we used in Chapter Six to illustrate the use of flowcharts and decision tables. The "Salesmen Gross Pay" program performs the following tasks:

1. Computes the sales commissions and gross pay of each salesman of a business firm.

2. Produces a report which shows the name, sales, quota, salary, commissions, and gross pay of each salesman.

3. Tallies the number of salesmen in each of the three following categories:

FIGURE 15–5

Sample Program Three

```
IBM                              FORTRAN CODING FORM

PROGRAM  SALESMEN GROSS PAY
PROGRAMMER  ABLE T. PROGRAMMER

C      SAMPLE PRØGRAM THREE: SALESMEN GRØSS PAY
       DIMENSIØN KNTR(3)
01     DØ 02, I=1,3
02     KNTR(I)=0
03     TØTAL=0.0
04     WRITE (2,05)
05     FØRMAT (1H1,10X,'SALESMEN GRØSS PAY REPØRT' // 'SALESMEN
      1SALES      QUØTA      SALARY  CØMMISSIØN   GRØSS PAY')
06     READ (1,07,END=23) ANAME,BNAME,CNAME,SALES,QUØTA,SALARY
07     FØRMAT (3A5,3F10.2)
08     IF (SALES.GT.0.0) GØ TØ 12
09     KNTR(1) = KNTR(1)+1
10     CØMMIS = 0.0
11     GØ TØ 18
12     IF (SALES-QUØTA)13,16,16
13     KNTR(2) = KNTR(2)+1
14     CØMMIS = SALES * 0.1
15     GØ TØ 18
16     KNTR(3) = KNTR(3)+1
17     CØMMIS = QUØTA * 0.1 + (SALES-QUØTA) * 0.2
18     GRSPAY = SALARY + CØMMIS
19     WRITE (2,20) NAME1,NAME2,NAME3,SALES,QUØTA,SALARY,CØMMIS,GRSPAY
20     FØRMAT (1X,3A5,5F10.2)
```

```
IBM                              FORTRAN CODING FORM

PROGRAM
PROGRAMMER

21     TØTAL = TØTAL + SALES
22     GØ TØ 06
23     SMEN  = KNTR(1) + KNTR(2) + KNTR(3)
24     AVRAGE = TØTAL / SMEN
25     WRITE (2,26) TØTAL,AVRAGE
26     FØRMAT (// ' TØTAL SALES = $',F10.2,5X,'AVERAGE SALES = .$',F10.2,)
27     WRITE (2,28) KNTR(1),KNTR(2),KNTR(3)
28     FØRMAT (' NUMBER ØF SALESMEN BY PERFØRMANCE CATEGØRY',/
      1'   NØ SALES: ',I3,'   BELØW QUØTA: ',I3,'   ABØVE QUØTA: ',I3)
29     STØP
30     END
```

a. Salesmen who have not made any sales.
b. Salesmen who have not equaled their sales quota.
c. Salesmen who have equaled or exceeded their sales quota.

4. Computes and prints the total amount of sales and the average value of sales made.

The program, flowchart, input data card format, and output report format of sample program three is shown in Figures 15–5, 15–6, 15–7 and 15–8. Let us examine the important features of this program.

Analysis of the Program

The first line of the program is *not* a FORTRAN statement but is an explanatory "comment" that describes the name of the program. Such comments are not executed by the computer. A *"C"* is required in column one of the program card for each comment.

The first four FORTRAN statements initialize three counters and an accumulator, i.e., KNTR (1), KNTR (2), and KNTR (3), and TOTAL. Note that the counters are really elements of a one-dimensional array named KNTR. The term "initialize" refers to operations which reserve space in memory for counters and accumulators and clear them to zero. We use a DIMENSION statement and a DO loop of two statements to initialize the counters in order to illustrate one way these statements can be used. *Statements 04 through 05* cause the printing of the title and the column headings of the Salesmen Gross Pay Report.

Statements 06 and 07 read punched cards containing the name, sales, quota, and salary of each salesman. Statement 07 contains three variable names (ANAME, BNAME and CNAME) which allow the name of each salesman to be read from a 15-position name field on the input data card. This assumes a FORTRAN compiler which limits an "A specification" to five positions. Thus, statement 08 utilizes three A specifications of five positions each to define the format of the name field.

Statements 08 through 18:

1. Identify whether a salesman has had no sales, sales below quota, or sales equal to or above quota.

2. Increment counters to tally the number of salesmen in each performance category.

3. Compute commissions (except for no sales) and calculate gross pay by adding salary to commissions.

FIGURE 15–6

Flowchart of Sample Program Three

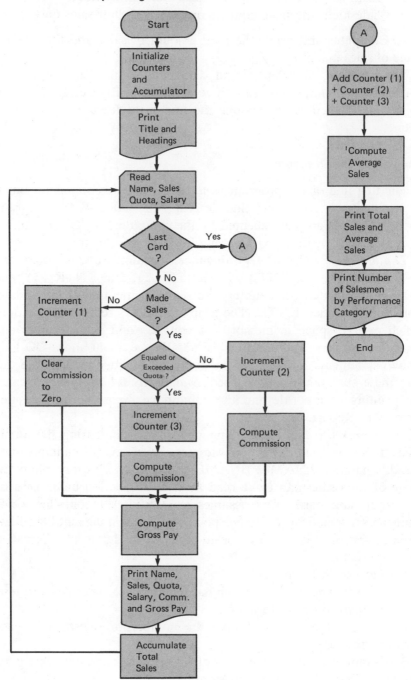

FIGURE 15–7

Input Data Card Format of Sample Program Three

Card Name **SALESMAN - CARD**

	1 2 3 4 5 6 7 8 9 10 11 12 13 14 15 16 17 18 19 20 21 22 23 24 25 26 27 28 29 30 31 32 33 34 35 36 37 38 39 40 41 42 43 44
Print	
	Print Line 1
	Tier 1
Punch	*NAME* *SALES* *QUOTA* *SALARY*
Program Control Card	1 2 3 4 5 6 7 8 9 10 11 12 13 14 15 16 17 18 19 20 21 22 23 24 25 26 27 28 29 30 31 32 33 34 35 36 37 38 39 40 41 42 43 44 45
	A N D E R S O N R T 1 2 5 0 0 . 0 0 1 0 0 0 0 . 0 0 1 0 0 0 . 0 0

Statement 19 prints the name, sales, quota, salary, commission, and gross pay for each salesman utilizing the format of *statement 20*. *Statement 21* accumulates the total value of all sales made.

Statement 22 transfers control back to the READ statement.

Statement 23 is the first statement outside the program loop. It is executed when all data cards have been read. It computes the total

FIGURE 15–8

Output of Sample Program Three

SALESMAN GROSS PAY REPORT

SALESMAN	SALES	QUOTA	SALARY	COMMISSION	GROSS PAY
ANDERSON R T	12500.00	10000.00	1000.00	1500.00	2500.00
BAKER D A	8000.00	10000.00	1000.00	800.00	1800.00
CALLISON W E	18500.00	20000.00	2000.00	1850.00	3850.00
DAWSON F L	0.00	5000.00	500.00	0.00	500.00
FERRANTE J S	9500.00	10000.00	1000.00	950.00	1950.00

TOTAL SALES = $657500.00   AVERAGE SALES = $9700.00

NUMBER OF SALESMEN BY PERFORMANCE CATEGORY:

NO SALES: 2   BELOW QUOTA: 28   ABOVE QUOTA: 6

number of salesmen whose data cards have been processed. It adds together the contents of the three counters and converts the resulting sum to the real variable mode. This sum is then used in *Statement 24* to compute the average sales per salesman.

Statements 25 and 26 print the amount of total sales and average sales along with appropriate descriptive headings. *Statement 27 and 28* print the number of salesmen in each performance category along with descriptive headings. Notice that statement 28 requires that a number (other than zero) be punched in column six of a second program card, since this statement is too long for a single card. *Statements 29 and 30* terminate the program.

Programming Alternatives

We mentioned in Chapter Six that programmers will frequently develop different programs to solve the same data processing problem. Such differences in programs may be based on differences in programming skill, but much of it arises simply from differences in the personal preferences of the programmers involved. Much of it is also based on the differences in the features and limitations of the different computers and compilers that may be used. This is also true of the statements utilized in Sample Program Three. Let us briefly mention a few alternatives that could have been utilized.

The first three statements initialized three counters through the use of a DIMENSION statement and a two-statement DO loop. This could also have been accomplished by the use of statements such as KNTR1 = 0, KNTR2 = 0, and KNTR3 = 0. However, this method would become impractical if we had to initialize many counters. Thus, the DIMENSION statement allows us to form an array which reserves places in memory for many variables without specifying individual names for each variable. The DO loop allows us to initialize each element of the array (or operate on it in some other way) without having to write a separate statement for each variable. Thus, the use of a DIMENSION statement and a DO loop added both power and flexibility to the FORTRAN program.

We could have utilized an alternative method of providing flexibility to the DO loop. An integer variable could have been used as the maximum value of the loop variable. (For example: DO 02,I = 1,N). The value of N would have to be established each time the program was used. Frequently a "header" card at the beginning of the data cards will be read which contains the number that is to be used as the maximum value of the DO loop for a particular run.

A final example of an alternative programming method for Sample Program Three concerns the statements utilized for "alphameric" (alphabetic, numeric, and special characters) data input/output. We could have utilized the "H" specification of the FORMAT statement to read salesmen's names. However, such use is severely restricted by most FORTRAN compilers and is therefore not widely used.

PREPARING FORTRAN PROGRAMS

In Chapter Six we showed that computer programming requires the activities of *programming analysis* and *program design* before *program coding* can be properly accomplished. *Checking, testing,* and *correcting* activities are then required to properly "debug" a newly written program. In this chapter, we have concentrated on the fundamentals of *program coding* in FORTRAN. However, developing effective FORTRAN programs requires the accomplishment of most of the programming activities mentioned in Chapter Six.

Before writing a FORTRAN program, you should take the time to analyze each data processing problem you are asked to program and attempt to design the processing procedures required for its solution. You should begin by developing a general program flowchart of your proposed solution. This should help you identify the input/output, logical, and computational steps required to carry out your data processing assignment. You should also determine the format of the input (frequently on punched cards) and the output (frequently a printed report). This can be accomplished by using input/output layout forms or informal "rough layouts" which detail the format of proposed input and output media.

The FORTRAN Coding Form

Once these steps have been accomplished, program coding can begin. Most programmers use a *program coding form* to assist their programming efforts and facilitate the keypunching of their program. Figure 15–5 illustrated the use of a FORTRAN coding form for Sample Program Three. The *program cards* of the program are keypunched using the coding form as a guide. Each space on the coding form corresponds to one column of a punched card. Each line of the coding form is punched into a single program card. The following is a summary of the purpose of each column of a FORTRAN program card.

1. A *"C"* in column 1 identifies a "comment" which is not executable by the computer. There are no restrictions on the characters that can be used in the other columns of a comment card. Comments are printed as part of the listing of the program and therefore are used to explain and document some aspect of the program.

2. FORTRAN statement numbers can be punched into *columns 1–5* of FORTRAN statements. Statement numbers are required only for statements which are referred to by other statements. Statement numbers can range from one to 99999 and can be in any order.

3. A character other than zero can be punched into *column 6* of "continuation cards" when a FORTRAN statement is too long for a single program card. The first program card for such a statement must contain a blank or a zero in column 6.

4. The FORTRAN statement is keypunched in *columns 7–72* of the program card. Remember that FORTRAN uses only upper case (capital) letters and ignores blank spaces (except in Holerith specifications).

5. The FORTRAN compiler ignores *columns 73–80* of program cards. These are sometimes used to number and identify each card in the program "source deck" for the benefit of the programmer.

Coding the FORTRAN program on the coding form should be done by following the program flowchart you have developed. You will probably make changes in both the flowchart and the program statements during this process. Make frequent reference to the rules for FORTRAN statements in the chapter. When you have written a complete program, go over your program and flowchart several times in order to "desk check" the program. Keypunch the program into program cards using the coding form as a guide.

Executing the Program

Once the program cards have been prepared, the input data can be keypunched into *data cards* according to the specifications of the FORMAT statements of your program. The program "source deck" and the data cards should be desk checked for possible errors. The program, data, and "job control" cards can then be submitted to your computer center for compiling and execution.

Most computer centers have different procedures for the use of the "*job control cards*" that are required for every program that is to be processed. Job control cards may be needed at the beginning and end of your program deck and data cards. The job control cards are required by the operating system or other control programs of the computer system. They identify your program as a FORTRAN program and specify other details required for compiling and execution. Consult your computer center for the proper format and arrangement of job control cards.

Your program may fail to execute on its first attempt. Use the program listing and the "diagnostic" listing of *error statements* to help you *debug* the program. Errors should be corrected by keypunching corrected FORTRAN statements into new program cards. The program should be resubmitted until it can be successfully *compiled* and *executed*. When this finally occurs, you will have successfully directed an electronic computer in the accomplishment of a data processing assignment.

Interactive FORTRAN Programming

Many computer systems with time-sharing capabilities now support *interactive* versions of FORTRAN. Several versions resemble the BASIC programming language which is described in Chapter 17. This is an interesting commentary on the success of the BASIC language, for it has frequently been described as a simplified version of FORTRAN.

If you wish to use interactive versions of FORTRAN, you should utilize most of the fundamental rules of FORTRAN programming explained in this chapter. The major exceptions to these rules are usually in the area of input/output statements which resemble those of BASIC. For example, some interactive versions of FORTRAN allow "free-form" input/output statements and do not require FORMAT statements. Therefore, you should refer to the material on the BASIC language in Chapter 17, especially the section on the INPUT and PRINT statements, and the section entitled *Preparing and Using BASIC Programs*. The later section explains and illustrates *interactive programming* utilizing a *time-sharing terminal* and should be quite helpful. Of course, you should consult a reference manual for

FIGURE 15–9

Simple Program
in Interactive
FORTRAN

```
10  INPUT, Y, Z
20  X = Y + Z
30  PRINT, X
40  STOP
50  END
```

specific information on the rules and capabilities of the interactive FORTRAN version that is available to you.

Figure 15–9 is an interactive FORTRAN version of a program to calculate $X = Y + Z$ and print X. Compare it to the batch processing version of Figure 15–1 and the BASIC version of Figure 17–1. Notice how similar all of these programs are. Therefore, you should not have much trouble writing simple interactive programs in FORTRAN.

KEY TERMS AND CONCEPTS

Arithmetic statements, 483, 486–488
Input/output statements, 484, 488–489
Specification statements, 484, 489–492
Control statements, 484, 493–496
Subprogram statements, 485
Constant, 486
Integer, 486
Real number, 486
Variable, 486
Array, 492–493

Subscript, 492
DO loop, 495–496
END option, 498
Counter, 499
Initialize, 503
FORTRAN coding form, 507–508
Program cards, 507
Job control cards, 509
Interactive FORTRAN programming, 509–510

ASSIGNMENTS

1. Review the key terms and concepts above and reread the appropriate chapter material to reenforce your understanding where necessary.

2. Briefly describe the purpose of the five basic types of FORTRAN statements and the functions of the fundamental statements in each category.

3. Review the sample FORTRAN programs of the chapter to deepen your understanding of the statements that are utilized in a complete FORTRAN program to accomplish a specific data processing assignment.

4. Discuss why Sample Program Three is supposedly more "powerful, flexible, and user-oriented" than the other sample programs.

5. Identify several programming alternatives that could have been utilized in the sample programs.

6. Review the activities involved in preparing and executing a FORTRAN program.

7. Write a simple FORTRAN program similar to Sample Program One which performs one or more mathematical calculations.

8. Write a simple FORTRAN program similar to Sample Program Two which will compute and print the average (arithmetic mean) of the scores received on an exam by an undetermined number of students in a class.

9. Write a simple FORTRAN program similar to Sample Program Three which will perform the following tasks:
   a. Computes the regular pay, overtime pay, and total gross pay for an undetermined number of hourly paid employees.
   b. Produces a report which shows the following information for each employee: (1) name, (2) social security number, (3) regular hours worked (40 or less), (4) overtime hours worked (excess over 40 hours), (5) regular pay, (6) overtime pay, and (7) total gross pay.
   c. Computes and prints (1) the grand total of gross pay for all employees, (2) the average gross pay earned, and (3) tallies the number of employees that *did* and *did not* work overtime.

Chapter Outline

Purpose of the Chapter

Introduction

Fundamental Structure of COBOL
The COBOL Divisions, Outline of a COBOL Program

Fundamental Rules of COBOL
COBOL Words and Symbols: COBOL Characters,
    COBOL Words, Literals
The IDENTIFICATION DIVISION; The ENVIRONMENT
    DIVISION; The DATA DIVISION: The FILE SECTION,
    The WORKING-STORAGE SECTION;
The PROCEDURE DIVISION:
Input/Output Statements: The OPEN Statement, The CLOSE
    Statement, The READ Statement, The WRITE Statement.
Data Movement Statements: The MOVE Statement.
Arithmetic Statements: The COMPUTE Statement, The
    ADD, SUBTRACT, MULTIPLY, and DIVIDE Statements.
Control Statements: The GO TO Statement, The PERFORM
    Statement, The IF Statement, The STOP Statement.

Sample COBOL Programs
Sample Program One, Sample Program Two,
    Analysis of the Program.

Preparing COBOL Programs
The COBOL Coding Form, Executing the Program.

Key Terms and Concepts

Assignments

COBOL Acknowledgement

16

Fundamentals of COBOL Programming

Purpose of the Chapter
To promote a basic understanding of COBOL programming by:
1. Reviewing the basic vocabulary and rules of COBOL,
2. Analyzing several COBOL programs;
3. Writing simple programs in COBOL.

INTRODUCTION

COBOL is the most widely used programming language for business data processing. As we mentioned in Chapter Six, COBOL (COmmon Business Oriented Language) was specifically designed to handle the input, processing, and output of large volumes of alphameric data from many data files that is characteristic of business data processing. COBOL was developed and is maintained by the Conference on Data Systems Languages (CODASYL) which is composed of representatives of large computer users, government agencies, and computer manufacturers. The specifications of the COBOL language are therefore subject to periodic revision and updating. The American National Standards Institute (ANSI) has developed standards for COBOL which recognize different "levels" and "modules" of COBOL. Standards for a "Minimum Standard" COBOL and "Full Standard" COBOL have also been developed.

In this chapter we will concentrate on fundamentals and will not attempt to cover the advanced features of the various levels of

COBOL. This should enable us to learn quickly to write several simple COBOL programs which can be run on a wide variety of computer systems. *This kind of programming knowledge is sufficient for most computer users.* Persons wishing to become professional programmers should build on this foundation by additional study and practice, utilizing programming texts or manuals that provide an in-depth coverage of the advanced features of COBOL.

We can begin our study of COBOL by analyzing it as we would any language, i.e., by analyzing its "vocabulary" and its "grammar." COBOL has a vocabulary of words and symbols and a grammar of rules for writing computer instructions. It is essential that we learn the fundamental vocabulary and grammatical rules of COBOL if we wish the computer to properly accomplish specific data processing tasks. Therefore, in this chapter we will organize our study of COBOL in the manner shown below.

1. *Fundamental structure of COBOL.* We first take a brief look at the basic structure of COBOL programs.
2. *Fundamental rules of COBOL.* We then summarize the basic rules for writing COBOL statements.
3. *Sample COBOL programs.* Several examples of simple COBOL programs are presented and discussed.
4. *Preparing COBOL programs.* Instructions on the mechanics of writing and processing COBOL programs are presented.
5. *COBOL programming assignments.* The only way to really learn a language is to use it. Therefore, you are asked to write one or more simple COBOL programs at the end of the chapter.

In Chapter Five we showed how the COBOL statement: ADD SALARY, COMMISSIONS GIVING GROSSPAY illustrates how close to the English language a COBOL statement can be. The use of such English-like statements facilitates programming, makes it easy for a nonprogrammer to understand the purpose of a particular COBOL program, and gives a "self-documenting" capability to COBOL programs. Thus, COBOL is widely utilized for business data processing and can be used by the computer systems of most manufacturers. Of course, COBOL does have several limitations. It is a "wordy" programming language which is more difficult for non-professional programmers to utilize than other languages such as FORTRAN or BASIC. Since it has a business data processing and batch processing orientation, it is limited in its applicability to scientific data processing and interactive processing.

FUNDAMENTAL STRUCTURE OF COBOL

Like other high-level compiler languages, COBOL has "reserved words" and symbols which are utilized to write computer instructions called "statements" that are translated by the COBOL compiler into machine-language instructions and executed by the computer. A fundamental vocabulary of reserved words and symbols will be discussed in the pages that follow. This "limited instruction set" is sufficient for the purposes of this chapter.

Every computer program written in the COBOL language must contain four major parts called "divisions." We shall discuss a fundamental COBOL vocabulary that consists of the reserved words and symbols that are utilized in the four COBOL divisions of simple computer programs. The four COBOL divisions are summarized below.

The COBOL Divisions

1. The Identification Division.   Identifies the program by listing such information as the name of the program, the name of the programmer, the date the program was written, and other comments which identify the purpose of the program.

2. The Environment Division. Specifies the type of computer and peripheral equipment that will be used to process the program.

3. The Data Division.   Describes the organization and format of the data to be processed by the program.

4. The Procedure Division.   Contains the COBOL statements (called "commands") which describe the procedure to be followed by the computer in accomplishing its data processing assignment.

Outline of a COBOL Program

A standard outline or "skeleton outline" of a COBOL program is shown in Figure 16–1. It illustrates the structure and statements that are commonly used in COBOL programs. You should utilize this outline as a reference to assist you in correctly writing a COBOI program.

Notice that the ENVIRONMENT, DATA, and PROCEDURE divisions are subdivided into *"sections,"* each of which is identified by a "section name" such as the "INPUT-OUTPUT SECTION." Also notice that the sections of COBOL divisions are composed of *"paragraphs"* which consist of one or more *"sentences."* Notice that each

FIGURE 16–1

Standard Outline of a COBOL Program

IDENTIFICATION DIVISION.
PROGRAM-ID. program-name.
[AUTHOR. sentence . . .]
[INSTALLATION. sentence . . .]
[DATE-WRITTEN. sentence . . .]
[SECURITY. sentence . . .]
[REMARKS. sentence . . .]

ENVIRONMENT DIVISION.
CONFIGURATION SECTION.
SOURCE-COMPUTER. computer-name.
OBJECT-COMPUTER. computer-name.
[SPECIAL-NAMES. forms-control IS mnemonic-name . . .].
[INPUT-OUTPUT SECTION.]
$\lceil$ FILE-CONTROL.
    SELECT file-name ASSIGN TO input-or-output device.
      .
      .
$\lfloor$.

DATA DIVISION.
$\lceil$ FILE SECTION.
    FD file-name DATA $\begin{Bmatrix} \text{RECORD IS} \\ \text{RECORDS ARE} \end{Bmatrix}$ record-name [record-name . . .]
        LABEL RECORDS ARE OMITTED.
    01   record-name.
            description of record
              .
              .
$\lfloor$.

[WORKING-STORAGE SECTION.]
[REPORT SECTION.]

PROCEDURE DIVISION.
[section-name SECTION.]
paragraph-name. sentence. . . .
[paragraph-name. sentence. . . .]
$\lceil$[section-name SECTION.] $\rceil$ . . .
$\lfloor$[paragraph-name. sentence . . .] . . .$\rfloor$

paragraph must have a "paragraph name." For example, a PRO-CEDURE DIVISION paragraph consisting of COBOL input/output statements (sentences) could be given the paragraph name of "IN-PUT-OUTPUT." The paragraphs of the IDENTIFICATION and ENVIRONMENT DIVISIONS, on the other hand, have fixed paragraph names such as "SOURCE-COMPUTER."

The use of capital letters, underlining, brackets, etc. in the skeleton outline is not accidental. Most COBOL manuals utilize such notation to identify the mandatory and optional parts of a COBOL program. For example, all *underlined* items in the outline are mandatory, unless they are in brackets. All *capitalized* words are COBOL "reserved words," while words supplied by the programmer are not capitalized. Finally, only one of the items in each set of braces, { }, can be included in a COBOL program.

FUNDAMENTAL RULES OF COBOL

Like any programming language, COBOL has specific grammatical rules which must be followed if the computer is correctly to process a program. If these rules are not followed, clerical errors will result which will cause the computer to do one or more of the following:

1. Reject the program without compiling or processing it,
2. Print diagnostic error messages,
3. Produce incorrect or invalid results.

We will confine our discussion in this chapter to fundamental rules of COBOL that are sufficient for the programs which we will illustrate and which you will be asked to write. We shall organize these fundamental rules into categories that are related to the basic divisions of COBOL. In order to make the task of programming easier for beginners, we will simplify our presentation by omitting some of the details concerning the forms and restrictions governing the use of various COBOL statements. Persons wishing to make full use of all the features of COBOL in their programming should consult the many COBOL texts and manuals that are available.

COBOL WORDS AND SYMBOLS

We will utilize the four divisions of COBOL to organize our explanation of its fundamental rules. However, before we begin to discuss the rules that must be followed in developing each COBOL division, we should discuss some general requirements for the use of words and symbols in COBOL programming.

COBOL characters.   Cobol utilizes the 26 letters of the alphabet, the digits 0 through 9, and the characters shown below.

.	Period or decimal point	+	Plus sign
,	Comma	—	Hyphen or minus sign
;	Semicolon	/	Division symbol
'	Quotation mark	*	Multiplication symbol
( )	Parenthesis	**	Exponentation symbol
$	Dollar sign	>	Greater than symbol
=	Equal sign	<	Less than symbol

COBOL uses only upper case (capital) letters. *Commas* and *semicolons* are optional and are only utilized to improve readability of the program coding. Therefore, they are ignored by the COBOL compiler. *Blank spaces* in COBOL statements are also ignored unless they are part of a "nonnumeric literal" or are related to the period or minus sign as discussed below.

A *period* must be utilized at the end of each COBOL "entry," i.e., a division, section, or paragraph heading or a COBOL sentence. The COBOL compiler distinguishes between a *period* and a *decimal point* by the presence of a blank space after a period. Therefore, a decimal point cannot be followed by a space, while a period must always be followed by a space. Similarly, a *minus sign* is used in an arithmetic statement and must have spaces before and after it. A *hyphen* is used as a character in certain reserved words and in programmer supplied names and cannot be preceded or followed by a space.

COBOL words.   COBOL words are either predefined by the COBOL compiler ("reserved words") or are defined by the programmer ("programmer-supplied names"). COBOL reserved words have a specific meaning to the COBOL compiler and cannot be used as a programmer-supplied name. A list of common COBOL reserved words is shown in Figure 16–2. However, it should be noted that the reserved words in COBOL may vary slightly depending on the specific COBOL compiler used.

Most programmer-supplied names are either "data-names" or paragraph and section names. Data names are defined in the DATA DIVISION and identify specific data elements such as data records and files. Section and paragraph names identify the sections of the four COBOL divisions and the paragraphs of the PROCEDURE DIVISION.

Programmer-supplied names have to conform to a few basi/ However, programmers are encouraged to write COBOL sta.. that utilize names which help describe the data processing tasks the program is designed to accomplish. Thus, the statement COMPUTE GROSS-PAY = SALARY + COMMISSION is more descriptive than COMPUTE X = Y + Z.

Programmer-supplied names may utilize alphabetic characters, numeric digits, and hyphens and can be up to 30 characters in length. However, names cannot begin or end with a hyphen and must not contain any blank spaces within the name ("imbedded blanks"). Data names must contain at least one alphabetic character, but paragraph and section names may be completely numeric.

Hyphens are frequently utilized within programmer-supplied names to avoid the use of names with imbedded blanks. Hyphens and numeric characters are also utilized to avoid the use of COBOL reserved words, since most reserved words do not contain hyphens or numeric characters. For example, a programmer might utilize GROSS-PAY and RECORD2 as legitimate data names.

Literals. A "literal" is a numeric or alphameric value that is defined by the programmer. A numeric literal (also known as a "constant") consists of up to 18 numeric digits and is not enclosed in quote marks. A plus or minus sign may be used as its leftmost character, though it is assumed to be positive if a sign is absent. It may contain a decimal point anywhere except in its rightmost position. Numeric literals are frequently utilized to provide a program with numeric constants. For example, -213.5 is a numeric literal.

A nonnumeric literal must be enclosed in quote marks and may utilize up to 120 characters. Any type of characters can be utilized except other quotation marks. Even COBOL reserved words can be included in a nonnumeric literal. Nonnumeric literals are frequently utilized to provide report headings for the output of a program. For example 'THE TOTAL IS' might be used as a nonnumeric literal.

THE IDENTIFICATION DIVISION

The IDENTIFICATION DIVISION is the simplest COBOL division. As a minimum, the IDENTIFICATION DIVISION must contain the division heading, the paragraph name PROGRAM-ID, and a programmer-supplied name for the program.[1]

---

[1] Some COBOL compilers require that the program name be in quotes and limit its size to eight positions. *Example:* 'PAYROLL.'

FIGURE 16–2

COBOL Reserved Words

ABOUT	ELSE	LOWER-BOUND	RECORD-COUNT
ACCEPT	END	LOWER-VALUE	RECORDING
ADD	ENDING		REDEFINES
ADDRESS	ENDING-FILE-LABEL	MEMORY	REEL
ADVANCING	ENDING-TAPE-LABEL	MEMORY-DUMP	REEL-NUMBER
AFTER	END-OF-FILE	MINUS	RENAMES
ALL	END-OF-TAPE	MODE	RENAMING
ALPHABETIC	ENTER	MODULES	REPLACING
ALPHANUMERIC	ENVIRONMENT	MOVE	RERUN
ALTER	EQUAL	MULTIPLE	RESERVE
ALTERNATE	ERROR	MULTIPLIED	REVERSED
AN	EVERY	MULTIPLY	REWIND
AND	EXAMINE		RIGHT
APPLY	EXCEEDS	NEGATIVE	ROUNDED
ARE	EXIT	NEXT	RUN
AREA	EXPONENTIATED	NO	
AT		NO-MEMORY-DUMP	SAME
	FD	NOT	SECTION
BEFORE	FILE	NOTE	SELECT
BEGINNING	FILE-CONTROL	NUMERIC	SENTENCE
BEGINNING-FILE-LABEL	FILLER		SENTINEL
BEGINNING-TAPE-LABEL	FIRST	OBJECT-COMPUTER	SEQUENCED
BITS	FLOAT	OBJECT-PROGRAM	SIGN
BLANK	FOR	OCCURS	SIGNED
BLOCK	FORMAT	OF	SIZE
BY	FROM	OFF	SOURCE-COMPUTER
		OMITTED	SPACE
CHARACTER	GIVING	ON	SPECIAL-NAMES
CHECK	GO	OPEN	STANDARD
	GREATER	OPTIONAL	STATUS

CLASS
CLOCK-UNITS
CLOSE
COBOL
COMPUTATIONAL
COMPUTE
CONFIGURATION
CONSTANT
CONTAINS
CONTROL
COPY
CORRESPONDING

DATA
DATE-WRITTEN
DECLARATIVES
DEFINE
DEPENDING
DIGIT
DISPLAY
DIVIDE
DIVIDED
DIVISION
DOLLAR

HASHED
HIGH VALUE

IF
IN
INCLUDE
INPUT
INPUT-OUTPUT
INTO
I-O-CONTROL
IS

JUSTIFIED

LABEL
LEADING
LEAVING
LEFT
LESS
LIBRARY
LINE
LOCATION
LOCK

OR
OTHERWISE
OUTPUT

PERFORM
PICTURE
PLACE
PLUS
POINT
POSITION
POSITIVE
PREPARED
PRIORITY
PROCEDURE
PROCEED
PROTECT
PURGE-DATE

QUOTE

RANGE
READ
RECORD

STOP
SUBTRACT
SUPERVISOR
SUPPRESS
SYNCHRONIZED

TALLY
TALLYING
TAPE
TEST-PATTERN
THAN
THEN
THROUGH or THRU
TIMES
TO

UNEQUAL
UNTIL
UPON
UPPER-BOUND
USAGE
USE

VALUE
VARYING

WHEN
WITH
WORD
WORKING-STORAGE
WRITE

ZERO (ZEROS, ZEROES)

Example: IDENTIFICATION DIVISION.
PROGRAM-ID.   PAYROLL.

COBOL allows up to six other paragraph names which provide additional paragraphs to describe and identify a COBOL program. These are: AUTHOR, INSTALLATION, DATE-WRITTEN, DATE-COMPILED, SECURITY, and REMARKS. The use of such paragraph names will be illustrated in a sample COBOL program later in the chapter.

The ENVIRONMENT DIVISION

The ENVIRONMENT DIVISION usually contains a CONFIGU-RATION SECTION and usually includes an INPUT-OUTPUT SEC-TION. The CONFIGURATION SECTION provides the name of the computer on which the program is to be compiled (the SOURCE-COMPUTER) and the computer which will execute the program (the OBJECT-COMPUTER). The computer name is frequently the same for both sections, and the form is specified by the COBOL compiler being used.

The INPUT-OUTPUT SECTION usually includes a FILE CON-TROL paragraph which assigns the data files that are to be used in the program to specific input/output devices of the computer system. The format of each sentence in the FILE CONTROL paragraphs consists of the reserved word SELECT followed by the name of a data file and then the term ASSIGN TO followed by the name of the input/output device as specified by the computer manufacturer. An example of a simple ENVIRONMENT DIVISION is shown below. Note that the FILE-CONTROL sentences specify the required names for the IBM 2501 card reader and 1403 printer.

ENVIRONMENT DIVISION.

CONFIGURATION SECTION.
SOURCE–COMPUTER.   IBM–370.
OBJECT–COMPUTER.   IBM–370.

INPUT–OUTPUT SECTION.
FILE–CONTROL.
    SELECT PAYROLL–FILE ASSIGN TO SYS001–UR–2501–S.
    SELECT PAY–REPORT ASSIGN TO SYS012–UR–1403–S.

The DATA DIVISION

The DATA DIVISION usually contains a FILE SECTION and a WORKING-STORAGE SECTION. The FILE SECTION describes the input/output files which are to be used by the program. It also contains descriptions of the data records and fields in each file. Remember that in Chapter Two we defined a data "field" or data "item" as a grouping of characters, (such as a "name field"); a data "record" as a grouping of related fields (such as an "employee record"); and a data "file" as a grouping of related records (such as a "payroll file"). The WORKING-STORAGE SECTION defines primary storage "work areas," data records and data constants which will be developed internally by the computer.

The FILE SECTION. The FILE SECTION is composed of "file description entries," "record description entries," and "item description entries," which describe the records and fields in each file. The general form of the FILE SECTION is shown below.

FD   File-name

$$\text{LABEL RECORD IS} \begin{cases} \text{OMITTED} \\ \text{STANDARD} \\ \text{data name} \end{cases}$$

$$\text{DATA} \begin{cases} \text{RECORD IS} \\ \text{RECORDS ARE} \end{cases} \text{data name, data name, ...}$$

01   Record-name.

$$\text{02   Data-item name} \begin{cases} \text{PIC} \\ \text{PICTURE} \\ \text{PICTURE IS} \end{cases} \text{picture.}$$

A file description entry begins with the characters "FD" which is a reserved word that indicates the beginning of a *file description*. The remainder of the file description consists of:

1.   The name of the file, such as SALES-FILE.
2.   An entry that specifies whether the file contains a "label record." Sometimes the first record in a file is not a *data record* but is a *label record* which identifies the contents of the file. In this chapter we will assume the absence of labels and utilize the entry:

LABEL RECORD IS OMITTED

3. An entry which specifies the names of the data records in the file, such as:

DATA RECORD IS SALES-RECORD.

After the file description entries are completed, the *record description entries* are coded. These identify the format of data fields and other data elements of the records in a file. The first part of a record description is the "level number" of the record, which is always 01, followed by the name of the record.

Example: 01 SALES-RECORD.

The next part of the record description consists of *"item description entries"* which specify the level number and name of each data field and data element in the record. A level number of 02 is utilized for data fields, 03 for subdivisions of data fields, 04 for subdivisions of the 03 level, etc. The general form of an item description entry is:

$$\text{Level number} \qquad \text{data-item name} \begin{cases} \text{PICTURE} \\ \text{PIC} \\ \text{PICTURE IS} \end{cases} \text{picture.}$$

Each item description entry must be followed by a *"data description picture"* which specifies the format of the data element. For example, the size of a data field, the use of numeric or alphabetic characters, and the position of a decimal point must be specified. This is accomplished by utilizing the reserved words PICTURE IS, PICTURE, or PIC, followed by a *"picture"* of the data field as described by a string of characters. For example, the description entry of a SALES-AMOUNT data field might be:

02 SALES-AMOUNT IS 9999V99.

This entry indicates that SALES-AMOUNT is a numeric data field which has a maximum size of six positions, with two positions to the right of an "assumed" decimal point. Figure 16–3 summarizes the basic characters used in data description pictures.

A few basic hints for utilizing the characters in a data description picture are outlined below.

1. The X is usually used instead of the A because it can represent alphabetic characters as well as numbers and other characters.
2. The V indicates where the decimal point for input data "should" be. COBOL assumes that the decimal point is not recorded on input data.

FIGURE 16–3

Basic Characters in Data Description Pictures

Character	*Meaning*
9	Numeric data
X	Alphanumeric data
A	Alphabetic data
V	"Assumed" decimal location for input
Z	Replace leading zero with blank in output
$0,.	Characters to appear in output
(n)	Repeat character *n* times

3. A "repeat number" inside a parenthesis can be utilized to avoid a long string of picture characters. For example, X(5) is equivalent to XXXXX.

4. The Z suppresses leading zeroes but not other numeric characters. For example, if the output data had a value of 0275, the picture ZZ99 would cause the output to be printed as 275.

5. The $ can be used in place of the Z or nine to suppress zeroes and commas and "float" the dollar sign to the position in front of the first nonzero digit. For example, if the output data had a value of 000328, the picture $$$9.99 would cause the output to be printed as $3.28.

6. Unused portions of a data record must be specified by a FILLER entry. For example, if ten positions of a punched card are to be skipped, the item description entry would be:

02 FILLER PICTURE X(10).

A simple example of a complete file description is shown below. It describes a file named SALES-FILE where each data record is a punched card named SALES-RECORD. Each punched card consists of a salesman's name (SALESMAN), sales quota (SALES-QUOTA), and sales amount (SALES-AMOUNT) data fields, with the rest of the 80 columns of the punched card being ignored by using the FILLER entry.

```
FD   SALES-FILE
     LABEL RECORD IS OMITTED
     DATA RECORD IS SALES-RECORD.
01   SALES-RECORD.
     02   SALESMAN PICTURE IS X(20).
     02   SALES-QUOTA PICTURE IS 99999V99.
     02   SALES-AMOUNT PICTURE IS 99999V99.
     02   FILLER PICTURE IS X(46).
```

Before closing our description of the FILE SECTION we should mention the frequent practice of COBOL programmers to define *only one data record and data item when specifying the file to be utilized for the printing of output reports.* This is done when several types of lines with different formats must be printed (titles, headings, detail lines, totals, etc.). Rather than writing several record description entries in the FILE SECTION, programmers define a single output record for the print file that equals the printer line size (frequently 132 or 133 print positions). The different types of print lines in a report are then defined in the WORKING-STORAGE SECTION. An example of such a file description in the FILE SECTION is:

```
FD   PRINT-FILE
     DATA RECORD IS OUTPUT-LINE.
01   OUTPUT-LINE PICTURE X(132).
```

The WORKING-STORAGE SECTION. The WORKING-STORAGE SECTION has two parts, one for describing independent data items in working storage areas, the other for describing data records and their data fields. The general form of the WORKING-STORAGE SECTION is shown below.

WORKING-STORAGE SECTION.

$$77 \text{ data-item name} \begin{cases} \text{PIC} \\ \text{PICTURE} \\ \text{PICTURE IS} \end{cases} \text{picture.}$$

$$01 \text{ Record-name.}$$
$$02 \text{ data-item name} \begin{cases} \text{PIC} \\ \text{PICTURE} \\ \text{PICTURE IS} \end{cases} \text{picture.}$$

Notice that the description of *independent data items* begins with the level number 77, while *record description entries* utilize the level numbers 01, 02, etc., as in the FILE SECTION. The use of data description pictures is also similar to the FILE SECTION.

The data items in the WORKING-STORAGE SECTION can be given initial values by the use of the reserved words VALUE or VALUE IS in an item description, followed by the actual values that are desired.

Example: 77 COUNTER PICTURE 999 VALUE 000.

This item description entry would specify a three-position numeric field named COUNTER and set its initial value to zero.

COBOL provides several reserved words to help simplify the use of the VALUE clause. These are summarized below.

1. The words ZERO, ZEROS, or ZEROES, and SPACE or SPACES can be used to fill a field with zeros and blank spaces, respectively.

   Example: 77 COUNTER PICTURE 999 VALUE ZEROS.

2. The word ALL can be used to fill a data field with other characters. For example, we could fill a 10-position nonnumeric literal field with asterisks with the following entry:

   02 INDICATOR PICTURE X(10) VALUE ALL '*'.

3. The VALUE clause is frequently utilized within a FILLER entry to specify headings in output reports. For example, the heading of a sales report (assuming 133 print positions on a print line) might be specified by the following example.

01 HEADING-LINE

   02 FILLER PICTURE X(60) VALUE SPACES.
   02 FILLER PICTURE X(12) VALUE 'SALES REPORT'.
   02 FILLER PICTURE X(61) VALUE SPACES.

The PROCEDURE DIVISION

The PROCEDURE DIVISION usually consists of several paragraphs which may be grouped into sections. There must be at least one paragraph in the division, but sections are optional. Each paragraph begins with a paragraph name and includes one or more sentences. A sentence is a "statement" or "command" which specifies actions to be accomplished. A paragraph may be established to identify several commands that perform a particular data processing task. A paragraph is also established when there is a need to make reference to a command or group of commands in a sentence in another part of the program.

We will now discuss several basic reserved words which are utilized as "verbs" to write commands in the PROCEDURE DIVISION. Learning to use such verbs will allow you to write the PROCEDURE DIVISION of simple COBOL programs. We will organize our discussion of these verbs according to the four categories outlined below.

1. *Input/Output.* OPEN, CLOSE, READ, WRITE.
2. *Data movement.* MOVE.
3. *Arithmetic.* COMPUTE, ADD, SUBTRACT, MULTIPLY, DIVIDE.
4. *Control.* GO TO, IF, PERFORM, STOP.

INPUT/OUTPUT STATEMENTS

The OPEN statement.   The OPEN statement is utilized to prepare files to be read or written. All files must be opened before they can be used for the first time in a program. The general form of the OPEN statement is:

$$\text{OPEN} \begin{Bmatrix} \text{INPUT} \\ \text{OUTPUT} \\ \text{I-O} \end{Bmatrix} \text{file name, file name.} \ldots$$

Example: OPEN INPUT SALES-FILE, PAYROLL-FILE.
              OPEN OUTPUT PRINT-FILE.
              OPEN INPUT SALES-FILE OUTPUT PRINT-FILE.

The CLOSE Statement.   The CLOSE statement terminates the processing of a file in a program. All files which were opened must be closed before the program is terminated. The general form of the CLOSE statement is:

CLOSE   file name, file name. . . .

Example: CLOSE SALES-FILE, PRINT-FILE.

The READ Statement.   The READ statement reads a single record from a file that is named in the statement. This command utilizes an input device such as a card reader, magnetic tape unit, or magnetic disk drive to read the next record from a file that must have been defined in the DATA DIVISION. The general forms of the READ statement are:

READ file name.
READ file name RECORD.

Example: READ SALES-FILE.
              READ SALES-FILE RECORD.

The READ statement frequently includes a provision for recognizing when the last record of a file has been read. The reserved words AT END are utilized to recognize this "end-of-file" condition. The computer then executes the command that follows the AT END phrase. This frequently involves terminating the program with "end-of-job" activities such as closing files, taking totals, etc. In the example below END-OF-JOB would be the paragraph name for a group of sentences which would perform such activities.

The general form of the READ statement with an AT END clause is:

READ file name AT END command.

Examples: READ SALES-FILE AT END STOP RUN.
READ SALES-FILE AT END GO TO END-
OF-JOB.

The WRITE statement.   The WRITE statement writes a single record that is named in the statement onto an open output file. The record must have been defined in the FILE SECTION of the DATA DI-VISION. The output device utilized (card punch, printer, magnetic tape, etc.) must have been assigned to the output file in the FILE-CONTROL SECTION of the ENVIRONMENT DIVISION. The general form of the WRITE statement is:

WRITE record-name.

Example: WRITE SALES-RECORD.

Spacing control for printed reports can be furnished by the following form of the WRITE statement:

WRITE record name $\begin{Bmatrix} \text{BEFORE} \\ \text{AFTER} \end{Bmatrix}$ ADVANCING integer LINES.

For example, the statement WRITE SALES-RECORD AFTER ADVANCING 2 LINES will print the contents of SALES-RECORD after double-spacing.

Another frequently used version of the WRITE statement is:

WRITE record name FROM record name.

It is utilized whenever the FILE SECTION OF THE DATA DIVI-SION has defined the output file as a single record that equals the printer line size (132 or 133 print positions). In this case, the WRITE statement specifies that the *output file* must utilize one of the several types of *output print lines* defined in the WORKING-STORAGE SECTION. For example, assume that one of the several types of print lines defined in the WORKING-STORAGE SECTION had a record name of TOTALS-LINE, and that the output file defined in the FILE SECTION was a single record of 133 print positions named OUTPUT-LINE. The WRITE statement to print TOTALS-LINE would be:

WRITE OUTPUT-LINE FROM TOTALS-LINE.

DATA MOVEMENT STATEMENTS

The MOVE statement.   The MOVE statement transfers data from one area of storage to another. It is frequently utilized to copy the contents of a storage location, to initialize a data location with a specified value, or to move data to an output line. The general form of the MOVE statement is:

$$MOVE \begin{Bmatrix} \text{data-name} \\ \text{literal} \end{Bmatrix} TO \text{ data name, data name. . . .}$$

Examples: MOVE ZEROES TO COUNTER.
MOVE HEADING-LINE TO OUTPUT-LINE.

The MOVE statement is regulated by specific rules, many of them related to the PICTURE statements which defined data locations in the DATA division. For example, data can be moved from an alphabetic area to an alphanumeric area but not vice versa. Numeric data can be moved to a numeric or alphanumeric area but not to an alphabetic area. Data moved to an alphanumeric area will be left adjusted, with extra positions left blank. Data moved to numeric area is aligned according to the decimal point, with extra positions filled with zeros. *Truncation* (loss of characters) will result if a "receiving" area is shorter than the data being moved.

ARITHMETIC STATEMENTS

The COMPUTE statement. The COMPUTE statement is utilized to perform arithmetic operations that are expressed in the form of a mathematical formula. The use of mathematical symbols to the right of an equal sign allows the COMPUTE statement to perform the arithmetic operation of addition $(+)$, subtraction $(-)$, multiplication $(*)$, division $(/)$, and exponentation $(**)$. The COMPUTE verb can therefore be used in place of the ADD, SUBTRACT, MULTIPLY and DIVIDE verbs. The general form of the COMPUTE statement is:

$$COMPUTE \text{ data-name} = \begin{Bmatrix} \text{data name} \\ \text{literal} \\ \text{arithmetic expression} \end{Bmatrix}$$

Examples: COMPUTE X = (Y/Z) ** 2.
COMPUTE GROSS-PAY = SALARY
+ COMMISSIONS.

The order of computation in a COMPUTE statement follows standard mathematical practice and is similar to that used in FORTRAN. Computations are performed from left to right in the following order of priority: (1) exponentation, (2) multiplication and division, and (3) addition and subtraction. Parentheses are utilized to emphasize or change the normal order of computations. Additionally, a space before and after each arithmetic symbol is required.

The COMPUTE statement:

$$\text{COMPUTE X} = \text{Y} + \text{Z} * \text{A}/\text{B} ** 2 - \text{C}.$$

is executed like the mathematical equation:

$$X = Y + \left(\frac{ZA}{B^2}\right) - C$$

The COMPUTE statement:

$$\text{COMPUTE X} = (\text{Y}+\text{Z}) * (\text{A}/\text{B}) ** 2 - \text{C}.$$

is executed like the mathematical equation:

$$X = (Y+Z)\,(A/B)^2 - C$$

The ADD, SUBTRACT, MULTIPLY, and DIVIDE statements. The ADD, SUBTRACT, MULTIPLY and DIVIDE statements perform the arithmetic computations indicated by their verbs. They can be utilized in two basic forms illustrated below.

COBOL form	*Arithmetic equivalent*
1. ADD A, B TO C.	$C = A + B + C$
2. ADD A, B GIVING C.	$C = A + B$
1. SUBTRACT A FROM B.	$B = B - A$
2. SUBTRACT A FROM B GIVING C.	$C = B - A$
1. MULTIPLY A BY B.	$B = A \times B$
2. MULTIPLY A BY B GIVING C.	$C = A \times B$
1. DIVIDE A INTO B.	$B = B \div A$
2. DIVIDE A INTO B GIVING C.	$C = B \div A$

We can understand the distinction between the two forms of these statements by analyzing the ADD statement. The first form *adds* the data-items *preceding* the word TO to the data-item *following* the word TO. The second form *replaces* the value in the data-item *following* the word GIVING with the sum of the data-items *preceding* the word GIVING. Thus, if A had a value of 2, B a value of 3, and C a value of 4, the first ADD statement would result in C having a value of 9; the second statement would result in C having a value of 5.

The basic forms of arithmetic statements are frequently amended by the word ROUNDED. If we wish the result of an arithmetic statement to be rounded (rather than truncated) we can utilize the word ROUNDED in the statement.

Example: MULTIPLY HOURS BY RATE GIVING
             PAY ROUNDED.

Arithmetic statements are regulated by several rules. Only numeric literals or numeric data-names can be used. Numeric data-names must have been defined by PICTURE clauses in the DATA DIVISION as independent or elementary data items. Finally, the maximum size of numeric literals or data names is 18 digits.

CONTROL STATEMENTS

Control statements control the order in which a program is executed, perform comparisons and test conditions, change the sequence of a program through a branching process, or stop a program.

1. GO TO and IF statements alter the sequential execution of program statements by transferring control to another statement.
2. The PERFORM statement transfers control temporarily to another part of the program.
3. The STOP statement temporarily or permanently halts the execution of the program.

The GO TO statement.   The general form of the *"unconditional"* GO TO statement is:

$$\text{GO TO} \begin{cases} \text{paragraph name} \\ \text{section name} \end{cases}$$

Example: GO TO TOTAL-CALC.

Explanation: Transfer control to paragraph TOTAL-CALC.

The general form of the *"conditional"* GO TO is:

GO TO procedure-name-1, procedure-name-2, . .procedure-
    name-3 DEPENDING ON . . data-name.

Example: GO TO SINGLE, MARRIED DEPEND-
                ING ON STATUS.

Explanation: Transfer control to the SINGLE procedure if STATUS has a value of one, and to the MAR-RIED procedure if STATUS has a value of two. If STATUS has some other value, execute the next sequential instruction.

The PERFORM statement. The general form of the PERFORM statement is:

$$PERFORM \begin{cases} \text{paragraph name} \\ \text{section name} \end{cases}$$

Example: PERFORM TOTAL-CALC.

Explanation: Transfer control to the TOTAL-CALC pro-cedure until it is completed. Then return control to the statement that follows the PERFORM statement.

The PERFORM statement can be modified by the use of the TIMES and THRU words.

Example: PERFORM TOTAL-CALC 12 TIMES.

Explanation: Perform the TOTAL-CALC procedure twelve times before returning to the statement after the PERFORM statement.

Example: PERFORM TAX-CALC THRU TOTAL-CALC.

Explanation: Perform the procedures in the program from the TAX-CALC through the TOTAL-CALC pro-cedures before returning to the statement after the PERFORM statement.

The IF statement. IF statements perform comparisons and test con-ditions. They cause alternative processing activities in the program to occur depending on the results of the comparison or test. A basic form of the IF statement is:

IF condition, statement.

Example: IF COUNTER IS EQUAL TO 15, GO TO TOTAL-CALC.

Explanation: If the value of COUNTER equals 15 transfer control to the TOTAL-CALC procedure. (If not, continue with the normal execution sequence of the program.)

An extended form of the basic IF statement utilizes the words ELSE or OTHERWISE to transfer control to another statement if the condition specified is not true. The general form is:

$$\text{IF condition, statement-1} \begin{Bmatrix} \text{ELSE} \\ \text{OTHERWISE} \end{Bmatrix} \text{statement-2.}$$

Example: IF SALES > QUOTA, GO TO BONUS-CALC, OTHERWISE GO TO COMMIS-SION-CALC.

Explanation: If the value of SALES "is greater than" the value of QUOTA, transfer control to the BONUS-CALC procedure. If not, transfer to the COMMISSION-CALC procedure.

The *"condition"* portion of an IF statement has the general form of:

$$\begin{Bmatrix} \text{Data name} \\ \text{Literal} \\ \text{Arithmetic expression} \end{Bmatrix} \text{relational operator} \begin{Bmatrix} \text{Data name} \\ \text{Literal} \\ \text{Arithmetic expression} \end{Bmatrix}$$

The *"relational operators"* utilized depends on the type of condition being tested. For example, a *"relational"* condition utilizes the relational operators shown below.

IS EQUAL TO	or	=
IS NOT EQUAL TO	or	NOT=
IS GREATER THAN	or	>
IS NOT GREATER THAN	or	NOT>
IS LESS THAN	or	<
IS NOT LESS THAN	or	NOT<

A *"sign"* condition may be included in an IF statement utilizing the relational operators shown below.

$$\text{IS (NOT)} \begin{Bmatrix} \text{POSITIVE} \\ \text{NEGATIVE} \\ \text{ZERO} \end{Bmatrix}$$

Example: IF BALANCE IS POSITIVE, ADD 1 TO COUNTER.

A *"class"* condition may also be included in an IF statement if we wish to test for a numeric or alphabetic condition. The following relational operators would be used.

$$\text{IS (NOT)} \begin{Bmatrix} \text{ALPHABETIC} \\ \text{NUMERIC} \end{Bmatrix}$$

Example: IF INPUT-RECORD IS ALPHABETIC,
GO TO ERROR-ROUTINE.

The STOP statement. The general form of the STOP statement is:

$$\text{STOP} \begin{Bmatrix} \text{literal} \\ \text{RUN} \end{Bmatrix}$$

The STOP statement can cause a temporary or permanent halt in the execution of the program. If the STOP literal form is used, the program will be halted temporarily and the literal will be displayed on the operator's console. When the operator restarts the program, it will begin with the statement following the STOP statement. If the form STOP RUN is used, the program will terminate permanently.

SAMPLE COBOL PROGRAMS

No one expects a programmer (much less a beginning programmer) to remember all of the rules of COBOL. With practice, many of the rules become "second nature," but most programmers still have to refer occasionally to "langauge specification manuals" to assist their programming efforts. Even then, the presence of "bugs" in many programs when they are first written is evidence that a programmer may have inadvertently violated some of the rules of COBOL. Therefore, be sure to consult the COBOL rules in the previous section to assist you in correctly writing the programs that are assigned at the end of this chapter.

Sample Program One

Let us now analyze two examples of COBOL programs before you "take the plunge" and attempt your first program. We will begin with a very simple data processing assignment that requires the performance of the following tasks:

1. Read the values Y and Z from an undetermined number of punched cards.
2. Add Y and Z together to produce X. ($X = Y + Z$).

3. Print each resulting sum of X on the printer of the computer.
4. Accumulate the calculated values of X.
5. After all the data cards are read, compute and print the total and average (arithmetic mean) value of X.

Figures 16–4 and 16–5 illustrate the program and flowchart of Sample Program One. Let us briefly examine the statements of this program.

FIGURE 16–4

Sample Program One

```
00001    IDENTIFICATION DIVISION.
00002    PROGRAM-ID. COMPUTE-X.

00003    ENVIRONMENT DIVISION.
00004    CONFIGURATION SECTION.
00005    SOURCE-COMPUTER.    IBM-370.
00006    OBJECT-COMPUTER.    IBM-370.
00007    INPUT-OUTPUT SECTION.
00008    FILE-CONTROL.
00009        SELECT YZ-FILE ASSIGN TO SYSOO1-UR-2501-S.
00010        SELECT X-FILE ASSIGN TO SYS012-UR-1403-S.

00011    DATA DIVISION.
00012    FILE SECTION.
00013    FD YZ-FILE LABEL RECORD IS OMITTED
00014        DATA RECORD IS YZ-CARD.
00015    01  YZ-CARD.
00016        02 Y PICTURE IS 999V99.
00017        02 Z PICTURE IS 999V99.
00018        02 FILLER PICTURE IS X(70).
00019    FD X-FILE LABEL RECORD IS OMITTED
00020        DATA RECORD IS OUTPUT-LINE.
00021    01  OUTPUT-LINE.
00022        02 DATA-X PICTURE IS ZZZZ99.99.
00023        02 FILLER PICTURE IS X(123) VALUE IS SPACES.
00024    WORKING-STORAGE SECTION.
00025    77  COUNTER-X PICTURE IS 999 VALUE IS ZEROS.
00026    77  TOTAL-X PICTURE IS 999999V99 VALUE IS ZEROS.
00027    77  AVERAGE-X PICTURE IS 999V99.

00028    PROCEDURE DIVISION.
00029        OPEN INPUT YZ-FILE OUTPUT X-FILE.
00030    READ-CARD.
00031        READ YZ-FILE AT END GO TO FINISH.
00032    X-CALC-PRINT.
00033        COMPUTE X = Y + Z. ADD X TO TOTAL-X.
00034        ADD 1 TO COUNTER-X. MOVE X TO DATA-X.
00035        WRITE OUTPUT-LINE. GO TO READ-CARD.
00036    FINISH.
00037        MOVE TOTAL-X TO DATA-X. WRITE OUTPUT-LINE AFTER
00038        ADVANCING 2 LINES. DIVIDE COUNTER-X INTO TOTAL-X
00039        GIVING AVERAGE-X. MOVE AVERAGE-X TO DATA-X.
00040        WRITE OUTPUT-LINE AFTER ADVANCING 2 LINES.
00041        CLOSE YZ-FILE, X-FILE. STOP RUN.
```

FIGURE 16–5

Flowchart of the PROCEDURE DIVISION
—Sample Program One

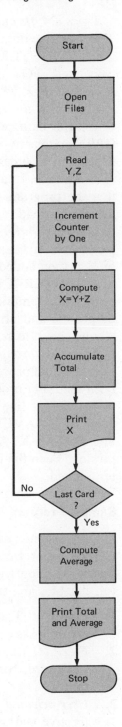

Lines 1 and 2 meet the minimum requirements for the IDENTIFICATION DIVISION. Sample Program One is given the name of COMPUTE-X.

Lines 3 through 10 are the statements of the ENVIRONMENT DIVISION. The CONFIGURATION SECTION specifies that an IBM 370 computer will compile and execute the program. The INPUT-OUTPUT SECTION assigns the INPUT file of data cards (called YZ-FILE) to an IBM 2501 card reader. The output file of the program (called X-FILE) will be printed on an IBM 1403 printer.

Lines 11 through 27 are the statements of the DATA DIVISION. Statements 13 through 18 of the FILE SECTION specify that the input card file does not have special label cards and that each card in the file constitutes a single data record. Each data card is specified as having Y and Z data fields, each field having a size of five numeric positions with an "assumed" decimal location before the last two positions. The remaining 70 positions of the data card are to be ignored by the card reader.

The printed output file of the program is described by *lines 19 through 23*. X-FILE does not have any label records and each output line constitutes a data record. Each output line consists of a numeric data field (called DATA-X) of eight digits and a decimal point with the rest of the print line being left blank. Notice that zero suppression is specified for the first four positions.

Lines 24 through 27 specify the WORKING-STORAGE SEC-TION. Three data fields are established in the primary storage of the CPU. COUNTER-X will count the number of times X values are calculated. TOTAL-X will accumulate a running total of X values. AVERAGE-X will store the average value of X after it is calculated.

Lines 28 through 41 comprise the PROCEDURE DIVISION where the data processing tasks of the computer are specified. An OPEN statement opens the input and output files. The READ-CARD paragraph includes a READ statement which directs the computer to read a punched card from the input file. The statement also specifies that the program should branch to the FINISH paragraph after the last card is read.

Lines 32 through 35 are the statements of the X-CALC-PRINT paragraph. A value of X is computed by adding Y and Z. This value of X is then added to the running total called TOTAL-X. The value of COUNTER-X is increased by one each time a value of X is computed. The computed value of X is moved to the DATA-X field in the output file and printed by the WRITE statement. Then the program "loops" back to read another data card.

Lines 36 through 41 constitute the FINISH paragraph which outlines the final processing tasks of the program after all data cards have been read and processed. The total accumulated value of X is moved to the output line and printed (after double-spacing). The average value of X (AVERAGE-X) is computed by dividing COUNTER-X into TOTAL-X. AVERAGE-X is then moved to the output line and printed. Then the input and output files are closed and the program is terminated.

Sample Program Two

Our second sample program demonstrates some features of COBOL that we have not utilized in the previous program. This makes the program more complex, but it also makes it more "powerful, flexible, and user-oriented."

1. *Powerful.* The program can efficiently perform more data processing tasks.
2. *Flexible.* The program can handle changes in input/output volume, size, format, etc., without major modifications being required.
3. *User-oriented.* The program can produce output that is more attractive and usable for persons who will utilize its results. In this case, the program reads and prints the names of people and pro-

vides appropriate descriptive titles and headings for the output report.

The sample program is based on the examples we used in Chapter Six to illustrate the use of flowcharts and decision tables. The "Salesmen Gross Pay" program performs the following tasks:

1. Computes the sales commissions and gross pay of each salesman of a business firm.
2. Produces a report which shows the name, sales, quota, salary, commissions, and gross pay of each salesman.
3. Tallies the number of salesmen in each of the three following categories:
   a. Salesmen who have not made any sales.
   b. Salesmen who have not equaled their sales quota.
   c. Salesmen who have equaled or exceeded their sales quota.
4. Computes and prints the total amount of sales 'and the average value of sales made.

The program, flowchart, input data card format, and output report format of Sample Program Two is shown in Figures 16–6, 16–7, 16–8 and 16–9. Let us examine the important features of this program that were not present in the previous sample program.

FIGURE 16–6

Sample Program Three

COBOL Coding Form

SYSTEM	SALESMEN COMPENSATION		PUNCHING INSTRUCTIONS		PAGE / OF 5
PROGRAM	SALESMEN GROSS PAY		GRAPHIC	CARD FORM #	*
PROGRAMMER	ABLE T. PROGRAMMER	DATE	PUNCH		

```
001  IDENTIFICATION DIVISION.
002  PROGRAM-ID.SALESMEN-GROSS-PAY.
003  AUTHOR.ABLE T.PROGRAMMER.
004  INSTALLATION. COMPUTER CENTER.
005  SECURITY. CONTROLLER ACCESS.
006  DATA-WRITTEN.NOVEMBER,1974.
007  REMARKS.THIS IS A PROGRAM TO PREPARE A SALESMEN GROSS PAY REPORT.

008  ENVIRONMENT DIVISION.
009  CONFIGURATION SECTION.
010  SOURCE-COMPUTER.IBM-370.
011  OBJECT-COMPUTER.IBM-370.
012  INPUT-OUTPUT SECTION.
013  FILE-CONTROL.
014      SELECT SALESMEN-FILE ASSIGN TO SYS001-UR-2501-S.
015      SELECT GROSSPAY-FILE ASSIGN TO SYS001-UR-1403-S.

016  DATA DIVISION.
017  FILE SECTION.
018  FD  SALESMEN-FILE LABEL RECORD IS OMITTED
019      DATA RECORD IS SALESMAN-CARD.
020  01  SALESMAN-CARD.
021      02  SALESMAN-NAME PIC X(15).
022      02  SALES PIC 999999V99.
023      02  QUOTA PIC 999999V99.
```

FIGURE 16–6 (continued)

COBOL Coding Form

SYSTEM		PUNCHING INSTRUCTIONS		PAGE 2 OF 5
PROGRAM		GRAPHIC		CARD FORM #
PROGRAMMER	DATE	PUNCH		

```
023      02  QUOTA PIC 999999V99.
024      02  SALARY PIC 99999V99.
025  FD  GROSSPAY-FILE LABEL RECORD IS OMITTED
026      DATA RECORD IS OUTPUT-LINE.
027  01  OUTPUT-LINE PIC X(132).
028  WORKING-STORAGE SECTION.
029  77  COUNTER-1 PIC 99 VALUE ZEROS.
030  77  COUNTER-2 PIC 99 VALUE ZEROS.
031  77  COUNTER-3 PIC 99 VALUE ZEROS.
032  77  SALESMEN PIC 999 VALUE ZEROS.
033  77  COMMISSIONS PIC 99999V99.
034  77  GROSS-PAY PIC 999999V99.
035  77  TOTAL-SALES PIC 999999999V99.
036  77  AVERAGE-SALES PIC 999999V99.
037  01  REPORT-TITLE.
038      02  FILLER PIC X(50) VALUE SPACES.
039      02  FILLER PIC X(25) VALUE 'SALESMEN GROSS PAY REPORT'.
040      02  FILLER PIC X(57) VALUE SPACES.
041  01  HEADING-LINE.
042      02  FILLER PIC X(79) VALUE '           SALESMAN           SALES
043  -      \      QUOTA        SALARY       COMMISSION     GROSS PAY'.
044      02  FILLER PIC X(53) VALUE SPACES.
045  01  DATA-LINE.
046      02  NAME PIC X(15).
```

COBOL Coding Form

SYSTEM		PUNCHING INSTRUCTIONS		PAGE 3 OF 5
PROGRAM		GRAPHIC		CARD FORM #
PROGRAMMER	DATE	PUNCH		

```
047      02  FILLER PIC X(5) VALUE SPACES.
048      02  XSALES PIC ZZZZ9.99.
049      02  FILLER PIC X(5) VALUE SPACES.
050      02  XQUOTA PIC ZZ9999.99.
051      02  FILLER PIC X(5) VALUE SPACES.
052      02  XSALARY PIC Z9999.99.
053      02  FILLER PIC X(5) VALUE SPACES.
054      02  XCOMMISSIONS PIC ZZZZ9.99.
055      02  FILLER PIC X(5) VALUE SPACES.
056      02  XGROSS-PAY PIC ZZ9999.99.
057      02  FILLER PIC X(49) VALUE SPACES.
058  01  TOTAL-AVERAGE-LINE.
059      02  FILLER PIC X(14) VALUE 'TOTAL SALES = '.
060      02  XTOTAL-SALES PIC ZZ9999999.99.
061      02  FILLER PIC X(21) VALUE '         AVERAGE SALES = '.
062      02  XAVERAGE-SALES PIC ZZZZ9.99.
063      02  FILLER PIC X(86) VALUE SPACES.
064  01  PERFORMANCE-LINE.
065      02  FILLER PIC X(68) VALUE 'NUMBER OF SALESMEN BY PERFORMANCE
066  -      \      CATEGORY:        NO SALES: '.
067      02  XCOUNTER-1 PIC 99.
068      02  FILLER PIC X(13) VALUE 'BELOW QUOTA: '.
069      02  XCOUNTER-2 PIC 99.
070      02  FILLER PIC X(13) VALUE 'ABOVE QUOTA: '.
```

FIGURE 16–6 (continued)

COBOL Coding Form

SYSTEM		PUNCHING INSTRUCTIONS	PAGE 4 OF 5
PROGRAM		GRAPHIC	*
PROGRAMMER	DATE	PUNCH	CARD FORM #

```
071        02  XCØUNTER-3 PIC 99.
072        02  FILLER PIC X(32) VALUE SPACES.
073   PRØCEDURE DIVISIØN.
074        ØPEM INPUT SALESMEN-FILE ØUTPUT GRØSSPAY-FILE.
075        WRITE ØUTPUT-LINE FRØM REPORT-TITLE BEFØRE ADVANCING 5 LINES.
076        WRITE ØUTPUT-LINE FRØM HEADING-LINE BEFØRE ADVANCING 2 LINES.
077   READ-CARD.
078        READ SALESMEN-FILE AT END GØ TØ TØTAL-AVERAGE.
079   NØ-SALES.
080        IF SALES IS GREATER THAN ZERØ, GØ TØ BELØW-QUØTA. ADD 1 TØ
081        CØUNTER-1. ADD ZERØS TØ CØMMISSIØNS. GØ TØ CALC-PRINT.
082   BELØW-QUØTA.
083        IF SALES IS EQUAL TØ QUØTA, ØR SALES IS GREATER THAN QUØTA,
084        GØ TØ ABØVE-QUØTA. ADD 1 TO
085        CØUNTER-2. MULTIPLY SALES BY 0.1 GIVING CØMMISSIØNS.
086        GØ TØ CALC-PRINT.
087   ABØVE-QUØTA.
088        ADD 1 TØ CØUNTER-3. CØMPUTE CØMMISSIØNS = QUØTA * 0.1 +
089        (SALES - QUØTA) * 0.2.
090   CALC-PRINT
091        ADD SALARY TØ CØMMISSIØNS GIVING GRØSS-PAY. ADD SALES TØ
092        TØTAL-SALES. MØVE SALESMAN-NAME TØ NAME. MØVE SALES TØ
093        XSALES. MØVE QUØTA TØ XQUØTA. MØVE SALARY TØ XSALARY.
094        MØVE CØMMISSIØNS TØ XCØMMISSIØNS. MØVE GRØSS-PAY TØ
095        XGRØSS-PAY. WRITE ØUTPUT-LINE FRØM DATA-LINE.
```

COBOL Coding Form

SYSTEM		PUNCHING INSTRUCTIONS	PAGE 5 OF 5
PROGRAM		GRAPHIC	*
PROGRAMMER	DATE	PUNCH	CARD FORM #

```
096        GØ TØ READ-CARD.
097   TØTAL-AVERAGE.
098        ADD CØUNTER-1, CØUNTER-2, CØUNTER-3 GIVING SALESMEN.
099        DEVIDE SALESMEN INTØ TØTAL-SALES GIVING AVERAGE-SALES.
100        MØVE TØTAL-SALES TØ XTØTAL-SALES. MØVE AVERAGE-SALES TØ
101        XAVERAGE-SALES. WRITE ØUTPUT-LINE FRØM TØTAL-AVERAGE-LINE
102        AFTER ADVANCING TWØ SPACES.
103   PERFØRMANCE.
104        MØVE CØUNTER-1 TØ XCØUNTER-1. MØVE CØUNTER-2 TØ XCØUNTER-2.
105        MØVE CØUNTER-3 TØ XCØUNTER-3. WRITE ØUTPUT-LINE FRØM
106        PERFØRMANCE-LINE AFTER ADVANCING 2 SPACES.
107        CLØSE SALESMEN-FILE, GRØSSPAY-FILE. STØP RUN.
```

FIGURE 16–7

Flowchart of the PROCEDURE DIVISION—Sample Program Two

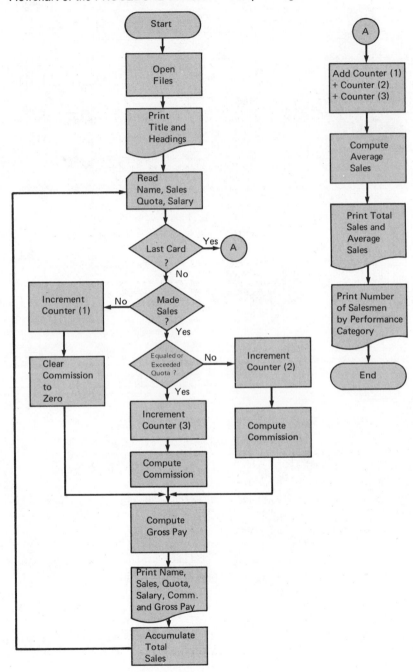

FIGURE 16-8

Input Data Card Format of Sample Program Two

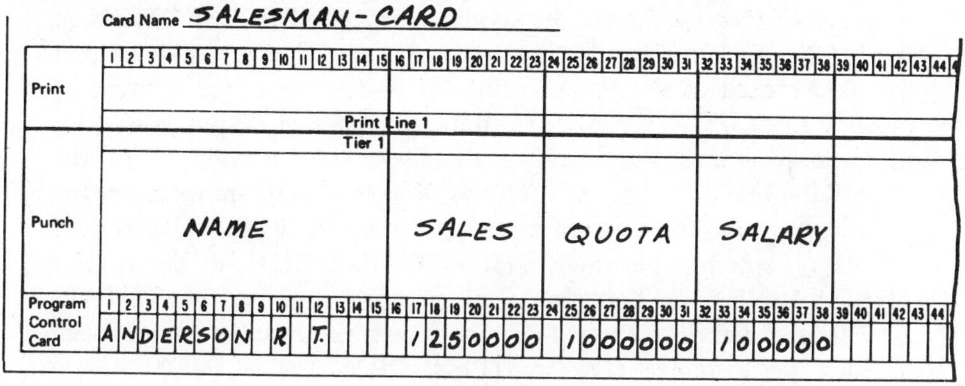

Card Name _SALESMAN - CARD_

	1 2 3 4 5 6 7 8 9 10 11 12 13 14 15	16 17 18 19 20 21 22 23	24 25 26 27 28 29 30 31	32 33 34 35 36 37 38 39	40 41 42 43 44
Print					
		Print Line 1			
		Tier 1			
Punch	*NAME*	*SALES*	*QUOTA*	*SALARY*	
Program Control Card	A N D E R S O N R T.	1 2 5 0 0 0 0	1 0 0 0 0 0 0	1 0 0 0 0 0	

FIGURE 16-9

Output of Sample Program Two

SALESMAN GROSS PAY REPORT

SALESMAN	SALES	QUOTA	SALARY	COMMISSION	GROSS PAY
ANDERSON R T	12500.00	10000.00	1000.00	1500.00	2500.00
BAKER D A	8000.00	10000.00	1000.00	800.00	1800.00
CALLISON W E	18500.00	20000.00	2000.00	1850.00	3850.00
DAWSON F L	0.00	5000.00	500.00	0.00	500.00
FERRANTE J S	9500.00	10000.00	1000.00	950.00	1950.00

TOTAL SALES = $657500.00   AVERAGE SALES = $9700.00

NUMBER OF SALESMEN BY PERFORMANCE CATEGORY:

NO SALES: 2   BELOW QUOTA: 28   ABOVE QUOTA: 6

Analysis of the Program

The first seven lines of the program are an extended version of the IDENTIFICATION DIVISION and provide much information to identify the program. *Lines 08 through 15* specify computer con-

figurations and file assignments that are similar to those in the EN-
VIRONMENT DIVISION of Sample Program One.

Lines 17 through 27 are the statements of the FILE SECTION of
the DATA DIVISION. An important feature of this section is that
the data record of the output print file is defined as the entire 132
position print line. Therefore, the different types of output print lines
in these programs are specified by *Lines 37 through 72* of the
WORKING-STORAGE SECTION. Figure 16–9 shows that the
output report has five types of print lines, a report heading (REPORT-
TITLE), column headings (HEADINGS-LINE), a detail line
(DATA-LINE), a line for total and average sales (TOTAL-
AVERAGE-LINE), and a line that shows the number of salesmen
in each performance category (PERFORMANCE-LINE).

Lines 29 through 36 establish several data fields in primary storage.
Three counters are established to keep track of the number of salesmen in each of the three performance categories. A running total of
sales is accumulated in TOTAL-SALES. The other data fields hold
the results of other calculations made by the program.

The PROCEDURE DIVISION (*lines 73–106*) begins with the
opening of input and output files, the printing of the report title and
column headings, and the reading of a data card. The next three paragraphs outline what processing should occur if a salesman has not
made any sales for the period (NO-SALES), has made sales below
his quota (BELOW-QUOTA), or has exceeded his sales quota
(ABOVE-QUOTA). Notice how the use of IF statements and GO
TO statements provides for three different types of processing depending on the sales performance of each particular salesman. Salesmen without sales do not receive a commission while salesmen below
quota earn a 10 percent commission. Salesmen above quota receive
a 10 percent commission on sales up to the quota amount, and a
20 percent commission on sales above quota.

The CALC-PRINT paragraph (*lines 89–95*) directs the computation of gross pay and the printing of the detail lines which show
the name, sales, quota, salary, commissions, and gross pay of each
salesman. Notice how the contents of each data field must be moved
to its proper place on the DATA-LINE and then printed from the
OUTPUT-LINE. Also accomplished in this paragraph is the accumulation of TOTAL-SALES.

The TOTAL-AVERAGE and PERFORMANCE paragraphs
(*lines 96–106*) outline the processing that occurs after the last data
card has been read and processed. The contents of the three counters

are added together to compute the total number of salesmen processed (SALESMEN). The average sales of the salesmen is then computed. The TOTAL-AVERAGE-LINE is then printed, followed by the printing of the PERFORMANCE-LINE and the termination of the program.

PREPARING COBOL PROGRAMS

In Chapter Six we showed that computer programming requires the activities of *programming analysis* and *program design* before *program coding* can be properly accomplished. *Checking, testing,* and *correcting* activities are then required to properly "debug" a newly written program. In this chapter, we have concentrated on the fundamentals of *program coding* in COBOL. However, developing effective COBOL programs requires the accomplishment of most of the programming activities mentioned in Chapter Six.

Before writing a COBOL program, you should take the time to analyze each data processing problem you are asked to program and attempt to design the processing procedures required for its solution. You should begin by developing a general program flowchart of your proposed solution. This should help you identify the input/output, logical, and computational steps required to carry out your data processing assignment. You should also determine the format of the input (frequently on punched cards) and the output (frequently a printed report). This can be accomplished by using input/output layout forms or informal "rough layouts" which detail the format of proposed input and output media.

The COBOL Coding Form

Once these steps have been accomplished, program coding can begin. Most programmers use a *program coding form* to assist their programming efforts and facilitate the keypunching of their program. Figure 16–6 illustrated the use of a COBOL coding form for Sample Program Two. The *program cards* of the program are keypunched using the coding form as a guide. Each space on the coding form corresponds to one column of an 80-column punched card. Each line of the coding form is punched into a single program card. The following is a summary of the purpose of each column of a COBOL program card.

1. Coding line sequence numbers can be punched into *columns 1–6* of a program card. The use of such line numbers is optional.
2. A hyphen in *column 7* identifies "continuation cards" which are utilized when a COBOL statement is too long for a single program card.
3. COBOL coding is keypunched into *columns 8–72*. Some COBOL coding must begin on column 8 (called the "A margin") while other coding begins on column 12 (called the "B margin"). For example, the names of divisions, sections, and paragraphs, and the FD, 01 and 77 level numbers of the DATA DIVISION, all begin at the A margin. On the other hand, file and record names, 02 level numbers, and the COBOL statements of the PROCEDURE DIVISION all begin at the B margin.
4. The COBOL compiler ignores *columns 73–80* of program cards. These are sometimes used to number and identify each card in the "source deck" for the benefit of the programmer.

Coding the COBOL program on the coding form should be done by following the input/output layouts and program flowchart you have developed. You will probably make changes in both the flowchart and the program statements during this process. Make frequent reference to the rules for COBOL statements in the chapter. When you have written a complete program, go over your program and flowchart several times in order to "desk check" the program. Keypunch the program into program cards using the coding form as a guide.

Executing the Program

Once the program cards have been prepared, the input data can be keypunched into *data cards* according to the specifications of the PICTURE statements of your program. The program "source deck" and the data cards should be desk checked for possible errors. The program, data, and "job control" cards can then be submitted to your computer center for compiling and execution.

Most computer centers have different procedures for the use of the *"job control cards"* that are required for every program that is to be processed. Job control cards may be needed at the beginning and end of your program deck and data cards. The job control cards are required by the operating system or other control programs of the computer system. They identify your program as a COBOL program and specify other details required for compiling and execution. Consult your computer center for the proper format and arrangement of job control cards.

Your program may fail to execute on its first attempt. Use the program listing and the "diagnostic" listing of *error statements* to help you *debug* the program. Errors should be corrected by keypunching corrected COBOL statements into new program cards. The program should be resubmitted until it can be successfully *compiled* and *executed*. When this finally occurs, you will have successfully directed an electronic computer in the accomplishment of a data processing assignment.

KEY TERMS AND CONCEPTS

Identification Division, 515, 519, 522
Environment Division, 515, 522
Data Division, 515, 523
Procedure Division, 515, 527–535
Sections, 515
Paragraphs, 515
Sentences, 515
Reserved word, 518, 520–521
Programmer-supplied name, 518
Data name, 518
Literal, 519

Configuration Section, 522
Input/Output Section, 522
File Section, 523–526
Working-Storage Section, 526–527
Input/Output statements, 528–529
Data movement statements, 529–530
Arithmetic statements, 530–532
Control statements, 532–535
COBOL coding form, 545–546
Program cards, 545
Job control cards, 546

ASSIGNMENTS

1. Review the key terms and concepts above and reread the appropriate chapter material to reenforce your understanding where necessary.

2. Identify and briefly describe the purpose of:
   a. The four divisions of COBOL
   b. The sections of the Environment and Data Divisions
   c. The four basic categories of statements used in the PROCEDURE division and the fundamental statements in each category

3. Review the sample COBOL programs of the chapter to deepen your understanding of the statements that are utilized in a complete COBOL program to accomplish a specific data processing assignment.

4. Discuss why Sample Program Two is supposedly more "powerful, flexible, and user-oriented" than the other sample program.

5. Review the activities involved in preparing and executing a COBOL program.

6. Write a simple COBOL program similar to Sample Program One which will compute and print the average (arithmetic mean) of the scores received on an exam by an undetermined number of students in a class.

7. Write a simple COBOL program similar to Sample Program Two which will perform the following tasks:

 a. Computes the regular pay, overtime pay, and total gross pay of an undetermined number of hourly paid employees.

 b. Produces a report which shows the following information for each employee: (1) name, (2) social security number, (3) regular hours worked (40 or less), (4) overtime hours worked (excess over 40 hours), (5) regular pay, (6) overtime pay, and (7) total gross pay.

 c. Computes and prints (1) the grand total of gross pay for all employees, (2) the average gross pay earned, and (3) tallies the number of employees that *did* and *did not* work overtime.

COBOL ACKNOWLEDGMENT

COBOL is an industry language and is not the property of any company or group of companies or any organization or group of organizations.

No warranty, expressed or implied, is made by any contributor or by the COBOL Committee as to the accuracy and functioning of the programming system and language. Moreover, no responsibility is assumed by any contributor, or by the committee, in connection therewith.

Procedures have been established for the maintenance of COBOL. Inquiries concerning the procedures for proposing changes should be directed to the executive committee of the Conference on Data Systems Languages.

The authors and copyright holders of the copyrighted material used herein FLOW-MATIC (Trademark of Sperry Rand Corporation); *Programming for the Univac (R) I and II. Data Automation Systems,* copyrighted 1958, 1959, by Sperry Rand Corporation; *IBM Commercial Translator,* Form No. F28–8013, copyrighted 1959 by IBM; *FACT,* DSI 27A5260–2760, copyrighted 1960 by Minneapolis-Honeywell, have specifically authorized the use of this material in whole or in part, in the COBOL specifications. Such authorization extends to the reproduction and use of COBOL specifications in programming manuals or similar publications.

Chapter Outline

Purpose of the Chapter

Introduction

Fundamental Vocabulary and Rules of BASIC
Arithmetic Statements: Constants, Variables, The LET
Statement, Priority of Arithmetic Operations,
Mathematical Functions
Input/output Statements: The READ Statement, The DATA
Statement, The INPUT Statement, The PRINT Statement
Control Statements: The GO TO Statement, The IF . . .
THEN Statement, The FOR and NEXT Statements,
The END Statement
Other Statements and Rules: The REM Statement, The
RESTORE Statement, The GO SUB and RETURN
Statements, The DIM Statement, Arrays and Subscripted
Variables, The STOP Statement, Statement Numbers

Sample BASIC Programs
Sample Program One, Sample Program Two, Sample
Program Three, Analysis of the Program

Preparing and Using BASIC Programs
Program Coding, Batch Processing, Real-Time
Processing: Activating the Terminal, Getting Ready,
Program Coding, Debugging and Execution

Key Terms and Concepts

Assignments

17

Fundamentals of
BASIC Programming

Purpose of the Chapter

To promote a fundamental understanding of BASIC programming by:

1. Reviewing the fundamental vocabulary and rules of BASIC,
2. Analyzing several BASIC programs,
3. Writing simple programs in BASIC.

INTRODUCTION

BASIC is a widely used programming language for time-sharing applications and interactive programming. As we mentioned in Chapter Six, BASIC (Beginner's All Purpose Symbolic Instruction Code) was developed in the early 1960s at Dartmouth College as a simple easily learned langauge that would allow students to engage in interactive (conversational) computing utilizing a time-sharing computer system. BASIC resembles a shortened and simplified version of FORTRAN. With only a few hours of instruction, a computer user can solve small problems by "conversing" with a computer utilizing a time-sharing terminal. BASIC has proven so easy to learn and utilize that it has quickly become a widely used time-sharing language.

Several versions of BASIC have been developed, including a batch processing version developed at the University of Washington. Such "extensions" of BASIC have transformed it into a more powerful language which can handle a wide variety of data processing assignments utilizing either batch processing or real-time processing systems.

The extensions of BASIC have not been standardized and differences exist in the BASIC compilers developed by many computer manufacturers and large computer users. However, the specifications for the most essential and widely used parts of BASIC (sometimes called "Basic" BASIC) are fairly well-standardized. Versions with more advanced features (frequently called "Extended" BASIC) are more likely to contain differences in specifications and usage.

In this chapter we will concentrate on the fundamentals of BASIC and will not attempt to cover the advanced features of Extended BASIC. This should enable us to quickly learn to write several simple BASIC programs which can be run on a wide variety of computer systems. *This kind of programming knowledge is sufficient for most computer users.* Persons wishing to become professional programmers should build on this foundation by additional study and practice utilizing programming texts or manuals that provide an in-depth coverage of the advanced features and statements of Extended BASIC.

We can begin our study of BASIC by analyzing it as we would any language, that is by analyzing its "vocabulary" and its "grammar." BASIC has a small vocabulary of words and symbols and a simple grammar of rules for writing computer instructions. It is essential that we learn the fundamental vocabulary and grammatical rules of BASIC if we wish the computer to properly accomplish specific data processing tasks. Therefore, in this chapter we will organize our study of BASIC in the manner shown below.

1. *Fundamental vocabulary and rules of BASIC.* We first take a brief look at the basic words and symbols utilized in BASIC programming and summarize the rules for writing BASIC statements.
2. *Sample BASIC programs.* Several examples of simple BASIC programs are presented and discussed.
3. *Preparing and using BASIC programs.* Instructions on the mechanics of writing and processing BASIC programs are presented.
4. *BASIC programming assignments.* The only way to really learn a langauge is to use it. Therefore, you are asked to write several simple BASIC programs at the end of the chapter.

FUNDAMENTAL VOCABULARY AND RULES OF BASIC

A fundamental vocabulary of "key words and symbols" in the BASIC language is discussed in this section. This "limited instruction set" is sufficient for the purposes of this chapter. Like other high-level compiler langauges, BASIC has "reserved words" and symbols which are utilized to write computer instructions called "statements" that are translated by the BASIC compiler into machine-language instructions and executed by the computer.

There are three major categories of statements in fundamental versions of BASIC: (1) *arithmetic,* (2) *input/output,* and (3) *control* statements. We shall organize our fundamental vocabulary by grouping the key words and symbols into these three categories plus a fourth "other" category as outlined below.

1. *Arithmetic.* LET and PRINT.
2. *Input/Output.* READ, DATA, INPUT, and PRINT.
3. *Control.* GO TO, IF . . . THEN, FOR, NEXT, and END.
4. *Other.* REM, RESTORE, GO SUB, RETURN, DIM and STOP.

Figure 17–1 illustrates several types of statements in a simple BASIC program which accepts values of Y and Z as input and computes and prints the result X.

FIGURE 17–1

Types of Statements in an Actual BASIC Program

```
10 INPUT Y, Z          Input/Output Statement
20 LET X = Y + Z       Arithmetic Statement
30 PRINT X             Input/Output Statement
40 END                 Control Statement
```

The grammatical rules of BASIC are fewer and simpler than those of most other programming languages. It is, therefore, easy to write error-free programs in BASIC. However, if the rules of BASIC are not followed, clerical errors will result which will cause the computer to do one or more of the following:

1. Halt processing of the program.
2. Print diagnostic error messages.
3. Produce incorrect or invalid results.

We will confine our discussion in this chapter to fundamental rules of BASIC that are sufficient for the programs which we will illustrate and which you will be asked to write. We shall organize these fundamental rules into categories that are related to the four categories of BASIC statements. In order to make the task of programming easier for beginners, we will simplify our presentation by omitting some of the details concerning the forms and restrictions governing the use of some BASIC statements. Persons wishing to make full use

of all of the features of BASIC in their programming should consult
the many BASIC texts and manuals that are available.

Arithmetic Statements

Arithmetic statements specify the arithmetic operations which are to
be performed. This is usually accomplished through the use of the
reserved word LET followed by an equal sign and an arithmetic expression, such as the LET $X = Y + Z$ statement of the program in
Figure 17–1. Arithmetic expressions may also be contained in a
PRINT statement which we will discuss in the next section. The
mathematical symbols utilized to perform arithmetic operations are
shown below.

Symbol	*Operation*
+	Addition
−	Subtraction
*	Multiplication
/	Division
↑	Exponentiation

Before we discuss the form of arithmetic statements, let us briefly
review the rules for constants and variables in BASIC.

Constants. Constants are known quantities written in numerical
form. A minus sign identifies a negative constant. An unsigned constant is treated as positive; therefore, the use of a plus sign is optional.
Constants can be written in either the "integer" or "real" modes. An
integer is a number *without* a decimal point. (It is also called a "whole
number" or "fixed-point" number.) A *real number* is a number *with*
a decimal point. (It is also called a "floating-point" or "double precision" number.) Real numbers are usually written in decimal form
unless they exceed the maximum limit of the particular BASIC compiler being used. Then they are written in an exponent form (also
known as floating-point or double precision format.) This form uses
a real number in decimal form followed by the letter E and an integer
exponent. The exponent is the power of ten by which the real number
is to be multiplied. Examples of each of these modes are shown below.

Integer Constant:　　463

Real Constant
　　Decimal form:　　463. or 463.0
　　Exponent form:　　4.63E2

Most BASIC compilers accept integers and real numbers (decimal form) with up to seven digits. Real numbers in exponent form can usually range between 10^{-15} and 10^{15}. Many compilers accept numbers of much greater size.

Variables. A variable is an unknown quantity or a quantity that can possess varying values. Variables are identified by names which consist of a single alphabetic letter (*A, B, X,* etc.) or a single letter followed by a single numeric digit (*A2, B5, X9,* etc.). The acceptable range for the numeric values of variables is similar to that of constants.

The LET statement. The general form of the LET statement is:

$$\text{LET } v = e$$

The "*v*" is a variable name and "*e*" is an arithmetic expression. The equal sign is *not* a symbol of mathematical equality. The statement LET $v = e$ means that "*the variable v is assigned the value of the arithmetic expression e.*" Thus, LET statements in BASIC are frequently called "assignment" or "replacement" statements. Only a single variable name may be on the left of the equal sign, while the right-hand side must be an arithmetic expression that consists of one or more constants, variables, and appropriate symbols.

Example: LET X = Y + Z

Explanation: The current value of *X* is replaced by the result of adding *Y* and *Z*.

Example: LET X = 5

Explanation: Assign the value 5 to the variable *X*.

Example: LET X = X + 1

Explanation: Increase the current value of *X* by one.

Priority of arithmetic operations.

1. Arithmetic operations in a statement are executed from left to right according to the following order of priority (hierarchy):

> First priority   —exponentation
> Second priority—multiplication and division
> Third priority   —addition and subtraction

2. Parenthesis must be used in pairs and overrule the normal order of priority. Thus, operations in parenthesis are performed first. When

a statement contains parenthesis inside another parenthesis, the operations in the innermost parenthesis are executed first.

3. Examples:

The BASIC arithmetic statement:

LET X = Y + Z * A/B↑ 2 − C

is executed like the mathematical equation

$$X = Y + \left(\frac{ZA}{B^2}\right) - C$$

The BASIC arithmetic statement:

LET X = (Y+Z) * (A/B) ↑ 2 − C

is executed like the mathematical equation:

$$X = (Y + Z)(A/B)^2 - C$$

Mathematical functions.   Most BASIC compilers provide several mathematical functions for use in arithmetic statements. Some examples are square root (SQR), logarithmic (LOG), and trigonometric (SIN,COS) functions. An example of the use of such "built-in" functions in an arithmetic statement is shown below.

Example: LET X = SQR (Y + Z)

Explanation: $X = \sqrt{Y + Z}$

Input/Output Statements

Input/Output statements direct the computer to transfer data between the CPU and input/output terminals. Fundamental input/output words are READ, DATA, INPUT, and PRINT.

1. READ statements read the contents of specific input data fields from storage.
2. DATA statements provide the input data to be read by the READ statement.
3. INPUT statements accept input data directly from the terminal.
4. PRINT statements type output onto a terminal.

The READ statement. The general form of the READ statement is:

READ variable, variable, . . . variable

The READ statement includes a list of variable names separated by commas that are in the order they are to be read. These variable names are assigned (in order) to the next available input data values provided by the DATA statements of the program.

Example: READ A, B, C

Explanation: Read the values for the variables *A*, *B*, and *C* from the input data provided by the DATA statements of the program.

The DATA statement.   The general form of the DATA statement is:

DATA constant, constant, . . . constant

The DATA statement includes a list of constants separated by commas that are in the order they are to be read. DATA statements thus provide the input data values for the READ statements of a program.

Example: DATA 75, 42, 81

Explanation: Provides three values for the variables in READ statements.

The data provided by the DATA statements of a program is stored in a "stack," "string," or "block" in computer storage. Data is stored in the order specified by their DATA statement *line numbers* and position in a DATA statement. The first READ statement of a program thus reads as many data values from the stack as there are variable names in the statement. The next READ statement in the program will read the next available data values, and so on. If there are *more* data values in the data stack than READ statement variables, the excess constants will not be used. If there are *fewer* data values than READ statement variables, then the computer will indicate that it is "out of data" and will terminate the program.

DATA statements are usually placed near the end of a program (in front of the END statement) for the convenience of the programmer since this spotlights and documents the data being provided by the program. This also minimizes the renumbering of line numbers if new DATA statements have to be added to a program. Most compilers limit the number of input data values that can be provided by a single DATA statement. A maximum of nine constants in one DATA statement is allowed by many compilers. Therefore, several DATA statements may be necessary for a program which requires a lot of data.

The INPUT statement.   The general form of the INPUT statement is:

INPUT variable, variable, . . . variable

The INPUT statement includes a list of variable names which are assigned to input data values to be provided by the user of the program via the terminal, rather than through the use of DATA statements. When the INPUT statement is executed, the computer usually types a question mark character ? on the terminal and waits for the input of data specified in the INPUT statement. The user then types in appropriate values (separated by commas) and depresses the RETURN key of the terminal. The computer will then continue with the execution of the program.

For example, the statement:

INPUT A, B, C

will cause the computer to print ? and wait for the user to type in values for A, B, and C, such as:

? 75, 42, 81

The PRINT statement.   The general form of the PRINT statement is:

PRINT list

The "list" of a PRINT statement can be:

1. A list of variables. This will cause the printing of the current values of the variables. For example:

PRINT A, B, C

2. A list of constants. This will cause the printing of one or more constants. For example:

PRINT 5, 10, 15

3. One or more mathematical expressions. This will cause the printing of the results of the expressions. For example:

PRINT X = Y + Z, A = B + C

4. Nonnumeric literals. This provides headings and labels for output. For example:

PRINT "THE ANSWER IS"

5. Left blank. This results in the skipping of a line (the printing of a blank line). For example:

PRINT

Many BASIC compilers severely limit the format of output. A print line on most terminals is divided into five "zones" of fifteen spaces each. The output of most PRINT statements is thus printed five to a line in the order specified by the statement. Printing starts in the leftmost zones and continues to the rightmost zones. If the PRINT statement has less than five output values, the rightmost zones will be left blank. If the PRINT statement has more than five output values, the excess values are printed on succeeding lines.

A *comma* in the PRINT statement causes a move to the next print zone. However, when a comma is the last character of a PRINT statement, it will cause the next PRINT statement to continue typing on the same print line. Many BASIC compilers provide for "packing" the print line by using *semicolons* instead of commas in the PRINT statements. The use of semicolons to separate output values in a PRINT statement will "override" the normal five-zone format. Output values will be printed in zones that may vary from six spaces to 12 spaces in width, depending on the size of the output data and the compiler used.

The format of numeric output values is also determined by the BASIC compiler. For example, a maximum of six significant digits are printed in many versions of BASIC. If a number is larger than six significant digits, it is automatically printed in exponent form. Most compilers do not print a decimal for a whole number and omit the "trailing zeros" of numbers that include a decimal.

Control Statements

Control statements control the order in which a program is executed, perform comparisons and test conditions, change the sequence of a program through a branching process, or stop a program. Fundamental control words are GO TO, IF . . . THEN, FOR, NEXT, and END.

1. GO TO and IF . . . THEN statements alter the sequential execution of program statements by transferring control to another statement.
2. FOR statements command the computer to repeatedly execute a series of statements (a "program loop") that are part of the computer program.
3. NEXT statements are used to end program loops formed by the FOR statement.
4. An END statement is the last statement of a BASIC program and informs the compiler that the program is completed.

The GO TO statement.   The general form of the GO TO statement is:

$$\text{GO TO } n$$

where *n* is a statement number which will be executed next. The GO TO statement (frequently written as GOTO) transfers control *"unconditionally"* to a statement other than the next sequential statement.

Example: GO TO 45

Explanation: Execute statement 45 next.

The IF . . . THEN statement.   The general form of the IF . . . THEN statement is:

$$\text{IF} \begin{Bmatrix} \text{variable} \\ \text{expression} \end{Bmatrix} \text{relation} \begin{Bmatrix} \text{variable} \\ \text{numeric literal} \\ \text{expression} \end{Bmatrix} \text{THEN } n$$

The IF . . . THEN statement is a *"conditional"* transfer of control because control is transferred only if a condition is satisfied. In the general form, *n* is the statement number of the statement that will be executed next if a specific condition is satisfied, i.e., is *true. If not,* that is, if *false,* the computer will execute the next sequential statement.

The *condition* specified consists of a comparison between a variable or expression and another variable, numeric literal, or expression utilizing the "relational symbols" outlined below.

$=$	Equal to
$<$	Less than
$>$	Greater than
$<>$	Not equal to
$<=$	Less than or equal to
$>=$	Greater than or equal to

Example: IF A $>=$ (B $+$ 100) THEN 45

Explanation: If the variable *A* is greater than or equal to the expression (*B* $+$ 100) execute statement 45 next. If not, execute the next sequential statement.

The FOR and NEXT statements.   The FOR and NEXT statements are utilized together to form a *"program loop."* The FOR statement is used at the beginning of the loop to specify the conditions of the loop. The NEXT statement is the last statement of such a program loop. The general form of the FOR statement is:

$$\text{FOR i} = \text{j TO k STEP m}$$

1. The *"i"* is a variable name that represents the "counter" or "index" of the program loop.
2. The *"j"* is a numeric literal, variable, or expression that establishes the *initial value* of the loop counter.
3. The *"k"* is a numeric literal, variable, or expression that is the *maximum value* that the loop counter can attain.
4. The *"m"* is a numeric literal, variable, or expression that is the *incremental value* by which the counter is to be modified for each trip through the program loop. The STEP portion of the statement can be omitted if *m* has a value of 1.

Example: FOR A = 1 TO 100

Explanation: All statements following this FOR statement will be executed up to and including a NEXT A statement. This process will be repeated 100 times.

The initial value of *A* is set to one and is increased by an increment of one each time the program loop is executed until *A* reaches a value of 100. Then the computer "exits from the loop" and executes the statements that follow the NEXT A statement.

The general form of the NEXT statement is:

$$\text{NEXT i}$$

where *"i"* corresponds to the variable name utilized for the counter of a corresponding FOR statement.

Example: NEXT A

The END statement.   The general form of the END statement is:

$$\text{END}$$

It must be the last statement of a BASIC program and can appear only once in a program. It notifies the compiler that the program is completed and causes termination of the program.

Other Statements and Rules

A few other types of BASIC statements should be briefly described at this time since they are frequently utilized even in simple BASIC programs.

The REM statement. REM statements are not translated by the compiler or executed by the computer. They are merely remarks and comments of the programmer which help document the purpose of the program and only appear in the program listing.

Example: REM PAYROLL PROGRAM

The RESTORE statement. The general form of the RESTORE statement is:

RESTORE

RESTORE statements restart the use of the input data provided by DATA statements. A BASIC program will terminate if it runs out of data values when executing a READ statement. However, a RESTORE statement allows the computer to read the same data several times in a program. It directs the computer to start over at the top of the "data stack" on the next READ statement.

GO SUB and RETURN statements. The GO SUB statement transfers control of the program to a subroutine. Its general form is:

GO SUB n

where n is the statement number of the first statement of the subroutine. The subroutine is a group of statements which ends with a RETURN statement that is outside of the main flow of the program. The RETURN statement transfers control back to the main program statement which follows the GO SUB statement. The general form of the RETURN statement is:

RETURN

The DIM statement. The DIM statement is utilized in BASIC to specify the "dimensions" (rows and levels) of "arrays" of data items. It reserves the memory locations required to store each element in an array. DIM statements are usually the first statements of a BASIC program since a DIM statement must be made before any other statement can reference the array that it defines. The general form of the DIM statement is:

DIM (array dimensions)

The "array dimensions" is a list of the maximum number of rows and/or columns for each array specified by the DIM statement.

Example: DIM A(20), B(10,5)

Explanation: The dimensions of two arrays (named *A* and *B*) are specified and the computer is directed to reserve the memory locations required to store each item in the arrays. *A* is a single list of 20 items and *B* is a "matrix" of ten rows and five columns.

Arrays and subscripted variables. An "array" can be defined as an arrangement of items. A *list* of items is a "one-dimensional array." A *table* or "matrix" of items arranged in rows and columns is a "two-dimensional" array. The dimensions of an array are specified by stating the maximum number of rows and columns in the array. For example, array B in the DIM statement above is a *ten-by-five array* or *matrix* since it has ten rows and five columns. (Rows are mentioned first, then columns.) Any item in an array is identified by integer numbers called "subscripts" which indicate the position of the item in an array, i.e., the number of its row, and/or column. For example, an item in the *seventh row* and the *third column* of array B would be identified as $B_{7,3}$ in mathematical notation and B(7,3) in BASIC notation.

In BASIC an array is identified by a "subscripted variable" such as B(10,5). Only a single letter of the alphabet can be utilized as a variable name. Subscripts can be integer variables and expressions, as well as integer constants such as B(K,I). However, only integer constants can be used as subscripts in DIM statements.

Arrays in BASIC are not only defined in DIM statements but can be specified "automatically" by the BASIC compiler. The compiler will automatically reserve memory locations for ten data values when a variable with a single subscript is mentioned in a statement, such as: READ A(J). Space for 100 data values (ten-by-ten) is reserved when a variable with two subscripts is utilized in a statement, such as: READ B(K,L).

The STOP statement. The general form of the STOP statement is:

STOP

The STOP statement terminates a program. It is an optional statement that can appear several times in a program and has the same effect as a GO TO statement which transfers control to the END statement.

Statement numbers. In order to simplify our presentation of BASIC statements, we have not utilized statement numbers in our examples.

However, each BASIC statement must have a unique *"line number,"* which may have from one to five digits. The computer executes the statements in the order specified by the line numbers rather than in the order that the statements appear in the program. Statements are usually not numbered consecutively but are numbered in increasing order in increments of five or ten such as 10,20,30,40, etc. This facilitates inserting a new statement in the program without having to renumber the statements that are to follow the execution of the inserted statement. Thus, a statement which must be added to a program can be placed at the end of the program as long as its line number correctly indicates its position in the order of execution.

If two or more statements have the same statement number, only the last one in the program will be compiled and executed. Thus, one can correct or replace a statement in a program by writing a new statement with the same statement number later in the program. If a statement is too long to fit on one line, it cannot be continued on another line. Instead, the statement must be subdivided into two or more statements with unique line numbers.

At least one blank space should be left between a line number and the beginning of a statement. However, spaces in BASIC statements are utilized to improve readability and are ignored by the compiler, unless they are part of a "literal" and are enclosed in quotation marks.

SAMPLE BASIC PROGRAMS

No one expects a programmer (much less a beginning programmer) to remember all of the rules of BASIC. With practice, many of the rules become "second nature," but most programmers still have to refer occasionally to "language specification manuals" to assist their programming efforts. Even then, the presence of "bugs" in many programs when they are first written is evidence that a programmer may have inadvertently violated some of the rules of BASIC. Therefore, be sure to consult the BASIC rules in the previous section to assist you in correctly writing the programs that are assigned at the end of this chapter.

Sample Program One

Let us now analyze a few examples of BASIC programs before you "take the plunge" and attempt your first program. We will begin with the very simple problem of adding two quantities together and printing the result $(X = Y + Z)$ that we have used as an example several times in Chapters Five and Six. Refer back to Figure 17–1 for a BASIC program that can accomplish this simple task. Since that program utilizes an INPUT statement, the values of Y and Z we wish to add must be furnished by the user of the program through the keyboard of the terminal when the program is executed. The computer will type a question mark and wait for the data values of Y and Z to be typed in by the user. For example: ? 27,53. The computer then calculates and prints X (in this case it would have a value of 80) and terminates the program.

We could perform the same calculation by using the READ and DATA statements for input. Figure 17–2 illustrates a program where

FIGURE 17–2

Sample Program One

```
10 READ Y,Z
20 LET X = Y + Z
30 PRINT X
40 DATA 27,53
50 END
```

values for Y and Z are furnished by a DATA statement and read by a READ statement. As in the previous program, the value of Y is 27 and the value of Z is 53, so the value of X that would be calculated and printed when the program is run would be 80.

Sample Program Two

The second sample program modifies program one by adding the following tasks:

1. The program must be able to process an undetermined number of DATA values for Y and Z.
2. The computed values of X are to be accumulated in the computer as well as printed.
3. After all the DATA values are read, the total of all the X values and the average value (arithmetic mean) of X must be computed and printed.

Figure 17–3 illustrates the program and flowchart of program two. Let us briefly analyze the statements of this program.

The first statement is a REM statement which identifies the purpose of the program. *Statements 20 and 30* "clear" the contents of a

FIGURE 17–3

Program and Flowchart of Sample Program Two

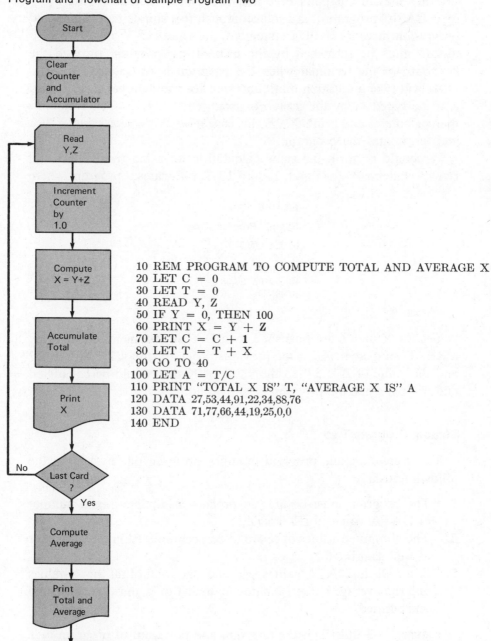

```
10 REM PROGRAM TO COMPUTE TOTAL AND AVERAGE X
20 LET C = 0
30 LET T = 0
40 READ Y, Z
50 IF Y = 0, THEN 100
60 PRINT X = Y + Z
70 LET C = C + 1
80 LET T = T + X
90 GO TO 40
100 LET A = T/C
110 PRINT "TOTAL X IS" T, "AVERAGE X IS" A
120 DATA 27,53,44,91,22,34,88,76
130 DATA 71,77,66,44,19,25,0,0
140 END
```

counter named C and an accumulator named T that we are reserving for later use. We accomplish this "initializing" routine by setting C and T to zero. *Statement 40* reads the first values of Y and Z provided by DATA *statements 120 and 130*.

Statement 50 tests for a Y value equal to zero. This is the "end-of-data" signal that we have devised which indicates that control should be transferred to *statement 100* for the computation of the average of X. This feature allows the program to process an undetermined amount of data each time it is used simply by adding more DATA statements. Of course, we must be sure that zero is not a possible value of Y before we use it as an end-of-data "flag."

Statement 60 is a PRINT statement that both computes and prints each value of X by adding Y and Z. *Statement 70* increments a "counter" by one each time a new value of X is calculated. This keeps track of the number of X values that are computed (C) and will be used to calculate an average value of X. *Statement 80* accumulates the total value of all X values (T).

Statement 90 instructs the computer to repeat the "program loop" by branching back to the READ statement and reading the next values of Y and Z that are in the "data stack." This process continues until an end-of-data condition is sensed when $Y = 0$. Then control is transferred out of the main program loop to *statement 100* which computes the average value of *X*. *Statement 110* then causes the printing of the total and average values of X and *statement 140* terminates the program.

Sample Program Three

Our final sample program demonstrates some features of BASIC that we have not utilized in the two previous programs. The program is based on the examples we used in Chapter Six to illustrate the use of flowcharts and decision tables. The "Salesmen Gross Pay" program performs the following tasks:

1. Computes the sales commissions and gross pay of each salesman of a business firm.
2. Produces a report which shows the salesman number, salary, commissions, and gross pay of each salesman.
3. Tallies the number of salesmen in each of the three following categories:
   a. Salesmen who have not made any sales.
   b. Salesmen who have not equaled their sales quota.
   c. Salesmen who have equaled or exceeded their sales quota.

4. Computes and prints the total amount of sales and the average value of sales made.

The program, flowchart, and output report of sample program three is shown in Figures 17–4, 17–5, and 17–6. Let us examine the important features of this program.

FIGURE 17–4

Sample Program Three

```
10 REM SALESMEN GROSS PAY PROGRAM
20 LET K1 = 0
30 LET K2 = 0
40 LET K3 = 0
50 LET T = 0.0
60 PRINT "SALESMEN GROSS PAY REPORT"
70 PRINT
80 PRINT "SALESMAN NO." "BASE PAY," "COMMISSION," "GROSS PAY"
90 FOR J = 1 TO 100
100 READ N, S, Q, B
110 IF S < 0.0 THEN 150
120 K1 = K1 + 1
130 C = 0.0
140 GO TO 210
150 IF S > = Q THEN 190
160 K2 = K2 + 1
170 C = S * 0.1
180 GO TO 210
190 K3 = K3 + 1
200 C = Q * 0.1 + (S − Q) * 0.2
210 G = B + C
220 T = T + S
230 PRINT
240 PRINT N, B, C, G
250 NEXT J
260 M = K1 + K2 + K3
270 A = T/M
280 PRINT
290 PRINT "TOTAL SALES:" T; "AVERAGE SALES:" A
300 PRINT "NO SALES:" K1; "BELOW QUOTA:" K2; "ABOVE QUOTA:" K3
310 DATA 001, 12500.00, 10000.00, 500.00
320 END
```

Analysis of the Program

Statements 20 through 50 initialize three counters and an accumulator, that is K1, K2, K3, and T. The term "initialize" refers to operations which reserve space in memory for counters and accumulators and clear them to zero. *Statements 60 through 80* cause the printing of the report title and column headings with appropriate spacing. *Statement 90* is a FOR statement which directs the operations of a

FIGURE 17–5

Flowchart of Sample Program Three

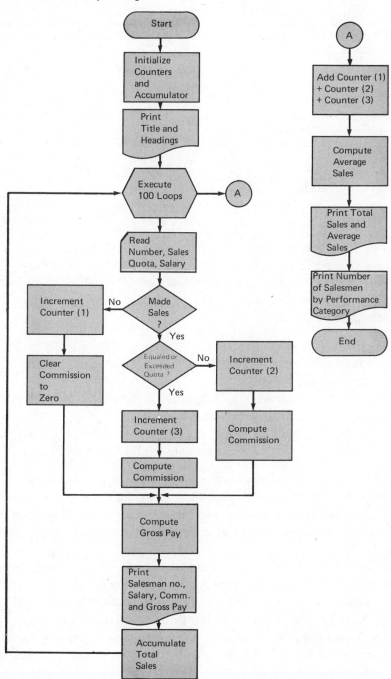

FIGURE 17–6

Output of Sample Program Three

SALESMAN GROSS PAY REPORT

SALESMAN NO.	BASE PAY	COMMISSION	GROSS PAY
001	500.00	1500.00	2000.00
↓	↓	↓	↓

TOTAL SALES = \$657500.00   AVERAGE SALES = \$9700.00

NO SALES: 2   BELOW QUOTA: 28   ABOVE QUOTA: 6

program loop that includes all *statements from 90 through 250.* This loop is to be repeated 100 times. *Statement 100* reads salesmen data provided by DATA statements like *statement 310,* which contains the employee number (N), sales (S), quota (Q), and base salary (B) of each salesman.

Statements 110 through 210:
1. Identify whether a salesman has had no sales, sales below quota, or sales above quota.
2. Increment counters (K1, K2, and K3) to tally the number of salesmen in each performance category.
3. Compute commissions (C) (except for no sales) and calculate gross pay (G) by adding base salary (B) to commissions.

Statement 220 accumulates the total value of all sales made (T). *Statements 230 and 240* space and print the employee number, salary, commission, and gross pay for each salesman. *Statement 250* is a NEXT statement that marks the last statement of the program loop.

Statement 260 is the first statement outside the program loop. It is executed following 100 trips through the loop. It computes the total number of salesmen whose data has been processed (M) by adding together the contents of the three counters. This sum is then used in *Statement 270* to compute the average sales per salesman.

Statements 280 and 290 space and print the amount of total sales (T) and average sales (A) along with appropriate descriptive headings. *Statement 300* prints the number of salesmen in each performance category along with descriptive headings. *Statement 310* is an example of the kind of DATA statements that would be used to provide data for each salesman. *Statement 320* terminates the program.

PREPARING AND USING BASIC PROGRAMS

In Chapter Six we showed that computer programming requires the activities of *programming analysis* and *program design* before *program coding* can be properly accomplished. *Checking, testing,* and *correcting* activities are then required to properly "debug" a newly written program. In this chapter, we have concentrated on the fundamentals of *program coding* in BASIC. However, developing effective BASIC programs requires the accomplishment of most of the programming activities mentioned in Chapter Six.

Before writing a BASIC program, you should take the time to analyze the data processing problem you are asked to program and attempt to design the processing procedures required for its solution. You should begin by developing a general program flowchart of your proposed solution. This should help you identify the input/output, logical, and computational steps required to carry out your data processing assignment. You should also determine the format of the input (usually in DATA statements) and the output (such as a printed report). Once these steps have been accomplished, program coding can begin.

Program Coding

Program coding in BASIC for short programs is usually accomplished at a computer terminal. Each line of a program is entered into the computer system via the keyboard of the terminal. When the complete program has been "typed in," the program is then executed and the output typed or displayed (if using a CRT device) on the terminal.

Program coding of longer programs is frequently accomplished by writing program statements on paper before typing them on a terminal. Since the rules for the form of BASIC statements are so simple, no special coding form is necessary, though they are available. Writing out the statements of lengthy programs helps the programmer follow the logic of his program flowchart and facilitates consideration of various alternative program statements without tying up a computer terminal. Writing program statements in advance is also the usual procedure for BASIC programs that are to be keypunched into punched cards for batch processing. (Paper tape prepared by an "off-line" device may also be used.) The written program statements facilitate the "desk checking" and keypunching processes.

Batch Processing

If the BASIC program statements have been keypunched into "program cards" for subsequent batch processing, they should be desk checked for possible errors. The program and "job control" cards can then be submitted to your computer center for compiling and execution. Most computer centers have different procedures for the use of the "job control cards" that are required for every program that is to be processed. Job control cards may be needed at the beginning and end of your program deck. The job control cards are required by the operating system or other control programs of the computer system. They identify your program as a BASIC program and specify other details required for compiling and execution. Consult your computer center for the proper format and arrangement of job control cards.

Your program may fail to execute on its first attempt. Use the program listing and the "diagnostic" listing of error statements to help you debug the program. Errors should be corrected by keypunching corrected BASIC statements into new program cards. The program should be resubmitted until it can be successfully compiled and executed.

Real-Time Processing

BASIC is most widely used as a time-sharing language that relies on a central computer to provide a "conversational computing" or "interactive processing" environment for many computer users at remote terminals. Such an environment allows a BASIC program to be coded, debugged, and executed in "real-time," frequently called *"interactive programming."* An example of conversational computing utilizing a "canned program" in BASIC was provided at the end of Chapter Six. However, in this chapter we wish to write our own BASIC programs utilizing a time-sharing terminal. Therefore, let us examine the procedures involved in such interactive programming.

The exact procedures for using a terminal for interactive programming depend on the particular computer system, BASIC compiler, and terminal that is utilized. However, the following example should illustrate the general procedures that are involved.

Activating the terminal. Some terminals are "activated" (connected on-line to the computer) by merely turning on a switch. Other terminals require that the terminal user "call" the computer by utilizing the procedures that follow.

1. Depress the TALK button on the data set and listen for the dial tone.
2. Dial the time-sharing service number and wait for a shrill tone.
3. Depress the DATA button and hang up the receiver.

Getting ready. Once the terminal has been activated, it will begin to type or display messages. The user will respond, using the keyboard of the terminal. Most systems require a "user code" or *identification code*. You should obtain one from your computer center. The computer may also ask what programming language you wish to use and whether you wish to use a previously written program or write a new one. Some systems also require that you assign a name to the program you wish to write. Then the computer will signal that it is ready for you to begin programming. In many systems the word READY is displayed to indicate this condition.

Figure 17–7 is an illustration of the terminal entries and responses

FIGURE 17–7

Getting Ready for BASIC Programming

PLEASE LOGON	(The computer wants you to "log on" to the system with your identification code.)
LOGON USER-JAO	(You key in your identification code. In this example, USER-JAO is the code used.)
LOGON ACCEPTED FROM LINE #021 AT 1310 ON 06/11/74	(Your LOGON is accepted from your terminal which is on data communications line 21 at the time and date shown.)
EXEC BASIC	(You ask the computer to execute the program you are going to write using the BASIC compiler since the program is written in the BASIC language.)
BASIC, NEW OR OLD	(The computer wants to know if you want to use a previously written program in BASIC or write a new one.)
NEW	(You want to write a new program.)
NEW PROGRAM NAME	(What is the name of the program you want to write asks the computer?)
X-CALC	(You key in the program name.)
READY	(The computer is ready for you to begin.)

of the *"getting ready"* stage. The user's entries and responses are underlined to distinguish them from the computer's messages and output. The author's comments are on the right in parentheses. It should be noted that most systems require that the RETURN key of the terminal be depressed each time the user has completed typing in an entry.

Program coding, debugging, and execution. The terminal user now begins to code his program by typing each line of his program on the keyboard of the terminal, depressing the RETURN key after each line is completed. This positions the typing element at the beginning of the next line and transmits the line of coding to the central computer where it is analyzed by the BASIC compiler. The computer may interrupt program coding to print *error messages* which indicate that the transmitted line of coding is in error:

For example:

INVALID VARIABLE NAME

When this occurs the programmer can correct the error by re-typing a corrected BASIC statement with the same line number as the erroneous statement. When the complete program has been coded, many programmers request a corrected listing of the program by using the system command: LIST. This results in a complete listing of the program which deletes statements that have been replaced and lists the program in line number order.

The program is now ready for execution. In most systems the system command RUN is keyed in to signal the computer to execute the program. The computer will then type or display the output of the program. Some systems will indicate that processing is complete by a message such as DONE or RUN COMPLETE. The user then usually indicates that he no longer wishes to use the BASIC compiler and/or the terminal by commands such as GOODBYE, BYE, or LOGOFF. Such "sign-off" commands will disconnect the terminal from the computer after the sign-off time and the amount of computer time that was consumed is typed or displayed.

Figure 17–8 illustrates the terminal output for sample program one. It consists of the listing and output of the program and appropriate system commands and messages.

FIGURE 17-8

Executing Sample Program One

LIST	(You ask for a listing of the program)
X-CALC	(The program name)
10 READ Y, Z 20 LET X = Y + Z 30 PRINT X 40 DATA 27, 53 50 END	(Sample Program One)
RUN	(You ask that the program be executed)
80	(The output-result of the program)
DONE	(Processing is completed)
BYE	(You end your use of the BASIC compiler.)
LOGOFF	(You terminate your conversation with the computer.)
LOGOFF AT 1315 ON 06/11/74 CPU TIME USED: 1.0017 SECONDS	(The computer notes the time you finished your conversation and the amount of CPU time you used.)

KEY TERMS AND CONCEPTS

Arithmetic statements, 554–556
Input/output statements, 556–559
Control statements, 559–561
Constant, 554
Integer, 554
Real number, 554
Variable, 555

Array, 563
Subscripted variable, 563
Counter, 567
End of data flag, 567
Initialize, 568
Batch processing in BASIC, 572
Interactive programming in BASIC, 572–575

ASSIGNMENTS

1. Review the key terms and concepts above and reread the appropriate chapter material to reenforce your understanding where necessary.
2. Briefly describe the purpose of the three fundamental types of BASIC statements and the functions of the statements in each category.
3. Review the sample BASIC programs of the chapter to deepen your understanding of the statements that are utilized in a complete BASIC program to accomplish a specific data processing assignment.
4. Review the activities involved in preparing and executing a BASIC program utilizing either batch processing or real-time processing.
5. Write a simple BASIC program similar to Sample Program One which performs one or more mathematical calculations.
6. Write a simple BASIC program similar to Sample Program Two which will compute and print the average (arithmetic mean) of the scores

received on an exam by an undetermined number of students in a class.

7. Write a simple BASIC program similar to Sample Program Three which will perform the following tasks:

    a. Computes the regular pay, overtime pay, and total gross pay of an undetermined number of hourly paid employees.

    b. Produces a report which shows the following information for each employee: (1) social security number, (2) regular pay, (3) overtime pay, and (4) total gross pay.

    c. Computes and prints: (1) the grand total of gross pay for all employees, (2) the average gross pay earned, and (3) tallies the number of employees that *did* and *did not* work overtime.

Chapter Outline

Purpose of the Chapter

Introduction to PL/1

Fundamentals of PL/1
Program Structure, Types of Statements

Sample PL/1 Program

Introduction to RPG

Fundamentals of RPG
Specifications Forms, Indicators, Program Generation

Sample RPG Program

Key Terms and Concepts

Assignments

18

Introduction to PL/1 and RPG

Purpose of the Chapter

To introduce computer users to PL/1 and RPG by reviewing their basic structure and characteristics and analyzing sample programs in each langauge.

INTRODUCTION TO PL/1

PL/1 (Programming Language 1) was developed by IBM in 1965 as a general purpose language which could be used by new generations of "general purpose" computers for both business and scientific applications. As we mentioned in Chapter Six, PL/1 was designed to include the best features of FORTRAN and COBOL as well as some of the capabilities of assembler languages and ALGOL. PL/1 is not as widely used as COBOL and FORTRAN, primarily because only a few software suppliers (besides IBM) have developed PL/1 software. However, growth in the use of PL/1 is expected to continue as more computer users adopt it as their primary programming language.

PL/1 has been criticized as being difficult to learn and inefficient to program, though even its critics agree it is a highly flexible general purpose language. PL/1 attains its flexibility by providing features which support business, scientific, real-time, and systems programming applications and by utilizing a "modular" design and a "default interpretation" capability. Thus, PL/1 is organized into modules (or "subsets") which are tailored to specific applications or levels of complexity similar to the levels and modules of ANSI COBOL.

The default interpretation feature simplifies PL/1 programming, since it allows a programmer to ignore the specifications of the PL/1 modules he is not using. The PL/1 compiler will automatically select the "default interpretation" for each specification that is required by a program unless it is specified by the programmer. Such "default specifications" are usually the specifications of modules that are utilized by programs that do not require the advanced features of PL/1.

The modular design and default interpretation features of PL/1 facilitate its use by former users of FORTRAN, COBOL, and ALGOL and by computer users with either simple or complex EDP requirements. PL/1 can also be utilized by both large and small computers, since PL/1 compilers are available in modules that are tailored to the various PL/1 language subsets.

Another feature of PL/1 that contributes to its flexibility and facilitates program coding is a *free-form format* for program coding. No special coding form is required, and more than one statement can be written on a line. Also, different "modes" of data (integer, real, etc.) can be mixed in an expression. The PL/1 compiler automatically performs the necessary conversions so that proper results are obtained. Finally, PL/1 allows free-form formatting of input and output (as in BASIC), though the format of the data can also be specified as in FORTRAN and COBOL.

FUNDAMENTALS OF PL/1

Program Structure

A PL/1 *"statement"* is defined as a string of characters terminated by a semicolon. A PL/1 program consists of several statements which are grouped into *"blocks"* or "groups." One or more blocks make up a *"procedure";* while one or more procedures make up a complete PL/1 *program*. The general form of a PL/1 program that consists of a single "main" procedure is shown below.

```
label:    PROCEDURE OPTIONS (MAIN);
          statement; statement; statement;
          statement; statement; statement;
          statement; statement; . . . ;
END label;
```

This general form illustrates the program structure of most simple PL/1 programs. The procedure *"label"* identifies the procedure; for example, the label "PAYROLL" might be used for a payroll calculation procedure. The PROCEDURE statements: PROCEDURE OPTIONS (MAIN), identifies a program as a simple *"main"* program, as opposed to a complex program with several procedures (subroutines) and other options. The END statement must be the last statement of a PL/1 program.

Statements in PL/1 resemble those in FORTRAN. However, *variable names* may be up to 31 characters in length and may utilize a "break" character (as in GROSS_PAY) instead of a hyphen. PL/1 also has two character sets of 48 and 60 characters, respectively. Both sets include the ten decimal digits and the 26 upper case letters of the alphabet. Other symbols include those shown in Figure 18–1.

FIGURE 18–1

Selected PL/1 Symbols

Arithmetic Operators

+	Addition, plus prefix
−	Subtraction, minus prefix
*	Multiplication
/	Division
**	Exponentiation

Comparison Operators

>	Greater than
> =	Greater than or equal to
=	Equal to
| =	Not equal to
< =	Less than or equal to
<	Less than

Special Characters

%	Percent
#	Number
$	Dollar
@	At cost
?	Question
—	Break
/*	Indicates beginning of a comment
*/	Indicates end of a comment

Note that those symbols include those used at the beginning and end of nonexecutable "comments," such as:

/* THIS IS A SAMPLE PL/1 PROGRAM*/

Types of Statements

Five basic categories of statements utilized in simple PL/1 programs are outlined below.

1. *Assignment* or *Arithmetic* statements assign values and per-

form arithmetic and logical operations. Unlike FORTRAN, several variables can appear on the left side of the statement. Examples are:

$$X = Y + Z$$
$$J, K, L = 0;$$
$$GROSS\_PAY = SALES + COMMISSIONS;$$

2.   *Input/output* statements transfer data between the CPU and input/output devices. When input/output is in the form of discrete data records in a file, the READ or WRITE statements are utilized. When input/output takes a "free-form" FORMAT in the form of a continuous "stream" of characters, the GET and PUT statements are utilized. Examples are:

READ FILE (PAY) INTO SALARY;
WRITE FILE (PAY) FROM GROSS_PAY;
GET LIST (Y, Z);
PUT LIST (X);

3.   *Control* statements control the execution sequence of the statements in a program. They perform comparisons and test conditions, transfer control within a program through a "branching" process, and direct the repetitive execution of statements by forming "program loops." Examples are:

GO TO PAYROLL;
IF HOURS > 40.0 THEN GO TO OVERTIME;
DO PAYROLL = 1 TO 100 BY 1;

4.   *Data Declaration* statements specify the "mode" and format of data variables. The mode of variables can be specified as fixed-point (FIXED) or floating-point (FLOAT). The format of the data is frequently specified by identifying the number of positions in a data field and the number of places to the right of the decimal point (if any). *DECLARE* statements also specify the number of rows and columns in "arrays" of data and the "levels" of data fields in a data record. Examples are:

DECLARE V FLOAT;
DECLARE (J, K, L) FIXED;
DECLARE (SALARY, COMMISSION, GROSS_PAY) FIXED
                                             DECIMAL (8, 2);
DECLARE A(5, 10), B(10, 10);
DECLARE 1 ITEM, 2 TYPE, 2 CLASS, 2 NUMBER;

The third example above specifies three fixed-point variables that have a field width of eight positions with two places after the decimal point. The fourth example statement specifies an array named "A" that consists of five rows and ten columns and an array named "B" that is a ten-by-ten matrix. The final statement specifies a data record named ITEM that consists of three data fields named TYPE, CLASS, and NUMBER.

5.   *Program Structure* statements identify and specify the types of program segments being utilized. We have previously described the PROCEDURE and END statements, which are two basic program structure statements of simple PL/1 programs. Also utilized in simple programs are labels which identify individual statements that will be referenced by other statements in the program. Examples are:

> PAYROLL: PROCEDURE OPTIONS (MAIN);
> START: GET LIST (Y, Z);
> END: PAYROLL;

SAMPLE PL/1 PROGRAM

We are now ready to analyze a simple PL/1 program that performs the calculation $(X = Y + Z)$ that we have used as an example several times in Chapters Five and Six. Figure 18–2 illustrates the program and flowchart of a simple PL/1 program that (1) reads an undetermined number of values of Y and Z from an input device (card reader, magnetic tape unit, etc.), (2) calculates $X = Y + Z$, and (3) writes each resulting sum of X on an output device (printer, magnetic tape unit, etc.). Let us closely examine the flowchart and statements of this program.

The *first line* of the program is a nonexecutable "comment" which helps document the purpose of the program. The *second line* of the program is a PROCEDURE statement that identifies the program as a "main" procedure. The *third line* is a GET statement that transfers a value of Y and a value of Z (utilizing a free-form "stream" input format) from an input device to the CPU. This statement is given the label START because it will be referenced by a later program statement.

The *fourth line* of the program is an IF . . . THEN statement which is utilized as a "end of data" test. In this program we will utilize a value of 999 for Y as a signal that there are no more values of Y and Z to read. If the computer senses a Y value of 999 (which must not be a valid Y value), the program will branch to the END statement and terminate.

The *fifth line* calculates $X = Y + Z$. The *sixth line* is a PUT

FIGURE 18–2

Sample PL/1 Program and Flowchart

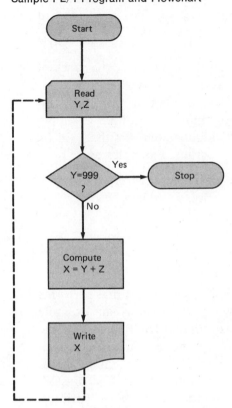

```
/* SAMPLE PL/1 PROGRAM */
X_CALC: PROCEDURE OPTIONS (MAIN);
START: GET LIST (Y, Z);
IF Y = 999 THEN GO TO END;
X = Y + Z;
PUT LIST (X);
GO TO START;
END: X_CALC;
```

statement that transfers the resulting value of X to an output device, utilizing a free-form "stream" output format. The *seventh line* is a GO TO statement which transfers control of the program back to the statement labeled START. Therefore, a "program loop" is formed which will repeat the execution of the statements on lines *three through seven* until the end-of-data signal is sensed. The program will then branch to the END statement on the *eighth line* and terminate.

The simple program we have just analyzed does not reveal the power, flexibility, and extensive capabilities of PL/1. However, it should help you gain a basic understanding of the general form of simple PL/1 programs. Persons who wish to learn how to use the many advanced features of PL/1 should consult the many PL/1 texts and manuals that are available.

INTRODUCTION TO RPG

RPG (Report Program Generator) is a simple "problem-oriented" language which was originally designed to generate programs that produced printed reports. However, several versions of RPG have been developed (such as RPG I and RPG II) which have made RPG a widely used language for report preparation, file maintenance, and other business data processing applications of small computer users. As we mentioned in Chapter Six, RPG cannot handle large complex applications which require a "procedure-oriented" language (such as COBOL, FORTRAN, and PL/1) and a large computer system. However, RPG can easily handle many types of straightforward business applications and can be used with small computer systems that do not have the storage capacity required by procedure-oriented languages.

Since it is *problem-oriented* rather than *procedure-oriented,* RPG does not require the use of statements which outline the procedure to be followed by the computer. Instead, a person using RPG fills out a few simple "specification sheets" which are used to describe (1) the form of the input data, (2) the input/output devices and data files to be used, (3) the format of output reports, and (4) the calculations that are required. Given these specifications, the RPG translator program generates a machine-language program that can perform the necessary data processing operations and produce required reports. RPG is comparatively easy to learn and simple to use, which adds to its popularity with small computer users. For example, RPG II is utilized for business data processing applications by thousands of small computers like the IBM System/3.

FUNDAMENTALS OF RPG

Specification Forms

Programming in RPG usually involves the use of at least three of the four specifications forms described below. See Figure 18–3.

1. File description specifications. This form defines the data files to be utilized. It identifies a file as input and/or output, specifies its basic characteristics, and assigns it to a particular input/output device.

2. Input specifications. This form specifies the format of data records contained in an input file. It identifies and describes the records in the file, and the data fields that make up each record.

FIGURE 18–3

RPG Specification Forms

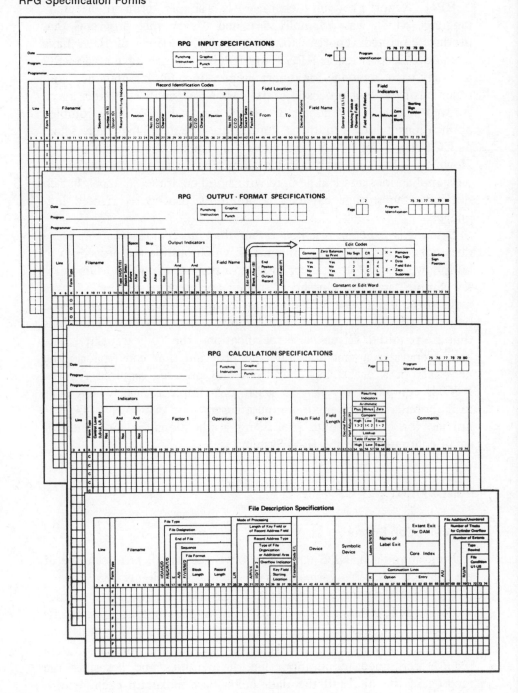

3. Output specifications. This form specifies the format of the output report. It identifies and describes output data records and their fields. It may also specify: (1) the use of titles and headings, (2) printer carriage control, (3) editing operations, and (4) the conditions which govern the writing of each type of output record.

4. Calculation specifications. This form is utilized whenever a program requires mathematical operations, such as addition, subtraction, multiplication, and division. It specifies the mathematical operations to be performed and identifies the types of data which are to be utilized in each calculation.

In addition to the specification forms described above, two other forms are sometimes used for specialized applications. The *"file extension specification"* form provides additional information required by the more complex methods of file organization utilized by direct access files. The *"line counter specification"* form is utilized for print line control when reports are written on magnetic tape or disc for subsequent printing by the printer of a computer system.

Indicators

RPG specification forms include columns which are utilized to specify various special "indicators." These indicators can be set "on" or "off" before or during the *execution* of a program by the occurrence of certain specific conditions. The indicators are tested during the running of a program to determine what operations must be performed. Examples of selected RPG indicators are summarized below.

1. *Resulting indicators* on the input specifications form might indicate which type of input records must be utilized in calculations or appear in an output report.
2. *Output indicators* on the output specifications form might indicate a first page or page overflow condition.
3. *Calculation indicators* on the calculation specifications form might indicate program control conditions caused by the results of completed calculations. Such indicators usually control program loops and branching based on specified variable parameters, control totals, and error conditions.

Program Generation

The completed specification forms represents the RPG "source program." The source program is then keypunched into punched cards utilizing the format of each specification sheet. Each line of a specifications form is punched into a single program card. The source program cards are then combined with appropriate "job control cards" and entered into the computer system.

The RPG compiler then translates the source program into an "object program" which consists of machine-language instructions that represent the data processing procedures required by the specifications forms. Thus, the RPG compiler has *"generated a program"* that can produce reports and carry out other data processing assignments when appropriate input data are entered into the computer system.

SAMPLE RPG PROGRAM

We will conclude our introductory analysis of RPG by analyzing a simple RPG program that performs a calculation similar to the $(X = Y + Z)$ that we have utilized as a simple example several times in the text. In order to emphasize the business data processing nature of RPG, let us convert this calculation to one that computes GROSS PAY as the sum of SALARY + COMMISSIONS. However, many RPG compilers limit the size of data names and file names to six characters. Therefore, we shall shorten our data names to comply with such restrictions.

Figure 18–4 illustrates the specifications forms of a simple RPG program that (1) reads an undetermined number of "salesman payroll cards" containing the name, salary, and commissions of each salesman, (2) calculates GRSPAY = SALARY + COMISN, and (3) prints the name and gross pay of each salesman. Let us closely examine the specification forms of this program.

The *file description specifications* form defines the input file of salesman payroll cards (SPAY) and the output print file of salesmen gross pay amounts (GPAY). Notice that SPAY is defined as an input file by an I in *column 15,* while GPAY is designated as an output file by an O in the same column. Other columns (1) designate SPAY as a primary file (P in *column 16*), (2) indicate that both files utilize fixed-length records (F in *column 19*), (3) specify block and record length (*columns 20–27*), and (4) indicate the input/ output devices to be used (*columns 40–52*).

The *input specifications* sheet specifies the data fields of the records in the input file SPAY. The AA in columns 15 and 16 indicate that sequence control is not applicable. The 99 in columns 19–20 will

FIGURE 18–4

Sample RPG Program

File Description Specification

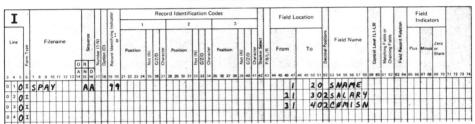

RPG   INPUT SPECIFICATIONS

RPG   CALCULATION SPECIFICATIONS

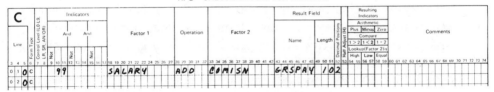

RPG   OUTPUT   SPECIFICATIONS

turn on "resulting indicator" 99 whenever an input card is read. This will control calculation and printing of output and will be explained in the next two paragraphs. Columns 44–58 define the names and card column positions of the input data fields. The name of each salesman (SNAME), his salary (SALARY) and his commission amount (COMISN) are the data fields that are defined.

The *calculation specifications* form specifies that factor one (SALARY) is to be added (ADD) to factor two (COMISN) to produce the result field (GRSPAY). This calculation is to be performed each time a card is read, as indicated by indicator 99 in columns 10–11. Since GRSPAY is a data field created as the result of a calculation, its field length and decimal positions are specified in columns 49–52.

The *output specifications* sheet specifies the form and position of the output data in the output print file (GPAY). Each line of output is a "detail record," (D in column 15) rather than a "header" (H) or a "total" (T) record. The 2 in column 18 specifies double-spacing. The 99 in columns 24–25 indicates that a line will be printed whenever an input record is read, i.e., when indicator 99 is turned on. Columns 32–43 specify the names and print line positions of the output records SNAME and GRSPAY. Columns 45–70 are utilized to specify output constants and editing. Thus, we specify the use of a dollar sign, zero suppression, and a decimal point for GRSPAY.

The sample RPG program results in a printed listing of the names and gross pay amounts of each salesman. It does not reveal the full capabilities of RPG. However, it should help you gain a basic understanding of the fundamentals of RPG programming. Consult the many RPG texts and manuals that are available if you wish to learn about the many other features of the RPG language.

KEY TERMS AND CONCEPTS

Modular design, 579
Default interpretation, 580
PL/1 procedure, 581
Assignment statements, 581
Input/Output statements, 582
Control statements, 582
Data declaration statements, 582
Program structure statements, 583

Problem-oriented language, 585
File description specifications, 585
Input specifications, 585
Output specifications, 587
Calculation specifications, 587
Indicators, 587
Program generation, 587–588

ASSIGNMENTS

1. Review the key terms and concepts above and reread the appropriate chapter material to reenforce your understanding where necessary.

2. Explain how modular design and default interpretation provide flexibility to the PL/1 language.

3. Briefly describe the purpose of the five basic types of PL/1 statements.

4. Explain how programming with a problem-oriented language like RPG differs from programming with procedure-oriented languages like FORTRAN, COBOL, or PL/1.

5. Briefly describe the purpose of the four main types of specification forms utilized in RPG programming.

6. Describe the purpose of indicators in RPG.

7. Explain the importance of the program generation phase of RPG programming.

8. Review the sample PL/1 and RPG programs of the chapter to deepen your understanding of the basic structure and statements required to accomplish simple data processing assignments.

Glossary for
Computer Users

The following extensive glossary includes terms which are fundamental to effective understanding and communication between *business computer users* and *computer professionals*. Most definitions used are consistent with those published by several official sources.[1] However, the form of such definitions is *not* designed to express exact standards for computer professionals, but to assist the beginning computer user in business.

---

[1] Two major standard glossaries are:

1. American National Standards Institute, *American National Standard Vocabulary for Information Processing,* USA Standard X3.12–1970 (New York, 1970).
2. International Federation for Information Processing, Ian Gould, Editor, *IFIP Guide to Concepts and Terms in Data Processing* (Amsterdam: North Holland Publishing Company, 1971).

Glossary For Computer Users

Absolute Address. An address that is permanently assigned by the computer designer to a particular physical storage location.

Absolute Coding. Coding that uses machine instructions and absolute addresses.

Access Time. The time interval between the instant that the CPU requests a transfer of data to or from a storage device and the instant such an operation is completed.

Accounting Machine. In punched card data processing, an electromechanical machine which accepts data from punched cards, processes the data through arithmetic and logical operations, and prints various accounting reports and documents.

Accumulator. A register in which the results of arithmetic or logic operations are formed.

Acoustic Coupler. A modem which converts digital data into a sequence of tones which are transmitted by a conventional telephone hand set to a receiving modem which transforms the data back to digital form.

Adaptive System. An "open cybernetic system" which possesses the feedback-control characteristic of cybernetic systems but also interchanges input and output and receives feedback from the environment. Adaptive systems therefore have the ability to adjust themselves to their environment, as well as to adjust themselves to an internally established goal.

Address. A name, number, or code that identifies a particular location in storage or any other data source or destination.

Address Modification. The process of altering the address portion of a machine instruction.

ADP. Automatic Data Processing. Data processing performed by electronic or electrical machines with a minimum of human assistance or intervention. The term is applied to both punched card data processing and electronic data processing.

ALGOL. ALGOrithmic Language. An international procedure-oriented language that is widely used in Europe. Like FORTRAN it was designed primarily for scientific-mathematical applications.

Algorithm. A set of well-defined rules or processes for the solution of a problem in a finite number of steps.

Alphanumeric. Pertaining to a character set that contains letters of the alphabet, numeric digits, and special characters such as punctuation marks. Also called "alphameric."

Analog Computer. A computer that operates on data by measuring changes in continuous physical variables, such as voltage, resistance, and rotation. Contrast with Digital Computer.

ANSCII. American National Standard Code for Information Interchange. A standard code used for information interchange among data processing systems, communication systems, and associated equipment. The coded character set consists of seven-bit coded characters (eight-bits including a parity check bit.)

ANSI. American National Standards Institute.

APL. A Programming Language. A mathematically-oriented language originated by Kenneth E. Iverson of IBM. Real-time and interactive versions of APL are being utilized in many time-sharing systems.

Arithmetic-Logic Unit. (ALU). The unit of a computing system that contains the circuits that perform arithmetic and logical operations.

Array. An arrangement of elements in one or more dimensions.

Assemble. To translate a symbolic language program into a machine language program by substituting absolute operation codes for symbolic operation codes and absolute or relocatable addresses for symbolic addresses.

Assembler. A computer program that assembles.

Associative Storage. A storage device in which storage locations are identified by their contents, not by names or positions.

Asynchronous Computer. A computer in which each operation starts as a result of a signal generated by the completion of the previous operation or by the availability of the parts of the computer required for the next operation. Contrast with Synchronous Computer.

Audio-response Unit. An output device of a computer system whose output consists of the spoken word.

Audit Trail. The presence of data processing media and procedures which allow a transaction to be traced through all stages of data processing, beginning with its appearance on a source document and ending with its transformation into information on a final output document.

Automation. The automatic transfer and positioning of work by machines or the automatic operation and control of a work process by machines, i.e., without significant human intervention or operation.

Auxiliary Operation. An off-line operation performed by equipment not under control of the central processing unit.

Auxiliary Storage. Storage that supplements the primary storage of the computer. Same as Secondary Storage.

Background Processing. The automatic execution of lower priority computer programs when higher priority programs are not using the resources of the computer system. Contrast with Foreground processing.

Backup. Standby equipment or procedures for use in the event of failure, damage, or overloading of normally used equipment and facilities.

Base Address. A given address from which an absolute address is derived by combination with a relative address.

BASIC. Beginners All-purpose Symbolic Instruction Code. A programming language developed at Dartmouth College which is widely utilized by time-sharing systems.

Batch Processing. A category of data processing in which data is accumulated into "batches" and processed periodically. Contrast with Real-time Processing.

Binary. Pertaining to a characteristic or property involving a selection, choice, or condition in which there are two possibilities, or pertaining to the number system which utilizes a base of two.

Bit. A contraction of "binary digit" which can have the value of either 0 or 1.

Block. A grouping of contiguous data records or other data elements which are handled as a unit.

Blocking. Combining several data records or other data elements into blocks in order to increase the efficiency of input, output, or storage operations.

Bootstrap. A technique in which the first few instructions of a program are sufficient to bring the rest of itself into the computer from an input device. Contrast with Initial Program Loader (IPL).

Branch. (1) A transfer of control from one instruction to another in a computer program that is not part of the normal sequential execution of the instructions of the program. (2) The set of instructions that are executed between two successive decision instructions.

Buffer. Temporary storage used to compensate for a difference in rate of flow of data or time of occurrence of events, when transmitting data from one device to another.

Bug. A mistake or malfunction.

Business Data Processing. Use of automatic data processing in accounting or management.

Business Information System. Information systems within a business organization that support one of the traditional "functions of business," such as marketing, finance, production, etc. Business information systems can be either operational or management information systems.

Business System.   The business firm as a system of interrelated components which must be controlled and coordinated toward the attainment of organizational goals such as profitability and social responsibility.

Byte.   A sequence of adjacent binary digits operated upon as a unit and usually shorter than a computer word. In many computer systems, a byte is a grouping of eight bits which can represent one alphabetic or special character or be "packed" with two decimal digits.

Calculator.   A data processing device suitable for performing arithmetical operations which requires frequent intervention by a human operator.

Call.   To transfer control to a subroutine.

Cathode Ray Tube. (CRT).   An electronic vacuum tube which displays the output of a computer system.

Central Processing Unit. (CPU).   The unit of a computer system that includes the circuits which control the interpretation and execution of instructions. In many computer systems, the CPU includes the arithmetic-logic unit, the control unit, and the primary storage unit. The CPU is also known as "the central processor" or the "main frame."

Chain.   A list of data records which are linked by means of pointers. Though the data records may be physically dispersed, each record contains an identifier by which the next record can be located.

Channel.   A path along which signals can be sent. More specifically, a small special purpose processor which controls the movement of data between the CPU and input/output devices.

Check Bit.   A binary check digit, for example, a parity bit.

Check Digit.   A digit in a data field which is utilized to check for errors or loss of characters in the data field as a result of data transfer operations.

Check Point.   A place in a program where a check, or a recording of data for restart purposes is performed.

Clock.   (1) A device that generates periodic signals utilized to control the timing of a synchronous computer. (2) A register whose content changes at regular intervals in such a way as to measure time.

COBOL. COmmon Business Oriented Language.   A business data processing language.

CODASYL. Conference of DAta SYstems Languages.   The group of representatives of users and computer manufacturers who developed and maintain the COBOL language.

Coding.   Developing the programming language instructions which direct a computer to perform a data processing assignment.

Collate.   To combine items from two or more ordered sets into one set having a specified order not necessarily the same as any of the original sets.

Compile. To translate a high-level programming language into a machine language program.

Compiler. A program that compiles.

Computer. A data processing device that can perform substantial computation, including numerous arithmetic or logic operations without intervention by a human operator during the processing.

Computer Application. The use of a computer to solve a specific problem or to accomplish a particular operation. For example, common business computer applications include sales order processing, inventory control, and payroll.

Computer Industry. The industry composed of firms which supply computer hardware, software, and EDP services.

Computer Professional. Persons whose occupation is related to the providing of computer services in computer-using organizations or in the computer industry. For example, systems analysts, programmers, computer operators, etc.

Computer Program. A series of instructions or statements, in a form acceptable to a computer, prepared in order to achieve a certain result.

Computer System. Computer hardware and software as a system of input, processing, output, storage, and control components. Thus, a computer system consists of input and output devices, primary and secondary storage devices, the central processing unit, and the control units within the CPU and other peripheral devices. Computer software can also be considered as a system of programs concerned with input/output, storage, processing, and control.

Computer User. Anyone who uses the output of a computer system.

Conditional Transfer. A transfer of control in the execution of a computer program that occurs if specified criteria are met.

Console. That part of a computer used for communication between the operator and the computer.

Control. (1) The systems component that evaluates "feedback" to determine whether the system is moving toward the achievement of its goal and then makes any necessary adjustments to the input and processing components of the system to insure that proper output is produced. (2) Sometimes synonymous with feedback-control. (3) A management function that involves observing and measuring organizational performance and environmental activities and modifying the plans and activities of the organization when necessary.

Control Card. A punched card that contains input data required for a specific application of a general routine. For example, "job control cards" are a series of cards coded in "job control language" (JCL) which direct an operating system to load and begin execution of a particular program.

Control Panel. A panel that contains manual controls or external wiring which governs some of the operations of a computer or other data processing machine.

Control Program. A program that assists in controlling the operations and managing the resources of a computer system. It is usually part of an "operating system."

Control Unit. A subunit of the central processing unit which controls and directs the operations of the entire computer system. The control unit retrieves computer instructions in proper sequence, interprets each instruction, and thus directs the other parts of the computer system in the implementation of a computer program.

Conversational Computing. A type of real-time processing involving frequent man-machine interaction. A dialogue occurs between a computer and a user, in which the computer directs questions and comments to the user in response to the questions, comments, and other input supplied by the user.

Counter. A device such as a register or storage location used to represent the number of occurrences of an event.

Cryogenics. The study and use of devices utilizing properties of materials near absolute zero in temperature.

Cybernetic System. A system that uses feedback and control components to achieve a self-monitoring and self-regulating capability.

Cybernetics. That branch of learning which brings together theories and studies on communication and control in living organisms and machines.

Cylinder. An imaginary vertical cylinder consisting of the vertical alignment of data tracks on each surface of magnetic disks which are accessed simultaneously by the read/write heads of a disk storage device.

Data. A representation of facts, concepts, or instructions in a formalized manner suitable for communication, interpretation, or processing by humans or machines.

Data Bank. (1) A comprehensive collection of libraries of data utilized by an organization. (2) A centralized common data base which supports several major information systems of an organization. Also known as a "common data base," a "central data base," and a "central information file."

Data Base. (1) The data and information upon which a system is "based," i.e., all of the data and information that could be used to support an organization or function, such as the "management data base," or the "marketing data base." (2) A "superfile" which consolidates and integrates data records formerly stored in several separate data files, i.e., a "personnel data base" might consolidate data formerly contained in several files such as the "payroll file," "employee skills file," "personnel action file," etc.

Data Communication. Pertaining to the transmitting of data over electronic communication links between a computer system and a number of terminals at some physical distance away from the computer.

Data Communication System. An electronic data processing system that combines the capabilities of the computer with high-speed electrical and electronic communications.

Data Management. Control program functions which provide access to data sets, enforce data storage conventions, and regulate the use of input/output devices.

Data Management System. (DMS). A generalized set of computer programs which control the creation, maintenance, and utilization of the data bases and data files of an organization. Also called "data base management system" (DBMS).

Data Medium. The material in or on which a specific physical variable may represent data.

Data Processing. The execution of a systematic sequence of operations performed upon data. Synonymous with information processing.

Data Processing System. A system which accepts data as input and processes it into information as output.

Debug. To detect, locate, and remove errors from a program or malfunctions from a computer.

Decision Table. A table of all contingencies that are to be considered in the description of a problem, together with the actions to be taken.

Diagnostics. Messages transmitted by a computer during language translation or program execution which pertain to the diagnosis or identification of errors in a program or malfunctions in equipment.

Digital Computer. A computer that operates on digital data by performing arithmetic and logical operations on the data. Contrast with Analog Computer.

Direct Access. (1). Pertaining to the process of obtaining data from, or placing data into, storage where the time required for such access is independent of the location of the data. (2) Pertaining to a storage device in which the access time is effectively independent of the location of the data. Synonymous with random access. Contrast with Serial Access.

Direct Access Storage Device. (DASD). A storage device that can directly access data to be stored or retrieved. For example, a magnetic disk unit.

Direct Address. An address that specifies the storage location of an operand.

Disk Pack.   A removable unit containing several magnetic disks which can be mounted on a magnetic disk storage unit.

Display.   A visual presentation of data.

Document.   A medium on which data has been recorded for human use, such as a report or invoice.

Documentation.   A collection of documents or information which describes a computer program, information system, or required data processing operations.

Double Precision.   Pertaining to the use of two computer words to represent a number.

Down Time.   The time interval during which a device is malfunctioning or inoperative.

Dump.   To copy the contents of all or part of a storage device, usually from an internal device onto an external storage device.

Duplex.   In communications, pertaining to a simultaneous two-way independent transmission in both directions.

Duplicate.   To copy so that the result remains in the same physical form as the source. For example, to make a new punched card with the same pattern of holes as an original punched card.

Dynamic Relocation.   The movement of part or all of an active computer program and data from one part or type of storage to another without interrupting the proper execution of the program. This technique is essential to advanced multiprogramming and virtual memory systems.

EBCDIC. Extended Binary Coded Decimal Interchange Code.   An eight-bit code that is widely used by current computers.

Echo Check.   A method of checking the accuracy of transmission of data in which the received data are returned to the sending device for comparison with the original data.

Edit.   To modify the form or format of data; for example, to insert or delete characters such as page numbers or decimal points.

Effective Address.   The address that is derived by applying indexing or indirect addressing rules to a specified address to form an address which is actually used to identify the current operand.

Electrical Accounting Machine. (EAM).   An electromechanical data processing machine which utilizes punched cards as a data medium and is controlled by an externally wired control panel. Also called a tabulator.

Electronic Data Processing. (EDP).   The use of electronic computers to process data automatically.

Emulation.   To imitate one system with another so that the imitating system accepts the same data, executes the same programs, and achieves the same results as the imitated system. Contrast with Simulation.

Executive Routine. A routine that controls the execution of other routines. Synonymous with supervisory routine.

Facilities Management. The use of an external service organization to operate and manage the electronic data processing facilities of an organization.

Feedback. (1) Information concerning the components and operations of a system. (2) The use of part of the output of a system as input to the system.

Feedback-Control. A systems characteristic that combines the functions of feedback and control. Information concerning the components and operations of a system (feedback) is evaluated to determine whether the system is moving toward the achievement of its goal, with any necessary adjustments being made to the system to insure that proper output is produced (control).

Field. A subdivision of a data record that consists of a grouping of characters which describe a particular category of data. For example, a "name field" or a "sales amount field." Sometimes also called an "item" or "word."

File. A collection of related data records treated as a unit. Sometimes called a "data set."

File Label. A unique name or code that identifies a file.

File Maintenance. The activity of keeping a file up to date by adding, changing, or deleting data.

File Processing. Utilizing a file for data processing activities such as file maintenance, information retrieval, or report generation.

Fixed-Length Record. A data record that always contains the same number of characters or fields. Contrast with Variable-Length Record.

Fixed-Point. Pertaining to a positional representation in which each number is represented by a single set of digits, the position of the radix point being fixed with respect to one end of the set, according to some convention. Contrast with Floating-Point.

Fixed Word-Length. Pertaining to a computer word or operand that always has the same number of bits or characters. Contrast with Variable Word Length.

Flag. Any of various types of indicators used for identification.

Flip-flop. A circuit or device containing active elements, capable of assuming either one of two states at a given time. Synonymous with toggle.

Floating-Point. Pertaining to a number representation system in which each number is represented by two sets of digits. One set represents the significant digits or fixed-point "base" of the number, while the other set of digits represents the "exponent" which indicates the precision of the radix point.

Flowchart. A graphical representation in which symbols are used to represent operations, data, flow, logic, equipment, etc. A "program flow-chart" illustrates the structure and sequence of operations of a program, while a "system flowchart" illustrates the components and flows of data processing or information systems.

Foreground Processing. The automatic execution of the computer programs that have been designed to preempt the use of the computing facilities. Usually a real-time program. Contrast with Background Processing.

Format. The arrangement of data.

FORTRAN. FORmula TRANslator. A high-level procedure-oriented programming language widely utilized to develop computer programs that perform mathematical computations for scientific, engineering, and selected business applications.

Function. A specific purpose of an entity or its characteristic action.

General Purpose Computer. A computer that is designed to handle a wide variety of problems. Contrast with Special Purpose Computer.

Generate. To produce a machine-language program by selecting from among various alternative subsets of coding the subset that embodies the most suitable methods for performing a specific data processing task based upon parameters supplied by a programmer or user. For example, a "report program generator" (RPG) will generate the machine-language program to produce a report based upon specifications supplied by a programmer.

Generator. A computer program that performs a generating function.

GIGO. A contraction of "Garbage In, Garbage Out," which emphasizes that data processing systems will produce erroneous and invalid output when provided with erroneous and invalid input data or instructions.

Graphic. Pertaining to symbolic input or output from a computer system, such as lines, curves, geometric shapes, etc.

Hard Copy. A data medium or data record that has a degree of permanence and that can be read by man or machine. Similar to Document.

Hardware. Physical equipment, as opposed to the computer program or method of use, such as mechanical, magnetic, electrical, or electronic devices. Contrast with Software.

Hash Total. The sum of the numbers in a data field which is not normally added such as account numbers or other identification numbers. It is utilized as a "control total," especially during input/output operations of batch processing systems.

Header Card. A card that contains information related to the data in cards that follow.

Header Label. A machine-readable record at the beginning of a file containing data for file identification and control.

Heuristic. Pertaining to exploratory methods of problem solving in which solutions are discovered by evaluation of the progress made toward the final result. It is an exploratory trial-and-error approach guided by rules-of-thumb. Contrast with Algorithmic.

Hexadecimal. Pertaining to the number system with a radix of sixteen. Synonymous with sexadecimal.

High-level Language. A programming language utilizing macro instructions or statements which is oriented toward the problem to be solved or the procedures to be used. Also called "higher-level language" and "compiler language." Contrast with Machine Language and Assembly Language.

Hollerith. Pertaining to a particular type of code or punched card utilizing 12 rows per column and usually 80 columns per card. Named after Herman Hollerith, who originated punched card data processing.

Hybrid Computer. A computer for data processing which utilizes both analog and digital representation of data.

Index. An ordered reference list of the contents of a file or document together with keys or reference notations for identification or location of those contents.

Indexing. The use of "index registers" for address modification in stored-program computers.

Index Register. A register whose contents may be added to or subtracted from the operand address prior to or during the execution of a computer instruction.

Index Sequential. A method of data organization in which records are organized in sequential order and also referenced by an index. When utilized with direct access file devices, it is known as "index sequential access method" or ISAM.

Information. (1) Data that has been transformed into a meaningful and useful form for specific human beings. (2) The meaning that a human assigns to data by means of the known conventions used in their representation.

Information Processing. Same as Data Processing.

Information Retrieval. The methods and procedures for recovering specific information from stored data.

Information System. A system which collects and processes data and disseminates information in an organization. An information system may utilize several kinds of data processing systems as subsystems in order to collect and process data and disseminate information.

Information Theory.   The branch of learning concerned with the likelihood of accurate transmission or communication of messages subject to transmission failure, distortion, and noise.

Initialize.   To set counters, switches, addresses, and variables to zero or other starting values at the beginning of or at prescribed points in a computer program.

Input.   Pertaining to a device, process, or channel involved in the insertion of data into a data processing system. Opposite of output.

Input/Output. (I/O).   Pertaining to either input or output, or both.

Input/Output Control System. (IOCS).   Programs which control the flow of data into and out of the computer system.

Inquiry.   A request for information from a computer system.

Installation.   (1) The process of installing new computer hardware or software. (2) A data processing facility such as a "computer installation."

Instruction.   A grouping of characters that specifies the computer operation to be performed and the values or locations of its operands.

Instruction Cycle.   The phase in the execution of a computer instruction during which the instruction is called from storage and the required circuitry to perform the instruction is readied.

Integer.   A whole number as opposed to a "real number" which has fractional parts.

Integrated Circuit.   A complex microelectronic circuit consisting of interconnected circuit elements which cannot be disassembled because they are placed on or within a "continuous substrate" such as a ceramic "chip."

Integrated Data Processing.   Data processing in which the coordination of data acquisition and all other stages of data processing is integrated into a coherent system.

Interactive Language.   A programming language designed to allow a programmer to communicate with the computer during the execution of the program.

Interactive Processing.   See Conversational Computing.

Interactive Program.   A computer program that permits data to be entered or the flow of the program to be changed during its execution.

Interactive Programming.   Developing a computer program in real-time with the assistance of a computer. A programmer can design, code, compile, test, debug, and develop alternatives for a new program utilizing a computer terminal and the real-time assistance of a computer system.

Interface. A shared boundary, such as the boundary between two systems. For example, the boundary between a computer and its peripheral devices.

Interpreter. A computer program that translates and executes each source language statement before translating and executing the next one.

Interrupt. A condition that causes an interruption in a data processing operation during which another data processing task is performed. At the conclusion of this new data processing assignment, control may be transferred back to the point where the original data processing operation was interrupted or to other tasks with a higher priority.

Item. Same as Field.

Iterative. Pertaining to the repeated execution of a series of steps.

Job. A specified group of tasks prescribed as a unit of work for a computer.

Job Control Cards. See Control Card.

Job Control Langauge. (JCL). A language for communicating with the operating system of a computer to identify a job and describe its requirements.

Justify. (1) To adjust the printing positions of characters toward the left or right-hand margins of a data field or page. (2) To shift the contents of a storage position so that the most or the least significant digit is at some specified position.

K. An abbreviation for the prefix "kilo," that is 1,000 in decimal notation. When referring to storage capacity it is equivalent to two to the tenth power, or 1,024 in decimal notation.

Key. One or more characters within an item of data that are used to identify it or control its use.

Keypunch. (1) A keyboard actuated device that punches holes in a card to represent data. Also called a card-punch. (2) The act of using a keypunch to record data in a punched card.

Label. One or more characters used to identify a statement or an item of data in a computer program or the contents of the data file.

Language. A set of representations, conventions, and rules used to convey information.

Library. A collection of related files or programs.

Library Routine. A proven routine that is maintained in a program library.

Line Printer. A device that prints all characters of a line as a unit. Contrast with Character Printer.

Linear Programming.   In operations research, a procedure for locating the maximum or minimum of a linear function of variables that are subject to linear constraints.

Linkage.   In programming, the coding that connects two separately coded routines.

List.   (1) An ordered set of items. (2) A method of data organization which uses indexes and pointers to allow for nonsequential retrieval.

List Processing.   A method of processing data in the form of lists.

Load.   In programming, to enter data into storage or working registers.

Location.   Any place in which data may be stored.

Log.   A record of the operations of a data processing system.

Logical Data Elements.   Data elements that are independent of the physical data media on which they are recorded. For example, portions of the same "logical record" may be located on several different "physical records" such as punched cards. Also, a collection of several logical records constitutes a "logical file" which may be stored in several different "physical file" devices.

Loop.   A sequence of instructions that is executed repeatedly until a terminal condition prevails.

Machine Instruction.   An instruction that a computer can recognize and execute.

Machine Language.   A language that is used directly by a computer.

Macro Instruction.   An instruction in a source language that is equivalent to a specified sequence of machine instructions.

Magnetic Card.   A card with a magnetic surface on which data can be stored.

Magnetic Core.   Minute doughnut-shaped rings composed of iron oxide and other materials that are strung on wires which provide electrical current that magnetizes the cores. Data is represented by the direction of the magnetic field of groups of cores. Widely utilized as the primary storage media in second and third generation computer systems.

Magnetic Disk.   A flat circular plate with a magnetic surface on which data can be stored by selective magnetization of portions of the flat surface.

Magnetic Drum.   A circular cylinder with a magnetic surface on which data can be stored by selective magnetization of portions of the curved surface.

Magnetic Ink.   An ink that contains particles of iron oxide which can be magnetized and detected by magnetic sensors.

Magnetic Ink Character Recognition. (MICR).   The machine recognition of characters printed with magnetic ink. Contrast with Optical Character Recognition.

Magnetic Tape.   A tape with a magnetic surface on which data can be stored by selective magnetization of portions of the surface.

Management Information System. (MIS).   An information system that provides the information required to support management decision-making.

Management System.   An integrated network of planning, organizing, staffing, directing and controlling activities that directs the operations of a business system.

Manual Data Processing.   (1) Data processing requiring continual human operation and intervention which utilizes simple data processing tools such as paper forms, pencils, filing cabinets, etc. (2) All data processing that is not automatic, even if it utilizes machines such as typewriters, adding machines, calculators, etc.

Mark-sensing.   The electrical sensing of manually recorded conductive marks on a nonconductive surface.

Mass Storage.   (1) Devices having a large storage capacity, such as magnetic disks or drums. (2) Secondary storage devices with extra large storage capacities (in the hundreds of millions of bytes) such as magnetic strip and card units.

Master File.   A data file containing relatively permanent information which is utilized as an authoritative reference and is usually updated periodically. Contrast with Transaction File.

Mathematical Model.   A mathematical representation of a process, device, or concept.

Matrix.   A two-dimensional rectangular array of quantities.

Mechanical Data Processing.   Data processing which utilizes mechanical, electrical, or electronic devices which require significant human operation and intervention. It utilizes such devices as typewriters, adding machines, calculators, copying machines, dictating equipment, etc.

Memory.   Same as Storage.

Merge.   To combine items from two or more similarly ordered sets into one set that is arranged in the same order.

Message.   An arbitrary amount of information whose beginning and end are defined or implied.

Microprogram.   A small set of elementary control instructions called "microinstructions" or "microcodes."

Microprogramming.   The use of special software (microprograms) to perform the functions of special hardware (electronic control circuitry). Microprograms stored in a read-only storage (ROS) module of the control unit interpret the machine-language instructions of a computer program and decode them into elementary microinstructions which are then executed. Thus, elementary microfunctions of the

CPU that had formally been executed by the "hard-wired" circuitry of the control unit are now executed by the microprograms of the ROS.

Minicomputer. A very small (for example, "desk-top size") electronic, digital, stored-program, general purpose computer.

Mnemonic. The use of symbols which are chosen to assist the human memory, which are typically abbreviations or contractions, such as "MPY" for multiply.

Modem. MOdulator-DEModulator. A device which converts the digital signals from input/output devices into appropriate frequencies at a transmission terminal and converts them back into digital signals at a receiving terminal.

Module. A unit of hardware or software that is discrete and identifiable and designed for use with other units.

Monitor. Software or hardware that observes, supervises, controls, or verifies the operations of a system.

Multiplex. To interleave or simultaneously transmit two or more messages on a single channel.

Multiplexor. A device which makes multiplex operations possible.

Multiprocessing. Pertaining to the simultaneous execution of two or more computer programs or sequences of instructions by a computer or computer network.

Multiprogramming. Pertaining to the concurrent execution of two or more programs by a computer by overlapping or interleaving their execution.

Nanosecond. One-billionth of a second.

Nest. To embed subroutines or data in other subroutines or data at a different hierarchical level such that the different levels of routines or data can be executed or accessed recursively.

Noise. (1) Random variations of one or more characteristics of any entity such as voltage, current, or data. (2) A random signal of known statistical properties of amplitude, distribution, and special density. (3) Any disturbance tending to interfere with the normal operation of a device or system.

Normalize. To multiply a variable or one or more quantities occurring in a calculation by a numerical coefficient in order to make an associated quantity assume a value that does not exceed desired parameters.

Numeral. A discrete representation of a number.

Numeric. Pertaining to numerals or to representation by means of numerals. Synonymous with numerical.

Numerical Analysis. The study of methods of obtaining useful quantitative solutions to problems that have been expressed mathematically, including the study of the errors and bounds on errors in obtaining such solutions.

Numerical Control.   Automatic control of a process performed by a device that makes use of all or part of numerical data generally introduced as the operation is in process.

Object Program.   A compiled or assembled program composed of executable machine instructions. Contrast with Source Program.

Octal.   Pertaining to the number representation system with a radix of eight.

Off-line.   Pertaining to equipment or devices not under control of the central processing unit.

On-line.   Pertaining to equipment or devices under control of the central processing unit.

Operand.   That which is operated upon. That part of a computer instruction which is identified by the address part of the instruction.

Operating System.   Software that controls the execution of computer programs and that may provide scheduling, debugging, input/output control, accounting, compilation, storage assignment, data management, and related services.

Operation.   A defined action, namely, the act of obtaining a result from one or more operands in accordance with rules that specify the result for any permissible combination of operands.

Operation Code.   A code that represents specific operations. Synonymous with instruction code.

Operational Information System.   An information system that collects processes and stores data generated by the operational systems of an organization and produces data and information for input into a management information system or for the control of an operational system.

Operational System.   A basic subsystem of the business system which constitutes its input, processing, and output components. Also called a physical system.

Operations Research. (OR).   The use of the scientific method to provide criteria for decisions concerning the actions of people, machines, and other resources in a system.

Optical Character Recognition. (OCR).   The machine identification of printed characters through the use of light sensitive devices.

Optical Scanner.   A device that optically scans printed or written data and generates their digital representations.

Output.   Pertaining to a device, process, or channel involved with the transfer of data or information out of a data processing system.

Overflow.   That portion of the result of an operation that exceeds the capacity of the intended unit of storage.

Overlapped Processing. Pertaining to the ability of a computer system to increase the utilization of its central processing unit by overlapping input/output and processing operations.

Overlay. The technique of repeatedly using the same blocks of internal storage during different stages of a program. When one routine is no longer needed in storage, another routine can replace all or part of it.

Pack. To compress data in a storage medium by taking advantage of known characteristics of the data in such a way that the original data can be recovered.

Page. A segment of a program or data, usually of fixed length, that has a fixed virtual address but can in fact reside in any region of the internal storage of the computer.

Paging. A process which automatically and continually transfers pages of programs and data between primary storage and direct access storage devices. It provides computers with advanced multiprogramming and virtual memory capabilities.

Parallel. Pertaining to the concurrent or simultaneous occurrence of two or more related activities in multiple devices or channels.

Parity Bit. A check bit appended to an array of binary digits to make the sum of all the binary digits, including the check bit, always odd or always even.

Parity Check. A check that tests whether the number of ones or zeros in an array of binary digits is odd or even.

Pass. One cycle of processing a body of data.

Patch. To modify a routine in a rough or expedient way.

Pattern Recognition. The identification of shapes, forms, or configurations by automatic means.

Peripheral Equipment. In a data processing system, any unit of equipment, distinct from the central processing unit, that may provide the system with outside communication.

PERT. Program Evaluation and Review Technique. A network analysis technique utilized to find the most efficient scheduling of time and resources when developing a complex project or product.

Physical Data Element. The physical data medium which contains one or more logical data elements. For example, a punched card is a single physical record which may contain several logical records.

Picosecond. One-trillionth of a second.

PL/1. (Programming Language 1). A procedure-oriented high-level general purpose programming language designed to combine the features of COBOL, FORTRAN, ALGOL, etc.

Plot. To map or diagram by connecting coordinate values.

Plugboard. A perforated control panel into which plugs are manually inserted to control the operation of equipment.

Pointer. A data item associated with an index, a record, or other set of data which contains the address of a related record.

Position. In a string, each location that may be occupied by a character or binary digit and maybe identified by a serial number.

Precision. The degree of discrimination with which a quantity is stated.

Privileged Instruction. A computer instruction whose use is restricted to the operating system of the computer and is not available for use in ordinary programs.

Problem-oriented Language. A programming language designed for the convenient expression of a given class of problems.

Procedure. The course of action taken for the solution of a problem.

Procedure-oriented Language. A programming language designed for the convenient expression of procedures used in the solution of a wide class of problems.

Process. A systematic sequence of operations to produce a specified result.

Process Control. The use of a computer to control an ongoing physical process such as industrial production processes.

Processor. A hardware device or software system capable of performing operations upon data.

Production Run. A computer run involving actual data as opposed to test data.

Program. (1) A series of actions proposed in order to achieve a certain result. (2) An ordered set of computer instructions which cause a computer to perform a particular process. (3) The act of developing a program.

Program Library. A collection of available computer programs and routines.

Programmed Check. A check procedure designed by the programmer and implemented specifically as part of his program.

Programmer. A person mainly involved in designing, writing, and testing computer programs.

Programming. The design, writing, and testing of a program.

Programming Language. A language used to prepare computer programs.

Punched Card. A card punched with a pattern of holes to represent data.

Punched Tape. A tape on which a pattern of holes or cuts is used to represent data.

Punch Position.   A defined location on a card or tape where a hole may be punched.

Queue.   A waiting line formed by items in a system waiting for service. To arrange in or form a queue.

Queuing Theory.   A form of probability theory concerned with queues.

Radix.   In positional representation, that integer by which the significance of the digit place must be multiplied to give the significance of the next higher digit place. For example, in decimal notation, the radix of each place is ten.

Random Access.   Same as Direct Access.

Random Data Organization.   A method of data organization in which logical data elements are distributed randomly on or within the physical data medium. For example, logical data records distributed randomly on the surfaces of a magnetic disk file.

Read.   To acquire or interpret data from a storage device, a data medium, or any other source.

Read-Only Storage. (ROS).   A storage device into which data cannot be written by the computer with which it is used. This condition can be temporary or permanent.

Real-time.   Pertaining to the performance of data processing during the actual time a process transpires in order that results of the data processing can be used in guiding the process.

Real-time Processing.   Data processing in which data is processed immediately rather than periodically. Contrast with Batch Processing.

Record.   A collection of related items or fields of data treated as a unit.

Register.   A device capable of storing a specified amount of data such as one word.

Relative Address.   The number that specifies the difference between the absolute address and the base address.

Remote Access.   Pertaining to communication with the data processing facility by one or more stations that are distant from that facility.

Reproduce.   To prepare a duplicate of stored data or information.

Rounding.   The process of deleting the least significant digits of a numeric value and adjusting the part that remains according to some rule.

Routine.   An ordered set of instructions that may have some general or frequent use.

RPG. Report Program Generator.   A problem-oriented language which utilizes a generator to construct programs that produce reports and perform other data processing tasks.

Run. A single continuous performance of a computer program or routine.

Scale. To adjust the representation of a quantity by a factor in order to bring its range within prescribed limits.

Scan. To examine sequentially, part by part.

Secondary Storage. Storage that supplements the primary storage of a computer. Synonymous with auxiliary storage.

Segment. (1) To divide a computer program into parts such that the program can be executed without the entire program being in internal storage at any one time. (2) Such a part of a computer program.

Self-adapting. Pertaining to the ability of a system to change its performance characteristics in response to its environment.

Sequence. An arrangement of items according to a specified set of rules. Contrast with Random.

Sequential Access. A sequential method of storing and retrieving data from a file. Contrast with Random Access.

Sequential Data Organization. Organizing logical data elements according to a prescribed sequence.

Serial. Pertaining to the sequential or consecutive occurrence of two or more related activities in a single device or channel.

Serial Access. Pertaining to the process of obtaining data from or placing data into storage, where the access time is dependent upon the location of the data most recently obtained or placed in storage. Contrast with Direct Access.

Service Program. A program that provides general support for the operation of a computer system, such as input/output, diagnostic, and other "utility" routines.

Set. (1) A collection. (2) To place a storage device into a specified state, usually other than that denoting zero or space character. Contrast with Clear.

Setup. To arrange and make ready the data or devices needed to solve a particular problem.

Setup Time. The time required to setup the devices, materials, and procedures required for a particular data processing application.

Signal. A time-dependent value attached to a physical phenomenon which conveys data.

Significant Digit. A digit that is needed for a certain purpose, particularly one that must be kept to preserve a specific accuracy or precision.

Sign Position. A position, normally located at one end of a numeral, that contains an indication of the algebraic sign of the number.

Simplex.   Pertaining to a communications link that is capable of transmitting data in only one direction. Contrast with Duplex.

Simulation.   The representation of certain features of the behavior of a physical or abstract system by the behavior of another system. Contrast with Emulation.

Skeletal Coding.   Sets of instructions in which some addresses and other parts remain undetermined. These addresses and other parts are usually determined by routines that are designed to modify them in accordance with given parameters.

Software.   A set of computer programs, procedures, and possibly associated documentation concerned with the operation of a data processing system. Contrast with Hardware.

Solid State.   Pertaining to devices whose operation depends on the control of electric or magnetic phenomenon in solids, such as transistors, diodes, etc.

Sort.   To segregate items into groups according to some definite rules.

Source Program.   A computer program written in a language that is an input to a translation process. Contrast with Object Program.

Special Character.   A graphic character that is neither a letter, a digit, nor a space character.

Special Purpose Computer.   A computer that is designed to handle a restricted class of problems. Contrast with General Purpose Computer.

Statement.   In computer programming, a meaningful expression or generalized instruction in a source program, particularly in high-level programming languages.

Storage.   Pertaining to a device into which data can be entered, in which they can be held, and from which they can be retrieved at a later time.

Storage Allocation.   The assignment of blocks of data to specified blocks of storage.

Storage Protection.   An arrangement for preventing access to storage for either reading, for writing, or both.

Store.   To enter or retain data in a storage device. Sometimes synonymous with storage device.

Stored Program Computer.   A computer controlled by internally stored instructions that can synthesize, store, and in some cases alter instructions as though they were data and that can subsequently execute these instructions.

String.   A linear sequence of entities such as characters or physical elements.

Subprogram.   A part of a larger program.

Subroutine.   A routine that can be part of another routine.

Subsystem. A system that is a component of a larger system.

Switch. A device or programming technique for making a selection.

Symbol. A representation of something by reason of relationship, association, or convention.

Symbolic Address. An address expressed in symbols convenient to the computer programmer.

Symbolic Coding. Coding that uses machine instructions with symbolic addresses.

Synchronous Computer. A computer in which each event, or the performance of any basic operation, is constrained to start on, and usually to keep in step with, signals from a clock. Contrast with Asynchronous Computer.

System. (1) A group of interrelated or interacting elements. (2) A group of interrelated components that seeks the attainment of a common goal by accepting inputs and producing outputs in an organized process. (3) An assembly of methods, procedures, or techniques united by regulated interaction to form an organized whole. (4) An organized collection of men, machines, and methods required to accomplish a set of specific functions.

Systems Analysis. (1) Analyzing in detail the components and requirements of a system. (2) Analyzing in detail the information needs of an organization, the characteristics and components of presently utilized information systems, and the requirements of proposed information systems.

Systems Development. (1) Conceiving, designing, and implementing a system. (2) Developing information systems by a process of investigation, analysis, design, programming, implementation, and maintenance.

Table. A collection of data in which each item is uniquely identified by a label, by its position relative to the other items, or by some other means.

Table Look-up. A procedure for obtaining the function value corresponding to an argument from a table of function values.

Tabulate. To form data into a table or to print totals.

Telecommunications. Pertaining to the transmission of signals over long distances. Similar to data communications.

Terminal. A point in a system or communication network at which data can either enter or leave. Also, an input/output device at such a point in a system.

Thin Film. A data medium consisting of an extremely thin layer of magnetic material which is deposited on plates or wires.

Throughput.   The total amount of useful work performed by a data processing system during a given period of time.

Time-sharing.   Providing computing services to many users simultaneously, while providing rapid responses to each user.

Track.   The portion of a moving storage medium, such as a drum, tape or disk, that is accessible to a given reading head position.

Transaction File.   A data file containing relatively transient data to be processed in combination with a master file. Synonymous with detail file.

Transducer.   A device for converting energy from one form to another.

Translator.   A device or computer program that transforms statements from one language to another, such as a compiler or assembler.

Transmit.   To send data from one location and to receive the data at another location.

Truncate.   (1) To terminate a computational process in accordance with certain rules. (2) To remove characters from the beginning or ending of a data element, especially digits at the beginning or ending of a numeric quantity. Contrast with Rounding.

Turnaround Time.   The elapsed time between submission of a job to a computing center and the return of the results.

Unconditional Transfer.   Pertaining to an unconditional departure from the normal sequence of execution of instructions in a computer program.

Unit Record.   Pertaining to a single physical record that contains a single logical record.

Update.   To incorporate into a master file the changes required to reflect the most current status of the records in the file.

Utility Program.   A standard set of routines which assists in the operation of a computer system by performing some frequently required process such as sorting, merging, etc.

Variable.   A quantity that can assume any of a given set of values.

Variable-Length Record.   Pertaining to data records which contain a variable number of characters or fields.

Variable Word Length.   Pertaining to a machine word or operand that may consist of a variable number of bits or characters. Contrast with fixed-word length.

Verify.   To determine whether a transcription of data or other operation has been accomplished accurately.

Virtual Machine.   Pertaining to the simulation of one type of computer system by another computer system.

Virtual Memory. The use of secondary storage devices as an extension of the primary storage of the computer, thus giving the "virtual" appearance of a larger "virtually unlimited" main memory than actually exists.

Word. (1) A character string or bit string considered as an entity. (2) An ordered set of characters handled as a unit by the computer.

Word Processing. Pertaining to the use of automated and centralized typing, addressing, dictating, copying, and filing systems that are utilized in modern offices.

Write. To record data on a data medium.

Zero Suppression. The elimination of nonsignificant zeros in a numeral.

Selected Bibliography

Selected Bibliography

Fundamentals of Computers and Data Processing

AWAD, ÉLIAS M. *Business Data Processing*. 3d ed. Englewood Cliffs, N.J.: Prentice-Hall, Inc., 1971.

BARTEE, THOMAS C. *Digital Computer Fundamentals*. 3d ed. New York: McGraw-Hill Book Co., 1972.

BERNSTEIN, JEREMY. *The Analytical Engine: Computers—Past, Present, and Future*. New York: Random House, Inc., 1963.

BOYES, R. L., SHIELDS, R. W., and GREENWELL, L. G. *Introduction to Electronic Computing: A Management Approach*. New York: John Wiley & Sons, Inc., 1971.

CHAPIN, NED. *Computers: A Systems Approach*. New York: Vannostrand Reinhold Co., 1971.

DAVIS, GORDON B. *Introduction to Electronic Computers*. 2d ed. New York: McGraw-Hill Book Co., 1971.

DIPPEL, GENE, and HOUSE, WILLIAM C. *Information Systems: Data Processing and Evaluation*. Glenview, Ill.: Scott, Foresman and Co., 1969.

EADIE, DONALD. *Modern Data Processors and Systems*. Englewood Cliffs, N.J.: Prentice-Hall, Inc., 1971.

ELLIOTT, C. ORVILLE and WASLEY, ROBERT S. *Business Information Processing Systems: An Introduction to Data Processing*. 4th ed. Homewood, Ill.: Richard D. Irwin, Inc., 1975.

FAVRET, ANDREW G. *Digital Computer Principles and Applications*. New York: Vannostrand Reinhold Co., 1972.

FORKNER, I. and McLEOD, R. *Computerized Business Systems*. New York: John Wiley & Sons, 1973.

Introduction to IBM Data Processing Systems: Student Text. 4th ed. (GC20–1684–3). White Plains, N.Y.: International Business Machines Corp., 1970.

LAURIE, EDWARD J. *Modern Computer Concepts*. Cincinnati: Southwestern Publishing Co., 1970.

MADER, CHRIS and HAGIN, ROBERT. *Information Systems: Technology, Economics, Applications.* Chicago: Science Research Associates, Inc., 1974.

SANDERS, DONALD H. *Computers in Business: An Introduction.* 2d ed. New York: McGraw-Hill Book Co., 1972.

THIERAUF, ROBERT J. *Data Processing for Business and Management.* New York: John Wiley & Sons, 1973.

VAZSONYI, ANDREW. *Introduction to Electronic Data Processing.* Homewood, Ill.: Richard D. Irwin, Inc., 1973.

WALKER, CARRIE M. and COTTERMAN, WILLIAM W. *An Introduction to Computer Science and Algorithmic Processes.* Boston: Allyn and Bacon, 1970.

Information Systems Development

BOCCHINO, WILLIAM A. *Management Information Systems: Tools and Techniques.* Englewood Cliffs, N.J.: Prentice-Hall, Inc., 1972.

BOOTH, GRAYCE M. *Functional Analysis of Information Processing.* New York: John Wiley & Sons, 1973.

BOUTELL, WAYNE S. *Computer-oriented Business Systems.* 2d ed. Englewood Cliffs, N.J.: Prentice-Hall, Inc., 1973.

BURCH, JR., JOHN G. and STRATER, JR., FELIX R. *Information Systems: Theory and Practice.* Santa Barbara, Calif.: Hamilton Publishing Co., 1974.

CHANDOR, ANTHONY, GRAHAM, JOHN, and WILLIAMSON, ROBIN. *Practical Systems Analysis.* New York: G. P. Putnam's Sons, 1970.

CLIFTON, D. H. *Systems Analysis for Business Data Processing.* Princeton: Auerbach Publishers, Inc., 1970.

COUGER, J. DANIEL, and KNAPP, ROBERT W. *System Analysis Techniques.* New York: John Wiley & Sons, 1974.

DANIELS, ALAN and YEATES, DONALD. *Systems Analysis.* Palo Alto: Science Research Associates, Inc., 1971.

DeMASI, RONALD J. *An Introduction to Business Systems Analysis.* Reading, Mass.: Addison-Wesley Publishing Co., 1969.

GLANS, T. B., GRAD, B., HOLSTEIN, D., MEYERS, W. E., and SCHMIDT, R. N. *Management Systems.* New York: Holt, Rinehart and Winston, Inc., 1968.

HARE, JR., VAN CORT. *Systems Analysis: A Diagnostic Approach.* New York: Harcourt Brace & World, Inc., 1967.

HEANY, DONALD F. *Development of Information Systems.* New York: The Ronald Press Co., 1968.

HONEYWELL INFORMATION SYSTEMS. *Business Information Systems Analysis & Design*. Minneapolis: Student Reference Guide, 1971.

HOPEMAN, RICHARD J. *Systems Analysis and Operations Management*. Columbus, O.: Charles E. Merrill Publishing Co., 1969.

JOSLIN, EDWARD O. ed. *Analysis, Design and Selection of Computer Systems*. Arlington, Va.: College Readings, Inc., 1971.

KINDRED, ALTON R. *Data Systems and Management: An Introduction to Systems Analysis and Design*. Englewood Cliffs, N.J.: Prentice-Hall, Inc., 1973.

KIRK, FRANK G. *Total System Development for Information Systems*. New York: John Wiley & Sons, 1973.

MCMILLAN, CLAUDE, and GONZALEZ, RICHARD F. *Systems Analysis: A Computer Approach to Decision Models*. Homewood, Ill.: Richard D. Irwin, Inc., 1973.

MARTIN, JAMES. *Design of Real-Time Computer Systems*. Englewood Cliffs, N.J.: Prentice-Hall, Inc., 1967.

MEADOW, CHARLES T. *The Analysis of Information Systems*. 2d ed. Los Angeles: Melville Publishing Co., 1973.

ROTHSTEIN, MICHAEL F. *Guide to the Design of Real-Time Systems*. New York: John Wiley & Sons, 1970.

ROSOVE, PERRY E. *Developing Computer-based Information Systems*. New York: John Wiley & Sons, 1967.

Applying Computers to Business and Management

ALEXANDER, M. J. *Information Systems Analysis: Theory and Applications*. Palo Alto: Science Research Associates, Inc., 1974.

BASSLER, RICHARD A. and JOSLIN, EDWARD O. *Applications of Computer Systems*. Arlington, Va.: College Readings, Inc., 1974.

BASSLER, RICHARD A. and JOSLIN, EDWARD O. *An Introduction to Computer Systems*. 2d ed. Arlington, Va.: College Readings, Inc., 1972.

BIRKLE, JOHN and YEARSLEY, RONALD B., eds. *Computer Applications in Management*. Princeton: Brandon Systems Press, 1970.

BOORE, WILLIAM F., and MURPHY, J. R. *The Computer Sampler: Management Perspectives on the Computer*. New York: McGraw-Hill Book Co., 1968.

BOWER, JAMES B. and WELKE, WILLIAM R. *Financial Information Systems: Selected Readings*. Boston: Houghton Mifflin Co., 1968.

DAVIS, GORDON B. *Management Information Systems: Conceptual Foundations, Structure, and Development*. New York: McGraw-Hill Book Co., 1974.

DEARDEN, JOHN. *Computers in Business Management.* Homewood, Ill.: Dow Jones-Irwin, Inc., 1966.

DEARDEN, JOHN and McFARLEN, F. WARREN. *Management Information Systems: Text and Cases.* Homewood, Ill.: Richard D. Irwin, Inc., 1966.

DEARDEN, JOHN, McFARLEN, F. WARREN, and ZANI, WILLIAM M. *Managing Computer-based Information Systems.* Homewood, Ill.: Richard D. Irwin, Inc., 1971.

DESMONDE, WILLIAM H. *Computers and Their Uses.* 2d ed. Englewood Cliffs, N.J.: Prentice-Hall, Inc., 1971.

ELIASON, ALLEN L. and KITTS, KENT D. *Business Computer Systems and Applications.* Chicago: Science Research Associates, Inc., 1974.

HARRISON, THOMAS. *Handbook of Industrial Control Computers.* New York: John Wiley & Sons, 1972.

HEAD, ROBERT V. *Manager's Guide to Management Information Systems.* Englewood Cliffs, N.J.: Prentice-Hall, Inc., 1972.

HODGE, BARTOW and HODGSON, ROBERT N. *Management and the Computer in Information and Control Systems.* New York: McGraw-Hill Book Co., 1969.

JOHNSON, RICHARD A., KAST, FREMONT, E. and ROSENZWEIG, JAMES E. *The Theory and Management of Systems.* 3d ed. New York: McGraw-Hill Book Co., 1973.

KANTER, JEROME. *Management Guide to Computer System Selection and Use.* Englewood Cliffs, N.J.: Prentice-Hall, Inc., 1970.

KANTER, JEROME. *Management-oriented Management Information Systems.* Englewood Cliffs, N.J.: Prentice-Hall, Inc., 1972.

KELLY, JOSEPH F. *Computerized Management Information Systems.* New York: The MacMillan Co., 1970.

KENNEVAN, WALTER J. and JOSLIN, EDWARD O. *Management and Computer Systems.* 2d ed. Arlington, Va.: College Readings, Inc., 1973.

LUCAS, JR., HENRY C. *Computer-based Information Systems in Organizations.* Chicago: Science Research Associates, Inc., 1973.

MOCKLER, ROBERT J. *Information Systems for Management.* Columbus, O.: Charles E. Merrill Publishing Co., 1974.

MURDICK, ROBERT G. and ROSS, JOEL E. *Information Systems for Modern Management.* Englewood Cliffs, N.J.: Prentice-Hall, Inc., 1971.

O'BRIEN, JAMES A. *The Impact of Computers on Banking.* Boston: Bankers Publishing Co., 1968.

O'BRIEN, JAMES A. *Managing and Marketing Bank Computer Services.* Boston: Warren, Gorham & Lamont, 1971.

O'BRIEN, JAMES J. *Management Information Systems: Concepts, Techniques and Applications.* New York: Van Nostrand, Reinhold Co., 1970.

PRINCE, THOMAS R. *Information Systems for Management Planning and Control.* 3d ed. Homewood, Ill.: Richard D. Irwin, Inc., 1975.

SMITH, SAMUEL V., BRIEN, RICHARD H. and STAFFORD, JAMES E. *Readings in Marketing Information Systems.* Boston: Houghton Mifflin Co., 1968.

WEISS, ERIC A., ed. *Computer Usage Applications.* New York: McGraw-Hill Book Co., 1970.

Managing the Computer in a Dynamic Environment

BRANDON, DICK H. *Management Planning for Data Processing.* Princeton: Brandon Systems Press, 1970.

BRANDON, DICK H. and GRAY, MAX. *Project Control Standards.* Princeton: Brandon Systems Press, 1970.

CANNING, RICHARD G. and SISSON, ROGER L. *The Management of Data Processing.* New York: John Wiley & Son, 1967.

FOY, NANCY S. *Computer Management: A Common Sense Approach.* Philadelphia: Auerbach Publishers, Inc., 1972.

HAMMING, RICHARD W. *Computers and Society.* New York: McGraw-Hill Book Co., 1972.

Organizing the Data Processing Activity. 2d ed. (GC20–1622–1) White Plains, N.Y.: International Business Machines Corp., 1973.

PYLYSHYN, ZENON W., ed. *Perspectives on the Computer Revolution.* Englewood Cliffs, N.J.: Prentice-Hall, Inc., 1970.

ROTHMAN, STANLEY and MOSMANN, CHARLES. *Computers and Society.* Chicago: Science Research Associates, Inc., 1972.

ROTHERY, BRIAN. *Installing and Managing a Computer.* New York: Brandon Systems Press, 1969.

SANDERS, DONALD H. *Computers and Management in a Changing Society.* 2d ed. New York: McGraw-Hill Book Co., 1974.

The State of the Computer Industry in the United States. Montvale, N.J.: American Federation of Information Processing Societies, 1973.

TAVISS, IRENE, ed. *The Computer Impact.* Englewood Cliffs, N.J.: Prentice-Hall, Inc., 1970.

Unlocking the Computer's Profit Potential. New York: McKinsey & Co., Inc., 1968.

WOFSEY, MARVIN M. *Management of ADP Systems.* Philadelphia: Auerbach Publishers, Inc., 1973.

Computer Programming Languages

BASIC

BARNETT, EUGENE H. *Programming Time-Shared Computers in BASIC.* New York: John Wiley & Sons, 1972.

DIEHR, GEORGE. *Business Programming with BASIC.* New York: John Wiley & Sons, 1972.

GROSS, JONATHAN L. and BRAINARD, WALTER S. *Fundamental Programming Concepts.* New York: Harper & Row, 1972.

HARE, JR., VAN CORT. *Introduction to Programming: A BASIC Approach.* New York: Harcourt, Brace, & World, Inc., 1970.

MURRILL, PAUL W. and SMITH, CECIL W. *BASIC Programming.* Scranton: International Textbook Co., 1971.

PEGELS, C. CARL. *BASIC: A Computer Programming Language with Business and Management Applications.* San Francisco: Holden-Day, 1973.

SHARPE, WILLIAM F. and JACOB, NANCY L. *BASIC: An Introduction to Computer Programming Using the BASIC Language.* rev. ed. New York: The Free Press, 1971.

COBOL

McCAMERON, FRITZ. *COBOL Logic and Programming.* 3d ed. Homewood, Ill.: Richard D. Irwin, Inc., 1974.

McCRACKEN, DANIEL D., and GARBASSI, UMBERTO. *A Guide to COBOL Programming.* 3d ed. New York: John Wiley & Sons, 1970.

MURACH, MIKE. *Standard COBOL.* Chicago: Science Research Associates, Inc., 1971.

MURRILL, PAUL W. and SMITH, CECIL L. *An Introduction to COBOL Programming.* Scranton: International Textbook Co., 1971.

SMITH, MARILYN Z. *Standard COBOL: A Problem-Solving Approach.* Boston: Houghton Mifflin Co., 1974.

DAVIS, GORDON B. and LITECKY, CHARLES R. *Elementary COBOL Programming: A Step by Step Approach.* New York: McGraw-Hill Book Co., 1971.

FORTRAN

ANTON, HECTOR, R. and BOUTELL, WAYNE S. *FORTRAN and Business Data Processing.* New York: McGraw-Hill Book Co., 1968.

COUGER, J. DANIEL, and SHANNON, LOREN E. *FORTRAN IV: A Programmed Instruction Approach* rev. ed. Homewood, Ill.: Richard D. Irwin, Inc., 1972.

KEROS, JOHN W. *Computers, FORTRAN IV, and Data Processing Applications.* Boston: Allyn & Bacon, Inc., 1972.

MAY, PHILIP T. *Programming Business Applications in FORTRAN IV*. Boston: Houghton Mifflin Co., 1973.

MALCOM, ROBERT E. and GOTTERER, MALCOM H. *Computers in Business: A FORTRAN Introduction*. Scranton: International Textbook Co., 1968.

McCRACKEN, DANIEL D. *A Simplified Guide to FORTRAN Programming*. New York: John Wiley & Sons, 1974.

NIELSEN, GORDON L. *FORTRAN Primer for Business and Economics*. Braintree, Mass.: D. H. Mark Publishing Co., 1968.

RAUN, DONALD L. *An Introduction to FORTRAN Computer Programming for Business Analysis*. Belmont, Calif.: Dickenson Publishing Co., 1968.

SASS, C. JOSEPH. *FORTRAN IV Programming and Applications*. San Francisco: Holden-Day, Inc., 1974.

SILVER, GERALD A. *Simplified FORTRAN IV Programming*. New York: Harcourt, Brace, Jovanovich, Inc., 1971.

TEAGUE, ROBERT. *Computing Problems for FORTRAN Solution*. San Francisco: Canfield Press, 1972.

VELDMAN, DONALD J. *FORTRAN Programming for the Behavioral Sciences*. New York: Holt, Rinehart & Winston, 1967.

PL/1 and RPG

ANGER, ARTHUR L. and others. *Computer Science: The PL/1 Language*. New York: John Wiley & Sons, 1972.

BRIGHTMAN, RICHARD W. and CLARK, JOHN R. *RPG I and RPG II Programming*. New York: The MacMillan Co., 1970.

DAVIDSON, MELVIN. *PL/1 Programming with PL/C*. Boston: Houghton Mifflin Co., 1973.

HUGHES, JOAN K. *PL/1 Programming*. New York: John Wiley & Sons, 1973.

SEEDS, HARICE L. *Programming RPG and RPG II*. New York: John Wiley & Sons, 1971.

VAZSONY, ANDREW. *Problem-Solving by Digital Computers with PL/1 Programming*. Englewood Cliffs, N.J.: Prentice-Hall, Inc., 1970.

IBM Application Manuals

(Selected data processing application manuals of the International Business Machines Corp., White Plains, New York.)

Accounts Payable. (GE20–8030–2)

Basic Accounting Concepts and Introduction to Punched Card Accounting Applications. (E20–8058)

Bank Cost Accounting and Profitability Analysis. (E20–0011–1)

Bank Investment Portfolio. (E20–0401–0)

IBM System/3: Card System Introduction. (C21–7505–0)

Computer Approach to Marketing Applications for Consumer Packaged Goods Manufacturers. (GE20–0351–0)

Consumer Goods Business Information System: Manufacturing. (G320–1258–0)

Consumer Goods Business Information System: Marketing. (G320–1259–0)

Consumer Goods Business Information System: Physical Distribution. (G320–1260–0)

IBM Financial Analysis Program. (E20–0002)

Guide to General Ledger. (E20–0323–0)

Guide to Inventory and Material Accounting. (E20–0321–0)

Guide to Order Writing, Billing, Inventory, Accounts Receivable, and Sales Analysis. (E20–0320–0)

Guide to Payroll. (E20–0322–0)

IBM 3650 Retail Store System: Introduction. (GA27–3075–0)

Life Insurance and Related Applications Using the IBM System/360 Model 20. (GK20–0485–0)

Management Information System for Retailers. (GE20–0186–0)

Management Reports in Today's Business. (G320–1129–1)

Personnel Data System. (E20–0193–1)

Retail Impact-Inventory Management Program and Control Techniques. Application Description. (GE20–0188–5)

Retail Store System: Merchandise Processing System Concepts. (GE20–0411–1)

The Production Information and Control System. (GE20–0280–2)

Recommended Periodicals

(Periodicals which cover the fields of computers, data processing, and information systems and are a vital source of information on current developments.)

Abstracts of Computer Literature. Burroughs Corp. Plant Library, 460 Sierra Madre Villa, Pasadena, Calif., 91109.
Bimonthly abstracts on various aspects of computing (free).

Automation-Data in State and Local Government. Michigan Dept. of Education, Bureau of Educational Services, Library Div., 735 E. Michigan Ave., Lansing, Mich., 48913.
Monthly review of published articles on EDP (free).

Communications of the ACM.   Assn. for Computing Machinery, 1130 Avenue of the Americas, New York, N.Y., 10036.
Monthly journal of technical articles on computers.

Computer Characteristics Quarterly.   Adams Associates, 128 The Great Road, Bedford, Mass., 01730.
Quarterly presentation of key characteristics on computers, peripheral devices, etc.

Computer Decisions.   Hayden Publishing Co., 50 Essex St., Rochelle Park, N.J., 07662.
Monthly data processing articles on general interest (free to educators in data processing and other qualified individuals).

Computer Digest.   North American Publishing Co., 134 N. 13 St., Philadelphia, Pa., 19107.
A monthly digest of recent articles on computers.

Computer Education.   Data Processing Horizons, Inc., P. O. Box 99, South Pasadena, Calif., 91030.
A monthly journal covering current developments in the teaching of data processing.

Computers and Automation.   Berkeley Enterprises, Inc., 815 Washington St., Newtonville, Mass., 02160.
A monthly magazine covering EDP topics of general interest.

Computerworld.   Computerworld, Inc., 129 Mt. Auburn St., Cambridge, Mass., 02138.
A weekly newspaper oriented towards developments in EDP and the computer industry.

Computing Newsletter for Schools of Business. University of Colorado, Colorado Springs, Colo., 80907.
Monthly newsletter on developments in computers and information systems education that affects education in business.

Computing Reviews. Assn. for Computing Machinery, 1130 Avenue of the Americas, New York, N.Y., 10036.
Monthly reviews of books, articles, and films on various aspects of computing.

Data Base.   ACM Special Interest Group on Business Data Processing, 1130 Avenue of the Americas, New York, N.Y., 10036.
Quarterly publication devoted to articles on various aspects of business EDP.

Data Processing Magazine.   North American Publishing Co. 134 N. 13 St., Philadelphia, Pa., 19107.
Monthly magazine concentrating on topics of general interest in data processing.

Data Processing Digest.   Data Processing Digest, Inc., 1140 S. Robertson Blvd., Los Angeles, Calif., 90035.
Monthly coverage of general topics in data processing.

Datamation.   Technical Publishing Co., 1301 S. Grove Ave., Barrington, Ill., 60010.
Monthly covering developments in the data processing field (free to educators in data processing and other qualified individuals).

EDP Analyzer.   EDP Analyzer, 134 Escondido Ave., Vista, Calif., 92083.
Monthly analysis of specific EDP topics.

EDP Weekly.   Industry Reports, Inc., 514 Tenth St., N. W., Washington, D.C., 20004.
Covers weekly developments in data processing.

IBM Data Processor.   IBM Corp., Data Processing Div., 112 E. Post Rd., White Plains, N.Y., 10601.
Monthly review of IBM computer applications and services.

IBM Systems Journal.   IBM Corp., Armonk, N.Y., 10504.
Quarterly publication of technical articles on hardware and software.

Information Processing Journal.   Cambridge Communication Corp., 1612 K St., N. W., Washington D.C., 20006.
Quarterly journal that provides critical evaluations of articles and books on various aspects of data processing.

Infosystems.   Business Press International, Inc., 288 Parks Ave., West Elmhurst, Ill., 60126.
Monthly articles on business EDP topics.

Journal of the Association for Computing Machinery.   Assn. for Computing Machinery, 1130 Avenue of the Americas, New York, N.Y., 10036.
A quarterly publication devoted mainly to technical papers (free to members).

Journal of Data Management.   Data Processing Management Assn., 505 Busse Hwy., Park Ridge, Ill., 60068.
Monthly publication of articles on management and applications in business data processing.

Journal of Systems Management.   Assn. for Systems Management, 24587 Bagley Rd., Cleveland, O., 44138.
Monthly journal covering analysis and design of information and management systems (free to qualified subscribers).

Management Advisor.   American Institute of Certified Public Accountants, 666 Fifth Ave., New York, N.Y., 10019.
Bimonthly articles relating to computer and systems planning and analysis.

Software Age.   Press-Tech, Inc., 1020 Church St., Evanston, Ill., 60201.
Bimonthly coverage of software developments and other related topics at a nontechnical level (free to qualified subscribers).

index

Index

M

N

O

This book is set in 11 and 10 point Times Roman, leaded 2 points. Part numbers are 24 point (small) Helvetica Italic and chapter numbers are 30 point Helvetica Medium. Part and chapter titles are 24 point (small) Helvetica Regular. The size of the type page is 27 x 46 picas.